THE
NEW BOOK
OF
KNOWLEDGE

THE
NEW BOOK
OF
KNOWLEDGE

Grolier Incorporated, Danbury, Connecticut

VOLUME 2

B

The publishers wish to thank the following for permission to use copyrighted material:
Abington Press for excerpts from *The Bible Story for Boys and Girls, Old Testament,* and *The Bible Story for Boys and Girls, New Testament,* by Walter Russell Bowie, copyrights 1952 and 1951 by Pierce & Smith.

Trademark
THE BOOK OF KNOWLEDGE
registered in U.S. Patent Office

B, the second letter of the English alphabet, was also the second letter of the Phoenician, Hebrew, and Greek alphabets. The Phoenicians and Hebrews called it *beth*. The Greeks called it *beta.*

Many scholars believe that the Phoenician letters were pictures of objects. *Beth*, they say, was probably a simple picture of a house. It looked like this: ⋈.

The Greeks borrowed this basic form for their *beta*, but they made a double-looped version. Since the Greeks wrote from left to right instead of from right to left like the Phoenicians, the *beta* was also reversed. By the 5th century B.C. it looked like this: Β.

In adapting the Greek alphabet, the Romans kept the form of the *beta* but changed its name to *be*—the name it still has today in most European alphabets.

The B is most frequently pronounced as in *baseball* or *bishop*, although in some English words, such as *comb* or *debt*, the letter is silent.

The English B stands for many things. It has even been used in punishment. In Europe during the Middle Ages, and in the United States at the time of the Puritans, anyone who spoke against God was called a blasphemer. Sometimes a B was branded on the foreheads of the guilty ones as a sign of their sinfulness.

In chemistry B stands for the element boron. In a list of things, it labels the second item. On a report card it means above-average work. In music B is the name of a note as well as an abbreviation for bass, the lowest part in a musical composition.

B occurs in abbreviations. The college degree bachelor of arts is shortened to B.A. When used in dates, B.C. means "before Christ," as in "48 B.C." Some B abbreviations employ the small b. "Born," for instance, is indicated before dates by a small b, as in "Queen Elizabeth I, b. 1533."

> Reviewed by MARIO PEI
> Author, *The Story of Language*

See also ALPHABET.

BABBITT, NATALIE. See CHILDREN'S LITERATURE (Profiles).

SOME WAYS TO REPRESENT B:

The **manuscript** or printed forms of the letter (left) are highly readable. The **cursive** letters (right) are formed from slanted flowing strokes joining one letter to the next.

The **Manual Alphabet** (left) enables a deaf person to communicate by forming letters with the fingers of one hand. **Braille** (right) is a system by which a blind person can use fingertips to "read" raised dots that stand for letters.

The **International Code of Signals** is a special group of flags used to send and receive messages at sea. Each letter is represented by a different flag.

International Morse Code is used to send messages by radio signals. Each letter is expressed as a combination of dots (•) and dashes (––).

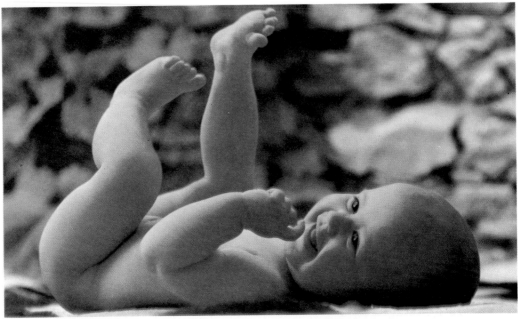

Newborn babies can do very little by themselves, but by the age of a few months, they are alert and interested in what they see—and they learn to smile.

BABY

A baby cat is called a kitten, and a baby dog is called a puppy. A human baby is often referred to as an infant. All of these babies are mammals.

Mammals are animals whose young, or offspring, are born alive after a period of development inside the mother. (Only two primitive types lay eggs.) After birth the offspring depend on their mother's milk for survival. Mammals may be very large, like the elephant, or very small, like the mouse.

▶BEFORE THE BABY IS BORN

By the time the human mammal, or baby, enters the world, it has spent 9 months in a complicated process of growth and development. This process begins when the **ovum,** or egg, of the mother unites with the **sperm,** or seed, of the father. The fertilized egg begins to grow inside the mother's **uterus,** or womb. In about 3 weeks various organs begin to form. The tiny fertilized egg is then known as an **embryo.** The embryo continues to develop. Later it is called a **fetus.** When the fetus is 3 months old, it is about 3 inches long (8 centimeters) long. By 4 months, it is about twice this length.

When the fetus is 4 or 5 months old, the fetal heartbeat may be heard through a stetho-scope placed on the mother's abdomen. At about the same time, the mother may become aware of little movements within her body. These movements bring her great joy, for she knows she has begun to ''feel life.''

The fetus is developing and moving around in the bag, or sac, of fluid that surrounds and protects it. Inside the sac, the fetus is attached at the belly (abdomen) to the placenta by a cord containing blood vessels. The placenta is a pancake-shaped organ through which the mother's blood flows to give nourishment to the fetus until it is ready to be born.

After 9 months in the uterus of the mother, the fetus is ready to come into the world. More than 90 percent of all babies are born after 9 months, known as full term.

If the fetus is born too soon, or prematurely, it may be difficult for it to survive. Medical advances have made it possible for more than half of all babies born after 20 weeks in the uterus to survive. However, the risk of long-term defects increases as the fetus spends less time in the uterus before birth. The biggest problem faced by premature babies is breathing, because their lungs are immature, and they lack a crucial substance (surfactin) that helps them absorb oxygen into their lungs. That is why they are placed in incubators (special beds in which the environment can be controlled) that provide extra oxygen.

For many months, the baby's parents wonder what their infant will be like. Will it be a boy or girl? What color hair and eyes will it have? Will it inherit any diseases? These and other matters are determined long before the baby's birth. The father's sperm and mother's egg contain the ingredients (called chromosomes) that carry all the characteristics the baby will inherit from its parents. The sex of the baby is determined by chromosomes in the father's sperm. These chromosomes are present in the amniotic fluid that surrounds the fetus before it is born. An analysis of this fluid can identify certain medical disorders, and the sex of the baby, before birth.

▶AFTER THE BABY IS BORN

At last the baby is born. If it is an average baby, it weighs about 7 or 8 pounds (3 or 3.5 kilograms), and it is about 20 inches (about 51 centimeters) long. Male babies are slightly larger than female babies.

The healthy baby's first action after birth is to utter a sharp cry. With a good loud cry the baby's lungs expand and adapt to the outside world. The lungs enable the baby to breathe the air that now surrounds it. The cry also indicates that the baby is off to a good start.

Most human mothers give birth to a single baby. In about 1 out of every 80 births twins are born. Some twins are **identical.** This means that they have developed from a single fertilized egg. Other twins are **fraternal,** which means that two eggs may have been fertilized at the same time. Identical twins are usually very much alike. Fraternal twins may be quite different from one another. Triplets are born about once in 6,400 births, quadruplets about once in 500,000. Quintuplets, five babies born at one time, are very rare indeed.

Healthy infants have a strong tendency to suck. For the first months of life, sucking enables babies to obtain the nourishment necessary for their growth.

During the months of pregnancy, the mother's breasts have been getting ready to make milk. If the mother chooses not to feed the baby with her own milk, the use of a "formula" is recommended. The formula is usually made of cow's milk mixed with a form of sugar and water. Sometimes vitamins are added. It is put into a bottle that has a nipple made to resemble the nipple of the mother's breast. When the baby's mouth is put to the nipple of the breast, or to the bottle, the strong sucking reflex makes it possible for the infant to suck and swallow this first important food.

Growth and Development

Although babies vary a great deal, there is a general timetable for their growth and development, especially during the first year.

The newborn period in a baby's life is the first month after birth. This is a period of great change not only for the baby, but also for the rest of the family who have awaited the arrival for 9 months.

Newborn babies can do some things by themselves. They can breathe, cry, sleep, and move their arms and legs. They can suck and swallow food, and their bodies can take care of eliminating waste products. But since human babies have little control over these simple actions, they are completely dependent on others for their care.

Very young babies sleep most of the time, about 16 hours per day. When they are awake they are usually eating or crying. Their hearing is good, especially for human voices, and they will react to loud noises. Newborns have trouble focusing but see best at a distance of about 7 to 9 inches (18 to 23 centimeters). They also are the most alert when they are held upright; in that position they can absorb the most information (smells, lights, sounds). When babies are about 2 weeks old, their eyes will follow light and fix on an object. At about the age of 2 months, babies can see colors and, to the delight of their parents, begin to smile.

Babies must be carefully guarded against illness. People with colds or other infections should not handle the baby or get close to it, especially if the baby is premature or delicate. If the baby is bottle-fed, the formula must be prepared carefully. The bottle and nipple should be sterile (free of germs).

Small babies, especially premature infants, have a very limited capacity to control their temperature. They are poorly insulated because they do not have much fat. So it is important to keep babies warm.

After the first few months the baby should be examined by a pediatrician (a doctor who specializes in treating babies and older children), who will discuss the baby's progress with the parents or other caretaker. The pediatrician may suggest the addition of vitamins

The development of babies is the object of extensive research. Doctors and psychologists are attempting to find out what infants know at birth and how they organize and use that knowledge during their early years.

and some foods, such as cereal, fruits, and vegetables, to the baby's diet. The pediatrician will also give the baby "shots," or oral vaccines that will protect the baby from certain diseases, such as measles, whooping cough, and polio.

Two- or three-month-old babies can hold their heads up. But babies cannot sit up alone until they are about 6 or 7 months old. By about 9 months, most learn to stand while holding on to something. By this time, babies are quite good at crawling around and exploring their world. The baby usually can take a few steps at about the time of its first birthday.

When do babies learn to talk? Well, if you listen carefully, you will notice that they begin to make sounds when they are still very young. We call these sounds "baby talk." Unfortunately, we do not understand baby talk very well, but we enjoy listening to it and talking back to the baby. Babies start to babble consistently, with some indication of meaning, around 6 to 9 months of age. They start to vocalize in response to others much earlier.

They learn the words of their own language by listening and copying. The process of using and understanding language depends on individual development.

Most babies have a few teeth by the time they are a year old. When babies are born, they have no teeth. But even at birth a baby's teeth are under the gums in the form of tooth buds. As the baby grows, the teeth begin to show through the gums.

▶ ARE YOU A SIBLING?

Brothers and sisters in a family are called **siblings.** Siblings have an important role to play when a new baby arrives, just as parents do.

Parents sometimes worry that older siblings might be jealous of a new baby. Older children often feel that some of their parents' love and attention will have to be shared. Usually, however, siblings also welcome the arrival of a baby. They are proud of the newcomer and quickly discover the excitement of watching an infant grow.

Children who have the opportunity to live with a baby in the family gain valuable experience. If they are old enough, their parents will let them help take care of the new baby. They will learn to help feed the baby, change the diapers, and take the younger child for a walk in the carriage. All of this experience will help siblings to become good baby-sitters when they are old enough. It will also help them become good parents when they are adults.

In a family where love, tenderness, and respect for each member are important, babies and older siblings will thrive. Although no one really remembers what it was like to be a baby, what happened to all of us in our early years will probably have a great effect on us as we grow up.

JEAN PAKTER, M.D., M.P.H.
Director, Bureau of Maternity Services
and Family Planning
New York City Department of Health
Reviewed and updated by MICHAEL E. LAMB,
PH.D.
Professor of Psychology,
Psychiatry, and Pediatrics
University of Utah

BABYLONIA

Babylonia was a region in what is now southern Iraq where a talented people built a great civilization almost 4,000 years ago. Among their accomplishments, the Babylonians developed the exact sciences, especially mathematics and astronomy. Because the Babylonians sought to use their science to predict the future, their astronomy gave way to astrology, a belief that the motion of the heavenly bodies affects the course of human events. Thus, while the Babylonians laid a foundation for modern science, it remained for the later Greeks to separate science from superstition.

The Babylonians were a Semitic people whose language was related to Hebrew and Arabic. They were influenced by a people who lived earlier in the region, the Sumerians. Like the Sumerians, they used a style of writing called cuneiform (''wedge-shaped'') and developed a culture built around large cities.

The Tower of Babel. The most distinctive type of Babylonian building was the ziggurat, a towerlike temple, built in stages and topped by a religious shrine. Though the ziggurat was first developed by the Sumerians, the Babylonians carried on the tradition. The most famous ziggurat is the Tower of Babel mentioned in the Bible. The god of the Babylonians was Marduk, whose cult spread with the growth of the Babylonian Empire.

The capital of Babylonia was the city of Babylon, situated near the Euphrates River where it approaches the Tigris River, not far from present-day Baghdad, the capital of Iraq.

The Code of Hammurabi. Babylon became important after 1800 B.C. under a succession of kings known as the First Dynasty of Babylon. The most famous monarch in that line was Hammurabi (Hammurapi), who ruled from about 1792 to 1750 B.C. By the use of shrewd diplomacy and strong armies, he defeated his rivals, the kings of other city-states, and carved out the most powerful empire of his day. Hammurabi also established a code of laws that regulated society strictly, with justice but little mercy. For example, a builder was to be executed if the house he built collapsed and killed the homeowner. And an incompetent surgeon who cost a patient his or her eye or life was to have his operating hand cut off. Though harsh, Hammurabi's laws protected his subjects from injustice.

Hammurabi's Code, one of the world's oldest sets of laws, was inscribed about 4,000 years ago on this tablet. The seated figure is that of Hammurabi, king of Babylon.

Nebuchadnezzar II. The next great king of Babylon arose a thousand years later. Nebuchadnezzar II, who reigned from 605 to 562 B.C., made Babylon the greatest city on earth. He beautified his capital with structures such as the Hanging Gardens, famed as one of the Seven Wonders of the Ancient World. Nebuchadnezzar conquered many nations, including the Jews, whose Temple in Jerusalem he destroyed in 586 B.C.

The long rule of Babylon ended with its capture by the Persians under Cyrus the Great in 539 B.C. At least one great monument of the Babylonians survives, however. The development of modern Iraq is due in large measure to its restoration of the ancient irrigation canal system built by the Babylonians, which made the region between the Tigris and Euphrates rivers the most fertile in the world.

CYRUS H. GORDON
New York University
Author, *Hammurapi's Code*

A brilliant composer and organist, Bach wrote much of his music for the church. His work influenced such great musicians as Mozart, Haydn, and Beethoven.

BACH, JOHANN SEBASTIAN (1685–1750)

Johann Sebastian Bach was born on March 21, 1685, in Eisenach, Germany. He was the greatest member of a renowned musical family of more than 50 musicians who lived in central Germany between 1500 and the 1800's.

At the age of 10, Bach was left an orphan and went to live with his older brother, a church organist at Ohrdruf. When he was 15, Bach went to Lüneburg, where a scholarship allowed him to attend school. There he sang in the choir and learned much of the best music of the time. He also studied with the great organist George Böhm.

In 1703, Bach became church organist at Arnstadt and immediately began to compose for the organ, the harpsichord, and voices. He went to Mühlhausen in 1707, and while he was an organist in that city he married his cousin, Maria Barbara Bach. The following year they moved to Weimar, where Bach remained in the service of the Duke of Weimar for ten years.

Most of Bach's music at Weimar was composed for the organ and church choirs. When Bach wanted to change jobs again, the Duke put him in jail to try to make him stay. But Bach was determined to leave and journeyed to Cöthen, where he entered the service of Prince Leopold of Anhalt. During his six years at Cöthen, Bach composed many of his best-known instrumental works, such as the *Brandenburg* concertos, the English and the French suites for harpsichord, and much chamber music.

Bach's wife died in 1720. The following year he married Anna Magdalena Wilcken. Bach became the father of 20 children, and several of his talented sons became well-known composers.

Bach changed jobs for the last time in 1723 and became director of music at St. Thomas' Church and School in Leipzig. Though he was not happy with the post, he remained there for 27 years, until his death. Most of Bach's greatest religious works were composed during these years, including the *Magnificat*, the *St. John* Passion, the *St. Matthew* Passion, the B-minor Mass, and many cantatas. In Leipzig, Bach also completed *The Well-Tempered Clavier,* a collection of 48 preludes and fugues in all the keys. Like most of Bach's music, it was not published until long after his death. Bach was well known as an organist, but during his lifetime he never became a celebrated composer like his famous contemporary, George Frederick Handel.

In 1747, Bach journeyed to Potsdam to visit his son Karl Philipp Emanuel, who was a musician at the court of King Frederick II of Prussia. The King admired Bach and wanted to hear him play. To the King's delight Bach improvised on a melody that the King had given him. When Bach returned to Leipzig, he repaid the royal friendship by composing the *Musical Offering* based on the King's theme and dedicating it to the King.

Bach then turned to his last great work, *The Art of Fugue,* which remained unfinished at his death. It is the fruit of Bach's lifelong study of a musical technique called counterpoint. As Bach grew older his eyesight became increasingly poor, until toward the end of his life, he was totally blind. He died in Leipzig on July 28, 1750. It was not until almost 100 years later that the world recognized Bach as one of its greatest composers.

Reviewed by KARL GEIRINGER
Author, *The Bach Family*

BACKGAMMON

Backgammon is a game of luck and skill played with dice and checkers on a special board. The game was probably introduced into Europe by the Crusaders. In the eastern Mediterranean area, it has been played with such enthusiasm that for many years the better players of this region were the best in the world. But excellent players have developed elsewhere as the game's popularity has spread.

▶ **EQUIPMENT**

Each player has a set of 15 checkers. The checkers can be of any two different colors, but usually one set is dark and the other is light in color. Each player also has two dice and a cup in which to shake them.

The backgammon board is a rectangle. It is divided into two halves by a vertical line called the *bar.* One half of the board is called the *inner,* or home, *table.* The other half is called the *outer table.*

Twelve triangles, called *points,* stick out from each of the two long sides of the board. Six points are on each side of the inner table, and six points are on each side of the outer table. The players, usually identified as Black and White according to the color of their checkers, sit on opposite sides of the board.

▶ **OBJECT OF THE GAME**

At the start of the game, the checkers are arranged as shown in Diagram 1. Each player

tries to move all his checkers to his own inner table by advancing according to the numbers rolled on the dice. The white checkers move clockwise and the black move counterclockwise. Each player is moving his checkers from the opponent's inner table around the board by way of the two outer tables and then to the inner table on his own side of the board. After all checkers are in a player's own inner table, the player *bears off* (removes the checkers from the board). The first player to bear off all of his checkers is the winner.

▶ **NOTATION**

Each point on the backgammon board has a number as shown on the outer rim of the board in the diagrams below. The numbers are used by writers of books and columns on backgammon to describe the moves that the players have made. These numbers do not appear on a real backgammon board, but a beginning player might find it helpful to lightly pencil them onto the board. This would enable the player to follow a written game or instructions move by move.

The points on both sides of the board are numbered from 1 through 12, going from the inner table to the outer. The initials B and W, referring to Black and White, indicate which side of the board the point is on. When a move is described, it indicates the point moved from, followed by the point moved to. For example, assume that White throws a 6 and a 1 as an opening move and chooses to move

Diagram 1. A board set up for play. White will move in direction of arrows, black the opposite direction.

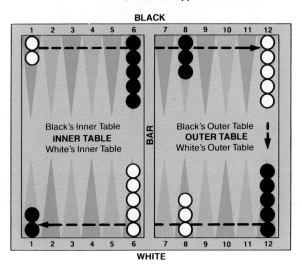

Diagram 2. White rolled a 6 and a 1 and has made an opening move. The notation is White: B12—W7, W8—W7.

the checkers as indicated in Diagram 2. White has moved one checker from Black's 12 point to White's 7 point and another from White's 8 point to White's 7 point. The move would be notated as follows: White: B12–W7, W8–W7.

▶START OF THE GAME

To begin a game, each player rolls one die. The player who throws the highest number plays first by using the numbers on both his and his opponent's dice. After this, the players take turns rolling their dice onto the board from their cups and moving their checkers.

▶THE PLAY OF THE GAME

The numbers on the two dice, taken separately, show the number of points over which the player's checkers may be moved. When one checker has been moved the number of points indicated by one die, the number on the other die may be used to move the same checker further—or it may be used to move a different checker. For example, if a player throws a 5 and a 6, the player could choose to move one checker 5 points and a different checker 6 points, or he could opt to move one checker 11 points. No other combinations are possible—in other words, the total of 11 cannot be divided into moves of 7 and 4 or 8 and 3. The split can only be made according to the numbers on the individual dice.

If a player should happen to roll doubles (both dice the same), the player may move twice as many points as the total shown on the dice. For example, a roll of 3–3 counts as four 3's rather than the two 3's shown. The player can move a total of 12 points rather than 6. This move can be made in units of 3 using as many as four checkers. A possible opening move for White throwing double 3's might be: White: B1–B7 (2). The (2) shows that two separate checkers made the same move.

▶MOVES

If a player has two or more checkers on a point, he has *made* that point. White has made point W7 in Diagram 2. His opponent can pass over that point but cannot land on it. A player can, however, land on a point on which the opponent has only a single checker. Such a point is called a *blot*. When a checker of the opposite color lands on a blot, the checker that was originally there has been *hit* and is re-

moved from the board and placed *on the bar*. A player who has a checker on the bar may re-enter the game by throwing a number that will place the hit checker on any open point on the opponent's inner table. All checkers on the bar must be entered before the player can move any of his other checkers.

Whenever possible, a player *must* move his checkers using both (or all four, in the case of doubles) numbers thrown. There will be cases, however, where the opponent's points prevent a player from moving any of his checkers. In this case, the play passes to the opponent. If only one number of a roll is usable, it must be the higher one.

▶BEARING OFF

When a player has advanced all 15 of his checkers to his own inner table, he may begin to bear off.

A checker is borne off a point that matches the number rolled on one die. For example, on a 4–2 roll, a checker may be removed from the 4 point and another from the 2 point. When a number on one die is higher than the highest point on which a player has checkers, the player takes the checker off the highest occupied point. That is, if the player throws a 5, and the 5 point is empty but there is a checker on the 4 point, the player bears off the checker from the 4 point. It is not permitted to bear off a checker from a point higher than the number on the die.

If all the player's checkers are in his inner table, it is not required that they be borne off with each roll of the dice. Instead, they could be moved further into the inner table.

If a player's checker is hit during the bearing off, it is put on the bar. The checker must re-enter the game and move all the way around the board again to its inner table before bearing off can start again. In other words, a player can bear off *only* if all of his checkers are in his own inner table.

The winner is the first player to bear off all his or her checkers. If the loser has not borne off a single checker, this player is *gammoned* and loses a double game. If the loser has a checker on the bar or in the opponent's inner table, she or he is *backgammoned* and loses a triple game.

CHARLES H. GOREN
Author, *Goren's Modern Backgammon Complete*
BACKPACKING. See HIKING AND BACKPACKING.

BACON, FRANCIS (1561–1626)

Francis Bacon, an English statesman, philosopher, and essayist, was born in London on January 22, 1561. He showed great brilliance as a child and at the age of 12 entered Cambridge University. After two years at Cambridge, he began the study of law.

Bacon completed his law studies, and in 1584 was elected to Parliament. Ambitious as well as intelligent, he rose to political prominence under King James I. He was knighted and appointed attorney general. In 1618 he was made Baron Verulam and named lord chancellor, the highest legal post in England. He was created Viscount St. Albans in 1621.

Bacon was one of the King's closest advisers. But in 1621 he was charged with accepting gifts from persons whose cases were waiting to be tried in the courts. Since giving and receiving gifts was a common practice at the time, it was obvious that Bacon's political enemies were using the charge in order to rid the kingdom of his influence. He was convicted and imprisoned in the Tower of London. After a few days he was released, but his political career was over.

Bacon had begun to write his famous essays and other works during his busy years as a man of public affairs. Now he devoted the remainder of his life to philosophical and scientific writing. He had planned a long work that would reform philosophical and scientific study. "I have taken all knowledge as my province," he stated. But he was able to finish only two parts of the great work. Among his completed writings are *The Advancement of Learning*, *History of Henry VII*, and the collected *Essays*. Bacon made the essay a popular literary form in England.

Bacon's scientific curiosity led to his death. One winter day, it occurred to him that food could be preserved by cold. To demonstrate this, he bought a chicken and stuffed it with snow. While working in the snowy weather, he caught cold. The illness grew worse, and he died on April 9, 1626.

Reviewed by ELIZABETH S. WRIGLEY
Director, The Francis Bacon Library

BACON, ROGER (1214?–1292?)

Roger Bacon, an English scientist and philosopher, helped lay the foundations of modern scientific thinking. He recognized the need for research and accurate methods of scientific study at a time when many people still relied on myths and superstitions to explain events in the world around them.

Little is known for certain about Bacon's life. He was born sometime between 1214 and 1220, the son of a well-to-do family in Ilchester, England. He may have entered Oxford University as early as the age of 13. In the 1240's he taught at the University of Paris.

Europe during Bacon's lifetime was having a revival of learning, based on the discovery of great written works from ancient Greece and Rome. Most scholars simply accepted and taught this knowledge from the ancient world. But Bacon did something different. He learned from living people and from the world around him, as well as from ancient wisdom.

Bacon also conducted his own experiments. He spent years studying how the eye works. He sprayed water into the air to study the nature of rainbows. He tested superstitions by performing experiments with the actual materials.

About 1250, Bacon returned to England, entered the Franciscan order of monks, and began to teach science at Oxford. But his experiments made his superiors angry. In 1257 they sent Bacon back to Paris. He was told to write and teach only what they approved.

Nevertheless, Bacon secretly obtained a commission from Pope Clement IV to write a report on the importance of science. One part of it, the *Opus majus* ("Greater Work"), was an outline of scientific knowledge. The importance of this report lies in Bacon's emphasis on the need to observe, test, and measure.

In 1278, Bacon's religious superiors imprisoned him in Paris for his unusual ideas. He was freed in 1290, but he had become a weak old man. He returned to England and is thought to have died in Oxford in 1292. Today Bacon's ideas—unusual for their time—are considered an important part of modern science.

JOHN S. BOWMAN
Author and science editor

Few creatures other than bacteria can survive in such harsh environments as a hot spring (*left*) or a sea vent buried deep within an ocean trench (*right*).

BACTERIA

Although they are typically too small to be seen without a microscope, bacteria are the most common life-forms on Earth. They are everywhere in our world—even places where conditions are so extreme that plants and animals cannot survive. These small, simple creatures can be found in sea vents on the ocean floor, where the temperature climbs to 230°F (110°C)—higher than the boiling point of water! Others have been discovered in the frozen ice of the Antarctic and the dry, salty world of Death Valley. Some bacteria can even live in places without oxygen. Most bacteria live in the milder conditions found on the Earth's surface or on living or dead plants and animals. Large numbers of bacteria live on our skin and in our throat and intestine. In fact, there are more bacterial cells living on and in the human body than there are human cells making up the body.

▶ THE CHARACTERISTICS OF BACTERIA

Bacteria (plural of bacterium) are believed to have been the first life-forms on Earth. Fossils suggest that bacteria were present more than 3.5 billion years ago. While we are not sure what these first living organisms were like, they were probably small,

simple creatures, much like the bacteria that now exist.

Size. A unique feature of bacteria is its size. Most bacteria can only be seen with a microscope that magnifies objects about 1,000 times their actual size. The internal parts of a bacterium are studied using an electron microscope, which magnifies objects several thousands of times. Bacteria are so very small—about 500 average bacteria could be placed side by side across the period at the end of this sentence—they are measured in units called micrometers (a micrometer is one-millionth of a meter). Typical bacteria are 0.3 to 2.0 micrometers in diameter. Because of its size, food, water, and waste products can pass quickly into and out of the bacterial cell.

Structure. Most bacteria have a thick, protective wall around their cell. This rigid layer, which is made of chemicals unique to bacteria, gives the bacterial cell its shape. A thin skinlike covering called a cell membrane lies just inside the cell wall. Within the cell membrane are all the essential molecules and fluid

Fossil microbes found in ancient rock establish bacteria as the first—and for about 2 billion years the only—form of life on Earth.

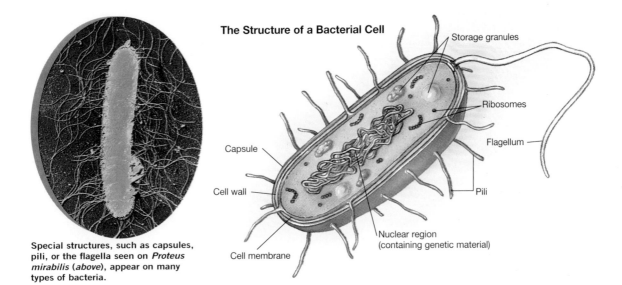

The Structure of a Bacterial Cell

Storage granules

Ribosomes

Flagellum

Capsule

Cell wall

Pili

Nuclear region
(containing genetic material)

Cell membrane

Special structures, such as capsules, pili, or the flagella seen on *Proteus mirabilis* (*above*), appear on many types of bacteria.

that the cell needs to carry on its life processes. Unlike other living organisms, a bacteria does not have its cell substances contained in a nucleus or in other membrane-covered bodies. Instead, its essential materials are scattered throughout the cell. These materials include genes—the basic units of heredity that can transfer the traits of organisms to the next generation.

Special structures can be found on some bacteria. These structures allow the bacteria to survive in special environments. Some bacteria make a sticky slime layer, or capsule, around their cell walls. This layer allows the bacteria to attach to surfaces. Bacteria that cause tooth decay attach to the surface of teeth with this sticky capsule. The capsule also allows some bacteria to produce diseases, such as pneumonia.

Some bacteria have long, whiplike tails, called flagella, coming out of their cells. Flagella turn like motorboat propellers and help the bacteria move with a swimming motion. Other bacteria glide on surfaces or travel using a corkscrew motion. Bacteria move to

get to the food, air, or light that they need to grow.

Short, straight hollow tubes called pili or fimbriae are also seen on some bacteria. These hairlike structures form a border or fringe around the cell. Fimbriae help the bacteria attach to surfaces, such as the cells in our throats. Special types of pili can transfer genes from one bacterial cell to another.

Reproduction. Living cells, including bacteria, must be able to reproduce themselves. Bacteria do this by a simple process in which one cell increases in size and then divides into two equal cells. This form of asexual reproduction is called binary fission because one mother cell splits into two daughter cells. Instructions for copying itself are contained in the genes. The cell also contains the basic chemicals, cell machinery, and energy needed to complete the manufacturing process.

With abundant nutrients, bacteria will grow and reproduce very quickly. Some bacteria can divide every 20 minutes, if conditions are right. That means that a starting bacteria could multiply into a million bacteria in less than 7 hours. Fortunately, the Earth will not be overgrown by bacteria because inadequate food supplies and harmful conditions keep them in control.

Obtaining Food. Some bacteria can

Each daughter cell that results from this dividing mother cell will be able to live independently, even though the cells may stay together, growing in chains or clusters.

The many thousands of species of bacteria are typically classified according to whether they are rod shaped (*Salmonella, left*), round (*Streptococcus, center*), or spiral (*Rhodospirillum, right*).

make their own food and cell parts from basic materials such as carbon dioxide and water. These bacteria are called autotrophs, meaning "self-feeders." From sunlight or simple chemicals found in their environment, these independent creatures get the energy needed to synthesize organic nutrients. Other bacteria get nutrients and energy from foodstuffs originally made by other organisms. These heterotrophs, meaning "other-feeders," commonly break down plant and animal cells into simple organic nutrients. All animals and many bacteria are heterotrophs. For example, human beings, as well as bacteria that live in the intestinal tract, digest a meal of grains, vegetables, and meat to get nutrients and energy needed for growth.

KINDS OF BACTERIA

The many different species, or kinds, of bacteria are grouped together in the Kingdom Monera. **Microbiologists**, the scientists who study bacteria and other microscopic organisms, have identified and described more than 10,000 species. There are several different ways to classify bacteria. They can be grouped based on how they reproduce, how they obtain food, or what kind of environment they inhabit. But the most common way to group bacteria is by how they are shaped. Although there are some unusual bacteria that are star shaped, triangular, or square, bacteria viewed under the microscope generally appear either rod shaped, round, or spiral.

The names of bacterial shapes come from Latin words. A rod-shaped bacterium is called a **bacillus**. A round bacterium is called a **coccus**. A spiral bacterium is called a **spirillum**. Some variations in bacterial

shape and arrangement can occur. The rod-shaped bacteria can be cigar shaped or have pointed ends. Cocci can be oval or bean shaped. The spiral bacteria can be wavy or corkscrew shaped in pairs, chains, or clusters. For example, the organism *Streptococcus*, which can cause sore throats, is a type of round bacterium that is linked together in chains.

▶ THE IMPORTANCE OF BACTERIA

Although bacteria can be found everywhere, we notice them because of the infections they cause, like sore throats, or from the foods they spoil. While some bacteria can cause serious disease or threaten those people who have weakened immune defenses, most bacteria are harmless, and many are very helpful. Bacteria are the source of food for the many animals in our oceans, lakes, and rivers. They also recycle nutrients in the soil so plants can grow. These small creatures maintain the proper balance of chemicals in our world. Harmless bacteria living on us keep us healthy by competing with disease-producing bacteria. Some bacteria in our intestine even supply us with some vitamins. We enjoy the tasty foods that bacteria help to make, such as sourdough bread, cheese, yogurt, and pickles. In addition, bacteria can be modified in a process called genetic engineering to make substances that they normally do not produce. These modified bacteria can then help digest oil spills, recycle waste, make soil more fertile, or make drugs to treat disease.

CYNTHIA V. SOMMER
University of Wisconsin at Milwaukee

See also ANTIBIOTICS; DISEASES; FERMENTATION; FOOD PRESERVATION; GENETICS; MICROBIOLOGY.

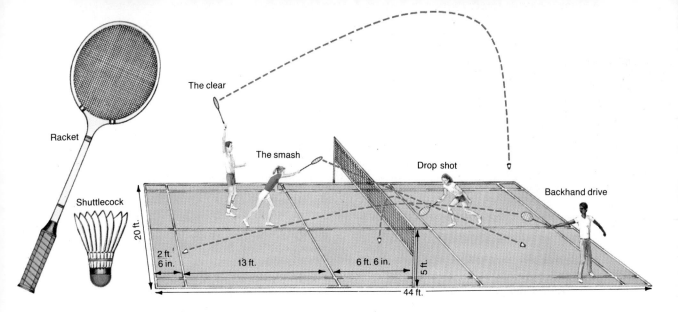

Racket

The clear

The smash

Drop shot

Backhand drive

Shuttlecock

20 ft.

2 ft. 6 in.

13 ft.

6 ft. 6 in.

5 ft.

44 ft.

BADMINTON

Badminton is a fast game played with rackets and a shuttlecock on a wood, dirt, or grass court. The court is somewhat like a tennis court, but smaller. The shuttlecock, often called simply the shuttle, or "bird," is hit back and forth over a net 5 feet (1.5 meters) high. It must be returned before it strikes the court. The game can be played by two persons (singles) or four persons (doubles). It can be played both indoors and outdoors. Official tournaments are played indoors.

Badminton developed from Battledore and Shuttlecock, an ancient game that was popular with children. There are several explanations of how the modern game began; one is that about the year 1870, English army officers brought a version of it to England from India, where it was called Poona. The new game took its name from the Duke of Beaufort's estate, Badminton, where the game was probably played indoors for the first time. Badminton became popular in England, and in the 1890's the Badminton Association was formed. In 1934 the International Badminton Federation was organized. The two international badminton championships are the Thomas Cup competition for men and the Uber Cup for women.

▶PLAYING BADMINTON

The game starts with the player in the right service court serving to an opponent in the diagonally opposite right service court. Allowed only one serve at the start of each point, the server continues serving to alternate courts until the rally is lost. If a rally is lost, a point is not lost, only the serve. This is called side out. An opponent then takes a hand at serving.

Any of the following is called a fault, and results in side out if committed by the serving side or loss of a point if committed by a receiver:

Server
(1) Serving outside the service court.
(2) Contact with the serve anyplace above the waist.
Server or receiver
(1) Hitting the shuttle out of bounds, or twice in succession on the same side of the net, or under or through the net, or before it crosses the net.
(2) Carrying the shuttle with the racket.
(3) Touching the net or its supports during play.
(4) Serving or receiving the serve with the feet on the line, or with both feet not in contact with the floor until the shuttle is hit.
A shuttle falling on a boundary line is good.

▶SCORING

Points can be scored only while serving. A game is won by the first player or side to score 15 points, except in women's singles, in which game is 11 points. If a tie score of 13 all is reached (9 all in women's singles), the side that reached the tie score first may, if it chooses, set the game at 5 (or 3 in women's singles). This means that game will not be reached until either side has scored 5 (or 3) more points. Similarly, if the score becomes tied at 14 all (or 10 all in women's singles), game may be set at 3 (or 2) more points.

The side that wins a game serves first in the next game. The opposing sides change ends of the court after each game.

THE BASIC STROKES

Overhead shots are played from above the head; underhand shots are those played from below waist level. Any stroke hit on the right-hand side of the body is a forehand; on the left-hand side of the body, a backhand. The descriptions and instructions in this article are for right-handed players. If you are left-handed, substitute "left" for "right" and "right" for "left."

The serve is the most important stroke because it puts the shuttle in play at the start of each point.

The smash, or kill shot, is the principal point-winning stroke in badminton. It is hit downward from an overhead position with as much speed as possible.

The clear is a shot that sends the shuttle high to the opponent's back boundary line.

The drop shot causes the shuttle to drop close to the net in the opponent's court. It may be hit either overhead or underhand.

The drive sends the shuttle skimming low over the net in a line parallel to the floor.

Several auxiliary shots are often useful in badminton. The hairpin and crosscourt net shots can be used to return a drop shot with a drop shot. They can be hit from one side of the court to the other (crosscourt), or directly back over the net (hairpin).

The round-the-head shot is an overhead backhand played as a forehand. It is protection against a weak backhand. The half smash is used to angle the shuttle downward sharply.

GRIPS AND FOOTWORK

There are different grips for holding the racket to make the various shots.

For the forehand and serve grip, hold the throat of the racket with your left hand. Keep the face of the racket perpendicular to the floor. Then place your right hand on the handle, as if shaking hands with it. Your fingers should be slightly spread.

For backhand shots the hand is turned slightly to the left, the thumb placed flat along the back of the handle, not around it.

Keep your wrist firm and yet flexible, not stiff and tense. The wrist must be cocked back at the beginning of the backswing. As the arm comes forward the wrist snaps or whips the racket head to meet the shuttle.

Good footwork enables you to move quickly in any direction and to have your feet properly placed while stroking. The weight must be on the balls of the feet, and the knees should be mobile. For forehand strokes the left foot is advanced toward the net and the left side faces the net. On the backhand the right foot is advanced and the right side faces the net. These same principles apply to overhead forehands and backhands.

TACTICS AND STRATEGY

The object of the game is to win the required number of points by forcing opponents to make errors. If opponents do not make outright errors they can be forced to make weak returns that can be put away—that is, placed beyond their reach.

Basic strategy in singles involves forcing your opponent to "set up" the shuttle high in the forecourt, where it can be put away with a smash. Use the clear and drop shots to run an opponent to the corners of the court. If an opponent is in the backcourt, try to drop shot. Use a clear shot against an opponent in the forecourt. Drive the shuttle to give an opponent less time.

Generally the singles serve is hit high and deep to the back boundary line. In doubles it should skim over the net and drop near the short service line. The value of a good low serve in doubles cannot be overestimated.

In doubles, attack by hitting the shuttle downward whenever possible. The shuttle is placed strategically to force the opponents to hit upward, or defensive, shots. In mixed doubles the woman usually plays the shots in the front half of the court. The man stands behind her and plays the shots coming to the backcourt.

WHAT MAKES A CHAMPION?

The outstanding characteristic of a champion at badminton is the ability to react in split-second time with eyes, mind, feet, and hands. Becoming a champion takes physical and mental effort at all times. Constant practice, physical fitness, reading instructional books, and observing expert players help make a winner. Habits of concentration, confidence, and self-determination are necessary. The great players of the game almost always have been good sports. This is apparent in their conduct on and off the court.

MARGARET VARNER
Former World Badminton Champion

BAGHDAD

Baghdad is the capital and largest city of Iraq. It is situated in a region of the Middle East called the Cradle of Civilization, a fertile area whose history dates back more than 4,000 years. Approximately 4.5 million people live in the city proper, which covers an area of 254 square miles (658 square kilometers).

The City. Baghdad spreads out on both sides of the historic Tigris River, which is spanned by twelve bridges.

The ancient city of Baghdad has been the capital of Iraq since the nation became a republic in 1958. In recent decades, the city's economy and culture have suffered as a result of regional warfare.

Wide boulevards, high-rise buildings, and colleges and universities give much of Baghdad a modern appearance. The main thoroughfares, notably Rashid and Sadun streets, come together in Tahir Square, the hub of the city.

Economic Activity. Baghdad is Iraq's main center of manufacturing. Chief industries include petroleum refining and the production of petrochemicals, textiles, processed foods, construction materials, and engineering equipment. The city is also noted for its handicrafts of gold, silver, brass, and copper.

History. Baghdad was created in the A.D. 700's by Abdullah al-Mansur (ruled 754–75), a caliph of the Abbasid dynasty of Muslim rulers, who ordered 100,000 workers to build the city for him. For the next 500 years, Baghdad was one of the great cities of the world, attracting merchants and goods from India, Persia (Iran), Egypt, and the Mediterranean region. Under the Caliph Harun al-Rashid (ruled 786–809), the city saw the flowering of Arab culture. Grand palaces, imposing mosques (Muslim houses of worship), colleges, well-paved streets, and public baths reflected the city's wealth, splendor, and high level of sophistication.

In 1258, Baghdad was almost destroyed by invading Mongols. For centuries thereafter it was largely a provincial town, first under the administration of the Persian and then the Ottoman empires.

After the defeat of the Ottoman Empire in World War I (1914–18), Baghdad came under British rule. In 1921 it was designated the capital of the newly established kingdom of Iraq, which became an independent monarchy in 1932. When the monarchy was overthrown in 1958, Baghdad became the capital of the present Republic of Iraq.

Baghdad's economy was strained by Iraq's long war with Iran (1980–88). The city also suffered severely from U.S. and allied bombings during the 1991 Persian Gulf war, which followed Iraq's invasion of Kuwait. Economic sanctions imposed on the country destroyed the city's trade and left many people in poverty. Baghdad sustained further damages in the late 1990's when the United States targeted local military installations in retaliation for Iraq's refusal to honor its postwar agreements with the United Nations.

BALKRISHNA G. GOKHALE
Director, Asian Studies Program
Wake Forest University

BAGPIPE. See WIND INSTRUMENTS.

BAHAMAS

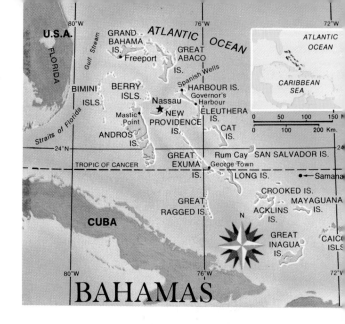

BAHAMAS

The Bahamas is a nation made up of many small islands in the Atlantic Ocean. They form an archipelago (a chain of islands) lying between the Florida coast of the United States and the Caribbean islands of Cuba and Hispaniola.

Christopher Columbus is believed to have first stepped ashore on one of the islands of the Bahamas during his voyage to the Americas in 1492. San Salvador (Watling Island) is long thought to have been the island. Recently, however, some scholars have suggested that Columbus may have first landed on another site in the Bahamas, Samana Cay.

▶ THE PEOPLE

Most of the people of the Bahamas are blacks whose ancestors were brought to the islands as slaves. Over half of the people live on New Providence Island, mostly in the area of Nassau, the capital city. Nassau's fine hotels, quaint streets and houses, and a variety of shops selling goods from all over the world at low prices attract many tourists. The only other city of any size is Freeport on Grand Bahama, the second most populous island.

The country has an extensive primary and secondary school system, which contributes to its high literacy rate. School is free and compulsory for all children between the ages of 5 and 14. Students seeking higher education generally attend the College of the Bahamas on New Providence or the University of the West Indies in Jamaica or study in the United States, Canada, or Britain.

▶ THE LAND

There are about 700 islands and 2,000 tiny sand cays (keys) and exposed bits of coral reef in the Bahamas. The islands extend in an arc for some 1,200 kilometers (750 miles) to the northern edge of the Caribbean Sea. They are formed largely of coral and are mostly low-lying. The highest elevation is almost 120 meters (400 feet). Only a relatively small number of the islands are permanently inhabited.

The climate of the Bahamas is semitropical. Temperatures vary little with the seasons and are moderate in both winter and summer. Rainfall averages about 1,270 millimeters (50 inches) a year, which is enough for most types of farming. On the smaller islands there is less rainfall, and often there are shortages of fresh drinking water. The islands are subject to hurricanes in the fall. The heavy rains and strong winds that accompany these violent storms occasionally cause severe damage.

Eleuthera has some of the loveliest beaches in the Bahamas.

THE ECONOMY

The mainstay of the economy is the tourist industry. Well over 1,000,000 visitors a year are attracted by the climate, beautiful beaches, and clear water. Nassau and Freeport are the most popular tourist spots. But the waters near the Bimini Islands off the coast of Florida are famous for big game fishing. In the spring anglers gather there for annual fishing tournaments.

Nassau is also a center of finance because the tax laws of the Bahamas have encouraged the growth of international banking there. Nassau's importance to the Bahamas is so great that the islands other than New Providence are called Out Islands and their people are called Out Islanders.

Petroleum refining has become an important source of income for the Bahamas. Petroleum and petroleum products now rank as one of the country's leading exports. The islands are also a transfer point for petroleum being shipped to the United States.

Manufacturing and agriculture play a relatively small role in the economy. There is light manufacturing on Grand Bahama Island, where a deepwater port has been dredged at Freeport. Alcoholic beverages, tobacco, textiles, chemicals, paper, rubber goods, and plastics are produced.

Only about 1 percent of the land is cultivated, and this is used mostly for growing crops for domestic use. Eleuthera Island, one of the first islands to be settled, is an important farming area. Vegetables, pineapples, and dairy and poultry products are shipped from Eleuthera to Nassau. At Rock Sound, a prosperous farming community on Eleuthera, beef cattle are raised and shipped to New Providence.

Although the waters of the islands teem with fish, only crayfish (spiny lobster) are caught commercially. The country has little in the way of mineral resources except for salt, which is produced on the southernmost island, Great Inagua. There seawater is channeled into shallow basins. When the sun evaporates the water, the salt is left behind. Straw handicrafts provide additional income for the islanders. New ways to expand the economy and provide more jobs are constantly being sought. An influx of Haitian refugees has added to unemployment problems.

FACTS AND FIGURES

THE COMMONWEALTH OF THE BAHAMAS is the official name of the country.

CAPITAL: Nassau.

LOCATION: Archipelago in the Atlantic Ocean off the coast of Florida. **Latitude**—20° 50' N to 27° 25' N. **Longitude**—72° 37' W to 80° 32' W.

AREA: 13,935 km^2 (5,380 sq mi).

POPULATION: 230,000 (estimate).

LANGUAGE: English.

GOVERNMENT: Constitutional monarchy. **Head of state**—British monarch, represented by governor-general. **Head of government**—prime minister. **International co-operation**—United Nations, Commonwealth of Nations, Organization of American States (OAS).

NATIONAL ANTHEM: "March On, Bahamaland."

ECONOMY: **Agricultural products**—vegetables, pineapples, dairy and poultry products. **Industries and products**—tourism, textiles, cloth, paper, rubber goods, plastics, petroleum refining, chemical products. **Chief exports**—petroleum and petroleum products, cement, alcoholic beverages, pulpwood, crayfish, salt. **Chief imports**—food, drink, tobacco, raw materials. **Monetary unit**—Bahamian dollar.

HISTORY AND GOVERNMENT

The Spanish explored the islands in the 1500's but made no serious efforts to colonize them. The few Indians who lived there were shipped to the West Indies to work in mines and on plantations. In the 17th century the British gained control of the Bahamas and began to settle some of the larger islands. During the United States Civil War, Nassau was a meeting place for blockade runners from the Confederate states and ships from England. There cotton from the South was traded for English goods.

The Bahamas became self-governing in 1964, although Britain still handled foreign affairs, defense, and internal security. When complete independence came in 1973, the Bahamian Government took over the management of these affairs.

The government of the Bahamas is headed by a prime minister, while a governor-general represents the British monarch, who is head of state. Parliament has two houses—the elected House of Assembly and the Senate, to which members are appointed.

JOHN F. LOUNSBURY
Arizona State University

BAHRAIN

BAHRAIN

Bahrain is a country made up of a group of islands lying in the Persian Gulf off the coast of Saudi Arabia. It is the smallest in area of all the states of the Arabian Peninsula. Indeed, it ranks among the smallest of the world's nations. In spite of its size, however, Bahrain has for centuries been one of the more flourishing states of the region. Its location made it important as a port and a center of trade for the countries bordering the gulf. It was famed for its pearls and for the skill of its boatbuilders. The discovery of oil brought further prosperity to Bahrain, although its reserves of oil are not nearly so large as those of some of its neighbors. Over the years Bahrain has used its income from oil to establish an extensive social welfare program for its citizens and to continue its economic development toward the day when its oil will be completely gone.

▶THE PEOPLE

Bahrain is by far the most densely populated country of the Arabian Peninsula. Most of the people are Arabs, some of whom have immigrated to Bahrain from neighboring countries. There are sizable numbers of Pakistanis, Iranians, and Indians, some of whom work as merchants in the cities. It is estimated that about 30 percent of the people are non-Bahraini. Many came to Bahrain because of the relatively high standard of living and to work in the oil industry. The foreign communities include Europeans (mainly British) and Americans. The Arabs are Muslims, about equally divided between the Sunni and Shi'a sects, the two main branches of Islam.

About half the population is concentrated in the two leading cities of Manama and Muharraq. Manama is the largest city, the capital, and chief port. It is connected with Muharraq, which is on another island, by a 2.5-kilometer (1½-mile) causeway. The two cities present interesting contrasts. Manama,

a commercial city, has been modernized, while Muharraq, with its old houses and narrow streets, retains a traditional look. The port of Muharraq is the center of Bahrain's boatbuilding industry. The boats are dhows, rather small vessels with triangular sails once common throughout the Arab world.

Traditional ways of life in the Arab states of the Persian Gulf began to change when oil was discovered. Bahrain was the first of the gulf states in which oil was found, and the effects of modernization are most evident here. The country has a growing middle class and a skilled work force. This is largely a result of Bahrain's emphasis on education. Schooling is free and compulsory for all children between the ages of 6 and 16. Schools of higher education include Gulf Polytechnic and the University College of Arts, Science, and Education. These are being combined to form a National University of Bahrain. A Gulf University also is being built.

Revenue from oil provides Bahrainis with a number of social welfare programs. These include free medical and hospital care and low-cost housing.

▶THE LAND

Bahrain is made up of about 33 islands, islets, and sandbars, most of them uninhabited. The largest island is Bahrain, from which the country takes its name. Other important islands include Muharraq, Sitra, Umm Nasan (Umm Na'san) and Hawar, which lies near Qatar. The land is mainly flat desert, with the only fertile area in the north. The highest elevation, 137 meters (450 feet), is at Jabal Dukhan on Bahrain

Island. Most of Bahrain Island is barren. However, a narrow strip of land in the north, watered by springs and wells, can be cultivated. The main crops grown here are dates, vegetables, and alfalfa, used to feed livestock. The waters of the Persian Gulf have abundant fish and are one of the world's richest sources of natural pearls.

Bahrain's climate is extremely hot and humid in summer. Winters are relatively cool. Rainfall is slight, averaging less than 100 millimeters (4 inches) a year.

▸ **THE ECONOMY**

Most of Bahrain's income is derived from oil. Bahrain had the first oil refinery in the Middle East and refines not only its own crude oil but also oil from nearby Saudi Arabia. Before oil was discovered in 1932, Bahrain depended on commerce and trade, agriculture, fishing, pearling, and boat building. The development in Japan of cultured, or artificially induced, pearls led to the decline of Bahrain's industry. Shrimp abound in the gulf. Harvesting and freezing them for export is an important part of the fishing industry.

Oil experts predict that Bahrain's deposits of oil, never very large to begin with, will eventually be exhausted. To help diversify the economy, the government has encouraged foreign investment.

Bahrain is becoming a major transportation and commercial center for the Persian

Gulf. A new aluminum smelting plant and other industrial plants have been constructed. Port and storage facilities and ship repair yards are being enlarged at Mina Sulman, southeast of Manama. The Bahrain airport handles the largest planes. Engineering and international banking are developing rapidly.

▸ **HISTORY AND GOVERNMENT**

Bahrain's history goes back to very ancient times. In the northern part of Bahrain Island are many thousands of burial mounds, some extremely large, which indicate that people lived here perhaps as long ago as 3000 B.C. The Sumerians had contacts with ancient Bahrain. Later the Greeks and Romans visited the islands.

Bahrain was colonized by the Portuguese in the 1500's and then fell under the rule of the Persians. In the 1700's the al-Khalifa family, who came from the Arabian mainland, became the ruling sheikhs of Bahrain and for a time exercised control over neighboring Qatar. Their descendants rule as emirs, or princes, in Bahrain today.

Early in the 1800's, Bahrain came under British influence. Several treaties were negotiated with Britain that were similar to the treaties Britain had signed with other gulf states. In return for British protection, Bahrain agreed, among other things, not to engage in slavery or piracy. Bahrain remained a British protectorate until 1971, when it gained complete independence.

Bahrain is ruled by an emir, who is the head of state and governs through an appointed prime minister and cabinet. A legislature, the National Assembly, was dissolved by the emir in 1975.

In 1986, Bahrain completed a 25-kilometer (15½-mile)-long causeway, linking Bahrain Island with its neighbor Saudi Arabia. Bahrain was a member of the allied coalition against Iraq in the 1991 Persian Gulf War. Sheik Isa bin Salman al-Khalifa, who had been emir since 1961, died suddenly in 1999. He was succeeded by his eldest son, Hamad bin Isa al-Khalifa.

Reviewed by MAJID KHADDURI
Director, Center for Middle East Studies
Johns Hopkins University

BAKER, JOSEPHINE. See MISSOURI (Famous People).

BAKING. See BREAD AND BAKING.

FACTS and figures

STATE OF BAHRAIN is the official name of the country.

LOCATION: Persian Gulf near Saudi Arabia.

AREA: 240 sq mi (622 km²).

POPULATION: 700,000 (estimate).

CAPITAL AND LARGEST CITY: Manama.

MAJOR LANGUAGE: Arabic.

MAJOR RELIGIOUS GROUP: Muslim.

GOVERNMENT: Emirate. **Head of state**—emir. **Head of government**—prime minister (appointed by the emir). **Legislature**—Consultative Council (appointed).

CHIEF PRODUCTS: Oil, shellfish, fish, dates, refined aluminum.

MONETARY UNIT: Dinar (1 dinar = 1,000 fils).

Balboa was the first European to sight the Pacific Ocean. Stepping into its waters, he claimed the great ocean and all the land it touched for Spain in 1513.

BALBOA, VASCO NÚÑEZ DE (1475–1519)

Vasco Núñez de Balboa, a Spanish explorer and adventurer, was the first European to see the Pacific Ocean.

Balboa was born at Jerez de los Caballeros, Spain, in 1475. Little is known about his early life until about 1500, when he joined an expedition to seek his fortune in America. Finding no gold, he settled as a farmer on the island of Hispaniola (now Haiti and the Dominican Republic). Balboa soon found himself deeply in debt. To escape his creditors, he hid in a large barrel and was carried on board a ship bound for the settlement of San Sebastián, in Colombia.

When the ship was safely at sea, Balboa came out of hiding. The commander of the expedition, Martín Fernández de Enciso, was furious at the stowaway and threatened to abandon him on a desert island. However,

Enciso allowed him to remain after Balboa convinced the crew that he would be valuable to them as a soldier.

This proved to be true, for when the expedition reached San Sebastián, they found it in ruins. Balboa took charge and led the survivors to Panama. There they started a new colony, which he called Darien.

But soon a quarrel broke out between Balboa and Enciso over who should be in command. Enciso was overthrown and sent back to Spain, and Balboa became governor of the new colony.

Balboa then set out to explore the surrounding country, hoping to find gold. His generosity won him the friendship of the Indians, who ordinarily distrusted and fought the Spaniards. The Indians had little use for gold. But seeing that Balboa prized it so highly, they told him of a marvelous land to the south where people ate from golden plates and drank from golden cups. They also said that just beyond the mountains lay a great sea. Balboa did not know that only a narrow strip of land (the Isthmus of Panama) lay between the Atlantic and Pacific oceans. He thought that this sea might be the route to Cathay (China), which Columbus had sought in vain.

Meanwhile, Enciso had returned to Spain and angrily complained about Balboa to King Ferdinand. Anxious to regain the King's favor, Balboa set out to discover the great sea the Indians had described. With 190 Spaniards and 1,000 Indians he cut his way across the jungle-covered mountains of Panama. On September 25, 1513, Balboa left his companions and climbed the last mountain peak by himself. From its summit he saw the gleaming Pacific Ocean stretching as far as the eye could see. He named it the South Sea and claimed it and all the land it touched for the King of Spain.

Balboa then planned to explore Peru—the land of gold. Before he could carry out his plans, a new governor, Pedrarias Dávila, arrived from Spain. Pedrarias, jealous of Balboa, had him arrested on a false charge of treason. And in 1519, not far from the colony he had founded and the ocean he had discovered, Balboa was executed.

Reviewed by KENNETH S. COOPER
Author, *World Ways*

BALDWIN, JAMES (1924–1987)

James Baldwin was a black American novelist, playwright, and essayist. He was a leading literary voice in the civil rights movement of the 1950's and 1960's.

Baldwin was born in New York City on August 2, 1924, the oldest of nine children. His father, a Baptist preacher, was a violent man who died when James was a teenager. A gifted student, James read widely and displayed a talent for writing. By his early twenties, he was writing essays and reviews for *The Nation* and other respected periodicals.

Baldwin's first novel, *Go Tell It on the Mountain* (1953), is perhaps his best. The partly autobiographical work tells of a black teenager and his struggles with a tyrannical stepfather at home and with racial injustice in the outside world. Baldwin continued to explore racial conflict in his later works, including the novels *Another Country* (1962), *Tell Me How Long the Train's Been Gone* (1968), and *Just Above My Head* (1979), and the play *Blues for Mister Charlie* (1964).

Noted writer James Baldwin explored the experiences of black Americans.

Baldwin's essays, which reached a wide audience, were highly acclaimed for their insights into black experience in a white-dominated society. His most important essay collections were *Notes of a Native Son* (1955), *Nobody Knows My Name* (1961), and *The Fire Next Time* (1963). *The Evidence of Things Not Seen* (1985) is an essay on the murders of 28 black children in Atlanta in 1980 and 1981.

After 1948, Baldwin lived mainly in France, returning to the United States to teach and lecture. He died in St. Paul de Vence on December 1, 1987.

Reviewed by PETER CONN
Author, *Literature in America: An Illustrated History*

BALDWIN, MATTHIAS WILLIAM. See RAILROADS (Profiles).

BALFOUR, ARTHUR JAMES (1848–1930)

Arthur James Balfour is considered one of the most brilliant and intellectual of all the British prime ministers. A member of Parliament (MP) for 48 years, he served as Conservative prime minister from 1902 to 1905.

Born on July 25, 1848, at Whittingehame in the Scottish border country, Balfour was 6 when his father died. He was greatly influenced by his mother, whose brother, the Marquess of Salisbury, would later serve four terms as prime minister.

At Cambridge University it was thought that Balfour would become a philosopher. In 1874, however, he chose to enter politics. At first he seemed to be little more than a lightweight, witty conversationalist, whose career advanced in his uncle's shadow. But he rapidly won a reputation for firmness and fairness in his political dealings.

As government leader in the House of Commons (1891–92 and 1895–1902), Balfour became especially skillful in debate. He was the natural choice to succeed Salisbury as Conservative prime minister in July 1902.

Balfour's government achieved school reforms brought about by the Education Act of 1902, but little else. Disputes over tariff reform caused the Conservatives to lose the 1906 general election to the Liberals. Despite criticism, Balfour continued to lead his party in opposition until 1911.

The Balfour Declaration

During World War I, Balfour returned to government office as foreign secretary (1916–19). His most famous achievement was to issue the Balfour Declaration (1917), a statement pledging British support for the establishment of a Jewish homeland in Palestine following the war (providing the non-Jewish communities already living there would be safeguarded). Balfour also helped draw up the Treaty of Versailles (1919) and other postwar settlements. Later, as Earl Balfour, he served in Stanley Baldwin's cabinet (1925–29).

ALAN PALMER
Author, *The Penguin Dictionary of Modern History*

BALKANS

The Balkans are a region of southeastern Europe of great strategic and historical importance. Physically, the region consists of a peninsula jutting southward into the Mediterranean Sea. The peninsula is bounded on the west and southeast by the Adriatic, Ionian, and Aegean seas (arms of the Mediterranean) and on the east by the Black Sea. Politically, the Balkans usually include the countries of Albania, Bulgaria, Greece, Romania, Yugoslavia (now consisting of Serbia and Montenegro), and the new nations—formerly part of Yugoslavia—of Bosnia and Herzegovina, Croatia, Macedonia, and Slovenia.

THE BALKANS

The Land. The word *balkan* is of Turkish origin and means "wooded mountain range." The name is apt, for rugged mountains are the dominant feature of the Balkan landscape. There are several great mountain chains. The Carpathians in Romania extend, as the Balkan Mountains, into Bulgaria. The Dinaric Alps run parallel to the Adriatic coast in Yugoslavia and Albania and continue, as the Pindus Mountains, into Greece. The Rhodope range forms the boundary between Bulgaria and Greece.

The mountains isolated the different peoples of the region and tended to create a number of small states, which were often in conflict with one another. At the same time, certain valleys and rivers, particularly the Danube, the region's chief river, provided access for foreign invaders. The mountainous terrain also limited the amount of land that could be used for farming, although the valleys can be fertile.

The climate ranges from the continental, with long, cold winters and relatively short summers, to the Mediterranean, with mild winters and long, hot summers.

The People. The Balkan Peninsula is home to varied peoples. The majority are Slavs, the descendants of South Slavic peoples who arrived in the region in the A.D. 500's and 600's. Greeks, Romanians, Albanians, and Magyars (Hungarians) are the main non-Slavic groups, and there are Turkish, German, Macedonian, and other minorities.

The six major languages of the region are Serbo-Croatian, Slovenian (both spoken chiefly in Yugoslavia), Albanian, Bulgarian, Greek, and Romanian. Serbo-Croatian, Slovenian, and Bulgarian are Slavic languages.

Romanian is a Romance language, derived from Latin. It is a legacy of the time when Romania was a Roman colony.

Most Balkan peoples traditionally have belonged to the Roman Catholic or Eastern Orthodox churches. There is a considerable Muslim population as well, a reminder that the region was long ruled by the Ottoman Turks.

Early History. The first great civilization in the region was that of ancient Greece, followed, in the 300's B.C., by the short-lived empire of Alexander the Great. The Balkans became part of the Roman Empire in the A.D. 100's and 200's. With the division of the Roman world in 395, the region came under the rule of the Eastern Roman, or Byzantine, Empire, centered in Constantinople (modern Istanbul).

The arrival of the Slavs and the decline of Byzantine power permitted the development of distinct Balkan nationalities, the forerunners of today's Balkan states. There were, at different periods, large Bulgarian and Serb empires. Between the late 1300's and the mid-1500's, the region was conquered by the Ottoman Turks. As Ottoman power itself began to wane in the late 1600's, parts of the Balkans fell to an expanding Austria.

The Struggle for Independence. The struggle for Balkan independence began in earnest in the early 1800's, with the rise of Serbia and the liberation of Greece from Turkish rule. Over the next century, Montenegro, Bulgaria, and Romania won independence. In 1912 an alliance of Serbia, Bulgaria, Greece, and Montenegro defeated Turkey in the First Balkan War. As a result, Albania gained its independence and Turkey was forced to give up almost all of its remaining European lands. Disputes over territorial claims, however, led to the Second Balkan War in 1913, in which Bulgaria was defeated by its former allies, joined by Turkey.

The Modern Balkans. Meanwhile, the great European powers, particularly Britain, France, Austria-Hungary, and Russia, had also become entangled in Balkan affairs. World War I (1914–18) arose out of a Balkan issue—the ambition of Serbia to take Bosnia and Herzegovina from Austria-Hungary. The war brought about the destruction of the Austro-Hungarian empire. As a result a new nation, Yugoslavia, was formed from Serbia, Bosnia and Herzegovina, Montenegro, and other states, and the present-day Balkan states came into being. The war also led to the final collapse of the old Ottoman Empire.

The Balkans fell under Nazi German domination between 1941 and 1945, during World War II. After the war, a Communist political system was imposed on the Balkan countries, except for Greece. As Communism crumbled in the late 1980's and early 1990's, the regimes were replaced by popularly elected governments. In Yugoslavia the changeover led to the breakup of the country and to civil war. The fighting was most severe among Serbs, Croats, and Muslims in Bosnia and Herzegovina and between Serbs and ethnic Albanians in the Yugoslav province of Kosovo.

ARTHUR CAMPBELL TURNER
University of California, Riverside

See also articles on individual countries.

BALL

All over the world, people play ball and have done so since prehistoric times. Some early people wove reeds into rounded shapes. Others used leather stuffed with feathers for ball playing. Later, Greeks and Romans used an air-filled leather ball called a *follis* in games of catch. They also inflated balls of larger sizes, with which they played a kind of soccer and other kicking games.

Balls have been made from many materials. Native Americans used balls made of deer hide, while across the world from them, Japanese children played with balls of tightly wadded tissue paper wrapped with string. It is said that Columbus found the Indians of Central America playing with solid, black balls made of vegetable gum and took some of these rubber balls back to Europe.

We learn from the history of people and their folklore that some of our modern ball games started as religious and magical ceremonies. The Egyptians seem to have been among the first people to have ceremonial ball games. Each spring two large groups of people, each representing one of their gods, acted out a contest that used a round, wooden ball and crooked sticks. The object was to drive the ball through the opposing goal. The side that knocked the ball past the defenders won.

Today a ball and stick are used in playing such games as polo, field hockey, and lacrosse. Each team tries to score while keeping the other side from scoring goals.

At first, ball games were played mainly to develop skill in tossing and catching. Over time, many different sticks, bats, and rackets were added to strike or otherwise control the motion of the ball, and many special games were invented. Today there are more than thirty major sports in which a ball is the key object used in the game. These range from the oval football to the tiny table-tennis ball.

The ball has played a part in many other customs unrelated to sports. The ballot, used in voting, is named after the Italian *ballotta* ("little ball"), from the ancient Greek custom of casting votes with small balls. Often, white and black balls were used—white to vote yes and black to vote no. The word "blackball," meaning to exclude someone from membership by casting a negative vote, goes back to this practice.

The ball belongs to everyone, so it is difficult to find out who invented it or from what country it first started to roll to the four corners of the world.

JACQUE HETRICK
Spalding

BALL, LUCILLE. See NEW YORK (Famous People).

BALLADS

The ballad is a type of folk song that tells a story using simple words and a simple melody. The words are often in the form of a dialogue between two people.

The ballad developed in Europe during the Middle Ages. The name comes from the Latin word *ballare* ("to dance"). Originally ballads were dancing songs, but by the 1200's they had become solo songs. Today they may or may not be danced or performed with an instrumental accompaniment, but they always emphasize the story and are sung in a way that stresses the words over the melody. Ballad melodies are, nevertheless, beautiful and varied. They range from those based on Gregorian chants in Western Europe to Slavic types in Eastern Europe.

Scholars once believed that the ballad dated back to primitive times and was composed by groups of people. Since then, experts have decided that it has far more recent and sophisticated beginnings. Ballads were composed by individuals with some artistic background and training. As the songs were passed from singer to singer and from generation to generation, they were varied, shaped, and recreated to reflect the concerns, beliefs, and tastes of the time.

The ballads sung in America can be divided into three groups: traditional British ballads, later products of British city presses, and native American narrative songs.

Traditional ballads were first created in Great Britain six or seven centuries ago. Passed on by word of mouth, they usually rhyme and are divided into stanzas. The best ones are strikingly beautiful and moving. The traditional ballads are sometimes called Child ballads, named after Professor Francis James Child, who collected 305 of them in his classic five-volume book, *The English and Scottish Popular Ballads* (1882–98). "Lord Randal," "Sir Patrick Spens," "Barbara Allen," and "The Twa Corbies" are some well-known Child ballads.

Ballads from the British presses of the 1600's to the 1800's are known as broadside ballads. Many were printed on large sheets of paper called broadsides and were sold for a penny. Others were printed in small books called chapbooks. These songs usually recounted tales of mistaken identity, disguised lovers, or cruel crimes. Often the broadsides were based on traditional ballads. They were performed and sold by professional singers on city streets and at country fairs.

Using these British songs as models, Americans composed ballads about outlaws like Jesse James and Billy the Kid, folk heroes like John Henry, and tragic young women like Young Charlotte and Naomi Wise. Sometimes these songs are American versions of British stories.

English-speaking countries are not the only ones with highly developed ballad traditions. Scandinavia has a large stock of ballads, many of which are variants of well-known British and American songs. In countries that made up the former Yugoslavia, the ballad is an important form of literature, preserving many legends. The ballads of Bulgaria and Ukraine are also outstanding.

French and Italian ballads often stress emotion and melody instead of story. Ballads are less common in Germany and the Low Countries; Germany, however, has many ballad-like pieces based on political and religious themes.

Spain's ballads, called *romances*, are frequently semihistorical, focusing more on personality than on factual details. Many of them consist of groups of songs on a single theme.

Russian *byliny* are narrative songs, like British ballads. They usually deal with the exploits of fabulous heroes. *Byliny* do not rhyme and are not divided into stanzas.

Traditional ballads continue to survive from ages past. The old songs are reshaped and new songs are created from the older models. These songs spread to more distant areas, where they continue to undergo change. Thus the ballads that people sing are a good indication of their present concerns, beliefs, and musical tastes.

TRISTRAM P. COFFIN
American Folklore Society
Revised by MELVIN BERGER
Author, *The Story of Folk Music*

See also FOLK MUSIC.

Rudolf Nureyev and Margot Fonteyn in *Romeo and Juliet*, based on the play by Shakespeare.

BALLET

A ballet is theatrical entertainment combining dance with other art forms, usually stage design and music. It may tell a story or merely depict an idea or mood. Ballet is a French word that comes from the Italian *ballo,* "a dance."

The exercises, or techniques, of ballet are designed to display the human body in the most elegant and harmonious way possible. Ballet technique is strict, and the training is strenuous. But the result on stage is natural and beautiful.

Ballet is nearly 500 years old. Yet it is very young compared with dance itself, which began with primitive people. Ballet began in Italy about the time of Columbus' voyages to America. It was quite different then from what it is today. At that time ballet was a court entertainment for the amusement of the nobility at lavish balls and banquets. Dancing, music, pantomime (acting without words), poetry, and drama were combined. The first ballet dancers were the royalty and nobles of the court, since there were no professional dancers. The steps were modeled on the elegant but rather simple social dances of the day.

Ballet as we know it is the product of many countries. The French organized the technique and gave it liveliness. The Russians added strength and passion. The English gave it delicacy and tenderness. The Americans gave it speed and variety.

▶ BALLET IN FRANCE

Queen Catherine de Médicis of France was familiar with the elaborate dance productions of Italy, her native land. In 1581, she ordered a grand entertainment—a ballet—to celebrate a royal wedding. The result was most spectacular. Thousands of people witnessed its lavish blending of dance, dramatic scenes, music, and complex scenery. Hundreds of dancers, singers, and actors took part, portraying the goddess Circe and all of her friends and enemies. Huge machines and stage effects were moved about the room so that the audience, seated on three sides, could see them.

All this was the work of an Italian musician best known by his French name, Balthasar de Beaujoyeulx. He was probably the first choreographer, or maker of dances, as we know the word today. He called his work *Le Ballet Comique de la Reine* ("The Queen's Comic Ballet"). Ever since then, performances of this kind have been called ballets.

Catherine's grandson, Louis XIV, loved to dance. He received lessons daily. At the age of 13, he danced in the *Ballet de Cassandre.*

1st position   2nd position   3rd position

The ballets in King Louis' time were formal and quite solemn. Usually they dealt with mythology or history. For a while only members of the court danced in them, but the King soon tired of their lack of skill. He had already brought together professional writers like Molière, Philippe Quinault, and Isaac de Benserade; the composer Jean-Baptiste Lully; and the choreographer Pierre Beauchamp. To improve the dancing, King Louis organized the Royal Academy of Dance in 1661. This academy was the beginning of the Paris Opera Ballet and today's Paris Opera Ballet School.

By 1681, France had its first prima ballerina, the leading female dancer in a ballet company. She was Mademoiselle Lafontaine. Pictures of the time show her to be lovely and very dignified in her long, stiff gown, her high-heeled slippers, and her plumed headdress. She danced that year in *Le Triomphe de l'Amour* (''The Triumph of Love''), with choreography by Beauchamp and music by Lully. Mademoiselle Lafontaine was the first of a series of professional ballet dancers. Each of these experts brought something new to the art of ballet.

In a children's ballet class, a teacher helps a young student position his body correctly. The long wooden railing, called a barre, helps dancers keep their balance while practicing.

4th position   5th position

Several names stand out in the history of ballet in the 1700's. Marie Camargo boldly shortened the ballet costume to mid-calf. She also removed the heels from her slippers. Thus she could move more quickly and perform small, intricate steps like the *entrechat-quatre*, a double crossing of the feet in midair. Gaetan Vestris was the first male dancer to show in his *jetés* (leaps) and *tours en l'air* (turns in the air) that men could develop a ballet style very different from that of women. Danish and Russian dancers later stressed this difference even more.

But no matter how versatile they are, dancers depend on the imagination of choreographers. The great choreographer Jean Georges Noverre looked at the productions around him and saw that ballet was deteriorating into a mere display of technique. He believed that ballet should express strong emotions. After his reforms, ballet became more like drama. Noverre's ballets are not danced today. But his book, *Letters on Dancing and Ballets*, is still widely read by choreographers.

Marie Taglioni (1804–84)

All of us have at some time wished to fly. The female dancers of the early 1800's felt that way, too. As imaginary creatures like ondines (water sprites) or sylphides (tree sprites), they were actually attached to wires so that they could soar above the stage. More often they gave the illusion of lightness by rising to the very tips of their toes. Pictures of Marie Taglioni, one of the foremost dancers of the time, show her this way.

In 1832, Taglioni's father, Filippo Taglioni, created a ballet especially for her. Called *La Sylphide,* it was about a mysterious' forest creature so playful and so touching that she lured a young Scot, James, away from his fiancée on his wedding day. Poets and composers of this period, known as the romantic age, loved sadness. In *La Sylphide,* as in most romantic ballets, the end was tragic. The sylphide died, leaving James alone in the forest to mourn her.

Carlotta Grisi (1819–99)

While Taglioni was touring in Russia, an Italian dancer, Carlotta Grisi, arrived at the Paris Opera. Jules Perrot, a celebrated dancer, fell in love with her, as did the poet Théophile Gautier. Gautier wrote a ballet story for her. It was *Giselle* (1841), the tragedy of a gentle peasant girl who loved to dance. Jean Coralli was the choreographer, but *Giselle's* variations (special solos) were made by Perrot.

A scene from *La Sylphide,* a romantic 19th-century ballet, is performed by members of the American Ballet Theatre.

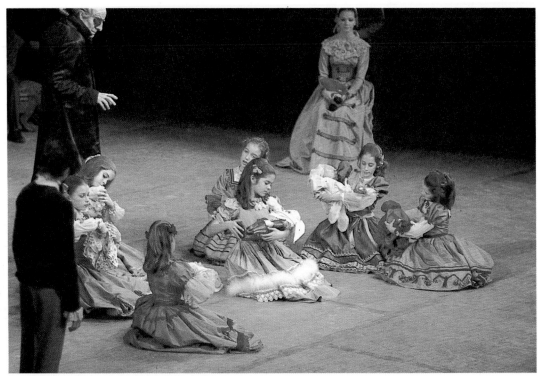

A scene from *The Nutcracker*, which is often danced during the Christmas season.

Giselle is even more tragic than *La Sylphide* because Giselle is a real girl and not a sprite. She is wooed by the handsome Albrecht. She falls deeply in love with him, not knowing that he is a count in disguise and can never marry her. To make matters worse, he is already engaged to the Countess Bathilde. When Giselle learns of the betrayal, she goes insane and dies. Later, she rises from her tomb to dance with the remorseful Albrecht and to protect him from being destroyed by the Wilis, spirits of young girls who died before marriage.

▶**RUSSIAN BALLET**

If you were to ask a friend to name two favorite ballets, the answers might be *Swan Lake* and *The Sleeping Beauty* or *Scheherazade* and *Petrouchka*. These—and many more—came from Marius Petipa and Michel Fokine, two Russian choreographers whose ballets are now performed all over the world.

Marius Petipa (1819–1910)

Petipa, born in France, won fame as a choreographer in St. Petersburg. In 1862 he devised a three-act spectacle called *The Pha-*

raoh's Daughter*. Like his later ballets, it took all evening to perform and had a complicated plot. This gave plenty of opportunity for a stilted kind of mime that described what was going on but told the audience very little about the person doing the mime. There were also interludes of beautiful pure dance, usually solos, called variations. They had little or nothing to do with the story. But they were beautifully made and were perfectly suited to the music.

For his most celebrated ballets, Petipa was fortunate to have the composer Peter Ilyich Tchaikovsky. His music was so inspired and so perfectly made that it could stand on its own when played separately from the ballets. The grandest collaborations of Petipa and Tchaikovsky were *The Sleeping Beauty* (1890) and *Swan Lake* (1895). In *Swan Lake*, Petipa shared the choreography with his assistant, Lev Ivanov. This ballet returned to a theme very popular during the romantic period—that of a young prince falling in love with a bewitched creature. And like the romantic ballets, *Swan Lake* ends in death. Two of its variations, the *White Swan Pas de Deux* and the *Black Swan Pas de Deux,* are very often danced separately from the ballet. (A pas de deux is a dance for two people.)

Petipa planned the action of *The Nutcracker* (1892) and gave complete musical instructions to Tchaikovsky. But the choreographer fell ill, and Ivanov actually staged the ballet. It has become a favorite for the Christmas season, and children often have starring roles.

When Petipa planned a new ballet, he did not care whether the costumes and sets were suited to the period and place of the story. They were done according to a formula. This bothered Michel Fokine, who was a student at the Imperial School of Ballet when Petipa was director of its company.

Michel Fokine (1880–1942)

Many of the students at the Imperial School of Ballet were satisfied merely to learn technique and dance in Petipa's ballets. But Fokine had a lively, curious mind. He studied history and painting and spent hours in museums.

One day Fokine wrote a letter to the director of the school and said that he would like to make a new kind of ballet. The mime and the variations would not be separate. They would be part of the action. The style of movement and the style of the costumes and sets would be suited to the period of the ballet. And the stories of the ballets would be simple and believable.

Fokine was not allowed to go ahead, so he began to work on his own. His smallest dance, a five-minute solo called *The Dying Swan* (1905), became his best known. It was made for his classmate Anna Pavlova to dance at a charity ball. To this day it is associated with her.

Then, to show that he knew his craft and that he knew the styles of different periods, Fokine created a ballet in the romantic style, *Les Sylphides.* He borrowed the atmosphere but not the story of *La Sylphide.* The music was a series of piano pieces by Frédéric Chopin. The delicacy of this ballet and the ease with which the movement flows along with the music have made it Fokine's best-known and most performed ballet.

Fokine was staging ballets outside of the Imperial Ballet in Russia. But his first important opportunities came when Sergei Diaghilev formed his Ballets Russes in Paris.

Sergei Diaghilev (1872–1929)

In St. Petersburg, the home of the Imperial Ballet, a group of young authors, painters, and composers often met in the evenings to talk about their work. They started a magazine called *The World of Art,* with Sergei Diaghilev as its editor.

Diaghilev could not write or paint or compose. But he had exquisite taste, and he knew how to bring the right people together to make interesting things happen. He arranged an exhibit of Russian painting in Paris in 1906, and he produced the opera *Boris Godunov* in Paris in 1908. In 1909 he put together his own ballet company. He turned to Fokine as his chief choreographer, and he gave Fokine four of the world's greatest dancers as the principals for his ballets. They were Anna Pavlova, Tamara Karsavina, Vaslav Nijinsky, and Adolph Bolm.

Given this freedom, Fokine's imagination began to soar. In quick succession he turned out the wild *Polovtsian Dances* from the opera *Prince Igor;* the playful *Carnaval;* the lush *Scheherazade,* with its brilliant leaping dance for Nijinsky as the Golden Slave; the myste-

Anna Pavlova in a 1910 production of *The Dying Swan,* the role she made famous.

Marina Kondratieva and Maris Lieta in the Bolshoi Ballet's production of *Spring Water*.

rious Russian fairy tale *Firebird;* and *Petrouchka,* a touching story of puppets brought to life. The last two ballets introduced a new ballet composer, Igor Stravinsky.

Diaghilev was restless. One choreographer was not enough for him. He was constantly searching for new talents in the different arts, and he combined them imaginatively. For example, the choreographer Léonide Massine worked with the painter Pablo Picasso and the composer Manuel de Falla for *The Three-Cornered Hat*. The choreographer George Balanchine worked with the painter Georges Rouault and the composer Sergei Prokofiev for *The Prodigal Son*. Nijinsky, as choreographer, came together with the painter Nicholas Roerich and the composer Igor Stravinsky for *The Rite of Spring*.

Other ballets that were made famous by the Ballets Russes include Massine's *La Boutique Fantastique* and Balanchine's *Rossignol*, in which 12-year-old Alicia Markova danced the nightingale.

Diaghilev's company was disbanded after his death, but the ballets he produced are still presented. Russian dancers have continued to play an important part in ballet. Some, such as Vladimir Vasiliev, Yekaterina Maximova, Galina Ulanova, and Maya Plisetskaya, danced with the Bolshoi Ballet, Russia's leading company. Others, such as Rudolf Nureyev, Natalia Makarova, Aleksandr Godunov, and Mikhail Baryshnikov, left to live and work in other countries.

▶ **BALLET IN ENGLAND**

When the Diaghilev company was disbanded, several of its dancers settled in London, where the company had often toured. Two of them, the Irish-born Dame Ninette de Valois and the Polish-born Dame Marie Rambert, became the pillars of British ballet.

Like Diaghilev, Marie Rambert liked to take chances on young and unknown artists. Thus she gave a first start to two of England's finest 20th-century choreographers, Sir Frederick

Ashton and Antony Tudor. Their first ballets appeared in Rambert's tiny Mercury Theatre.

Ninette de Valois was an organizer. She wanted a national ballet company and would settle for nothing less. In 1933 she became head of the Vic-Wells Ballet. Alicia Markova was its ballerina. The company grew in size and support to become the Sadler's Wells Ballet. For this company, De Valois gambled on an unknown 16-year-old dancer, who made her debut as the Swan Queen in *Swan Lake.* She was Margot Fonteyn, who later became one of the world's best-loved dancers. Finally, in 1957, De Valois saw her dream come true. As Dame Ninette, she was artistic director of Britain's Royal Ballet.

In the meantime, she had engaged Frederick Ashton as choreographer for the company. His ballets—whether witty, as in *A Wedding Bouquet,* or serious, as in *Ondine*—showed a refined, poetic style and respect for the classical tradition. They provided Fonteyn with some of her finest roles. Ashton's style is shown at its best in two works produced after his retirement as the company's artistic director in 1970. They were *Enigma Variations,* created

to music by Edward Elgar, and *A Month in the Country*. In these ballets, every detail of movement was not only precisely made but seemed perfectly suited to the person performing it.

▶ DANISH BALLET

In the 1950's, the Royal Danish Ballet began to travel outside Denmark. It had a tremendous impact. The Danes gave special attention to the acting parts of ballets. In the hands of artists such as Niels Bjorn Larssen and Gerda Karstens, standard roles came alive in a new way.

The Danes had an interesting tradition from the 1800's. It came from the teaching and choreography of August Bournonville, which the Danes had lovingly preserved. The Bournonville style stressed the differences between men and women dancers. It featured strong movements and brilliant leaps for the men and intricate *terre-à-terre* (close to the ground) steps for the women. Because he traveled much during his career, Bournonville created ballets in a variety of styles. Many are performed today, among them *Napoli, Far from Denmark, Flower Festival at Genzano,* and *La Ventana.*

La Fille Mal Gardée (The Unchaperoned Girl) is a comic ballet with a happy ending.

George Balanchine's ballet *Jewels* is in three parts: *Emeralds*, *Rubies*, and *Diamonds*.

Some present-day Danish dancers combine the Bournonville style with the stronger Russian style. They have made their mark on companies in other parts of the world where they have gone to live and work. Among them are Toni Lander, Erik Bruhn, Peter Martins, Helgi Tomasson, and Peter Schaufuss.

▶ **BALLET IN CANADA**

The Royal Winnipeg Ballet is Canada's oldest company. It began as the Winnipeg Ballet Club in 1938 and became a fully professional company in 1949. Today it is famous for performing the works of 20th century choreographers such as Gweneth Lloyd, Arnold Spohr, Brian MacDonald, and Michel Conte.

The National Ballet of Canada, based in Toronto, was established in 1951. The company is noted for its performances of original works by Grant Strate and David Adams. Les Grands Ballets Canadiens began in Montreal in 1952 as a television troupe. The company performs classics and original works.

▶ **BALLET IN THE UNITED STATES**

In the 1800's, the United States produced such fine ballet dancers as George Washington Smith, Mary Ann Lee, and Augusta Maywood. But it was not until the 1900's that ballet began to find a wide and enthusiastic public. It all began with the tours of Anna Pavlova between 1910 and 1930. Pavlova was tireless. She went to every community that would have her. She did not encourage daring choreography. The members of her company were often modestly trained young dancers acquired along the way. But to many people of the United States, Pavlova was ballet.

Two years after Pavlova's death in 1931, the Ballet Russe de Monte Carlo arrived in the United States. Some of its dancers were from Diaghilev's company. Others were new. Audiences fell in love with stars such as Alexandra Danilova, Natalie Krassovska, Mia Slavenska, Irina Baronova, Tatiana Riabouchinska, Tamara Toumanova, and Igor Youskevitch.

At first the Ballet Russe depended on Russian choreographers such as Léonide Massine, David Lichine, and Michel Fokine. Gradually it turned to Americans such as Agnes de Mille, whose *Rodeo* (1942) gave an image of cowboys and ranchers that audiences still enjoy when it is performed today.

Dancers and choreographers of the United States soon began to found their own companies. Lincoln Kirstein, a wealthy young Harvard graduate with a strong writing talent, lured former Diaghilev choreographer George Balanchine to New York. The promises were a company of his own with a school behind it to train the dancers. It took time. Their modest company first performed in 1933. The company grew and in 1948 became the New York City Ballet.

The repertory of the New York City Ballet is extremely varied. Yet it is dominated by Balanchine and by the United States choreographer Jerome Robbins, who has blended jazz and modern dance with more traditional elements in ballets such as *Fancy Free*. Outstanding artists such as Maria Tallchief, Melissa Hayden, Suzanne Farrell, Jacques D'Amboise, Edward Villella, and Mikhail Baryshnikov have danced with the company.

In 1940 another major company, Ballet Theatre (later called the American Ballet Theatre), was created. It has developed the careers of many choreographers, among them Agnes de Mille, Jerome Robbins, and Eliot Feld. While developing new talents, it has kept the classics alive. Antony Tudor, the British choreographer who began his career with Marie

Two great stars of ballet, Mikhail Baryshnikov and Natalia Makarova, in *The Sleeping Beauty*.

Rambert in London, was associated with the company from its earliest days.

In the United States, the American Ballet Theatre and the New York City Ballet are the equivalent of the great national companies of Europe and the former Soviet Union. But smaller companies contribute to dance in the United States. Among them are the Dance Theater of Harlem, a classically oriented company of black dancers, and the Joffrey Ballet. The Joffrey Ballet has presented the works of its resident choreographer, Gerald Arpino. It has also staged 20th-century classics such as Kurt Jooss's *Green Table* and modern works such as José Limón's *The Moor's Pavane*.

While these companies have made New York City a world center of dance, the entire country has come alive with companies such as the Boston Ballet, the Pennsylvania Ballet, the Houston Ballet, and the Minnesota Dance Theatre. These and many more hold the key to the future of ballet in the United States.

DORIS HERING
Critic-at-large, *Dance Magazine*

See also DANCE.

BALLOONS, RESEARCH. See BALLOONS AND BALLOONING.

Karen Brown and Keith Saunders of the Dance Theater of Harlem, in *Allegro Brillante* by George Balanchine.

BALLOONS AND BALLOONING

Have you ever wondered what it would be like to float on the wind, drifting silently above your town? You could find out—if you were a balloonist. Every flight would be an adventure because in ballooning, you must travel where the wind takes you.

Balloons are aerostats, or lighter-than-air craft. A modern balloon is a bag made of a light material such as nylon or plastic. Air is blown into the bag and is then heated by a burner. Or the bag may be filled with a gas such as helium or hydrogen. The gas or hot air causes the balloon to rise. The pilot and passengers ride in a basket or gondola suspended underneath the balloon.

Not all balloons carry passengers. Scientists launch balloons carrying instruments to study the upper atmosphere and to gather information about the weather. And balloon satellites orbit the earth. Today balloons have two main uses—as tools in research and as a means of recreation in the sport of ballooning.

▶ HISTORY

Early in the 18th century Bartholomeu de Gusmão, a Portuguese priest, developed a small hot-air balloon. But the first big balloon was built by two French brothers, Joseph Michel and Jacques Étienne Montgolfier, in 1783. They made a huge bag of paper and cloth, which they held over a fire. When they released the smoke-filled balloon, it soared into the sky.

Encouraged by their success, the Montgolfier brothers built a balloon with a basket underneath to carry passengers. In the basket they put a rooster, a duck, and a young sheep. The balloon was filled with hot air from a fire and was released. The basket, with its animal passengers, floated upward. High above the earth the warm air inside the balloon cooled off, and the balloon slowly floated to earth. Live passengers had been carried into the air and returned safely for the first time in history.

This feat inspired two men to become the first human beings to fly above the earth. They were Jean François Pilâtre de Rozier, a French physician, and François Laurent, the Marquis d'Arlandes. A huge blue and gold hot-air balloon carried them aloft over Paris on November 21, 1783.

Colorful balloons rise into the air at the beginning of a race in Iowa. Ballooning is best in open country, far from tall buildings, traffic, and high-tension wires.

Fire was always a danger at these early balloon launchings. One spark could send a balloon up in flames. But in the same year that the hot-air balloon was developed, Jacques A. C. Charles, a French scientist, invented the gas balloon. Charles built a sphere of rubberized silk and filled it with hydrogen, a gas that is lighter than air without being heated. The balloon soared into the air and landed in a field near Paris, where it was destroyed by frightened farm workers.

With the help of others, Charles later developed a balloon that could carry passengers. To rise higher, the balloonist released sand from bags tied to the side of the basket. To come down, the balloonist pulled a rope that opened a valve located at the top of the balloon. The open valve allowed hydrogen to escape, so that the balloon would slowly deflate and return to earth.

The Age of Ballooning

The popularity of the safer gas balloons soon surpassed that of the hot-air type, and a ballooning craze swept Europe. Balloonists of this period were daring souls whose exploits were memorable.

In 1785, Jean Pierre Blanchard, a French balloonist, and John Jeffries, an American, crossed the English Channel in a gas balloon. Blanchard later made the first free flight in the United States, in Philadelphia, on January 9, 1793. President George Washington was among those who watched his ascension. On this occasion, Blanchard carried the first airmail letter and made scientific observations of the effects of altitude on the human body. For example, he discovered that his heart beat more rapidly at high altitudes. And he brought bottles filled with air back to earth. When the air was studied, it was found to contain less oxygen than air near the ground.

Blanchard's wife, Madeline-Sophie, was famous for spectacular ascensions at night. In 1819 she was killed when fireworks she had carried aloft ignited her balloon.

Ballooning was furthered by several inventions. In 1797 a French balloonist, André Garnerin, astonished spectators by leaping from a balloon and floating safely to the earth. In secret, he had invented the first practical parachute. In 1839, John Wise, an American, invented the rip line. By pulling this line, a

Above: The balloon that carried two French balloonists on the first piloted flight in 1783. Below: Preparing for the first successful piloted balloon flight in the United States—in Philadelphia, 1793.

balloonist near the ground could open a large panel in the balloon and deflate it quickly in an emergency.

The jet streams—long currents of air moving at high altitudes—had not been discovered in Wise's time. But he was convinced that a balloon could cross the Atlantic Ocean by traveling on rivers of wind.

Balloons in War

Balloons became important in military operations during the U.S. Civil War (1861–65) and the Franco-Prussian War (1870–71). Balloonists were sent up in tethered balloons—balloons anchored to the ground by long lines—to observe the enemy troops and even to report descriptions of battles from an aerial position. From their high positions, they could direct cannon fire more accurately. Balloons were also used to carry messages.

During World War I (1914–18), balloons were again used for observation. In both world wars, barrage balloons were anchored by long cables along Britain's coast to block enemy aircraft. During World War II (1939–45), Japan sent balloons carrying bombs across the Pacific Ocean toward the northwestern coast of North America. But few of the balloons completed the trip, and most of those that did landed in remote areas.

Reaching for Height and Distance

Balloonists have ventured to the limits of their endurance to learn about the upper atmosphere and to discover how high and how far balloons can travel.

In 1862, James Glaisher, an English scientist, and Henry Coxwell, his balloon pilot, rose to a height of 30,000 feet (more than 9,000 meters) without oxygen. But early high-altitude research could be dangerous. At high altitudes, the air contains so little oxygen that a person can suffocate. In 1875, three French balloonists floated up in a balloon called the *Zenith*, carrying bottles of oxygen with them. But they lost consciousness at about 25,000 feet (7,500 meters), before they could use their equipment. When the *Zenith* returned to the earth, only one was alive.

In 1927, an American military balloonist, Captain Hawthorne Gray, also died during a high-altitude ascension. He lost consciousness at about 44,000 feet (13,400 meters), although he was wearing an oxygen mask. Notes made

by Gray gave valuable information about the atmosphere at high altitudes.

Auguste Piccard, a Swiss scientist and inventor, developed a way to explore the upper atmosphere safely in a balloon. He invented an airtight aluminum gondola that was round, like a ball. Inside it he put oxygen and pressure tanks. In 1931 he ascended to more than 51,000 feet (15,500 meters) and became the first person to look without a telescope into the black depths of outer space. Piccard made many other ascents into the upper atmosphere, as did his brother, Jean Piccard. They brought back information about cosmic rays and high-altitude electricity. Since then, balloons have risen higher and higher. In 1961, Malcolm Ross and Victor A. Prather, Jr., of the U.S. Navy, reached a height of over 113,500 feet (34,500 meters).

Balloonists have attempted to set records in distance as well. But the dream of crossing the Atlantic was not realized until 1978. Three U.S. balloonists—Ben Abruzzo, Maxie Anderson, and Larry Newman—made the crossing. Their helium balloon, *Double Eagle II*, traveled from Maine to France. In 1981, four balloonists crossed the Pacific. Ben Abruzzo, Larry Newman, Ron Clark, and Rocky Aoki flew the *Double Eagle V* from Japan to California, a distance of 6,000 miles (9,500 kilometers).

The first nonstop balloon flight around the world was achieved in 1999. Bertrand Piccard and Brian Jones piloted the *Breitling Orbiter 3* westward from Switzerland, landing 19 days later in the Egyptian desert.

What makes a balloon rise?

A big balloon soars up into the sky because it is filled with a gas that is lighter than air.

Air itself is made up of gases, the chief ones being oxygen and nitrogen. Certain other gases are lighter than air. One of these is helium, and that is why a balloon filled with helium rises.

Hot air will also make a balloon rise because hot air is lighter than cold air. It is lighter because as air is heated, its gas particles spread out and become less dense.

You can demonstrate with this simple experiment that air expands as it is warmed. Snap the open end of a small balloon over the top of an empty soda bottle. The balloon hangs limp. Now set the bottle in a pan of hot water. The hot water heats the bottle and warms the cold air inside it. Gradually the warm air in the bottle pushes its way into the balloon. The balloon slowly fills with air and begins to inflate.

▶ BALLOONS IN SCIENTIFIC RESEARCH

Balloons are of value in scientific research because they can go very high and stay up a relatively long time. Rockets can go higher, but they stay up only briefly and so cannot collect as much information as balloons can.

Three types of gas balloons are most commonly used in scientific research today—extensible balloons, zero-pressure balloons, and superpressure balloons. They are made of various kinds of plastic. Tethered hot-air balloons are sometimes used as observation platforms—to study the skies, for example, or to locate archeological sites.

Extensible balloons are small. As a balloon of this type rises, the gas inside it expands because the pressure of the surrounding air is less at high altitudes. When the balloon reaches a certain height, the pressure inside it causes it to burst. A parachute opens and carries the instruments back to the earth.

Zero-pressure balloons are among the largest balloons. They can carry heavy loads to high altitudes. They are only partly filled with gas when they are launched. But as they rise, the gas expands to fill the balloon. Excess gas escapes through a vent. Zero-pressure balloons usually stay aloft for several days.

Superpressure balloons can remain aloft for months. Like zero-pressure balloons, they are launched partly filled with gas. But then they are sealed, so that the expanding gas will not escape. The excess pressure that builds up as the balloon rises keeps it aloft at a constant altitude.

The instruments sent up in these balloons include devices that measure the temperature, pressure, humidity, and chemical composition of the air. The information they provide is used in studying the atmosphere and the weather. Communications equipment is also sent aloft in balloons.

Radiation—in the form of visible light, X rays, gamma rays, cosmic rays, or infrared or ultraviolet radiation—gives us information about space. But the earth's atmosphere blocks much of the radiation from space. From the edge of the atmosphere, instruments in a balloon can gather more information about the sun, the planets, and distant stars—their temperatures, speed and direction of motion, chemical composition, and so on—than can be gathered on the earth. The instruments in-

Research balloons help scientists gather information not easily obtained on earth. This balloon, shown during launching, carries an infrared telescope.

clude telescopes, spectroscopes, photometers, and cosmic ray counters.

During the 1950's, balloons paved the way for people to enter outer space. Balloons as tall as 50-story buildings rose to gather information about cosmic rays and other radiations from outer space. Monkeys were sent aloft in balloons as a test of what happens to the body at high altitudes. Guided missiles were carried aloft by balloons and then fired from the edge of space out into space. Since then, several balloon satellites have been launched into orbit by rocket. New equipment is often tested in balloons before being sent up in rockets or space probes.

In 1978, *Double Eagle II* carried three United States balloonists on the first flight across the Atlantic Ocean.

▶ THE SPORT OF BALLOONING

Ballooning has become popular as a sport that offers competition and the enjoyment of floating freely above the earth. Many rallies and events are held each year. In one of the best-known events, balloonists from all over the world travel over the Alps from Switzerland to Italy.

Competition takes various forms. There are long-distance races, in which the winner is the balloonist who travels farthest. There are cross-country and spot-landing contests, in which the pilot must take off and land within a specified time. In the cross-country event, the balloonist who travels farthest is the winner. In spot-landing contests, balloonists attempt to land at a designated point. In a hare-and-hounds chase, a single "hare" bal-

loon flies off, followed minutes later by the other balloons, or "hounds." The hound balloon that lands closest to the hare wins.

Both gas and hot-air balloons are used in competition. Modern hot-air balloons that carry propane burners to heat the air have been widely used since the early 1960's. Several hot-air balloons that rely on the heat of the sun have also been developed.

Sport balloons vary in size. The smallest are flown by a pilot dangling in a harness beneath the balloon. The average sport balloon can carry three people.

To inflate a typical hot-air balloon, the ground crew assembles the gondola, lays the balloon (a huge nylon bag) flat on the ground, and attaches the gondola to it. A fan is directed into the mouth of the balloon until the balloon is almost half filled with cold air. Then a propane burner is lighted, and the flame is directed into the mouth of the balloon to heat the cold air. As the air in the balloon is heated, the balloon begins to drift upward. The ground crew lets the balloon rise slowly until it has reached the necessary height. The gondola is held on the ground until the pilot has finished a preflight inspection and is ready for takeoff.

The propane burners are carried at the mouth of the balloon, above the gondola. They enable the pilot to regulate the air temperature. In this way the pilot can control the altitude of the balloon—but nothing else. Balloons travel where the wind takes them. The pilot can do nothing except change the altitude of the balloon to take advantage of air currents blowing in different directions.

In the United States, both the balloon and the pilot must be licensed by the Federal Aviation Agency. You may obtain a student balloon license when you are 14 years old. A student balloonist may fly alone but may not carry passengers. When you are 16 years old, you may become a private balloon pilot. To earn the license, you must have ten hours of instruction in balloons, including one ascent to 3,000 feet (915 meters) and a solo flight. You must also pass a flight test and an examination on weather conditions and on federal aviation rules.

Balloon Federation of America

BALLOT. See ELECTIONS.
BALTIC SEA. See OCEANS AND SEAS OF THE WORLD.

BALTIMORE

Baltimore is the largest city in Maryland and one of the major ports of the United States. It lies on the banks of the Patapsco River near Chesapeake Bay, 40 miles (about 65 kilometers) northeast of Washington, D.C. Baltimore is a center of industry, culture, education, and transportation. To visitors, it has the flavor of both an old southern city and a modern industrial community.

Through the years, manufacturing industries grew along with shipping and other port activities. Today the chief industries turn out steel and other metal products, chemicals, electronic equipment, and processed foods. Nearly 740,000 people live in the city proper. Baltimore's greater metropolitan area contains more than half the population of the state.

Baltimore was chartered in 1729 and was named after the Lords Baltimore who founded the Maryland colony. The Continental Congress met in Baltimore during the Revolutionary War. The Cumberland Road brought prosperity to the city in the early 1800's. But when the Erie Canal opened in 1825, Baltimore was threatened with a loss of trade. The city met this threat by building the first railroad in the United States—the Baltimore and Ohio.

Many monuments and landmarks reflect the city's long and colorful history. The oldest U.S. warship still afloat, the wooden frigate *Constellation*, is anchored not far from where it was launched in 1797. During the War of 1812, Fort McHenry in the Baltimore harbor was heavily bombarded by the British fleet. This event inspired Francis Scott Key to write "The Star-Spangled Banner" (1814). Baltimore also contains such landmarks as the nation's first Roman Catholic cathedral and the home and burial place of writer Edgar Allan Poe.

Since the 1950's the city has been a leader in urban renewal. Rows of handsome red brick houses have been restored, and a civic center and modern office and apartment complexes have been built in the heart of the city. One of the most ambitious projects has been the redevelopment of the Inner Harbor. A popular attraction of the Inner Harbor is the National Aquarium in Baltimore where visitors can view many kinds of exotic plant and animal life.

Among the city's many universities is Johns Hopkins University, which has a world-famous school of medicine. Residents and visitors enjoy the city's symphony orchestra and opera company and the outstanding art collections at the Walters Art Gallery and the Baltimore Museum of Art. Sports fans cheer baseball's Orioles at Oriole Park and watch horses run in the Preakness each spring at Pimlico Racetrack.

GEORGE BEISHLAG
Towson State University

See also MARYLAND.

Shops, restaurants, and commercial buildings line Baltimore's Inner Harbor, where the warship *Constellation* is anchored. At the far right is the National Aquarium in Baltimore.

BALZAC, HONORÉ DE (1799–1850)

The French writer Honoré de Balzac is known around the world for the novels and shorter works of fiction that he collected under the general title *La Comédie humaine (The Human Comedy)*. His ambition in this great work was to describe all of French society.

Balzac was born on May 20, 1799, in Tours, where his father was a civil servant. At the age of 8, he was sent to boarding school. He was an undisciplined child, and he was often sent to detention, or "kept in." He looked on this punishment as a blessing in disguise because it gave him all the time he wanted for reading. When his family moved to Paris in 1814, he went to school there.

For a while Balzac studied law, but he had no taste for legal work. He wanted to write plays, but his first play, *Cromwell* (1819), was a failure. He turned to writing sensational novels under various pen names. Realizing that he would never make his fortune this way, he went into business as a publisher and later as a printer. But he earned only debts.

In 1829, Balzac started the novels that made him famous. Some were fantastic, like *The Wild Ass's Skin* (1831). This novel tells how a young man acquires a magic piece of leather that grants his every wish but shrinks a little every time he uses it. He knows he will die when the leather has shrunk to nothing. Others were realistic, like *Eugénie Grandet* (1833), the story of a miser who loves his gold more than his daughter.

Balzac lived extravagantly, and he was always in debt. His many women friends inspired the sensitive portraits of women in his novels. Just before his death, he married a Polish countess, Eveline Hanska.

Balzac worked as intensely as he lived. By writing as much as 16 hours a day, he published over 80 titles between 1829 and 1847. This great labor brought on a serious illness before he was able to complete *The Human Comedy*. But when he died in Paris on August 18, 1850, he left a vivid record of his time.

F. W. J. HEMMINGS
Author, *Balzac: An Interpretation of La Comédie humaine*

BAMBOO. See GRASSES.

BANANA

The banana is a tropical fruit. People used it as a food even before history began to be written. The armies of Alexander the Great found bananas growing in India in 327 B.C. No doubt they grew there long before that time. Because of an old story that the sages of India rested in the shade of the plant and ate its fruit, the banana is often called the "fruit of the wise men."

Plant scientists believe that roots of banana plants were carried to the east coast of Africa by a people who moved there in ancient times. From there the banana plant was carried across the African continent to the Guinea Coast by early Arab traders.

When Portuguese explorers discovered the Guinea Coast of Africa in 1482, they found bananas growing there. These explorers took roots of the plant, and its African name, banana, to the Portuguese colonies in the Canary Islands. The next step in the journey of the banana plant was across the Atlantic Ocean to the New World. In 1516, only a few years after Columbus' famous voyages of discovery, a Spanish missionary brought this useful plant to the Caribbean island of Hispaniola. Other missionaries followed his example and planted bananas on the other islands of the Caribbean and on the tropical mainland. Thus, the banana plant had to go more than halfway around the world to reach Central America, where so many of the world's bananas are grown today.

It was not until the latter part of the 19th century that bananas were brought into the United States in quantities for sale in stores. Before that time, very few Americans other than those who had traveled in tropical countries had ever seen or tasted a banana. Even after banana schooners began entering New Orleans, Boston, and other ports, only people who lived in or near the port cities were able to eat bananas. The banana is perishable. Unlike some other fruits, it cannot be stored. Within a period of ten to twenty days, bananas must be harvested, shipped several thousand kilometers, ripened, and sent to the stores where they are sold. Today's modern transportation —fast, refrigerated ships, trains, and trucks— makes it possible for families in Chicago, in the United States, or Calgary, in Canada, to eat bananas every day of the year.

▶THE BANANA PLANT AND ITS GROWTH

The banana plant is often called a tree. But it is not a real tree because there is no wood in the stem that rises above the ground. The stem is made up of leaves growing very close together, one inside the other. The leaves that spread out at the top of the stem usually are from 2.5 to 3.5 meters (8 to 12 feet) long and more than 0.5 meters (about 2 feet) wide. These leaves spread out and rise in the air, making the banana plant look like a palm tree. When the plant is old enough to bear fruit, it is from 4.5 to 9 meters (15 to 30 feet) tall.

Bananas grow in bunches. Each bunch consists of 9 to 16 clusters of fruit, called "hands," and each hand contains from 12 to 20 separate bananas, called "fingers." A bunch of bananas usually weighs from 25 to 45 kilograms (55 to 100 pounds).

The size of the plant and the size of the bunch of fruit depend on the climate and the kind of soil in which the plant grows. Bananas grow best where the soil is deep and rich and the climate is warm and moist. They cannot be grown satisfactorily in any place where temperatures fall below 13°C (55°F). For good fruit, the temperature should not go below 21°C (70°F) for any length of time.

Bananas grow in all the moist, tropical areas of the world. Most of the bananas sold in North America and Europe are grown in Central America, northern South America, tropical Africa, and the Caribbean islands. Bananas are grown in Taiwan and the Philippines for sale in Japan. In other tropical areas, bananas are grown mainly for local use.

To grow new banana plants, pieces of rootstock (bits cut from the base of growing plants) are planted in holes about 3 meters (10 feet) apart. Each piece of rootstock must have one or more sprouts, or "eyes," like the eyes of a potato. Green shoots appear above the ground three or four weeks later. Only the strongest shoot is allowed to become a plant. This plant forms its own rootstock, from which other plants continue to grow. Careful pruning

Bananas grow well in tropical Costa Rica. This bunch will be cut while still green and sent to far-off markets.

ensures that one strong, fruit-producing plant follows another.

Banana plants need care and attention to produce fruit of good quality. They must be provided with water by irrigation if the normal rainfall does not supply at least 250 centimeters (100 inches) per year. The leaves must be sprayed to prevent damage by insects and diseases. The area around the plants must be kept free of weeds and grass. The plants must be fertilized with nitrogen and potash. On a large plantation, many workers are required to care for the plants and harvest the fruit.

About eight to ten months after planting, a flower appears on the banana plant. This flower is at the end of a long stalk, which grows from the base up through the center of the stem and turns downward when it emerges from the top. Small bananas form on this flower stalk as it grows downward. Bananas really grow upside down. As the small bananas form on the stalk, they point downward, but as they grow they turn and point upward. In three months they are plump and ready to harvest. Bananas are harvested while they are still green. Even when they are to be eaten where they are grown, they are not allowed to ripen on the plant. A banana that turns yellow on the plant loses its flavor. Also, the peel bursts open and insects get into the fruit. The finest flavor develops only when the fruit is cut while green and ripened afterward. The bananas sold in stores in the United States, Canada, and Europe are shipped there under refrigeration while still green. They are then ripened in special rooms where cool tempera-tures of 16 to 21°C (60 to 70°F) and moist air combine to allow the best-tasting fruit to be developed.

Each banana plant bears only one bunch of fruit. When the bunch is harvested, the plant is cut down. But as the plant has been growing to maturity and producing fruit, an-other plant has been growing beside it from the same rootstock. Soon this plant's fruit will be ready to harvest. This cycle of production will continue for years, if the plants are not destroyed by diseases, high winds, or floods.

NORWOOD C. THORNTON
Formerly, United Fruit Company

BANDS AND BAND MUSIC

Everyone loves a band. No football game, parade, circus, or Fourth of July celebration would be quite complete without a rousing march. Not only does everyone love to hear a band, but almost everyone loves to play in one. In the United States alone there are mil-lions of people who play in bands now or who have played in school, college, or town bands.

The word **band** is a broad term that de-scribes a group of musicians performing on wind and percussion instruments. One thinks immediately of a brightly uniformed marching band, perhaps part of an army or navy unit or the band of a college or high school.

Aside from marching bands and bands that entertain at fairs, public ceremonies, and in-formal social gatherings, there are other bands that exist only to perform music in a concert, just as an orchestra does. Such bands are known as concert or symphonic bands, or wind ensembles. What all bands have in com-mon is that they are composed of wind and percussion instruments in various combina-tions. Bands usually have at least 50 players.

Since bands often perform out-of-doors, they require instruments whose sounds carry easily. Trumpets, trombones, tubas, horns, drums—all are instruments capable of mak-ing plenty of noise with little effort on the part of the player. The large family of woodwinds, including clarinets, oboes, bassoons, and flutes (and their relatives, bass clarinets, Eng-lish horns, saxophones, and piccolos), also has this advantage.

A second requirement is that the instru-ments be easy to carry. It is impossible to march while playing a cello or a double bass; even the violin is not easy to play while one is walking. But one can easily play brass and woodwind instruments while marching. And of course the band has always required in-struments that create the proper military ex-citement. For this the brass and percussion instruments are perfect.

There is a special type of band called a brass band. As its name implies, it uses only brass instruments and no woodwinds. Many excellent Salvation Army bands are of this type. They usually have 24 players and pro-duce a good, well-blended sound despite their limits of tone quality and range.

A fife and drum band from Newport, Rhode Island.

EARLY HISTORY

Bands of some sort have existed almost from biblical times. Armies have always marched to the beat of drums, and soldiers have always taken their signals from the sounds of a trumpet or bugle of some sort. Little groups of wind-instrument players have sounded the hours of the day. (In 16th-century Germany the players assembled on the tower of the town's tallest building for this.) Bands have added to the beauty and impressiveness of church services and accompanied all kinds of outdoor public ceremonies.

Until the middle of the 18th century, however, there were practically no regularly organized bands. The combination of instruments used for any occasion was determined by whatever instruments were available in the town and whatever players were free at the moment and could be assembled for the occasion. New instruments were being invented (the clarinet, for instance, appeared around 1700) and old ones improved. Great excitement was created in Europe when, around 1750, a whole family of new percussion instruments was introduced by traveling bands from Turkey. Composers were soon busy writing "Turkish music," with parts for tambourines, cymbals, triangles, bass drums, and other clanging and beating instruments.

In 1763 King Frederick the Great of Prussia was the first to regulate the kinds and number of instruments used in his bands. He ordered that all of his military bands have at least two oboes, two clarinets, two horns, and two bassoons. To this basic group other instruments, including flute, trumpet, and drum, were gradually added. By the end of the 18th century, the bands were playing regularly not only for military parades but also for special court functions and popular outdoor concerts.

BEGINNINGS OF THE MODERN BAND

The modern band was born in the year 1789 as a result of the French Revolution. In that year Bernard Sarrette (1765–1858) founded the Band of the National Guard in Paris. This group of 45 players was immediately in demand for the popular demonstrations and numerous public ceremonies of the new government. By 1790 this band had 70 players and led to the formation of many military and town bands throughout Europe.

Many of the leading composers of the time served as bandmasters and wrote pieces for their bands. François Joseph Gossec (1734–1829) served for a time as bandmaster of the National Guard Band, with Charles Simon Catel (1773–1830) as his assistant. Their symphonies and overtures are still played by bands today. Others who composed for band included Luigi Cherubini (1760–1842), Ferdinando Paër (1771–1839), Etienne Mehul (1763–1817), and even the great composer Ludwig van Beethoven (1770–1827). The French band tradition reached its highest point in the great *Funeral and Triumphal Symphony* of Hector Berlioz (1803–69). It was written for a band of 208 players for the dedication of the Bastille Column in 1840.

WILHELM WIEPRECHT (1802–72)

Wilhelm Wieprecht was chiefly responsible for organizing the band as we know it today. A forward-looking musician, he experimented with mechanical improvements for the instruments. It was through his example that the use of horns and trumpets with valves, or keys, became universally accepted. It was then possible to play these instruments in more difficult kinds of music, and a greater variety of sound in band music resulted. This and the work of Adolphe Sax (inventor of the saxophone) and Theobald Boehm (who developed the modern flute) contributed to the development of the modern band and its music.

Wieprecht was responsible for the first of the massed-band festivals and band contests, forerunners of today's school and college band festivals. In 1838 he organized a grand festival in which over 1,000 players plus 200 extra side drummers performed. The occasion was the visit of the Russian Emperor Nicholas to the King of Prussia. What a royal welcome it must have been!

By the middle of the 19th century, bands in Europe had become an important part of every country's musical as well as military life. Among the most famous bands in England were the band of the Royal Horse Guards and the band of the Grenadier Guards led by Sir Daniel Godfrey (1831–1903). Godfrey was probably the best-known bandmaster of his time. His many arrangements for band are still performed in England and America. .

BANDS IN THE UNITED STATES

The development of bands and band music in the United States is one of the most colorful stories in American history. The earliest American bands were based on British models, and even before the American Revolution there is record of a band led by Josiah Flagg, of Boston. He was one of the first organizers of concerts in the American colonies. It is an interesting fact that Flagg's *Collection of the Best Psalm Tunes* was engraved by Paul Revere.

Although there is little historical record of bands in America before 1800, we know there was a wealth of band music composed in Revolutionary times and shortly thereafter. People, then, must have enjoyed band concerts and employed small bands for military purposes and public celebrations. Every American schoolchild knows the famous painting *The Spirit of '76.*

Marches were composed to celebrate patriotic occasions. The *Federal March* of Alexander Reinagle, performed in 1788, was written for the Fourth of July procession in Philadelphia celebrating the ratification of the United States Constitution. There were also many marches written in honor of the country's leading citizens and military heroes, such as *General Washington's Grand March* and *Jefferson's March.* During this period almost every town had its local band, attached to the town's militia.

PATRICK SARSFIELD GILMORE (1829–92)

Patrick S. Gilmore, born in County Galway, Ireland, in 1829, arrived in the United States at the age of 19. He was a man of enormous energy and vivid imagination and a born showman. In 1859 he took over the Boston Brigade Band, clad the players in bright new uniforms, rehearsed them over and over, and began an enormous schedule of performances. His band played for concerts, parades, and public ceremonies of all kinds. Also, as was the custom then, he provided dance music for balls and other events.

During the Civil War Gilmore conceived the idea of a huge band festival. With the help of the Army, he organized a Grand National Band consisting of 500 Army bandsmen plus a number of additional drum and bugle players. They were accompanied by a chorus of 5,000 schoolchildren. As a crowning touch Gilmore added 36 cannons, firing them by pushing hidden electric buttons. The great event took place in New Orleans on March 4, 1864.

Spectacular as this event was, it was only a hint of greater things to come. Returning to Boston after the war, Gilmore began to work on his next celebration, the National Peace Jubilee, given in 1869. This time he used an orchestra of 500, a band of 1,000, a chorus of 10,000, two batteries of cannons, and 100 firemen with hammers and anvils. The Jubilee lasted 5 days.

But Gilmore had even grander ideas. For 10 days, in 1872, he presented a World Peace Jubilee. His performers included an orchestra of 1,000, a band of 2,000, a chorus of 20,000, cannons, anvils, organ, and bells.

In 1873 Gilmore moved to New York, where he became leader of the 22nd Regiment Band. This became known as Gilmore's Band. He made several tours with the band in the United States, Canada, and Europe. He died in 1892.

JOHN PHILIP SOUSA (1854–1932)

John Philip Sousa was perhaps the greatest bandsman who ever lived. Trained as a violinist, he was only 24 years old when he was asked to take over the United States Marine Band. During Sousa's 12 years as director of the Marine Band, it achieved a national reputation for brilliance of performance that it retains to this day.

In 1892 Sousa left the Marine Band and formed a band of his own. He then toured extensively throughout the United States, Canada, and Europe. Sousa's band was probably the greatest band in the history of America. Its members included the leading virtuoso players of the day. His band had something that no band before him had and that every band since his has depended upon: Sousa's own marches. Brilliant in sound, rousing in spirit, and absolutely perfect for a band, they still form the backbone of band music everywhere. In fact, when most people think of band music, it is the sound of a Sousa march that they usually have in mind. Sousa wrote about 140 marches, including the famous *Stars and Stripes Forever, The Washington Post,* and *El Capitan.*

The United States Marine Band at Washington, D.C.

EDWIN FRANKO GOLDMAN (1878–1956)

In the 20th century the nature of the band changed. The great touring bands of Sousa's time disappeared. Movies, television, and radio took the place of the old-time touring band that gave concerts wherever it went.

There is, however, no lack of popularity for the concert band, the kind that does not go on tours. The leading band of this type in the United States is the Goldman Band, founded in 1911 by Edwin Franko Goldman. Trained as a trumpet player, Goldman was for 10 years a member of the Metropolitan Opera Orchestra, in New York City. While he was playing there, he conceived the idea of forming a permanent concert band. By 1918 he was giving a regular series of outdoor summer band concerts; his players were among the leading musicians of the day. The summer concerts he started have become a tradition in the musical life of New York. They are now given under the direction of his son, Richard Franko Goldman.

Edwin Franko Goldman was the first bandmaster to encourage leading composers of the day to compose original works for band. It is through his efforts that today we are able to hear a large variety of music composed especially for bands.

RICHARD FRANKO GOLDMAN

See also PERCUSSION INSTRUMENTS; WIND INSTRUMENTS.

The Band of the Canadian Guards at Ottawa, Ontario.

Left: Tourists take in a view of the Bow River and the surrounding area from atop Sulphur Mountain in Banff National Park in Alberta. Banff is Canada's oldest national park.

Below: Banff National Park features spectacular mountains, emerald green forests, and glacial lakes. Boating on Moraine Lake is just one of the many ways to enjoy the scenery.

BANFF NATIONAL PARK

Banff National Park in Alberta is the oldest and one of the largest of Canada's national parks. Engineers were surveying a route for the Canadian Pacific Railway in 1883 when they discovered hot springs on the eastern slopes of the Rocky Mountains, at the spot where the town of Banff now stands. When the discovery of these springs amid the beautiful snowcapped peaks became known, the Canadian government decided to preserve the mountain scenery and wildlife of the area as a public park. In 1887 an area around Banff was set aside as Rocky Mountains National Park. Later it was renamed Banff National Park. The area has been expanded over the years; it now covers more than 2,500 square miles (6,500 square kilometers).

Through the deep valleys of Banff National Park, between such famous mountains as Castle, Rundle, and Temple, glacier-fed streams flow into crystal-clear lakes. The main river is the Bow, which runs southeastward through most of the park. The most famous lake is Louise, renowned for its magnificent natural setting. The towns of Banff and Lake Louise are two world-famous resorts located in this park. People come long distances to enjoy such sports as skiing and tobogganing in winter and hiking, golf, and mountain climbing in summer. Banff's popular swimming pool uses water from the hot springs at the foot of Sulphur Mountain. Because wild animals are protected from hunters, tourists may get to see moose, elk, mountain sheep, and bears close by the highways.

Lake Louise is on the main Canadian Pacific Railway line at the east end of Kicking Horse Pass. Banff is also on the Canadian Pacific Railway and on the Trans-Canada Highway as well.

The Banff Center, now a part of the University of Calgary, was established at Banff in 1933 as a summer school to teach subjects connected with the theater. Since then it has grown tremendously. It offers courses in drama, ballet, opera, creative writing, and fine arts. Every summer students come from many countries to attend this unusual school.

JOHN S. MOIR
University of Toronto

BANGKOK (KRUNG THEP)

Bangkok is the capital, largest city, and cultural center of Thailand and one of the leading cities of Southeast Asia. It lies in a bend of the broad Chao Phraya River, not far from the Gulf of Siam (Gulf of Thailand). Bangkok is famous for its beautiful Buddhist temples. Today, the glittering spires of more than 300 temples rise on the skyline beside modern skyscrapers.

In 1982, Bangkok celebrated the 200th anniversary of the Thai royal family, the Chakri dynasty. The first Chakri king, Rama I, moved the capital from Thonburi (now part of Bangkok) across the river to the tiny village known as Bangkok. The Thais call their capital Krung Thep—sometimes translated as "city of angels"—a shortened form of the name Rama I gave his new capital.

People once moved about Bangkok mainly by boat—and many still do. As the city spread outward from the riverbanks, canals were built to provide transportation links to the river. Streets on land were often only narrow lanes for walking and for use by bicycles and carts. People went to market, visited neighbors, and transported goods by water. Shops and houses crowded the banks of the canals.

After World War II, the number of cars and trucks increased, and new streets were needed. Many of the canals were filled in and paved. Road building has changed the face of Bangkok more than any other kind of construction.

Bangkok is a city with no single center. Instead, it has many centers that developed as the city grew. In the oldest part of the city is the Grand Palace. It is almost a small city itself, with many buildings inside a high wall. They include the famous Temple of the Emerald Buddha, which houses a statue of Buddha that is the most sacred of all objects for the Buddhists of Thailand. The lovely emerald-green statue is actually carved from a piece of jasper. Across the river is another landmark, the Temple of the Dawn.

Near the Grand Palace are many large government buildings, theaters, museums, and Silpakorn and Thammasat universities. To the north is the palace where the present king lives. To the south is the old Chinese part of the city, where Thai merchants and artisans of Chinese ancestry own small stores and shops. In the newer parts of the city, modern shopping centers have been built. Tall office and apartment buildings and hotels rise many stories above much older shops and houses.

Bangkok is Thailand's center of industry and banking, its busiest port, and a hub of international air and railroad transportation. Factories in the city and in new industrial areas in the suburbs turn out a wide variety of goods. These include processed foods, metal and electrical goods, pharmaceuticals, textiles, and jewelry.

The population of Bangkok's metropolitan area, which includes Thonburi, is approximately 5,400,000. Like other big cities, Bangkok faces traffic jams, pollution, and other problems, such as lack of jobs and housing. Parts of the low-lying city are subject to floods, especially during times of heavy rain. But Bangkok is still a showcase of Thai culture and an exciting place to live in or visit.

JAMES BASCHE
Author, *Thailand: Land of the Free*

The Bangkok skyline, with its gilded temples and modern skyscrapers, reflects the mixture of past and present.

BANGLADESH

Bangladesh is a nation in South Asia almost entirely surrounded by the territory of its giant neighbor, India. Though small in area, Bangladesh is one of the most heavily populated, and one of the poorest, countries in the world. Formerly known as East Pakistan, Bangladesh declared its independence from Pakistan following a civil war in 1971.

▶THE PEOPLE

Bangladesh means "Bengal Nation," and the vast majority of the people are Bengalis who are related to the Bengalis of neighboring India. The largest minority groups are the Biharis, who emigrated from India, and the tribal people of the Chittagong Hills. Most of the people are Muslims. There are a sizable number of Hindus and some Buddhists and Christians. The hill tribes practice traditional religions. Bengali (or Bangla) is the official language, but English is also widely spoken.

FACTS
and figures

PEOPLE'S REPUBLIC OF BANGLADESH is the official name of the country.

LOCATION: South Asia.

AREA: 55,598 sq mi (143,998 km²).

POPULATION: 115,600,000 (estimate).

CAPITAL AND LARGEST CITY: Dhaka.

MAJOR LANGUAGES: Bengali, or Bangla (official); English.

MAJOR RELIGION: Muslim.

GOVERNMENT: Republic. **Head of state**—president. **Head of government**—prime minister. **Legislature**—Jatiya Sangsad (National Assembly).

CHIEF PRODUCTS: Agricultural —jute, rice, tea, sugarcane, fruits, oilseeds, wheat. **Manufactured**—jute products, cotton textiles, refined sugar, leather goods, fertilizer, paper. **Mineral**—natural gas.

MONETARY UNIT: Taka (1 taka = 100 poisha).

Bengalis place great value on education, and almost every village has one or more local schools. The government provides free primary school education for five years. Bangladesh has a number of colleges and universities. The oldest and largest is the University of Dhaka, founded in 1921, which is located in Dhaka, the capital.

The basic unit of life in Bangladesh is the village. It is usually located along the course of a river or canal with rice fields nearby. Communication between villages is chiefly by boat. There are thousands of boats, of all sizes and shapes, and they travel up and down the rivers carrying people and goods.

The everyday diet in Bangladesh consists of rice and fish with some vegetables. The typical house is built of reeds, bamboo, and mats and is plastered with clay or mud. Men usually wear the lungi, a length of colored cotton cloth worn wrapped around the waist and stretching to the ankles. At work the lungi is tucked up to the knees. Women often wear saris—long, colorful garments draped around the body from the shoulder to the ankles. Traditionally, Muslim women cover their faces, especially around strangers.

▶THE LAND

Bangladesh is a land largely of low plains crisscrossed by rivers. The most important rivers are the Ganges and the Brahmaputra and their tributaries. In the south the rivers, by depositing sediment, have created areas of very rich soil.

The only elevated areas are in the southeast, in the Chittagong Hills. This hill country, the home of the tribal people, is covered with dense tropical forest.

Bangladesh is a tropical country. The average temperatures range from over 60°F (16°C) to over 90°F (32°C). It is also a land of torrential monsoon rains, which fall from June to September. In addition, violent winds called cyclones (or typhoons) regularly bring heavy flooding to the region, causing many deaths and widespread devastation. Since Bangladesh's independence alone, cyclones have killed hundreds of thousands of people and left many millions more homeless.

▶THE ECONOMY

Bangladesh is an agricultural country. The main food crop is rice. Jute is the major

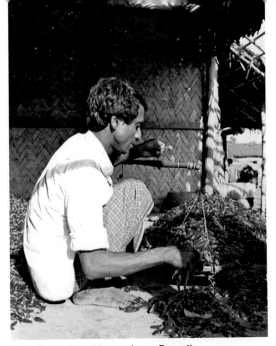

Most of Bangladesh's people are Bengalis.

BANGLADESH

commercial crop. Bangladesh is one of the world's leading producers and suppliers of jute, a plant fiber used to make burlap, sacking, and twine. Exports of jute are the country's chief source of income. Tea, grown in the hill region, is the second most important cash crop. Other crops include sugarcane, wheat, mangoes, coconuts, pineapples, and oilseeds, from which cooking oil is derived.

The manufacture of jute products is Bangladesh's chief industry. Other manufactured goods include cotton textiles, refined sugar, leather goods, fertilizer, and paper and paper products.

Aside from natural gas, Bangladesh has few useful mineral resources. It has deposits of coal, but they are difficult to mine.

The average farm is small, and the farming methods usually do not enable farmers to produce large crops. Bangladesh is one of the most densely populated areas in the world, and the population is rising very rapidly. Unless agriculture is modernized and effective means of population control are adopted, the country will face problems in attempting to feed its people adequately.

The many rivers and canals are both a blessing and a problem. They provide the chief means of transportation of people and goods. But to be used efficiently, they require effective methods of flood-control and mechanization. The great hydroelectric potential of the country can be utilized for industrial growth only if the rivers are harnessed. This

A farmer watering his rice fields. Rice is the staple food in Bangladesh.

Left: Riverboats are a common form of transportation.
Above: A typical small Bangladesh village.

would enable Bangladesh to provide power for industrialization. But such projects require vast amounts of money, which the country cannot easily supply.

▶CITIES

There are fewer than a dozen major urban centers in Bangladesh. The most important of these is Dhaka, the capital and largest city. Formerly the capital of East Pakistan, the city has many historic buildings and is an educational and cultural center. It is also the nation's chief industrial area. Chittagong, on the Karnafuli River east of the Bay of Bengal, has a good natural harbor and is the nation's chief port. It is also a major industrial and rail center.

▶HISTORY AND GOVERNMENT

Bangladesh is a young nation, but the history of the region goes back to ancient times. In the beginning, Bangladesh was part of the larger Bengal region of eastern India. It was ruled by successive groups of invaders—the Turks, the Moguls, and the British. In 1947, India gained its independence from Britain. East Bengal (now Bangladesh) became part of Pakistan. This new nation was created because the Muslim League demanded an independent and separate nation for the parts of the former British Indian Empire where the Muslims were a majority.

Pakistan was born with built-in flaws. It was made up of two parts, East Pakistan and West Pakistan, which were separated by about

Bicycles and pedicabs crowd the busy city of Dhaka, the capital of Bangladesh.

1,000 miles (1,600 kilometers). India lay between them. The two parts of Pakistan were quite different in their peoples and cultures. Groups from West Pakistan soon took control of the new nation. East Pakistan turned out to be a good place for commercial investments. But the Bengalis charged that most of the profits were drained off to West Pakistan. The West Pakistani leaders were accused of neglecting the interests of the eastern region and treating it as a colony. The East Pakistanis also complained that they were not receiving their fair share of political power. They believed they were entitled to a greater voice because they made up more than 55 percent of the nation's total population.

Other issues led to frustration and discontent among the Bengalis of Pakistan. The government at first refused to accept Bengali as one of the national languages. Popularly elected local governments in the East were dismissed on charges of wanting to secede from Pakistan. Bengali leaders were imprisoned as traitors. There were frequent riots, and a long period of military rule (from 1958 to 1971) created dangerous tensions in the East.

The Birth of Bangladesh

The climax came in the elections of 1970. The Awami League, led by Sheikh Mujibur Rahman (Mujib), won most of the seats in the East Pakistani provincial legislature and a majority in the national legislature. The victory would have given Sheikh Mujib a decisive role in Pakistani politics. This situation was unacceptable to General Yahya Khan, the leader of the national government, and Zulfikar Ali Bhutto, the leader of the Pakistan People's Party, the majority party in West Pakistan. They objected especially to the Awami League's Six Point Program, which included self-government for the eastern region. West Pakistani leaders believed this would lead to the breaking up of Pakistan.

The two parts of Pakistan tried to form a plan for restoring civilian rule and drafting a new constitution. Their failure to do so set off riots in the East. The West Pakistani army brutally suppressed the riots. It is charged that millions of people lost their lives and hundreds of villages were destroyed. Some 10,000,000 Bengalis, mostly Hindus, fled to India. This placed a great economic burden on India. Incidents mounted until, in December 1971, India and Pakistan went to war. The war was swift. In less than two weeks, the Indian Army, with the aid of the Bengali guerrillas, had compelled the Pakistani forces to surrender.

Sheikh Mujibur Rahman, who had been arrested and imprisoned in West Pakistan, was released. On January 10, 1972, he arrived in Bangladesh and became prime minister of the new nation. He later became its president.

Recent History

Bangladesh faced enormous problems. Millions of people had become refugees. The economy had been disrupted, and the country was torn by political quarrels. In 1975 the government was overthrown by army officers, and President Mujib was killed.

Bangladesh was governed under martial, or military, law by General Ziaur Rahman (known as Zia). In 1978, Zia was elected president. Martial law was lifted in 1979, and elections were held for the legislature. In 1981, Zia was killed during an attempted coup.

In 1982, General Hussain Mohammed Ershad seized power and reimposed martial law. In 1986 he was elected president and he later lifted martial law. His opponents, charging widespread fraud, had refused to take part in the elections. Elections held in 1988 also were boycotted by the opposition. Political protests forced Ershad to resign in 1990. In elections held in 1991, the Bangladesh Nationalist Party won the largest number of seats, and the party leader, Khaleda Zia, widow of the former president, became prime minister. Continuing political unrest, however, compelled her, in 1994, to step down until new elections were held in 1996. Her party was victorious because the Awami League, the main opposition, refused to take part, charging fraud. Widespread demonstrations forced new elections that same year, in which the Awami League won the largest number of seats. Hasina Wazed, daughter of the late President Mujib, was named prime minister.

BALKRISHNA G. GOKHALE
Director, Asian Studies Program
Wake Forest University

See also INDIA; PAKISTAN.

BANGOR. See MAINE (Cities).
BANJO. See STRINGED INSTRUMENTS.

The Bank of the United States, which received its charter in 1791, was the country's first federal bank. In 1797 it moved into this building, which is considered to be the oldest U.S. bank building. The bank stayed in business only until 1811 when its charter expired, but the building still stands on South Third Street in Philadelphia.

BANKS AND BANKING

What can you do when you have money that you do not want to spend, or carry around, or keep at home? You could deposit the money at a bank in a checking or savings account. On the other hand, if you didn't have enough money to meet your needs, you could ask a bank to lend you money. By providing these two functions—holding money and lending money—banks play a very important role in the United States economy. They make the money in bank accounts available to people who need to borrow money.

When you deposit money in a bank as savings, you also earn interest. The interest is a fee paid to you for the use of your money. Suppose, for example, that you deposit $100 in a bank offering an interest rate of 5 percent on savings. At the end of one year the amount of money in your account would be $100 plus the additional interest.

Money deposited in a bank as savings is loaned to borrowers at a higher interest rate than is paid to savers. For example, a bank that pays 5 percent interest on savings may charge 10 percent interest on the money when it is loaned to borrowers. The interest the bank receives is income for the bank. It is used to pay interest to depositors, as well as to pay for the salaries of bank employees, and for equipment, supplies, and other costs of operating the bank.

Banks are owned by stockholders who have invested money in the bank. Part of a bank's total assets are the funds invested by these stockholders. But most of a bank's assets come from money that people have deposited and from interest paid on loans.

▶HISTORY OF BANKING

Banking activities are almost as old as the earliest civilizations. The earliest bankers were moneychangers or moneylenders. These people had strongboxes in which to keep money, and people left money with them for safekeeping or borrowed money from them in exchange for a fee. As early as A.D. 534 the ancient Romans had laws and regulations concerning moneylending and banking activities.

Today most banks have safe-deposit boxes in their vaults, which customers may rent and use to store important papers and other valuable items.

Modern banking is generally thought to have begun in Italy during the late 1500's. In fact, the word "bank" comes from the Italian word *banco*, which means bench. The term became associated with banking because many early Italian bankers conducted their business from benches in the street.

In England during the 1600's it became common practice for people to give their gold and silver to local goldsmiths for safekeeping. These goldsmiths, who made jewelry and other items, had strong vaults in which they kept precious metals. It was only natural that people who did not have safe places for their valuables would want to keep their gold and silver in these vaults. The goldsmiths issued paper receipts, or notes, to the people who left precious metals with them. Eventually, people began to use these paper notes as money; the goldsmiths became bankers.

As trade flourished in Europe in the 1600's and 1700's banking became so important that commercial banks were set up. These commercial banks were privately owned, and their chief business was to help merchants finance trading activities. They accepted deposits of money, made loans, collected bills, and acted as places of exchange in which money from one country could be converted into the money of another country.

Banking in the United States

The first banks established in the United States were state banks. In 1781, the Bank of North America, the first bank to receive a charter, or license to operate, was organized in Philadelphia. Other states soon issued charters to banks of their own. The first national bank, the Bank of the United States, was established in 1791 and had branches in several cities.

During the late 1700's and early 1800's many state banks in the United States followed unsound banking practices. They issued far too many loans in the form of paper bank notes (paper money). The Bank of the United States had the authority to control the amount of paper money issued by the state banks, but in 1811 its charter expired and the Bank of the United States no longer had any control.

Increasing numbers of people became concerned about the value of their paper notes and asked state banks to exchange the notes for gold and silver coin (called **specie**). Many banks, however, did not have enough precious metals to back the notes and they stopped exchanging gold and silver for paper notes. As a result, the notes quickly lost their value. This dangerous financial situation led to the failure of many banks. When the banks failed, depositors lost their life savings.

The National Bank Act of 1863, which was amended in 1864, created a national banking system in the United States. Under the provisions of this system, the state banks were driven out of the business of issuing paper notes. The national banks were allowed to continue issuing bank notes until 1935. Federal laws then gave the power to issue paper notes solely to a centralized banking system called the Federal Reserve.

Bank tellers help customers with many different transactions, including making deposits to and withdrawals from their accounts and taking care of bills such as loan payments.

▶ THE AMERICAN BANKING SYSTEM

The banking system in the United States today is made up of many banks operating at different levels. All these banks, however, must operate under the jurisdiction and rules of the Federal Reserve System, the centerpiece of American banking.

The Federal Reserve System

The Federal Reserve System was established by Congress in 1913 in an effort to correct some serious problems that existed in American banking. Prior to the establishment of the Federal Reserve System, the United States experienced several severe financial panics during which many businesses failed and many banks were forced to close. The national banking system at the time was unable to deal with these crises. It was decided that major reforms were needed, and the Federal Reserve System was the result.

The Federal Reserve System—or the Fed, as it is commonly called—is made up of three levels of organization. The top level consists of the Board of Governors, the Federal Open-Market Committee, and the Federal Advisory Council. The Board of Governors is the most important of these three groups. It is the central policy-making body of the Federal Reserve System. It consists of seven members appointed by the president and confirmed by the Senate. Each member is appointed for a 14-year term and is ineligible for reappointment. The Board of Governors remains relatively independent of politics. Board decisions do not have to be approved by the president or Congress, and board members do not have to fear losing their jobs when a new president is elected.

The second level of the Federal Reserve System consists of the Federal Reserve Banks. The United States is divided into twelve districts, and there is a separate Federal Reserve Bank for each district. The twelve Federal Reserve Banks are located in Boston, New York, Philadelphia, Cleveland, Richmond, Atlanta, Chicago, St. Louis, Minneapolis, Kansas City, Dallas, and San Francisco. The activities of these Federal Reserve Banks are coordinated by the Board of Governors. The Federal Reserve Banks do not deal directly with the public. They are "bankers' banks" that deal only with other financial institutions and the government.

The third level of the Federal Reserve System consists of other financial institutions, including commercial banks, savings and loan associations, credit unions, and savings banks. These financial institutions utilize the services of the Federal Reserve System and are subject to reserve requirements established by the Fed. They perform the regular day-to-day business of banking in the nation.

The Federal Reserve System performs many important functions, the most important of which is controlling the nation's money supply. It also plays a major role in clearing checks. The Fed supervises member banks and serves as a depository for the money that banks are required to keep as reserves. The Fed is also responsible for supplying the nation's paper money in the form of Federal Reserve Notes.

Types of Banks

There are several different types of financial institutions in the United States that are commonly thought of as banks.

Commercial Banks. Commercial banks make up the largest banking group in the United States. At one time, commercial banks could easily be distinguished from other financial institutions by the fact that only they could

The Savings and Loan Crisis of the 1980's

Before the 1980's, savings and loan institutions were allowed to make loans only to individuals to buy houses. This changed in 1982 with the enactment of a deregulation act that changed the way the savings and loan industry operated. The deregulation of the industry led to one of the worst financial disasters since the Great Depression and was one of the worst scandals in American history.

As a result of deregulation, an estimated $250 billion of depositors' money was lost through poor management practices or, in some cases, fraud. Questionable construction projects — shopping centers in the desert, suburban developments with almost nobody to live in them, and unneeded high-rise office buildings — were financed by the savings and loan industry. A massive building binge occurred, and buildings of all types were built, often on pure speculation; that is, on the chance that buyers would be found.

When developers could not sell these properties, they defaulted on (could not repay) their loans. Since the savings and loan institutions could not sell these properties either, many went bankrupt. The government took over these bankrupt institutions and the unneeded real estate became the property of the American taxpayers. Most of the property will probably be sold eventually at a fraction of its cost, and taxpayers will have to absorb an estimated loss of at least $250 billion.

Savings and loan associations, which have always offered loans to their customers for building or buying houses or for buying real estate, now provide many other types of loans and services, including checking accounts.

offer checking accounts. However, changes in the banking laws now allow other financial institutions to offer checking accounts as well.

Commercial banks can be established and operated only after being granted a charter by either the federal government or a state government. Commercial banks chartered by the federal government are called national banks. Those chartered by one of the states are called state banks. The primary functions of commercial banks are to receive deposits, make loans, and provide checking and other services to customers. Commercial banks primarily make short-term commercial loans to businesses and personal loans to individuals.

Savings and Loan Associations. Savings and loan associations are owned and operated by individuals who, as shareholders, elect a board of directors to manage the organization. Historically, savings and loan associations primarily made long-term loans—twenty years or longer—to individuals for the purpose of building homes or buying existing homes and other real estate. Today, however, savings and loan associations make many other types of loans as well. They also make checking account services available to depositors.

Savings Banks. Savings banks specialize in individual savings accounts. These banks may be owned by stockholders, although most function as **cooperatives**, or **mutuals**, and are owned by their depositors. Mutual savings banks originated in the United States in the early 1800's when commercial banks were not interested in handling the small savings deposits of wage earners. By pooling their savings in a mutual savings bank, wage earners with individual savings could find profitable investment opportunities for their money.

Credit Unions. Credit unions are cooperative nonprofit associations owned and operated by their members. They are often organized by the employees of large companies or the members of labor unions for the benefit of their membership. The primary purpose of credit unions is to offer high-interest savings accounts and low-interest loans to members.

Investment Banks. Investment banks specialize in distributing the **securities**, or stocks and bonds, of corporations to the public. Investment banks purchase newly issued stocks and bonds from companies and then resell these securities to individual investors in smaller quantities. Investment banks buy securities from a company at a particular price with the intention of reselling them at a higher price. The difference between the purchase price and the sale price is the investment bank's profit. Investment banks provide companies with the money they need without the companies having to wait for the general public to buy stock.

The World Bank. While some of the nation's major banks do business with foreign countries, there are a few specialized banks that deal exclusively in international finance. One of these, the International Bank for Reconstruction and Development (IBRD), more commonly known as the World Bank, officially began operating in 1944. The original purpose of the World Bank was to help finance the reconstruction of areas of the world damaged during World War II. Since that time, the World Bank has also assisted in the economic growth of underdeveloped countries by providing them with long-term loans. In 1956, the World Bank established the International

Bank customers often find themselves in long lines during their lunch hours or just before bank closings on Fridays. This is when many people deposit or cash paychecks, or make withdrawals for weekend trips.

Finance Corporation (IFC), the purpose of which is to stimulate private investments in developing countries. While the World Bank lends money only for public, or publicly sponsored, projects, the IFC helps to finance private enterprise.

Banking Services

Banks provide many services to the public and the government. But most of the regular business of a bank involves accepting deposits from savers and making money available to borrowers in the form of loans.

Time Deposits. In time deposits, money usually stays in an account for an extended period of time. Savings accounts are a type of time deposit. Most people who put money in a savings account plan to leave it there until it is needed—perhaps to buy a house, to pay for a child's education, or to use during retirement. Banks pay interest on the money deposited in a savings account, so the amount of money left in an account will gradually increase.

A person who deposits money in a savings account often receives a savings passbook. This passbook shows the amount of money in the deposit. When money is deposited or withdrawn from the account, the balance in the passbook will be updated. Periodically, the bank will add the interest that has been earned on the account to the balance.

People who have large amounts of money to deposit as savings often put the money in a special account called a **certificate of deposit (CD)**. An advantage of certificates of deposit is that they usually pay higher interest rates than passbook savings accounts. However, certificates of deposit are only payable at a definite date in the future, called the maturity date. This maturity date might range from 30 days to several years. If a person withdraws money from a certificate of deposit before the maturity date, he or she will have to pay a penalty in the form of lost interest.

Demand Deposits. Demand deposits are checking accounts, which allow individuals to deposit, withdraw, and transfer their money whenever they want. Checking accounts pro-

CLEARING A CHECK

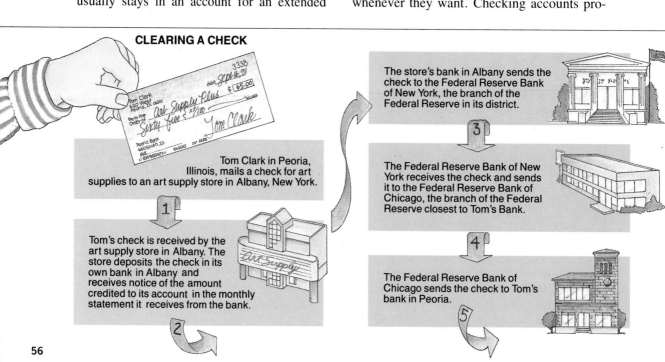

Tom Clark in Peoria, Illinois, mails a check for art supplies to an art supply store in Albany, New York.

1

Tom's check is received by the art supply store in Albany. The store deposits the check in its own bank in Albany and receives notice of the amount credited to its account in the monthly statement it receives from the bank.

2

The store's bank in Albany sends the check to the Federal Reserve Bank of New York, the branch of the Federal Reserve in its district.

3

The Federal Reserve Bank of New York receives the check and sends it to the Federal Reserve Bank of Chicago, the branch of the Federal Reserve closest to Tom's Bank.

4

The Federal Reserve Bank of Chicago sends the check to Tom's bank in Peoria.

5

vide a convenient way for people to have access to their money without having to carry it around as cash. A person can write checks against a checking account at any time. These checks can be made payable to oneself to withdraw money, or they can be made payable to someone else to transfer money to that person. Banks sometimes pay interest on checking accounts, usually with the provision that a minimum amount of money be kept in the account at all times.

Each month banks send detailed statements to customers with checking accounts. These statements show how much money was deposited during the month, the number of checks written and the amount of each, and the current balance of the account. Enclosed with the statement will be the checks that were written, cashed, and returned to the bank during the month. These checks, for which money has been withdrawn from the checking account, are called cancelled checks. They can serve as receipts for any bills paid by check.

Loans. Banks make many types of loans to individuals or businesses. One major type of loan is a home mortgage loan, which is provided to people who want to buy or build a home. Home mortgage loans usually require repayment over a loan term, perhaps as long as twenty to thirty years. After the buyer pays a down payment on the home, the bank finances the balance of the cost. The buyer then pays off this amount, plus interest, in periodic (usually monthly) installments. On a large

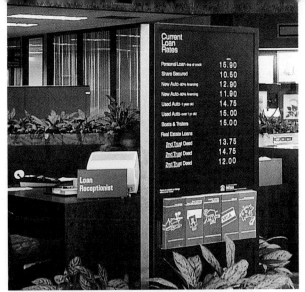

Many banks post the rates they offer for making loans to customers for different items. Customers may compare the rates of different banks to find which one offers the best rate for their needs.

loan repaid over many years, the buyer will pay a large amount of interest as a part of each payment.

Banks make many short-term loans to both individuals and businesses. For example, a person might borrow $1,000 from a bank for a period of six months. The person signs a note promising to repay the money borrowed in addition to interest charged by the bank for the use of its money. Usually, the person must also offer something of value, such as an automobile, as security, or collateral. If the person fails to repay the loan, the bank can take possession of this collateral.

The rate of interest that banks charge depends on the type and length of the loan. The **prime rate** is the rate of interest that large city banks charge their best customers (large businesses that have excellent credit ratings). The rate of interest paid by the average borrower is usually higher than the prime rate.

Other Services. Banks also provide many other services to their customers. Most banks have safe-deposit boxes in their vaults, which they rent to customers for safekeeping of valuable possessions. Banks also provide financial advice to their customers, sell traveler's checks, and issue credit cards.

Financial experts in a bank's trust department provide a variety of services. They manage real estate and collect rents, invest money in stocks and bonds, sell securities, give advice on drawing up wills, and manage company pension and health-insurance plans. Money left to charities is often handled by the

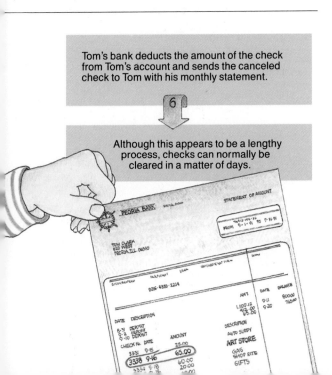

Tom's bank deducts the amount of the check from Tom's account and sends the canceled check to Tom with his monthly statement.

6

Although this appears to be a lengthy process, checks can normally be cleared in a matter of days.

trust departments of banks as well. Of course, the bank charges a fee for all of these services.

Many banks also offer bank credit cards to their customers. These credit cards enable people to buy items on credit by charging the items on their cards. The banks pay the merchants for the purchases and then bill the credit card holders, who make payments to their banks. The banks charge interest only on the amounts of the monthly bills that are not paid on time. Bank cards can also be used by customers to get cash advances from banks.

Many banks today have automatic teller machines (ATM's) that let customers have access to their accounts 24 hours a day. The bank customer inserts a special card into the machine and then enters a secret identification number. Once this is done, the customer has access to his or her bank account and can deposit, withdraw, and transfer money without the assistance of a bank employee.

Another service offered by many banks is electronic funds transfer (EFT). An electronic funds transfer system moves money into or out of a customer's account electronically. For example, some employees have their salaries electronically credited to their accounts, eliminating the need to cash or deposit paychecks. Electronic funds transfer speeds service to customers and also eliminates much of the paperwork involved in various banking services.

Safety of Bank Deposits

During the Great Depression of the 1930's many people lost their life savings when banks failed. In order to prevent that from happening again, government insurance funds were created. These insurance funds guaranteed that depositors would be paid the full amount of their deposits if a bank failed.

Prior to 1989, accounts in savings and loan associations were insured by the federal Savings and Loan Insurance Corporation (FSLIC), and accounts in commercial banks were insured by the Federal Deposit Insurance Corporation (FDIC). In the late 1980's, however, the failure of many savings and loan associations caused the bankruptcy of the FSLIC insurance fund. As a result, beginning in 1989, the FDIC became responsible for insuring accounts in both commercial banks and savings and loan associations.

To handle all these accounts, two separate insurance funds were established within the FDIC—the Banking Insurance Fund (BIF) and the Savings Association Insurance Fund (SAIF). The BIF insures deposits in commercial banks up to $100,000 per deposit. The

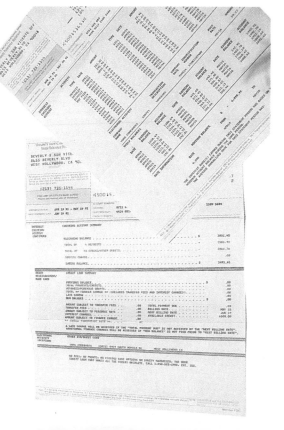

Above: By using automatic teller machines (ATM's), customers have quick and easy access to their accounts day or night. *Right:* Banks provide statements to their customers every month that show opening and closing balances, cancelled checks, and transactions such as deposits, withdrawals, and service charges.

SAIF insures deposits in savings and loan associations up to a total of $100,000. If a bank or savings and loan association has financial troubles and is unable to repay depositors, repayment will be made out of the insurance funds. Credit union deposits are also insured up to $100,000 by insurance funds.

▶ BANKING IN CANADA

Attempts to establish a Canadian bank go back to the late 1700's. But it was not until 1817 that the first bank in Canada was successfully launched. Early banks in Canada were established as private partnerships, by provincial law, or by royal charters obtained in England. However, by 1867 the federal government had assumed sole responsibility for the country's banking system.

Canada's central bank, the Bank of Canada, is the centerpiece of Canadian banking. It was founded in 1934 and nationalized in 1938. In addition, there are five large banks chartered under Canadian law, each of which has a nationwide network of branch banks.

The Bank of Canada is directed by law to regulate credit and currency in such a way as to promote the best interests of the Canadian economy. It carries out banking policies by changing rates of interest on loans, altering the amount of reserves that must be held by chartered banks to back up deposits, buying and selling securities, and responding to changes in foreign exchange rates. Canadian banks provide basically the same services as American banks. There are differences, however, in policy and in the services provided.

▶ CAREERS IN BANKING

Most of the people working in banks are either bank officers or clerical workers. Bank officers, depending on their rank, usually have some authority to make business decisions involving the bank. Bank officers might include positions such as president, vice president, and comptroller. Some, such as loan and trust officers, head specific departments.

Clerical workers in banks include secretaries, bank tellers, bookkeepers, and various other employees who do clerical work. These positions generally outnumber bank officers by a ratio of about six to one.

ALLEN SMITH
Professor of Economics
Eastern Illinois University

See also CREDIT CARDS; ECONOMICS; INFLATION AND DEFLATION; MONEY.

BANNEKER, BENJAMIN. See WASHINGTON, D.C. (Famous People).
BANSHEES. See FAIRIES.

BANTING, SIR FREDERICK GRANT (1891–1941)

Frederick Grant Banting, a Canadian doctor and scientist, was born on November 14, 1891, in Alliston, Ontario. He is remembered for his contribution to the control of diabetes, a serious disease in which the pancreas, a large gland near the stomach, produces too little insulin. Insulin is a chemical needed by the body to use and store sugar. Scientists knew that insulin from a healthy animal could help human patients, but no one—until Frederick Banting—knew how to obtain it.

Banting earned a medical degree at the University of Toronto and served with the Canadian Army Medical Corps in World War I (1914–18). After the war Banting returned to his medical practice and to teaching in London, Ontario. While preparing a lecture on the pancreas, he suddenly realized how he might obtain insulin. Working in the laboratory of Professor John J. R. Macleod at the University of Toronto, Banting set to work in May 1921. He was assisted by Charles H. Best, a young graduate student.

Within weeks Banting and Best obtained the first insulin from a dog pancreas. By January 1922, after many tests, they gave insulin to a diabetic, who immediately improved. Other patients also improved when given insulin. Another researcher, James B. Collip, perfected the method of preparing insulin.

In 1923, Banting and Macleod were awarded the Nobel Prize, which they shared with Best and Collip. The University of Toronto set up a new medical research institute named after Banting, and he was knighted in 1934. Banting was killed in an airplane crash in Newfoundland on February 21, 1941.

JOHN S. BOWMAN
Author and Science Editor

BARBADOS

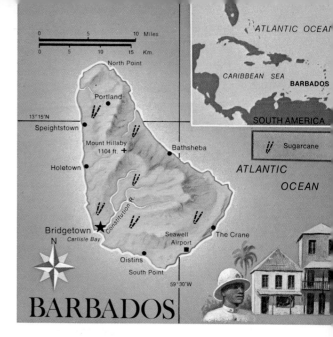

BARBADOS

Barbados is an island nation in the West Indies. Although it has been independent of Britain since 1966, there are many reminders of over 300 years of British rule. People play cricket, a British game, and take afternoon tea. Drivers use the left-hand side of the road, as the British do, and the hills are dotted with tiny cottages that remind one of Britain.

The People and Economy. Most of the people are descendants of slaves brought from Africa centuries ago. The rest are mainly of British origin. English is the official language but is spoken in a distinctive, lilting way. The people are known as Barbadians, though they often call themselves Bajans.

Barbados has a high standard of living compared to other developing countries; still, overpopulation is a major problem. The island's economy was once dominated by sugar and related industries, such as the production of rum and molasses. But Barbados' fine beaches and pleasant climate have made tourism the chief source of the country's income.

The Land. Barbados lies in the Atlantic Ocean but it is considered the easternmost of the islands of the Caribbean Sea. From its highest point—Mount Hillaby, 1,104 feet (336 meters)—the island slopes gently down to the sea. The Atlantic coast is rugged, with a high surf. The Caribbean coast has smooth, wide beaches and calm, blue waters. Bridgetown, the capital, is located on the Caribbean side of the island. The climate is warm, but the trade winds have a cooling effect on the temperature. Rainfall is abundant, especially in the north.

History and Government. Barbados was uninhabited when the Portuguese Pedro a Campos landed there in the early 1500's. He named the island Barbados, meaning "bearded," probably for the beardlike vines or moss that hung from the trees.

The British established the first permanent settlement in 1627. Slaves were imported to work on the tobacco, cotton, and sugarcane plantations, until slavery was abolished in the 1800's. Barbados gained self-government in 1961 and full independence in 1966.

Barbados recognizes the British monarch, represented by a governor-general, as the head of state. Real political authority, however, rests with the Barbadian Parliament. It is made up of the House of Assembly, elected by popular vote, and the Senate, whose members are appointed by the governor-general. The prime minister is chosen from the majority party in the House of Assembly.

BRANFORD M. TAITT
Former Consul General of Barbados

BARBAROSSA. See FREDERICK (Holy Roman Emperors: Frederick I).

FACTS and figures

BARBADOS is the official name of the country.

LOCATION: West Indies.

AREA: 166 sq mi (430 km²).

POPULATION: 259,000 (estimate).

CAPITAL AND LARGEST CITY: Bridgetown.

MAJOR LANGUAGE: English (official).

MAJOR RELIGIOUS GROUP: Christian (Protestant).

GOVERNMENT: Constitutional monarchy. **Head of state**—British monarch, represented by a governor-general. **Head of government**—prime minister. **Legislature**—Parliament (consisting of the House of Assembly and the Senate).

CHIEF PRODUCTS: Agricultural—sugarcane, sweet potatoes, corn, cassava, beans. **Manufactured**—sugar, rum, molasses, cotton clothing, pharmaceuticals.

MONETARY UNIT: Barbados dollar (1 dollar = 100 cents).

BARCELONA

Barcelona is the second largest city of Spain and the capital of the autonomous region of Catalonia. With about 1.7 million people (nearly 5 million in the metropolitan area), it is exceeded in population only by Madrid, the national capital. Barcelona is situated in northeastern Spain, on the Mediterranean Sea. Economically, it is the country's chief port and an important industrial city, accounting for one-quarter of Spain's manufactured goods.

The City. As the capital and largest city of Catalonia, Barcelona has long been at the center of Catalan history and culture. The older part of the city, which lies just above the harbor, dates from the 1100's. Its main thoroughfare is the Ramblas, a handsome promenade lined with trees, flower stands, cafés, and bookstores. The Ramblas leads past the Gothic Quarter, site of the cathedral and other buildings from the Middle Ages, and ends at the Plaza Catalonia, a hub of commercial activity.

Roughly northwest of the plaza is the famous church of the Sagrada Familia (Holy Family), designed by Antonio Gaudí in the late 1880's. Other examples of Gaudí's work include the Casa Milá and the Güell Park. Two

other major figures of modern art, Pablo Picasso, who came to Barcelona as a boy, and Joan Miró, who was born here, are celebrated with museums devoted to their paintings, sculptures, and other works. The city is also a center of literary life. Among its institutions of higher education is the University of Barcelona, founded in 1450.

History. Barcelona traces its origins to the Phoenicians and their successors, the Carthaginians, who founded the settlement of Barcino in the 200's B.C. The city was later ruled by Romans, Visigoths, Muslim Moors, and the Franks of Charlemagne, before an independent Catalan state was established under the counts of Barcelona in the A.D. 1000's. Following Catalonia's federation with the neighboring kingdom of Aragon in the next century, Barcelona controlled a Mediterranean empire that included the Balearic Islands and Sicily. But its power declined when Aragon was incorporated into a united Spain in 1517.

The later history of Barcelona was stormy. It rebelled against Spain in 1640 and again in 1705, and from 1808 to 1813, it was ruled by France. By the mid-1800's, the Catalan language and culture had almost disappeared, but an improved economy helped bring about a cultural rebirth and the dream of independence. A center of resistance to the Nationalists during the Spanish Civil War (1931–39), Barcelona suffered under the postwar government of General Francisco Franco. But with Franco's death in 1975, Catalonia's cultural aspirations revived, and in 1979, autonomy, or local self-rule, was approved. Barcelona's selection as the site of the 1992 Summer Olympics was a symbol of the city's renewal.

ROBERT W. KERN
University of New Mexico
Editor, *Historical Dictionary of Modern Spain*

BARKLEY, ALBEN. See VICE PRESIDENCY OF THE UNITED STATES.

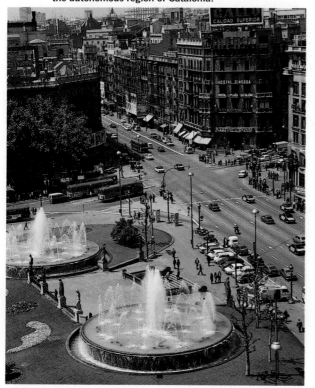

The Plaza Catalonia is a hub of commercial activity in Barcelona, Spain's second largest city and the capital of the autonomous region of Catalonia.

BARLEY

Barley is a cereal grain belonging to the grass family, which includes wheat, oats, rye, and rice. It is an important cereal grain because it is able to thrive in a variety of climates. From the Arctic to the Andes, from the Himalayas to Ethiopia, in climates that are too cold or too dry for other cereal grains, barley grows.

Barley was the first grain cultivated by people. Although wild barley was probably domesticated by several early civilizations, some of the earliest archeological evidence indicates that it was cultivated 10,000 years ago along the Euphrates River in what is now Syria. Cultivated barley seeds were carried from place to place and bred with other wild barley of the area to make the barley more suitable for growing in a specific region. By 5,000 years ago, barley was a staple crop in Ethiopia, Tibet, China, and India. Columbus introduced barley to the Americas on his first voyage there. Today, leading producers of barley are Russia, Canada, and the United States.

The Barley Plant. Barley is similar in appearance to other members of the grass family. Like all grasses, it flowers and produces seeds. Grain heads form at the top of stems. The plant usually reaches a height of about 30 inches (76 centimeters). Size, color, length, and stiffness of the head are just a few of the characteristics that vary among the many hundreds of varieties of cultivated barley that exist worldwide. But no matter what their special characteristics, all types of barley can be classified by the arrangement of the grains in the head. The most important commercial barleys are the two- and six-row types.

Growing and Harvesting Barley. Barley grows best in the world's temperate regions. It is well suited to a climate where the ripening period is long and cool, the soil is well drained, and the growing period has moderate rainfall and humidity. Different types of barley are grown depending on the altitude, climate, and whether the barley will be used for food, ground as grain, or to produce malt for brewing beer. Planting takes place in the spring and fall. Spring barley is usually planted in early spring and harvested in summer. Winter barley, which is planted in the fall, grows throughout the winter and is harvested the following spring.

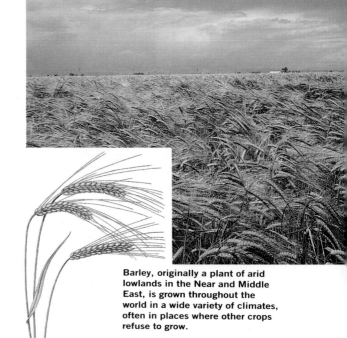

Barley, originally a plant of arid lowlands in the Near and Middle East, is grown throughout the world in a wide variety of climates, often in places where other crops refuse to grow.

Diseases and pests can attack and damage barley as it grows, causing serious losses in crop production. A variety of methods are used to prevent damage. The main methods for controlling diseases are the planting of disease-resistant varieties and the use of fungicide seed treatment. Insect damage can be avoided by planting those varieties that are resistant to insects, varying the time of planting, introducing predators and parasites that feed on the insects, and using insecticides.

While some countries continue to harvest barley by hand, the fastest and most common method in the developed world is to harvest the dry, fully ripe grain with machines called combines. Sometimes barley is cut when it is less ripe, while the straw is still slightly green. Then the barley is cut and tied into bundles (shocks) or left in cut rows (windrows). The grain is allowed to dry and is threshed out later. This method is preferred when it is important to have undamaged kernels.

Uses of Barley. Most of the barley produced is used for animal feed. The barley is processed and mixed with other ingredients to produce different kinds of feeds. Barley is also important in the production of food. It is made into the malt that is used in brewing beer. Other foodstuffs, such as soups and bread, are also made with barley.

ETHEL M. DUTKY
University of Maryland

See also BEER AND BREWING; PLANTS.

BARNARD, CHRISTIAAN (1922–   )

Christiaan Barnard is the South African surgeon who performed the first human heart transplant. This historic operation took place on December 3, 1967. Barnard removed the healthy heart of a young woman who had been fatally wounded in an automobile accident. He transplanted her heart into the chest of Louis Washkansky, a 55-year-old man whose heart was failing. Washkansky lived for 18 days with the transplanted heart.

Although Washkansky died of pneumonia soon after the transplant, the operation was considered a success—Washkansky's new heart beat strongly until the end. Barnard performed his second heart transplant operation a month after the first one. This time, the recipient of the transplanted heart lived for 18 months. Barnard continued doing transplant operations with critically ill patients. His innovative surgical procedures included another first. In 1974, he transplanted a second heart in a human being. The hearts were linked together, forming a kind of double pump to circulate blood throughout the body.

Christiaan Barnard was born on November 8, 1922, in a small town called Beaufort West, South Africa. His father was a minister and the family was quite poor. Barnard's mother had high expectations of her children and urged them to work hard and strive to be the best in their classes. Barnard studied hard and was admitted to medical school in Cape Town, South Africa. He received advanced training in heart surgery at the University of Minnesota in the United States. It was in 1958 that Barnard returned to South Africa and introduced the revolutionary new technique of operating directly on the heart—the procedure called open-heart surgery.

Barnard retired as a surgeon in 1983. The effects of chronic arthritis eventually made it difficult for him to operate. Since retiring, Barnard has continued doing research related to transplant operations and has authored several books on health and medical topics. His writings also include his autobiography, *Christiaan Barnard: One Life* (1970).

ELIZABETH KAPLAN
Science Writer

See also HEART.

BARNUM, PHINEAS TAYLOR (1810–1891)

Phineas T. Barnum was an American showman with a genius for staging and promoting unusual events. His claims about his shows were often exaggerated or false, and he considered himself a master of the art of "humbug," or fooling the people. Nevertheless, he was one of the first entrepreneurs to recognize the importance of publicity, using techniques such as brass bands and sensational newspaper advertisements to draw attention to his shows.

P. T. Barnum was born on July 5, 1810, in Bethel, Connecticut. He began his show business career in New York City, where at the age of 25 he exhibited an aged woman named Joice Heth, claiming she had been George Washington's nurse. Hundreds of people paid to see Heth, said to be 161 years old.

In 1841, Barnum acquired the American Museum in New York City, where he displayed amusing and astonishing oddities—both genuine and fake—including sword swallowers, giants, bearded ladies, and the midget known as General Tom Thumb. In 1850 he promoted and managed a highly successful American concert tour by the famous Swedish singer Jenny Lind.

In 1871, Barnum launched a traveling circus that he billed as the "Greatest Show on Earth." Ten years later he joined his circus with that of a competitor, James A. Bailey. Under Barnum and Bailey the spectacular three-ring circus became an American institution. The Barnum and Bailey Circus was purchased by the Ringling Brothers in 1907.

Barnum published an autobiography in 1855. He also was a member of the Connecticut state legislature and served one term as mayor of Bridgeport, Connecticut. He died in Bridgeport on April 7, 1891.

Reviewed by ROBERT S. PELTON
Curator, The Barnum Museum

BAROMETER

The air around you is made up of tiny molecules of gas that are constantly in motion. Pulled by the Earth's gravity, these air molecules also press down on the Earth and everything on it. In fact, about 1 ton of air presses down on each square foot (about 10 metric tons on each square meter) of the Earth's surface. The force of the air pressing down on the surface of the Earth is called **air pressure**. A barometer is an instrument that measures air pressure.

You may have seen a barometer hanging on a wall. Inside it there is a small box, or chamber, with thin metal walls. Most of the air has been drawn out of this chamber so its thin walls will move in or out slightly when there is an increase or decrease in the air pressure outside of it. A pointer on the front of the barometer, which is connected by a series of levers to the chamber walls, indicates these small changes. The pointer moves in front of a dial that is marked off in units of air

An Aneroid Barometer

pressure. These units are usually measured in inches or centimeters.

Air pressure is important in weather forecasting. A change in air pressure usually means a change in weather. A drop in pressure often means that bad weather is coming. A rise in pressure usually means that clear weather is on the way.

Air pressure also changes when you move from sea level to higher altitudes. It is usually greater at the surface of the Earth near sea level than it is at mountaintops or above as you move through the upper levels of our atmosphere. When you climb a mountain, for example, you will find that because the air presses down less strongly it feels "thinner." Airplane pilots often use barometers called **altimeters** to tell them how high they are above the ground.

The barometers you have read about so far are called aneroid barometers. Aneroid means "without liquid." There are other barometers that do use liquids. The very first barometer was of this type. An Italian scientist named Evangelista Torricelli (1608–47) designed it in 1643. He took a long glass tube that was closed at one end and filled it with mercury. He turned this tube upside down in a pan that contained more mercury. The mercury in the tube started running out, of course. Soon the mercury stopped running out because the weight of the mercury in the tube was balanced by the pressure of air on the mercury outside the tube.

Mercury barometers are still used today. Scientists read a mercury barometer by seeing how high the column of mercury in the tube is. When air pressure increases, the mercury column goes up. When the pressure decreases, the column goes down.

Mercury barometers are very accurate. But they are clumsy to move around, and they have to be kept upright so that the liquid stays level. That is why ordinary barometers used in homes or the barometers used on ships and airplanes are aneroid barometers. Mercury barometers are used mainly in weather stations and scientific laboratories.

Reviewed by SERGE A. KORFF
New York University

See also WEATHER.

A Fortin Mercury Barometer ►

Mercury level

Reading scales

Cross Section of an Aneroid Barometer ▼

Hollow metal box

Thermometer

Mercury cup

Springs

Levers

Pointer

The Triumph of Divine Providence, a ceiling fresco by the Italian artist Pietro da Cortona, has the swirling shapes and rich detail characteristic of some baroque art.

BAROQUE ART
AND ARCHITECTURE

The term baroque is used by art historians to describe European painting, sculpture, and architecture created in the period from about 1600 to 1750. When first applied to the visual arts, at the very end of this period, the term conveyed a rather negative attitude toward its subject, suggesting bizarre or simply bad taste. Only in modern times was the term baroque freed from such unflattering associations and used to describe art produced in the period between the end of the Renaissance in the 1500's and the beginnings of modernism in the later 1700's. The baroque period is so rich and so diverse, however, that no single term can accurately describe all of the art produced in these years.

▶CHARACTERISTICS

The diversity of baroque art is the result of several factors. The first is geographical. While Renaissance culture originated in Italy about 1400 and gradually spread from Flor-

ence throughout much of Europe, baroque art appeared almost at the same time in nearly every European capital. In the early 1600's, artists of several nationalities working in several different countries—Spain, France, and the Netherlands as well as Italy—created works of great originality.

Although there were shared preferences among artists from different nations with respect to subject matter and style, there were also significant differences. In each country there was a considerable variety of styles from which to choose. An earthy realism that copied life was one choice; a more refined manner that revived the classical styles of ancient Greece and Rome and of the Renaissance was another; and a dramatic, emotionally charged style that sought to represent the supernatural was yet a third. Choices of subject matter frequently went hand in hand with such choices of style.

Religious beliefs and practices played perhaps the greatest role in the various expressions of baroque art. The Reformation of the mid-1500's divided Europe into Catholic

In *The Calling of St. Matthew*, the Italian artist Caravaggio set a biblical story in his own day. Christ, at the far right of the painting, calls on Matthew, who points at himself questioningly, to follow him. The costumes and setting are those of Caravaggio's Rome, not of the time of Christ. Only the dramatic lighting suggests the sacred subject matter.

countries and Protestant countries. In most Protestant countries, including Germany and England, art was considered an unnecessary luxury and was suppressed. But in one Protestant country, Holland, an entirely new kind of art was created. It was based on the routines of everyday life, while still following the Calvinist doctrine of banning images that depicted religious subjects. In Catholic countries such as Italy, Spain, and France, on the other hand, painters and sculptors continued the long-standing practice of using biblical stories as their primary subject matter.

▶ITALY

The first painter who might be called baroque was Michelangelo Merisi da Caravaggio. Caravaggio, as he was known, worked mostly in Rome, where he painted a number of large canvases that depicted religious subjects from the New Testament. But if his subject matter remained traditional, his realistic treatment of the human figure and the setting was radically new. In such paintings as *The Calling of St. Matthew* (1599–1602), Caravaggio set the story not at the time of Christ but in his own time. The costumes of the fig-

ures as well as the architecture and furnishings of the interior setting are based on contemporary Roman fashions. Sometimes the figures in his paintings can be identified as his friends. The only element in Caravaggio's religious paintings that suggests a divine presence is his use of **tenebrist** light, a sharply contrasting spotlighting that resembles stage lighting.

Caravaggio's realistic depiction of biblical stories was very different from the approach taken by his contemporary Annibale Carracci. Carracci's paintings return to the clarity of design and balanced composition of such High Renaissance artists as Raphael. Most of Carracci's paintings were of religious subjects, but his most famous works, the frescoes on the ceiling of the Farnese Gallery in Rome (1597–1605), illustrate mythological scenes from the writings of the Roman poet Ovid. Many of the figures are based on classical statues or the paintings of Raphael and Michelangelo. Although they appear lifelike, they are so idealized that they could never be confused with real figures in real settings.

A third approach to art was taken by Pietro da Cortona, who excelled as both an architect and a painter. His large ceiling fresco *The*

Triumph of Divine Providence (1633–39) in the Palazzo Barberini, Rome, is a dazzling composition of loosely arranged, colorful figures that swirl freely overhead. In style as well as in subject, this is far removed from the realism of Caravaggio or the timelessness of Carracci. Cortona's *Triumph* is, in fact, a representation of the supernatural, an imaginary vision of the ascent to immortality of a living person, Pope Urban VIII Barberini.

One artist who seemed to capture the spirit of his time in all its diversity and vitality was the sculptor Giovanni Lorenzo Bernini. His statue *David* (1623), done when he was still a young man, expresses most of the characteristic features of baroque art. While its pose imitates sculpture from the ancient past, it is also very realistically rendered. Like many works of art

In works such as *David*, the Italian sculptor Giovanni Lorenzo Bernini captured the vitality of the baroque age. The sculpture, based on a biblical story, depicts the young David in the act of hurling a stone at the giant Goliath. The figure imparts a sense of movement and drama that draws the viewer into the action of the story.

from this period, it represents one moment in a continuous action, in this case David hurling a stone from his sling at Goliath. Finally, it draws the spectator into the action, making him or her an active participant in the story being told.

Although he preferred sculpture, Bernini also designed a number of architectural projects that contribute to the magnificence of Rome. Chief among these was his completion of the rebuilding of St. Peter's Basilica, the most important church in the Catholic world. In addition to sculpting a number of works for the interior of the great church, in the 1650's he designed and built the enormous open square that stands in front of it. This square, or piazza, consists of two curving colonnades that are shaped like arms that reach out to gather in the faithful, a symbolic gesture that Bernini noted in writings that accompanied his plans. Walking through St. Peter's Square today, one still experiences the majesty, the authority, and the self-confidence of the baroque popes.

▶ SPAIN

Spain also experienced a Golden Age during the 1600's. In art as in literature, a simple and humble realism emerged just after the turn of the century. In Seville and Madrid, painters and sculptors created works so lifelike that at times one cannot tell the difference between art and reality. Sculpture in particular frequently blended the two—statues were made of carved and painted wood, rather than the white marble used in Italy, and often were clothed in actual garments.

The greatest Spanish artist of the period was Diego Velázquez. Velázquez began his career in Seville as a painter of scenes of everyday

Spanish artist Francisco de Zurbarán specialized in realistic portrayals of saints. His painting *St. Serapion* depicts a monk who died for his beliefs.

life and while still a young man moved to Madrid, where he was appointed court painter to King Philip IV. His masterpiece, *The Maids of Honor* (1656), depicts the artist himself at work in his studio on what seems to be a portrait of the Infanta Margarita Teresa, daughter of the king and queen. Servants attend the little girl, the family dog rests by her side, and the furnishings of the studio are precisely detailed. Among the framed paintings that hang on a dark rear wall is a mirror in which the likenesses of Philip IV and his queen are recognizable. When a viewer stands in front of the painting, he or she occupies the same space as the king and queen. Art and reality are so perfectly blended that the experience of looking at this picture is positively magical. A reproduction of *The Maids of Honor* appears in the article SPAIN, ART AND ARCHITECTURE OF in Volume S.

Catholicism was a powerful influence in Spanish life of this period, and paintings of religious subjects became ever more popular. Velázquez' contemporary Francisco de Zurbarán specialized in painting realistic portrayals of Christ and the saints. The figures are highlighted with sharply contrasted tenebrist light that gives them intense spiritual power.

▶FRANCE

Baroque art in France was for the most part an expression of the values of the French crown, especially of King Louis XIV. The great palace of Versailles (1669–85) was built by Louis a few miles outside of Paris as a symbol of his absolute authority. The design

The palace of Versailles was built for France's King Louis XIV. The design of the palace and its gardens conveys the power and grandeur of the French crown.

of the palace and of the surrounding parkland is the product of a rational and rigidly disciplined approach that echoes the king's control of government. The architecture and the painting and sculpture that decorate the palace are purely classical in style, conveying to all a sense of the orderly and timeless truths of the king's political policies.

Not every artist in France was content to work for the government. Many painters chose to leave the country rather than place their creativity in the service of politics. Indeed, the two greatest French painters of the baroque period, Nicholas Poussin and Claude Lorrain, spent their entire careers in Italy. Both artists turned to the gentle Roman landscape for inspiration. Claude, as he is known, painted the poetry of the lovely countryside, populated with grazing flocks of sheep and picturesque ruins of ancient monuments. Poussin depicted some of the same features of the Roman countryside, but his paintings were intended to do more than delight the viewer. He used the classical setting as a stage for presenting the drama of human history. His paintings instruct as well as delight. The purpose of his art was to elevate the mind to its highest and most moral state.

▶THE NETHERLANDS

In the northwestern part of Europe, political and religious differences led to the division of the region then known as the Netherlands into two independent states. The southern provinces, called Flanders (comprising present-day Belgium and part of northern France), were in the 1600's part of the Spanish Empire. The northern provinces, known as Holland (the present-day Netherlands), broke away from Spain at the end of the 1500's, establishing an independent democracy that was one of the first of its kind.

Flemish Art. The art of Flanders in the baroque period continued to reflect the religious beliefs of Catholicism and the rigid class distinctions of Spanish society. Peter Paul Rubens expressed the values of this culture better than anyone. His painting *The Adoration of the Magi* (1624) depicts the birth of Christ as an aristocratic pageant, with none of the simplicity usually found in Nativity scenes. Instead of humble shepherds in a rustic stable, there are splendidly costumed Magi in a grand setting offering expensive gifts.

Left: The Adoration of the Magi, by Flemish artist Peter Paul Rubens, portrays the birth of Christ as an elegant pageant, with richly costumed Magi bearing expensive gifts. *Above:* Dutch baroque artists often depicted scenes from daily life rather than religious subjects. *Woman Pouring Milk*, by Jan Vermeer, finds a simple beauty in the routines and surroundings of everyday life.

Rubens' younger contemporary Anthony Van Dyck specialized in painting portraits of members of the same upper class that would have appreciated the material finery of *The Adoration*. Van Dyck was so successful at flattering the aristocracy that his works were in demand in all the courts of Europe, especially England. The ladies and gentlemen in his pictures are always taller, slimmer, more elegant, and more graceful than they were in life. Some of the artist's methods are still used in fashion advertisements today, while the pointed beard and mustache worn by many of his male sitters remain known as a Vandyke.

Dutch Art. Life was very different in the northern Netherlands during this period. Along with political and economic freedom, the Dutch insisted on religious freedom. Catholicism was abolished as the official religion, and most of the population followed the Protestant teachings of John Calvin. Although Calvinism left no place for art in religious practice, the art of painting did not disappear in Holland. Instead the arts flourished, with an increasing number of painters turning to Dutch life itself for their subject matter.

Jan Vermeer specialized in painting the interiors of simple middle-class households in his native town of Delft. There are no biblical or mythological subjects in Vermeer's paintings to distract us from their plain compositions and pure colors. A work such as *Woman Pouring Milk* (about 1660) is surprisingly modern in its simple design and its reflection of the mood of the artist's own daily life.

Other Dutch painters specialized in outdoor scenes, in landscape, in still lifes of flowers, fish, or fruit, or in portraiture. Frans Hals painted only portraits, and a comparison of his informal likenesses with the society portraits of Anthony Van Dyck reveals the deep cultural differences between Holland and neighboring Flanders in this period.

The greatest Dutch artist of the baroque period was Rembrandt van Rijn. Rembrandt spent most of his life in Amsterdam, where his

Left: The Syndics of the Cloth Merchants' Guild, by the Dutch artist Rembrandt van Rijn, captures the individuality of each of the prosperous Dutch businessmen it portrays. This emphasis on the individual is typical of baroque art.

Below: St. Paul's Cathedral, in London, was built by the architect Christopher Wren in an English version of the baroque style. Its massive dome is modeled on the dome of St. Peter's Basilica in Rome.

imagination and curiosity led him to explore a far wider range of subjects than did most of his contemporaries. He painted many biblical scenes, not for churches and not as aids to religious worship, but as imaginary records of significant moments in human history. Human feeling in all its mystery and complexity is the true subject of his work. Many of his most moving paintings are portraits—most of individuals, some of groups, and many of himself. His *Syndics of the Cloth Merchants' Guild* (1662), a group portrait of five Amsterdam businessmen, is typical in the way it creates unity out of informality, preserving the indi-

viduality of each member of the group while knitting their personalities together into a coherent whole. The soft coloring, mellow light, and sketchy brushwork of Rembrandt's paintings contribute to the sense of unity found in his work. While these are personal elements that distinguish him from other artists of his time, Rembrandt's interest in capturing a fleeting moment and his emphasis on the inner life of individuals who share their thoughts and moods with the viewer are characteristics found throughout baroque art.

▶ENGLAND

In geography and culture, England has always remained apart from the rest of Europe. Like many Protestant countries, England was suspicious of the power of visual images. Painting all but died out during the 1600's. Architecture, on the other hand, flourished in London after the Great Fire of 1666. St. Paul's Cathedral was rebuilt by Christopher Wren not in the Gothic style of the old cathedral but in the up-to-date baroque manner. If its plan and interior remain recognizably English, its impressive facade and stately dome are based on the architectural styles of Paris and Rome. Like so many works of art from the period around 1700, St. Paul's speaks a truly international language, pronounced, however, with a distinct regional accent.

JOHN VARRIANO
Mount Holyoke College
Author, *Italian Baroque and Rococo Architecture*

A performance of an opera at the palace of Versailles, France, in the 1600's. Opera was one of many important musical forms developed during the baroque period.

BAROQUE MUSIC

Baroque is the term used to describe the music of the period extending roughly from 1600 to 1750. The baroque era includes all the music from the time of Italian composer Claudio Monteverdi in the late 1500's to German composers Johann Sebastian Bach and George Frederick Handel in the 1700's. Many of the most important musical forms were developed during this period, including the sonata, symphony, concerto, suite, opera, oratorio, and many others.

The composers of the baroque era tried to use their music to express intense emotions. As a result, music became much more dramatic than it had ever been before. Further, secular (nonreligious) music was considered to be as important as sacred music in the baroque era. While most of the best music of earlier times was composed for the church, much baroque music was written for other purposes.

In baroque music we can see the beginnings and early development of modern harmony. Before the beginning of the baroque period, the most common type of music was **polyphonic music**, in which two or more melodies are sounded together. Baroque composers developed a style of vocal music, called **monody**, with only one melody and a supporting harmony. This innovation encouraged composers to invent new and interesting harmonies.

The importance of harmony led to a new kind of musical notation called the **figured bass**. It was used so widely during the baroque era that the period is sometimes called the figured-bass period. Only the melody line and a simple bass part were written out in the musical score. The composer indicated the harmony by writing figures—numbers and symbols—under the bass part below the staff. The performer playing accompaniment (usually the keyboardist) filled in the harmony according to the figures. The figures suggested a general harmonic outline but allowed room for improvisation by the performer. Figured bass was used first in vocal music and later spread to instrumental music.

▶VOCAL MUSIC

Opera was developed in Florence, Italy, near the end of the 1500's. A group of amateur poets, musicians, and painters, known as the Florentine Camerata, wanted to revive ancient classical Greek drama, which they knew had been accompanied by music. They decided to write plays based on classical subjects and to set the plays to music. But instead of reproducing the drama of ancient Greece, they invented something new—the opera.

New vocal forms were invented for this new kind of music. **Recitative** imitates the inflections of speech. It consists of a single melodic line for solo voice with a simple instrumental accompaniment. With recitative, words could be clearly expressed and the story could be easily followed. The **aria** is a more lyrical form for solo voice, used to show the emotional state of a character rather than to move the story along. Arias are usually in A-B-A form; that is, the first part is repeated after the end of the contrasting second, or middle, part. These are called *da capo* arias, a form that became very popular in baroque vocal music. *Da capo* means to repeat from the beginning of a piece. In the *da capo* aria, singers often have an opportunity to show off their vocal skills.

The world's first opera was *Dafne,* which had its premiere performance in 1598. It was the work of two members of the Florentine Camerata, the poet Ottavio Rinuccini and the composer Jacopo Peri. Most of the music for *Dafne* has been lost, but all of Peri's second opera, *Euridice* (1600), still exists. Both operas were popular successes.

In 1607, ten years after the first performance of *Dafne,* Italian composer Claudio Monteverdi wrote *Orfeo,* an opera that is still performed today. Monteverdi was the first to write ensemble numbers such as duets and trios, and to give an important role to the orchestra. He made expressive use of colorful orchestral effects. He enlarged the orchestra and developed new performance techniques. For this reason many people consider Monteverdi the father of the symphony orchestra.

The opera developed rapidly. In Naples, Italy, Alessandro Scarlatti established many of the traditions of Italian opera that later composers followed. In France, Jean-Baptiste Lully laid the foundations of French opera. Lully emphasized the drama in his operas and gave the orchestra a more important role. He also established the ballet in French opera. In England, Henry Purcell composed *Dido and Aeneas* (1689), which has remained one of the most important English operas.

The Oratorio and the Passion. Baroque musicians also enriched church music with new vocal forms such as the oratorio and the Passion. These required choruses, recitatives, solo and ensemble numbers, and orchestral interludes and accompaniment. Both the oratorio and the Passion were dramatizations of Bible stories. They were usually meant to be performed without scenery or costumes.

The first composer to write a fully developed oratorio was Italy's Giacomo Carissimi. His oratorio *Jephte* (before 1649) established some of the traditions that later oratorio composers followed: It was one of the first to leave out scenery and costumes; it had a narrator, who kept the story moving; and it had dramatic and expressive choruses. For these reasons, Carissimi's *Jephte* is considered the first modern oratorio.

The Passion was a musical setting of the suffering and death of Christ. It had been used occasionally by Renaissance composers as a piece for unaccompanied chorus, but it underwent great change in the baroque era. The baroque Passion added solo voices and orchestra. It also added a chorale, a four-part setting of a hymn tune, which the church congregation joined in singing. Germany's Heinrich Schütz was the first important composer of Passions. Schütz studied in Italy, and he was strongly influenced by the Italian composers, especially Monteverdi.

The Cantata. The cantata was another major musical form that developed in the ba-

A painting by Dutch artist Jan Vermeer shows a woman playing a virginal (an early type of harpsichord). Much baroque music was written for keyboard instruments.

roque era. It began as a secular form of music and later was introduced into the church. The cantata was a small composition that required fewer musicians than large works like the oratorio. Cantatas were composed for one or two solo voices accompanied by a small instrumental group. They usually began with an introduction for instruments alone, followed by contrasting sections of recitatives and arias.

Church cantatas were based on biblical texts and became very popular in the 1600's and 1700's. The form was perfected by German composer Dietrich Buxtehude. Many of Buxtehude's cantatas use chorale melodies of the Lutheran Church. The most famous Italian composer of cantatas was Alessandro Scarlatti, who is better known for his operas. Scarlatti wrote some 600 cantatas in addition to more than 100 operas and about 35 oratorios.

▶ INSTRUMENTAL MUSIC

Probably nothing else in the baroque period has had more far-reaching effects than the development of instrumental music. For the first time, instrumental music was regarded as equal in importance to vocal music. As in vocal music, many baroque instrumental forms began in Italy.

Renaissance composers had written many pieces for the organ. But they wrote them in the polyphonic vocal style, as though the organ were a combination of human voices rather than an instrument. Baroque composers of organ music, on the other hand, began to develop a distinctly instrumental style of writing. They emphasized the tonal qualities for which the organ was best suited. Italian composer Girolamo Frescobaldi perfected some of the chief forms of organ music. These included the organ toccata, fugue, and partita. Dietrich Buxtehude was another important composer of organ music. With Buxtehude, organ music reached a stage of development that remained unsurpassed until Johann Sebastian Bach.

Music for instruments other than the organ also had to develop a nonvocal style before it became independent from vocal music. Instrumental music developed rapidly because brilliant new stringed instruments were being made by the famous violin-making families of Cremona, Italy. First the Amati family and later the Guarneri and Stradivari families made wonderful new violins, violas, and cellos.

These instruments have never been surpassed for their beautiful rich tone and finely crafted construction.

The Sonata and the Concerto. Early in the baroque era, a new musical idea emerged for which a new term was invented—sonata. A sonata was a composition that could be performed only on an instrument, just as the cantata was a piece of music that was meant only to be sung. Once composers started making this distinction, they began to develop a strictly instrumental style that was completely different from vocal music.

The first master to do so was Italy's Arcangelo Corelli. Corelli was the foremost violin virtuoso of his time and the first important composer of violin music. He produced two landmark works. One of these consisted of

Italian violinist and composer Arcangelo Corelli was influential in the development of the sonata and the concerto, two leading instrumental forms.

twelve sonatas for violin and keyboard accompaniment. In these sonatas a new style of violin performance was demonstrated fully for the first time. His second great contribution was a set of twelve *concerti grossi* (grand concertos) for a combination of instruments. Corelli's violin sonatas and concertos were the ancestors of the later solo sonata and the classical concerto.

The practice of contrasting the tone color, or timbre, of instruments with each other was a baroque invention. For the first time on a large scale, the special tone quality of individual instruments was fully used. This formed the basis on which modern orchestral writing was built. Baroque composers wrote many concertos for violin, flute, cello, and keyboard. Later in the period, concertos for other instruments such as the horn and the oboe also became popular.

The sonata and the concerto developed rapidly. The leading composers were Italy's

An engraving (*left*) portrays the baroque composer George Frederick Handel presenting his *Water Music* to King George I of England. The set of orchestral suites was first performed on a barge during a royal procession down the River Thames. Handel and Johann Sebastian Bach (*below*) were two giants of the baroque age. Their works, which represent the pinnacle of baroque music, paved the way for the achievements of the classical period that followed.

Antonio Vivaldi, Giuseppe Tartini, and Domenico Scarlatti, the son of Alessandro. Scarlatti was the first important composer in Italy to write sonatas for a keyboard instrument. He also created a brilliant new style of keyboard writing and perfected a new technique of performing on the harpsichord.

The Dance Suite. Outside Italy, too, great advances were being made in instrumental music. Composers were creating a treasury of smaller pieces for keyboard instruments. These pieces often were based on dances. Composers began to arrange them in groups called suites. The dance suite consisted of several dance movements contrasting in mood, tempo, and rhythm. The basic arrangement consisted of four dances: an allemande in moderate tempo; a courante, or running dance; a slow and stately sarabande; and a quick and lively gigue, or jig. Composers often added dances between the sarabande and gigue, such as the minuet or gavotte. Outstanding composers of dance suites and other beautiful keyboard pieces were Germany's Johann Froberger, England's Henry Purcell, and France's François Couperin and Jean-Philippe Rameau.

▶**HANDEL AND BACH**

Baroque music reached a climax with two of the greatest composers who ever lived: George Frederick Handel and Johann Sebastian Bach. With these creative giants, baroque music came to its final fulfillment. With Handel, opera in the old Italian tradition reached its highest development. Henceforth opera would develop in completely new directions. With Handel, too, the oratorio—and with Bach, the Passion—reached a stage of near perfection. See the biographies of Bach and Handel in volumes B and H.

Few composers before Bach and Handel wrote instrumental music with such expressiveness, emotion, and beauty. Both of these masters composed sonatas, concertos, suites, and solo instrumental music that fully achieved all the possibilities of the baroque style. They also pointed the way for the future. The works of Bach and Handel not only represent the end of the baroque era, they look forward to the beginnings of the classical period that followed.

DAVID EWEN
Music Historian
Reviewed by KENNETH NOTT
Hartt School, University of Hartford

BARRIE, SIR JAMES MATTHEW
(1860–1937)

James Matthew Barrie, the creator of Peter Pan, was born in the Scottish town of Kirriemuir on May 9, 1860, the son of a local weaver. When James was 6, his older brother David was drowned in a skating accident. Their mother was heartbroken but consoled herself with the idea that in dying so young, David would remain a boy forever. It was this idea that Barrie later turned into his most famous play, *Peter Pan*.

Barrie knew from an early age that he wanted to be a writer. He graduated from Edinburgh University in 1882, and in 1885 he moved to London and began writing novels. The most famous was *The Little Minister* (1891). But Barrie is best known as a writer for the stage. His first successful play, *Walker, London* (1892), was followed by *The Admirable Crichton* (1902), *What Every Woman Knows* (1908), and *Dear Brutus* (1917).

Barrie married the actress Mary Ansell in 1894, but they had no children of their own. One day in the summer of 1898, while walking his dog in Kensington Gardens, Barrie met three young brothers, George, Jack, and Peter. Their parents, Arthur and Sylvia Llewelyn Davies, and the Barries soon became friends. The story of Peter Pan had been in Barrie's mind since childhood, and now he started writing it as a play to entertain the Davies boys. But instead of making Peter a tragic boy who *could* not grow up, Barrie changed him into the carefree boy who *would* not grow up. *Peter Pan* was first performed in London on December 27, 1904, and it has been a favorite of children ever since. The story has been retold in books and as an animated cartoon.

Barrie was made a baronet in 1913. In 1929 he donated the entire copyright in *Peter Pan* to a London children's hospital. He died on June 19, 1937.

ANDREW BIRKIN
Author, *J. M. Barrie and the Lost Boys*

▶PETER PAN

Peter Pan and the fairy Tinker Bell flew from Never-Never Land, where Peter was leader of the Lost Boys, right into the Darling children's nursery. Peter told Wendy, John, and Michael Darling about Never-Never Land

Peter, Tinker Bell, and the three Darling children fly over the rooftops of London in this illustration from an early edition of James M. Barrie's *Peter Pan*.

and about the mermaids, pirates, and Indians who lived there. He said he would teach the Darlings to fly if they would go back with him.

Just then Liza, the Darlings' maid, and Nana, the Newfoundland dog who was the children's nursemaid, came into the nursery. The children hid until they left. This excerpt picks up the story from there.

"It's all right," John announced, emerging from his hiding-place. "I say, Peter, can you really fly?"

Instead of troubling to answer him Peter flew around the room, taking the mantelpiece on the way.

"How topping!" said John and Michael.

"How sweet!" cried Wendy.

"Yes, I'm sweet, oh, I am sweet!" said Peter, forgetting his manners again.

It looked delightfully easy, and they tried it first from the floor and then from the beds, but they always went down instead of up.

"I say, how do you do it?" asked John, rubbing his knee. He was quite a practical boy.

"You just think lovely wonderful thoughts," Peter explained, "and they lift you up in the air."

He showed them again.

"You're so nippy at it," John said "couldn't you do it very slowly once?"

Peter did it both slowly and quickly. "I've got it now, Wendy!" cried John, but soon he found he had not. Not one of them could fly an inch, though even Michael was in words of two syllables, and Peter did not know A from Z.

Of course Peter had been trifling with them, for no one can fly unless the fairy dust has been blown on him. Fortunately, as we have mentioned, one of his hands was messy with it, and he blew some on each of them, with the most superb results.

"Now just wriggle your shoulders this way," he said, "and let go."

They were all on their beds, and gallant Michael let go first. He did not quite mean to let go, but he did it, and immediately he was borne across the room.

"I flewed!" he screamed while still in mid-air.

John let go and met Wendy near the bathroom.

"Oh, lovely!"

"Oh, ripping!"

"Look at me!"

"Look at me!"

"Look at me!"

They were not nearly so elegant as Peter, they could not help kicking a little, but their heads were bobbing against the ceiling, and there is almost nothing so delicious as that. Peter gave Wendy a hand at first, but had to desist, Tink was so indignant.

Up and down they went, and round and round. Heavenly was Wendy's word.

"I say," cried John. "why shouldn't we all go out?"

Of course it was to this that Peter had been luring them.

Michael was ready: he wanted to see how long it took him to do a billion miles. But Wendy hesitated.

"Mermaids!" said Peter again.

"Oo!"

"And there are pirates."

"Pirates," cried John, seizing his Sunday hat, "let us go at once."

BARRYMORE FAMILY

Ethel Barrymore said of herself and her brothers Lionel and John: "We became actors not because we wanted to go on the stage, but because it was the thing we could do best."

The Barrymores were a noted family of actors who traced their connection with the stage back to Shakespeare's day. Ethel, Lionel, and John appeared together on film only once—in *Rasputin and the Empress* (1932). Separately, they displayed the acting talent that made the name Barrymore a synonym for actor.

Ethel Barrymore (1879–1959) became a star at the age of 21 in *Captain Jinks of the Horse Marines*. She appeared in a series of comedies and later in plays by Barrie, Ibsen,

and Shakespeare. She crowned her stage career in 1940 as the spirited schoolteacher in Emlyn Williams' *The Corn is Green*. She also acted in films, winning an Academy Award for *None But the Lonely Heart* (1944).

Lionel Barrymore (1878–1954) preferred painting to acting. He disliked romantic roles and established himself as a skillful character actor. In 1918 he made a great hit in *The Copperhead*, followed by *The Jest* in 1919 (with his brother), *Macbeth* (1921), and *The Claw* (1921). After that he devoted most of his time to motion pictures. Troubled in his later years by a hip injury, he remained active in films, performing from a wheelchair.

Stunning portrayals of Richard III and Hamlet established **John Barrymore** (1882–1942) as one of the greatest actors of the English-speaking stage. In the 1920's, he went to Hollywood, where he starred in a variety of films, including *Grand Hotel* (1932) and *Twentieth Century* (1934). His charm, his classic profile, and his headline romances added a new chapter to the Barrymore legend —a legend that lives on in younger generations of Barrymores.

JAMES KOTSILIBAS-DAVIS
Author, *The Barrymores*

BARTLETT, JOSIAH. See NEW HAMPSHIRE (Famous People).

From left: Actors Lionel, Ethel, and John Barrymore in costume for *Rasputin and the Empress*, the only film in which all three siblings appeared together.

BARTÓK, BÉLA (1881–1945)

Béla Bartók, the great modern composer, was born in Nagyszentmiklós, Hungary (now in Romania), on March 25, 1881. At age 5 he was given his first piano lessons by his mother. Four years later he began to compose.

In 1899, Bartók was admitted to the Academy of Music in Budapest as an advanced student in piano and composition. During 1903, his last year at the academy, he won much praise for his brilliant piano recitals. His symphonic poem *Kossuth*, written in the same year, brought him international recognition.

As a young man, Bartók was greatly influenced by the spirit of Hungarian nationalism. In 1905 he began making field trips to the Hungarian countryside to learn about the folk music of his land. There he discovered that the villagers had often taken the music of neighboring areas of Eastern Europe and mixed it with their own. He began to use the melodies and rhythms of these mixed styles in his compositions, combining them with a new approach to harmony for which he would become famous. Later he collected folk songs from other countries and wrote books on the special features of folk music. His work encouraged other composers to make use of folk music in their own compositions.

In 1907, Bartók was appointed professor of piano at the Academy of Music. Shortly afterward he began to compose the first of his six string quartets, which were completed between 1909 and 1939. They are thought to be among the finest string quartets ever written.

During the 1920's, after studying old Italian keyboard music, Bartók achieved a completely original style of composing. He combined the sounds and rhythms of folk music with the techniques of composers such as Frescobaldi, Beethoven, and Debussy, as in the First Piano Concerto. He also began his *Mikrokosmos*, pieces for piano students.

Political unrest in Hungary caused Bartók to settle in the United States in 1940. For a time he was associated with Columbia University, where he was able to continue his study of folk music. Bartók was also a successful pianist until ill health forced him to stop performing in public. But he made recordings and continued to compose. His popular Concerto for Orchestra was written in 1943. Bartók died in New York City on September 26, 1945.

BENJAMIN SUCHOFF
Author, *Guide to the Mikrokosmos of Béla Bartók*

BARTON, CLARA (1821–1912)

Clara Barton devoted most of her life to helping people. Her greatest accomplishment was the founding of the American Red Cross.

Clarissa Harlowe Barton was born on Christmas Day, 1821, on a farm near Oxford, Massachusetts. The youngest of five children, she received her early education from her brothers and sisters. At the age of 15, Clara became a teacher.

After 18 years of teaching, Clara Barton moved to Washington, D.C., where she worked in the Patent Office. When the Civil War broke out, reports on the suffering of wounded soldiers troubled her. She urged people to contribute medicines and bandages. She often took these supplies to the battlefield herself, caring for the wounded during action.

When the war was over, Clara Barton headed a group that searched for missing soldiers. She also gave lectures on her war experiences. After four years of this work, she became ill and went to Switzerland to recuperate. There she first learned of the international Red Cross, an organization for the relief of suffering caused by war. When the Franco-Prussian War began in 1870, she remained in Europe to work with the Red Cross.

In 1873, Clara Barton returned to the United States. Although she was not well, she devoted all her energy to establishing an American branch of the Red Cross. In 1881 she succeeded, becoming its first president. As a result of her efforts, the work of the Red Cross was enlarged to aid victims of peacetime disasters such as earthquakes and floods. In 1904, at the age of 83, Clara Barton retired. She died eight years later, on April 12, 1912, at Glen Echo, Maryland.

Reviewed by ALLEN F. DAVIS
Temple University

See also RED CROSS.

BASALT. See ROCKS (Igneous Rocks).

BASEBALL

Baseball is called the American national pastime. Every spring and summer, millions of fans watch professional major-league games in ballparks or on television. There are also professional minor leagues, which serve as a training ground for the majors, as well as thousands of college, high school, Little League, and other amateur teams. In addition to organized competition for every age group, the game is played on an informal basis in parks, school yards, and sandlots. Hardly a child in the United States has grown up without playing baseball in one form or another, and hardly an adult is not familiar with at least some of the rules, terms, and stars of "the great American game."

Baseball began in the United States during the mid-1800's. Through the years, baseball has developed a rich and colorful history. The popularity of the game today owes much to its tradition and folklore. Many fans spend hours recalling dramatic moments and great achievements of the past, reciting statistics, and comparing old-time and present-day stars. Some fans root for the same team for their whole lives, watching games or reading about them in the newspaper every day.

Baseball is so much a part of American life that its terms have been adopted into the everyday speech of the people. "Pinch-hit," "going to bat," "three strikes you're out," and scores of other baseball terms and sayings are used even by people who are not well acquainted with the game.

As baseball became the national pastime of the United States, it also spread to other countries. Today the sport is popular in Latin America, Canada, Japan, and elsewhere.

Colorful, exciting, and rich in tradition, baseball is often called the American national pastime. During the spring and summer, millions of fans flock to major league stadiums to root for their favorite teams. Before the game starts, some youngsters are lucky enough to get the autograph of a star player. When the action begins, attention focuses on the batter (*top right*), the pitcher (*bottom right*), and the fielders and base runners (*bottom left*).

▶ HOW BASEBALL IS PLAYED

The basic rules of baseball have undergone little change in more than 100 years. Two teams, consisting of nine or ten players each, play the game on a large field. During the course of the game, the two teams alternate between **batting** (offensive play) and **fielding** (defensive play). The equipment needed to play baseball includes a bat, a ball, and padded gloves worn by players in the field. The object of the game is to score more **runs** than the opposing team. Generally, a run is scored when a batter hits the ball with the bat and runs safely around four bases, starting from home plate. The fielders try to catch the batted ball and halt the runner's progress to prevent the runner from reaching a base safely.

Field and Equipment

A baseball field has two main sections—the **infield** and the **outfield**. The infield is often called the diamond because it contains four bases—called **home plate**, **first base**, **second base**, and **third base**—that are arranged in the shape of a diamond. The outfield extends to a fence or a grandstand that encloses the entire playing area.

The infield and outfield are contained within two straight lines extending diagonally from home plate. One line goes past first base, and the other line goes past third base; they each extend all the way to the outfield fence or grandstand. These two lines are called foul lines. The area between them is **fair territory**; the area outside them is **foul territory**.

OUTFIELD

Left Fielder

Center Fielder

Right Fielder

Umpire

Foul line

Shortstop

Second base

Second Baseman

First Baseman

Umpire

Foul line

Umpire

Third Baseman

90'

Third base

Pitcher

INFIELD

Pitcher's mound

First base

Pitching rubber

Coach's box

60'6"

90'

Coach's box

FOUL TERRITORY

Batter

Home plate

FOUL TERRITORY

On-deck circle

Umpire

Catcher

420

home plate
17 in x 17 in

right
handers
batter's
box

6 ft.

left
handers
batter's
box

5 ft.

8 ft.

4 ft.

catcher's box

3 ft. 7 in

Defensive players occupy nine positions on the field: pitcher, catcher, first base, second base, shortstop, third base, left field, center field, and right field. The batter (offensive team) stands in the batter's box (*left*) at home plate and tries to hit the ball beyond the reach of the fielders. Base runners try to advance to home plate, thereby scoring a run.

cowhide, is stitched on with thick red thread. The ball weighs between 5 and 5¼ ounces (142 and 149 grams) and is 9 to 9¼ inches (23 to 24 centimeters) in circumference.

Until recently, all bats had to be made of wood (usually ash but sometimes hackberry or hickory). Today aluminum bats are permitted at every level of competition up to the minor and major leagues, where wood is still required. A bat must be no more than 2¾ inches (7 centimeters) in diameter at the thickest part and no more than 42 inches (107 centimeters) long.

The nine defensive players all wear padded leather gloves, or mitts, when they go out in the field. The gloves allow them to catch the ball without hurting their hands. Different fielders use different kinds of gloves.

Baseball uniforms usually include a cap, jersey, knicker-style pants, socks, and shoes. The shoes have metal spikes or rubber cleats on the soles to give the player a solid footing. Batters are required to wear a hard plastic helmet to prevent injury if the ball hits them in the head.

In a standard baseball diamond, each base is 90 feet (27.4 meters) apart. The size of the outfield varies from field to field. In major league stadiums, the outfield fence or grand-stand is generally between 300 and 450 feet (91 and 137 meters) from home plate. Except for dirt areas around each base, most of the infield and all of the outfield is grass. (Some major league stadiums use artificial grass.)

An official baseball has a cork center, sur-rounded by layers of rubber and tightly wound yarn. The outer cover, made of bleached white

BASIC BASEBALL EQUIPMENT

The basic equipment used in baseball includes a wooden or metal bat (1), a ball (2), and leather gloves for fielding. Most fielders use a standard five-fingered glove (3); a first baseman's mitt (4) has a larger "pocket"; a catcher's mitt (5) is round and heavily padded. Other gear includes a batting helmet (6); spiked or cleated shoes (7); and a mask (8), chest protector (9), and leg guards (10) for the catcher.

Players and Positions

Each of the nine players in the field occupies a specific position and performs a specific defensive role. Together they try to keep the team at bat from getting on base and scoring runs.

The main defensive player is the **pitcher**. From a dirt mound in the middle of the diamond, the pitcher throws the ball to the batter. In an effort to keep the batter from hitting it, the pitcher may use a variety of overarm or sidearm pitches—fastballs, curveballs, knuckleballs, and others. The pitcher also fields batted balls (catches and throws them to a teammate), keeps a watchful eye on base runners so they will not advance, and covers first base or home plate when necessary. The pitcher has the most responsibility for seeing that the team at bat does not score. If the pitcher loses control of the game and lets too many opposing players get on base and score

Throwing different kinds of pitches at different speeds, the pitcher tries to keep the batter from hitting the ball. With one foot on the rubber, the pitcher winds up, takes a long stride toward home plate, and hurls the ball with full force. The motion should be smooth and easy, with a strong follow-through. It is important to end up in a balanced position, ready to field a batted ball.

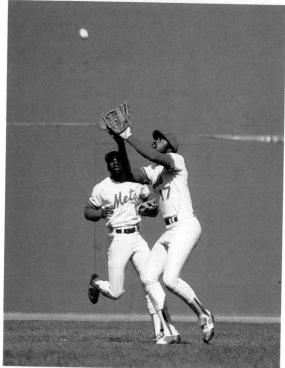

Teamwork in the field is an essential ingredient of winning baseball. *Above:* With the infielder in perfect position, a throw arrives at third base just ahead of the sliding runner. *Below:* An outfielder catches a fly ball as his teammate tries to avoid a collision.

ners who try to score, and to field batted balls that fall near home plate. The catcher must play in close harmony with the pitcher. The catcher studies opposing batters and gives signals to the pitcher indicating what type of pitches to throw. The catcher wears a metal face mask, a padded chest protector, and plastic shin guards to prevent injury from balls tipped by the bat. The catcher's mitt is very thickly padded because pitches are thrown very fast.

Four other members of the defensive team are called infielders. These players try to catch any balls hit by the batter within the infield. The **first baseman** guards first base and the area around it. The **second baseman** plays on the side of second base toward first, while the **shortstop** plays on the other side of second base; together they defend the middle of the infield. The **third baseman** covers third base and the area around it.

Finally, three players called outfielders try to catch any balls hit over or past the infielders. These players are the **left fielder** (on the third-base side), the **center fielder**, and the **right fielder**.

For the offensive team, players take their turns at bat in an order listed before the game starts. This batting order, or **lineup**, normally consists of nine players who also have positions in the field. But because pitchers are not usually good hitters, the American League in 1973 decided to allow another player—the designated hitter—to bat instead of the pitcher. This created a ten-player team. The designated hitter does not play a fielding position.

If substitute batters, called **pinch hitters**, come into the game, they normally bat in the same places in the lineup as the players they replace. But if two or more substitutes (other than pinch hitters) enter at the same time, they can be inserted in any vacant spots in the lineup.

The person in charge of the players and strategies for each team is the **manager**, often a former player. The manager sets the team's lineup, makes substitutions, and directs many plays on the field. The manager also has several coaches, who help train members of the team in skills and strategies. During a game, coaches stand just outside first base and third base, where they make hand signals to base runners and batters.

runs, the starting pitcher may be replaced by a relief pitcher.

The next most important defensive player is the **catcher**, who crouches in a boxed area behind home plate. The catcher's job is to catch all the pitcher's throws that are not hit by the batter, to guard home plate against run-

Every batter has his or her own way of standing at the plate, gripping the bat, and swinging. All good batters assume a balanced position and concentrate fully on the pitch. In the split second it takes the ball to reach home plate, the batter must decide whether or not to swing. If the batter decides to swing, the bat begins to level out as the ball approaches. When contact is made, the batter's head should be down, eyes still focused on the ball. A quick snap of the wrists and a full follow-through add power and distance to the hit. Once contact has been made and the swing is completed, the hitter drops the bat and runs toward first base.

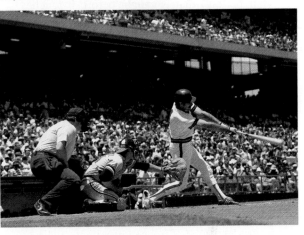

Conduct of Play and Basic Rules

The visiting team takes the first turn at bat. It remains at bat until the home team, fielding, has gotten three **outs**, or put out three visiting players. The home team then bats until three of its players have been put out. When each team has had a turn at bat and a turn in the field, one **inning** is over.

A complete baseball game normally consists of nine innings. However, if the home team is ahead after eight and a half innings or takes the lead in the last half (or bottom) of the ninth inning, then the home team is automatically the winner, and the game is over. Also, if play is stopped because of rain or any other reason after five innings (four and a half innings if the home team is ahead), the game is considered complete; if play is stopped before five innings of play, the game is continued at a later date. Finally, if the score is tied at the end of nine innings, the game goes on until the tie is broken and both teams have had an equal number of times at bat.

The focus of action in any baseball game is the confrontation between pitcher and batter. The batter stands in a boxed area on either side of home plate, depending on whether he or she bats right-handed or left-handed. The

The strike zone is the area directly over home plate between the top of the shoulders and the top of the uniform pants to the top of the knees. If the batter does not swing at a pitch in this zone, the umpire calls a strike. If the pitch is outside the strike zone, the umpire calls a ball.

pitcher throws the ball toward the batter, and the batter tries to hit it. The pitcher aims the ball at an area called the **strike zone**. To be in the strike zone, the ball must pass over home plate within an area extending from the midpoint between the top of the batter's shoulders and the top of the uniform pants to the top of the knees. If the pitch passes through the strike zone and the batter does not swing, a **strike** is called on the batter. A strike is also called if the batter swings at the ball and misses, or if the batter hits the ball into foul territory. The batter is out when three strikes have been made. (A foul ball is not counted as the third strike unless it is a foul bunt or a foul tip caught by the catcher before it touches the ground.)

There are other ways in which a batter can be put out. If the batter hits a ball in the air (fair or foul) that is caught before it touches the ground, the batter is said to have flied out. If the batter hits a fair ground ball that is caught by a fielder and then thrown or carried to first base before the batter gets there, the batter is said to have grounded out.

There are also a number of ways in which a batter can get on base. If a batted ball lands in fair territory and the batter reaches first base before the fielder gets the ball there, the batter has made a **single**. If the batter can reach second base safely on the same hit, it is a **double**. If the batter can reach third base, it is a **triple**. A fair ball hit over the fence or into the stands is a **home run**. The batter can also make a home run by hitting a fair ball onto the playing field and running around all the bases before the fielders get the ball back to home plate. This exciting (and rare) play is called an inside-the-park home run. Any single, double, triple, or home run is called a **hit**.

A batter sometimes can proceed to first base without getting a hit. Each pitch to the batter that passes outside the strike zone is called a **ball**. After four balls, the batter is credited with a **walk** and advances freely to first base. The batter also is awarded first base if hit by a pitched ball; if interfered with by the catcher; or if the catcher drops the ball on a third strike and fails to throw it to first base before the batter arrives there.

In addition to pitching, fielding, and batting, **base running** is an important part of the game of baseball. Once a batter gets on base, the object is to advance to each of the next bases and finally to score a run by reaching home plate. Base runners may advance to the next base any time they think they can do so safely. Usually they wait until the batter hits the ball and then decide whether or not to try to advance. On a fly ball, however, they must wait, or **tag up** at the last base they held until the ball is caught; after tagging up, they may run to the next base. If a runner advances to the next base without the aid of a batted ball or a fielder's error, the runner is said to **steal** a base.

But base runners must always be alert because the fielding team can put them out in several ways. Base runners are out if they are tagged with the ball by a fielder when they are off base or if they go outside the base lines to avoid being tagged. Base runners also can be forced out. For example, if the runner is on first base and the batter hits a ground ball, the runner must advance to second base so that

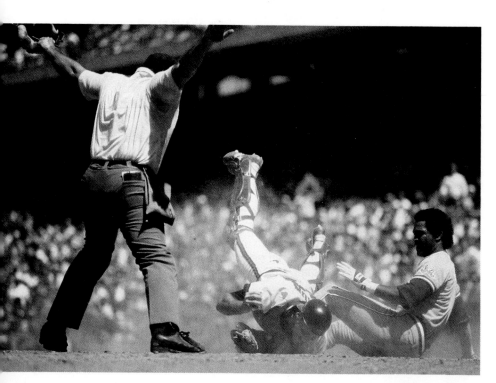

A play at the plate is one of the most thrilling in baseball. As a base runner slides into home, the catcher receives a throw from another fielder and tries to tag the runner before his foot touches the plate. The two players collide in a cloud of dust, and the umpire signals "safe" (*as left*) or "out."

BASEBALL TERMS

Assist: A play by one fielder that makes it possible for another to make a put-out.

Balk: An illegal motion by the pitcher, entitling base runners to advance one base each.

Bases loaded: When there is a runner at each base.

Battery: A team's pitcher and catcher.

Batting average: Number of hits divided by times at bat (as: 18/60 = .300). If a batter reaches base safely on an error or fielder's choice, the batter does not get credit for a hit. If the batter hits a sacrifice or gets a base on balls or is hit by a pitched ball, the batter is not charged with a time at bat.

Bullpen: A special area where relief pitchers warm up.

Bunt: A batted ball tapped with the bat rather than hit with force.

Doubleheader: Two games played consecutively on a single day.

Double play (DP): A play in which the batter and a runner, or two runners, are put out.

Dugout: The seating area, often below the level of the playing field, reserved for players, managers, and coaches.

Earned run: Any run scored except one that results from a fielding misplay.

Earned run average (ERA): Number of earned runs charged against a pitcher divided by total innings pitched times 9 (as: $10/50 \times 9 = 1.80$).

Error: Any play on which a fielder misses a reasonable opportunity to put out a batter or runner, or a misplay that allows a runner to advance.

Fielder's choice: An attempt by the fielder of a fair ground ball to put out a runner instead of the batter who hit the ball.

Fielding average: Total put-outs and assists divided by total chances (put-outs, assists, and errors)
(as: $\frac{66 + 33}{66 + 33 + 1} = \frac{99}{100} = .990$).

Force play: A play in which a runner is put out when forced to advance to the next base to make room for the next runner.

Full count: When there are three balls and two strikes on the batter.

Grand slam: A home run with the bases loaded.

Infield fly: A fair fly ball hit above the infield when there are runners on first and second or on all three bases and there is not more than one out. The umpire declares "infield fly," and the batter is automatically out.

Line drive: A ball hit in the air but on a straight line, usually not far off the ground.

No-hitter: A game in which the pitcher does not give up a single hit.

Passed ball: A failure of the catcher to hold a pitched ball (other than a wild pitch), permitting a runner to advance; not scored as an error.

Percentage (team or pitcher): Number of games won divided by total games won and lost
(as: $\frac{15}{15 + 9} = \frac{15}{24} = .625$).

Pickoff: A throw by a pitcher or catcher to another fielder, catching a runner off base.

Rookie: A player in his first year in the major leagues, or a young player trying out for a big-league team.

Runs batted in (RBI): A run that scores and is credited to a batter as a result of the batter's safe hit, sacrifice, or infield out; or the batter's reaching first base on a fielder's choice; or the batter's getting a base on balls or being hit by a pitched ball with the bases full, forcing in a run.

Sacrifice: A successful attempt by the batter (before two are out) to advance a runner or runners by means of a bunt or a long fly out.

Shutout: A game in which a team fails to score.

Spring training: The period before the start of the regular season when major league teams train and play exhibition games to prepare for the season. Many teams hold their spring training camps in Florida or Arizona.

Squeeze play: An attempt to bring home a runner from third base by means of a bunt.

Stolen base: The act of a runner in advancing one base without the aid of the batter or any misplay by the defending team.

Switch-hitter: A player who can bat right-handed or left-handed.

Wild pitch: A pitch too high, low, or wide for the catcher to handle, allowing a base runner to advance.

---

first base will be left open for the batter. If the ground ball is caught and thrown to a fielder at second base before the runner arrives, the runner is forced out.

On the same play, if the fielder at second base then throws the ball to a fielder at first base and the ball arrives there before the batter, then the batter is out as well. This is called a **double play**, because two outs were made on one batted ball. A double play also can occur if a fielder catches a fly ball and throws the ball to a base before the runner gets back to it. Sometimes the fielding team can even get three outs on one batted ball—a rare **triple play**.

A Game of Inches

Baseball is often called a game of inches. For example, a speedy ground ball may pass within an inch or two of a infielder's reach, making the difference between a hit or an out. Sometimes even a fraction of an inch can determine whether a pitch is a ball or a strike, whether a batted ball is fair or foul, or whether a base runner is safe or out. Even one close play can decide the outcome of a whole game.

The job of making these decisions and enforcing the rules of the game falls on a group of **umpires** stationed around the field. Major league games usually have four umpires—one each at home plate, first base, second base, and third base. The home plate umpire decides whether pitches are balls or strikes and whether runners attempting to reach home plate are safe or out. The other umpires rule on plays at or near their designated bases.

While some rules of baseball may seem complicated, a good player should know every detail, understand many strategies, and react quickly to every situation. Almost every play is different, presenting batters, fielders, and base runners with a variety of choices and opportunities. To play well requires speed, power, pinpoint accuracy, split-second timing, and a special instinct for the game.

▶**LEAGUES AND COMPETITION**

Millions of Americans play organized baseball, participating on teams that play regularly against one another and that usually compete in groups called leagues. All the teams in a league play each other at least once during the course of a season. The team that has won the most games in a league at the end of the season becomes the champion. Sometimes the top several teams in a league compete in a special post-season tournament to determine the champion. There are baseball leagues for nearly every age group. Adult players who are paid to play on a team are called professionals. The top professionals play in the major leagues. Most people who play baseball, however, are unpaid amateurs who play for enjoyment and competition. Amateur programs range from Little League for youngsters to high school, college, and adult leagues.

Major Leagues

There are 30 teams in major league baseball today—28 based in U.S. cities and two in Canadian cities. These teams are divided into two leagues: 14 in the **American League** and 16 in the **National League**. Each league consists of an Eastern Division, a Central Division, and a Western Division.

A major league season starts in April and lasts until October. Every team plays a total of 162 games during the **regular season**. Most games are played between teams in the same league, but some interleague play was begun during the 1997 season. Each team plays half of its games at its home ballpark and half of them away at the ballparks of other teams. There are day and night games, and occasion-

ally teams play two games in one day—a **doubleheader**. At the end of the regular season, the three top teams in each division and a fourth team, a wild-card team—the team in the league with the next best record—compete for the league title, or **pennant**. The two pennant winners then play in the **World Series**, which is sometimes called the Fall Classic because it usually takes place in October. The winner of the World Series is then recognized as the world champion.

Another highlight of the major league season is the all-star game, a special game between the best players in the American League and the National League. The game has no effect on the standings, but fans enjoy seeing the top stars compete against each other.

Minor Leagues

Major league teams get many of their players from the minor leagues. Each major league club provides financial support to minor league teams. Promising players receive training and experience on these teams, which are often called farm teams. When a minor league player performs well, the parent team usually brings the player up to its major league team.

The minor leagues are generally classified into three groups according to the level of play —Class A, Class AA, and the highest level, Class AAA. There are also winter leagues and leagues for rookies, or first-year players, some of which are in Mexico and other Latin American countries.

MAJOR LEAGUE TEAMS

National League

Eastern Division	Central Division	Western Division
Atlanta Braves	Chicago Cubs	Arizona Diamondbacks
Florida Marlins	Cincinnati Reds	Colorado Rockies
Montreal Expos	Houston Astros	Los Angeles Dodgers
New York Mets	Milwaukee Brewers	San Diego Padres
Philadelphia Phillies	Pittsburgh Pirates	San Francisco Giants
	St. Louis Cardinals	

American League

Eastern Division	Central Division	Western Division
Baltimore Orioles	Chicago White Sox	Anaheim Angels
Boston Red Sox	Cleveland Indians	Oakland Athletics
New York Yankees	Detroit Tigers	Seattle Mariners
Tampa Bay Devil Rays	Kansas City Royals	Texas Rangers
Toronto Blue Jays	Minnesota Twins	

Amateur Competition

Organized amateur baseball begins with Little League, for youngsters age 9 to 18. The Little League rules are similar to those of the major leagues. The biggest difference is that, for the younger players, the diamond is smaller and the pitcher's mound is closer to home plate. Also, Little League games last six innings instead of nine. (See LITTLE LEAGUE BASEBALL in Volume L.)

American Legion and Babe Ruth leagues also offer teenagers the opportunity to continue playing competitive baseball. Most high schools and colleges also have baseball teams and leagues. In addition, local groups such as park and recreation boards, boys' clubs, and others frequently offer baseball programs for people of all ages.

▶ AN INTERNATIONAL GAME

Although baseball is regarded as the American national pastime, the game is popular in other countries. Minor leagues in Canada and Mexico have been sending players to U.S. professional teams for many years. In 1969 the Montreal Expos became the first major league team based outside the United States. Another Canadian team, the Toronto Blue Jays, was added in 1977. In 1992 the Blue Jays became the first team outside the United States to win the World Series.

Baseball is also widely played and followed enthusiastically in Puerto Rico, the Virgin Islands, and many Latin American countries such as the Dominican Republic, Cuba, Venezuela, Panama, and Nicaragua. These countries have, in fact, developed a number of great players who became stars in the major leagues in the United States—Roberto Clemente, Juan Marichal, Tony Oliva, Orlando Cepeda, Moises Alou, and a host of others. Because competition at all levels is held year-round in these countries, during the winter months many U.S. professionals go to them to take part in competitive league play.

Baseball was introduced to Japan by an American teacher, Horace Wilson, in 1873. The level of play in Japanese baseball is very high, and it has produced its own stars. The most famous was Sadaharu Oh of the Yomiuri Giants, who hit 868 career home runs. A number of American players also have played professionally in Japan.

The game also is popular, especially with youngsters, in Asian countries such as Taiwan and South Korea. Since the 1960's, Asian teams have won the most Little League World Series championships.

Because of its worldwide popularity, baseball became a demonstration sport in the 1984 Summer Olympics and an official medal sport in 1992.

SELECTED MAJOR LEAGUE RECORDS

Highest batting average, lifetime: .367, Ty Cobb; .358, Rogers Hornsby; .349, Dan Brouthers.

Highest batting average, season: .438, Hugh Duffy (1894); .432, Willie Keeler (1897); .429, Ross Barnes (1876).

Most hits, lifetime: 4,256, Pete Rose; 4,191, Ty Cobb; 3,771, Hank Aaron; 3,630, Stan Musial; 3,515, Tris Speaker.

Most hits, season: 257, George Sisler (1920); 254, Lefty O'Doul (1929) and Bill Terry (1930).

Longest consecutive-game hitting streak: 56 games, Joe DiMaggio (1941); 41 games, George Sisler (1922).

Most runs batted in, lifetime: 2,297, Hank Aaron; 2,212, Babe Ruth; 1,995, Lou Gehrig; 1,961, Ty Cobb; 1,951, Stan Musial.

Most runs batted in, season: 191, Hack Wilson (1930); 184, Lou Gehrig (1931); 183, Hank Greenberg (1937).

Most home runs, lifetime: 755, Hank Aaron; 714, Babe Ruth; 660, Willie Mays; 586, Frank Robinson.

Most home runs, season: 70, Mark McGwire (1998); 66, Sammy Sosa (1998); 65, Mark McGwire (1999).

Most stolen bases, lifetime: 1,334 Rickey Henderson (end of 1999 season); 938, Lou Brock; 937, Billy Hamilton.

Most stolen bases, season: 130, Rickey Henderson (1982); 118, Lou Brock (1974); 110, Vince Coleman (1985).

Most runs scored, lifetime: 2,245, Ty Cobb; 2,174, Hank Aaron and Babe Ruth; 2,165, Pete Rose.

Most runs scored, season: 196, Billy Hamilton (1894); 177, Babe Ruth (1921); 170, Tom Brown (1891).

Most consecutive games played: 2,632, Cal Ripken, Jr. (1982–98); 2,130, Lou Gehrig (1925–39).

Most games won by a pitcher, lifetime: 511, Cy Young; 417, Walter Johnson.

Most games won by a pitcher, season: 41, Jack Chesbro (1904); 40, Ed Walsh (1908); 37, Christy Mathewson (1908).

Most strikeouts, lifetime: 5,714, Nolan Ryan; 4,136, Steve Carlton; 3,701, Bert Blyleven; 3,640, Tom Seaver.

Most strikeouts, season: 383, Nolan Ryan (1973); 382, Sandy Koufax (1965); 367, Nolan Ryan (1974).

PENNANT AND WORLD SERIES WINNERS—YEAR-BY-YEAR RECORD
The winner of the World Series is indicated by an asterisk (*).

Year	American League	National League	Games Won–Lost		Year	American League	National League	Games Won–Lost	
1903	*Boston	Pittsburgh	5	3	1953	*New York	Brooklyn	4	2
1905	Philadelphia	*New York	4	1	1954	Cleveland	*New York	4	0
1906	*Chicago	Chicago	4	2	1955	New York	*Brooklyn	4	3
1907	Detroit	*Chicago	4	0	1956	*New York	Brooklyn	4	3
1908	Detroit	*Chicago	4	1	1957	New York	*Milwaukee	4	3
1909	Detroit	*Pittsburgh	4	3	1958	*New York	Milwaukee	4	3
1910	*Philadelphia	Chicago	4	1	1959	Chicago	*Los Angeles	4	2
1911	*Philadelphia	New York	4	2	1960	New York	*Pittsburgh	4	3
1912	*Boston	New York	4	3	1961	*New York	Cincinnati	4	1
1913	*Philadelphia	New York	4	1	1962	*New York	San Francisco	4	3
1914	Philadelphia	*Boston	4	0	1963	New York	*Los Angeles	4	0
1915	*Boston	Philadelphia	4	1	1964	New York	*St. Louis	4	3
1916	*Boston	Brooklyn	4	1	1965	Minnesota	*Los Angeles	4	3
1917	*Chicago	New York	4	2	1966	*Baltimore	Los Angeles	4	0
1918	*Boston	Chicago	4	2	1967	Boston	*St. Louis	4	3
1919	Chicago	*Cincinnati	5	3	1968	*Detroit	St. Louis	4	3
1920	*Cleveland	Brooklyn	5	2	1969	Baltimore	*New York	4	1
1921	New York	*New York	5	3	1970	*Baltimore	Cincinnati	4	1
1922	New York	*New York	4	0	1971	Baltimore	*Pittsburgh	4	3
1923	*New York	New York	4	2	1972	*Oakland	Cincinnati	4	3
1924	*Washington	New York	4	3	1973	*Oakland	New York	4	3
1925	Washington	*Pittsburgh	4	3	1974	*Oakland	Los Angeles	4	1
1926	New York	*St. Louis	4	3	1975	Boston	*Cincinnati	4	3
1927	*New York	Pittsburgh	4	0	1976	New York	*Cincinnati	4	0
1928	*New York	St. Louis	4	0	1977	*New York	Los Angeles	4	2
1929	*Philadelphia	Chicago	4	1	1978	*New York	Los Angeles	4	2
1930	*Philadelphia	St. Louis	4	2	1979	Baltimore	*Pittsburgh	4	3
1931	Philadelphia	*St. Louis	4	3	1980	Kansas City	*Philadelphia	4	2
1932	*New York	Chicago	4	0	1981	New York	*Los Angeles	4	2
1933	Washington	*New York	4	1	1982	Milwaukee	*St. Louis	4	3
1934	Detroit	*St. Louis	4	3	1983	*Baltimore	Philadelphia	4	1
1935	*Detroit	Chicago	4	2	1984	*Detroit	San Diego	4	1
1936	*New York	New York	4	2	1985	*Kansas City	St. Louis	4	3
1937	*New York	New York	4	1	1986	Boston	*New York	4	3
1938	*New York	Chicago	4	0	1987	*Minnesota	St. Louis	4	3
1939	*New York	Cincinnati	4	0	1988	Oakland	*Los Angeles	4	1
1940	Detroit	*Cincinnati	4	3	1989	*Oakland	San Francisco	4	0
1941	*New York	Brooklyn	4	1	1990	Oakland	*Cincinnati	4	0
1942	New York	*St. Louis	4	1	1991	*Minnesota	Atlanta	4	3
1943	*New York	St. Louis	4	1	1992	*Toronto	Atlanta	4	2
1944	St. Louis	*St. Louis	4	2	1993	*Toronto	Philadelphia	4	2
1945	*Detroit	Chicago	4	3	1994	World Series canceled by a strike.			
1946	Boston	*St. Louis	4	3	1995	Cleveland	*Atlanta	4	2
1947	*New York	Brooklyn	4	3	1996	*New York	Atlanta	4	2
1948	*Cleveland	Boston	4	2	1997	Cleveland	*Florida	4	3
1949	*New York	Brooklyn	4	1	1998	*New York	San Diego	4	0
1950	*New York	Philadelphia	4	0	1999	*New York	Atlanta	4	0
1951	*New York	New York	4	2	2000	*New York	New York	4	1
1952	*New York	Brooklyn	4	3					

▶ HISTORY OF BASEBALL

Games with a stick and ball were played as early as 5,000 years ago as part of religious rites in ancient Egypt. Later, the Christian church in France popularized a game in which a ball was swatted with two sticks by two teams of worshipers. This custom spread throughout Europe, giving rise in England to a children's game called rounders. Rounders was surprisingly similar to modern baseball. A batter hit a thrown ball and ran around one or more bases, which were in the form of rocks, sticks, milk stools, or wooden posts. In rounders, fielders threw the ball at base runners. A runner struck by a thrown ball while off base was out. In the 1880's, Americans called the game town ball. When there were not enough players for two entire teams, they played one old cat, two old cat, or three old cat, depending on the number of bases used.

Origins and Early Growth

According to a popular legend, baseball was invented in 1839 by a young West Point cadet named Abner Doubleday at Cooperstown, New York. Most baseball historians now dispute that story, emphasizing the evolution of the sport from such earlier bat-and-ball games as rounders and town ball. The person generally given credit for the biggest role in the evolution of modern baseball is Alexander J. Cartwright. In 1845, Cartwright drew up some rules that are very much like those followed today. Cartwright's rules set four bases 90 feet apart. They also established the foul lines, the strikeout, three-out innings, and nine-player teams. But the ball had to be pitched underhand, runs were called aces, and 21 or more aces made a game.

Cartwright also helped organize the first regular baseball team, the New York Knickerbockers. On June 19, 1846, the Knickerbockers lost the first recorded game to the rival New York Nine, 23–1, in four innings, at Hoboken, New Jersey. After that, amateur baseball spread to other eastern cities. Baseball attracted wide interest during the Civil War (1861–65), when soldiers took up the game.

The Rise of Professional Baseball

By the 1860's, baseball teams were paying some of their players a share of the money paid by fans to watch games. But the first professional team to pay a regular salary to all its players was the Cincinnati Red Stockings of 1869.

Modern professional baseball got its true start in 1876, when the eight-team National League was founded. A rival American Association was formed in 1881 but it disbanded after ten years. The American League, also originally founded with eight teams, had its first season in 1901.

The rivalry that developed between the National League and the American League greatly increased popular interest in baseball. In 1903 the championship teams of the two leagues met in the first World Series, which was won by the Boston Red Sox.

Baseball today is played much as it was in the late 1800's (*above*), when the first professional leagues were organized. One major difference is the vast stadiums, some with plastic domes and artificial grass. Houston's Astrodome (*right*) was the first indoor ballpark.

GREAT PLAYERS IN THE HISTORY OF BASEBALL

The National Baseball Hall of Fame was established in 1936 and dedicated in 1939. It is located in Cooperstown, New York, which is regarded as the home of baseball. Many of the best players in baseball history are honored in the Hall of Fame. They are chosen by an annual secret ballot of the Baseball Writers' Association or by the Committee on Veterans. All players profiled here have been elected to the Hall of Fame. Biographies of three important members, Lou Gehrig, Jackie Robinson, and Babe Ruth, can be found in the appropriate volumes. Consult the Index to find more information on other important players and managers, including Yogi Berra, *Roy Campanella, *Roberto Clemente, Dizzy Dean, *Bob Gibson, *Josh Gibson, *Roger Maris, *Pete Rose, and *Tom Seaver. (An asterisk indicates players whose pictures appear later in this article.)

HANK AARON (1934–) broke Babe Ruth's home run record in 1974 when he hit his 715th home run. By the end of his career, he had set a new lifetime record of 755 home runs. Aaron played for the NL's Milwaukee Braves, later the Atlanta Braves, and the AL's Milwaukee Brewers. He was the NL batting champion for two years and was named MVP in 1957. Aaron was elected to the Hall of Fame in 1982.

HANK AARON

GROVER CLEVELAND ALEXANDER (1887–1950) was one of baseball's greatest pitchers. During his 20-year career with NL teams (Philadelphia, Chicago, and St. Louis), he won 373 games and lost only 208, winning 30 or more games in three consecutive seasons, a league record he shares with Christy Mathewson. In 1916 he pitched 16 shutouts, a major league record. He was elected to the Hall of Fame in 1938.

GROVER CLEVELAND ALEXANDER

GEORGE BRETT (1953–) spent his entire major league career with the Kansas City Royals, where he established himself as one of the best hitters in the history of the game. Brett was named the Royals' Player of the Year eight times, was an All-Star 13 times, won three batting titles, and was named the AL's MVP in 1980 when he batted .390. He retired after the 1993 season with a lifetime batting average of .305 and was elected to the Hall of Fame in 1999.

GEORGE BRETT

ROD CAREW

STEVE CARLTON

TY COBB

JOE DIMAGGIO

BOB FELLER

ROD CAREW (1945–), a left-handed hitting infielder, played for the Minnesota Twins and the California Angels. In 1977, his best season, Carew had a .388 batting average and won the AL's MVP award. By the end of his career he had 3,053 hits and a .328 batting average. He won seven batting titles. He was elected to the Hall of Fame in 1991.

STEVE CARLTON (1944–), known as Lefty for his excellence as a left-handed pitcher, was the first pitcher to win four Cy Young Awards. He is second in career strikeouts (4,136) and second in wins for left-handers (329). Playing for the Philadelphia Phillies, Cleveland Indians, St. Louis Cardinals, San Francisco Giants, Chicago White Sox, and Minnesota Twins, Carlton had six 20-win seasons and won 27 games in 1972. He was elected to the Hall of Fame in 1994.

TY COBB (1886–1961), nicknamed the Georgia Peach, holds the highest lifetime batting average (.367) in baseball history and is one of the leaders in hits (4,191), runs (2,245), total bases (5,863), runs batted in (1,961), and stolen bases (892). Cobb played outfield for 24 seasons. He played most of his career with the Detroit Tigers but played the last two years with the Philadelphia Athletics. In 1936, Cobb was the first player elected to the Hall of Fame.

JOE DIMAGGIO (1914–99) played outfield for the New York Yankees from 1935 to 1943 and again from 1946 to 1951. He was named the AL's MVP three times and set a major league record for hitting safely in 56 consecutive games. DiMaggio compiled a lifetime batting average of .325 and a slugging percentage of .579. He was elected to the Hall of Fame in 1955.

BOB FELLER (1918–) was known for his strikeouts while pitching for the Cleveland Indians (1936–41 and 1945–56). During his career he won 266 games and lost 162. He also pitched three no-hit games. Feller was nicknamed Rapid Robert because of his fastball, which was clocked at 98.6 miles (158.7 kilometers) per hour. He was elected to the Hall of Fame in 1962.

HANK GREENBERG (1911–86) was a first baseman and

outfielder for the Detroit Tigers (1933–46) and first baseman for the Pittsburgh Pirates (1947). Twice named the AL's MVP, Greenberg hit 331 career home runs, including 58 in 1938. His slugging percentage of .605 is the fifth best in the history of major league baseball. Greenberg was elected to the Hall of Fame in 1956.

ROBERT MOSES "LEFTY" GROVE (1900–75) was primarily a fastball pitcher. During his career with the Philadelphia Athletics (1925–33) and the Boston Red Sox (1934–41), Grove won 300 games and lost 141, and he struck out more than 2,000 players. He was elected to the Hall of Fame in 1947.

ROGERS HORNSBY (1896–1963) was a right-handed hitter whose .358 career batting average is second only to that of Ty Cobb. Hornsby, usually a second baseman, played for the St. Louis Cardinals, New York Giants, Boston Braves, Chicago Cubs, and St. Louis Browns. During his career he won seven NL batting titles, including a single-season record .424 in 1924. His slugging record of .577 is one of the ten best. He was elected to the Hall of Fame in 1942.

REGGIE JACKSON (1946–) was a left-handed slugger who was an outfielder and a designated hitter. Jackson played for the Oakland A's, Baltimore Orioles, New York Yankees, and California Angels. During his career he hit 563 home runs, the sixth highest in baseball history. During the 1977 World Series he set a record by hitting five home runs. Jackson was elected to the Hall of Fame in 1993.

WALTER JOHNSON (1887–1946) was nicknamed the Big Train because of his size and overpowering fastball. During his career as a right-handed pitcher for the Washington Senators, Johnson won 416 games, struck out 3,508 batters, and pitched 113 shutouts (the most in major league baseball history). His record of 416 lifetime wins is second only to that of Cy Young. In 1936 Johnson was elected as one of the five original members of the Hall of Fame.

HANK GREENBERG

LEFTY GROVE

ROGERS HORNSBY

REGGIE JACKSON

WALTER JOHNSON

SANDY KOUFAX

MICKEY MANTLE

CHRISTY MATHEWSON

WILLIE MAYS

SANDY KOUFAX (1935–) was a left-handed pitcher for the Brooklyn (and later Los Angeles) Dodgers from 1955 to 1966. During his career he hurled four no-hit games and won the Cy Young award as the NL's best pitcher in 1963, 1965, and 1966. Koufax retired after the 1966 season because of arthritis in his pitching arm. His lifetime record is 165 wins and 87 losses. Koufax was elected to the Hall of Fame in 1972.

MICKEY MANTLE (1931–95) was an outstanding centerfielder and hitter for the New York Yankees from 1951 to 1968. He was voted the AL's MVP three times (1956, 1957, and 1962) and won the Triple Crown in 1956 for leading the league in batting average, home runs, and runs batted in. Mantle's 536 career home runs are the eighth best in major league baseball history. Mantle was elected to the Hall of Fame in 1974.

CHRISTY MATHEWSON (1880–1925), a right-handed pitcher, played most of his career for the New York Giants. Mathewson set an NL record with 373 lifetime wins, the third best in major league history. He helped the Giants win four pennants and the 1905 World Series. Known for his fastball and "fadeaway," or screwball, Mathewson won a record 37 games in 1908. His three World Series shutouts in 1905 are still a record. In 1936, Mathewson became one of the original five players elected to the Hall of Fame.

WILLIE MAYS (1931–) was an outstanding batter, outfielder, and base runner. His record of 660 career home runs ranks third behind those of Hank Aaron and Babe Ruth. After joining the New York Giants, later the San Francisco Giants, in 1951, he was named Rookie of the Year. He was the NL's MVP in 1954 and 1965. In 1972 Mays joined the New York Mets and retired at the end of the 1973 season. He was elected to the Hall of Fame in 1979.

STAN MUSIAL (1920–), an outfielder and first baseman for the St. Louis Cardinals, was voted the NL's MVP three times (1943, 1946, and 1948). He won seven league batting titles. Nicknamed Stan the Man, Musial ended his 22-year career with a .331 lifetime batting

AL	American League
MVP	Most Valuable Player
NL	National League

average, compiling 3,630 career hits. He is one of baseball's all-time career leaders in total bases (6,134), runs (1,949), runs batted in (1,951), games played (3,025), and consecutive games (895). Musial was elected to the Hall of Fame in 1969.

MEL OTT (1909–58) was one of the NL's most feared batters. In 22 years with the New York Giants, he hit 511 home runs and had a career batting average of .304. Ott is also an all-time career leader in runs (1,859) and runs batted in (1,861). He was chosen for the All-Star team eleven times. After retiring as a player, Ott managed the Giants from 1942 to 1948. He was elected to the Hall of Fame in 1951.

SATCHEL PAIGE (1906?–1982), a right-handed pitcher, spent 20 years in the Negro Leagues at a time when blacks were not allowed in major league baseball. In 1948, at the age of 42, he joined the Cleveland Indians and became the first black pitcher in the AL. Although past his prime, he won six of seven games for Cleveland, helping them win the pennant. Paige was elected to the Hall of Fame in 1971.

FRANK ROBINSON (1935–) was a star outfielder and right-handed slugger who became the first black manager in the major leagues. Robinson's 586 lifetime home runs rank the fourth best in baseball. He is the only player in history to be named MVP in both the NL and the AL. Most of his playing career was with the Cincinnati Reds (NL) and Baltimore Orioles (AL). He also was a manager with the Cleveland Indians, San Francisco Giants, and Baltimore Orioles. Robinson was elected to the Hall of Fame in 1982.

NOLAN RYAN (1947–) was a right-handed pitcher best known for his blazing fastball. In 1973 Ryan set a record for the most strikeouts in a season (383), and in 1989 he became the first pitcher to strike out 5,000 batters. His 5,714 career strikeouts are a major league record. Ryan played for the New York Mets,

STAN MUSIAL

MEL OTT

SATCHEL PAIGE

FRANK ROBINSON

NOLAN RYAN

WARREN SPAHN

HONUS WAGNER

TED WILLIAMS

CY YOUNG

California Angels, Houston Astros, and Texas Rangers. He was inducted into the Hall of Fame in 1999.

WARREN SPAHN (1921–) was an outstanding pitcher for the Boston Braves, later the Milwaukee Braves, New York Mets, and San Francisco Giants. Spahn won a total of 20 games in 13 different seasons and threw two no-hitters. His 363 career wins are a record for left-handed pitchers and the all-time fifth best among all pitchers. Spahn also ranks among the top ten best in innings pitched (5,246). He was elected to the Hall of Fame in 1973.

HONUS WAGNER (1874–1955), nicknamed the Flying Dutchman because of his deceptive speed, is considered by many to be the greatest shortstop and one of the greatest all-around players in baseball history. His career batting average of .328 includes 3,430 hits, 651 doubles, and 252 triples. Wagner was one of the original five players named to the Hall of Fame in 1936.

TED WILLIAMS (1918–) was a natural-born hitter. Williams played with the Boston Red Sox from 1939 to 1960 (except when he was in the Armed Forces during World War II and the Korean War). He won six batting championships, batted .406 in 1941, and was twice voted the AL's MVP. His career batting average (.344), slugging percentage (.634), and home runs (521) are among the best in baseball history. His slugging percentage is surpassed only by that of Babe Ruth. Williams was elected to the Hall of Fame in 1966.

CY YOUNG (1867–1965) was the first person in modern baseball to pitch a perfect game. During his 22-year career, he pitched in 906 games, winning a major league record 511. He also holds the record for innings pitched (7,357) and is fourth best in shutouts (76). Young played for NL teams in Cleveland, St. Louis, and Boston, and AL teams in Boston and Cleveland. He was elected to the Hall of Fame in 1937. Baseball's annual pitching awards are named for him.

The Modern Era

Baseball became the "great American game" during the early 1900's. Stadiums were built that could seat thousands of spectators, and soon games were broadcast on radio. Record-setting performances, dramatic World Series games, memorable plays, and colorful personalities became part of a history and folklore that continue to grow.

The period from 1900 to 1919 is sometimes called the dead ball era in baseball history. The balls used during that time were used until they were battered out of shape. Very few home runs were hit, and games usually ended with low scores. Nevertheless, these early years produced some of the greatest players in the history of the game—Cy Young, Walter Johnson, Grover Cleveland Alexander, Christy Mathewson, Ty Cobb, Honus Wagner, Tris Speaker, Nap Lajoie, and others.

The leading teams during this period were the Chicago Cubs and New York Giants in the National League, and the Philadelphia Athletics and the Boston Red Sox in the American League. The Cubs, featuring the fabled double-play combination of "Tinker to Evers to Chance," played in four World Series in five years, winning in 1907 and 1908. The Athletics, managed by the legendary Connie Mack, appeared in four of five World Series from 1910 through 1914, winning three.

Baseball's darkest moment came in 1919, when the Cincinnati Reds defeated the heavily favored Chicago White Sox in the World Series. It was later discovered that eight White Sox players had accepted bribes from gamblers to lose the series. In what became known as the Black Sox Scandal, the eight players were banned from baseball for life.

The next two decades, from 1920 to 1939, have been called the golden era of major league baseball. In 1920 the New York Yankees purchased a hard-hitting player named Babe Ruth from the Boston Red Sox. Many still regard "The Babe" as the greatest baseball player ever. In 1920, Ruth hit an amazing 54 home runs. In 1921 he hit 59 home runs, and in 1927 he hit 60—a record that lasted 34 years. The era of the dead ball was over. Fans flocked to games to see The Babe play.

In addition to the great feats of Babe Ruth, several off-the-field developments boosted the image and popularity of professional baseball. In 1921, Judge Kenesaw Mountain Landis be-

The exploits of Babe Ruth (*above*), including his 714 home runs in 22 seasons (1914–35), increased baseball's popularity. His record of 60 home runs in a year, set in 1927, lasted until 1961, when Roger Maris (*right*) hit 61.

came the major league's first commissioner. Landis helped restore honesty and integrity to the game in the aftermath of the Black Sox Scandal. Meanwhile, many radio stations began broadcasting play-by-play accounts of games, bringing baseball to vast new audiences during the Roaring Twenties.

In the 1930's, more milestones were reached. The first all-star game was played in 1933 at Comiskey Park in Chicago. The first night game was played in 1935 in Cincinnati. The Hall of Fame was dedicated in 1939, and the first television broadcast of a baseball game was made in 1939 from Ebbets Field in Brooklyn.

Besides Babe Ruth, other stars such as Lou Gehrig, Rogers Hornsby, Lefty Grove, Dizzy Dean, and Mel Ott attracted thousands of fans to ballparks. Ruth, Gehrig, and others led the New York Yankees in one of the greatest sucsional baseball, black players had been barred from competing in the major leagues. They competed in what were called the Negro Leagues, which produced some of the game's best players, including Satchel Paige, Josh Gibson, and "Cool Papa" Bell. The breaking of the color line by Robinson in 1947 opened the door to the major leagues for other black players. (Admission rules to the Hall of Fame were changed in 1971 so that great players from the Negro Leagues could be admitted.)

The 25 years after World War II gave fans the treat of watching a galaxy of stars. Among the many top hitters of the era were Hank Greenberg, Joe DiMaggio, Ted Williams, Stan Musial, Ralph Kiner, Duke Snider, Hank

Among the great Hall of Fame catchers are Josh Gibson (*top*), considered the greatest hitter in the black baseball leagues of the 1930's and 1940's; Roy Campanella (*far left*), named Most Valuable Player in the NL three times during the 1950's; and Johnny Bench (*left*), a fine slugger and fielder who won ten consecutive Gold Glove awards from 1968–77 as the NL's best defensive catcher.

cess stories in professional sports history. From 1921 through 1939, the "Bronx Bombers," as they were called, won eleven American League pennants and eight World Series. Another strong team of this era was the New York Giants, who won seven pennants and three World Series.

Over the next three decades, major league baseball continued to grow and change. An important breakthrough occurred in 1947, when 28-year-old Jackie Robinson signed a contract with the Brooklyn Dodgers and became the first black player in the major leagues. From the very beginning of profes-

Aaron, Mickey Mantle, Willie Mays, Ernie Banks, Eddie Mathews, Roberto Clemente, and Frank Robinson. Great pitchers included Whitey Ford, Warren Spahn, Bob Feller, Robin Roberts, Bob Lemon, Early Wynn, Sandy Koufax, Don Drysdale, Juan Marichal, and Bob Gibson.

Another important change after World War II was the movement of existing franchises, or teams, to different cities and the addition of new ones. Among the teams that changed cities during the 1950's were the Brooklyn Dodgers, who moved to Los Angeles, and the New York Giants, who went to San Francisco.

In 1961 the American League expanded to ten teams with the addition of the Washington Senators. In 1962 the National League added the New York Mets and Houston Colt .45's (now called the Houston Astros). In 1977, the Seattle Mariners and Toronto Blue Jays joined the American League.

Meanwhile, new stars were born and new records were set. In 1951, Bobby Thomson clinched the pennant for the Giants with a dramatic ninth-inning home run in a playoff game against the Dodgers. In 1956, Don Larsen pitched the only perfect game (no batters reach first base) in World Series history. Between 1941 and 1964, the Yankees won an amazing 18 pennants and 12 World Series.

major leagues in 1998, the Arizona Diamondbacks in the National League and the Tampa Bay Devil Rays in the American League.

The mid-1960's also marked the end of the old Yankee dynasty. Since then, only a few teams have repeated as world champions: the Oakland Athletics in 1972, 1973, and 1974; the Cincinnati Reds in 1975 and 1976; the Yankees in 1977 and 1978 and again in 1998 and 1999; and the Toronto Blue Jays in 1992 and 1993.

Some of baseball's most cherished records have fallen. In 1974, Hank Aaron hit his 715th home run, surpassing Babe Ruth's all-time mark. Pete Rose reached and then passed Ty Cobb's record of 4,191 lifetime base hits. Sev-

No list of the game's Cy Young award winners for outstanding pitching would be complete without Roger Clemens (*left*), who won the award a record five times (1986–87, 1991, 1997–98). Tom Seaver (*right*) won three Cy Young awards (1969, 1973, 1975), and Bob Gibson (*below*), who led the Cardinals to two World Series titles in 1964 and 1967, won two (1968, 1970).

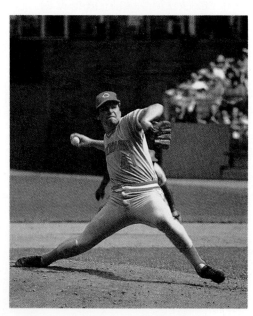

The late 1960's signaled another new era in baseball. The leagues expanded, new ballparks opened, attendance climbed yearly, and baseball became big business. In 1965 the first of many indoor stadiums with artificial turf—the Houston Astrodome—was opened. With the expansion of the two leagues in 1969, the present post-season play-off format, called the League Championship Series, was introduced. In 1973 the American League adopted the designated-hitter rule, and in 1993 two new teams, the Colorado Rockies and the Florida Marlins, were added to the National League. Two more teams joined the

Baseball's outstanding hitters include Pete Rose *(far left)*, who had a record-setting 4,256-hit career, and Roberto Clemente *(left)*, who won 4 NL batting titles (1961, 1964–66). Rose was the only player to get 200 or more hits in ten different years, while Clemente won twelve Gold Glove awards as the NL's best right fielder.

eral pitchers have exceeded Walter Johnson's career total of 3,508 strikeouts, with the record now held by Nolan Ryan, the strikeout king of baseball. Cal Ripken, Jr., surpassed Lou Gehrig's record of most consecutive games played, 2,130, during the 1995 season. And in 1998, Roger Maris' single-season home run record was broken by two players: Mark McGwire, who hit 70, and Sammy Sosa, who hit 66.

A key change came in 1976. For the first time, players with at least six years of experience in the majors could become **free agents**. Players who once had to stay with the same team until traded, sold, or released now could offer their services to any team. With franchise owners bidding against each other, veteran stars can often sign multimillion-dollar contracts to move from team to team.

The 1994 baseball season ended when a dispute between players and club owners over salary issues led to a players' strike on August 12, 1994. It lasted for 34 days, until the club owners canceled the rest of the regular season and all post-season play. The dispute was still not resolved by the spring of 1995, and the 1995 season did not begin until April 26, 23 days late and shortened by 18 games. A new wild-card playoff format was introduced in 1995 to stimulate fan interest by keeping more teams involved in the pennant race. The dispute was finally resolved in late November 1996.

Reviewed by PETER V. UEBERROTH
Former Commissioner of Baseball

See also LITTLE LEAGUE BASEBALL; ROBINSON, JACK ROOSEVELT (JACKIE); RUTH, GEORGE HERMAN (BABE).

Many fans are avid collectors of baseball cards. Among those sought after are cards of exceptional third-baseman, George Brett; record-setting base stealers Lou Brock and Rickey Henderson; slugger Ernie Banks; premier pitcher Sandy Koufax; and Ken Griffey, Jr., one of today's all-around stars both at bat and in the field.

Basketball is an exciting, fast-paced sport in which success often depends on the ability of five strong individuals with special athletic skills to work together as a team.

BASKETBALL

Basketball is the most popular indoor sport in the world. It is also one of the few sports whose year of birth and originator can be traced accurately. The game was invented in 1891 by Dr. James A. Naismith. Although basketball grew and developed in the United States, the game today is played and watched in more than 150 countries.

Two teams, of five players each, play the game on a court. At each end of the basketball court is a round metal rim, or hoop, placed 10 feet (3 meters) above the floor. The rim is attached to a backboard made of wood or fiberglass. Hanging from the rim is a white cord net. The rim and net together are called the basket, or goal.

The object of the game is to score points by shooting a large ball through the basket while preventing the other team from scoring points. The winning team is the team that has scored the most points during the course of the game.

Basketball is a fast-paced, exciting game. Much of its appeal lies in its unique blend of teamwork and individual athletic skills. Speed, strength, stamina, quick reflexes, leaping ability, and shooting accuracy are just some of the important skills for a basketball player to possess. Taller players generally have an advantage over shorter players because taller players can reach closer to the bas-

ket. Shorter players, however, can be valuable for their quickness, ball-handling ability, and other contributions. For any player, the most important asset is the ability and willingness to play in close harmony with the other players on the team. Above all, basketball is a team sport, not an individual sport. At any level of competition—from playground to professional—the most successful teams are the teams that work together as a unit.

When Dr. Naismith invented the game of basketball, he was a physical education instructor at the International Training School of the Young Men's Christian Association (YMCA) in Springfield, Massachusetts. It was winter, and his students needed a fast-action game that could be played indoors. He decided on a game in which the players would have to throw a ball into baskets. So he attached a couple of old wooden peach baskets to the ends of the gym balcony and established some basic rules.

Although the rules laid down by Dr. Naismith are still basic to the game, basketball has come a long way since it was first played in the Springfield YMCA. Every four years, amateur players from all over the world compete in an Olympic basketball tournament. In the United States, millions of fans attend games in sports arenas and gyms. Many millions more watch on television. The top male players compete as professionals. Colleges and high schools sponsor teams for both male and female players. Recreational centers and youth organizations run leagues for younger players.

Part of basketball's popularity stems from the fact that it can be played in many ways. Although organized competition calls for five-player teams, the game can be played for practice or recreation with any number down to "one-on-one." It can even be played alone. In addition, basketball does not cost much money to play, as little equipment is required —only a ball and a hoop.

▶ THE COURT AND EQUIPMENT

A full-size, regulation basketball court is 94 feet (28.7 meters) long and 50 feet (15.2 meters) wide. However, a smaller court is generally used for competition up through the high school level. Indoor courts have a hardwood surface, while outdoor courts are made of asphalt or some other weather-resistant material. The boundaries of a basketball court are marked by two pairs of parallel lines called the side lines and end lines (or baselines). The court is divided in half by a midcourt line parallel to the end lines. Other lines on the court mark off special areas, such as the free-throw lanes, free-throw circle, and center circle.

The basket at each end of the court is attached to a backboard suspended above the floor. The backboard is set midway between the side lines and parallel to the end line. The backboard is usually rectangular in shape, but a fan-shaped backboard also can be used. Painted on the backboard, directly above the rim, is a large rectangle. This helps a player aim when trying to bounce the ball off the backboard and into the basket.

The metal rim should be exactly 10 feet (3 meters) above the floor. It is 18 inches (45.7 centimeters) in diameter, nearly wide enough to fit two basketballs at the same time. The net hanging from the rim is open at the bottom so the ball can fall through.

A regulation basketball is 30 inches (76.2 centimeters) in circumference and weighs from 20 to 22 ounces (567 to 624 grams). (The ball used in the women's game is slightly smaller.) The surface of the ball is made of leather or rubber, usually orange or brown in color. It has a pebble grain for easy gripping. The ball is inflated with air so that it bounces easily.

The only other equipment really needed to play basketball are a pair of athletic socks and sneakers with rubber soles. In formal competition, the two teams also wear uniforms. Each team wears a different color uniform. The standard basketball uniform includes shorts and a sleeveless jersey or T-shirt. On the back of each jersey is a number to identify the player.

Basketball Court

▶HOW THE GAME IS PLAYED

Each team defends the basket at its own end of the court (backcourt) and tries to shoot the ball into the basket at the other end (front-court). The team in possession of the ball, and trying to score, is said to be on **offense**. The team without the ball, and trying to prevent the other team from scoring, is said to be on **defense**. Players can advance the ball up and down the court only by passing (throwing) it or dribbling (bouncing) it.

The Team

The five players on the court for each team normally are a **center**, two **forwards**, and two **guards**. The center is usually the tallest player and takes a position close to the basket. A good center can dominate a game by scoring baskets, rebounding (grabbing missed shots), and blocking the opponents' attempts at the basket. The two forwards are stationed to the sides of the center, along the end lines or farther out on the wings. They are strong players who try to maneuver for close shots at the basket; they should also be good rebounders. The two guards are usually smaller and quicker than the center and forwards. They also play farther away from the basket. The main responsibilities of the guards are to guide the offense and set up the plays. The guards should be good dribblers, passers, and outside shooters.

Although the center, forwards, and guards have somewhat different roles, their positions are not fixed or stationary. They can move anywhere on the court and perform any role in the offense or defense. In fact, a team can change the positions at any time. For example, it might use three forwards and two guards, or two centers and three guards.

In addition to the five players on the court, a basketball team has several substitute players. The substitutes are brought into the game to give the other players a rest or to take advantage of their own special abilities. For example, a substitute who is especially good at defense may be brought into the game to guard the other team's best shooter. Or the team's best shooter may be brought into the game when scoring is especially needed.

Coaches

The coach organizes the basketball team, instructs the players in important skills, and

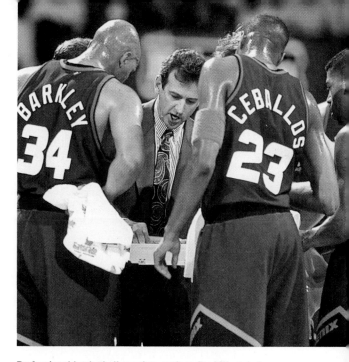

Professional basketball coaches such as Paul Westphal (*above*) must prepare their teams well for league competition and be ready to outline new strategies during a close game to strengthen a team's defenses or increase its scoring opportunities.

holds regular sessions to drill the team and to prepare for each game. The coach also designs plays and strategies to use against opposing teams. During a game the coach determines which players to use, tells them what to do, and decides when to call time outs. The coach of a college or professional team often has at least one assistant coach.

Over the years, there have been a number of well known college and professional coaches in the sport. Adolph Rupp won a record 879 games as coach at the University of Kentucky from 1930–72 and led the team to four national championships. He also coached the 1948 Olympic gold-medal team. "Red" Auerbach led the Boston Celtics to nine league championships. The 767 career wins of Hank Iba, coach of Oklahoma A&M from 1934–70, is the second best record after the record of Adolph Rupp. Other memorable coaches are Frank McGuire, Pete Newell, Joseph Lapchick, Dean Smith, Lenny Wilkens, and Bobby Knight.

Officials

The conduct of play is controlled by two officials on the court. (Sometimes three are used.) They ensure that the game is played

Good ball handlers like John Stockton (*above left*) find ways to dribble around formidable defenders. Two strong centers, Patrick Ewing and Hakeem Olajuwon (*above*), vie for a jump ball to tip to a teammate who could help the team score early during a game in the 1994 NBA championship series.

according to the rules. The officials carry whistles. When a player has committed a foul or violation, an official will blow the whistle to stop play and assess the appropriate penalty. The head official has the final decision in any dispute. Otherwise, the officials have the same duties. The officials are assisted by a scorekeeper and a timekeeper. They sit at a table alongside the court.

Time

The team that scores more points in the specified amount of time wins the game. A high school basketball game is played in four 8-minute quarters, while younger teams play 6-minute quarters. College games are divided into 20-minute halves, professional games into 12-minute quarters. There is a rest period at halftime. (In the second half of the game, the teams "trade" ends of the floor, and each now shoots for the basket that it had defended during the first half.) In case of a tie score at the end of the last period, overtime periods are played—3 minutes in high school games, 5 minutes in college and professional games.

During the course of a game, the clock is stopped when the buzzer sounds to end a quarter or half or when an official blows the whistle for any reason. For example, an official will blow the whistle when the ball goes out of bounds, or to signal that a foul or violation has been committed, or when a team calls a time-out. Each team is allowed only a limited number of time-outs during the game.

The Action

The game begins with a "jump ball" at the center of the court. Two opposing players, usually the centers, face each other at the mid-court line. Their teammates get in position around the center circle. The referee tosses the ball in the air between the two facing players. Each one jumps up and tries to tap the ball to a teammate.

As soon as one team gains possession of the ball, it goes on the offense and advances toward the other team's basket. A shot for the basket may be made from anywhere on the court. It is best, however, to move the ball as close to the basket as possible before shooting.

Players may pass the ball back and forth or from side to side in order to confuse the defensive players. If this happens, one member of the offensive team can get under the basket for a clear, easy shot. Passes do not have to stay in the air—the bounce pass is commonly used. But the ball must stay on the playing court. Should it go out-of-bounds, the official decides which player touched it last. The ball is then awarded to the opposing team.

Kenny Anderson (*above left*) keeps his head up while dribbling, searching for a teammate closer to the basket to whom he can pass the ball. Important points can also be scored at the free throw line. Mahmond Abdul-Rauf (*above center*), a good shooter, gets ready to put one up. Grabbing rebounds, as Dennis Rodman does here (*above right*), is essential to a winning effort.

The only other legal way a player can move the ball is by bouncing it along the floor with one hand. This is called **dribbling**. Once a player stops dribbling and holds the ball with both hands, it must be either passed or shot for a basket. If the player dribbles again, before another player touches the ball, or walks or runs while holding the ball (**traveling**), the ball is turned over to the other team.

When a basket is scored, the opposing team gains possession of the ball and passes it inbounds from behind the end line. That team goes on offense and tries for a basket at the other end of the court. The team that just scored now becomes the defensive team. Defensive players try to guard their opponents very closely. They will attempt to steal the ball, intercept a pass, block a shot, or force the team on offense to take only a difficult shot.

A very important part of the game of basketball is **rebounding**. Every missed shot results in a rebound (unless the missed shot goes out-of-bounds). Whichever team can catch the rebound keeps possession of the ball and goes on the offense. Tall players generally get the most rebounds because they are positioned close to the basket and they can reach very high. But smaller players can also grab rebounds if they get in a good position and can legally block their opponents.

Rules and Scoring

Players may not interfere with the progress of an opponent by holding, pushing, slapping, or tripping. Such violations are called **personal fouls**. If a player commits five personal fouls (six in professional competition), that player is disqualified from the game and replaced by a substitute. Another kind of foul is called the **technical foul**. A technical foul is assessed for unsportsmanlike conduct or such other violations as delaying the game, calling too many time-outs, or having too many players on the court.

In basketball, points are scored on either a **field goal** or a **free throw** (also called a "foul shot"). A field goal is a basket made from the court during normal play. A field goal counts 2 points. In professional basketball, 3 points are counted for a field goal shot from beyond a line marked in an arc 22 feet (6.7 meters) from the basket. In men's college basketball,

3 points are counted for a field goal shot from beyond a line 19 feet 9 inches (6.0 meters) from the basket.

A free throw is awarded to a player after certain fouls. The player who is fouled takes a free (unguarded) shot from the free-throw line, which is 15 feet (4.6 meters) from the basket. The other players line up along the free-throw lane to await a rebound. A successful free throw counts 1 point. Two free throws are allowed for a personal foul against a player in the act of attempting a field goal. (If the field goal is made, it counts 2 points, and the fouled player gets one free throw.) In some situations, a **one-and-one** free throw is allowed. That is, if the first free throw is made, the shooter is awarded a second free throw. (The one-and-one free throw is not used in professional basketball.) In professional basketball, three foul shots are awarded to a player fouled while attempting a three-point field goal. Free throws are also awarded to a team if the opposing team commits a technical foul.

Several rules in basketball concern time limitations. From out-of-bounds, a player has 5 seconds to pass the ball inbounds to a teammate. If a team gains possession of the ball in the backcourt, that team has 10 seconds to advance the ball across the midcourt line. Once the ball is across the midcourt line, it may not be passed or dribbled back behind the midcourt line. In high school and college games, no guarded player may hold the ball for more than 5 seconds without dribbling or passing. In any game, no offensive player may stay inside the free-throw lane for more than 3 seconds. In professional basketball, the offensive team has 24 seconds, from the moment of gaining possession of the ball, to attempt a field goal; in a men's college game, the limit is 45 seconds; in a women's college game, the limit is 30 seconds. (There is usually no such restriction in high school basketball.) If time-limit violations occur, the official stops play and gives the ball to the opposing team.

A defensive player may block a shot that is on its way up. But the defensive player may not block a shot that is on its way down; knock the ball off the rim or away from the area above the basket; pin the ball against the backboard; or block a shot that has already hit the backboard. Any of these illegal blocks, called **goaltending**, results in the shooting team being awarded a field goal.

▶ASPECTS OF OFFENSE

In trying to score a basket, the offensive team works together to free one player for a good shot. The guards, forwards, and center move around constantly, trying to get free of the defense. They pass the ball among themselves and dribble when necessary while trying to create an opening for someone to shoot. Breaking through an opponent's defense is sometimes very difficult, and usually requires skillful passing, clever fakes, and acrobatic shooting.

There are two basic styles of offensive play. One is called the **set-pattern** offense. This is a deliberate, pre-arranged series of movements and passes. Each player begins from an assigned spot on the court and follows a specified route through or around the area in front of the basket. Such a pattern can be very complicated. Sometimes the pattern has to be altered or rerun several times, with many passes, before any player gets free for a shot. In a set-pattern offense, **picks** and **screens** are very effective in getting someone free. In a pick or screen, an offensive player takes a firm, stationary position to block the path of one or more defensive players. Another offensive player can then get away for a clear shot. Set-pattern offenses are designed to include many picks and screens.

The other basic style of offense is called the **fast break**, or **running game**. In a fast break, the offensive team tries to score as quickly as possible after gaining possession of the ball. A fast break begins with a rebound at the defensive basket. Then the offense moves the ball downcourt as fast as it can, trying to beat the defensive players to the basket.

▶ASPECTS OF DEFENSE

Good defense is as important as good offense to the success of a basketball team. When the other team has the ball, all five players must work hard on defense to keep the opponents from scoring.

There are two basic types of basketball defense. One is **man-to-man**, in which each defensive player is assigned a certain offensive player to guard. Sometimes a defender will have to help a teammate guard a particular offensive player. This is called "double teaming." The other basic defensive system is called **zone defense**. In this type, each defensive player is assigned a certain area of the

The physical strength required of basketball players on both offense and defense can be seen in this moment when Magic Johnson is trying to power by Michael Jordan on his way to the basket.

court to protect. The player guards any opponent who enters that area. In a zone defense, the players can be arranged in several different ways. The various arrangements have such names as "2-1-2," "1-3-1," "2-3," and "3-2." For example, in a "2-1-2" zone defense, two defensive players are positioned between the free-throw line and midcourt, one is positioned near the free-throw line, and two are positioned close to the basket.

Zone defenses are used in high school and college basketball along with man-to-man defense. Teams often will switch their defense during a game, perhaps changing from one zone to another or from a zone to a man-to-man, trying to confuse their opponents. In professional basketball, however, zone defenses are illegal, and only the man-to-man defense is allowed.

▶ HINTS ON PLAYING BASKETBALL

For the individual player, success in basketball depends on the ability to perform certain basic skills. Coaches call these the **fundamentals** of the game. Young players should concentrate on learning the fundamentals. Even experienced players should practice them often. The most important areas are footwork, dribbling, passing, shooting, and defense.

Exceptional playmaker Scottie Pippin always executes the fundamentals of basketball well. Here he snaps a chest-high pass up court to a teammate who could be headed for a score.

Footwork. Good footwork is important in every aspect of the game. Balance, speed, quick changes of direction, and the ability to stop and go suddenly give any player a big advantage. To be in a position to move fast, stand with one foot slightly forward. Your knees should be bent slightly, your shoulders a bit forward. Hold your arms out a little, with the fingers spread. When you start to run, use your rear foot as a spring. Take short steps. To move to the side or rear, pivot on the back foot. Use the front foot to guide you in whatever direction you want to go.

Dribbling. Dribbling must be done with one hand. Any player should be able to dribble with the right hand or the left hand. Always keep your head up while dribbling so you can be alert for a teammate to whom you can pass.

When you are unguarded and dribbling the ball down court, use the high, or normal, type of dribble. Lean forward a little and bend your knees slightly. The hand that controls the ball should have the fingers spread wide. Your other hand should be at your side for balance. The ball should be bounced about waist high.

If a defender is near, use a low dribble and protect the ball with your body. The stance is the same as for the high dribble except that you bend your knees more. When you are crouching, keep the ball closer to the floor, bouncing it easily as you move around.

Passing. The fastest way to get the ball down court is by passing it. Passing is the key ingredient in offensive play. There are several different kinds of passes, but it is always best

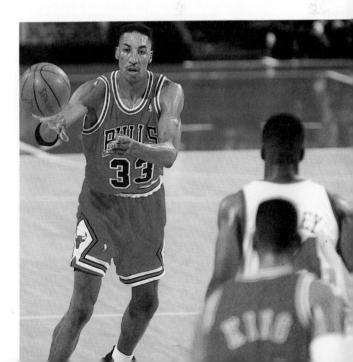

to use the simplest pass you can to complete the play.

The **chest pass** is the most widely used for short, quick throws. Hold the ball chest high with both hands, fingers forward, thumbs behind the ball. As you get ready to pass, bring the ball back toward your chest, turning it so that your thumbs are now under the ball. Then step out with your forward foot while pushing your arms straight ahead. With your wrists snap the ball to the receiver.

The **bounce pass** is effective when your defender keeps his or her hands in the air. With your knees bent, hold the ball waist high with both hands. When you see that your receiver is clear, bend your back knee almost to a kneeling position. Straighten your arms and flip the ball downward on a single bounce toward your receiver.

To throw high to a teammate, you can use the **two-hand overhead pass**. Hold the ball as you would for a chest pass, but with your fingers a little more behind the ball. Keep your feet just apart, and bend your knees slightly. Lift your hands above and a little in front of your head. Take a step forward and bend your wrists back. Then push the ball forward with a quick snap of the wrists.

For getting the ball to a teammate on the run, the best choice might be a **shovel pass**. This is a two-handed underhand pass. It should be short and soft, with no spin on the ball.

To make a long pass, especially on a fast break, you may use the **football pass**. It is made with one hand, the ball cocked behind your head. As you begin to throw, step forward with the opposite leg—just as if you were throwing a football. (Interestingly, this pass is also called the baseball pass, because a baseball is thrown the same way.)

It is also important to learn how to fake. Look high, pass low. Look low, pass high. Fake a pass one way and then pass another. When you have mastered the basic passing techniques, you can try more difficult passes. Just make sure the ball gets to your teammate.

Shooting. No basketball skill is more important than shooting for the basket. In trying to make a basket, a player can choose any of several different kinds of shots. Always choose the easiest shot for the situation. Whatever the shot, maintain good balance, concentrate on the rim, and do not rush. To become a good shooter, practice, practice, and practice some more.

The easiest shot in basketball is the **lay-up**. Dribbling the ball, stride hard toward the basket and jump off one foot. In the air, lay the ball gently off the backboard and into the hoop. When you take a lay-up, push off the floor with the foot opposite your shooting hand. Practice taking lay-ups with either hand, from either side of the basket.

The **dunk** is the most spectacular shot in basketball. The player leaps high in the air,

Reggie Miller (*below*), known for his accurate shooting, prepares to put a good spin on his outside jump shot. Shaquille O'Neill (*right*) completes another of his spectacular slam dunks.

bringing the ball well above the rim. Then the player simply slams it down through the hoop. Usually, only very tall players can reach high enough to perform a dunk. But shorter players who are extremely good leapers can often perform dunks, too.

Another shot for tall players is the **hook shot**. Use the hook only when you are near the basket. After getting the ball, turn so that you are sideways to the basket. With the hand farther from the basket, raise the ball in a circular motion above your head. At the highest point, release the ball with a quick snap of the wrist.

Shots taken farther away from the basket are called "outside" shots. There are two basic ways of shooting from the outside. One is the **set shot**. The two-hand set is best for younger players. Keep your feet slightly apart, knees bent. Hold the ball on each side, with the seams running horizontally. Keep your fingers spread and thumbs back. As you raise the ball near your chin, bend your knees a bit more. Bring your wrists back so that the ball is cupped in your hands. Then straighten your knees and arms, pushing the ball toward the basket with a snap of the wrists. For a one-hand set shot, put the weight of the ball on one hand and use the other hand to guide the ball as you raise it toward the basket.

For more experienced players, the **jump shot** is the most commonly used outside shot.

It is taken like a one-hand set shot, except that the player jumps before shooting. Bend your knees and jump slightly off the floor with both feet. At the peak of your jump, release the ball toward the basket with the same wrist-snapping action.

Always try to take an outside shot the exact same way. Maintain good balance and rhythm. Feel comfortable. It is very important to concentrate on the basket. Snap your wrists, putting backward spin on the ball. Follow through on the release, as if guiding the ball after it has left your hands.

Defense. Guarding an opponent well requires as much concentration as shooting does. Always know where the ball is. Always know where your opponent is. Also know your opponent's abilities and playing habits. Can this player make long shots? Can this player dribble well with either hand? Also be alert for a teammate who needs defensive help. Most of all, work hard and hustle.

When on defense, always keep your knees bent. In guarding, spread your feet with one slightly in front. If your left foot is forward, hold your left arm head-high with fingers spread. Hold out your right arm to the side, between knee and hip. When your opponent has the ball, stand in front and move your arms constantly. Your object is to block any pass and keep a shot from being taken. The

A well-executed hook shot, like this one of Dikembe Mutombo's (*below left*), is an effective scoring tool near the basket. Mark Price (*below right*) gets ready to release a classic one-handed set shot.

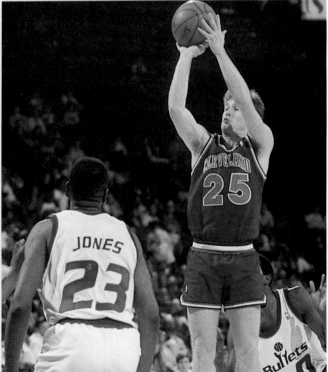

GREAT PLAYERS IN THE HISTORY OF BASKETBALL

The Basketball Hall of Fame elected its first members in 1959. However, it was not opened to the public until 1968. The Hall of Fame is located in Springfield, Massachusetts, the birthplace of the sport. A number of the players profiled here have been elected to the Basketball Hall of Fame.

KAREEM ABDUL-JABBAR (LEW ALCINDOR) (1947–   ) began his NBA career in 1969 after playing college ball at UCLA. He played for the Milwaukee Bucks (1969–75) and the Los Angeles Lakers (1975–89). The leading scorer in NBA history (38,387 points), he was named the league's MVP six times. He also scored 10 or more points in more than 600 consecutive games. He retired in 1989 and was elected to the Hall of Fame in 1995.

RICK BARRY (1944–   ) was named Rookie of the Year when he joined the San Francisco Warriors, later the Golden State Warriors, in 1965. During Barry's 14-year career in the ABA and NBA, he became the only player to lead both leagues in scoring (the NBA in 1967 and the ABA in 1969). In 1975 he led the Golden State Warriors to the NBA championship and was named MVP in the Finals. Barry was elected to the Hall of Fame in 1986.

ELGIN BAYLOR (1934–   ) was one of the leading scorers in NBA history. He joined the Minneapolis Lakers in 1958 and was named Rookie of the Year in 1959. Baylor remained with the Lakers when they moved to Los Angeles in 1960 and retired from the team in 1972. In the 1962 NBA Finals, Baylor scored 284 points, the most ever by one player in a playoff series. An All-Star ten times, he was elected to the Hall of Fame in 1976.

LARRY BIRD (1956–   ), an All-American at Indiana State University, played professionally for the Boston Celtics. Considered by some to be the greatest all-around basketball player in history, Bird was named the NBA's MVP for three consecutive years (1984–86). He

KAREEM ABDUL-JABBAR

RICK BARRY

ELGIN BAYLOR

LARRY BIRD

WILT CHAMBERLAIN

BOB COUSY

DAVE COWENS

JULIUS ERVING

led the Celtics to three league championships (1981, 1984, 1986) and played on the 1992 U.S. Olympic championship team. He retired in 1992. In 1997 Bird became head coach for the Indiana Pacers. He was elected to the Hall of Fame one year later.

WILT CHAMBERLAIN (1936–99) played with the Philadelphia Warriors, the Philadelphia 76ers, and the Los Angeles Lakers. Chamberlain was the NBA's leading scorer for seven consecutive seasons (1959–65). He holds the NBA record for career rebounds and was named MVP four times. He holds the NBA record for the most points (100) scored in one game. Chamberlain retired in 1973 and was elected to the Hall of Fame in 1979.

BOB COUSY (1928–   ), a guard with the Boston Celtics, was one of the NBA's finest players. A brilliant playmaker, he led the league in assists for eight consecutive seasons. His Celtics won six NBA championships, and he was chosen for the NBA All-Pro team ten years in a row. After retiring in 1963, Cousy coached at Boston College and for the NBA's Cincinnati Royals. In 1969 he was a player and coach for seven of the Royals' games. Cousy was elected to the Hall of Fame in 1971.

DAVE COWENS (1948–   ) played with the Boston Celtics for ten seasons. He was chosen for the NBA All-Stars seven consecutive times (1972–78) and was named MVP in the NBA in 1973. Cowens was the Celtics' player and coach for 68 games during the 1978–79 season. After his retirement in 1980, Cowens played one season (1982–83) with the Milwaukee Bucks. He was elected to the Hall of Fame in 1991.

JULIUS ERVING (1950–   ), nicknamed Dr. J, became known for his spectacular leaping ability and acrobatic moves. Erving played for the Virginia Squires and New York Nets in the ABA and the Philadelphia 76ers in the NBA. He led the ABA in scoring in 1973 and 1974 and the NBA in 1976. Erving was named MVP in the ABA three times and once in the NBA. He retired in 1987 and was elected to the Hall of Fame in 1993.

JOHN HAVLICEK (1940–) joined the Boston Celtics in 1962 and spent his entire career with the team. He averaged 20.8 points per game during his 16-season career and was one of the top scorers in NBA history with 26,395 career points. For four consecutive years he was named to the first team NBA All-Pro. He also helped the Celtics win eight NBA titles and was named MVP in the playoffs in 1974. Havlicek was elected to the Hall of Fame in 1983.

ELVIN HAYES (1945–) was named College Player of the Year in 1968 while at the University of Houston. During a 16-year NBA career, Hayes averaged 21.0 points per game. He is the sixth leading scorer in league history with 27,313 career points and the fourth leading rebounder with 16,279 rebounds. An NBA All-Star in 1975, 1977, and 1979, Hayes was elected to the Hall of Fame in 1989.

EARVIN "MAGIC" JOHNSON (1959–) joined the Los Angeles Lakers in 1979. He was named league MVP three times (1987, 1989, 1990) and won five NBA championships with the Lakers (1980, 1982, 1985, 1987, and 1988). He is second in NBA career assists (10,141). In 1992 Johnson retired from basketball after testing positive for the HIV virus. Since then he has worked to promote AIDS awareness. He played on the 1992 U.S. Olympic gold medal team.

MICHAEL JORDAN (1963–) spent his entire career with the Chicago Bulls and has been hailed as one of the greatest players of all time. His career began with Rookie of the Year honors in 1985. He was MVP five times and an All-Star eleven times; set an NBA record by leading the league in scoring for ten seasons (seven of which were consecutive seasons); and holds the Bulls' record for total points scored (29,277). Jordan retired briefly from basketball in 1993 to try his hand at professional baseball, spending just over a season in the minor leagues. He returned to the NBA in 1995, helping the Bulls to win three more championships before retiring a final time in 1999.

JOHN HAVLICEK

ELVIN HAYES

MAGIC JOHNSON

MICHAEL JORDAN

GEORGE MIKAN

BOB PETTIT

OSCAR ROBERTSON

BILL RUSSELL

JERRY WEST

GEORGE MIKAN (1924–) was considered the first outstanding tall center in professional basketball. In 1950, sports writers voted him the greatest basketball player of the first half of the 20th century. As a center for the Minneapolis Lakers, he was a three-time NBA scoring leader and helped lead his team to five league championships. In 1959 Mikan became one of the first players elected to the Basketball Hall of Fame.

BOB PETTIT (1932–) was the first player in NBA history to score 20,000 points. When Pettit retired from the Milwaukee Hawks, later the St. Louis Hawks, in 1965, he had amassed 20,880 points. At 6 feet 9 inches, Pettit was also a leading rebounder. He was elected to the Hall of Fame in 1970.

OSCAR ROBERTSON (1938–), an All-American at the University of Cincinnati, was named Rookie of the Year when he joined the Cincinnati Royals in 1960. He went on to become one of the leading scorers in NBA history with a career total of 26,710 points. With a total of 9,887 assists, he ranks third on the NBA's all-time list. Robertson retired in 1974 and was elected to the Hall of Fame in 1979.

BILL RUSSELL (1934–), played on the gold-medal–winning U.S. basketball team at the 1956 Olympics. He then joined the Boston Celtics and led them to eleven NBA championships. Named MVP five times, Russell became a player and coach for the Celtics in 1966, the first black to coach a major professional sports team. Russell became a TV sportscaster in 1969. Then he coached the Seattle SuperSonics and later the Sacramento Kings. He was elected to the Hall of Fame in 1975.

JERRY WEST (1938–) was one of the leading scorers in NBA history, with 25,192 points during his career. He played guard with the Los Angeles Lakers during his entire professional career, and was selected to play in 13 consecutive NBA All-Star games. After retiring as a player, West coached the Lakers from 1976 to 1979 and then became their general manager in 1982. He was elected to the Hall of Fame in 1979.

ABA	American Basketball Association
MVP	Most Valuable Player
NBA	National Basketball Association
NCAA	National Collegiate Athletic Association

hand on the side is for blocking a pass. The raised hand is for blocking a shot or high pass. If your opponent tries to get away from you by dribbling to the side, move in the same direction with a shuffle, or side step.

When your opponent is in scoring territory, guard as closely as possible. But be careful not to foul. When your opponent is out in the middle of the court or beyond, you can stay a few feet away. If your opponent is awaiting a pass near the basket, stand a bit behind in a straddle position and keep one hand in front to knock away the ball.

In guarding an opponent, try never to leave your feet. Work hard with your legs, not your hands. If your opponent shoots, put both arms straight in the air. Try not to jump—if you do, you will probably foul your opponent. If you must jump, make sure to jump straight up, not toward your opponent.

▶ **EARLY HISTORY**

When Dr. Naismith invented basketball in 1891, the game was played with peach baskets and a soccer ball. Every time a goal was made, someone had to climb a ladder to retrieve the ball. Over the next several years, changes were made to improve the game. In 1893, hoops with net bags began to be used. In 1894, backboards and a slightly larger ball were introduced. The standard metal rim and bottomless netting first appeared in the early 1900's. The modern seamed ball was developed by the 1930's.

When the game was first played, nine people formed a team. Later it was changed to permit nine, seven, or five to play. Standard rectangular courts were established in 1903. As the game spread and formal competition was organized, other regulations gradually were introduced. By the mid-1930's, most of the modern rules had been set.

▶ **MODERN COMPETITION**

Basketball today is still played most widely in the United States. There is organized league competition for boys and girls, men and women, amateurs and professionals. And the popularity of the game continues to grow, both in America and throughout the world.

High School

Most high schools in the United States today, whether public or private, sponsor bas-

ketball teams for both boys and girls. A school's top team is called the varsity. For freshmen and sophomores, many high schools also field a junior varsity squad. Schools within the same general area are organized into a league, with a full schedule of games among all the teams. In some states, high schools are divided into groups based on the number of students enrolled. After the regular season, a statewide tournament is held to determine the champion in each group. Large cities such as New York and Chicago also hold championship tournaments.

In the United States, the National Federation of State High School Associations is the governing body of organized basketball for high school players. The federation is made up of 50 state high school athletic associations, plus one for the District of Columbia, and determines the rules for high school competition.

College

The game of basketball began to catch on in American colleges and universities within only a few years after its invention. By the beginning of the 1900's, the game was being played by more than 50 U.S. colleges. By the 1930's, some intercollegiate games were attracting thousands of fans. Still, it was not until after World War II (1939–45) that college ball became extremely popular. Competition improved and rivalries developed. Some colleges began building big arenas and giving scholarships to good players. Then television brought the excitement into everybody's living room. Since the 1970's, women's college basketball has boomed along with men's.

The National Collegiate Athletic Association (NCAA) governs major college basketball competition. The largest schools compete in Division I; those with smaller enrollments compete in Division II and Division III. Certain other small colleges belong to the National Association of Intercollegiate Athletics (NAIA).

Most colleges also belong to conferences of 8 to 13 teams each. The schools in each conference are located in the same part of the country. Each team plays the other teams in the conference at least twice each year. Then there might be a tournament to determine the conference champion. Some of the

Some Common Basketball Terms

Assist — A pass to a teammate that leads directly to a field goal.

Backboard — The surface of wood or fiberglass to which the basket is attached.

Backcourt — The half of the court away from the basket under attack.

Basket — (1) The iron rim (or hoop) and the attached net through which goals are scored; (2) a field goal.

Blocking — A foul by a defensive player who blocks the legal path of an offensive player.

Charging — A foul by an offensive player who runs into a defensive player having legal position.

Dribbling — Continuous bouncing of the ball with one hand, the only legal way a player may move with the ball.

Fast break — A style of offense in which a team attempts to race to the offensive basket before the defense can get set.

Field goal — A basket made from the court during normal play. A field goal is worth 2 or 3 points, depending on the part of the court from which it is attempted.

Free throw — A free (unguarded) shot from the free-throw line, awarded to players after certain fouls by the opposing team.

Free-throw lane — The area on the floor bounded by the free-throw line, the end line under the basket, and connecting lines forming a 12-foot lane (high school and college) or 16-foot lane (professional). The free-throw lane is also called the "foul lane."

Free-throw line — A line, 15 feet from the basket, behind which the shooter must stand in attempting a free throw. The free-throw line is also called the "foul line."

Frontcourt — The half of the court in which the basket is under attack.

Goaltending — An illegal block of an attempted field goal.

Held ball — Possession of the ball by opposing players at the same time. In professional basketball, a jump ball determines which team will get possession of the ball; in college basketball, possession is determined on an alternating basis.

Jump ball — A means of putting the ball into play in which an official tosses it upward between two opposing players. Each player jumps and tries to tap the ball to a teammate.

Man-to-man defense — A style of team defense in which each player is assigned one specific opponent to guard anywhere on the court.

Offensive foul — A personal foul committed by a member of the offensive team, usually not involving a free throw as part of the penalty. Also called "player control foul."

Palming — An illegal means of carrying the ball while dribbling.

Personal foul — Any of a variety of body-contact fouls. A player who has committed five personal fouls (six in professional basketball) is disqualified from the game.

Pick — A legal method of providing shooting room for a teammate by taking a stationary position that "picks off" or blocks a defensive player.

Pivot — A position taken by a player with his or her back to the basket, at the head of or alongside the free-throw lane, from which the player can spin or shoot or pass the ball to teammates moving toward the basket.

Post — A synonym for pivot. "High post" means farther from the basket, "low post" means closer to the basket.

Press — A style of defense in which defensive players closely guard the offensive players. (A "full-court press" is applied all over the court; a "half-court press" is applied only after the ball is brought across the midcourt line.)

Rebound — The recovery of a missed field goal attempt.

Shot clock — A timer that indicates how much time remains for the offensive team to attempt a field goal. In professional basketball, for example, a team has 24 seconds to attempt a field goal after gaining possession of the ball.

Steal — The capture of the ball from the hands of a player by the defender; also, an intercepted pass.

Technical foul — foul imposed for misbehavior or some technical rule infraction. The penalty is a free throw (sometimes two free throws). In high school and college games, the team shooting the free throw also receives possession of the ball.

Ten-second rule — The rule that a team must bring the ball across the midcourt line within 10 seconds after gaining possession in the backcourt.

Three-point shot — A field goal made from behind a line marked in an arc a certain distance from the basket; such field goals are credited with 3 points.

Three-second rule — The rule that offensive players may not take set positions within the free-throw lane for more than 3 seconds.

Traveling — Running or walking with the ball without dribbling it. Also called "steps" or "walking."

Turnover — Loss of possession of the ball without attempting a field goal.

Violation — Any infraction of the rules that is not classified as a foul. The penalty is loss of possession of the ball.

Zone defense — A style of team defense in which each player is assigned to guard a designated floor area rather than a specific opponent.

Some signals used frequently by officials

Jump ball

Personal foul

Points scored
(1, 2, or 3 fingers)

Traveling

Illegal dribble

Offensive foul

best-known basketball conferences are the Big Ten, Atlantic Coast Conference, Big East, Big South, Southeastern Conference, and Pacific 10. During the regular season, a team also plays several schools from outside its own conference.

The highlight of the college basketball season is the NCAA championship, a tournament held after the regular season and conference championships. In men's Division I play, 65 teams are selected for the NCAA tournament; in women's play, 64 teams compete. Tournaments are also held in Divisions II and III, for both men and women.

The men's NCAA tournament has been held every year since 1939. The most successful team has been the University of California at Los Angeles (UCLA). Coached by the legendary John Wooden, UCLA won ten NCAA titles in the 1960's and 1970's. The first women's NCAA tournament was held in 1982.

International

Outside the United States, most formal competition is either amateur or semiprofessional. The rules used in international basketball are established by the International Basketball Federation (FIBA). The game is played basically as it is in the United States, though with certain minor differences. The free-throw lane, for example, is larger and shaped differently from the one used in American basketball.

The first official basketball competition in the Olympic Games was held in 1936, for men only. Women's basketball became an official Olympic sport in 1976.

Men's Professional Basketball

The first professional basketball teams also date from the early days of the game. The most famous early pro team was the Buffalo Germans. They were created in 1895 and lasted 30 years. During one stretch, the Germans won 111 straight games.

The greatest professional team of the 1920's was the Original Celtics of New York City. The Celtics were the first basketball team to sign players to

exclusive contracts. In the 1930's the Renaissance Big Five, or Rens, a team of black players, dominated the game.

Probably the best-known professional team of all time is the Harlem Globetrotters, formed in 1927 by Abe Saperstein. This team of black players is not part of any league. Instead, they tour the world playing exhibition games in which they use their skill and clowning routines to entertain spectators.

The National Basketball League was formed in 1937. It was composed of professional and industrial teams from small midwestern cities. Another proleague, the Basketball Association of America, was established in 1946.

In 1949, owners of Eastern hockey arenas wanted to sell seats when hockey was not

---

NATIONAL BASKETBALL ASSOCIATION

EASTERN CONFERENCE

Atlantic Division	Central Division
Boston Celtics	Atlanta Hawks
Miami Heat	Charlotte Hornets
New Jersey Nets	Chicago Bulls
New York Knickerbockers	Cleveland Cavaliers
Orlando Magic	Detroit Pistons
Philadelphia 76ers	Indiana Pacers
Washington Wizards	Milwaukee Bucks
	Toronto Raptors

WESTERN CONFERENCE

Midwest Division	Pacific Division
Dallas Mavericks	Golden State Warriors
Denver Nuggets	Los Angeles Clippers
Houston Rockets	Los Angeles Lakers
Minnesota Timberwolves	Phoenix Suns
San Antonio Spurs	Portland Trail Blazers
Utah Jazz	Sacramento Kings
Vancouver Grizzlies	Seattle SuperSonics

NATIONAL BASKETBALL ASSOCIATION CHAMPIONS

1951	Rochester Royals	1978	Washington Bullets
1952–54	Minneapolis Lakers	1979	Seattle SuperSonics
1955	Syracuse Nationals	1980	Los Angeles Lakers
1956	Philadelphia Warriors	1981	Boston Celtics
1957	Boston Celtics	1982	Los Angeles Lakers
1958	St. Louis Hawks	1983	Philadelphia 76ers
1959–66	Boston Celtics	1984	Boston Celtics
1967	Philadelphia 76ers	1985	Los Angeles Lakers
1968–69	Boston Celtics	1986	Boston Celtics
1970	New York Knickerbockers	1987–88	Los Angeles Lakers
1971	Milwaukee Bucks	1989–90	Detroit Pistons
1972	Los Angeles Lakers	1991–93	Chicago Bulls
1973	New York Knickerbockers	1994–95	Houston Rockets
1974	Boston Celtics	1996–98	Chicago Bulls
1975	Golden State Warriors	1999	San Antonio Spurs
1976	Boston Celtics	2000	Los Angeles Lakers
1977	Portland Trail Blazers		

being played. With these large arenas available, the National Basketball League merged with the Basketball Association of America to form the modern National Basketball Association (NBA). The American Basketball Association (ABA) began in 1967 as a league for cities without NBA teams. It was dissolved in 1976, and some of its teams and best players were absorbed into the NBA.

The NBA now has 29 teams (27 teams are in United States cities, and the other two teams are based in Canadian cities) divided into two conferences. The Eastern Conference consists of the Atlantic and the Central divisions; the Western Conference has the Midwest and the Pacific divisions. Each team plays a regular-season schedule of 82 games, many against teams in the same division. But all the teams play each other a few times every year.

At the end of the regular season, the top 16 teams compete in a series of playoffs to determine the NBA champion. The Boston Celtics, with 16 championships, have been the most successful team in NBA history. From 1959 to 1966 they took the crown eight years in a row. During the 1980's the Los Angeles Lakers won the NBA championship five times (1980, 1982, 1985, 1987–88). The 1990's were dominated by the Chicago Bulls, who won the championship six times (1991–93, 1996–98).

In 1998, a labor dispute between NBA owners and players resulted in the postponement of the 1998–99 season. However, an agreement was reached between the two sides in January 1999, just before the entire season was about to be canceled.

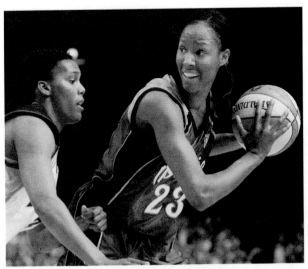

With talented players such as Chamique Holdsclaw (right), the WNBA has become as exciting and popular as the NBA.

Women's Professional Basketball

Women first played basketball in 1892, but the first women's pro league was not organized until 1978. This league, the Women's Professional Basketball League (WBL), did not prove to be popular and it ceased operating in 1981. A surge of interest in women's basketball led to the formation of a new women's pro league, the eight-team American Basketball League (ABL), in September 1995. This league also lasted only three years, declaring bankruptcy in 1998.

The Women's National Basketball Association (WNBA) is sponsored by the NBA and began play in June 1997. The WNBA has expanded from its original 8 teams to a total of 16, which are divided into an Eastern and Western Conference. Players who have risen to stardom in the WNBA's short history include Sheryl Swoopes and Tina Thompson of the Houston Comets, Chamique Holdsclaw of the Washington Mystics, and Teresa Weatherspoon of the New York Liberty. The Houston Comets have been the WNBA's most dominant team, winning the League's first four championships.

Reviewed by DAVE DEBUSSCHERE
Member, Basketball Hall of Fame

BASTILLE. See FRENCH REVOLUTION.

BASUTOLAND. See LESOTHO.

BATON ROUGE. See LOUISIANA (Cities).

WOMEN'S NATIONAL BASKETBALL ASSOCIATION

EASTERN CONFERENCE	WESTERN CONFERENCE
Charlotte Sting	Houston Comets
Cleveland Rockers	Los Angeles Sparks
Detroit Shock	Minnesota Lynx
Indiana Fever	Phoenix Mercury
Miami Sol	Portland Fire
New York Liberty	Sacramento Monarchs
Orlando Miracle	Seattle Storm
Washington Mystics	Utah Starzz

WOMEN'S NATIONAL BASKETBALL ASSOCIATION CHAMPIONS

1997–2000 Houston Comets

Bats are the only mammals that fly. They are also among the most social of mammals. Some species have been known to live in colonies of more than a million members.

BATS

In the animal kingdom, bats are classed as mammals. Like all mammals, bats nurse their young on milk. Like most mammals, they have hair and bear living young. But in one way, bats are different from all other mammals: Bats can fly.

There are mammals known as flying squirrels and flying lemurs, but they do not truly fly. Rather they glide from tree to tree. Bats are the only mammals that move through the air with wings.

A bat's wing is not like a bird's wing. While the bird's wing is formed chiefly of feathers, the bat's wing is a double layer of skin stretched over the thin bones of its arm and fingers. A bat's skeleton is the framework for these wings. The arm extends from a shoulder socket, bends at the elbow, and ends with long, slender fingers. The fingers are almost as long as the rest of the body. They support the main part of the wing and are covered with skin.

The wing covers all fingers except a short thumb, which is left free. A sharp claw on the end of the thumb forms a hook at the top of the wing. When its wings are folded, the bat uses its hooks to climb tree trunks, rocky walls, and other rough surfaces.

The skin connecting the webbed fingers is also attached to the bat's clawed feet. This makes the back part of the wings. Most bats have an extra flap of skin connecting their feet. While flying, many can fold this flap into a pocket for catching insects.

Since its leg bones and leg muscles are included in its wings, a bat can fly more easily than it can walk. But the feet are far from useless. Like human hands, a bat's feet can turn inward, which enables them to grasp objects like twigs and branches. Sharp claws hook securely into cracks or around bumps in the wall or ceiling of a cave. These claws are so strong that they support the bat's whole weight, even during sleep.

When resting, a bat can use its claws to cling to a wall or tree trunk—or it may hang upside down, suspended by its feet. Bats hang upside down because it is easier for them than perching upright.

Bats may be less than 1 inch (2.5 centimeters) in length or as long as 15 inches (38 centimeters). Their wing spread can be as wide as 5 feet (1.5 meters). Bats have fur that may be white, red, brown, gray, or black.

HOW BATS LIVE

There are nearly a thousand different species, or kinds, of bats. They live in almost every part of the world except the polar regions. Each kind of bat has different habits, though the various species also have many things in common.

Bat Colonies

Bats are usually social animals. That is, they live in groups. Often they can be found living in caves. If you see one bat flying into a cave, you can be reasonably sure there are other bats inside. In some caves thousands of bats crowd together on walls or ceilings. Smaller bat colonies numbering only ten or twelve bats may live in a hollow tree.

Caves and hollow trees are not the only places where bats live. Some bats simply roost in trees, hanging like leaves from twigs and branches. Two kinds of tropical bats make tents from palm leaves. Such a bat slits the leaf with its teeth, then hangs inside the folds.

Bats live in the pyramids of Egypt and in the fruit trees of Australia. In North America and Europe people sometimes share a house with bats and never know they are there. A bat can squeeze through narrow cracks and roost between layers of wall and ceiling.

Night Creatures

Most bats are nocturnal. This means that they are active only at night. They sleep in the daytime and come out at night to find food. Only a few kinds of bats venture out in bright sunlight. Bats are probably night creatures for the same reasons that most small mammals are. A small animal is in less danger at night. In the daytime it is in constant danger of being eaten by larger animals that sleep at night. Also, at night bats can catch insects with less competition from birds.

The Search for Food

Most bats live on insects alone. Some eat only fruit. Some eat both insects and fruit. A few kinds of bats eat other things—meat, fish, and even flower nectar.

In Canada and the United States, the most familiar bats are insect eaters, though there are nectar-feeding bats in Arizona and California. Probably the best-known fruit bats are the huge flying foxes. In Australia these giant bats have become a serious nuisance to fruit growers. They swarm over the orchards, devouring fruit at night and roosting in the trees by day.

In India one kind of bat has been seen eating mice, birds, and lizards. When captured, the large spear-nosed bats of tropical America will eat almost anything. They have been fed bananas, horsemeat, liver, and hamburger. They will even eat smaller bats.

The bats with the most unusual diets are found in the tropics. *Noctilio* bats of South and Middle America eat fish. They skim over a pond or lake, dragging their sharp claws

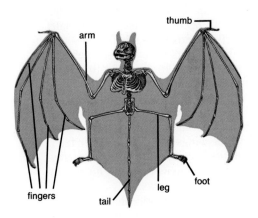

The bat's anatomy is specially adapted for flying. The hands and arms form the wings. The highly developed arm bones hold out flaps of skin from the bat's back and belly. A double layer of thin, flexible skin covers the elongated bones of the fingers.

Bats eat a wide variety of food, some species consuming up to half their weight each night. At left, a bat uses its long tongue to obtain nectar. At right, a mother and baby bat rest. Bats roost by hanging upside down with their wings folded over their bodies.

through the water to catch small fish swimming near the surface. Another group of jungle bats, the tiny hummingbird bats, eat chiefly the pollen and nectar of flowers.

Probably the most famous tropical bats are the vampires, found only in South and Middle America. The vampire bat has inspired legends, superstitions, and horror tales—all of them false. A vampire bat does bite other animals and drinks their blood. But a vampire bat may bite a sleeping horse, cow, or goat—or even a person—without being noticed. Its sharp teeth make a shallow cut. Then the bat simply laps up a small amount of blood and flies away. The chief danger to the victim is not loss of blood but rather infection. Vampire bats—as well as several other species—are known carriers of rabies.

Migration and Hibernation

Bats cannot survive in extremely cold weather. So some fly to warmer climates for the winter. When spring comes, these bats return to a favorite roost. They may make long flights, flying as far as 800 miles (1,287 kilometers) during a migration.

Instead of migrating, other bats avoid winter conditions by hibernating deep in caves, where the temperature changes very little from season to season. For many weeks hibernating bats hang head downward, sometimes packed together in thick clusters. They each have an extra layer of body fat that provides the fuel they need to keep alive until spring.

Birth of Young

Bats mate in the fall, before hibernating or flying away for the winter. When the weather begins to warm up, female bats gather in the roosts that will become nurseries. In late spring or early summer, the baby bats are born. Most mother bats have just one baby at a time. (Some have up to four, but this is as rare as twins in human families.)

When a baby bat is born, the mother forms a living cradle by hanging belly-up from the ceiling or a branch. She may hang by the hooks at the top of her wings as well as by her feet. The newborn bat rests in this cradle. The baby bat is able to hang on to its mother's fur, using its own sharp teeth and claws.

Young bats grow so rapidly that a 10-day-old bat can be too heavy for its mother to carry. Within a month after birth, the baby bat has grown to its full size. A bat born in June is flying on nightly hunting trips by August. It may live as long as 10 to 14 years, a remarkably long lifetime for a small mammal.

Ancestors of today's bats were flying about the earth at least 50 million years ago. Since that time some bats have changed very little. One 40 million-year-old bat fossil found in Europe looks very much like the skeleton of a modern bat.

Some scientists think that the first bats may have evolved from a tree-climbing mammal that could leap and glide after insects. Over millions of years the limbs of some gliding animals may have developed into wings. These winged animals would have been the first bats. Scientists are still looking for fossils that would prove this theory.

▶HOW DO BATS FIND THEIR WAY IN THE DARK?

For centuries people who studied bats wondered how they found their way in the dark. Many people thought that bats had unusually keen eyesight and could see by light too faint for human eyes to detect. Scientists now know that a bat's ability to navigate depends not on its eyes but on its ears and vocal organs.

The first steps toward understanding how bats navigate were taken in the 1780's. An Italian zoologist named Lazzaro Spallanzani suspected that bats could not see in the dark. To find out, he blinded some bats and released them into a room crisscrossed with silk threads. The bats flew through the maze without touching the threads. Then he tried plugging their ears with wax. The animals blundered about, flapping their wings helplessly and becoming entangled in the threads.

Spallanzani's work was almost forgotten until 1920. That year, at Cambridge University in England, Professor H. Hartridge suggested that bats sent out signals that were beyond the range of human hearing. (Such sounds are called **ultrasonic**.) He thought bats might use the echoes of these signals to navigate in the dark. But Hartridge could not prove his theory. He had no way of listening to ultrasonic sounds.

In 1941 two scientists in the United States proved that Spallanzani and Hartridge had been on the right track. Donald R. Griffin and Robert Galambos of Harvard University placed bats in front of a new electronic instrument that could detect ultrasonic sounds. The men could hear no sounds, but patterns on a screen showed that the bats were uttering high-pitched cries.

Griffin and Galambos strung a room with a network of wire and repeated some of Spallanzani's experiments. They added their own modern equipment—microphones and recording devices. Patterns on the electronic screen showed that the bats were constantly squeaking as they flew successfully through the maze of wires.

A bat sends out signals—high-pitched squeaks—that bounce off anything in its path. A sound that is bounced back, or reflected, is called an echo. The bat uses echoes to locate things in the dark. So scientists call this system **echolocation**. It is often compared to the radar and sonar systems used by people, which also use reflected signals to locate objects. But radar and sonar are newcomers. Bats have been using echolocation for millions of years.

BARBARA LAND
Columbia Graduate School of Journalism
Reviewed by KARL F. KOOPMAN
The American Museum of Natural History

See also ECHO; RADAR, SONAR, LORAN, AND SHORAN; SOUND AND ULTRASONICS.

A bat locates and judges distance to its prey by bouncing ultrasonic signals off it. The same technique, called echolocation, helps a bat navigate in the dark.

Batteries are made in many shapes and sizes to fit a variety of devices. Wristwatches, toys, radios, and flashlights are some of the things these batteries power.

Automobile battery

Lantern battery

D

C

AA

AAA

Button cells

9 Volt

Nickel cadmium (rechargeable)

BATTERIES

When you enjoy music from a portable radio or find your way in the dark with a flashlight, you are using the most common portable power source known—the battery.

Batteries are very much a part of our lives. Without them many toys would not work, automobiles would not start, and digital wristwatches would not tell time. Even satellites in orbit would stop relaying their signals to Earth.

▶WHAT IS A BATTERY?

A battery is a device that produces electrical energy, usually by means of a chemical reaction. This chemical reaction takes place in the part of the battery known as the **cell**. Cells are the battery's building blocks. Each battery contains one or more cells. The common transistor radio battery is made up of six cells. The common "D" battery is just a single cell.

Batteries can be either **primary** or **secondary** devices. Primary batteries are those that can be used only as long as the supply of chemicals inside them lasts. (The process of producing electricity uses up the chemicals.) When a primary battery stops producing power, it must be replaced. The "dead" battery should be taken to a recycling or waste-disposal center.

Secondary batteries, on the other hand, can be recharged. When these batteries are exhausted, an electrical current can be applied to the battery to reverse the chemical reaction that took place inside the cells. The result is a battery with a new supply of energy; it can be used until it runs down again.

▶HOW PRIMARY BATTERIES WORK

One of the most common primary batteries is the "D" battery, also known as the flashlight battery or the dry cell. The dry cell is not really dry. It contains a central carbon rod surrounded by a damp paste of chemicals. These are enclosed in a container made of zinc. When the battery is being used, the carbon, chemicals, and zinc react with each other to produce electricity.

To start the chemical reaction, the battery must be in an electrical circuit. Only when there is a demand for power will the battery produce electricity. When the "on" switch is moved—on a flashlight, for example—a complete path, or electrical circuit, is formed that includes the battery, switch, connecting wires, and bulb. Electricity can now flow through the circuit, and the flashlight bulb lights.

Often more than one battery is needed to provide sufficient power to run a device. Several batteries can be used together if they are lined up in a certain way. In a **series connection**, the positive end of one battery is in contact with the negative end of another battery. This arrangement multiplies the force that pushes the electricity (like a pump pushing water) through the device being powered.

Sometimes cells can be wired in a **parallel connection**, that is, positive end to positive end and negative end to negative end. When this is done, the "push" available is the same as from a single battery, but the amount of electricity is multiplied. This type of connection is used where heavy loads, such as electrical motors, must be powered.

Types of Primary Batteries

The flashlight battery is just one of many kinds of primary batteries. Another common type of dry cell is the 9-volt battery, also known as the transistor radio battery. This device is made up of six flat, 1.5-volt cells stacked one upon the other in a package that will easily fit the small spaces in pocket-size transistor radios and calculators. (These devices do not all use 9-volt batteries. Some take "A" or "AA" cells.) The battery's connecting posts, called **terminals**, are made into clips, and both are located on the top of the package. This helps avoid the problem of putting the battery into a device upside down.

Another type of primary battery is the alkaline battery, which is popular because of its longer life. Its operation is similar to that of the carbon-zinc dry cell, except for the chemicals used. Since the early 1980's, manufacturers have reduced the amount of mercury used in alkaline batteries because of concerns of mercury poisoning in the environment.

Other types of primary batteries are the silver-oxide battery used in electronic wristwatches and the very long-life lithium battery. These batteries are named for the chemicals they contain.

Because all primary batteries in time will run down and have to be replaced, they are most widely used in products or applications where low cost is important or where recharging is not practical, such as in a wristwatch.

▶ HOW SECONDARY BATTERIES WORK

Secondary batteries are often referred to as "wet cells" since many do contain liquids (unlike the dry or damp chemicals in primary batteries). Secondary batteries are also often called storage batteries because when they are being recharged, they are storing energy.

The most common secondary battery is the lead-acid automobile battery. This device is made up of six cells, each of which contains metal plates made of lead and lead dioxide. The plates are immersed in a weak solution of sulfuric acid and water. On the outside of the battery, positive and negative terminals are used to make the electrical connection to the metal plates and acid solution inside.

The automobile battery is turned on by the ignition switch in the car. This action forms a completed electrical circuit. As the battery is being used, or discharged, the lead plates chemically change into different compounds of lead. This process can provide electricity as long as enough lead is present on the plates.

When the battery runs low, however, it can be recharged by forcing electricity to flow into it in the reverse direction. This is the process called charging. It is carried out in a car by a device called an alternator, which is a small electrical generator run by the automobile engine. During charging, the chemical compounds change back into the original lead and lead dioxide. The life of such a battery is measured in years, because it can be charged thousands of times as it runs down.

Types of Secondary Batteries

Other types of secondary batteries are the nickel cadmium and nickel-metal hydride batteries, which are named for the chemicals they contain. Like lead-acid automobile batteries,

A Primary Battery

Metal cap
Wax seal
Plastic jacket
Zinc casing
Damp paste of chemicals
Carbon rod
Metal base

The carbon-zinc dry cell, or flashlight battery, is a common type of primary battery. A chemical reaction between the carbon, zinc, and damp chemical paste causes an electrical current to be produced.

A Secondary Battery

Positive terminal
Negative terminal
Negative lead plates
Positive lead dioxide plates
Sulfuric acid and water solution

The lead-acid automobile battery, a type of secondary battery, contains lead and lead-dioxide plates set in a solution of sulfuric acid and water. This kind of battery can be charged and used over and over again.

they can be charged many times. This is done with a charging device that plugs into an electrical outlet. These batteries can be used in the same applications as primary batteries. They also are used to power rechargeable flashlights, cellular phones, and a variety of battery-operated household appliances that are supplied with their own chargers.

In general, secondary batteries are used where large amounts of power are needed or where charging is practical to carry out. Though they initially cost more than primary batteries, secondary batteries can be very economical because they are not discarded and replaced every time they run down.

▶ HOW POWERFUL ARE BATTERIES?

The amount of power that a battery can deliver is directly related to the amount and type of chemicals it contains. This power depends on two measurements, amperes and volts. An ampere is the amount of electricity the battery can produce in 1 second. Volts are a measure of the "push" the battery can give to electricity flowing through a wire.

The amount of chemicals in a battery also influences the battery's size, so a large battery is more powerful than a small one. Small "AAA" penlight batteries (1.5 volts and $\frac{1}{8}$ ampere) will run a penlight for an hour or so. An automobile battery (12 volts and 50 amperes) will provide enough power to start a car or run an electric golf cart.

The life of a battery also depends on the amount of power it must deliver to the device it is running. An automobile battery can start a car and keep it running for a short while, but it will very quickly run down if the car's alternator (turned by the engine) does not begin to charge it. On the other hand, tiny button-size batteries will operate a digital wristwatch for a year or more. This is because the power requirements of a wristwatch are very small.

▶ NEW TYPES OF BATTERIES

All of the batteries described ultimately will run down and have to be replaced. Even rechargeable units will reach a point where they will not respond to charging. As a result, scientists are constantly trying to develop the ideal battery that will last for years (when not in use) and will deliver maximum power for long periods of time when needed. Two candidates are the solar cell and the fuel cell.

Solar Cells

Solar cells are unique because no chemical reaction occurs to use up material. Electricity is produced when light, particularly sunlight, strikes the surface of the cell. This surface is a thin wafer of specially treated, pure silicon.

The power produced by such cells is directly related to the amount of light present. With enough light, a 3-inch (8-centimeter) solar cell will produce about one-third the amount of electrical energy of a "AAA" penlight battery. It will do so, however, as long as light falls on the cell—even for years.

Individual solar cells are almost always connected together to form solar batteries. They are used in applications where it is impractical or even impossible to replace worn-out batteries. The power source for most artificial satellites circling Earth consists of large solar batteries that are made up of hundreds of individual cells. Solar batteries are also being used as inexpensive power sources for hand-held electronic calculators.

Fuel Cells

Another candidate for the ideal battery is the fuel cell. This device produces electricity from the interaction of two gases—typically hydrogen and oxygen. This battery works by passing hydrogen and oxygen gas over a heated substance in a specially constructed chamber. A complex chemical process combines the two gases and produces electricity as a result.

An interesting by-product of fuel cells is pure water. Because the gases are obtained inexpensively and the by-product is useful, fuel cells are suitable for space travel and may become a major source of power for our cities.

Nuclear Batteries

A third type of battery that exhibits extremely long life is the nuclear battery, which powers some space probes. It produces electricity as the result of the decay of radioactive material. A nuclear battery has a lifetime that is measured in hundreds or even thousands of years. However, the problem with this device is the danger of radioactive contamination. For this reason the widespread use of these batteries probably will not occur in the near future.

IRWIN MATH
Author, *Wires and Watts:*
Understanding and Using Electricity

See also ELECTRICITY.

BATTLES

A battle is an organized conflict between two or more competing armies, navies, or air forces that is fought to achieve victory at a particular location in the shortest possible amount of time.

The first armies were organized about 3000 B.C. to protect the civilizations that developed in the fertile river valleys of Mesopotamia (modern Iraq). Such armies fought back raiders with stone weapons, but they did not have armor to shield their bodies. Then about 2000 B.C., humans discovered how to make the copper and tin alloy called bronze, which could be sharpened and hammered to make long swords, axes, spearheads, and armor in the form of helmets and breastplates. Conflicts between bronze-equipped soldiers led to the first organized battles, in which they had to choose suitable ground, stand in line, and use their weapons in a disciplined way.

Cavalry soldiers on horseback were the dominant power in battle from about 500 B.C. to A.D. 1500. The most important cavalry armies were those of Attila the Hun, who attacked western Europe in the A.D. 400's; the Mongols under Genghis Khan, who created an empire from China to western Russia in the 1200's; and the Turks, who conquered the eastern Roman Empire (Byzantium) in the 1400's. Foot soldiers in China, India, the Middle East, Russia, and eastern Europe were easily defeated by the superior mobility of these horse soldiers.

While Asians were adapting the horse as an instrument of warfare, Europeans were perfecting iron weapons and armor, which made them equally fearsome on the battlefield. Iron, which had come into general use about 1000 B.C., was superior to bronze because it was cheap, plentiful, and easily worked into blades, helmets, and breastplates. The Greeks of the city-states, about 400 B.C., were the first to organize armies equipped with iron weapons, but it was the Romans who created the first large armies based on iron technology. By the first century A.D. the Roman Empire extended across the whole of western Europe, North Africa, and much of the Middle East.

The secret of Roman success was discipline on the battlefield. Legions of soldiers were drilled to fight in close formation. They were trained not to yield, no matter how terrifying

Superior weaponry enabled Alexander the Great to defeat Darius III at the Battle of Gaugamela (331 B.C.) and conquer the Persian Empire in the Middle East.

the attack. Occasionally Roman armies were overwhelmed, but for five hundred years, they proved generally invincible. It was only when the empire was pressed by huge numbers of German warriors in the 400's that the power of legions was broken and the Roman Empire destroyed.

Europeans nevertheless maintained the tradition of close-order combat with iron weapons. They also managed to adapt their style of warfare to fighting on horseback, which made them formidable opponents of the Mongols and Turks in battle. During the Crusades, from about 1095 to 1291, in which Christians tried to recapture the Holy Land from the Muslims, small armies of European knights on horseback frequently defeated much larger numbers of Muslim cavalry.

The principal contribution to fighting on the battlefield, however, came from the perfection of gunpowder weapons by the Europeans in the 1500's. Equipped with firearms and

The Scots Greys, a British cavalry regiment, charged the French infantry at the Battle of Waterloo in 1815.

25 of the World's Most Important Battles *(in historical sequence)*

Megiddo, 1469 B.C. The first recorded battle of history, fought between the Pharaoh Thutmose III of Egypt and rebel chieftains, took place near Mount Carmel in modern-day Israel.

In 1588, the English fleet defeated the Spanish Armada in the English Channel.

In 1863, Union forces (right) defeated the Confederates (left) on the third and final day of the Battle of Gettysburg. This battle turned the Civil War in the Union's favor.

Marathon, 490 B.C. The victory of the Greeks over the invading forces of the Persian emperor Darius I near Athens rescued Greek democracy from the threat of foreign tyranny.

Salamis, 480 B.C. In this first important naval battle of history, the Greek navy defeated the Persian fleet near Athens.

Gaugamela, 331 B.C. Alexander the Great's victory over the Persian Empire on the Tigris River in modern-day Iraq led to the establishment of Greek rule in the Middle East.

Cannae, 216 B.C. In the Second Punic War, Hannibal of Carthage invaded southern Italy, where he was badly outnumbered by Roman forces. Nevertheless, by using a deceptive battle strategy, he was able to encircle and defeat the Romans.

Alesia, 52 B.C. Roman general Julius Caesar established the Roman Empire by completing the conquest of Gaul (modern France) and capturing the Gaulish chief Vercingetorix.

Adrianople, A.D. 378 The Roman emperor Valens was killed and his army destroyed by German invaders. The western half of the Roman Empire then fell under German rule.

Châlons, 451 Attila the Hun's army of Central Asian horse soldiers was defeated in western Europe by the allied forces of Roman general Flavius Aëtius and Theodoric I, King of the Visigoths. The victory saved Europe from non-Christian domination.

Tours, 732 Charles Martel, the Christian king of France, defeated an Arab invasion coming northward from Spain, saving France from Muslim rule.

Talas, 751 The Chinese empire was defeated by Arabs in Central Asia, blocking the advance of Chinese rule toward the Middle East.

Hastings, 1066 William, Duke of Normandy, defeated the Anglo-Saxon king Harold. Normans then became the rulers of England.

Manzikert, 1071 The Turks of Central Asia defeated the army of Byzantium (the eastern Roman Empire) and captured modern Turkey.

Ain Jalut, 1260 The advance of the Mongol Empire into the Middle East was at last halted by the Turks.

Constantinople, 1453 The Turks captured the capital of the eastern Roman Empire, killed the last Christian emperor, and established Muslim rule in southeastern Europe.

Spanish Armada, 1588 The English fleet defeated the Spanish in the English Channel, saving England from invasion and preventing the conquest of Protestant northern Europe by the Catholics.

Vienna, 1683 An alliance of Christian kings halted the advance of Muslim Turks into central Europe.

Yorktown, 1781 British forces, under the command of General Charles Cornwallis, were forced to surrender to the Americans, led by General George Washington. This action guaranteed the independence of the American colonies.

Valmy, 1792 The armies of the French Revolution defeated an alliance of European monarchs, paving the way for the rise of Napoleon.

Waterloo, 1815 The combined forces of Britain and Prussia defeated Napoleon and brought down the French Empire.

Gettysburg, 1863 In this decisive battle of the U.S. Civil War, the Union army defeated the Confederacy and began the conquest of the South.

The Marne, 1914 At the outset of World War I, the Allies halted the advance of the invading German army outside Paris. A line of trenches was established, along which most of the rest of the war was fought.

The Meuse, 1940 In the first full year of World War II, German tanks broke the French line of defense and captured France in six weeks. The British army escaped to England from Dunkirk.

Midway, 1942 The American aircraft carrier fleet in the Pacific defeated the Japanese carrier fleet, avenging the attack on Pearl Harbor and beginning the defeat of Japan in World War II.

Stalingrad, 1943 A German army, which had invaded the Soviet Union in 1941, was surrounded on the Volga River and was forced to surrender. This victory led to the defeat of the Germans on the eastern front in World War II.

D-Day, 1944 An Allied force of American, British, and Canadian troops landed on the coast of France in Normandy. They drove back the Germans and began the advance which led to Hitler's defeat on the western front in World War II.

Allied troops invaded Normandy on D-Day, June 6, 1944.

horses, Europeans easily conquered the native peoples of the Americas in the New World, beat back the Turks in southeastern Europe, and extended their power into the Middle East, India, and Africa.

As the use of firearms spread, armies continually sought out new technologies and more sophisticated weaponry. Following the Napoleonic Wars in the early 1800's, steam power started to play a major role in military maneuvers. Ironclad steamships increased the efficiency of naval forces, and steam-powered railroads rapidly moved armies between battlefields. Heavy artillery, such as cannons, became larger and more powerful.

In the wars of the 1900's, technology increasingly dominated warfare. During World War I (1914–18), the introduction of the machine gun forced infantry units to dig and live in trenches to shield themselves from the constant barrage of bullets. In World War II (1939–45), one of the key weapons was the armored tank, which had been developed to withstand machine-gun fire. Aircraft also were adapted for armed combat against the tanks and became the dominant weapon at sea. Ordnance dropped from the air could cause crippling damage to surface ships and also could destroy submarines below the surface. The most terrifying weapon of all, the atomic bomb, threatened the survival of entire civilizations. Today battlefield technology is so highly developed that traditional battle styles have become increasingly obsolete.

JOHN KEEGAN
Author, *A History of Warfare*

BAUHAUS. See GERMANY, ART AND ARCHITECTURE OF.

BAUM, L. FRANK. See SOUTH DAKOTA (Famous People).

BEACH, AMY MARCY. See NEW HAMPSHIRE (Famous People).

A large bear is a powerful animal. If it is cornered or attacked, it can be very dangerous.

BEARS

A shaggy giant wades into a stream. Ducking its head, it lunges forward. Then it comes up, a big salmon flopping between its jaws. The huge beast clambers ashore to eat its meal in comfort. This expert catcher of fish is the Kodiak bear, one of the great Alaskan brown bears. It is the world's largest land-dwelling flesh eater, often measuring nearly 3 meters (about 9 feet) in length.

Alaskan brown bears feed almost entirely on fish when salmon are running upstream to spawn. At other times the bears make a meal of whatever is available. They may dig for roots and bulbs and eat grass, berries, fruits, eggs, and insects. Or they may burrow after squirrels and other small mammals.

▶ "BEASTS THAT WALK LIKE PEOPLE"

Although they eat many different kinds of food (and much of it vegetable), bears make up one family of the Carnivora, or meat-eating mammals. Raccoons and pandas are their close relatives, but bears also share a common ancestry with dogs. All bears have bulky bodies and stubby tails. Their legs are thick and powerful. When they walk, their heels touch the ground, just as ours do. The prints of their hind feet are remarkably like those of a huge, flat-footed human being. In fact, the American Indians called grizzly bears "the beasts that walk like people." Bears ordinarily move at a lumbering walk, but they can run at nearly 50 kilometers (about 30 miles) an hour when necessary. Some are skilled tree climbers. Bears live from 15 to 30 years in the wild and even longer in captivity.

In the wild, most bears are found in parts of Asia, Europe, and North America. There are no bears in Africa, Antarctica, or Australia, and only one species lives south of the equator. This is the South American spectacled bear. The main types that inhabit North America are big brown bears, grizzly bears, and American black bears. Polar bears live in the Arctic region.

▶ THE BLACK BEAR APPEARS IN SEVERAL COLORS

The American black bear, which weighs up to 225 kilograms (500 pounds), is the smallest of the North American bears. It is a wide-ranging species, found from Alaska and northern Canada to central Mexico. In spite of its name, the black bear appears in a variety of colors. In the eastern part of their range, most of these bears grow shiny black fur. To the west, many of them have brown or cinnamon-colored coats. Brown cubs are often born in the same litter with black ones. A race with grayish blue fur—the glacier, or blue, bear—lives in southern Alaska. The creamy white Kermode's bear appears on islands off British Columbia.

Like bears everywhere, the American black fills up on many different kinds of food during the summer and fall. By the time cold weather comes, the bear is very fat and ready for a long winter's nap. It curls up in a den under a ledge or under the roots of a tree and goes to sleep. Eating nothing and living off its fat, the bear usually stays in this snug retreat until spring. Once in a while it may wake up briefly and grumble. On mild days it may even leave its den for a short walk.

The bear's winter sleep is not true hibernation. The animal's temperature remains almost normal, and it breathes regularly four or five times a minute. In true hibernation a mammal's body temperature may drop close to freezing, while its heartbeat and breathing are very slow and faint. To all appearances, the animal seems to be dead. Woodchucks and many ground squirrels hibernate in this way, but bears do not.

Cubs are born in late January or early February while the mother is in her den.

Most bears appear even larger than they are because they have loose skin and dense, shaggy fur. Bears have an excellent sense of smell, but their eyesight and hearing are usually poor. Their ears are small and are set close to their heads.

Bears have five toes on each foot and a strong, curved claw on each toe for digging and climbing. The claws are not retractile (cannot be drawn in, as a cat's claws can), but they can pick up very small objects. The feet of tree-climbing bears have soles with a rough surface. Polar bears have thick fur on the soles of their feet to help them grip on ice.

SLOTH BEAR

BROWN BEAR   POLAR BEAR

Above, polar bears in northern Canada. They roam ice packs and coasts of the Arctic Ocean. Right, Alaska grizzly. Notice its shoulder hump. These bears have almost disappeared south of Canada.

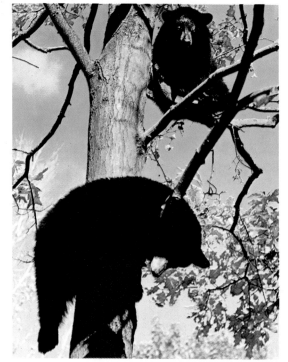

Left, black bears climbing a tree. They are the smallest North American bears. Below, Alaskan brown bear with salmon. When full-grown, these bears are the world's largest land-dwelling flesh-eaters.

Usually she has two cubs, but sometimes three or four are born. Their eyes are closed, and they are almost naked. Each one is less than 25 centimeters (10 inches) long and weighs under 0.5 kilograms (1 pound). They remain in the den with the mother until late March or early April. By then they are covered with thick coats of wooly hair. They come out and wander through the spring woods with her. The mother keeps a constant watch over the cubs. She teaches them how to hunt for food. If danger threatens, she sends them up a tree. If they disobey, she cuffs

them soundly. The cubs usually stay with the mother until they are 1½ years old.

▶ THE GRIZZLY, A VANISHING MONARCH

The grizzly bear weighs up to 450 kilograms (1,000 pounds). It is much larger than its cousin the black bear. The black bear has a straight profile, but the grizzly's face has a concave (curved-in) appearance. The grizzly also has a shoulder hump and very long, straight claws. In color it ranges from a yellowish shade to almost black. Some individuals have light-tipped hair, giving them the grizzled appearance for which these bears are named. Such bears are also called silvertips.

This mighty bear once ranged from Alaska to Mexico. Now grizzlies have almost disappeared south of the Canadian border. Only small numbers still roam wilderness areas of Idaho, Montana, and Wyoming. The most likely place to see a grizzly bear is in a national park in the American West.

Grizzlies are closely related to Alaskan brown bears. Some experts consider that the two are different races of the same species. Kodiak bears, which are larger than grizzlies, weigh up to 780 kilograms (1,700 pounds).

▶ THE GREAT WHITE BEAR

The polar bear roams the ice packs and coasts of the Arctic Ocean, all the way around the earth. This great white bear may weigh as much as 450 kilograms (1,000 pounds). It is a powerful swimmer and is sometimes found far at sea, traveling from one iceberg to another. The polar bear has keen eyes and an extra-sharp sense of smell. It is an expert hunter. It stalks seals, walrus pups, and other prey. Often it hides its black nose with its paws so that it will not be seen against the ice and snow.

The only polar bear that stays in a den during the Arctic winter is a female that is expecting cubs. Before winter comes, she travels inland and digs a den in deep snow. There she sleeps through the months-long night. And there her cubs, each about 25 centimeters (10 inches) long, are born. Like black bear cubs, they may stay with their mother until they are 1½ years old. Today, the hunting of polar bears for sport or for commercial purposes is limited by international agreement.

▶ BEARS IN OTHER PLACES

The spectacled bear lives in the Andes mountains of South America. Many variations of brown bears inhabit mountains in Europe and Asia. Asia also has such interesting species as the Himalayan black bear, which has a kind of mane; the insect-eating sloth bear of India and Sri Lanka; and the small, short-haired Malayan sun bear. All three have white or yellowish crescents on their chests.

ROBERT M. McCLUNG
Author, science books for children

The South American spectacled bear was named for the markings of light fur around its eyes.

The Himalayan bear is a hunter of livestock. It is black in color, with a light crescent marking.

The Beatles in 1966. *Clockwise from left:* John Lennon, Paul McCartney, George Harrison, and Ringo Starr.

BEATLES, THE

During most of the 1960's, the Western world seemed to move to the beat of four young rock musicians from Liverpool, England. They called themselves the Beatles.

John Lennon (1940–80), a guitarist and singer, was the original leader of the group. He explained the name Beatles in this way: "When you said it, it was crawly things [beetles]; when you read it, it was beat music." The other members were Paul McCartney (1942–   ) and George Harrison (1943–   ), also guitarists and singers, and the drummer and singer Ringo Starr (1940–   ), whose real name was Richard Starkey.

Before the Beatles, many people thought rock was American music that was not to be taken seriously. The Beatles proved them wrong.

Each Beatle brought different strengths to the group. John had a strong personality and a sharp wit. Paul was a showman, who charmed audiences with his melodic voice. George was known as a gifted and serious musician. Ringo was adored for his "goofy," down-to-earth personality.

Brian Epstein, a young record dealer, became their manager. He was a major force in their success. With great difficulty, he found a record company willing to sign the Beatles. Their first single recording, "Love Me Do"

(1962), quickly became popular. Their second record, "Please Please Me" (1963), was a big hit. Teenagers—in a frenzy known as "Beatlemania"—struggled to get close to their new heroes.

The Beatles appeared in New York for the first time in 1964. Their engaging personalities and energetic sound turned Britain's most popular rock group into an overnight success in the United States. Within weeks, the top five best-selling records there were all by the Beatles.

Before long, adults found it hard to ignore the Beatles' talents. John Lennon's first book, *In His Own Write,* and the group's first movie, *A Hard Day's Night,* won enthusiastic reviews. Beatles tunes like "Yesterday" were recorded by hundreds of other artists in many musical styles. In 1965, Queen Elizabeth II honored the Beatles by making them members of the Order of the British Empire.

As time went on, the words of their songs, written mainly by Lennon and McCartney, became more poetic. The subjects ranged from the haunting loneliness of "Eleanor Rigby" to the fantasy of "Yellow Submarine" (the theme song for the full-length cartoon of the same name). Their music changed, too. The Beatles began experimenting with electronic effects and instruments from around the world. And they invited jazz and classical musicians to perform on their recordings.

The Beatles made their last stage appearance in 1966. They produced their masterpiece, the album *Sergeant Pepper's Lonely Hearts Club Band,* in 1967, the year of their manager's death. Later that year, the four wrote and directed a film, *Magical Mystery Tour,* in which they toured the English countryside in search of wonder, magic, and fun.

The Beatles made several more recordings as a group, including the hit songs "Hey Jude," "Get Back," "Come Together," "Something," and "Let It Be." But the members had also begun to pursue separate interests, and in 1970 the group disbanded. All four continued to enjoy some success as solo artists during the 1970's. Many fans hoped for a reunion. But in 1980, John Lennon was assassinated in New York City. The "magical mystery tour" was truly over.

NICHOLAS SCHAFFNER
Author, *The Boys from Liverpool*

See also ROCK MUSIC.

BEAUMONT, WILLIAM (1785–1853)

William Beaumont was a frontier surgeon who discovered how the human stomach works. He made his discoveries in a remarkable way: by acquiring a patient with a hole in his stomach. His work ranks as a landmark in medicine. Yet compared with modern doctors, Beaumont had almost no training.

Born on November 21, 1785, in Lebanon, Connecticut, he was one of nine children. His father was a veteran of the Revolutionary War. Young William received some schooling, but no one knows how much. In 1806 he moved to upstate New York, where he taught school. Here he began to read many books about medicine. Four years later he became an apprentice to a doctor and did everything from sweeping floors to assisting in surgery. That was his first medical training. In 1812 he entered the army as a surgeon's assistant.

When the War of 1812 ended, Beaumont practiced medicine in Vermont for a few years. Then he re-enlisted in the army and was assigned to Fort Mackinac, an outpost in northern Michigan. Before going west in 1821, he married. In time he and his wife had three children.

Beaumont was post surgeon at the fort. One day in 1822 he was called to treat a wounded French-Canadian Indian named Alexis St. Martin. St. Martin, who was 18, had been accidentally shot. The bullet had both exposed his stomach and made a hole in it the size of a man's finger.

Beaumont placed him in the post hospital. There, for almost a year, Beaumont treated the wound and kept St. Martin alive. Later Beaumont took St. Martin into his own home and fed and clothed him.

By 1825 St. Martin was well enough to chop wood, but he still had a hole in his stomach. A small flap had grown over the hole, but it could be easily pushed aside. This meant Beaumont could study a human stomach at work and see how it digested food —if St. Martin would let him. Beaumont made an offer. If St. Martin would serve as a human laboratory, Beaumont would give him food, drink, and lodging.

St. Martin agreed, and Beaumont began ten years of experiments that were to make him famous. He tied bits of food to string

William Beaumont, as he appeared about 1821.

and held them in the opening. In this way, he discovered that the stomach produces gastric juice, which dissolves food. He collected the juice in bottles and noted that it continued to dissolve food there. He saw how the movements of the stomach muscles helped to shred the food. Beaumont also found that some meats were digested more easily than others and that small pieces were digested more easily than large ones. His studies still stand as the greatest single contribution to understanding digestion.

The army assigned Beaumont to various posts, and he always took St. Martin with him. But St. Martin often tired of being a human laboratory. He twice left and returned to his native Canada.

Beaumont received some help from other scientists and some support from the U.S. government. But for the most part he carried on the work on his own. He paid St. Martin's expenses even after St. Martin married and had children. When Beaumont finished writing his classic book about his work, he had to pay for publishing it.

In 1834 St. Martin left for the third time, and Beaumont could not persuade him to return. Still, the important discoveries had been made. Beaumont retired from the army in 1840 and settled in St. Louis as a private doctor. He died on April 25, 1853.

JOHN S. BOWMAN
Author and Science Editor

BEAUREGARD, PIERRE G. T. See CIVIL WAR, UNITED STATES (Profiles: Confederate).

The beaver is a talented lumberjack that uses giant chisel-like front teeth and well-developed chewing muscles to fell trees.

BEAVERS

Beavers inhabit ponds and streams in wooded areas from Alaska to northern Mexico. Their bodies are ideally constructed for their varied activities on land and in the water. A beaver's large hind feet are webbed for swimming. Its broad, flat tail is scaly and naked, except for a few bristles. The tail serves as a prop when the beaver stands up to gnaw on trees; it becomes an alarm signal when slapped against the water; it also is a rudder and an oar to aid in swimming.

Although they are air breathers, beavers are thoroughly at home in the water. They can remain submerged for 15 minutes at a time. When a beaver dives, flaplike valves in its ears and nostrils close, shutting out the water. Except for its tail, the beaver is clothed in a shiny coat of soft, thick underfur; this is overlaid with longer, coarser guard hairs. Glands on either side of the tail supply oil, which keeps the coat waterproofed and glistening. The two inner claws of the beaver's hind feet are grooved; they make efficient combs for grooming the coat and spreading the oil through it.

▶CHAMPION HEWERS OF WOOD

Beavers live in family groups, or colonies. The family usually consists of the parents and their young of the past two years. Together they cut trees, build and repair their dams and lodges, and store branches for the winter food supply. This work makes them the most remarkable engineers among the Rodentia, the order of gnawing mammals to which they belong. And among mammals, only human beings are better engineers than beavers.

For felling trees, a beaver uses its four front teeth—the orange-colored, chisel-edged gnawing teeth (incisors). With these sharp tools it takes only a few minutes to cut down a small willow tree. Occasionally beavers fell trees as big as 2 feet (0.6 meter) in diameter. Favorite beaver trees are softwoods like aspen, poplar, and willow. But the beaver also cuts birch, sugar maple, wild cherry, alder, hemlock, and pine.

Building dam

After selecting a tree to cut, the beaver gouges out first one chip and then another a few inches below. Next it tears out the middle chip of wood. Working in this way, the beaver girdles the tree, then cuts deeper and deeper until the tree falls. The beaver cannot control the direction in which the tree will fall. As it begins to totter the beaver dashes for safety.

When all is quiet, the work begins again. But first the beaver may make a meal of tender green bark, buds, and twigs. Holding a section of wood in its front paws, the beaver nibbles away like a person eating corn on the cob. Stomach full, it starts cutting the tree into convenient lengths for moving to the pond.

▶ BUILDING DAMS AND LODGES

In deep streams with high banks, beavers sometimes make underground dens in the bank instead of building lodges. Digging the entrance underwater, they tunnel upward beyond the water level. There they hollow out a living chamber in the bank. In such a den the beaver family is safe from most enemies. Even in shallow streams beavers often build bank dens when they first settle in an area. Then they start to dam the stream.

The dam blocks the flow of water and creates a pond where the beavers will live. The dam keeps the pond level constant during spring rains and summer droughts. It is deep enough not to freeze solid in winter.

To build a dam, the beavers drag branches to the place they have selected in the stream. The branches are laid side by side, parallel to the current. Their ends are often thrust into the bottom mud to anchor them. Mud and debris are piled on top. Layer upon layer, the dam is built up. To prevent leaks, the beavers plaster the upstream face with mud, leaves, and stones scooped up from the stream bottom.

Beaver dams vary considerably in size. They can be from 3 feet (1 meter) in length to more than 100 feet (31 meters). Exceptionally large dams may be as much as 10 feet (3 meters) in height.

In the pond that forms behind their dam the beavers usually build an island lodge. Pulling boughs and branches into the water, they build up a broad foundation of sticks and wood—sometimes more than 30 feet (9 meters) across. Making the huge pile slope inward, they construct mounds that may stand up to 8 feet (2.4 meters) above the pond's surface. When the outer structure is complete, the beavers plaster the chinks and holes with mud and debris. A section of the roof is left unchinked, as an air hole. Underwater entrances lead to

Beavers are industrious builders. They use wood, mud, and rocks to construct lodges and dams. Inside the lodge, beaver parents shelter their young. A beaver colony builds a dam to make sure the entrances to the lodge are safely hidden under the water's surface. Beavers also forge canals to make transporting supplies easier.

Air hole

Repairing lodge

Canal

Cutting tree

Canal

Kits

Pond surface

Food store

Bringing food to young

Tunnel entrance

Woody plants are important to the colony's way of life. Gnawing on a tender shoot (*left*) helps satisfy the beaver's nutritional needs. A beaver uses a tree branch (*above*) to make underwater repairs to the lodge.

the main living space. This chamber may be as big as 8 feet (2.4 meters) across and 5 feet (1.5 meters) high.

As time goes by, the beavers have to travel farther and farther from the pond to find suitable trees. Dragging branches and logs, they wear smooth paths, or "tote roads," through the woods. To make the going even easier, they dig canals from the pond to connect with the tote roads. Whenever the job of bringing wood in from increasing distances becomes too difficult, the beavers leave the area. Then in a new location, they start all over again.

▶ FAMILY LIFE OF THE COLONY

From early spring until late fall, all the members of the beaver colony are busy. They repair their dams after the spring floods. They build or enlarge their lodge. They stock food for winter eating. By the time ice and snow arrive, the beavers have a huge quantity of branches stored in the bottom of the pond, close to the lodge. These are thrust into the pond bottom, where they stay fresh.

When the surface of the pond freezes over, the beavers retire to their lodge. Whenever they are hungry, they simply swim out under the ice, cut a fresh branch from the food supply, and carry it into the lodge. Stripped of its tender bark, the branch is finally thrown out.

It may be used the next spring for repairing the dam or lodge.

As spring approaches, the expectant mother beaver prepares a soft nest of wood and bark shavings on the floor of the lodge. Here her young, usually three or four in number, are born during April or May, nearly four months after mating. When the female is expecting, the father beaver moves out for the time being. The year-old youngsters may move out with him. The 2-year-olds leave home for good at this time; they search for mates with whom they will live for the rest of their lives.

The baby beavers, called kits, weigh about 1 pound (0.5 kilogram) at birth. They are born with their eyes open, and they can move about. They grow rapidly and may reach 25 pounds (11 kilograms) in a year's time.

▶ THE BEAVER AND CONSERVATION

In a few areas beavers may become nuisances when their dams flood roads, croplands, or timber areas. But the beaver's good points far offset such problems. Beaver ponds act as fire guards in the forests. They provide homes and breeding places for fish, water birds, and other wildlife. Beaver dams help to control floods and conserve water. They keep soil from washing away. Rich silt backs up behind the dams year after year. When the beavers finally move on, the ponds gradually fill in. They become part of wide, gentle valleys covered with fertile soil.

ROBERT M. MCCLUNG
Author, science books for children

BECKET, SAINT THOMAS À
(1118?–1170)

Thomas à Becket was archbishop of Canterbury during the reign of Henry II of England. As archbishop, he clashed with the king over the rights of the church against the rights of the crown. The conflict led to Thomas' death. It has become one of the most famous episodes in English history and literature.

Thomas was born in London, probably on December 21, 1118. His father, a merchant, came from Normandy, in France. Thomas was educated in London and Paris. While in his 20's, he entered the service of Theobald, archbishop of Canterbury. In 1154, he was appointed archdeacon of Canterbury. That same year, 21-year-old Henry of Anjou came to the English throne as King Henry II. He made Thomas his chancellor, or chief official. Thomas served the king faithfully, and a warm friendship grew up between them. After Theobald died in 1161, Henry offered Thomas the office of archbishop. Thomas accepted reluctantly. He feared that the policies of the strong-willed king would conflict with his own views of his duty as head of the church.

In 1164, the king had a document prepared known as the Constitutions of Clarendon. Its purpose was to restore some of the power of the crown, which had been weakened during the period before Henry became king. Among other things, it provided that members of the clergy who were convicted of crimes by church courts were to be punished by civil courts. Previously, the church had both tried and punished its own members. Thomas refused to sign the document. This infuriated the king, who had expected his friend's support.

Thomas fled to France, where he continued to speak out on the rights of the church. In 1170, Thomas and the king were partly reconciled, and Thomas returned to England. But his refusal to lift the ban against two excommunicated bishops angered the king again. On December 29, 1170, four of Henry's knights murdered Thomas in the cathedral of Canterbury. Henry denied that he had ordered Thomas' death. But he did penance at Thomas' tomb in the cathedral, which at once became a shrine for pilgrims. In 1173, Thomas was made a saint.

Reviewed by ROBERT LACEY
Author, *Majesty*

BECQUEREL, ANTOINE HENRI
(1852–1908)

Antoine Henri Becquerel is known as the man who discovered radioactivity—a discovery that influenced the development of atomic weapons, nuclear energy, and radioactive medical treatments.

Becquerel was born on December 15, 1852, in Paris, France. Both his father, Alexandre Edmond Becquerel, and his grandfather, Antoine César Becquerel, one of the founders of electrochemistry, were physicists.

Becquerel worked as an engineer as well as a professor of physics. His discovery of radiation occurred in February 1896. A few months before, Wilhelm Roentgen had discovered X rays—invisible penetrating forms of radiation. Becquerel wanted to find out whether or not phosphorescent materials—materials that glow in the dark after being stimulated by sunlight—would also give off X rays. What he discovered was that certain substances, such as uranium, would give off X rays even when they had not been stimulated by light.

Soon scientists discovered that other elements give off energy in this way. These are the radioactive elements, whose atoms are decaying. Particles from the atoms break away and release the energy that held the atoms together. When harnessed, this produces the enormous energy needed to produce nuclear power.

In 1901, while experimenting with radium, Becquerel developed what looked like a reddish-brown sunburn on his skin. He reasoned that the burn was caused by the radium—that the rays emitted were able to penetrate and cause changes to living things. His discovery led to the controlled use of radioactivity in the treatment of some diseases. For his discoveries he was awarded, along with Marie and Pierre Curie, the Nobel prize in physics in 1903.

Becquerel died on August 25, 1908, in Le Croisic, France.

RACHEL KRANZ
Editor, Biographies
The Young Adult Reader's Adviser

See also CHEMISTRY, HISTORY OF; URANIUM.

BEECHER, HENRY WARD (1813–1887)

Henry Ward Beecher was the most famous American preacher of his time. He was born on June 24, 1813, in Litchfield, Connecticut. His father, Lyman Beecher, was a distinguished Presbyterian minister, and four of Henry's brothers also became clergymen. Among his sisters, Catharine Beecher was a notable educator, and Harriet Beecher Stowe won fame for her novel *Uncle Tom's Cabin*.

Beecher graduated from Amherst College, in Massachusetts, in 1834. He was not a disciplined student, but he loved literature and read widely. He was athletic, fun-loving and friendly, and a fine storyteller. After Amherst, he studied at Lane Theological Seminary, in Cincinnati, Ohio. In 1837, he married Eunice White Bullard and began his ministry. Soon he became pastor of a church in Indianapolis, Indiana. He developed his skill as a preacher and in 1847 moved to Brooklyn, New York, as minister of Plymouth Church of the Pilgrims (Congregational). He remained there until his death, on March 8, 1887.

Beecher's sermons were informal, impulsive, witty, emotional, and dramatic. They mirrored his warm personality and attracted between 2,000 and 3,000 people each week. He had a fine voice and a poetic command of language. His physical appearance helped make him a striking figure in the pulpit. He had a strong build and a lionlike head with hair that reached his coat collar. Beecher aimed for the hearts of his listeners and stressed God's love for sinners. He was tolerant of other views. For example, he defended the theory of evolution when most of the clergy attacked it. And he spoke out on the social and political issues of the day, opposing slavery and championing the right of women to vote.

ARI HOOGENBOOM
City University of New York,
Brooklyn College

BEER AND BREWING

Beer is an alcoholic beverage that has been drunk for thousands of years. The making, or brewing, of beer appears to have begun very early in many parts of the world. A beerlike beverage was made in Mesopotamia as early as 6000 B.C. Beer was also brewed in ancient Egypt, Greece, and Rome.

During the Middle Ages most beer was brewed by monks, and almost every monastery had a brew house. Eventually others took over this task and brewing grew into an industry with organizations, or guilds, of brewers. Beer in the Middle Ages was a thick, heavy beverage with a much higher alcohol content than today's beer. This thick, nourishing beer, almost as much a food as a drink, was an important item in people's daily diet.

In medieval England, beer, or ale, was often the chief drink at festivals and celebrations. It was such an important part of these revels that the word "ale" was sometimes used to mean a festival. Lamb-ales were celebrations held at lamb-shearing time. College-ales were parties at which students drank the ale they had brewed. The word "bridal" comes from "bride-ale," which was a wedding feast.

The knowledge of brewing beer was brought to the New World by the early colonists. At first, beer was made in small home breweries. However, as the colonies grew, brewing was established as an industry. One of the first breweries was built in 1683 at Pennsbury, Pennsylvania. Within a hundred years, the brewing industry had become an important part of the nation's economic life.

▶ HOW BEER IS MADE

The brewing of beer starts with grain, primarily barley, although corn or rice is sometimes used as well. The grain is mixed with water and is kept warm until it begins to germinate, or sprout. After a week, the grain is roasted and the germination stops. This partly sprouted grain is known as **malt**.

The malt is mixed with water and boiled to form a sweet liquid called **wort**. The dried seed cones of a plant called the hop vine are added to the wort and the mixture is boiled again. These seed cones, called **hops**, have a slightly bitter taste and give beer its characteristic tangy flavor. All solid matter is then filtered out of the mixture and **yeast** is added. Yeast contains microscopic organisms that

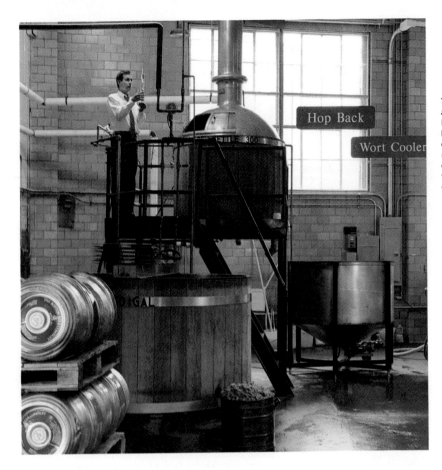

The copper brew kettle at left is located at the Boston Beer Company brewery. Here an employee carefully monitors the simmering of malt and water, which forms the liquid called wort.

feed on sugars and starches. As these organisms feed on the sugars of the wort they release alcohol as a waste product. The change from sugar to alcohol is called **fermentation**, the most important step in the brewing process. Fermentation also produces carbon dioxide gas, which gives beer its bubbles.

After fermentation, the beer is pumped into closed storage tanks where it ages. Then it is filtered again before it is put into barrels, bottles, or cans. From start to finish, the brewing process may take several months.

There are several common types of beer. **Lager beer** originated in Germany. Its name comes from the German word for "storage" (*lager*) because the beer is stored or aged before it is packaged. Lager is usually pale yellow in color, and it has an alcoholic content of about 3 or 4 percent. Special kinds of lager beer include **bock beer**, a darker and heavier type of lager, and **Pilsner**. **Light beer** is a type of lager with reduced carbohydrate contents and fewer calories. **Dry beer** is a lager that is specially brewed to be less sweet than other lagers. **Ale** has a paler color and sharper taste

than lager beer and has an alcoholic content of about 4 or 5 percent. **Porter** is a dark brown beer with a slightly sweet taste. **Stout** is one of the darkest, heaviest, and strongest beers. Its alcoholic content is about 5 to 6.5 percent.

In many parts of the world, people prefer to drink beer chilled. In some places, however, beer is served either at room temperature or slightly warmed. Differences in climate and culture may have something to do with this.

Despite their skill at brewing, old-time brewers could never be certain that each batch would be the same. Today, however, brewing is a highly scientific process—all ingredients are carefully tested and each step is closely controlled. As a result, today's beer is as uniform in quality as any other manufactured product. The amount of beer produced has also changed over the years. In the past, beer was usually brewed for personal use or in small quantities by professionals. Today, most beer is mass-produced in large quantities, although in some places home-brewing or small breweries have become quite popular.

UNITED STATES BREWERS ASSOCIATION

A honeybee (*left*) laden with pollen, which it has stored in special "pollen baskets" on its hind legs, burrows within dandelion petals to suck up the flower's sweet nectar. A beekeeper (*above*) collects the honey produced in a hive from the gathered nectar.

BEES

In a field of blooming flowers, bees are a familiar sight buzzing about seeking the rich stores of nectar and pollen held within the flower blossoms. Bees gather the nectar and pollen for food. They turn the nectar into delicious, sweet honey, which people eat. They also produce beeswax, which is used to make candles, crayons, and cosmetics. Many plants would not grow without their help. As bees fly about searching for food, they fertilize plants by spreading pollen from one plant to another. This allows the plants to reproduce.

There are about 20,000 different kinds, or species, of bees. They are found on every continent except Antarctica. There are two general groups of bees: **solitary bees**, which live alone, and **social bees**, which live together in large groups called **colonies**. A colony of bees can contain hundreds, sometimes thousands, of members.

▶THE BODY OF A BEE

Like all insects, the bee has three body parts: head, thorax, and abdomen. Its body looks fuzzy because it is covered with many fine hairs. Even its antennae, or feelers, are covered with tiny hairs. In addition to a pair of antennae on its head, the bee has five eyes and has chewing and sucking mouthparts. The bee uses its eyes—one pair of large compound eyes and three small eyes—to distinguish colors and different flower shapes. The antennae, or feelers, have sense organs that provide the bee with the senses of touch and smell. Along with the **mandibles** (jaws) that it uses to cut

and chew, the bee has a long tubelike tongue that it uses for sucking.

The thorax of the bee is composed of three segments. The bee has two pairs of wings on its thorax—a large front set and a smaller hind set. The wings, which move up and down and forward and backward, allow the bee to fly forward, backwards, and sideways, and even hover in midair. A pair of legs is attached to each of the thorax segments.

The abdomen of the bee has two very important features. One is a special sac called the **honey stomach**. In it, the bee carries the nectar it collects. The other is its sting. The sting is attached to the abdomen and is found only on female bees. Some species of bees have better developed stings than others. Within one species, there is also a difference between the sting of the female worker bee and that of the queen bee. The worker bee has a straight sting with hooks. The queen bee has a smooth, curved sting. The worker bee defends its life and home with its sting, while the queen bee only uses its sting to kill other queens.

SOCIAL BEES

The honeybee is the most social bee of all. An average honeybee colony has about 30,000 bees, but there may be up to 80,000. The bees live together in their home, called a **hive**, dividing the labor of the colony. Within the hive, the bees produce wax, which they use to build **honeycombs**. A honeycomb is made up of a mass of six-sided compartments, or **cells**.

The colony contains three different kinds of bees: the queen, the drones, and the worker bees. The **queen bee** is a large female who lays all the eggs in the colony. Although the queen lays eggs from January to November, the majority of eggs are laid between the first warm days of spring and the end of the summer.

At the height of the season, the queen may lay as many as 1,000 to 2,000 eggs a day. Since she lives about five years, she may lay up to 1 million eggs in her lifetime. The queen is the mother of the entire colony, and the whole hive is one big family of bees.

The **drones** are the males of the colony. They take no part in the work of the hive. They have only one function—to fertilize the eggs of a queen. A typical colony has several hundred drones.

The **worker bees** are all females. They are smaller in size than the queen. They are able to lay eggs, however, they usually do not lay eggs when the colony has a queen. Worker bees do all the labor in the hive necessary for

Within the bee colony, there are three different kinds of bees: (a) the female worker bee, (b) the male bee, called a drone, and (c) the queen bee.

The External Body Structures of a Honeybee

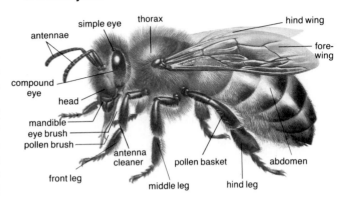

the maintenance and growth of the colony. Tens of thousands of worker bees live in a typical hive.

Inside the Hive. The beehive is a smoothly run, organized society. Each bee has a job to do. If you watch the entrance of a beehive, you will see the busy traffic of bees coming and going. One after another, bees fly out of the hive. Other bees, heavily loaded with the food needed to supply the colony, land and enter the hive.

Workers called **foragers** fly out to flowers and collect pollen and nectar. Pollen, necessary for the formation of seeds in plants, is a source of protein, vitamins, and minerals for bees. When the bees who collect pollen groom themselves, they put the pollen grains that cling to the fine hairs of their bodies into special "pollen baskets." These baskets are flattened areas on their hind legs surrounded by long hairs. Nectar is a sweet, sugary liquid. It is 40 to 80 percent water. The bee sucks it into its mouth with its flexible tongue and stores it in its honey stomach.

When a bee returns to the hive, it spits up its load of nectar through its mouth. The nectar is handed over to other worker bees that place it in empty cells. Special chemicals called **enzymes** are added to the stored nectar. As the nectar dries out, it changes into honey and is a great source of energy for the bees. The nectar gathered by one bee during its entire lifetime is enough to produce about 1.5 ounces (45 grams) of honey.

Duties of a Worker Bee. Some worker bees build the honeycomb. Some clean out empty cells and prepare them for the eggs that the

From An Egg to An Adult Bee

The queen bee (1) deposits one egg in the cell, and a wormlike larva (2) hatches from the egg. The larva grows as it is fed royal jelly or bee-bread. When the larva finishes spinning its cocoon, workers seal the cell with wax (3); the larva starts to pupate, its wormlike body changing into the form of an adult bee. With its growth complete, the young adult bee breaks through the wax cap and (4) emerges from its cell.

queen will deposit there. Some feed and nurse the growing young. Guard bees stand at the entrance to the hive and protect the hive against enemies, such as wasps, wax moths, and bees from other colonies. Fanning bees ventilate the hive. Still other worker bees take care of the nectar and pollen.

The task of a worker bee depends on its age. For the first three days of its life, the worker cleans a section of the hive called the **brood nest**, which is the part of the hive where the eggs are laid and the young bees are raised.

During the time the worker bee is preparing the brood nest for new eggs, special glands in its head are developing. Once the glands fully develop, they will secrete a creamy substance called **royal jelly**. Then the worker becomes a **nurse bee**, tending the developing larvae (wormlike grubs that hatch from the eggs) and feeding them royal jelly. After several days, the worker stops producing royal jelly and be-

gins to produce wax from glands in its abdomen. At about 12 days, the same bee is a builder of wax cells.

At about 16 days, some workers stop building and start standing guard at the entrance to the hive. There they defend the hive against intruders. Other workers this age receive the nectar and pollen brought by foragers. From the age of 3 weeks until the end of its life, the worker bee shifts to its last and longest job— the collecting of nectar and pollen.

Every bee gathers its own information about the needs of the hive. In any one day it spends part of its time patrolling the hive, inspecting cells and larvae, interacting with other workers, and looking over the building areas and the stores of food. From such inspection tours, new forms of activity start—nursing, building, or cleaning, as each need arises.

In summer when there is a lot of work in the hive, a worker bee may live to only 5 or 6

This page, left: The queen bee checks the brood nest for empty cells in which to lay her eggs. *Right:* Wormlike larvae hatch from the eggs the queen has deposited in the cells. *Opposite page, left:* After the larvae have spun cocoons, the worker bees crawl over the cells in the brood nest, sealing the cells with wax. *Right:* Breaking through the wax cap of its cell, a full-grown bee emerges.

weeks. During the fall and winter there is less work, so a worker may live several months.

The Mating Flight of the Queen. Each time the hive has a new queen, there is a mating flight. A new queen is needed when the old queen dies, leaves to establish a new hive, or becomes feeble. Special cells in the brood nest house developing queen bees. The first queen to emerge destroys those developing in other cells. If two queens emerge at the same time, they fight until one is killed. An old queen may fight the new queen or leave the hive. Only one queen will emerge from the battles.

When the new queen is about a week old, she leaves the hive for her mating flight. During the flight, she will mate with one or more drones. When they mate, the drone transfers sperm (male sex cells) into the queen's body. The queen stores the sperm until she is ready to lay eggs.

The drones die after mating and the queen returns to the hive. A few days later, the queen starts to move over the honeycombs, looking for empty cells in which to lay her eggs.

From Egg to Adult Bee. If the queen exposes her eggs to the sperm she is storing just before they are laid, the eggs will be fertilized. If she does not, the eggs will be unfertilized. All the unfertilized eggs become males (drones). All the fertilized eggs become females (either egg-laying queens or workers).

The eggs develop into larvae after three days. All the larvae receive the same food, royal jelly, for the first three days. Then some of the larvae receive a mixture of honey and pollen called **beebread**. The larvae that are fed beebread will become worker bees. Some lar-

WONDER QUESTION

Are there really "killer" bees?

The so-called "killer" bees are just very good at protecting themselves when bothered. They are the descendants of bees brought from Africa to South America as part of an effort to develop a stronger breed of honeybee. But before a breed could be developed, 26 queen bees escaped from the research hives.

The sting of the Africanized "killer" bee is no different from that of any other honeybee. However, the Africanized bees are quicker to attack and more of them will join in an attack. For the bees to actually kill anything, a mass stinging involving hundreds of bees would have to take place.

vae are selected to be fed only royal jelly. These larvae will develop into queen bees.

The nurse bees carefully tend the larvae, visiting each larva with food nearly 1,300 times a day. At 6 days, the larva starts to spin a cocoon, a shell of silk, inside its wax cell. When the cocoon is completed, the cell is sealed with wax by the worker bees. The larva changes into a pupa within the cocoon. During the pupa stage, the wormlike body of the larva changes into the form of an adult bee. A full-size queen bee emerges from the cell after 16 days. A full-size worker bee makes its way out of its wax cell in 21 days.

Unfertilized eggs go through the same

stages as fertilized eggs. They change into larvae and then become pupae. Full-size drones
emerge from the cells in 24 days.

With a queen laying 1,500 eggs a day, a
new bee emerges almost every minute to take
its place in bee society.

How Bees Communicate. Some foragers,
acting as "scouts," return from a food hunt
and tell other bees from their hive about the
food source they have found. The scouts pass
on their information by performing a "dance."
There are two basic dances that are used to tell
the direction and distance from the hive to a
source of nectar and pollen: a **round dance** and
a **waggle** dance. If the returning scouts do a
round dance, it means that food is near the
hive. The scouts use the **waggle dance** to describe the exact distance to the food and the
direction of the food in relation to the sun. The
faster the dances, the closer the food.

In the darkness of the hive, the other worker
bees surround the dancing scouts. Using the
sense organs on their antennae, the worker
bees pick up the flowers' nectar scent clinging
to the dancers. The worker bees become excited and start to follow the dancers.

After following the dance, the workers
leave the hive and—without the dancing bees
to lead them—fly directly to the area of the
food source. Once there, the workers search
the area for the flowers with the particular
scent that clung to the dancing scouts.

The bees form groups just large enough to
collect the available food. When the source of
the food is plentiful and rich, the worker bees
recruited by the scouts also dance on returning

While scouts search for a new location for the colony,
the queen and her group of workers cluster in a swarm
around a fence post.

to the hive. When the amount of food is reduced, the incoming bees simply deliver the
nectar and pollen and do not dance. In this
way many bees appear at a good source of
food and as the supply wanes, fewer and fewer
bees visit those flowers.

Bees also communicate information by the
secretions in their bodies. Bees that attend the
queen constantly lick a substance from her
body and share it with other members of the
colony. If the hive loses its queen, the other
bees of the colony become aware of her absence in a few hours. They look for her, and
if she cannot be found, they immediately set
about replacing her with a new queen.

Swarming. When a hive gets overcrowded,
the queen lays fewer and fewer eggs. The
worker bees build a new type of cell in the

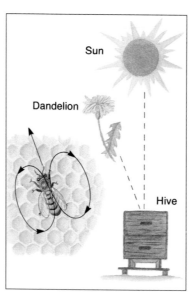

During the waggle dance
(which has a figure-eight
pattern), the scout tells others about the food source.
Here the scout shows the
relationship of the food
source, dandelion, to the
sun by starting the dance
facing toward the sun (*left*)
or away from the sun (*right*).

hive. These are much bigger than the other wax cells and are shaped somewhat like peanuts. Inside these special cells, the queen deposits the eggs from which a new queen will emerge. After the larvae develop from the eggs, the cells are covered with wax.

Soon after the cells are covered with wax, the old queen gathers many of the workers and leaves the hive to start a new colony. The departing queen and her group of workers is called a **swarm**. Their journey from the hive to find a new home is called a **swarming**. Left behind in the hive are workers that will tend the new queen and developing larvae.

Many scouts search for a new location for the colony. While the scouts search, the swarm gathers around a tree branch or other support. The scouts report back to the swarm using their "dance" language to describe the various locations they have found. The scouts then check out each site. Once one is chosen, the entire swarm travels to the new site.

Bumblebees are another familiar kind of social bee. Their colonies are not as large or complex as those of honeybees, and they do not produce as much honey. Also, the duties of the bumblebee queen are quite different from those of the honeybee queen.

Each spring the bumblebee queen must start a new colony because all of her workers die each year when winter comes. At first, the queen performs the work for the entire hive. She gathers pollen and nectar, builds wax cells, and feeds the young. Not until the larvae become adult workers does the queen have any help with her duties.

The hive thrives for a short time. In the fall, cold weather kills all but the new queens that hatched, and then mated, late in the season. The new queens hibernate and start new hives when the warm weather returns.

▶SOLITARY BEES

Many of the solitary bees have curious habits. **Carpenter bees** bite tunnels through solid wood. In the tunnels they make a series of cells, one on top of the other and separated by walls of tiny wood chips. **Mason bees** cement pieces of stone together, forming groups of cells that are attached to cliffs or stone walls. **Leaf-cutter bees** use their jaws like scissors and snip out pieces of leaves or flowers. They use this plant material to line their nests and make partitions between the cells. **Burrowing bees** tunnel into the ground.

Most solitary bees live alone. The female solitary bee puts pollen and nectar in the cells of the nest. She lays an egg on each lump of food, seals the cells, and flies away. She usually dies at the end of the summer. When the eggs hatch, the developing young feed on the food left for them. They are completely on their own, having no contact with the mother. When they are adults, male and female mate.

MILLICENT E. SELSAM
Author, science books for children
Reviewed by GENE E. ROBINSON
Department of Entomology
University of Illinois

See also FLOWERS; HONEY; INSECTS.

Nests of Solitary Bees

Mason bee

American carpenter bee

Leaf-cutter bee

BEETHOVEN, LUDWIG VAN (1770–1827)

The great composer Ludwig van Beethoven was born in Bonn, Germany, on December 16 or 17, 1770, and was baptized on December 17. His father, Johann, and his grandfather Ludwig van Beethoven were both musicians.

Beethoven revealed his own musical talents when he was very young. His father, an irresponsible drunkard, hoped the boy would be a profitable child prodigy like Mozart. Beethoven was often dragged out of bed in the middle of the night and forced to practice the piano. At the age of 7 he was playing in public. When Beethoven was 13, the elector of Cologne made him assistant organist at his chapel in Bonn.

In 1787 Beethoven traveled to Vienna and met his idol, Mozart. When Beethoven improvised on a melody that Mozart had given him, the great master was astounded.

But Beethoven could not stay in Vienna. His mother fell ill, and he rushed back to Bonn. The death of his mother left Beethoven and his brothers at the mercy of their drunken father. At the age of 18 Beethoven assumed full responsibility for the family.

In 1792 Beethoven returned to Vienna, where he spent the rest of his life. He became a pupil of Haydn. But he was dissatisfied with Haydn's method of teaching, which he considered not thorough enough. To avoid offending the famous master, he took lessons in secret from another composer, Johann Schenk.

Beethoven presented a strange appearance to the people of Vienna. He was a short, stocky man, untidily dressed, with dark, piercing eyes and a wild shock of black hair. Knowing himself to be a genius, he lived by his own rules. The German poet Goethe called him an "utterly untamed personality."

Nevertheless, he quickly became famous. Several princes became his patrons, and for a few years he was happy. Then, about 1800, tragedy struck. He discovered that he was slowly becoming deaf. This was the great crisis of his life.

After this, Beethoven's music became more profound. He developed a completely original style of composing. It reflected his violent emotions, his sufferings and joys. At this time Beethoven composed the most popular of all symphonies, his fifth. Other famous works of

Beethoven with the score of his great *Missa solemnis*.

this period are the *Eroica* and *Pastoral* symphonies, the *Appassionata* Sonata, the *Emperor* Concerto, his only opera, *Fidelio*, and the *Rasumovsky* string quartets.

In 1815 Beethoven became the guardian of his nephew Karl. Beethoven adored the boy, who gave his uncle nothing but trouble. Beethoven's hearing problems steadily increased; by 1820 he was almost totally deaf and had to carry on all conversation in writing.

Despite his deafness Beethoven now composed his greatest works. These include the last five piano sonatas, the *Missa solemnis*, the Ninth Symphony, with its choral finale, and the last five string quartets, which many people consider the finest of all his works.

In 1826 Beethoven became seriously ill. It is said that as he lay unconscious on his deathbed, on March 26, 1827, there was a loud clap of thunder. In response Beethoven sat straight up, shook his fist at the heavens, and fell back dead.

Beethoven is perhaps the most popular and revered of composers. He was a man of profound vision and his music has deeply moved its listeners for generations.

Reviewed by Karl Geiringer
University of California—Santa Barbara

Beetles vary greatly, not only in appearance but also in lifestyle. While the dung beetle (*left*) busily forms a dung ball to use as a nest for its eggs, the locust borer beetle (*above*) lays its eggs on plentiful goldenrod.

BEETLES

Wherever you look, on the ground, in the air, or in lakes and ponds, they can be found. They go busily about their daily tasks—whether it is nibbling on plant leaves, chewing wood from rotting logs, or cleaning the bones of dead animals. They are beetles, the most common of all the insects. In North America alone, there are more than 30,000 different kinds, or species, of beetles. Throughout the world, about 300,000 species of beetles can be found; and every year, new species are being discovered.

Beetles make up the insect order, or group, called Coleoptera. It is the largest order of the animal kingdom. The name Coleoptera, which means "sheath wing" in Greek, refers to the beetle's pair of hard, inflexible outer wings. The wings, called **elytra**, lock together down the beetle's back to provide a protective shell for the beetle.

Sometimes called the armored tank of the insect world, the beetle owes much of its ability to survive to the leathery elytra. With this tough outer shell, the beetle can live under stones and in other sheltered areas that insects with soft bodies cannot use, because they would be crushed. The beetle's shell also makes it resistant to dryness. This allows the beetle to live in places that are drier than the habitats of many other insects.

▶THE CHARACTERISTICS OF BEETLES

There is a great variety in the appearance of beetles. Some beetles are dark brown so that they blend in with the soil. Other beetles have bright colors or complex patterns on their elytra. Still others are iridescent, changing color in the sunlight. Although beetles vary greatly in size, shape, and color, they all share the same body plan. Like that of other insects, the beetle's body is divided into three main parts: the head, the thorax, and the abdomen.

Body Parts. The **head**, at the front of the body, holds the main sense organs (eyes and antennae), chewing mouthparts, and a primitive brain. Projecting from the head, the beetle's two antennae are covered with tiny hairs. The hairs are special sense organs that help the beetle detect sounds and odors. A pair of compound eyes, one on each side of the head, gives the beetle a well-developed sense of sight.

The chewing mouthparts of most beetles are designed to crush or break food into small pieces before the food actually enters the

The External Body Structures of a Beetle

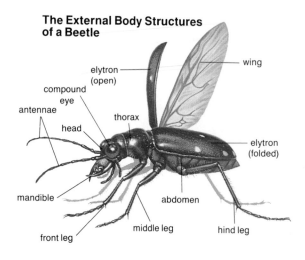

wing
elytron (open)
compound eye
antennae
thorax
head
elytron (folded)
mandible
abdomen
front leg
middle leg
hind leg

mouth. Plant-eating beetles have mouthparts that allow them to slice leaves, cut stems, bore under bark, or crush seeds. Beetles that eat other insects or animals have mouthparts that allow them to pierce, stab, or crush their prey. Some of these beetles can cause painful bites to an inexperienced insect collector.

The **thorax** forms the middle part of the body and holds the beetle's three pairs of legs as well as the elytra and a pair of hind wings. Different kinds of beetles have different kinds of legs. Many predatory beetles have long, slender legs that enable them to pursue their prey swiftly. Beetles that dig through the soil have legs that are flattened with toothed edges,

allowing the beetles to sweep large amounts of soil behind them.

The **abdomen** houses the organs that help the beetle digest food, get rid of waste, and produce offspring. The beetle does not have special organs, like our lungs, to help it breathe. Instead, holes called **spiracles** pierce the abdomen. Air enters the beetle's body through the spiracles and passes through tubes into open spaces in the abdomen and the rest of the body.

Locomotion. If the beetle needs to fly, it unlocks the elytra and the hind wings unfold. Only the hind wings are used for flight. When the beetle is not flying, the elytra cover and protect the thin, delicate hind wings.

Some beetles spend most of their life in water. An aquatic beetle has flattened legs that are used for paddles as it pushes through the water. A built-in air tank helps the beetle swim and dive underwater. The space between the elytra and the soft body underneath fills up with air. While the beetle is under water, it breathes using the stored air.

Behavior. Most beetles, unlike many types of bees, ants, wasps, and termites, are solitary insects. They live alone rather than in large nests or hives. Different types of beetles have

Two behaviors that are important to a beetle's survival are its ability to defend itself and its ability to reproduce. The bombardier beetle (*below*) effectively repels its enemies with a hot pulsing jet of chemicals. The mating blister beetle (*right*) provides for its offspring by laying its eggs near a larval food source.

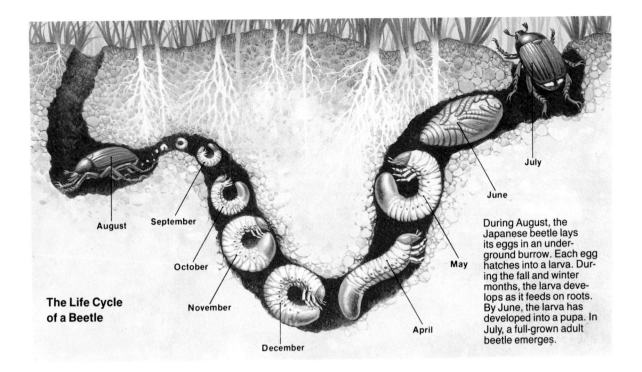

The Life Cycle of a Beetle

August

September

October

November

December

April

May

June

July

During August, the Japanese beetle lays its eggs in an underground burrow. Each egg hatches into a larva. During the fall and winter months, the larva develops as it feeds on roots. By June, the larva has developed into a pupa. In July, a full-grown adult beetle emerges.

different types of behavior that allow them to adapt to their environment, feed, defend themselves from predators, and breed.

People have been interested in some of the more unusual beetles for hundreds, even thousands, of years. In ancient Egypt, people were fascinated by the scarab, or dung beetle. This insect makes a ball of dung to lay its eggs in. Often the ball is as large or larger than the scarab itself. Some beetles make dung balls as big as softballs.

The Egyptians considered the ball of dung and the life of the scarab to be symbols for the world and the cycles of nature. So important was the scarab that it was used as a seal on many important Egyptian documents.

Another beetle with unusual behavior is the tortoise beetle. As it grows, it is protected by a collection of its own waste and shed skins. Stuck to its body, this material helps camouflage, or hide, the young beetle from predators. It also serves as a defense, because the foul odor of the pile of wastes discourages other insects and animals from coming close for an attack. Nicknamed the trash peddler, the young tortoise beetle develops into a brilliant, shiny metallic adult.

The bombardier beetle has an even more dramatic defense against predators. When an attacking animal approaches, the bombardier beetle raises its rear end into the air and shoots out a hot spray of burning liquid at the attacker. The spray is released with an explosion that is quite loud. The combination of the surprising sound and harmful spray wards off most animals that would prey upon this beetle.

▶ **THE LIFE CYCLE OF THE BEETLE**

Beetles, like many other insects, have a life cycle during which they pass through several different stages before becoming an adult. This process of growth and change is called **metamorphosis**.

The Egg. Most beetles begin the first stage of life as an egg. Beetle eggs are generally oval in shape with a tough but flexible outer shell. Inside the egg, the growing beetle feeds on the large yolk. The first stage ends when the developing beetle cuts its way through the shell, hatching into a beetle larva.

The Larva. The larval stage is the only one in which the beetle grows in size. Because beetles lay eggs on or in a food source, a newly emerged larva does not have to hunt for food. The larva, also called a grub, spends most of its time eating. When the larva grows too large for the hard shell (called an exoskeleton) that covers its body, the shell splits. The soft grub that emerges will quickly grow a new, larger exoskeleton. The new covering

Some Common Beetle Families

Firefly
Family: Lampyridae
Common name:
lightning bug or firefly
The name *Lampyridae* means "shining fire" in Latin. In some species, the eggs, larvae, pupae (plural of pupa) and adult fireflies all emit a glowing light.

Two-spotted Ladybug
Family: Coccinellidae
Common name: ladybird beetle or ladybug
The name *ladybug* originated in the Middle Ages. Named the beetle of Our Lady, this insect was dedicated to the Virgin Mary.

Colorado Potato Beetle
Family: Chrysomelidae
Common name: leaf beetle
There are more than 25,000 species of leaf beetles in the world. Both the larvae (plural of larva) and the adult leaf beetles feed on leaves. This makes many leaf beetles serious crop pests.

Dung Beetle
Family: Scarabaeidae
Common name: scarab
The scarab beetles are one of the largest families of beetles, with almost 1,300 North American species and 20,000 species in the world.

Striped Blister Beetle
Family: Meloidae
Common name: blister beetle
When a predator attacks a blister beetle, the beetle discharges a drop of blood containing an oily chemical. This chemical causes severe blistering of the skin.

Fiery Searcher Ground Beetle
Family: Carabidae
Common name: ground beetle
Almost all ground beetles are nocturnal, so they hide during the day and search for food at night. They are very aggressive predators, even climbing trees to get their prey.

Boll Weevil
Family: Curculionidae
Common name: snout beetle or weevil
With 40,000 species of snout beetles, this is the largest family of beetles in the world. These beetles get their name because they have a long snout, with their mouthparts attached at the farthest end.

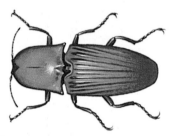

Click Beetle
Family: Elateridae
Common name: click beetle or snapping beetle
When attacked, the click beetle falls backward and plays dead. To right itself, the beetle bends at the thorax and hooks a long spine into an abdominal groove. It unhooks the spine with a click, throwing itself in the air and flipping end over end.

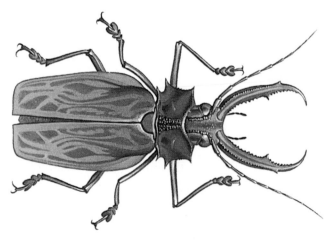

Giant Longhorn Beetle
Family: Cerambycidae
Common name: long-horned or wood-boring beetle
Larvae of this family are wood borers. They are easy to capture because they can be picked out of the wood with hooked sticks. Partly for this reason, the larvae are used as food in many parts of the world.

Tiger Beetle
Family: Cicindelidae
Common name: tiger beetle
Tiger beetle larvae wait for prey at the entrance of their vertical burrows. They attach themselves to the burrow wall with a hooklike spine on the abdomen that prevents them from being pulled out of the burrow when capturing large prey.

will also be shed as the larva continues to eat and grow. This process of growing and shedding the outer layer is called **molting**. A larva may molt three to seven times before it enters the next stage.

The Pupa. As it enters the pupal stage, the beetle buries itself underground or in a tree trunk or a plant so that it will not be attacked by predators. It usually forms a hard casing around itself for protection. Then it stops all movement for several days or weeks. On the outside it looks as if nothing is happening. But inside its case, the insect is transforming itself. The pupa forms legs, wings, and elytra. Its digestive system changes, and its reproductive system develops. When its development is complete, an adult beetle emerges and crawls or flies away.

The Adult. Although long-lived compared with most other insects, adult beetles live for less than a month. During this time they must mate, and the females must find a suitable place to lay their eggs. These ends accomplished, the adult beetle dies.

▶ **BEETLES AND THEIR ENVIRONMENT**

Many plant-eating beetles are considered serious pests because they feed on farm crops, trees, bushes, and other plants. One of the most destructive of these beetles is the boll weevil. Until 1843 the boll weevil lived only in Mexico, where it fed on a wild relative of the cotton plant. By 1892 the boll weevil had reached the southern tip of Texas, where there were vast fields of domesticated cotton. The boll weevil was able to spread quickly through the acres and acres of cropland, spreading northward into the southern United States at a rate of about 60 miles per year. Nothing the farmers could do prevented the expansion of this beetle's range.

One reason the boll weevil was able to spread so quickly is that a female boll weevil can lay as many as 300 eggs in her lifetime. The entire life cycle of the boll weevil takes only two or three weeks. Therefore, several generations of boll weevils can hatch in one summer, quickly increasing the population. Today, cotton farmers use a variety of methods to control the spread of the boll weevil, from insecticides and fertilizers to the introduction of sterile boll weevils that prevent the beetle from breeding successfully. But the boll weevil is a very adaptable insect. No method has

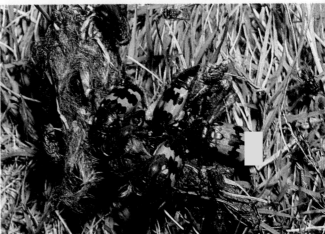

As a larva and an adult, the plant-eating Mexican bean beetle (*top*) is considered a pest. Carrion beetles (*above*) provide a beneficial service by feeding on animal wastes and dead animals.

enabled farmers to get rid of the boll weevil completely.

Other beetles are considered important in controlling insect pests on farm crops and in gardens. Ladybugs, or ladybird beetles, attack and eat aphids, scale insects, mites, and other pests. They have been used commercially since 1888 to control these insects in greenhouses and orchards. Many gardeners use ladybugs today to try to get rid of unwanted insects without using pesticides.

GAIL M. TERZI
Forest Biologist
Contributor, *Insect Biochemistry* journal

See also INSECTS; PLANT PESTS; VECTORS.

BEGIN, MENAHEM (1913–1992)

Menahem Begin, prime minister of Israel from 1977 to 1983, was the first Israeli leader to make a peace settlement with an Arab country. In a varied career, he was successively a law student, political agitator, terrorist, politician, and prime minister.

Begin was born on August 16, 1913, in Brest-Litovsk (now Brest, in Belarus). He grew up a Polish citizen and received a law degree from the University of Warsaw, although he never practiced law. While in his teens, he joined (and later became head of) Betar, a militant youth organization that sought to create a modern Jewish state in Palestine, then governed by Britain. In 1941, during World War II, he enlisted in the Polish forces operating under British command in the Middle East.

There, Begin used his military training against the British as leader of the Irgun Zvai Leumi, an extremist wing of the Jewish Underground, which he founded in 1943. Its most notorious terrorist act was the bombing of the King David Hotel in Jerusalem, site of British headquarters, in 1946. When the British departed and the state of Israel was established in 1948, Begin founded the Herut Party and won a seat in the Knesset, the Israeli parliament. Herut merged with other conservative political groups to form the Likud bloc, which Begin led to victory over Israel's long-ruling Labor Party in 1977 elections.

As prime minister, his greatest, and most surprising, achievement was a peace treaty with Egypt. In 1977 he invited a former enemy, Egyptian president Anwar el-Sadat, to come to Israel. This first meeting resulted in a treaty signed two years later. He and Sadat shared the Nobel Peace Prize for 1978. Begin's later years were less successful, culminating in the much-criticized Israeli military incursion into Lebanon, in an effort to destroy bases of the Palestine Liberation Organization (PLO), in 1982. He retired in 1983, after the death of his wife of 43 years, Aliza. He died in Tel Aviv on March 9, 1992.

ARTHUR CAMPBELL TURNER
University of California, Riverside
Coauthor, *Ideology and Power in the Middle East*

See also ISRAEL (History); SADAT, ANWAR EL-.

BEHRING, EMIL VON (1854–1917)

Emil Adolf von Behring was a pioneer in immunology, the science that explores how the human body protects itself from disease. For his innovative work, especially in the treatment of the diseases diphtheria and tetanus, he received the first Nobel Prize awarded for physiology or medicine in 1901.

Born in Hansdorf, Germany, on March 15, 1854, Behring spent the major part of his career engaged in intensive, and mostly solitary, research of his original ideas on serum therapy. He was particularly interested in combating infectious diseases through the use of antitoxins, the substances that neutralize disease toxins.

In experiments, Behring injected the blood serum from an animal that had recovered from tetanus into an uninfected animal. He discovered that the unaffected animal reacted by producing an antitoxin that made the animal immune to the disease. Behring was convinced that immunity could be passed on to other animals by using this antitoxin. Behring and his associate Shibasaburo Kitasato worked to isolate and define the antitoxin that provided the protection. Their success supported Behring's theories, theories which led to the development of preventive vaccinations against the dread diseases diphtheria and tetanus.

Behring's works, which are all published in German, include *The Practical Goals of Blood Serum Therapy* (1892) and *The History of Diphtheria* (1893). Behring contracted pneumonia and died in Marburg, Germany, on March 31, 1917.

GAIL KAY HAINES
Author, *Micromysteries: Stories of Scientific Detection*

BEIJERINCK, MARTINUS. See VIRUSES (The Discovery of Viruses).

BEIJING

Beijing (also spelled Peking) is the capital and cultural heart of the People's Republic of China. It is the country's second largest city, after Shanghai. Although known by various names, a city has existed on the site since ancient times. Its present name means "northern capital." Modern Beijing has the status of a municipality, which includes much of the surrounding area, and is administered directly by the national government. The population of the city proper is about 7 million; the metropolitan area has some 9.5 million people.

Location and Climate. Beijing is located at the northeastern edge of the North China Plain, the region where Chinese civilization began. Situated between the Pai and Yungting rivers, it lies about 100 miles (161 kilometers) inland from the Bo Hai, a gulf that forms part of the Yellow Sea. Some 35 miles (56 kilometers) to the north is the Great Wall, built centuries ago to protect China against nomadic invaders. Most of the landscape is mountainous, except for a lowland area on the southeast that merges into the plain.

Beijing has a variable climate. Autumns are pleasant, but summers can be quite hot, while in winter, temperatures average only 23°F (−5°C) and the city is frequently whipped by winds and sandstorms. The relatively little snow usually falls in early spring. Rainfall is moderate and occurs mainly in summer.

Layout of the City. The core of Beijing consists of two old sections, traditionally known as the Inner City and the Outer City. The Inner City, which is actually situated in the north, contains the former Imperial City, which was the seat of the government during the time of the emperors. Within the Imperial City stands the Forbidden City, with the palaces and shrines once used by the emperors and their families. Entry was forbidden to all but members of the imperial household. The buildings are now part of a museum, open to the public. The Legation Quarter, located in the southeastern corner of the Imperial City, was at one time the site of foreign embassies and other diplomatic residences.

Historically, the Inner and Outer Cities were fortified by massive stone walls. The walls of the Inner City, in particular, were pierced by nine great gates and surmounted by lofty guard towers. Most of the city walls have been torn down, but a few parts remain as

The Forbidden City (foreground) stands in the heart of Beijing, China's capital and second largest city. Surrounded by high walls, the Forbidden City was for centuries the seat of China's emperors, closed to all but the imperial household. It is now part of a museum, open to the public.

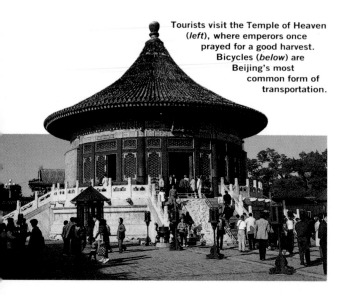

Tourists visit the Temple of Heaven (*left*), where emperors once prayed for a good harvest. Bicycles (*below*) are Beijing's most common form of transportation.

thoroughfares cross the two sections of the city, branching out into narrow lanes where the great majority of the people live. At most hours of the day, the streets are thronged by bicyclists, the bicycle being the most common form of transportation.

Beyond the city proper lie the suburbs, industrial districts, and farmlands that form part of the Beijing municipality. In all, the municipality encompasses an area of about 6,500 square miles (16,835 square kilometers).

Some Places of Interest. Near the southern edge of the Forbidden City is the vast Tiananmen (Gate of Heavenly Peace) Square. Situated in what is now the center of Beijing, it is frequently used for parades and other formal state occasions. The Great Hall of the People, where the country's legislature meets, stands on the western side of the square. On the eastern side are the Museum of the Revolution and the Chinese Historical Museum.

The most imposing of the palace buildings of the Forbidden City is the Hall of Great Harmony, which served as the imperial throne room. There are two places of particular interest in the southern part of the Outer City: the Temple of Heaven, where the emperors prayed at the time of the summer solstice to ensure a bountiful harvest, and the Temple of

monuments of the past. The walls and moat (a protective, water-filled trench) of the Forbidden City have been preserved.

The Outer City, in the south, is rectangular in shape. A colorful and lively district, it is largely commercial and residential. Its main entrance to the Inner City is by way of a broad, straight boulevard that passes through the enormous Qianmen (Front Gate). Other wide

Tiananmen Square (*left*) lies at the southern edge of the Forbidden City, which can be seen in the background. The vast square was the scene, in 1989, of massive protests by university students demanding democratic reforms. The emperor Kublai Khan (*below*), founder of the Yuan dynasty, made Beijing, then called Cambaluc, his capital in the 1260's.

Agriculture. The Summer Palace of the Qing emperors and Beijing University (one of the many educational institutions) are located in the northwestern suburbs. The Summer Palace is an especially popular tourist site, famed for its palaces, gardens, and lakes. The Beijing Zoo is noted for its pandas, animals native only to China. The numerous parks and artificial lakes add to the city's attractiveness.

Economic Activity. Beijing is not only the center of China's political and cultural life but one of its most important industrial regions as well. Among its chief manufactured products are iron and steel, machinery, chemicals, textiles, motor vehicles, and processed foods. Printing and publishing are other major industries. Beijing is also the hub of the nation's communications and transportation network. The city's own transportation system includes a subway, which was expanded in 1988.

History. Beijing has been a site of human settlement since before recorded history. Under the name of Chi, it was first established as a capital of the small kingdom of Yen in the 700's B.C. Destroyed and rebuilt a number of times as a result of war and conquest, it emerged as an important city under the Khitan Tatars in the A.D. 900's. As Cambaluc (Khanbalik), it became the capital of the emperor Kublai Khan, founder of the Yuan (Mongol) dynasty of Chinese rulers, in the 1260's. It was this city that the Venetian traveler and merchant Marco Polo visited and whose wealth and splendor he recounted on his return home. See the article on MARCO POLO in Volume P.

The architectural beauty of the city was greatly enhanced by succeeding dynasties, the Ming and the Qing (or Manchu), the last imperial dynasty. After the overthrow of the Qing and the founding of the Chinese republic in 1912, Beijing remained the capital until 1928, when the seat of government was moved to Nanjing (formerly Nanking), meaning "southern capital." Beijing was renamed Beiping (Peiping), or "northern peace."

Beijing's name and status as the national capital were restored in 1949, when the Communists gained control of the mainland and proclaimed the People's Republic in Tiananmen Square. The great square was also the scene of massive protests in 1989, when thousands of university students gathered to demand democratic reforms in China. The demonstrations, which lasted for more than six weeks, captured the attention of much of the world before they were crushed by the military.

HYMAN KUBLIN
City University of New York, Brooklyn College
Author, *The Rim of Asia*

BELARUS

Belarus, once known as Belorussia (also spelled Byelorussia), is a new nation of Eastern Europe. Formerly a part of the Soviet Union, it won its independence as a result of the breakup of the Soviet Union in 1991. Belarus is surrounded by five other nations—Poland on the west; Lithuania and Latvia on the northwest; Russia on the north and east; and Ukraine on the south. This location, at the crossroads of Eastern Europe, has played an important role in Belarus' history.

The People. The Belarusians trace their origins to Eastern Slavic tribes that settled in the region between the A.D. 500's and 600's. The name *Belarus* means "White Russia," but the origins of the name are lost in time. The Belarusian language belongs to the Eastern slavic language group, which also includes Russian and Ukrainian. Both Belarusian and Russian are official state languages.

Native Belarusians make up about 80 percent of the population. Russians are the largest minority, with about 13 percent. Poles and Ukrainians are the other major ethnic groups. Most of the people adhere to the Eastern (or Greek) Orthodox faith. There are smaller numbers of Roman Catholics and members of the Greek Catholic, or Uniate, Church, which recognizes the supremacy of the pope but observes the Orthodox rite. There is also a significant Jewish community.

At one time, the majority of Belarusians were engaged in agriculture and lived in small rural farming communities. Intensive development of the country's resources led to greater economic diversity. It also brought about great changes in where the people lived. The population today is concentrated mainly in the industrial central and northern parts of the country, especially around the cities of Minsk, the capital and largest city, Gomel, and Mogilyov.

The Land. Most of Belarus consists of flat or rolling plain. A small area of uplands near the city of Minsk reaches a height of about 1,135 feet (436 meters). The Pripet Marshes occupy most of the southern part of the country. A region of rivers, lakes, bogs, and woodlands, it is inhabited by a wide variety of wild animal life. Large parts of the marshes have been drained to create new farm land.

FACTS and figures

REPUBLIC OF BELARUS is the official name of the country.

LOCATION: Eastern Europe.

AREA: 80,154 sq mi (207,600 km²).

POPULATION: 10,300,000 (estimate).

CAPITAL AND LARGEST CITY: Minsk.

MAJOR LANGUAGE(S): Belarusian, Russian (both official).

MAJOR RELIGIOUS GROUP(S): Eastern Orthodox, Greek Catholic (Uniate), Jewish.

GOVERNMENT: Republic. **Head of state and government**—president. **Legislature**—Supreme Council.

CHIEF PRODUCTS: Agricultural—wheat, rye, and other grains, potatoes, sugar beets, and other vegetables, fodder, flax, hemp. **Manufactured**—processed agricultural products, textiles, machine tools heavy farm equipment, fertilizers. **Mineral**—oil, coal, potash.

Galloping horses enjoy a moment of freedom on a horse farm in western Belarus. The grassy plains that make up most of Belarus' land are especially suited to the raising of livestock, an important part of the country's agriculture.

About one-third of Belarus is covered with forests, one of its most important natural resources. Its mineral deposits include oil, coal, and potash. Peat, obtained from the southern bogs, is used as fuel.

The climate is moderately continental, with hot summers and cool winters.

The Economy. Before the collapse of the Soviet Union, Belarus had a Communist economic system, centrally planned and controlled by the state. Economic reforms now taking place are based on a market, or free-enterprise, system.

About two-thirds of the country's income comes from manufacturing, but agriculture is also important to the economy. Major crops include wheat, rye, and other grains; potatoes, sugar beets, and other vegetables; fodder, or feed for livestock; flax (from which linen is made); and hemp (used to make rope). The raising of cattle and other livestock is an important part of Belarusian agriculture. The chief manufactures include processed agricultural products, textiles, machine tools, heavy farm equipment, fertilizers, and other goods.

Early History: Polish Rule. By the A.D. 800's, Belarus was ruled by various princes who were linked to the ancient state of Kievan Rus (whose center was located in what is now Ukraine). The Kievan state was eventually destroyed by invading Mongols, and in the 1300's Belarus fell to Lithuania. For more than 400 years, Belarus was dominated first by Lithuania and then by Poland, which united with Lithuania in the 1500's. During this period the Belarusians, separated from the Eastern Slavs of Russia and Ukraine, developed their own language and culture, and emerged as a distinct people.

From Russian to Soviet Rule. When Poland was partitioned (divided) among its neighbors in the late 1700's, Belarus became a part of the Russian Empire. The Russian imperial government discouraged Belarusian cultural activities and prohibited the use of the Belarusian language in schools. This policy, however, did not succeed in destroying the idea that Belarus was a distinct nation with a history and tradition worth preserving.

During the social and political confusion caused by World War I and the Russian revolutions of 1917, Belarusian leaders issued a declaration of independence. But the infant state was crushed by political and military events and the attempt to establish independence failed. Under the Treaty of Riga (1921), Belarus was partitioned between newly independent Poland and Soviet Russia, the state that succeeded the Russian Empire. When the Union of Soviet Socialist Republics (or Soviet Union) was founded in 1922, Belarus—then called Belorussia—was one of its founding republics. In 1939, on the eve of World War II, the part of Belarus ceded to Poland in 1921 was taken over by the Soviet Union.

Independence. On July 27, 1990, as the Soviet Union began to break apart, the Belorussian parliament approved a declaration of sovereignty. The name Republic of Belarus was adopted in August 1991. In December 1991, with the complete collapse of the Soviet Union, Belarus and other former Soviet republics formed the Commonwealth of Independent States, with its administrative headquarters in Minsk.

A new constitution was adopted in 1996. It extended the term of elected president Aleksandr Lukashenko, who sought to restore a Soviet-style system, and greatly increased his powers. In 1997, Belarus and Russia signed a treaty in which they agreed to coordinate military, foreign, and economic policies.

PETER CZAP, JR.
Amherst College

BELFAST. See UNITED KINGDOM (Major Cities).
BELGIAN ART. See DUTCH AND FLEMISH ART.

BELGIUM

Since the Middle Ages, canals linked to the North Sea have brought trade and industry to the charming city of Bruges (*left*). Belgians are a mix of French-, Dutch-, and German-speaking peoples.

Belgium is a small nation located in northwestern Europe. Although not much larger than the state of Maryland in the United States, Belgium has always been more important than its small size suggests. This is due in part to its strategic location. Belgium shares borders with the Netherlands, Germany, Luxembourg, and France and is separated from Great Britain by just a narrow strip of the North Sea. Because of its location, Belgium historically has been caught up in the struggles and quarrels of its more powerful neighbors.

Belgium is a relatively young nation, having won its independence in 1830. But the region that is now Belgium has a long history. During the Middle Ages, it was one of the most prosperous parts of Europe, famous for its woolen textiles, lace, and great culture. Today Belgium is a highly industrialized country, sometimes known as the Workshop of Europe. The nation also plays an important role in the affairs of modern Europe.

▶ PEOPLE

Belgium is inhabited by approximately 10 million people, who are known as Belgians. They are divided into three groups.

The Flemings, who make up close to 60 percent of the population, live in the northern region called Flanders. The Flemings, descended from ancient Germanic peoples, speak Dutch.

The Walloons, who make up more than 30 percent of the population, speak French. Most Walloons live in Wallonia, a region in southern Belgium. They are descended from the Belgae, an ancient people whom the Romans conquered in the 1st century B.C.

German-speaking Belgians live in the eastern portion of the country, near the German border. They are a small minority, numbering about 60,000.

Language. Belgium is divided into distinct linguistic (language) regions. In Flanders, Dutch is the official language. French is the official language of Wallonia. Brussels, the capital, is officially bilingual; that is, both French and Dutch are used. Through the years disputes over the status and use of French and Dutch have caused considerable friction among Belgians. Some German is spoken in eastern Belgium.

Religion. Although Belgians are divided in language, they are united in their religion. Most of the people are Roman Catholics. Religious freedom, however, is guaranteed by the constitution.

Education and Libraries. All Belgian children between the ages of 6 and 18 are required to attend school. Private as well as public schools may receive financial support from the government.

Higher education is provided by several excellent universities. The Catholic University at Louvain, just east of Brussels, was founded in the 1420's and is the country's oldest university. The University of Antwerp and the Free University of Brussels place a high priority on scientific research.

Belgium's national library is the Royal Albert I Library in Brussels. Other important libraries include the Antwerp City Library and the University Library of Ghent.

Food and Drink. The Belgians are expert cooks and enjoy good food and pleasant dining. Every region of Belgium has its own specialties, but certain dishes are popular all over the country. A typical Belgian meal might begin with mussels (*moules*) or a chicken stew called *waterzooï de poulet*. The main course might be *carbonnade à la flamande*, a beef stew made with beer. Belgium is noted for its wide variety of superior beers.

▶ **LAND**

Belgium is shaped somewhat like a triangle. There is also a tiny 7-square-mile (18-square-kilometer) fragment of northern Belgium, called Baarle-Hertog, that is entirely surrounded by the Netherlands.

Land Regions. Belgium can be divided into three equal sections—the Lowlands, the Central Low Plateaus, and the Ardennes. The Lowlands in the north and west are practically flat. Parts of the northwestern lowlands were reclaimed from the sea and marshes during the Middle Ages. The northeastern lowlands are known as the Kempen.

The southern two-thirds of Belgium is more elevated. Central Belgium is part of the European Low Plateau. The hillier southern region belongs to the Rhine Massif.

In contrast to the almost flat coastal region, the Ardennes in the southeast feature plateaus, large forests, and picturesque rivers. Belgium's highest point, the Botrange, is located in this region.

Rivers. From northwest to southeast the principal Belgian rivers are the Leie, Schelde, Sambre, Meuse, Yser, and Ourthe.

Hiking is a popular activity in the Ardennes, a forested region in southeastern Belgium that borders Luxembourg and Germany.

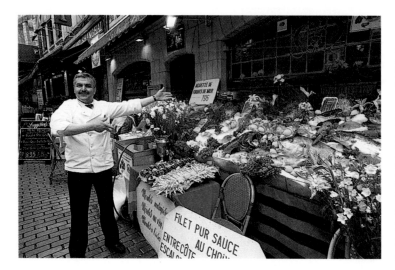

A merchant displays a variety of local seafood delicacies on a bustling side street in one of the oldest sections of downtown Brussels.

Most Belgian rivers are tributaries of the Schelde or Meuse. Northern and central Belgium are crisscrossed by many waterways, including artificial ones used for drainage and navigation.

Climate. Belgium's climate is known as marine west coast, which is typical of northwestern Europe. It has changeable and cloudy weather with frequent rains and moderate temperatures. Winters are generally mild except in the interior uplands. Summers are usually cool rather than warm. Daytime temperatures rarely rise above 80°F (27°C).

About 30 inches (760 millimeters) of precipitation—mostly in the form of rain—falls on northern Belgium in an average year. The Ardennes receive an even greater amount.

Natural Resources. Belgium is quite poor in natural resources. Coal was once plentiful, but today only phosphates, used in fertilizers, are found in large quantities. Sand and clay, used to make glass, brick, and cement, are also found.

▶ **ECONOMY**

Belgium is a highly industrialized nation with a generally high standard of living. The capital, Brussels, is the center of manufacture and commerce.

Services. Tourism throughout Belgium supports a wide range of service establishments, such as hotels, restaurants, and cultural institutions. The seashore, Brussels, and the Ardennes are among the most popular tourist destinations.

Manufacturing. Belgian industries depend to a large extent on imported raw materials.

For example, Belgian steel is made from iron ores imported from France and Luxembourg. Belgium produces more than 12 million tons of steel a year, making it one of the world's important steel-producing countries. Other leading industries include the manufacture of railroad equipment and armaments and the processing of such metals as zinc, copper, and lead.

The manufacture of woolens, lace, cloth, and other textiles has been important in Belgium since the Middle Ages. "Made in Belgium" also is found stamped on such products as glassware, foods, tobacco goods, timber, and paper products.

Agriculture. The major crops produced by Belgian farmers are wheat, oats, barley, potatoes, sugar beets, and rye. Flax, used for linen making, and tobacco are also grown. Belgium is also one of the biggest exporters of decorative flowers and plants.

Belgium's climate is good for grass growth, and as a result the country has a flourishing livestock industry. Dairy cattle, beef cattle,

---

FACTS and figures

KINGDOM OF BELGIUM (Royaume de Belgique in French and Koninkrijk België in Dutch) is the official name of the country.

LOCATION: Northwestern Europe.

AREA: 11,781 sq mi (30,513 km²).

POPULATION: 10,000,000 (estimate).

CAPITAL AND LARGEST CITY: Brussels.

MAJOR LANGUAGES: Dutch, French, German.

MAJOR RELIGIOUS GROUP: Roman Catholic.

GOVERNMENT: Constitutional Monarchy. **Head of state**—king. **Head of government**—prime minister. **Legislature**—parliament, consisting of the Senate and the Chamber of Representatives.

CHIEF PRODUCTS: Agricultural—wheat, oats, barley, potatoes, sugar beets, rye, flax, fruits, flowers, tobacco, livestock. **Manufactured**—iron and steel, textiles, machinery, railroad equipment, armaments, processed metals, processed food, lace, cut diamonds, glassware, chemicals, cement, tobacco products. **Mineral**—phosphates, coal.

MONETARY UNIT: Belgian franc (1 franc = 100 centimes).

and hogs are the most important. Livestock feed crops are widely grown and occupy about one-half of the cultivated acreage.

Trade. Belgian products are sold all over the world. Foreign trade is very important to the Belgian economy, which has widespread commercial interests, particularly in Europe. Belgium is a member of the European Union (EU). It also has trading connections with the United States. The Belgium Luxembourg Economic Union (BLEU), established in July 1921, maintains a system of monetary association between Belgium and Luxembourg.

Transportation. Belgium's farms and industries are served by an excellent transportation system. Roads reach every corner of the country. Belgium has one of the world's densest networks of railroad facilities and an extensive system of navigable rivers and canals.

Belgium has a small navy used for commercial purposes. Its national airline, Sabena, is partly owned by the government. Antwerp, Belgium's most important port, competes with Rotterdam in the Netherlands and Hamburg in Germany as northwestern Europe's leading port.

Communication. Belgium has six television broadcasting corporations—four public and two commercial. Three broadcast in Dutch and three in French. The number of regional television stations is growing. There are twelve public radio broadcasting companies—seven broadcasting in Dutch, four in French, and one in German—in addition to hundreds of local, private radio stations.

More than 30 newspapers are published daily. Those with the largest circulations include *De Standaard* and *Le Soir*.

▶ **CULTURAL HERITAGE**

Belgium has long been a rich center of cultural activities.

Music. Belgium's musical heritage began in the Middle Ages. In the 1800's, Flemish music was revived by Peter Benoit, a composer and teacher,

Flax, a fibrous plant used to make linen, is stacked to dry in the fields near Kortrijk. Flax has been grown in Flanders for more than a thousand years.

who founded the Flemish School of Music in Antwerp. Adolphe Sax, another Belgian, invented the saxophone in 1846. The best-known modern Belgian composer, César Franck, is remembered for such beautiful works as *Symphony in D Minor* (1889) and *Symphonic Variations* (1886). Jacques Brel, born in Brussels, was one of the most famous cabaret singers of the 1900's. For more information on Belgian music, see the article DUTCH AND FLEMISH MUSIC in Volume D.

Art and Architecture. Belgian artists have been world famous for many centuries. Many great Flemish artists lived between the 1400's and 1700's, including Jan van Eyck, Rogier van der Weyden, Hans Memling, Hieronymus Bosch, Pieter Brueghel the Elder and his son Jan, Peter Paul Rubens, Sir Anthony Van Dyck, and David Teniers the Younger. In modern times, the most acclaimed artists have been the expressionist James Ensor and the surrealists Paul Delvaux and René Magritte.

The architect Victor Horta was a pioneer of the Art Nouveau style. Among his most notable structures are Tassel House (1893) and his personal residence, now the Horta Museum. Other art museums include the Cinquantenaire Museum of Art and History and the Mu-

Surrealist painter René Magritte (1898–1967) was one of Belgium's most acclaimed artists. His paintings often include dreamlike images of men in bowler hats.

Brussels is the headquarters of the European Union (EU), a political and economic association of European nations. The city also serves as headquarters of the North Atlantic Treaty Organization (NATO).

seum of Modern Art, both in Brussels. For more information on Belgian art, see the article DUTCH AND FLEMISH ART in Volume D.

Literature. Belgians have also made important contributions to world literature. Among the most outstanding Belgian authors of the 1800's and 1900's were Charles de Coster, who wrote about the legendary prankster Till Eulenspiegel; Count Maurice Maeterlinck, winner of the Nobel Prize for literature in 1911; and Camille Lemonnier (1844–1913), the founder of the Belgian literary renaissance. Modern writers include Georges Simenon, the popular mystery story writer and creator of Inspector Maigret.

Cartoons. Many famous cartoonists have originated in Belgium. Hergé (Georges Remi) created *The Adventures of Tintin*, a series of stories featuring a world-famous boy reporter and his dog, Snowy. Peyo (Pierrot Culliford) created the little blue cartoon characters known as the Smurfs, which are popular in the United States and around the world.

▶ MAJOR CITIES

Brussels is the capital of Belgium and the nation's most populous city. Because it is headquarters of the European Union (EU) and the North Atlantic Treaty Organization (NATO), Brussels is also known as the capital of Europe. Many of the city's 1 million people are bilingual in Dutch and French.

Founded in the Middle Ages, Brussels was once the center of the cloth industry. In the 1500's it became the capital of the Spanish Netherlands. It has been Belgium's seat of government since the country became independent in 1830.

Brussels has many interesting sites. The Grand' Place, a square in the center of the oldest part of the city, is lined with exquisite guildhalls built in the baroque style of the 1600's. Another landmark is the Atomium. This enormous iron structure, built in the shape of a molecule, was the centerpiece of the 1958 World's Fair.

Antwerp, one of Europe's busiest seaports, is located on the Schelde River, which leads to the North Sea. Antwerp is also linked by canal to the Meuse River.

Founded in the early Middle Ages, Antwerp became the chief port of Flanders in the 1400's and later the financial capital of northern Europe. As trade grew, the city became the center of the diamond trade, and it remains so to this day.

▶ GOVERNMENT

Belgium is a hereditary, constitutional monarchy. The king is the head of the state and commander of the army. The king must approve all laws passed by Parliament.

Although the Belgian king would appear to have great powers, the actual government is headed by a prime minister, who is helped by other ministers. The Belgian Parliament is divided into two houses—the Senate and the Chamber of Representatives. The minimum voting age is 18. All qualified voters are required by law to vote.

▶ HISTORY

Julius Caesar wrote, "Of all the tribes of Gaul, the Belgae are the bravest." These words of the man who conquered the Belgic tribes in the 1st century B.C. have been echoed by others who tried to conquer Belgium during its long history.

Roman rule over Gallia Belgica lasted about 500 years. During the early Middle Ages, Belgium's history was closely interwoven with that of its neighbors. By the end of the Middle Ages, northern Belgium, under the rule of the counts of Flanders, had grown strong and prosperous. Commerce, manufacture, and the arts grew. Guilds and other trade organizations were established and run by a powerful and well-educated middle class.

Spanish, Austrian, French, and Dutch Rule. After being tied to the Austrian Empire for more than 200 years, Belgium passed to Spanish control in 1519. Then, in 1598, Belgium began a brief period of independence. This ended in 1621, when the Spanish once again took over the area they called the Spanish Netherlands. In 1713 Belgium was made a part of the Austrian kingdom, but in 1797 France annexed the country. After the final defeat of the French under the emperor Napoleon I at Waterloo (near Brussels) in 1815, Belgium and the Netherlands were set up as a united kingdom. The Belgians were unhappy about this union and on October 4, 1830, declared their independence.

Independence to World War I. The first king of independent Belgium was a German prince, Leopold of Saxe-Coburg-Gotha, an uncle of Britain's Queen Victoria. During his reign, Belgium began its industrial development. The late 1800's were also a period of active European colonization. Though at first Belgium did not participate directly, King Leopold II, acting more or less as a private individual, claimed a huge expanse of land in Africa's Congo River basin. In 1908 the Belgian Congo colony was placed under the direct control of the Belgian Parliament.

In 1909, Albert I became king. The early years of his reign were prosperous and happy ones for Belgium. But at the outbreak of World War I in 1914, German armies invaded and quickly occupied most of Belgium. Some of the bloodiest battles of the war were fought there, particularly at Ypres, Antwerp, Namur, and Mons. For more information, see the article ALBERT in Volume A.

World War II. In May 1940, during World War II, Belgium again became a European battleground. Belgian soldiers, aided by British and French allies, were unable to resist a German invasion.

Allied armies succeeded in driving the Germans out of Belgium in September 1944, but in December of that year, German armies re-entered the country. The savage Battle of the Bulge was fought in the Ardennes region during the winter of 1944–45. At last, in February 1945, Belgium regained its freedom. In 1951, King Leopold III, who had come to the throne in 1934, was forced to abdicate because many Belgians disapproved of his wartime behavior. He was succeeded by his son Baudouin. In 1957, Belgium became a founding member of the European Community (now the European Union).

The magnificent guildhalls surrounding the Grand' Place in the heart of Brussels were built in the 1600's. They served as meeting places for merchants and craftsmen.

Recent History. During the early 1960's, Belgium granted independence to the Belgian Congo and to Rwanda-Urundi (now the Democratic Republic of the Congo, Rwanda, and Burundi). At home, Parliament tried to settle a long-standing language dispute between the Flemings and the Walloons. Limited self-rule was granted to Dutch-speaking Flanders and to French-speaking Wallonia in 1980. Brussels, officially bilingual, was made a third federal region in 1989.

King Baudouin, after a reign of some 42 years, died in 1993. He was succeeded by his brother, Albert II.

KENNETH THOMPSON
University of California, Davis
Reviewed by CAROLINE LACOCQUE
Belgian-American Chamber of Commerce

See also DUTCH AND FLEMISH ART; DUTCH AND FLEMISH MUSIC.

BELGRADE

Belgrade is the capital and largest city of Yugoslavia and the capital of the republic of Serbia. Called Beograd by the Serbs, its name means "white fortress" or "white city."

With a population of more than 1 million (about 1.5 million in its metropolitan area), Belgrade is the major city of the central Balkans. It owes its existence and its importance to its strategic location. Situated on a height at the junction of two rivers, the Sava and the Danube, it lies astride the main travel routes between Central Europe and the lower Balkans. In addition to being an important river port, it is a rail center and manufacturing city.

The City. Although part of Belgrade was destroyed by the Germans during World War II (1939–45), most of its surviving historic buildings were undamaged. Among these is the Kalemegdan fortress. Dating from the Middle Ages, it stands on a high cliff overlooking the two rivers, with a commanding view of the city. The fortress is situated in a park and contains a military museum. Other important public buildings are the Orthodox cathedral, the former royal palace, a folklore museum, and the university, founded in 1863. The city has one remaining

mosque, or Muslim house of worship, of the many that once existed, a reminder of centuries of Turkish rule. Handsome, broad boulevards link the various parts of the city.

A rapidly developing suburb, Novi Beograd (New Belgrade), has grown up on the west bank of the Sava River. Many government buildings and the newer residential areas are located here.

History. Belgrade has had a long and tumultuous history. A fortified Roman settlement existed on the site until its destruction by invading Huns in the A.D. 400's. Subject to repeated invasion and conquest, the city had various rulers, including the Byzantine emperors, in the centuries that followed.

Belgrade became the Serbian capital in the 1400's, but in 1521 it fell to the Ottoman Turks. Except for a few brief periods, when it was controlled by the Austrians, the city remained under Turkish rule until 1867, when it was restored as the capital of an independent Serbia.

With the creation of a unified Yugoslav kingdom in 1918, Belgrade was made the national capital. It remained the capital of a smaller Yugoslavia when the country broke apart in 1991–92.

In 1999, NATO air strikes destroyed parts of Belgrade during the war against Serbian aggression in the province of Kosovo.

ARTHUR CAMPBELL TURNER
University of California, Riverside

The historic city of Belgrade lies on a height at the junction of the Sava and Danube rivers. Since the breakup of the Yugoslav federation in 1992, it has been the capital of a smaller Yugoslavia composed of Serbia and Montenegro.

BELIZE

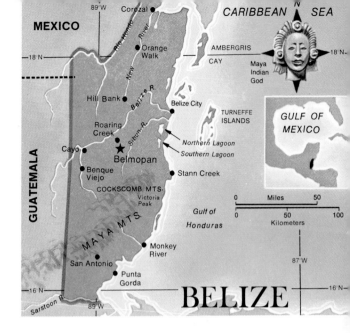

BELIZE

Belize is a small nation located on the eastern, or Caribbean, coast of Central America. Formerly a British colony known as British Honduras, it gained its independence in 1981. Belize is distinctive in being officially an English-speaking country in a region where Spanish is the common language.

▶ **THE PEOPLE**

Belize is the home of many different peoples. The Creoles form the largest ethnic group. They are chiefly descended from black Africans, who were originally brought to the region as slaves. Mestizos, or people of mixed Indian and European ancestry, make up the next largest group. There are smaller numbers of Maya and Carib Indians, East Indians, Europeans, Syrians, and Chinese.

While English is the official language, Spanish is also widely spoken. The Indians speak their own languages. Many Creoles speak an English dialect that contains numerous African words and is often difficult for other English-speaking people to understand. Over half the people are Roman Catholics. The remainder are Protestants.

Most of the people live along the Caribbean coast. About one-third of the population lives in Belize City, the largest city, chief port, and former capital.

▶ **THE LAND AND THE ECONOMY**

Belize has a long, swampy, and irregular coastline, fringed by small islands known as

Belize's long coastline on the Caribbean Sea (*left*) is fringed by numerous small islands called cays. Most are uninhabited. Parts of the interior (*below*) are mountainous and covered with dense rain forests.

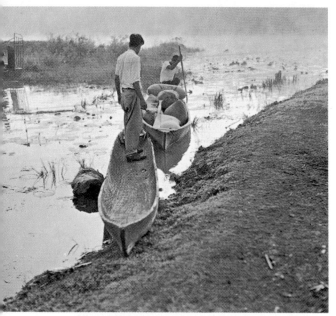

Most of Belize's rivers are shallow and not very long. But they provide transportation for small craft, such as dugout canoes, carrying village produce to market.

cays. The low coastal plain rises gradually toward the interior. In the south are the Maya Mountains and the Cockscomb Mountains. Victoria Peak, in the Cockscombs, rises to 3,681 feet (1,122 meters).

The hot and humid climate is cooled along the coast by northeast trade winds. In the south more than 170 inches (4,300 millime-

ters) of rain may fall each year. Belize lies within the Caribbean hurricane belt, and storms have caused great damage in the past. Belize City was nearly destroyed twice by hurricanes. For this reason a new capital, Belmopan, was built inland about 50 miles (80 kilometers) from Belize City. Belmopan has been the official capital since 1972.

Belize has many rivers, but most are shallow, and none is very long. The most important is the Belize River. A considerable part of the land is still covered with dense tropical forests. For much of Belize's history, lumbering was its most important economic activity. African slaves were brought to the territory to fell the valuable hardwood trees. Sugar is now the leading export.

▶HISTORY AND GOVERNMENT

Belize was once a part of the vast Maya Indian Empire. The first known European settlers were British sailors who had been shipwrecked off the coast in 1638. Other British settlers followed. For many years, Spain, which ruled the surrounding region, disputed Britain's possession of the territory. When Guatemala won independence from Spain in 1821, it assumed the Spanish claims.

British Honduras became a British crown colony in 1862. It was granted internal self-government in 1964, and in 1973 its name was changed to Belize, which came from an older name for the territory. Belize's movement toward independence was complicated by Guatemala's continued claims to the territory. Even after Belize won its independence in 1981, the territorial dispute was still not resolved. Relations between Belize and Guatemala have improved considerably in the years since, however. In 1991 diplomatic relations were established between the two countries.

The government of Belize is based on the British model. The British monarch, represented by a governor-general, is the head of state. Real political power, however, lies with the National Assembly, which is composed of an elected House of Representatives and an appointed Senate. The leader of the majority party in the House of Representatives becomes prime minister, or head of government.

Belize is a member of the Caribbean Community and Common Market (CARICOM).

Reviewed by SIR PETER STALLARD
Former Governor, Belize

FACTS and figures

BELIZE is the official name of the country.

LOCATION: Central America.

AREA: 8,867 sq mi (22,965 km²).

POPULATION: 170,000 (estimate).

CAPITAL: Belmopan.

LARGEST CITY: Belize City.

MAJOR LANGUAGE(S): English (official), Spanish.

MAJOR RELIGIOUS GROUP(S): Christian (Roman Catholic, Protestant).

GOVERNMENT: Constitutional monarchy. **Head of state**—British monarch, represented by a governor-general. **Head of government**—prime minister. **Legislature**—National Assembly (composed of a House of Representatives and a Senate).

CHIEF PRODUCTS: Agricultural—sugarcane, citrus fruits, bananas, rice, corn, beans. **Manufactured**—refined sugar, processed citrus fruits, lumber, clothing.

MONETARY UNIT: Belize dollar (1 dollar = 100 cents).

BELL, ALEXANDER GRAHAM
(1847–1922)

The date was March 10, 1876. The place was a small laboratory in a Boston boarding-house. A young man was working with an electrical instrument that was wired to one in another room. Suddenly the instrument spoke: "Mr. Watson, come here. I want you." Watson rushed into the other room, where his employer, Mr. Bell, had spilled some acid. Both men forgot the acid in their excitement over Watson's report: Bell's words, spoken near one instrument, had issued clearly from the other. These words had become the first spoken telephone message.

Alexander Graham Bell was born on March 3, 1847, in Edinburgh, Scotland. He was born into a family with an interest in speech and hearing. Both his grandfather and his father were teachers of correct speech. His father had developed "visible speech," a method of helping the deaf and hearing impaired to learn how to speak. From his mother, who was a portrait painter and an accomplished musician, he inherited a talent for music.

Bell's schooling was far from regular. In his early years he was taught at home along with his two brothers. At the age of 13 he spent a year in London with his grandfather. In his grandfather's library he read all he could about sound and speech—about the vibrations set up by the voice. He later recalled this year as the turning point of his life. By the age of 16, Graham, as he was called by his family and close friends, was teaching music and speech at a boys' school. Within a few years he was teaching his father's visible speech to deaf and hearing-impaired children.

While studying how the human voice works, Bell came upon the writings of Hermann von Helmholtz. Helmholtz was a German scientist who had used electric vibrations to make vowel sounds. Interested, Bell at once began to study electricity so that he could repeat Helmholtz's experiments.

Bell's family had moved to London, and he joined them there in 1868. But by 1870 both of Bell's brothers had died of tuberculosis, and his own life was in danger. Seeking a more healthful climate, the Bells left Britain and moved to Brantford, Ontario.

With his health improved, Bell went to Boston, Massachusetts, in 1871. There he again

Although Bell invented the telephone and made important contributions in many fields of science, he described his occupation as "teacher of the deaf."

took up his life's work of teaching the deaf and hearing impaired. Bell also continued his experiments. By now his work with electricity had led him to think about inventing a harmonic telegraph. This was a system that could carry several messages over one wire at the same time.

Bell needed money to carry on his experiments. It was given to him by two wealthy men, Gardiner Hubbard and Thomas Sanders. Hubbard had a deaf daughter, and Sanders a deaf son, both of whom were receiving instruction from Bell. It was arranged that the two fathers would share in any profits from Bell's work. Bell was now able to hire a skilled assistant, Thomas A. Watson.

It was during the summer of 1874 that Bell's thinking first went beyond his plan for a harmonic telegraph. What if an electric current could be made to vary, just as the air varies with sound waves? Then any sound—including human speech—could be carried by electricity. This was the idea of the telephone.

The next year was a busy one for Bell. Now that he had the idea of a telephone, he wanted to develop it. On June 2, 1875, Bell and Watson were experimenting with their telegraph, which made use of thin steel reeds. One of the reeds was stuck, and Watson plucked it with his finger. In another room Bell heard a reed in his instrument vibrate as if he himself had plucked it. The electric current had reproduced in this second reed the vibrations of the first.

If the current had done this, then surely it should also reproduce vibrations caused by the human voice. Bell now knew that the telephone was a practical idea. It was only a matter of time before he could perfect an instrument that would send words clearly. Success came on March 10, 1876, with the famous words, "Mr. Watson, come here. I want you."

By the end of 1877 the Bell Telephone Company had been formed, and many phones were in use. Bell himself did not take part in the telephone business that developed. Rather, he leased the right to build a company around his invention.

In the meantime Bell had married Mabel Hubbard, the deaf girl whom he had taught. They had two daughters. In 1882 Bell became a citizen of the United States. He divided his time between Washington, D.C., and his summer home, Beinn Bhreagh, on Cape Breton Island, Nova Scotia.

Bell had invented the telephone before he was 30. In the remaining 45 years of his life he applied his talents to many questions. He experimented with sending sound by light waves. He was interested in heredity and carried on breeding experiments with sheep. As early as the 1890's, Bell was experimenting with the problems of airplane flight. Throughout his life Bell continued working for the deaf and hearing impaired. His work in all these fields won him many honors. Bell died on August 2, 1922. He was so greatly admired that during the funeral the telephones of North America were silent in his honor.

JOHN S. BOWMAN
Author and Science Editor

See also ELECTRICITY; TELEPHONE.

BELLINI FAMILY

During the 1400's, Jacopo Bellini, a Venetian painter, owned one of the busiest workshops in Italy. He painted portraits for rich people and altars for the Church and taught

Madonna of the Trees (1487), by Giovanni Bellini.

young artists who came to study under him. Among his students were his sons, Gentile and Giovanni. Gentile was the elder.

Jacopo was born about 1400, and his sons were born about 1429 and 1430. The three artists worked in the shop for years, experimenting with a new medium, oil paint. The brothers continued to paint after Jacopo died (about 1470). In 1474, they began a series of historical paintings for the palace of the chief magistrate of Venice.

The sultan of Turkey asked the rulers of Venice to lend him one of their best painters. Gentile was chosen and was sent to Constantinople in 1479. Giovanni remained in Venice, working at the palace, teaching, and painting. He was the first of the great Venetian painters to capture a sense of open space and light. Today, he is regarded as the greatest of the Bellinis. When Gentile returned to Venice in 1480, the brothers worked together again.

Gentile died in 1507, and Giovanni in 1516. In 1577, a fire burned through the palace. It destroyed countless Bellini canvases—among the first masterpieces of oil painting.

Reviewed by ADRIANE RUSKIN BATTERBERRY
Author, *The Pantheon Story of Art for Young People*

BELLOW, SAUL (1915–   )

Saul Bellow is one of the foremost American writers of the period after World War II. His finely crafted novels of modern life won him the Nobel Prize for literature in 1976.

Bellow was born on July 10, 1915, in Lachine, Quebec, Canada. His parents, who were Jewish, had gone there two years before from Russia, where his father had been a businessman. Saul was the youngest of four children. Until he was 9, the family lived in Montreal, where he grew up learning four languages—French, English, Yiddish, and Hebrew. In 1924 the family moved to Chicago, and he afterward thought of that city as his hometown.

Bellow attended Chicago schools. He graduated with honors from Northwestern University and started graduate studies at the University of Wisconsin. But he left in his first year, determined to become a writer.

Bellow taught at colleges and universities and also worked as an encyclopedia editor. His first two novels, *Dangling Man* (1944) and *The Victim* (1947), are rather grim stories. His next novel, *The Adventures of Augie March* (1953), shows the humor for which he has become known. It was his first big success, and it won a National Book Award. *Henderson the Rain King*, about an American in Africa, followed in 1959.

In 1962, Bellow became a professor at the University of Chicago. Two later novels, *Herzog* (1964) and *Mr. Sammler's Planet* (1970), won National Book Awards. *Humboldt's Gift* (1975) won the Pulitzer Prize for fiction in 1976. Bellow has also written nonfiction and plays. *Him With His Foot in His Mouth and Other Stories* (1984) is a collection of his short stories.

Reviewed by JEROME H. STERN
Florida State University

BELLS AND CARILLONS

A bell is a hollow cup-shaped vessel that rings when struck. A bell may be struck on the outside by a hammer or mallet or by means of a clapper suspended inside the bell.

Most modern bells are made of metal—usually bronze, an alloy of copper and tin. In bell casting, two molds of baked clay are made. One forms the bell's interior, and the other forms the curved outside surface. Molten bronze is poured between the two molds. When the metal is cool and hard, the molds are removed. Bells are tuned by filing metal strips from their inside surfaces.

For centuries bells have been rung to mark the passing hours. But they have also been used for many other purposes: to sound an alarm, to announce a birth or a death, to call a congregation to worship, even to ward off evil spirits. The Egyptians wore bells on their ankles as a protection against lightning. In old England, folk dancers jingled bells to awaken the spirit of spring from a long winter's sleep.

In ancient Rome, bells announced public assemblies and church services. In the Middle Ages, bells woke the city at dawn, signaling morning prayers. Through the day, bells marked the hours, the half hours, and the quarters. They pealed for weddings and tolled for funerals and were heard at Easter and Christmas.

A modern-day bell tower in Atlanta, Georgia, holds a set of carillon bells. This carillon can be programmed by computer to play a sequence of tunes.

The First Bell Music.

The earliest attempts to make music with bells occurred in the Middle Ages, with the *cymbala*, or bell chime. This was a small set of bells hung from a rack.

The clock bell originated in the monastery. The bells rang from a tower, regulating not only life in the abbey but in the surrounding town as well. So necessary were the bells to a town that they became civic property.

Since the first clock bells could not ring by themselves, someone was hired to strike them at the proper times. The human bell ringer was soon replaced by clock machinery. It was then possible to ring many bells, and it became customary to ring a short tune as a warning that the hour bell was about to strike. This is known as a clock chime tune.

From Bells to Carillons.

A carillon is a set of bells with a range of between two and four octaves. Usually a carillon has at least 23 bells. The first carillons were made in the 1500's in Flanders (a region in present-day Belgium and northern France). At first the bells were rung automatically; later a keyboard, operated by a **carillonneur**, was added.

The carillon keyboard consists of levers and pedals. The levers resemble small broomstick handles. The carillonneur sits at a bench and strikes the levers with clenched hands while playing the foot pedals.

The oldest carillon in the world is in the Rijksmuseum in Amsterdam. It has 24 bells cast in 1554. A famous carillon is at Saint Rombold's Cathedral in Mechelen, Belgium. It has 49 bells. The first carillon in North America was installed at Notre Dame University in South Bend, Indiana, in 1856. The largest carillon in the world is at the Riverside Church in New York City. It contains six octaves of bells, of which the **bourdon**, or bass bell, weighs more than 18 tons.

Electronic carillons imitate the sound of bells through the use of electronic equipment; they are very different from true carillons.

JAMES R. LAWSON
Carillonneur, Riverside Church (New York City)

BEN-GURION, DAVID (1886–1973)

David Ben-Gurion became the first prime minister of Israel after the country became independent in 1948. He served as prime minister and minister of defense from 1949 to 1953 and from 1955 to 1963.

Ben-Gurion was born David Gryn on October 16, 1886, in Plonsk, Poland. His father, Avigdor Gryn, was a Zionist who inspired young David with the hope that some day a homeland for the Jewish people could be established in Palestine.

In 1906 David decided that the time had come for him to go to Palestine, then a part of the Turkish Empire. The new land was strange to someone who had always lived in Poland, but he soon found work as a farm laborer. In 1910 David became editor of the Palestine Labor Party's magazine. He signed one of his articles "Ben-Gurion," Hebrew for "son of the young lion." From then on he was known as David Ben-Gurion.

When World War I broke out in 1914, Ben-Gurion was arrested by the Turks and expelled from Palestine. First he fled to Egypt and later to the United States. In America he encouraged young people to emigrate to Palestine. One of these Americans was a nurse named Paula Munweis, who eventually became Ben-Gurion's wife. In 1917 Ben-Gurion helped organize the Jewish Legion to fight with the British Army against the Turks. In 1918 he returned to Palestine.

For the next 20 years Ben-Gurion devoted himself to Zionism and politics. He helped organize Histadrut (the General Federation of Jewish Labor). In 1935 he became chairman of the Jewish Agency for Palestine, an organization that assisted Jewish immigrants who wanted to settle in Palestine.

Israel declared its independence on May 14, 1948. Under Ben-Gurion's leadership the new nation became a modern democracy as well as a home for Jews seeking refuge. Ben-Gurion died in 1973, a national hero.

Reviewed by
HOWARD M. SACHAR
George Washington University

BENIN

Benin, formerly called Dahomey, is a small nation situated on the west coast of Africa. It traces its history back to the powerful kingdom of Dahomey in the 1600's. Later the region came under the control of France, which governed it until 1960. Unlike the old kingdom of Dahomey, however, Benin today is one of the poorest countries in Africa.

▶ PEOPLE

Most of the people in Benin live in the southern part of the country, which has the richest soil. The northern region is more sparsely populated. Of the many different ethnic groups in Benin, the most numerous are the Fon, the Adja, the Bariba, and the Yoruba. The majority of the people follow traditional African religions, but there are considerable numbers of Christians and Muslims. French is the official language, but Fon, Yoruba, and other African languages are widely spoken.

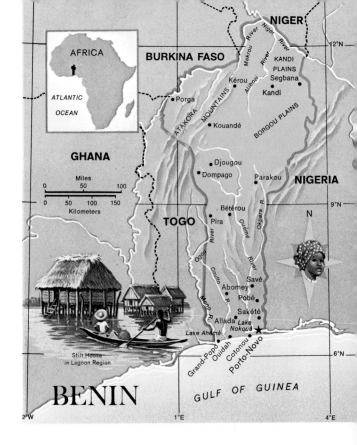

Stilt House in Lagoon Region

BENIN

FACTS and figures

REPUBLIC OF BENIN (République du Bénin) is the official name of the country.

LOCATION: West coast of Africa.

AREA: 43,484 sq mi (112,622 km²).

POPULATION: 6,200,000 (estimate).

CAPITAL: Porto-Novo (official).

LARGEST CITY: Cotonou (center of government administration).

MAJOR LANGUAGES: French (official), Fon, Yoruba, other African languages.

MAJOR RELIGIOUS GROUPS: Traditional African religions, Christian, Muslim.

GOVERNMENT: Republic. **Head of state and government**—president. **Legislature**—National Assembly.

CHIEF PRODUCTS: Agricultural—corn, sorghum, cassava, yams, beans, rice, cotton, palm oil, peanuts, poultry, livestock. **Manufactured**—palm oil, palm kernel oil, copra (dried coconut meat), shea butter, castor oil.

MONETARY UNIT: African Financial Community (CFA) franc (1 CFA franc = 100 centimes).

Most of the people are farmers who produce food chiefly for their own use. The main food crops are cassava, yams, beans, corn, sorghum, rice, and peanuts. Cassava is used in making bread and tapioca (*gari*). The farmers also keep poultry, cattle, sheep, and goats. Fish are an important source of food and one of the country's exports.

Improvement in education is essential to the country's development. Most schools are in the south, but the government is trying to provide education for the scattered population in the north. Most of the schools of higher education are located in Porto-Novo, the official capital, and Cotonou, the largest city and center of government administration.

▶ LAND

Benin occupies a long, narrow strip of land that includes both lowlands and highlands. It has a short coastline on the Gulf of Guinea, a part of the Atlantic Ocean.

The country has four geographical regions. In the south is a flat coastal area along the Gulf of Guinea. Next is a region of lagoons and lakes. Farther north the land rises to a broad plateau that reaches as high as 1,500 feet (460 meters). In the far north the land is divided between the Atakora Mountains and the broad plains of Borgou and Kandi. The major rivers are the Ouémé (the country's longest), the Mono, and the Couffo.

The northern and southern parts of the country have different climates. The south is hot and humid; the north is drier, with less rainfall.

▶ ECONOMY

Benin is a poor and underdeveloped country. Its economy is largely agricultural. The major industries are those that process the chief export crops—palm oil, palm kernels, and nuts. Palm products supply most of the country's exports. Palm oil is used in making soap and margarine. Copra (dried coconut meat), shea butter (the fat of shea tree nuts), cotton, peanuts, and castor oil are among the other important agricultural exports.

▶ HISTORY AND GOVERNMENT

The three great kingdoms of Ardra, Jakin, and Dahomey flourished in the early 1600's. During the 1700's, the strong kings of Dahomey gained control of Ardra and Jakin.

In 1738 the Yoruba from Nigeria seized Abomey, the capital of the kingdom of Dahomey, and forced the Dahomean rulers to pay tribute for nearly 100 years. In the late 1800's, the great Dahomean king Gezo reorganized the Dahomean Army, which included a famous band of female warriors. He succeeded in shaking off Yoruba control. Gezo signed the first trade agreement with the French in 1851, but the kings who came after him did not respect the agreement. In 1894, France forcibly deposed the last of the Dahomean kings, Béhanzin, and annexed the territory to French West Africa.

Gradually France began to give Dahomey and its other French African territories more control over their own affairs. Dahomey elected its own legislature in 1952. In 1960 it proclaimed its independence.

Dahomey then suffered years of political instability. Military coups through the early 1970's led to frequent changes of government. In 1972, Major (now General) Mathieu Kérékou came to power and established a Communist-style government, which he later renounced. In 1975 he changed the name of the country from Dahomey to Benin.

Kérékou governed as president and head of Benin's sole political party, the People's Revolutionary Party, until 1990, when anti-government demonstrations forced him to resign. In 1991, in the first free elections in more than twenty years, former prime minister Nicephore Soglo was elected president, defeating Kérékou. Kérékou regained power in 1996, however, defeating Soglo in a runoff election for president.

L. Gray Cowan
Columbia University

BENJAMIN, JUDAH PHILIP. See Louisiana (Famous People).

BENNETT, RICHARD BEDFORD. See Canada, Government of (Profiles).

BENNY, JACK. See Illinois (Famous People).

Once a powerful and wealthy African kingdom, Benin today is a small, developing nation. The northern part of the country is a region of plains and plateaus.

BENTON, THOMAS HART (1889–1975)

Thomas Hart Benton was a leader of the movement in American art known as **regionalism**. The subject of much of his work is life in the small towns and rural areas of the American Midwest.

Benton was born on April 15, 1889, in Neosho, Missouri, into a politically prominent

In *Arts of the West*, Thomas Hart Benton portrayed activities that he considered to be typical of the people of a particular region: the American West.

family. He studied at the Art Institute of Chicago from 1906 to 1907 and then went to Paris, where he became familiar with the latest trends in modern art. He returned to the United States in 1912. Gradually he rejected European modernism in favor of a realistic style and distinctly American themes.

After serving in the navy during World War I (1914–18), Benton traveled through the South and Midwest, painting the people and places he saw. Works such as *Boomtown* (1927), *Louisiana Rice Fields* (1928), and *Cotton Pickers* (1932) convey the vitality of the men and women who work the land and populate the towns and cities of America.

Benton used many of these same images in his murals, which he began to paint in the 1930's. Some of the best known are in the New School for Social Research, New York City (1930); the State Capitol, Jefferson City, Missouri (1935); and the Truman Library, Independence, Missouri (1959).

In 1935, Benton moved to Kansas City, Missouri, where he lived until his death on January 19, 1975. His autobiography, *An Artist in America*, was published in 1937.

Reviewed by KENNETH HALTMAN
New Britain Museum of American Art

BEOWULF

Beowulf is the longest and greatest poem that has come down to us from Old English, the ancient form of modern English. Only one manuscript of *Beowulf* has survived. It dates from about A.D. 1000, but the poem was probably composed about A.D. 700.

In the poem, Beowulf, a hero of a Germanic tribe from southern Sweden called the Geats, travels to Denmark to help defeat a terrible monster. Why was a poem about Danish and Swedish kings and heroes preserved in England? The English people are descendants of Germanic tribes called the Angles, Saxons, and Jutes. These tribes came from what is now southern Denmark. Thus, *Beowulf* tells a story about the old days in their homeland. The opening lines state:

Hwæt! We Gardena in geardagum
þeodcyninga þrym gefrunon
hu ða æþelingas ellen fremedon.

In modern English, this reads:

What! We have heard of the glory of the spear-
Danes in the old days,
of the people's kings,
how the princes did deeds of valor.

Old English poetry such as *Beowulf* is very different from modern poetry. It was probably recited, for few people at that time were able to read. Instead of rhyme, poets typically used **alliteration**—a technique in which the first sound of each word in a line is the same, as in "Peter Piper picked a peck of pickled peppers." A line of Old English poetry usually has three words that alliterate. The meter, or rhythm, of the poetry works together with the alliteration: The stress in a line falls on the first syllables of the words that alliterate, as in the line "**weo'x** under **wo'lc**num, **weo'rð**myndum þah." (He grew under the sky, he prospered in his glory.)

Beowulf, the hero of an Old English epic poem, had many adventures, including battles with dragons and other beasts. The poem was originally recited aloud.

Old English poets also used **kennings**, poetic ways of saying simple things. For example, a poet might call the sea the swan-road or the whale-road; a king might be called a ring-giver. There are many kennings in *Beowulf*. In fact, some scholars think the name Beowulf itself may be a kenning. It may mean "bee-wolf," a term for a bear, which attacks beehives the way a wolf attacks other animals.

▶ THE STORY

The story of *Beowulf* tells how King Hrothgar built a great hall called Heorot for his people. In it he and his warriors spend their time singing and celebrating, until a monster named Grendel, angered by their singing, attacks the hall and kills and eats many of Hrothgar's warriors. Hrothgar and his men, helpless against Grendel's attacks, have to abandon Heorot.

Beowulf, a young warrior, hears of Hrothgar's troubles and, with his king's permission, goes to help Hrothgar. Beowulf and his men spend the night in Heorot. After they fall asleep, Grendel enters the hall and attacks them, eating up one of Beowulf's men. Beowulf grabs Grendel's arm in a wrestling hold, and the two crash around in Heorot until it seems as though the hall will fall down with their fighting. Beowulf's men draw their swords and rush to his help, but there is a magic around Grendel that makes it impossible for swords to hurt him. Finally, Beowulf tears Grendel's arm from his body, and Grendel runs home to die.

The next night, after celebrating Grendel's death, Hrothgar and his men sleep in Heorot. But Grendel's mother attacks the hall, killing Hrothgar's most trusted warrior in revenge for her son's death. Hrothgar and Beowulf and their men track the monster to her lair under an eerie lake. Beowulf dives in and swims to the bottom. He finds Grendel's mother in a hideous cavern, along with her son's body and the remains of many men that the two have killed. Beowulf and Grendel's mother begin a fierce battle. Beowulf's sword breaks, but he finds another in the cavern, and with it he kills Grendel's mother. Taking Grendel's head with him, he returns to Heorot and is given many gifts.

Beowulf returns home and eventually becomes king of his own people. One day, late in Beowulf's life, a man steals a golden cup from a dragon's lair. When the dragon sees that the cup has been stolen, it leaves its cave in a rage, burning up everything in sight. Beowulf and his warriors come to fight the dragon, but only one of the warriors, a young man named Wiglaf, stays to help Beowulf. Beowulf kills the dragon with Wiglaf's help but dies from the wounds he has received. The dragon's treasure is taken from its lair and buried with Beowulf's ashes. And with that the poem ends.

Most scholars believe that *Beowulf* was written by a Christian poet. Grendel is called a descendant of Cain, and he and his mother have similarities to the devils and demons in medieval Christian stories. But the *Beowulf* poet was also very knowledgeable about pagan beliefs. The descriptions of Grendel and his mother, for example, owe as much to pagan beliefs about trolls as they do to Christian beliefs about demons. Beowulf's cremation at the end of the poem also refers to a pagan practice. But, even though Beowulf was a pagan, the poem's Christian audience could admire his heroic deeds. *Beowulf* is thus a product of the poet's knowledge of both Christian beliefs and the ancient history of his people. In combining them as he did, the *Beowulf* poet created a wonderful story.

DAVID E. GAY
Folklore Institute, Indiana University

BERG, ALBAN (1885–1935)

The Austrian composer Alban Berg was a leading figure in modern music. He combined contemporary techniques with traditional musical forms to create works of great power and emotion.

Berg was born in Vienna on February 9, 1885. He received no formal training in music until the age of 19, when he met the composer Arnold Schoenberg, who became his friend and teacher. Berg adopted Schoenberg's twelve-tone method of composition—in which every melody and harmony in a piece is drawn from a particular arrangement of twelve tones—for many of his later works.

Berg's early compositions included works for piano, string quartet, and orchestra. But his masterpiece is the opera *Wozzeck*, which had its premiere in Berlin in 1925. Based on an 1837 play by German dramatist Georg Büchner about a real-life criminal case, the opera was a worldwide success.

Berg died in Vienna on December 24, 1935, before completing his second opera, *Lulu*. The work, his only twelve-tone opera, was first

performed in 1937. A completed version based on Berg's manuscripts had its premiere in Paris in 1979.

Of Berg's instrumental works, the most important is probably his last completed work, a concerto for violin and orchestra (1935). Also notable are *Three Pieces for Orchestra* (1914–15), *Chamber Concerto* (1925) for violin, piano, and 13 wind instruments, and *Lyric Suite* (1926) for string quartet.

Reviewed by KENNETH NOTT
Hartt School, University of Hartford

BERGMAN, INGMAR.   See MOTION PICTURES (Profiles: Directors).
BERGMAN, INGRID.   See MOTION PICTURES (Profiles: Movie Stars).

BERING, VITUS (1680–1741)

In the early 1700's, many people still believed that a bridge of land connected Asia and North America. Vitus Bering, a Dane in the service of the czar of Russia, discovered that this land bridge did not exist. His explorations helped map what was at that time a little-known part of the world and led to the discovery of Alaska.

Bering was born at Horsens, Denmark, in 1680, and entered the Russian Navy when he was 23. In 1724, Czar Peter the Great named him to lead an expedition to the Kamchatka Peninsula on the northeast coast of Siberia.

The long journey across Siberia was filled with great hardships. After more than three years, the expedition finally reached a little village on Kamchatka. Bering had a ship built and in 1728 set sail across an uncharted sea, now called the Bering Sea. He discovered an island, which he named St. Lawrence Island. Then he sailed north through the strait (now called Bering Strait) that separates Asia and

North America. The discovery of this strait proved the two continents were not linked.

Bering returned to Russia in 1730 to report his findings and to plan a new expedition. In 1741 he sailed from Kamchatka again with two ships—his, the *St. Peter*, and the *St. Paul*, which was commanded by Aleksei Chirikov. The ships soon drifted apart, and on July 15–16 both Chirikov and Bering sighted the southern coast of Alaska from different points. The *St. Peter* stopped briefly at Kayak Island. But before exploring farther, Bering, who was ill, decided to return to Kamchatka for the winter. On the return voyage the *St. Peter* was buffeted by violent storms and wrecked on an uninhabited island off the coast of Kamchatka. Here, on December 8, 1741, Bering died and was buried. The island now bears his name.

Reviewed by HELEN DELPAR
Editor, *The Discoverers: An Encyclopedia of Explorers and Exploration*

BERLIN

The city of Berlin has long been a center of German political, economic, cultural, and intellectual life. Twice during the course of history it has served as the capital of a unified Germany.

Berlin first became the national capital in 1871, when the various German states were united into a single country. However, in the years that followed the defeat of the Nazi German regime in World War II (1939–45), Berlin—like Germany itself—was divided into two parts. East Berlin became the capital of East Germany (the German Democratic Republic), while West Berlin became one of the federal states of West Germany (the Federal Republic of Germany). During these years, the small university town of Bonn served as the capital of West Germany.

With the reunification of East and West Germany in 1990, however, the division of the city was ended, and Berlin once again became the official capital.

A sunny day draws Berliners to an outdoor café. In the background, the ruins of the old Kaiser Wilhelm Memorial Church stand as a stark reminder of the destruction of World War II.

Location, Area, and Population. Berlin is situated in northeastern Germany, on the Spree and Havel rivers. Its location has made it a traditional crossroads of trade between eastern and western and northern and southern Europe. Lying on the great sandy plain of the North German lowlands, the city has an average elevation of only about 112 feet (34 meters) above sea level.

Berlin makes up an urban area of about 441 square miles (1,142 square kilometers). With a population of nearly 3.5 million, it is the largest city in Germany and one of the ten largest cities in Europe. Yet the city's numerous parks, forests, lakes and other waterways give some of its districts a rustic, or country-like, setting.

Places of Interest. In the center of the former West Berlin the ruined tower of the Kaiser Wilhelm Memorial Church stands as a stark reminder of the destruction of World War II. Next to it is the new, modernistic church building, completed in 1961. The two structures are situated at the eastern end of the Kurfürstendamm, an elegant avenue of fashionable shops, restaurants, and theaters.

The reconstructed Reichstag, the old parliament building, is a landmark of historical importance. The original building was burned in 1933, soon after the Nazis took power. The present German parliament (or legislature) meets there on festive public occasions. Nearby is a Soviet war memorial, the Tiergarten, and the new Congress Hall. The Tiergarten, a park near the center of the city with a zoo and aquarium, is especially popular with Berliners. Other new buildings include the Berlin Philharmonic concert hall, the opera house, and several museums.

For years the wall that divided the city attracted millions of visitors. It was torn down in 1990, and all that remains of this relic of the Cold War is a swath of open space.

The Brandenburg Gate, one of Berlin's best-known monuments, is situated in the historic center of the city, in what was formerly East Berlin. A triumphal arch some 85 feet (26 meters) high, it faces the Tiergarten and stands at the western end of a tree-lined boulevard, Unter den Linden ("Under the Linden Trees"). This thoroughfare was once the site of military parades and the funeral processions of German rulers. Most of the government buildings, palaces, and foreign embassies that at one time lined the avenue were destroyed during World War II, but those that could be saved were restored.

At the eastern end of Unter den Linden is a giant square, which the East Germans named Marx-Engels-Platz, after the two major figures in the founding of Communism. It is also the site of the former royal palace. The huge Palace of the Republic, which once housed the East German parliament, stands nearby. Numerous museums are located on the appropriately named Museum Island.

Cultural Life. Berlin has been a cultural center of Germany for much of its modern history. During the Weimer period (1919–33), it was the entertainment capital of the world. Its numerous cabarets, theaters, and motion pictures enjoyed an international reputation, lost during the Nazi era that followed.

Top: East German border guards looked on calmly in 1989 as West Germans celebrated the coming reunification of the long-divided city. A reunited Berlin was soon followed by the reunification of Germany itself. *Right:* A poster for the German silent film classic *Metropolis* dates from 1926, when Berlin was famed as the popular entertainment capital of the world. *Far right:* This war memorial was dedicated to the thousands of Soviet troops killed in the 1945 battle for Berlin.

The city's division into eastern and western sectors from 1949 to 1990 meant that each developed its own distinct cultural life. Attempts were made, however, to preserve a common heritage. The great pre-war museum collections, for example, were divided between East and West Berlin's museums.

Berlin has recaptured some of its past glory through its Philharmonic Orchestra concerts, opera houses, theater groups, a yearly cultural festival, and jazz and rock performances. The Free University and Humboldt University play an important role in the city's intellectual life. Its many museums include the world-famous Pergamon Museum, noted for its collection of classical art.

The Economy. Before World War II, Berlin was a center of commerce and banking as well as an important industrial city. By the 1950's, West Berlin had recovered from the war's destruction and was in the midst of an economic boom. At the same time, East Berlin was integrated into the Communist economic system of East Germany. The standard of living was considerably higher in the West than in the East.

The major industries in the Greater Berlin area involve the production of electrical and electronic equipment, machinery and motor vehicles, engineering products, processed foods, chemicals, and clothing. The city also has the largest number of scientific and technological research institutions in the country.

Since the reunification of Germany in 1990, the federal government has provided substantial economic assistance to the former eastern sector.

The City's Origins. The city of Berlin developed out of two small trading settlements, Kölln and Berlin, which are first mentioned in documents of the 1200's. The two settlements merged in the 1300's. In 1486, Berlin became the seat of the electors (or rulers) of what was then the small state of Brandenburg. The Thirty Years' War (1618–48) laid waste to the city, but it was rebuilt by the Great Elector Frederick William.

Capital. In 1701, Berlin became the capital of the kingdom of Prussia, which had grown out of the original core of Brandenburg. In spite of military occupation by foreign armies during the wars of the 1700's and 1800's, Berlin, along with Prussia, grew steadily in importance. When the German states united around Prussia to form the German Empire in 1871, Berlin became its capital.

During World War II, much of Berlin was destroyed by bombing and in the

Above: Berlin was divided among the four victorious Allied powers in 1945, at the end of World War II. In 1949 the U.S., British, and French sectors were joined to form West Berlin. The Soviet sector became East Berlin. The city remained divided until 1989–90. *Left:* When the Soviet Union blockaded West Berlin in 1948–49, cutting off all land access to that part of the city, its people were supplied through a massive airlift by U.S. and British planes.

As onlookers cheer, a young Berliner adds his own blows to the crumbling wall that for nearly thirty years had physically divided the city. Erected in 1961, the Berlin Wall was designed to stop the flood of Germans escaping from Communist East Germany to West Germany, which had become a drain on the East German economy. The wall was also a symbol of the division of Germany itself, which lasted until 1990, when both Germany and Berlin were again united.

heavy ground fighting that took place in the closing weeks of the war in Europe. On May 2, 1945, Soviet armies captured the city. By agreement, U.S., British, French, and Soviet forces each occupied a sector of Berlin (see map). Germany as a whole was divided along the same lines. The United States, Britain, and France occupied the western part of the country (which later became West Germany). The Soviet Union controlled the eastern part (later to become East Germany). Berlin itself lay deep within the Soviet area of occupation of Germany. An inter-Allied governing authority administered the city jointly.

Blockade and Airlift. In 1948, Berlin became a focal point of the Cold War, the period of hostility that developed between the Soviet Union and the nations of the West after the war. The Soviets informally withdrew from the governing authority and tried to force the Western powers to end controls over their three sectors. When this failed, the Soviets cut off all land and water communications between western Germany and the three western sectors of Berlin in an effort to gain control over the entire city.

In response, the Western Allies launched a massive airlift of food and other supplies to the isolated western sectors. The blockade lasted eleven months, until May 1949, when the Soviets, not having gained their objective, lifted it.

The City Divided. In 1949 separate East and West Germanys were established. The U.S., British, and French sectors of Berlin were joined to form West Berlin; the Soviet sector became East Berlin. But the four Allied powers still had final control over the city.

In 1953 a revolt by workers in East Berlin against the East German government was crushed by Soviet tanks. Increasing numbers of East Berliners fled to West Berlin in subsequent years, until 1961, when the East German authorities erected a fortified wall, physically separating the two parts of the city.

Reunification. The easing of political tensions and a new agreement between the Western Allies and the Soviet Union in 1971 eased travel restrictions for Germans. Nevertheless, the Berlin Wall remained a symbol of a divided city and nation for nearly twenty more years. In November 1989, however, following widespread protests by its own people, the East German government opened the guarded crossing points of the wall.

As East Berliners poured into West Berlin in celebration, the dismantling of the wall and of a divided Germany was already underway. On October 3, 1990, the two Germanys were united, the special privileges of the four powers ended, and a separate West and East Berlin ceased to exist.

GERARD BRAUNTHAL
University of Massachusetts, Amherst

BERLIN, IRVING (1888–1989)

The American songwriter Irving Berlin helped define the modern American popular song. During his long career he wrote some 1,500 songs. Many—"Always," "Blue Skies," "Puttin' on the Ritz," and countless others—have become classics, recorded again and again by new generations of singers.

Berlin was born Israel Baline in Tyumen, Russia, on May 11, 1888, the youngest of eight children. He moved with his family to New York City at the age of 5. He had barely begun school when his father died, and he sold newspapers and sang in the streets to help support his family. He learned to play piano by ear and began to compose melodies by trial and error. He became Irving Berlin when his first song was mistakenly credited to "I. Berlin," and he decided to change his first name as well.

In 1909, Berlin got a job writing lyrics for a music publisher; he became world famous two years later for writing "Alexander's Ragtime Band," which sold more than one million copies of sheet music. Berlin formed his own music company in 1919. During the 1920's the composer developed his unerring touch for

U.S. songwriter Irving Berlin entertained generations of Americans with his popular tunes.

ballads. In 1935 he wrote *Top Hat*, the first of many film scores. In 1939 he composed "God Bless America," which became one of the country's best-loved patriotic songs.

Among Berlin's greatest successes was the song "White Christmas," which won an Academy Award in 1942 and became a modern Christmas carol. He also wrote hit Broadway musicals, notably *Annie Get Your Gun* (1946), with its rousing showstopper, "There's No Business Like Show Business."

Berlin's last major work was the Broadway show *Mr. President* (1962). He died in New York City on September 22, 1989, at 101 years of age.

Reviewed by CHARLES MORITZ
Editor, *Current Biography*

BERLIOZ, HECTOR (1803–1869)

Louis-Hector Berlioz, an innovative French composer, was born near Grenoble, France, on December 11, 1803. Because of pressure from his father, a physician, Hector went to Paris in 1821 to enroll in medical school. While there he attended many opera performances. He also studied music at the Paris Conservatory.

In 1824 the young student abandoned medical studies but continued to compose music. When his parents refused to support him, Hector taught music lessons and wrote articles. He completed his most individual work, *Symphonie fantastique*, in 1830. That year he also won a prestigious music prize that required him to live in Italy.

After his return to Paris in 1832, Berlioz met the Irish actress Harriet Smithson, whom he married the following year. Because his unusual compositions failed to win any recognition in France, Berlioz was forced to earn a

living as a music librarian and by writing essays and music criticism.

Finally, Berlioz did begin to win fame outside France. In 1843 he made a triumphant tour of Germany, conducting his own compositions. He had equally successful tours to Austria, Hungary, Russia, and England.

In Paris, though, his genius continued to go unrecognized. His great opera, *The Trojans at Carthage*, was only a partial success at its first performance in 1863. Discouraged, Berlioz stopped composing and writing. He died in Paris on March 8, 1869.

Since then his reputation has steadily grown. Berlioz is now regarded as one of the world's foremost composers, one of the first great orchestral conductors, and a very skilled writer on musical topics.

Reviewed by MARGERY MORGAN LOWENS
Peabody Conservatory of Music
The Johns Hopkins University

Bermuda is made up of many small islands situated in the western Atlantic Ocean. Their mild, sunny climate and natural beauty make the islands popular with vacationers, most of whom come from the United States.

BERMUDA

Bermuda, or the Bermudas, is a group of about 300 coral islands situated in the western Atlantic Ocean, about 670 miles (1,075 kilometers) southeast of Cape Hatteras, North Carolina. Most of the islands are small and only about 20 are inhabited. Also called Somers Islands, Bermuda is a British crown colony. The islands' natural beauty and their mild, sunny climate have made tourism the most important economic activity. Most vacationers come from the nearby United States.

The People. Bermuda has a population of about 58,000. About two thirds of the people are of black African or mixed ancestry, descendants of slaves brought to the islands in the 1700's. White Bermudians are largely of British ancestry. English is the official language. Most of the people are Christians, with the Anglican Church the largest Protestant denomination. The capital is Hamilton.

Part of the islands' charm is the unhurried tempo of life. Until 1946 automobiles were not permitted, horse-drawn carriages and bicycles being used instead. Even today the size and number of automobiles are limited.

The Land. Shaped roughly like a fishhook, Bermuda has a land area of about 21 square miles (54 square kilometers). The largest island, Bermuda (or Main Island), the site of Hamilton, is about 14 miles (23 kilometers) long. It is connected by causeways and bridges with other important islands. There are no natural lakes or streams, and Bermudians are dependent on collected rainwater for drinking.

The Gulf Stream gives Bermuda an unusually mild climate for a region so far north of the equator, allowing palm trees and other tropical vegetation to flourish. The average yearly temperature is about 70°F (21°C). Ocean breezes keep the summers from being oppressively hot.

Economy. Tourism, the mainstay of the economy, accounts for about half of Bermuda's income and provides about 65 percent of all employment. Some crops are grown for local use, and cut flowers, particularly Easter lilies, are cultivated for export. There is some light industry, chiefly ship repairing, boat building, and the manufacture of pharmaceu-

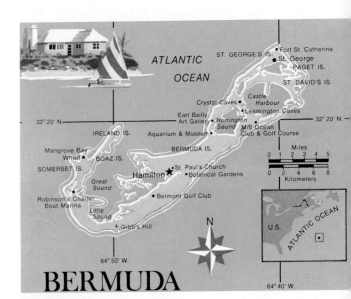

BERMUDA

ticals (medical drugs). Ship registry, finance, and insurance have become important sectors of the economy. Bermuda must import much of its food, fuel, and other necessities.

History and Government. The islands take their names from two ships' commanders—the Spaniard Juan de Bermúdez, who first sighted the islands in the 1500's; and Sir George Somers, whose ship, carrying English colonists to Virginia, was shipwrecked there in 1609. The first permanent English settlement of the then-uninhabited islands was made in 1612, at St. George. In 1815 the capital was transferred to Hamilton. The tourist industry developed in the 1900's. In 1941, during World War II, the British granted the United States a 99-year lease for naval and air bases on the islands. Several hundred U.S. military personnel are stationed on the islands.

Bermuda's constitution, which was amended in 1979, gives the colony considerable self-government. The British monarch is represented by an appointed governor, who is responsible for the islands' foreign affairs, de-

WONDER QUESTION

What is the Bermuda Triangle?

It is a triangular area of the Atlantic Ocean, with Bermuda, southern Florida, and Puerto Rico making up its approximate corners. It is also known, more ominously, as the Devil's Triangle, because of the numerous ships and airplanes that reportedly have vanished in the region, usually without trace. Some authors have sought to explain the disappearances as due to mysterious weather conditions in the area of the triangle. But this has not been borne out by any evidence.

fense, and police. The legislature consists of an appointed Senate and an elected House of Assembly. The leader of the majority party in the assembly serves as prime minister.

Reviewed by THOMAS G. MATHEWS
Secretary General, Association of Caribbean
Universities and Research Institutes

BERNINI, GIOVANNI LORENZO (1598–1680)

The sculptor, painter, and architect Giovanni Lorenzo Bernini was Italy's leading artist during the 1600's. His works, which include many of Rome's buildings, statues, and fountains, greatly influenced the development of Italian art of the baroque period.

The strong and graceful lines in the statue of King Louis XIV of France show both Bernini's technical skill and his ability to produce dramatic effects.

Bernini was born on December 7, 1598, in Naples. His father, a sculptor, received a commission from the pope and moved his family to Rome about 1605. Except for a short trip to Paris in 1665, Bernini spent his entire life in Rome. In 1639 he married Caterina Tezio; they had eleven children.

At 20, Bernini received his first important commission: a series of statues for the villa of Cardinal Borghese. Among them is the famous *David*. This figure, with its dramatic pose and expressive, flowing lines, sums up the ideals of the baroque style. Another of his great sculptures is the *Ecstasy of St. Teresa*, in the Cornaro chapel.

Some of Bernini's most powerful works were created for St. Peter's Basilica, including the square in front of the church, with its stately rows of columns and 162 statues.

Bernini died on November 28, 1680. He had been a painter, theatrical designer, and decorator. But he remains most famous for his sculpture and architecture.

Reviewed by HOWARD HIBBARD
Columbia University

BERNOULLI FAMILY

The Bernoulli family included several generations of prominent mathematicians and scientists. Because of religious persecution, the family fled Holland in 1583 and eventually settled in Switzerland. From the late 1600's to the mid-1700's, the Bernoulli family dominated European mathematics. The three most famous members of the family were Jakob I, Johann I, and Daniel. (Several Bernoullis had the same first names, so Roman numerals are often used to distinguish among them.) Jakob I and Johann I were the sons of Nikolas Bernoulli, a minor local official in Basel. Daniel was the son of Johann I.

Jakob (I) Bernoulli (1654–1705), the first member of the family to gain fame as a mathematician, was born in Basel, Switzerland. Jakob received a theology degree in 1676, but his real interest was mathematics. He traveled in Europe until 1683. Then he devoted his time to giving lectures, writing papers, and teaching himself more about mathematics. In 1687 he became professor of mathematics at the University of Basel, a position he held until his death. While at Basel, Jakob played an important part in developing both differential and integral calculus. His main contribution was showing how calculus could be applied to problems in many fields. Jakob also advanced the field of probability. A mathematical dispute with his brother Johann I led to their developing the calculus of variations.

Johann (I) Bernoulli (1667–1748), brother of Jakob I, received a degree in medicine from the University of Basel in 1694. He was drawn to mathematics as well, and in 1695 he gave up medicine to teach mathematics at the University of Groningen in the Netherlands. He returned to Basel after the death of his brother in 1705 and became professor of mathematics at the university. Johann's contributions to mathematics were greater than those of Jakob I. He became known for his work in both differential and integral calculus. He is also considered a cofounder, with his brother, of the calculus of variations. Johann's interests also extended to other fields, including physics, chemistry, and astronomy, and he sought to apply mathematical principles to these subjects.

Daniel Bernoulli (1700–82), son of Johann I, was born in Groningen. Of all the Bernoullis, he was perhaps the greatest mathematician. Daniel also had the widest interests, which included medicine, biology, physics, mechanics, and astronomy. Daniel originally planned a career in business and medicine. Like other family members, however, he was drawn to the field of mathematics. Between 1725 and 1732, he taught mathematics at the Academy of Sciences in St. Petersburg, Russia. He then went to the University of Basel, where he taught anatomy, botany, and then physics. Daniel's most important work was in mechanics. He was a founder of the science of hydrodynamics, the study of moving fluids. One of his main contributions in this area is Bernoulli's Principle, which states that the pressure in a fluid decreases as its velocity, or speed, increases. (This principle is explained in the article AERODYNAMICS in Volume A.) Daniel is also noted for his work in calculus and probability theory, especially as it applies to games. He is also considered one of the founders of the kinetic theory of gases, which helps explain the property and behavior of gases. Between 1725 and 1749, Daniel won many prizes for his work on astronomy, gravity, tides, magnetism, and ocean currents.

Several other Bernoullis were gifted mathematicians and scientists. **Nikolaus II** (1687–1759), nephew of Jakob I and Johann I, taught at many universities, including Padua and Basel. He was known for his work in probability theory. **Nikolaus III** (1695–1726), son of Johann I and brother of Daniel, also made contributions in probability theory while teaching at the Academy of Sciences in St. Petersburg, Russia. **Johann II** (1710–90), another son of Johann I, succeeded his father as professor of mathematics at Basel. He is known for his contribution to theories of heat and light. **Johann III** (1746–1807), son of Johann II, was known for his work in science. He became the royal astronomer at the Berlin Academy. **Jakob II** (1759–89), another son of Johann II, succeeded his uncle Daniel as professor of mathematics and physics at the Academy of Sciences in St. Petersburg. **Christoph** (1782–1863), grandson of Johann II and nephew of Johann III and Jakob II, was a naturalist who taught at the University of Basel.

Reviewed by BRYAN BUNCH
Coauthor, *The Timetables of Science*

BERRA, YOGI. See MISSOURI (Famous People).
BERRIES. See GRAPES AND BERRIES.
BERRY, CHUCK. See ROCK MUSIC (Profiles).

BESSEMER, SIR HENRY (1813–1898)

The industrial city of Bessemer, Alabama, is named in honor of Sir Henry Bessemer, the English inventor who made the steel industry possible. In 1855 and 1856 he patented a method of purifying iron so that it could be made into steel cheaply and easily. This method, called the Bessemer process, and a machine called the Bessemer converter are still used in steel manufacturing.

Henry Bessemer was born January 19, 1813, in the village of Charlton in southern England. His father, also an inventor, had a factory there for casting type. Young Henry spent his spare time in his father's workshop, learning to make use of his natural mechanical ability.

When he was 17 years old, Bessemer went to London, where he cast metal into artistic figures that were exhibited by the Royal Academy. Then he turned to embossing designs on cards and cloth. In 1833 he invented a method of canceling tax stamps so that they could not be used again.

During his busy life Bessemer worked out and patented 114 inventions. One of the most profitable was a method of making gold paint. The money from this invention enabled him to experiment and develop his steelmaking process, his most important invention.

The Bessemer process practically created the modern steel industry. Before the invention of this process, steel could be made only in small batches. As a result, it was very expensive. Bessemer's discovery made possible large-scale production of steel. It has been ranked with printing, the magnetic compass, and the steam engine as an invention that changed the world.

In 1879, Bessemer was knighted in reward for his tax-stamp canceling process. He died in London on March 15, 1898.

Reviewed by DAVID C. COOKE
Author, *Inventions That Made History*
See also IRON AND STEEL.

BETHUNE, MARY MCLEOD (1875–1955)

Mary McLeod Bethune rose from poverty to become a famous educator, a leader of women, and an adviser to presidents. She was born on July 10, 1875, near the small town of Mayesville, South Carolina. Her parents, Patsy and Sam McLeod, were recently freed slaves who made their living as farmers.

Even after the Civil War ended, there were not many schools for African American children in the South. Mary was 11 years old before a mission school was opened in Mayesville. She completed her education at the Moody Bible Institute in Chicago. When she was turned down for a post as a missionary in Africa, she went home to the South to teach. After her marriage to Albertus Bethune, a teacher, she moved to Florida. In 1904, she opened a school for African American girls in Daytona Beach.

The Daytona Normal and Industrial Institute for Negro Girls was only a shack, but its goals were high. The school's motto, "Enter to learn, depart to serve," described the aim of its founder, which was to educate girls to become teachers.

The early years of the school were difficult. Mary Bethune raised money by selling food to winter visitors in Daytona Beach. Before long, the institute received donations that made it possible to add a high school, a small hospital, and then a college. The institute was merged with a boys' school in 1923 and became Bethune-Cookman College in 1925.

In 1935, Mary Bethune founded the National Council of Negro Women. She helped President Franklin D. Roosevelt start the National Youth Administration, which provided employment for young people. She was a member of the President's unofficial "Black Cabinet," which advised him on ways to improve conditions for African Americans. During World War II, she served as a special assistant to the secretary of war to help end discrimination in the armed services.

The last years of Mary Bethune's life brought her many honors and awards. She died in Daytona Beach on May 18, 1955.

DANIEL S. DAVIS
Author, *Struggle for Freedom:
The History of Black Americans*

BHUTAN

The tiny kingdom of Bhutan lies high in the Himalaya mountains of South Asia. For most of its history, it was a forgotten and seldom-visited part of the world. Even today much of Bhutan remains largely undeveloped and remote from modern life.

▶ THE PEOPLE

The Bhotes (or Bhotias), who are related to the people of neighboring Tibet, make up a majority of Bhutan's population. They speak Dzongkha, a Tibetan dialect, and practice a form of Buddhism known as Lamaism, or Tibetan Buddhism. A few Bhutanese still follow the old religion of Bon—the worship of things in nature—that was common before the arrival of Buddhism. The Nepalese, who live in the south, are immigrants from the nearby country of Nepal. They practice the Hindu religion and speak Nepali.

Most Bhutanese are farmers or animal herders; others are skilled artisans. Settlements often cluster around a *dzong* (a fortresslike monastery). The people are extremely isolated, and travel is difficult in all parts of the country. There are no railroads and only a few good roads.

There are few towns; the largest is Thimbu, the capital. Most of the people live in widely scattered villages. A typical village house consists of a two-story building made of stone or mud-brick. The family lives on the upper floor, while farm animals occupy the lower floor. The yak, a long-haired ox, is the main beast of burden.

In the past, fewer than one person in a hundred in Bhutan could read and write. To correct this, the government has built elementary schools and is planning more. Most of the teachers come from India, which is helping to develop Bhutan. Most children of well-to-do Bhutanese attend school in India.

▶ THE LAND

In Bhutan the snowy Himalaya peaks and mountain highlands tower only a short distance away from dense jungles and valleys lush with rice fields. There are three distinct land regions—the High Himalayan region in the north, the Inner Himalayan region in central Bhutan, and the Duars plain in the south.

The High Himalayan region borders China. Many peaks in this part of Bhutan belong to

Towering mountains, lush valleys, and dense jungles make up the varied landscape of Bhutan. Most of its people live in the high, fertile valleys of central Bhutan.

the Great Himalayan range, which tower as high as 24,000 feet (7,300 meters). Even the lowest part of the region is more than half that height above sea level. Except for a few scattered Buddhist monasteries, the Great Himalayas are uninhabited.

Most Bhutanese live in the valleys of the Inner Himalayan region. These valleys can reach 8,000 feet (2,400 meters) above sea level. Rainfall is moderate, and the valleys are broad, fertile, and healthful. Paro, the former capital, and Thimbu, the new and still-developing capital, are both found here.

South of the Inner Himalayan region is a narrow strip of the Duars plain. The plain must be crossed to reach the narrow valleys that lead through the jungle-covered Himalayan foothills into the valleys of central Bhutan. The southern part of the Duars plain is covered with tall grass and bamboo. The north is rugged and heavily forested. There are many wild animals. Few people live on the Duars plain because of the heavy rainfall, dense vegetation, and malaria-ridden swamps.

The climate of Bhutan is as varied as the land. The high elevation gives the northern interior bitterly cold winters. But the lowlands of southern Bhutan have a humid, tropical climate throughout the year.

▶THE ECONOMY

Bhutan's economy is based on farming. Most farms are in the fertile valleys of the Inner Himalayas. The land is cultivated in a

BHUTAN

Rice   Wheat

series of terraces, each terrace bordered by a stone embankment. Rice and wheat are grown in the valleys and on the lower slopes. Rice is the country's leading export. Vast forests make timber an important resource.

Yaks, sheep, and goats are raised in all parts of Bhutan. The yak, besides being used as a beast of burden, provides meat, milk, and hides. Yak hair is used to make blankets. A creamy, yogurtlike cheese is prepared from yak milk.

▶HISTORY AND GOVERNMENT

Little is known about Bhutan's early history. According to old Tibetan manuscripts preserved in Buddhist monasteries, about 300 years ago a Tibetan lama, or priest, named Sheptoon La-Pha became the first man to proclaim himself king of Bhutan. During the 1700's and 1800's, the *penlops* (regional governors) acquired great power, and the king became a figurehead. In 1907 the most powerful of the *penlops*, Ugyen Wangchuk, became king. His descendants have continued as rulers of Bhutan. The present king, Jigme Singye Wangchuk, came to the throne in 1972.

Bhutan has no constitution, but it does have a legislative body, the Tshongdu, or National Assembly. Most of its members are elected directly by the people for 3-year terms; some seats are reserved for religious organizations; and the remaining members are appointed by the government. The king is assisted by the Royal Advisory Council and by the Council of Ministers, which serves as a kind of cabinet. In its foreign affairs, Bhutan traditionally has been guided by India.

P. P. KARAN
University of Kentucky

FACTS and figures

KINGDOM OF BHUTAN is the official name of the country.

LOCATION: South Asia.

AREA: 18,000 sq mi (46,620 km²).

POPULATION: 1,600,000 (estimate).

CAPITAL AND LARGEST CITY: Thimbu.

MAJOR LANGUAGES: Dzongkha (official), Nepali.

MAJOR RELIGIOUS GROUPS: Buddhist, Hindu.

GOVERNMENT: Monarchy. **Head of state and government**—king. **Legislature**—Tshongdu (National Assembly).

CHIEF PRODUCTS: Agricultural—rice, wheat, and other grains; fruit; livestock. **Manufactured**—handicrafts, processed food, timber, textiles.

MONETARY UNIT: Ngultrum (1 ngultrum = 100 chetrum).

BHUTTO, BENAZIR (1953–)

Benazir Bhutto was the first woman to head the government of a Muslim country. She inherited the political mission and passion of her father, Zulfikar Ali Bhutto, former Pakistani president and prime minister, and is the leader of the party he founded, the Pakistan People's Party (P.P.P.).

Benazir Bhutto was born in Karachi on June 21, 1953, into a wealthy landowning family that had been prominent in politics for three generations. She was educated at Radcliffe College in the United States and Oxford University in England, graduating with honors from Oxford in 1976. Soon after her return to Pakistan in 1977, her father was ousted as prime minister in a military coup. He was imprisoned and later executed.

Benazir, who had assumed with her mother, Nusrat, leadership of the P.P.P., spent most of the next four years under house arrest. In 1984 she went into exile in England. After military rule ended in Pakistan, she returned home in 1986 to popular acclaim. In 1988 elections, the P.P.P. won the largest number

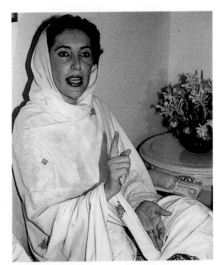

of seats and she became prime minister. Accused of corruption, she was removed from office in 1990. But she returned as prime minister after her party's strong showing in the elections of 1993.

In her domestic policy, Bhutto worked to free women from the restraints of traditional Pakistani society. In international affairs she refused to give up Pakistan's nuclear weapons development and signed an arms agreement with China. She was dismissed again in 1996, and her party did not win a majority in the 1997 elections.

ARTHUR CAMPBELL TURNER
University of California, Riverside

BHUTTO, ZULFIKAR ALI (1928–1979)

The career of Zulfikar Ali Bhutto, former president and prime minister of Pakistan, was cut short by his death. But, coming to power at a critical time for his country, he forever changed the landscape of Pakistani politics.

Bhutto was born on January 5, 1928, in Larkana. His father, Sir Shahnawaz Khan Bhutto, was a distinguished figure in the politics of the period. Zulfikar received a degree in political science from the University of California, Berkeley, and a law degree from Oxford University. Returning home in 1956, he practiced law but soon became more interested in politics.

Bhutto served as a delegate to the United Nations and in 1958, at the age of 30, was named minister of commerce. With intelligence, administrative ability, and charm, he advanced rapidly. He became foreign minister in 1963 but resigned from the government in 1966 over policy differences. In 1967 he founded the Pakistan People's Party (P.P.P.), which was his permanent legacy.

The political crisis that resulted from the breakaway of East Pakistan (now Bangladesh) in 1971, following a civil war, helped propel Bhutto to power. Elected president in 1971, he became prime minister under a new constitution in 1973. He launched far-reaching reforms at home and made Pakistan strongly independent in its foreign relations. However, a certain ruthlessness about him alienated many people. This, added to accusations of corruption, brought his rule to an end in 1977, when the army, headed by General Mohammed Zia ul-Haq, seized power.

Bhutto was imprisoned, charged with conspiracy to murder an opponent, and condemned to death. In spite of international appeals to spare him, he was hanged in Rawalpindi on April 4, 1979. He became a martyr to his followers and to his daughter Benazir, who would succeed him.

ARTHUR CAMPBELL TURNER
University of California, Riverside

See also PAKISTAN (History).

BIBLE

The Bible, a collection of diverse books written in ancient times, is one of the world's most famous pieces of literature. The English word "Bible" comes from the Greek word *biblia,* meaning "books," and aptly describes this library of religious writings. The books form the sacred scripture of Jews, Christians, and, to some extent, Muslims. The Bible has had more influence on art, drama, language, and other literature than any other single collection of books. It has been translated into more languages and published in more editions than any other single collection, and it has remained a best seller up to modern times.

The Bible may be divided into three major sections: the Old Testament, the New Testament, and the Apocrypha. "Testament" comes from the Latin word *testamentum,* meaning "will," "covenant," or "agreement," and described for ancient Israelites and early Christians the type of relationship that they had with their God.

The Old Testament, composed of 39 books, makes up the sacred literature of Judaism. In addition, Christianity also accepts the 27 books of the New Testament. The remaining 14 books, called the Apocrypha, are sometimes referred to as the Inter-Testament, since they fall chronologically between the Old Testament and the New Testament. Acceptance of this part of the Bible has varied from time to time among Christian groups.

Transmission and Translation

How did these collections come down to us from ancient times? This handing down of Biblical materials is properly called transmission. Since the Old Testament is the earliest part of the Bible, its transmission must be considered first. Ancient Hebrews, whose literature this was, began to tell of their God and his relation to them long before they began to write. As a result, the material that finally became the Bible began in oral form. Around the campfires, at the village gates, and in religious services, this sacred history had its beginning. After a while some of the material was put into written form, and other material was written and added. The collections grew and were reworked through the centuries as men felt they had new insights from God or about God. Eventually "books" were put together and became fixed in written form. These were finally accepted as authoritative for religious use. The list of such accepted books is called canon (from a word meaning "rule"). The making of such a list is called canonization and took place at various times for various books or collections of books. Since the apocryphal books were never accepted by Judaism, they did not form part of the official canon in the Hebrew Bible.

Transmission of the New Testament was considerably different. The reason is that by the time Christianity began, the civilized world was using written language as a means of communication. As a result, the stories about the life and ministry of Jesus, the missionary work of the Apostles, letters to churches, and similar material soon spread all over the Roman Empire in written form. In the course of time, individual collections of these materials were made, books were formed, and eventually the whole collection known as the New Testament came into being and was accepted as canonical by the early Christian Church. There is also a New Testament Apocrypha, but it has never been widely used by Christians because of the high esteem in which the canonical books were held.

Hebrew, except for some Aramaic in Ezra and Daniel, was the language in which the

Old Testament was written. The New Testament books were recorded in Greek ("everyday," or *koinē,* Greek). How did the Bible get into English, then, along with so many other languages? This, of course, came about through translations, called versions, from the original Hebrew and Greek. Thus there are as many versions of the Bible as there are translations of it. Some of these have become very famous. They were either very early, in a language that had a wide use, or became the Bible for a particular group.

Earliest translations were obviously of the Old Testament. Probably the most important of these was the Greek translation called the Septuagint. The name of this translation, meaning "seventy," was derived from the tradition that it had been done by 70 scholars (actually 72—6 from each tribe of Israel) at the request of one of the Ptolemies of Egypt in the 3rd century B.C. About a century earlier the Samaritans, who also followed Jewish law, had made a translation of the first five books of the Hebrew Bible (the Pentateuch). In the early Christian period, another important translation, called the *Peshitta,* was made from the Hebrew Bible by Syriac-speaking Christians. Jewish scholars likewise made translations for popular use (more properly a paraphrase with commentary) called the *Targumim,* in Aramaic.

Early Christians had adopted the Greek version of the Old Testament because it could be understood by most of them. After a while, however, a need was felt to have both the Old Testament and the New Testament in the language that was becoming more widely used—Latin. One very early Latin translation was made (using the Greek Old Testament for that part of the Bible), called the Old Latin, or Itala. The most famous early Christian translation, however, was that made by Saint Jerome in the early 4th century A.D. Since this was in the common ("vulgar") language of the day, the version is still called the Vulgate. Jerome used both the Hebrew and Greek versions for his translation. The Church accepted Jerome's translation, and it became the official version of the Bible, although the older Latin translation of certain books continued in use. The most famous edition of this version is the Sixtine edition, done at the order of Pope Sixtus V in 1590.

Christian missionaries had also gone to all parts of the ancient world and carried the Bible with them. In many places the Hebrew, Greek, and Latin versions were translated into the language of the people among whom they worked. As a result, translations appeared in Arabic, Gothic, Coptic, Ethiopic, Armenian, and a myriad of other languages.

All these translations were written by hand. When the printing press was invented about 1450, the production of individual translations of the Bible, as well as editions in the original languages, was tremendously advanced. In the 16th century the Christian Church was divided into Roman Catholic and Protestant branches by the Church dispute called the Reformation. From that time both Catholics and Protestants began to make their own translations independently.

Many printed editions of the Bible appeared. Of them, the German translation (1522–32) of Martin Luther set the pattern for many others. Just about the same time, an English printed edition was issued by William Tyndale but was quickly suppressed by the authorities in England. About 1535, however, Myles Coverdale published an English translation, probably in Zurich. This time the Church was less opposed to a "popular" version, and Coverdale's Bible became widely read. A whole series of English Bibles then began to appear, with the names of translators (Matthew's Bible, Taverner's Bible) or of the cities of publication (the Geneva Bible) or even with descriptive titles (the Great Bible, because of its size) to identify them. Finally an approved Bible called the Bishops' Bible (a revision of the Geneva Bible) was published in England in 1568.

In France a group of English-speaking Roman Catholics also felt the need for a translation of the official Latin version of the Bible. As a result, an English translation of the Vulgate was completed between 1582 and 1610 and is still known as the Rheims-Douai Version, in honor of the two cities in which it was done.

King James I called a conference at Hampton Court in 1604 in an effort to reconcile the religious parties of England. Out of this conference came the King James Version of the Bible, published in 1611. This is perhaps the best-known English Bible and has continued in use up to the present time. It was supposed to be only a revision of the Bishops' Bible, but other editions and newly discovered manuscripts in the original languages were also used.

As English changed and more new copies of ancient Biblical manuscripts (texts) were found, revisions of the King James Version were made from time to time. The English Revised Edition was completed in 1881; the American Revised Edition (or American Standard Version) appeared in 1901; and the Revised Standard Version was published between 1946 and 1952. At the same time a great number of independent translations were made of all, or part, of the Bible. These include many translations into modern speech as well as many versions for special use.

OLD TESTAMENT

In Hebrew the Old Testament is divided into three parts: the Law, the Prophets, and the Writings. These divisions are not followed exactly in the English Bible but make the contents of the Old Testament easier to summarize. Traditionally attributed to Moses, the first five books of the Old Testament make up the Law, or Pentateuch. In Hebrew they are named after the first word of each book, but in English the names are derived from the Greek Bible: Genesis, Exodus, Leviticus, Numbers, and Deuteronomy. These books trace the relationship of man to God, in a series of agreements, beginning with creation, through the division of people into nations, to the days of Abraham. Then the record of the special relation of the Hebrews to God is told, from the time of Abraham's call by God into the land of Canaan.

Abraham and his descendants, the patriarchs, traveled through Canaan until the family of Joseph finally entered Egypt. There they were ultimately enslaved, made their escape under Moses (the Exodus), and fled to the Sinai Peninsula, between the Mediterranean Sea and the Red Sea. At Mount Sinai the people, now properly called Israelites, received the Law from God and prepared to enter the Promised Land. Because of arguments among some of the people, they were all forced to wander for 40 years in the desert wilderness. At the end of that time the Israelites were permitted to enter Palestine under the leadership of Joshua.

This group of five books contains a great variety of literary styles and types. Some of the stories illustrate great religious truths: the creation, the fall of man, the flood, the Tower of Babel, the Passover and Exodus, the giving of the tablets of the Law, and other short narratives. Certain of the books contain great poetry: the Song of Lamech, the Blessings of the Patriarchs, the Song of Moses, and the Blessing of Moses. Others tell about specific people: Noah and his scoffing neighbors, Abraham's faith, Lot's inquisitive wife, the cunning of Jacob, and the frustration of Balaam when all his curses against Israel became blessings. The land, the nations, and the local customs are also described: the wilderness experience, the fire and smoke at Mount Sinai, the varied inhabitants of Canaan, the building of the Ark of the Covenant, the casting of metals and weaving of cloth, the marriage of Rebecca and Isaac, and other details of everyday living. In addition, long lists of ancestors and descendants, codes of law, rules for festivals and sacred ceremonies, are also presented. Yet with all this diversity, the entire Pentateuch is held together by the religious faith that the God of Israel cared for his people, from the first man to the birth of the Israelite nation, and that He had made a covenant, or agreement, with that people. Obedience to the covenant brought Israel to the promised land, but disobedience to its terms brought disaster.

Next in the Hebrew Bible is the group of books called the Prophets because it contains those books that the Jews considered to be the work of men speaking for God. The word "prophet" comes from the Greek word *prophetes,* "one who speaks forth." This division of the Bible is composed of the Former Prophets—Joshua, Judges, I and II Samuel, I and II Kings; and the Latter Prophets—Isaiah, Jeremiah, Ezekiel, and the Book of the Twelve. This last "book" contains the books of Hosea, Joel, Amos, Obadiah, Jonah, Micah, Nahum, Habakkuk, Zephaniah, Haggai, Zechariah, and Malachi. Some books that are generally found among the prophetical books in the English Bible are not included in the Hebrew Bible under that title but are placed among the Writings. Certain of the prophetic books also have slightly different names in the Hebrew and Greek Bibles and in the versions used by Roman Catholics and Protestants.

The Former Prophets are books that consider the history of Israel from the conquest of Canaan under Joshua down to the release from prison of Jehoiachin, Israel's last king, by the Babylonian king, Evilmerodach, in about 561 B.C. Here, then, is the great story of the wars fought, the settlement of the land, the rise of the monarchy under Saul, the history of King David, Solomon's reign and the building of the first Temple, the split of the united monarchy into the kingdoms of Israel in the north and Judah in the south, the fall of Jerusalem, and the Babylonian exile.

This part of the Bible is probably the most interesting to read as literature because it is a connective history and contains stirring tales of battles, stories of great people, the life of David, and tales of court intrigues and plots. It also tells of the sad downfall of the two kingdoms of Judah and Israel. Also, since Hebrew literature was in its classical period at this time, one can find some of the best examples of both poetry and prose.

The Latter Prophets are less easy to summarize, since each has its own specific message. Isaiah, Jeremiah, and Ezekiel make up the Major, or Greater, books because they are the longer ones in this section of the Bible. Historically these prophets span the period from King Uzziah in the 8th century B.C., to the time of the exile during the 6th century B.C. Isaiah is concerned with the religious and political problems of Judah in his day as relations with Assyria became more and more difficult for the people. A great promise of new hope for Israel has been added to Isaiah's words (Deutero-Isaiah) as a fitting climax to his book. Isaiah's "call" to prophecy (Chapter 6) is one of the most impressive accounts in ancient Hebrew literature.

Jeremiah lived at the end of the monarchial period, during the trying days of the destruction of the city of Jerusalem. He, too, speaks against the religious and social decay of his own day, but gives to the people going into exile the promise of a new covenant. God, says Jeremiah, has now made a covenant with Israel that shall not be kept on tablets of stone, but shall be in the heart of every man, no matter where he goes. This was a message of great hope to a people saddened by the loss of their great city and forced to live in a strange land.

Ezekiel might be called the planner of Judaism because he gave to the Israelites in exile a plan whereby they could keep their faith alive in times of strife and struggle. With the writings of Ezekiel, the religion of Israel became known as Judaism and was closely linked with the Law and the Temple. The God of Israel became known as the Holy One in Israel, and Jews tried to honor this holiness by strict observance of the proper religious ritual and duties.

Not less important, however, are the Minor, or Lesser, Prophets. Their books are just "smaller in size," the meaning of the Latin word *minor* used to describe them. In the Hebrew Bible the Book of the Twelve just fills one scroll of writing material, so these prophetical books have been put together for that reason. Here, again, each prophet has his own particular message, and each is a separate book in itself. Amos is really the oldest of the prophetic writers and is the first literary, or written, prophet. Amos, Hosea, and Micah all preach against the social, political, and religious abuses of their individual periods, and each one declares that God will punish His people for their evil. Nahum, Zephaniah, and Habakkuk give their attention to specific foes of Israel—the Assyrians, the Scythians, and the Neo-Babylonians—and use those threats to the nation to stress the need for the people to trust and obey God. A little later, in the 6th century B.C., the prophet Obadiah uses the example of the fall of Edom, one of Israel's neighbors, to illustrate the action of God in the world and to stress hope for the future of his own people. Jonah, with the famous story of the great fish, urges the Jews, now restored to their homeland, to reform themselves. In the same way, the prophets Haggai, Zechariah, and Malachi speak to the new generation. In Haggai religious duty is centered upon the rebuilding of the Temple, and in Zechariah there is hope offered of a better age to come. In Joel, the last book among the prophets in terms of date, hope is again given to the people during a new time of national disaster.

Thus, the prophetical books of the Old Testament furnish a great array of religious ideas, individual styles and approaches, and relate to many historical situations. From these books have come many of the religious beliefs of Judaism and Christianity as well as many influences upon other literature through the ages. In English, for example, there are many expressions in common use today that have their origin in the Old Testament: "the fat of the land," "a man after his own heart," "the skin of my teeth," "one among a thousand," "angels' food," "eat, drink, and be merry," "see eye to eye," "holier than thou," "no new thing under the sun," "to every thing there is a season."

The final division of the Old Testament in the Hebrew Bible might be called Miscellaneous. In the section known as the Writings are those books that the Jewish leaders considered to be of religious worth but not of the same type as those of the other two divisions. Therefore, in this category are found Psalms, a collection of hymns or religious poems said to be composed by David; Proverbs, which gives helpful advice on everyday living; Job,

in which the whole meaning of human suffering is considered; The Song of Solomon, a love song, once seen to have religious application; Ruth, a story of deep personal devotion as well as a protest against racial bigotry; Lamentations, a series of sorrowful reflections concerning the exile and the sad plight of the people; Ecclesiastes, a book of "wisdom," or religious philosophy; Esther, which explains the festival of Purim; Daniel, a book of stories of heroes, which urges religious faithfulness in a time of oppression; I and II Chronicles, Ezra, and Nehemiah, which summarize Israel's history up to the exile and then give an account of the events that followed.

Here, again, the individual books of this part of the Bible are all different and each one has its own special characteristics. Likewise, each of these books has had its own influence upon religious thought and upon the literature of the world. Psalms, for example, has furnished the basis for many hymns still sung in places of worship; Job has provided much material for modern literature; Ruth and Esther have given the world two great heroines; while Daniel and his friends have found their place in folk songs, art, and in such popular quotations as "the handwriting on the wall" or "into the lions' den."

PHILIP C. HAMMOND
Princeton Theological Seminary

APOCRYPHA

The Apocrypha were written between the 3rd and 1st centuries B.C. Although they have come down to us in Greek, Latin, and other translations, including the English of the King James Bible that was published in 1611, fragments of the Apocrypha in the original Hebrew and Aramaic have been found among the Dead Sea Scrolls from the caves around Qumran, in northwest Jordan.

For Catholics most of the Apocryphal books are sacred. For Protestants and Jews the Apocrypha are respected as instructive writings, but not as divinely inspired.

Judaism between the 3rd century B.C. and the 1st century A.D. was split into many sects. The rabbis felt it necessary to put an end to the developments that were dividing the peo-

ple. They chose a simple way out. By excluding all books written after the fall of the Persian Empire in the 4th century B.C., the rabbis removed the authority of all the later writings that were splitting the community. This is why the Old Testament does not include any books that were thought to come from the period after Alexander's conquest in the 4th century B.C.

The Apocrypha begin with the First Book of Esdras. This book has to do with the return of the Jews from their Babylonian exile to Palestine in the days of the Old Testament leaders Ezra and Nehemiah. The most famous passage from this book is the tale of the Three Guardsmen (3:1—5:6), showing that truth is the most powerful force in the world.

The Second Book of Esdras justifies God's ways through divinely inspired visions.

The Book of Tobit is a story about virtue and love. It has enough magic to make the tale doubly interesting. The dog appears as man's pet and companion in Tobit for the first time in Jewish literature.

The Book of Judith is about the trials of the Hebrew people. The heroine Judith saves her people by cutting off the head of the enemy general, Holofernes.

There are six additions to the Book of Esther. These additions, examples of how reverent the Apocryphal books are, add religious tone to the Old Testament Book of Esther, which never even mentions the name of God.

The most important literary books in the Apocrypha are known as Wisdom Literature. This type of writing has as its aim the improvement of men through virtuous and sensible living so that they may be respected in society and successful in their careers. The first of these Apocryphal books is The Wisdom of

An 11th-century Psalter (Book of Psalms) in Greek.

An illuminated page, in Latin, from the Gutenberg Bible. Johann Gutenberg invented printing from movable type.

This page from a Hebrew Bible begins the history of the Israelites in Egypt.

Jeremiah

Jonah

Paintings of famous prophets are a part of Michelangelo's work in the Sistine Chapel, St. Peter's, Rome.

Zechariah

Isaiah

Ezekiel

Solomon, which praises "Lady Wisdom," not a woman of flesh and blood, but wisdom treated as a divine person. The author of The Wisdom of Solomon is not only interested in teaching wise principles. He wants, in addition, to save the people from uncivilized heathenism.

The other book of Wisdom Literature is in many ways the finest composition in the Apocrypha. It is called Ecclesiasticus or The Wisdom of Jesus, Son of Sirach ("Jesus" is simply the Greek form of the old Hebrew name "Joshua"). Ecclesiasticus is a practical as well as a reverent teacher. While he advises us to turn to God with piety and prayer to save us from misfortune and illness, he reminds us that physicians and medicines have been created by God for our benefit (38: 1–15). He praises the practice of justice and reminds us that good character brings rich rewards. Life is short but a good name endures forever. Ecclesiasticus ends his book by telling us, "Work your work betimes, and in his time he will give you your reward."

The Book of Baruch is supposed to come from the pen of Baruch, the secretary of the Prophet Jeremiah. Among the books of the Apocrypha, this one comes closest to Old Testament prophecy. It ends with an appendix, The Letter of Jeremiah, in which the prophet tells the Jewish exiles in Babylonia to avoid worshiping idols.

There are three additions to the Old Testament Book of Daniel. (1) The story of Susanna tells how Daniel saved Susanna from the false accusations of two evil elders. (2) The story of the Three Children tells about Shadrach, Meshach, and Abednego, who according to the Book of Daniel were thrown into the fiery furnace. It is typical of Apocryphal literature to fill gaps in the "authoritative books." Since the Book of Daniel does not tell us what happened to the three men after they were thrown into the fiery furnace, a later author took advantage of the opportunity to write this story. (3) The story of Baal and the Dragon tells how Daniel proved to the king of Babylon that idols are false and God is true.

The Prayer of Manasseh is supposed to be the prayer recited, according to the Biblical II Chronicles 33:18, by the repentant King Manasseh of Judah. This composition is of high religious and literary quality.

The Apocrypha end with First and Second Maccabees. First Maccabees, covering the years 167–134 B.C., is a reliable historic account of the Jewish war against Antiochus Epiphanes and the developments that followed. Antiochus, whose empire included Palestine, tried to force the Jews to conform to Greek culture at the expense of their ancestral religion. The Jews rebelled under the leadership of the Maccabean brothers. Their victory is still celebrated by the Jews during the feast of Hanukkah.

Second Maccabees is more emotional than First Maccabees and is concerned with its special kind of Jewish viewpoint. Second Maccabees covers the period 175–160 B.C. It is not a continuation of First Maccabees but another account covering some of the same years.

CYRUS H. GORDON
Brandeis University

NEW TESTAMENT

The New Testament is that part of the Bible that is the heritage of Christians. It states a new relation between man and the God of Israel, in the person of Jesus of Nazareth. He is seen by the writers of the New Testament as the long-awaited Messiah of Israel and of the whole world, and is known by the Greek word for "Messiah," or "Saviour," which is "Christ."

The New Testament was written mainly in the days of the Roman Empire and covers the historical period from the last part of the reign of King Herod (37–4 B.C.) to just after the destruction of Jerusalem in A.D. 70. Often this period is referred to in Christian writings as "the fullness of time," because of the religious significance of the coming of Jesus. But it was a "full time" historically as well. Roman government had brought peace to most of the civilized world; Greek language had made international communication easy; and the weakening of the hold of old pagan gods on

For a Bible published in 1866 Paul Gustave Doré did this illustration of the miracle of the loaves and fishes.

the people had provided an atmosphere that welcomed a new faith.

Followers of Jesus, called the Apostles, began to spread the story of the risen Lord to all the world. The Apostles themselves went from town to town, preaching and teaching. From that activity the New Testament was born. First came collections of Jesus' own words; then the stories about his life and work, as well as letters to various individuals or groups explaining Christianity. Since writing had now become more common, these materials were written down very quickly or even appeared in written form originally (for example, the letters). As a result, the New Testament evolved into written form, then into collections of written books, and finally into the collection of canonical books, much more rapidly than the Old Testament did. Very soon these writings were considered to be equal in importance, in the religious sense, to the Old Testament, which Christians shared with their Jewish neighbors. Thus the New Testament was also regarded as holy, or sacred, literature for Christians.

When we examine the New Testament, we again see a collection of diverse books under one cover. Again divisions can be made in the material, just as the earliest Christians made them. In the New Testament the two main divisions consist of Gospels and Epistles, plus a single book called Revelation.

The Gospels are books that tell the story of Jesus—what he did, what he said, how he acted in relation to people. These books are four in number and bear the names of their writers, Matthew, Mark, Luke, and John. The early Church considered these to be the four best books of the many written about Jesus. Thus, they attributed them to Apostles or to close associates of the Apostles. They are called Gospels because that word means "good news"—the good news of Jesus' message and life for the world.

The Gospel of Mark stresses the human side of Jesus and explains many of the Jewish customs and words for Gentile readers. It is therefore referred to as the "human" Gospel or the "Roman" Gospel (to explain that it was written for non-Jewish readers). It begins the story of Jesus with his baptism in the river Jordan and ends with his appearances to the Apostles after his Crucifixion.

The Gospel of Matthew, on the other hand, is sometimes called the "Jewish" Gospel because of the arrangement of its material. In this book Jesus' teachings are carefully set down into categories for easy reference, just as the Jewish teachers in that period classified their teachings. There are really five such divisions in Matthew: Jesus' ancestry and birth, which introduces his baptism and temptation, leading up to his first "sermon"; stories of healing, with instructions to the disciples; Jesus' relation to John the Baptist and to other religious leaders, with a series of parables, or teaching stories; more healing stories, the feeding of the multitude, and the story of the Transfiguration; the Judaean ministry of Jesus, the triumphal entry into Jerusalem, parables, other teachings, and a conclusion that tells of his death and resurrection.

The Gospel of Luke is really a letter and should be read with Luke's other book, The Acts of the Apostles. Both books form what is called an apologia, or defense, of Christianity to the non-Christian world. Luke begins his Gospel with the birth of Jesus and a brief narrative of his boyhood, his ancestry, and his work. Since Luke tells so many stories about

Jesus' ministry to the common people, this Gospel is often spoken of as the "social" Gospel. In the Book of Acts the "history" of Jesus' message is continued, as it was carried out into the Gentile world by the Apostles and other missionaries. Again Luke is concerned with the effect of this message on people and their lives. The book therefore tells about the early Christian Church as it developed and grew from Jerusalem and other early centers of the ancient world.

The Gospel of John is quite a different book. It is not so much a story about Jesus as it is an interpretation of who and what he was. The language is more philosophical and is therefore harder to read. In early Christian art John was depicted as an eagle because his writings soared to such great height. John likes to contrast light and darkness, for example, in speaking about Jesus' relation to the world, and he likes to use many similes and metaphors. He begins his Gospel "In the beginning . . ." and shows how God entered the world because of his love for man. This view of Jesus is called the Incarnation (that is, God becoming man and living among men), and John stresses the reality and meaning of it for the world.

These four Gospels were written down to preserve the sayings and works of Jesus for future generations. They were all written relatively soon after his death, probably all before A.D. 100. At the same time that the Gospels were being put into writing, so were the Epistles, or Letters, which form the second main division of the New Testament. As people began to join the Christian sect questions were asked, problems came up, communications were sent, and disputes arose. Thus, letters began to be written by important Church leaders such as Paul, James, John, and others. They were carefully preserved by those who received them, often recopied, and were gradually collected. Since they dealt with important matters, they were finally joined with the Gospels and became part of the official literature of Christianity.

Traditionally the Epistles are classified into Pauline Epistles, attributed to the Apostle Paul, and General, or Catholic (in the sense of worldwide), Epistles, which were not addressed to any one particular church. To these are added the Epistle to the Hebrews, whose author is unknown, and the Book of Revelation.

The Pauline Epistles include the letters to individual churches: Romans, Galatians, I and II Thessalonians, I and II Corinthians, Philippians, Colossians, and Ephesians; along with letters to two young Church leaders named Timothy and Titus. Most of these letters are concerned with specific problems Paul wished to discuss with particular churches or groups, as well as answers to questions that they had asked him. One additional letter, however, known as Philemon, concerns a runaway slave.

In the letter to the Romans, Paul presented a system of Christian belief as he saw it, in order to instruct the people. To the Galatians, Paul wrote about the independence of Christians from some aspects of the Jewish law and gave warnings about falling away from the teachings that he, himself, had given them. Moral and theological problems arose in Thessalonika and Corinth, and Paul's letters to those people consider those issues, as well as matters of Church discipline and his own authority to deal with them. The letters to the Philippians, Colossians, and Ephesians stress the need for loyalty to Jesus' teachings and for loyalty within the Church itself. By this time

The German artist Albrecht Dürer created this engraving called *The Holy Family.*

some teachers had arisen in the Church who wished to modify or change the teachings of the original disciples of Jesus. As a result, Paul was often called upon to decide issues of faith and warn the people against false ideas. The letters to Timothy and Titus reflect somewhat the same problems. They are called pastoral letters, since Paul was giving advice to young men in charge of churches in regard to meeting theological problems, to conducting themselves, and to settling problems within their churches. The letter of Philemon stands by itself in the Pauline collection because it did not result from any question asked Paul, but from his own interest in a runaway slave, Onesimus, whom he had met. Paul sent Onesimus back to his master, Philemon, with a message stressing Christian brotherhood and freedom in Christ.

The anonymous letter to the Hebrews is unusual not only because it is unsigned, but the name of its author never seems to have been known in the early Church. Like the Gospel of John it is a more philosophical letter. Its purpose was to urge faithfulness to Christianity in a time of great persecution. It accomplishes its purpose by using much of the Old Testament to trace the history of faith down to the writer's own time, with Jesus seen as the fulfillment of the ancient promises of God.

Seven letters, the General Epistles, are known by their writers' names but were not addressed to any particular groups. These letters also arose from specific problems or from theological disputes in the Church, just as did the letters of Paul. The letter of James thus stresses good works along with faith, in order to keep Christians active as well as faithful. The two letters of Peter try to answer questions about suffering (I Peter) and to stress morality as an important Christian virtue (II Peter). John's first two letters meet problems arising out of false teachings by insisting on the "reality" of Jesus as human, as well as asserting his divine aspect. These letters thus mirror a controversy in the early Church concerning the nature of Jesus. Such controversies are termed Christological because they were about interpretations of Christ. The third letter of John is administrative and considers matters of Church government and authority. Jude returns to the matter of false teachings and again insists on the Christian interpretation of the life and ministry of Jesus. Many of the General Epistles relate to matters of interpretation, both of theological and administrative affairs. The early Church was growing rapidly, and many new converts had no background in the Old Testament viewpoints from which much of the thinking of Christianity had come. In addition, groups began to arise within the Church who wished to modify or change the words of Jesus, or to offer new interpretations. As these issues arose they had to be settled, reconciled, or denied by the leaders of the early Church.

The book called The Revelation of John is an apocalypse. That is a particular type of writing, full of hidden symbols and word pictures and often oriented toward some indefinite "end of time" sometime in the future. The symbols used by the writer of Revelation were such that they were familiar to Christians but hidden from non-Christians. When this book was written, Christians were undergoing persecution. The author therefore urged them to remain faithful, for Christianity would finally triumph over evil through Jesus, the Christ. The word pictures also helped to make the author's ideas alive—people could "see" what the author was trying to say in words. Since the Rome authorities could not understand the symbols and word pictures in the book, Christians could read it publicly and not be in danger of arrest. This book is very rich in beautiful allusions and has had a great effect on other Christian literature through the ages.

The Bible is a book of variety: the Old Testament gives us the record of ancient promise, while the the New Testament discusses its fulfillment for Christians in the person and message of Jesus. The period between the two is spanned in both history and ideas by the Apocrypha.

PHILIP C. HAMMOND
Princeton Theological Seminary

Entire article reviewed by JAMES I. McCORD
President, Princeton Theological Seminary

A. L. SACHAR
President, Brandeis University

MSGR. JOHN J. VOIGHT
Secretary of Education, Archdiocese of New York

See also BIBLE, PEOPLE IN THE; BIBLE STORIES.

The following is a brief description of some of the important people in the Bible.

Aaron was the older brother of Moses and the first Jewish high priest.

Absalom, one of the sons of King David, led a rebellion against his father and was slain by Joab, David's military general.

Adam and Eve were the first man and woman. God created Adam out of dust and Eve from one of Adam's ribs. They were expelled from the Garden of Eden for eating fruit from the tree of knowledge.

Barabbas was a criminal awaiting execution at the same time as Jesus. When the people of Judea were asked to choose who to free, they chose Barabbas.

Bathsheba, the wife of a Hittite army officer, fell in love with King David and married him after the death of her husband. One of their four sons, Solomon, succeeded his father as king.

Belshazzar was a king of Babylonia. During a feast, mysterious handwriting appeared on a wall and was thought to be a sign that Babylonia would fall. That night Belshazzar was killed and Babylonia was conquered.

Caiaphas was the high priest who presided at Jesus' trial before the Sanhedrin, Jerusalem's ruling council.

Cain and Abel were the sons of Adam and Eve. Cain killed his brother and was condemned by God to a life of wandering.

Daniel, an early Hebrew prophet, interpreted the handwriting on the wall at Belshazzar's feast.

Deborah was a prophetess and the only woman judge of the early Israelites.

Delilah was a Philistine who was loved by Samson. After discovering that the secret of Samson's strength was his hair, she cut it off and betrayed him.

Eli was a Hebrew judge and high priest. His two sons lost the sacred Ark of the Covenant in a battle with the Philistines.

Elizabeth was the mother of John the Baptist and a cousin of the Virgin Mary.

Enoch was the name of two biblical figures. One was the eldest son of Cain. The other was the father of Methuselah.

Esau, the son of Isaac and Rebekah, was the older twin brother of Jacob. He traded his birthright as eldest son to Jacob for a bowl of stew.

Esther, a Jewish woman who married the king of Persia, helped prevent the Persians from killing the Jews. This is celebrated in the Feast of Purim.

Gideon was a Hebrew judge who raised an army and saved Israel from the Midianites. Under his leadership, the tribes of Israel were united.

Hagar was one of Abraham's wives. She bore him a son, Ishmael. At the insistence of Abraham's first wife, Sarah, Hagar and Ishmael were cast out into the desert.

Hezekiah was a king of early Judah who instituted religious reforms, restored religious spirit, and abolished idolatry.

Ishmael, the son of Abraham and Hagar, was exiled into the wilderness with his mother. The Arab peoples are said to be descended from him.

Jacob, the younger twin son of Isaac and Rebekah, inherited the covenant given by God. He passed this covenant to his sons, who founded the 12 tribes of Israel.

Jephthah was a judge of Israel. Called to lead his people in battle, he vowed, if victorious, to sacrifice the first of his household to greet him on his return. He sacrificed his little daughter, his only child, in fulfillment of this vow.

Joel, an early Hebrew prophet, predicted a plague of locusts and events associated with the coming of the Messiah.

Jonathan was the eldest son of King Saul. A heroic military leader, he was a loyal friend of the future king, David. Jonathan was killed along with his father in the wars against the Philistines.

Judas Iscariot, one of Jesus' disciples, betrayed Jesus for 30 pieces of silver. He led soldiers to Gethsemane and identified Jesus with a kiss.

Lazarus was the brother of Mary and Martha. After he died, he was resurrected by Jesus.

Leah was the first wife of Jacob, who was supposed to marry Leah's sister Rachel. Their father tricked Jacob and substituted Leah for Rachel on the wedding night.

Martha, the sister of Mary and Lazarus, was gently reprimanded by Jesus for complaining that Mary listened to him instead of helping prepare their meal.

Mary Magdalene was a Galilean woman from whom Jesus cast out demons. She became a devoted follower of Jesus and was present at the Crucifixion.

Methuselah, the grandfather of Noah, was said to have lived 969 years.

Miriam, the sister of Moses and Aaron, was a prophetess. God rebuked her for being jealous of her brother Moses and she was stricken with leprosy.

Naomi and her family left their home in Bethlehem because of famine. After her husband and two sons died, she returned home with her daughter-in-law Ruth. She arranged Ruth's marriage to Boaz.

Nathan, a Hebrew prophet, served as advisor to King David and King Solomon.

Nicodemus was a member of the Jewish ruling council, the Sanhedrin. He became a secret disciple of Jesus and after the Crucifixion took expensive spices to cover the body of Jesus for burial.

Nimrod, the great-grandson of Noah, was a famous hunter and a mighty king of ancient Babylon.

Noah built a great ship, the Ark, and filled it with two of every kind of animal. When the great Flood came, Noah and his family were safe on the Ark. When they finally reached dry land they gave humanity and the animal kingdom a fresh start.

Pontius Pilate was the Roman governor of Judea who condemned Jesus to death.

Rachel was the best-loved wife of Jacob and the sister of Leah. Rachel bore Jacob two sons, Joseph and Benjamin.

Rebekah was the wife of Isaac. She bore him twin sons, Esau and Jacob. She helped Jacob, her favorite son, receive Isaac's blessing, which rightfully belonged to Esau.

Rehoboam, the son of King Solomon, caused Solomon's united kingdom to be divided into Israel and Judah. He then ruled Judah for some 17 years.

Ruth was the faithful daughter-in-law of Naomi. Her loyalty was rewarded by marriage to Boaz. Their first son was the grandfather of King David.

Salome, the daughter of Herod Philip and Herodias, danced for Herod Antipas, ruler of Galilee and Perea. As a reward, she demanded the head of John the Baptist.

Samson, a judge of Israel, had great strength, the source of which was his hair. When Delilah cut his hair, the Philistines captured him, blinded him, and chained him to their temple. As Samson's hair grew, his strength returned and he destroyed the temple, killing himself and many Philistines.

Samuel was Israel's last judge, a role that incorporated military, political, judicial, and spiritual leadership.

Sarah was the wife of Abraham and the mother of Isaac. After giving birth to Isaac, Sarah became jealous of Hagar, Abraham's other wife, and urged Abraham to banish Hagar and her son Ishmael into the desert.

Saul was the first king of Israel. Defeated and wounded in battle with the Philistines, Saul committed suicide rather than be captured.

Seth was the third son of Adam and Eve. According to the New Testament, Seth was an ancestor of Jesus Christ.

See also ABRAHAM; BIBLE; BIBLE STORIES; DAVID; ELIJAH; EZRA; ISAAC; ISAIAH; JESUS CHRIST; JEREMIAH; JOHN THE BAPTIST; JOSEPH; JOSHUA; MARY; MOSES; PETER; SOLOMON.

BIBLE STORIES

The Bible is great literature. Many writers have retold its stories for boys and girls. The following selections from the Old and New Testaments were adapted by Walter Russell Bowie.

▶ NOAH'S ARK

From the years far back, before the Bible was written, there had been handed down the tale that one time the earth had grown so wicked that there seemed nothing for God to do but to wash it clean and to start again.

God had to find someone fit to make the new start, and the one he found was Noah. God told Noah that there was going to be such a flood as had never been seen before. The waters would be so wide and deep that they would cover all the earth. God said that Noah must build a boat that would be big enough to take in all his family and also two of every sort of bird and animal he could find in the whole world. The boat was to be like a floating house, and it should be called the ark. It needed to be big, considering all that was going to be in it!

So Noah began to build the ark. It was a hard job to build such a tremendous boat, and it must have been all the harder when the neighbors stood around and laughed. "Who ever heard of building a boat in a dry meadow?" they asked. There the sun was shining down, and there was not enough water to float a stick, much less a thing like this huge ark. Noah must be crazy! But Noah kept on working.

Then one day it began to rain. Noah and his family went into the ark and took with them a male and female of every kind of living thing that came walking and running and creeping and flying from the face of the earth. As the water came up higher, the ark was lifted up and floated above the meadows.

When it started to rain, Noah, his family, and a male and female of every kind of animal went into the ark.

Goliath, armed with a sword, a spear, and a shield, came toward David. David drew back his arm and whirled his sling with deadly aim.

It kept on raining, and it rained harder. Day after day the water poured out of the sky as if the earth had been turned upside down and the ocean put on top. Forty days and forty nights it rained.

All the other people and creatures had climbed up to the tops of the hills to try to be out of the reach of the flood. But at last every spot of earth was covered, and nothing was left alive except Noah and his family and what they had with them in the ark.

At last the rain stopped and the sun came out, but for a hundred and fifty days the ark floated on the waters, above the empty earth. Then, little by little, the flood began to go down. One day Noah felt the bottom of the ark jolt on something, and there it was, scraping the top of the highest mountain that had been in all that part of the earth—Mount Ararat. No other land could be seen around it, but Noah knew that before long the rest of the earth would begin to be uncovered.

Noah went into the part of the ark where the birds were. He took a dove and opened a window and let the dove fly away. But presently the bird came fluttering back in the window again, because it had not found a single dry spot anywhere to rest.

A week longer Noah waited. Then he sent the dove out again. This time when the dove came back it carried in its bill a green olive leaf. Noah knew by this that somewhere the earth and the trees were rising above the water. Once more he sent the dove out. This time the dove did not

come back at all, and Noah knew that it had found a place to build its nest.

Then at last the ark itself settled down on solid ground. Noah opened the doors, and he and his family and all the beasts and birds and everything else came flying and running and scrambling out, glad to be back on the earth again.

Noah thanked God, and when he looked up he saw a rainbow in the sky. The rainbow was God's sign—the sign of his promise that "while the earth remaineth, seedtime and harvest and cold and heat and summer and winter and day and night shall not cease."

▶ DAVID AND GOLIATH

About that time the Philistines collected an army again and marched up into a valley in the land of Israel. They had with them a man who was as huge as a giant. His name was Goliath. On his head he wore a helmet of brass, and he had armor on his body and on his legs. His spear was as thick as a wooden beam, and his armor-bearer went before him with his great shield.

Every day Goliath came out into the valley between the camp of the Philistines and the camp of Israel and dared any man to come and fight him. But nobody dared, not even Saul. So Goliath shouted and strutted and shook his spear. "I defy the armies of Israel," he cried. "Give me a man that we may fight together!"

Now the three elder sons of Jesse, the brothers of David, were in Saul's army. David had gone back to Bethlehem for a while to take care of his father's sheep. One day, while the armies of Israel and of the Philistines were watching each other, Jesse decided to send his soldier sons some food—parched corn and bread and cheese. He told David to carry the food to the camp and give it to his brothers, and to find out how they were.

Early the next morning David left the sheep in charge of another shepherd, and started off. When he reached the camp of Israel there was a great stir in both armies, and a noise of shouting as of a battle about to begin.

David ran ahead until he found his three brothers. As he stood there talking with them, out came Goliath. He was shouting, as he always did, "What are you here for? I am a Philistine, and you are servants of Saul. Choose a man on your side, and let him come out and fight me. If he can kill me, we will be your slaves; but if I kill him, you shall be slaves to us. I defy you!"

The men around David drew back. None of them had any idea of going out to fight Goliath. They said to David, "You see that man? Whoever kills him will be rich. And Saul will give him his daughter to marry, and will make his family great in Israel."

As David looked at Goliath, he was filled with anger and contempt. "Who is this Philistine," he said, "that he should defy the armies of the living God?"

Eliab, his oldest brother, heard David say that, and was annoyed. "Why did you come down here?" he demanded. "And who have you left to keep those few sheep in the wilderness? I know your pride, and I know that you have come down here just to watch us fight."

David asked Eliab what he had done to make him speak like that. There was reason for his being there, and he would show it, too. He was not going to be frightened by Goliath, or by anyone else.

Presently the army began to talk of this young man, David, who had turned up in the camp, and word about him came to Saul. Saul sent for him. Here was the same lad who had been his armor-bearer and had played for him on the harp!

"Nobody need be troubled about Goliath," David said to Saul. "I will fight with this Philistine."

"You cannot fight with this Philistine," said Saul. "You are only a boy, and this man has been a fighter ever since he grew up."

But David had a different idea. "I have kept my father's sheep," he said, "and once there came a lion, and another time a bear, and took a lamb out of the flock. I went out after those beasts and killed them, and saved the lambs. Both the lion and the bear I killed, and this heathen Philistine shall be like them, since he has defied the armies of the living God. The Lord God who saved me from the paw of the lion and from the paw of the bear will save me from this Philistine."

Saul looked at David and thought for a moment. Then he said, "Go, and the Lord be with you." He put his own armor on David, helmet and breastplate and all, and he gave David his own sword. But David said he could not do anything in that heavy armor. He had never worn armor before, and he did not know how to handle a sword. He took them off, and gave them back to the king. Then David went down to a brook that ran through the valley. There he chose five smooth stones. He put these into the shepherd's bag which he wore at his waist. In one hand was his shepherd's staff, and in the other, his sling. With these David went out to meet the giant Philistine.

On came Goliath, with the man who carried his shield walking in front. When Goliath caught sight of David, he laughed. "Am I a dog," he shouted, "that you come to me with a stick?" And he cursed David by all his gods. "Come on," he said, "and I will give your flesh to the birds and beasts!"

But David answered: "You come to me with a sword, and with a spear, and with a shield; but I come to you in the name of the Lord of Hosts, the God of the armies of Israel, whom you have defied. This day the God of Israel will deliver you into my hands. I will kill you, and take your head from your body. The carcasses of the army of the Philistines I will give this day to the birds and the beasts, that all the earth may know that there is a God in Israel. Yes, all these people shall know that the Lord does not save with the sword and spear. The battle is the Lord's, and he will give you today into our hands."

The Philistine came on with heavy steps. David ran toward him. Putting his hand into his bag, David took out a stone and fitted it into his sling. His arm drew back and whirled with deadly aim. Out from the sling the smooth stone shot, and whistled through the air. It caught Goliath between the eyes and sank into his forehead. Goliath, the giant, pitched forward on his face.

As he fell, David ran and stood over him. He drew Goliath's own sword out of its sheath and cut off his head.

When the Philistines saw that, they fled in panic. The Israelites, shouting, poured after them along the valley and down across the country as far as the gates of Ekron. Then the army of Saul came back and took everything that was in the tents of the Philistines. But all David wanted was the armor of Goliath.

The sailors threw Jonah overboard. He had hardly touched the water when a whale came up and swallowed him.

▶ JONAH

Jonah was commanded by God to go and preach to the great and wicked city of Nineveh. This was the very city from which armies had often come to make war against the people of Israel.

Jonah did not want to go to Nineveh. Instead, he went down to the city of Joppa on the sea. There he found a ship that was going in the opposite direction from Nineveh. He paid his fare, went on board, and sailed away.

The ship had not gone far before a tremendous storm arose. The sailors were frightened and they began to pray. They threw overboard much of the cargo to lighten the ship and give it a better chance to keep afloat when the great waves broke over it. In spite of all the commotion, Jonah was asleep down below the decks. The captain went down and awoke him, and asked him to pray to God that they all might be saved.

But the sailors thought that this storm had come because there was an especially wicked person on the ship. They drew lots to see who it might be. The lot fell upon Jonah. Then the sailors asked him who he was, and what he had done, and why he was on the ship.

Jonah admitted that he was running away from God and from what God had told him to do.

The sailors tried to bring the ship to land. When they could not do this, they took Jonah and threw him overboard.

Hardly had Jonah touched the water, when up came a huge fish, like a whale, and swallowed him. Inside the fish, Jonah had plenty of time to think about God and to change his mind.

After three days, the fish came close to shore and cast up Jonah, unhurt, on the dry land. Now again Jonah heard the voice of God speaking in his heart. Once more it told him to go to Nineveh and preach there. This time he went. He preached that Nineveh and all its people would be destroyed unless they repented of their wickedness.

To Jonah's surprise, the people of Nineveh listened and repented. They fasted and put on sackcloth in sorrow for their sins. Even the king took off his royal robes, dressed himself in sackcloth, and sat down in ashes as a sign of being ashamed for the city's sins. And he gave a command that all the people should pray to God, and that everyone should turn away from whatever wickedness he had been doing.

But instead of being glad that his preaching had had such a great and wonderful result, Jonah was annoyed. He did not like Nineveh. He had not wanted to go there in the first place, and he did not want any good to come to Nineveh because of him. He began to complain to God. He said he had known that God was merciful and slow to anger and full of love and kindness, but he had not wanted God or anyone else to feel that way toward Nineveh. So far as he was concerned, he would rather die than see Nineveh blessed by God. So Jonah went outside the city. He made himself a little shelter and sat there alone and pouted, waiting to see what would happen.

It was very hot in the sun where Jonah sat. When God made a gourd vine to grow and cover Jonah's thin shelter with its cool green leaves, Jonah was pleased. But the next morning worms began to eat the gourd vine, and it withered.

When the sun rose there came a sultry east wind. The sun beat down so hot on Jonah's head that he fainted, and again he wished that he were dead.

At last God spoke to Jonah in a way to bring him to his senses. "You are angry because your gourd vine is withered," he said.

Jonah blurted out, "Yes, I am angry. I do well to be angry."

Then said the voice of God: "You did not make this gourd vine in the first place, and you did not make it grow. It was a thing that came up overnight and lasted only a day. And you are angry because it is gone. Yet here is Nineveh, the great city with more than a hundred thousand people in it and all the cattle upon which they depend, and you want to have it all destroyed."

So the Book of Jonah ends, and at least some men among the people of Israel began to appreciate its meaning: that God has pity upon all peoples, and that men must have pity too.

▶ DANIEL IN THE LIONS' DEN

Belshazzar was slain, and Darius, the king of Media, took his throne.

At first Daniel was honored by the new king even more than he had been honored before. Darius appointed a hundred and twenty princes as governors in the kingdom. Three of these he put in authority over all the others, and among these three Daniel stood first, so that he was next to the king.

That made the princes jealous. They did not want Daniel to be greater than they were. So they began to whisper among themselves, and to try to plan a way to get rid of Daniel. They knew that they could not find Daniel doing wrong. Everything that he did for the king was done well. But suppose they could persuade the king, without his thinking much about it, to make some law that Daniel would think was wrong. They knew that Daniel would not obey such a law. Then, if the king had solemnly declared that anyone who disobeyed it should be punished, they would have Daniel in a trap.

So the princes went to the king. They said to him that it was a dangerous thing to have people of other religions in his kingdom. Why could not everyone think as the king thought and believe what he believed? They suggested that the king give an order that for the next thirty days no one in the kingdom should pray to any god, or act as though even in heaven there could be anyone more important than the king.

The king, without stopping to understand just what might happen, gave the order and signed it with his royal seal. Then the princes who had persuaded him to do that persuaded him also to say that a law, signed and sealed in that fashion, would always be the law, and never could be changed.

Now they were ready to have their revenge on Daniel. When the law had been proclaimed, they watched to see what he would do. Daniel did just what they thought he would do. Law or no law, he went into his house at his regular times to pray. With the windows wide open, he knelt down, with his face turned toward Jerusalem, the Holy City, and prayed to God, just as he had always done.

The men who were trying to trap Daniel went off to tell the king. Had not the king made a law that for thirty days no one in his kingdom

Daniel was thrown into a den of lions, but the lions did not hurt him.

should pray to any god or make any petition to anyone except the king himself? And had it not been declared that any person who dared to disobey that law should be thrown into a den of lions? Well, there was one man who had paid no attention; one man who had gone right on praying as though what the king ordered did not matter.

"Who has done this?" the king wanted to know. And the princes told him it was Daniel.

Now the king was exceedingly sorry and distressed. All day long he thought and tried to find some way by which he could save Daniel. But he had made the law. Besides that, he had been persuaded into declaring that it should be one of the laws of the Medes and Persians that never could be changed. There was nothing left for him to do but to give the order that Daniel should be brought and thrown into a den of lions.

And so Daniel was put into the den where the lions were. The gate was fastened, and sealed with the king's own seal, so that no friend of Daniel could come and let him out.

The king grew more and more distressed. That night in his palace he would not eat, and he would not let any musicians play. When he lay down on his bed he could not sleep. Early the next morning he got up and went to the mouth of the den. In a miserable voice, hardly hoping for anything, he called, "Daniel, servant of the living God, has your God been able to save you from the lions?"

To his amazement and joy, he heard the voice of Daniel from the den, saying, "God has sent his angel and shut the lions' mouths so that they have not hurt me."

The king was filled with great joy. He ordered that Daniel should be taken out of the lions' den immediately. And there he was, safe and sound, not even scratched.

When the king thought of the men who had planned to have Daniel thrown into the den of lions, he ordered that they and everybody connected with them should be thrown in there themselves.

▶ **THE BOY JESUS**

When Jesus was twelve years old, he went with Joseph and Mary to Jerusalem to celebrate the Feast of the Passover. This was the greatest festival of the Jewish year. It had begun far back in the time of Moses, when the people of Israel were slaves in the land of Egypt. They had worked there making bricks for the temples and for the great monuments which Pharaoh, king of Egypt, commanded to be built. The story of all that happened then is written in the Old Testament Book of Exodus. The Feast of the Passover was the glad reminder of the way in which Moses helped the people of Israel to escape from Egypt and led them across the Red Sea to Palestine, the Promised Land. Everyone was happy when this festival came. It made men proud to remember God's help long ago, and it filled them with belief that God was with them still.

Jewish families always wanted to celebrate the Passover in Jerusalem, where the Temple was. Thousands and thousands of people, beyond anybody's counting, went up to the Holy City at Passover time. All of them were happy at the thought that they were going to see Jerusalem, the Holy City. They sang the beautiful old songs called the "pilgrim songs," which had first been written hundreds of years before.

One of them began:

"I was glad when they said unto me,
Let us go into the house of the Lord.
Our feet shall stand within thy gates,
    O Jerusalem."

And another song began:

"As the mountains are round about Jerusalem,
So the Lord is round about his people from
    henceforth even for ever."

Hardly anything could have been so exciting to Jesus as this first journey to Jerusalem. Joseph's family and their friends walked together in the midst of the growing crowds. The neighbors went too, and people from other towns along the way joined them. They stopped now and then by the roadside to eat the food they had brought with them. It was much more than one day's journey from Nazareth to Jerusalem. So at night they made a place to sleep on the ground and lay down under the open skies and the stars.

The Passover was in the spring, when the fruit trees were blossoming and the fields were bright with flowers. The road from Nazareth to Jerusalem led across the wide Plain of Esdraelon. Jesus knew the stories of the heroes who had walked on that same ground. Gideon had been there with his three hundred men; and David, and Jonathan, and Saul. Many armies had marched across it. Here and there in the earth one might come upon a broken sword blade or a piece of rusty iron from a chariot that had lain there for hundreds of years, left from some battle with the Philistines or the Egyptians or the terrible armies of the Assyrians.

After the pilgrims to Jerusalem had crossed the Plain of Esdraelon, they did not keep straight on. Instead, they crossed the Jordan River and

The young Jesus talked with the oldest and wisest teachers in the Temple court.

went through the country on the east side of the river. Jesus knew that this was because the people of Israel despised the Samaritans, who lived in the country just beyond the Plain of Esdraelon, and did not want to go into the Samaritans' land.

Along the valley of the Jordan River the roads ran south as far as the fords opposite the old city of Jericho. Here the travelers went back across the river. Then they began to climb up through the steep hills that led toward Jerusalem. Up and up they went, until at last they came to where they could see the Holy City.

Outside the walls of Jerusalem, and also within the walls, were green gardens that belonged to rich men's houses. On the highest hill was the splendid palace which Herod the king had built. But the most glorious thing was the Temple. It was even more magnificent than the Temple of Solomon which had stood on the same ground long before. The walls and columns were of colored marble, and great gates opened from each court to the court beyond. At the end of the farthest court there stood the holiest part of the Temple, so beautiful that hardly any other building in the world could be compared to it. Its marble walls were richly carved, and its roof was of shining gold.

Now that Joseph and Mary and Jesus had reached Jerusalem, they made ready for the Passover. Each family ate the Passover supper by itself. As the evening grew dark, a lamp was lighted, and the old, old prayers were said. Then the family ate a roasted lamb, and bread that had no yeast in it. They ate with their belts tightened and their sandals tied, because they were remembering the night when Moses had told the Hebrew people to be ready to leave

Egypt the instant he should give the word. The people of Israel were no longer in Egypt, but again they were not free. Rome ruled over them. Roman soldiers were there in the castle on the hill, next to the Temple. Many men who kept the Passover were hating the Roman rule and wishing to get rid of it.

Jesus may have been thinking that what they needed more was to get rid of their hatred and bitterness. Certainly he was thinking much about God and asking himself how he could know surely what God wanted for his people.

When the days of the Passover were finished, the people from Nazareth started for home. Again there was the great throng of friends and neighbors journeying along together. Joseph and Mary thought that Jesus was walking with some of the other groups. But when evening came and they stopped to camp for the night, they could not find Jesus anywhere. Then they were frightened. They went straight back to Jerusalem, looking for him. At last they came to the Temple. In one of the Temple courts some of the wisest teachers—teachers who knew most about the sacred books and the law of God— used to sit and let people ask them questions. There, in the midst of them, Mary and Joseph found Jesus. They were glad, and yet a little annoyed. Why had Jesus stayed there and let them be so worried?

"Son," said Mary, "why did you treat us so?"

Jesus was surprised. He thought they should have understood where he would be. "Did you not know," he answered, "that I must be in my Father's house?"

BICKERDYKE, MARY ANN BALL. See OHIO (Famous People).

Bicycling is enjoying a dramatic rise in popularity. Cyclists of all ages are taking to the roads for recreation, fitness, transportation, and sport.

BICYCLING

Bicycling is fun because it gives you the freedom of the road—freedom to travel almost anywhere under your own power. People have traveled around the world by bicycle. Cyclists have ridden to the heart of China, up mountains in Africa, and across the Australian desert. But it is not necessary to do anything quite so exotic to have fun on a bicycle. You can explore your neighborhood, your town, and your state by bicycle, discovering places and things you might never see from a car.

More than 85,000,000 Americans ride bicycles. Almost half of them are under the age of 16. They ride for many reasons. For children, a bicycle provides personal transportation—to school, to the store, and to friends' homes. Many adults consider the bicycle a means to better fitness. Bicycling strengthens the heart and lungs without putting severe strain on the body.

The chance to explore new places at a leisurely pace is another reason for bicycling. Bicycle tours are popular in Europe, and many countries have special bicycle paths and trails. In the United States, cycling groups such as those organized by the American Youth Hostels, Bikecentennial, and the League of American Wheelmen offer supervised outings for people of all ages. Bicycling is also a competitive sport, with races of various kinds.

▶ **TYPES OF BICYCLES**

The most familiar bicycles are probably the lightweight models designed for touring. They usually weigh about 25 pounds (11 kilograms) and have ten or more speeds, or gears, to make pedaling easier on hills and in other situations. They have narrow tires and hand brakes, operated by levers on the handlebars. Racing bikes are similar but lighter, weighing about 20 pounds (9 kilograms).

The turned-down handlebars on some racing and touring bikes shift the body forward, into an efficient pedaling position. Similar but heavier and sturdier bicycles, with one to five speeds and level handlebars, are popular for short trips. The high-riser, with raised handlebars and a banana-shaped seat, is a popular children's bicycle. The BMX (bicycle motocross) bicycle, which looks similar to a high-riser, is favored by many young riders because it has a strong frame and fat tires and can take a lot of heavy use. These bicycles have coaster brakes, which are operated by pedaling backward.

All-terrain bicycles (ATB's), also known as mountain bikes, are similar to BMX bicycles. ATB's are strongly built, with wide, knobby tires and up to 18 speeds. They were designed to be ridden on dirt trails, but many are now used on city streets. Other bicycles include folding bicycles, which can fit in the trunk of a car, and tandem bicycles, which carry two

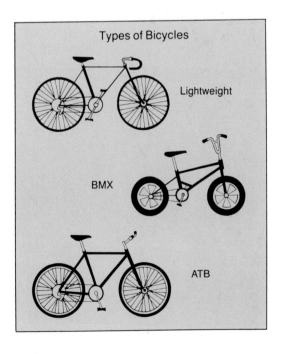

Types of Bicycles

Lightweight

BMX

ATB

people, one behind the other—each with a separate set of pedals. Still another type of bicycle is the recumbent, on which the rider sits in a reclining position and reaches forward in order to pedal.

Bicycles are available in different sizes, based on the diameter of the wheels and on the frame size, or distance from the top of the seat tube to the pedals. Adults are usually comfortable with 26- or 27-inch wheels, while 16 and 20 inches are typical sizes for a child's bicycle. (In countries that use the metric system, the corresponding sizes are 70 and 40 or 50 centimeters.) To choose the correct frame size, straddle the bicycle. For touring models,

there should be about 1 inch (3 centimeters) or so between your body and the horizontal bar that runs from the seat to the handlebars. For ATB's, there should be about 3 to 4 inches (8 to 10 centimeters). The seats of most bicycles can be adjusted to make the fit precise.

▶ BICYCLE RACING

The four main types of bicycle racing are road, track, off-road, and BMX racing. Road races are run over streets and highways, which are sometimes closed to other traffic. The racers use lightweight ten- to 15-speed bicycles with hand brakes. Track races are run on closed, banked tracks called velodromes. Cy-

Left: Track races take place on oval tracks called velodromes. The distance around the track ranges from about ⅒ of a mile to ⅓ of a mile (0.2 to 0.5 kilometer). *Below left:* Road racers ride over streets and highways on lightweight bikes. The course may be as short as 6.2 miles (10 kilometers) or as long as the Tour de France, which covers about 2,500 miles (4,000 kilometers). *Below:* BMX (bicycle motocross) is an off-road sport run on a bumpy, curvy dirt track, usually less than ¼ mile (400 meters) long.

Saddle · Dropped-style handlebars · Handlebar stem · Brake levers · Frame · Headset · Seat post · Rear brake · Gear shift levers · Front brake · Water bottle · Wheel · Fork · Front derailleur · Freewheel · Crankset · Hub · Rear derailleur · Bottom bracket · Chain · Pedal · Toe clip and strap

A well-maintained bicycle is a safe bicycle. **Every time you ride** — Check tire pressure; make sure brakes work; test lights, horn or bell; give a quick visual check for anything obviously wrong. **Every week** — Pump up tires and check pressure with gauge; check tires for cuts, bulges, or glass. **Every two weeks** — Clean and lubricate chain. **Every month** — Lubricate moving parts of derailleurs and brakes and check for worn brake pads; check adjustment of brakes and derailleurs and all bearings (headset, hubs, bottom bracket and pedals); check wheels for wobbling. **Every year** — Clean and lubricate both wheel hubs, bottom bracket, headset and pedal bearings; tighten all nuts and bolts.

clists compete on single-speed bicycles with no brakes. Off-road races, ridden on ATB's, are one of the newest cycling events. BMX racing, popular with young riders, is done on short dirt tracks with jumps, bumps, and curves.

Probably the best-known bicycle race in the world is the Tour de France. This yearly race lasts up to 25 days and covers about 2,500 miles (4,000 kilometers) or more. In 1986, Greg LeMond became the first U.S. cyclist to win the race. His victory did much to make bicycle racing more popular in the United States, as did the success of U.S. cyclists who won nine medals at the 1984 Olympics. By the late 1980's, some 250,000 Americans were riding bicycles in competition.

· On a worldwide basis, road and track racing is governed by the Union Cycliste Internationale, based in Switzerland. Road and track racing in the United States is under the authority of the U.S. Cycling Federation (USCF), which has some 500 affiliated (member) clubs. Based in Colorado Springs, Colorado, the USCF issues racing licenses, sponsors training programs, and oversees the U.S. Olympic cycling program. Riders as young as 9 may race in USCF-approved events.

Off-road races are usually authorized by the National Off-Road Bicycle Association. BMX events are overseen by the National Bicycle League or the American Bicycle Association.

▶ **THE HISTORY OF BICYCLES**

Sketches of a bicycle were made by the great 15th-century Italian artist and inventor Leonardo da Vinci. But the first working vehicle was designed by Baron Karl von Drais, of Germany, in 1818. It had no pedals—he pushed himself along with his feet. Similar machines were soon developed and came to be called **velocipedes,** from Latin words for speed and walking. In 1839, Kirkpatrick Macmillan, a Scottish blacksmith, added foot cranks connected by rods to the rear wheel of a velocipede. Later, Ernest Michaux, of France, put rotating pedals on the front wheel.

The first U.S. bicycles were produced after 1876 by Colonel Albert Pope of Massachusetts. They were **ordinaries,** a type of bicycle with a high front wheel and a tiny rear wheel. They cost more than $300 (over $1,500 in today's dollars). In the 1890's the **safety** bicycle replaced the ordinary. It had wheels of equal size and was driven by a chain. Basic bicycle design has changed little since then, but great improvements and refinements have been made.

Bicycling reached its peak in the United States in the late 1890's, when cyclists supported the Good Roads Movement for better highways to ride on. But as more cars took to the roads, bicycling declined. It became popular again in the 1970's, as a result of a gasoline shortage and increased interest in fitness.

Rules of the Road for Bicyclists

Follow lane markings. Do not turn left from the right lane. Do not go straight in a lane marked "Right turn only."

Ride in a straight line whenever possible and ride with traffic. Keep to the right, but stay about a car-door width away from parked cars.

Obey traffic signs and signals. Bicycles must behave like other vehicles if they are to be taken seriously by motorists.

Use hand signals. Hand signals tell motorists what you intend to do. Signal as a matter of law, of courtesy, and of self-protection.

Choose the best way to turn left. There are two ways to make a left turn: (1) Like a car. Look, signal, move into the left lane, and turn left. (2) Like a pedestrian. Ride straight to the far-side crosswalk. Walk your bicycle across.

Scan the road behind. Learn to look back over your shoulder without losing your balance or swerving left. Some riders use rearview mirrors. Always look back before changing lanes or changing positions within your lane, and only move when no other vehicle is in your way.

Ride a well-equipped bicycle. Always use a strong headlight and taillight at night and when visibility is poor. Be sure your bicycle is adjusted to fit you properly. For safety and efficiency, outfit it with bells, rearview mirrors, fenders (for rainy rides), and racks, baskets, or bicycle bags.

Go slow on sidewalks and bicycle paths. Pedestrians have the right-of-way. By law you must give pedestrians audible warning when you pass. Do not cross driveways or intersections without slowing to a walker's pace and looking very carefully for traffic (especially traffic turning right on a green light).

▶**BICYCLING SKILLS**

The traffic laws of every state say that people who ride bicycles have the same rights and duties as people who drive cars. In other words, a bicycle is a vehicle, and a bicyclist is a vehicle operator. Thus every bicyclist must know and follow the rules of the road.

Some important rules and tips for safe cycling appear in the boxes above. In addition, cycling is safer if you take these steps:

• Ride on routes with few cars, slow traffic, and easy intersections and on streets that have room for cyclists and motorists.

• Wear bright clothing that makes you stand out during the day. At night, wear white or reflective clothing (and make sure your bicycle is outfitted with a headlight, taillight, and reflectors). But remember that riding at night is dangerous, and avoid it.

• Wear a hardshell bicycle helmet with a sticker of approval from the American National Standards Institute (ANSI) or the Snell Memorial Foundation. It will shelter your head from the weather and make you more visible to motorists, and it may save your life. The USCF and other racing organizations require riders to wear helmets in their events.

• Ride a safe bicycle. A well-maintained bike is dependable and easy to ride. You can have a bicycle shop overhaul your bicycle once a year. Once a week or so, check to be sure that all nuts and bolts are tight, that the brakes stop the bicycle quickly, that the chain is lubricated, and that the pedals and hand-grips (or handlebar tapes) are tight. Check the tires for cuts and wear, and be sure they are inflated to the pressure shown on the sidewalls. See that the wheels spin freely and that there are no broken spokes.

Cycling is more fun, as well as safer, when you practice good cycling skills, wear a helmet, and ride a well-maintained bicycle.

JIM FREMONT
Education Director, Bicycle Federation of America

BIENVILLE, JEAN-BAPTISTE LE MOYNE, SIEUR DE. See LOUISIANA (Famous People).

How to rack balls for eight ball

Foot of table

Apex ball always sits on the Foot spot.

Head spot

Head string

Cue ball

Head of table

How to rack balls for rotation

Foot of table

Foot spot

How to rack balls for nine ball

Foot of table

Foot spot

Cue

Rack and object balls

Chalk

Cue ball

The various forms of the game of billiards are played on a rectangular cloth-covered table. Equipment includes a leather-tipped stick known as a cue, a white cue ball, and colored balls called object balls. The balls are racked (arranged) in different positions for different forms of the game.

BILLIARDS

Billiards is the general term for a number of different games played on cloth-covered rectangular tables on which balls are struck by sticks, called **cues**. The playing surface is always twice as long as it is wide and is lined by raised rubber cushions. On each turn, the leather tip of the cue is used to strike a white ball, called the **cue ball**, and drive it into what are called **object balls**. Points are scored in some versions by making the cue ball hit two or three object balls, sometimes striking the cushions in between hits; in other versions the goal is to drive object balls into openings, or **pockets**, in the cushions.

▶ FORMS OF THE GAME

The style of play most popular in the United States is called **pool**, or sometimes **pocket billiards** to separate it from the carom, or pocketless, games. Pool is played on a table 4½ feet (1.4 meters) wide by 9 feet (2.7 meters) long, or smaller. The most often played games are **eight ball**, **nine ball**, **rotation**, and **straight pool**. In England, Canada, Australia, and India, the favorite game is **snooker**. It is similar to pool but is played on a much larger table (usually 6 by 12 feet, or 1.8 by 3.7 meters) with smaller balls and smaller pockets.

▶ RULES OF GAMES

Only the highlights of major games are given here. In every game described, players shoot until they miss, they win the game, or they commit a foul. Examples of fouls are jumping a ball off the table or hitting the cue ball twice on a single stroke.

Eight Ball. The balls are **racked** (arranged with the aid of a triangular frame that is then removed) as shown in the diagram with the 8 ball in the center. One player is chosen to **break** the balls by driving the cue ball into the rack from a position behind the **head string**. When a ball goes into one of the pockets, the shooter is restricted for the rest of the game to the balls in the same group, either those numbered higher than eight (the stripes) or those numbered lower than eight (the solids), while the opponent must aim at only those balls in the other group. Each player tries to **pocket** all the balls in his or her group, which means driving them into any of the pockets with the cue ball. Once that is done, the player can shoot at the 8 ball, the pocketing of which wins the game. Pocketing the 8 ball out of order loses the game.

Nine Ball. In the last 20 years, nine ball has replaced straight pool (see below) as the game of choice for tournaments and matches for expert players. The balls, numbered one through

The cue stance should be relaxed and comfortable. The feet should form a line at about a 45-degree angle to the line of aim. The head should be directly over the cue, sighting as if through a gun sight. Keep the left arm straight and the feet in a comfortable position.

The bridge (position of the hand) must be solid to give firm guidance to the cue.

Another form of the bridge involves placing the fingers firmly on the table and using the thumb to guide the cue.

nine, are racked in a diamond shape as shown, with the 9 ball in the center and the 1 ball at the front. Whoever pockets the 9 ball wins. When breaking the balls, the cue ball must hit the 1 ball first. Players must always hit the lowest-numbered ball on the table first; if they do and any ball goes into a pocket, they shoot again. If a ball other than the lowest ball is contacted by the cue ball before other balls and a ball is pocketed, the pocketed ball is returned to the table on the foot spot and the next player shoots. If the 9 ball goes in on a legal shot, the game is over, even if other balls remain on the table.

Rotation. All 15 balls are racked in a triangle with the 1 ball in front and the 2 ball and 3 ball at the other corners. The 1 ball must be hit first on the break. On each shot, the cue ball must hit the lowest-numbered ball first; if it does and any ball goes in, the player shoots again. All balls pocketed during a player's turn at the table are totaled and credited to the player. Each ball is worth its number; for example, the 10 ball counts ten points. Since the numbers from 1 to 15 add up to 120 points, whoever scores 61 points or more wins.

Straight Pool. This game is considered the best test of skill by many top players. On each shot, the player must indicate which ball is intended for which pocket, a form of play termed "call shot." The numbers on the balls have no significance. Each legally pocketed ball counts one point, and a game consists of an agreed-on number of points. When only one ball remains on the table, the other 14 are racked in a triangle with the front ball missing. If the player can pocket the remaining ball and break the rack at the same time, that player can continue shooting.

Straight Billiards. Straight billiards is more popular than any other cue game in Europe, North Africa, Latin America, and Asia. A pocketless table and only three balls are used, a cue ball for each player and a red ball (sometimes two red balls). To start, the red ball is placed on the foot spot, one cue ball on the head spot, and the other cue ball 6 inches (15.2 centimeters) to one side of the head spot. A point is scored if the shooter can make the cue ball hit the other two balls, and the game is over when an agreed-on number of points is reached. By keeping the balls close together and near a cushion, experts can make hundreds, even thousands, of points in a row.

Three Cushion. In this difficult but beautiful game, points are scored by making the cue ball hit the other two balls; however, before it hits the second ball, it must contact three or more cushions. Many of the greatest players in the world prefer this game over all others. National championships are held in many countries, including the United States, and a world championship is held every year.

▶**TIPS FOR SUCCESS**

To become a good player, much practice is necessary and a great amount of thought and skill is required. The best way to learn is to take lessons from an accomplished player or to watch pool or billiards tournaments. You can also improve your game by reading books or magazines and by watching videotapes. These are readily available in libraries, bookstores, and billiard supply stores.

Robert Byrne
Author, *Byrne's Standard Book of Pool and Billiards*

BILLINGS. See Montana (Cities).

BILL OF RIGHTS

The Bill of Rights—the first ten amendments to the Constitution of the United States—ranks alongside the Constitution and the Declaration of Independence as one of the nation's most treasured documents. Since its adoption in 1791, the Bill of Rights has served as the cornerstone of basic American freedoms. Its laws specify the fundamental rights and most cherished liberties of the American people and protect them from the whims of popular majority opinions and abusive government officials.

The Bill of Rights became part of the Constitution of the United States on December 15, 1791. On the 150th anniversary of this event in 1941, President Franklin Roosevelt proclaimed December 15 as Bill of Rights Day. He wanted to make Americans aware of their rights and to remind them of their duties as citizens of the United States. On this day in 1991, Americans recognized the 200th anniversary of these important amendments that have proved so essential to the American political tradition.

The Bill of Rights, on display at the National Archives in Washington, D.C., summarizes the basic rights and freedoms of American citizens.

▶ WHY THE BILL OF RIGHTS WAS ADDED TO THE CONSTITUTION

At the Constitutional Convention of 1787, delegates rejected a motion made by George Mason, author of the Virginia Declaration of Rights (1776), to preface the Constitution of the United States with a bill of rights. The failure to mention basic rights soon became a major issue in the subsequent debates over whether or not the proposed Constitution would be ratified, or approved.

When the Constitutional Convention ended, delegates went back to their respective states to hold their own ratifying conventions. Each state would decide for itself whether or not to approve the new framework for the American government.

The debate over the need for a bill of rights was sparked by a proposal made by a dissenting minority in the Pennsylvania ratifying convention. Some delegates believed that guarantees of certain basic rights and liberties were missing from the proposed Constitution. They called for a number of amendments that would secure a wide range of liberties, such as the free exercise of religion, freedom of speech and press, and protection against unreasonable searches and seizures. Majorities in the ratifying conventions of New Hampshire, Massachusetts, New York, Maryland, Virginia, North Carolina and South Carolina also called for numerous amendments to the proposed Constitution. Although the substance of these recommended amendments differed from state to state, most contained provisions that would limit the powers of the new federal (national) government and protect the people from inconsistent and oppressive rule.

"....a bill of rights is what the people are entitled to against every government on earth, general or particular, and what no just government should refuse, or rest on inferences."

From a letter Thomas Jefferson wrote to James Madison, December 20, 1787.

The Anti-Federalists (those who were opposed to ratifying the Constitution) argued that the broad powers of the new federal government would threaten the powers of the individual states and the liberties of the people. However, the Federalists (those who supported ratification) argued that a bill of rights was unnecessary. Alexander Hamilton, for example, maintained that because the proposed federal government would possess only specifically assigned and limited powers, it could not endanger the fundamental liberties of the people. "Why," he asked, "declare that things shall not be done which there is no power to do? Why, for instance, should it be said that the liberty of the press shall not be restrained, when no power is given by which restrictions may be imposed?"

Nevertheless, the Federalists had to pledge their support for the addition of a bill of rights to the Constitution once the new government began operations. Otherwise they would risk endangering the Constitution's ratification in certain key states and face the possibility of another constitutional convention.

▶DRAFTING THE BILL OF RIGHTS

James Madison, the "Father of the Constitution," may also be considered the "Father of the Bill of Rights." In his campaign for a seat in the House of Representatives under the new Constitution, he promised his voters that he would energetically push for the adoption of a bill of rights. True to his word, he took the lead in the First Congress in pressing for the desired amendments.

On June 8, 1789, drawing from proposals made by the various state ratifying conventions, Madison proposed to the Congress nine amendments to the Constitution, containing nineteen specific provisions (many of which are now contained in the Bill of Rights). Madison and members of a House committee then went through the complex process of drafting a bill that would secure the necessary two-thirds approval of both houses of Congress. The House and the Senate modified some of Madison's proposals, eliminated others entirely, and added some new ones as well.

As it finally emerged from Congress, the proposed Bill of Rights consisted of twelve amendments and was offered to the states for ratification. The first two proposed amendments were never ratified by the states. (One was related to the size of the House of Representatives and the other to laws regarding the compensation, or payment, for senators and representatives.) On December 15, 1791, Virginia ratified the remaining ten amendments, and the Bill of Rights officially became part of the Constitution.

▶WHAT THE BILL OF RIGHTS SAYS

The first eight amendments of the Bill of Rights set forth specific guarantees and liberties. The Ninth Amendment acknowledges that the American people have rights that are not even specified in the Constitution or the Bill of Rights. (The Federalists argued for this particular amendment, stating that it would be impossible to list all of the rights and liberties that should be protected.)

The Tenth Amendment emphasizes the national character of the United States constitutional system. It declares that the states or people retain those "powers not delegated to the United States by the Constitution."

Most people, however, believe that their most important rights are those guaranteed by the First Amendment. Commonly called "First Amendment freedoms," these are the fundamental freedoms of religion, speech, and press, as well as the right of the people to assemble and to petition a government.

Other vital provisions contained in the first eight amendments also deal with the rights of individuals. They are designed to protect people against inconsistent or abusive government, particularly in criminal proceedings.

For example, the Fourth Amendment protects individuals from unreasonable searches and seizures (either of themselves or of their property and possessions) by law enforcement officials.

The Fifth Amendment prohibits double jeopardy, which means that someone cannot be tried twice for the same crime. The Fifth Amendment also states that people cannot be compelled to testify against themselves (self-incrimination), and it guarantees "due process," which means people accused of a crime must be properly notified of the charges and given a fair hearing.

The Sixth Amendment establishes the right of an accused person to a public trial by jury. The accused also has the right to have a lawyer, to confront hostile witnesses, and to obtain witnesses in his or her defense.

Finally, the Eighth Amendment prohibits the infliction of "cruel and unusual punishments" (either mental or physical) on those convicted of a crime.

The remaining amendments (the Second, Third, and Seventh) do not cover individual rights in criminal proceedings but address other specific concerns. The Second Amendment is the most noteworthy and controversial of these remaining amendments. After noting the need for a "well regulated militia" (a body of citizen soldiers called to serve during times of emergency or war), this amendment declares that the people's right ". . . to keep and bear Arms, shall not be infringed."

The Third Amendment prevents the government from making citizens shelter soldiers in their homes. This amendment was drafted in response to abuses by British forces during the Revolutionary War.

The Seventh Amendment was included to meet the demands of many Anti-Federalists who wanted to insure trial by jury in civil suits.

▶ **THE ORIGINS OF THE BILL OF RIGHTS**

The Virginia Bill of Rights (proclaimed in 1776, only days before the Declaration of Independence) was the first of ten such declarations by the states during the Revolutionary War period (1775–83). All of these declarations contained provisions that eventually found their way into the national Bill of Rights. Major portions of the First, Fourth,

---

The Bill of Rights

The First Ten Amendments to the Constitution of the United States
(Ratified December 15, 1791)

Amendment 1
Congress shall make no law respecting an establishment of religion, or prohibiting the free exercise thereof; or abridging the freedom of speech, or of the press; or the right of the people peaceably to assemble, and to petition the government for a redress of grievances.

Amendment 2
A well regulated Militia, being necessary to the security of a free State, the right of the people to keep and bear Arms, shall not be infringed.

Amendment 3
No Soldier shall, in time of peace be quartered in any house, without the consent of the Owner, nor in time of war, but in a manner to be prescribed by law.

Amendment 4
The right of the people to be secure in their persons, houses, papers, and effects, against unreasonable searches and seizures, shall not be violated, and no Warrants shall issue, but upon probable cause, supported by Oath or affirmation, and particularly describing the place to be searched, and the persons or things to be seized.

Amendment 5
No person shall be held to answer for a capital, or otherwise infamous crime, unless on a presentment or indictment of a Grand Jury, except in cases arising in the land or naval forces, or in the Militia, when in actual service in time of War or public danger; nor shall any person be subject for the same offense to be twice put in jeopardy of life or limb; nor shall be compelled in any criminal case to be a witness against himself, nor be deprived of life, liberty, or property, without due process of law; nor shall private property be taken for public use, without just compensation.

Amendment 6
In all criminal prosecutions, the accused shall enjoy the right to a speedy and public trial, by an impartial jury of the State and district wherein the crime shall have been committed, which district shall have been previously ascertained by law, and to be informed of the nature and cause of the accusation; to be confronted with the witnesses against him; to have compulsory process for obtaining witnesses in his favor, and to have the Assistance of Counsel for his defence.

Amendment 7
In Suits at common law, where the value in controversy shall exceed twenty dollars, the right of trial by jury shall be preserved, and no fact tried by a jury shall be otherwise re-examined in any Court of the United States, than according to the rules of the common law.

Amendment 8
Excessive bail shall not be required, nor excessive fines imposed, nor cruel and unusual punishments inflicted.

Amendment 9
The enumeration in the Constitution, of certain rights, shall not be construed to deny or disparage others retained by the people.

Amendment 10
The powers not delegated to the United States by the Constitution, nor prohibited by it to the States, are reserved to the States respectively, or to the people.

Fifth, Sixth, and Eighth amendments, for example, can be traced directly to the Virginia Bill of Rights.

The origins of many of the other rights and liberties contained in the Bill of Rights can be found in the English tradition, dating as far back as Magna Carta (1215), a document that marked the first step toward constitutional law in England. For example, the clause in the Fifth Amendment, which declares that individuals cannot be deprived of their "life, liberty, or property, without due process of law" is rooted in Chapter 39 of Magna Carta.

England's Petition of Right (1628) and Bill of Rights (1689) further expanded individual liberties and placed increased limitations on the ruler's powers and authority. English liberties and rights, such as trial by jury and protection against self-incrimination and unreasonable search and seizure, were, in fact, included in the charters establishing the American colonies. They were considered to be the "rights of Englishmen."

▶ ENFORCING THE BILL OF RIGHTS

The courts, both state and national, are responsible for enforcing the Bill of Rights, when instances of abuse are brought to their attention through proper legal channels. The Supreme Court of the United States, however, has the final word in determining whether or not the principles contained in the Bill of Rights have been violated.

Making such a determination is seldom an easy matter. The Court, for example, must answer such questions as, What constitutes "unreasonable" search and seizure? What limits can be placed on the free exercise of religion for reasons of public morality, safety, or health? Under what circumstances may speech be legally curtailed to prevent violence or property damage?

Originally, the Bill of Rights applied only to the laws and activities of the national government. It was not until after the Civil War that the Bill of Rights' provisions were applied to the states. The 14th Amendment (1868) was the first to declare that no state "shall . . . deprive any person of life, liberty, or property without due process of law."

Today, for all intents and purposes, the fundamental rights and liberties guaranteed by the Bill of Rights apply with equal force to both the national and the state governments.

▶ STATE BILLS OF RIGHTS

All of the fifty state constitutions contain a bill of rights. The Illinois Bill of Rights borrows from the Declaration of Independence in stating, "All men are by nature free and independent and have certain inherent and unalienable rights among which are life, liberty, and the pursuit of happiness." Some states' declaration of rights are even far more detailed than the national Bill of Rights. The California Declaration of Rights, for example, says, "A person may not be disqualified from entering or pursuing a business, profession, vocation, or employment because of sex, race, creed, color, or national or ethnic origin."

▶ THE CANADIAN BILL OF RIGHTS

The Canadian Charter of Rights and Freedoms, officially proclaimed by the Canada Act on April 17, 1982, applies to both the national and provincial governments. Sections of the charter deal with distinctly Canadian concerns, such as declaring the French and English languages to have equal status in official government proceedings.

The charter details major rights and liberties under the headings of **Fundamental Freedoms** and **Legal Rights**. The fundamental freedoms correspond to those found in the First Amendment in the American Bill of Rights, but they are more extensive. In addition to freedom for the press and media, peaceful assembly, and freedom of speech and religion, they include freedom of association, conscience, thought, belief, and opinion.

The legal rights of the charter are similar to those found in the Fourth, Fifth, Sixth, and Eighth amendments in the American Bill of Rights. These include, among others, protection against self-incrimination, double jeopardy, unreasonable search and seizure, and cruel and unusual punishment.

GEORGE CAREY
Author, *The Federalist: Design for a Constitutional Republic*

See also FEDERALIST, THE; FIRST AMENDMENT FREEDOMS; UNITED STATES, CONSTITUTION OF THE; UNITED STATES, GOVERNMENT OF THE; UNITED STATES, HISTORY OF THE.

BILLY THE KID. See NEW MEXICO (Famous People).

BILOXI. See MISSISSIPPI (Cities).

BINARY SYSTEM. See NUMERALS AND NUMERATION SYSTEMS.

BINGHAM, HIRAM. See HAWAII (Famous People).

BIOCHEMISTRY

Biochemistry forms the meeting ground of two great sciences: biology and chemistry.

There is a Greek word, *bios,* which means "life." For that reason **biology** is the name given to the study of living things—animals, plants, and microscopic forms of life. Biology takes in the description of living things. It takes in their ways of living and growing and reproducing.

Chemistry is the name given to the study of the composition of various substances. It includes the manner in which the composition changes or can be changed. Chemists are interested in all substances: those in rocks, in sea water, and even in distant stars.

Now suppose you combine biology and chemistry. You have the study of the substances that make up living things, their composition and the changes they undergo. This is **biochemistry**.

▶ THE ORIGINS OF BIOCHEMISTRY

Biochemistry is a fairly new science, but many of its processes are as old as life. The means by which green plants make their food is a biochemical process. So is digestion in human beings and in other animals. Long before people knew anything about science, they stumbled upon biochemical processes. Cooking is one. Some substances in food are changed when the food is cooked. The food is made tastier and easier to digest. Primitive people also found that if fruit juice was allowed to remain in a warm, dark place, certain changes took place in it. The juice fermented and changed to wine.

Such discoveries were accidental. People did not understand what happened during cooking or fermentation. They understood only that by certain methods they could change various substances. Then in the late 1700's modern chemistry was developed.

How Chemistry Led to Biochemistry

The early chemists were concerned with what we call inorganic chemistry, or the chemistry of nonliving things. For example, they were interested in minerals. Yet they could not ignore living things altogether. Certain substances existed both in living organisms and in the nonliving world. For instance, all creatures are made up mostly of water; this is the same water that we find all about us.

However, chemists also knew that many substances of living organisms are not at all like those of the nonliving world. One important difference has to do with what happens when they are heated.

When inorganic substances are heated, no basic change takes place in them. Iron that is melted is still iron. Water that is boiled is still water. If a copper bowl is broken up and melted down, a second bowl can be made of the material.

With organic substances the basic form is easily changed by heat. They char, smoke, or burn. And then they are no longer what they were to begin with. There is no way that a cooked or burned egg can be made back into a raw egg.

Because organic substances are easily changed, the chemists who studied them had to work more carefully and slowly than the chemists who studied rocks and minerals. Even so, between 1750 and 1850 chemists learned much about the nature of these substances. Organic chemistry, or the chemistry of living things, became the first approach to biochemistry.

Among the early discoveries were the three main kinds of organic substances that make up all living matter. Chemists called them carbohydrates, fats, and proteins. Examples of carbohydrates are starch and sugar; wood is mostly cellulose, which is another kind of carbohydrate. Butter and olive oil are examples of fats. Gelatin and egg white are examples of protein.

The human body uses carbohydrates and fats for energy. It uses protein to form new tissue.

Both fats and carbohydrates are made up of three elements. They are carbon, hydrogen, and oxygen. In the body these combine with oxygen from the air to supply energy. Before long, chemists discovered that proteins were far more complicated than either fats or carbohydrates. Protein contains not only carbon, hydrogen, and oxygen, but also nitrogen. The body uses nitrogen in building new tissue.

In spite of these discoveries, scientists still thought that organic matter had no connec-

Friedrich Wöhler (1800–82) proved that it was possible to make an organic substance from inorganic chemicals.

tion with inorganic chemicals. They believed it was impossible to change inorganic substances into organic substances.

Then in 1828 a German chemist named Friedrich Wöhler accidentally proved that false. While heating some inorganic chemicals he happened to make an organic substance, urea. Up to that time scientists believed that only a living body could make an organic substance.

Wöhler's discovery was the first real breakthrough into biochemistry. Scientists then realized there could be no clear dividing line between chemical processes and life processes. Chemists and biologists found that their work was overlapping more and more.

▶ WHAT BIOCHEMISTS STUDY

Biochemists today explore a great range of subjects. These fall into several main areas.

Pharmacology

One of the oldest branches of biochemistry is called **pharmacology.** It is the study of how chemicals affect living tissue. Everyone who orders drugs or a prescription from the pharmacist comes in touch with this branch of biochemistry.

The fact that certain plants could be used to cure various diseases had long been known. In the 1800's scientists began to learn about the chemical basis of these cures. They also learned to make new substances that resembled natural chemicals in many ways but were not found in living tissues. Some of these substances that they made had powerful effects on living tissue.

Among the great discoveries of the 1800's were the antiseptics, chemicals that could kill germs. Scientists also discovered chemicals that could deaden pain. These are the anesthetics.

Chemotherapy

Chemotherapy, a special branch of pharmacology, is the treatment of diseases with chemicals. In the 20th century laboratories made new chemicals that could destroy germs without hurting human beings. Other chemicals, called antibiotics, were obtained from microbes. They were even more deadly to germs. By the 1970's chemotherapy had brought many ancient diseases under control. Other diseases, such as cancer, were under constant attack by researchers.

Dietetics

Toward the end of the 1800's the science of **dietetics** became very important. This is the study of how the body makes use of foods. Biochemists began by using animals in experiments. They fed special diets to rats or guinea pigs and studied the effects on the animals.

By 1900 biochemists realized that it was not enough just to eat food. People had to have the proper foods. Certain substances were important to health and to life, even though these substances were present in the body only in tiny quantities. Many of these substances could not be made by the body, so they had to be present in the diet. Some of these substances were inorganic. Others were organic. They were given the name "vitamins."

If vitamins are missing from the diet, a person can develop a deficiency disease such as anemia or scurvy. The most common form

Hereditary substances, such as the DNA molecule (shown *at right* in the computer-generated drawing), can be manipulated in the laboratory (*above*) to produce enzymes and other body chemicals.

of anemia is caused by a lack of iron in the blood; scurvy is caused by a lack of vitamin C. Biochemists have learned not only what foods are necessary to fight such deficiency diseases but also how to make vitamins in the laboratory.

Endocrinology

Shortly after 1900 the biochemists discovered that certain organs in the body produce substances that keep the body in proper working order. These chemical substances are called hormones. The study of hormones is called **endocrinology.**

If the body's organs do not produce the proper amount of hormones, serious disorders can result. The most common disease of this sort is diabetes; it is caused by a lack of the hormone called insulin. Biochemists have learned how to take hormones such as insulin from the glands of animals. People with diabetes can use insulin that has been obtained from cattle. Diabetics can now lead almost normal lives if they use insulin carefully. And biochemists are learning how to make other hormones in the laboratory.

The Body's Chemistry

Since 1900 biochemists have concentrated more and more on the chemical changes that go on in people. The changes that can occur are so many and so complicated that it takes long, hard work for the biochemist to untangle all the threads.

The most complicated organic substances are the proteins. They are made of long chains of organic chemicals called amino acids. Although there are only about two dozen different kinds of amino acids, the body can put them together in millions of different ways. Each different protein has its own special purpose in the human body.

For example, there are special kinds of proteins called enzymes. Each of the millions of changes that take place in the body depends on one particular kind of enzyme. If this particular enzyme is missing from the body, then the body cannot change one substance into another. There are special enzymes, for example, that make it possible for food to be digested. Biochemists have also discovered that enzymes are responsible for the fermentation of bread dough and fruit juice.

▶FUTURE DEVELOPMENTS

The most exciting future developments in biochemistry lie in two directions.

Photosynthesis

For many years scientists wanted to work out the exact changes that go on in green plants when they combine the carbon dioxide of the air with water and form starch. The green plant uses the energy of sunlight to bring about this change, and the process is called **photosynthesis.**

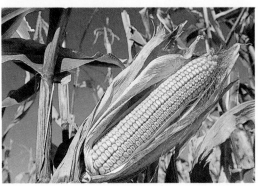

Biochemists study the effects of nitrogen deficiency on crops such as corn (*above*). Without nitrogen, plants yield stunted ears (*top right*); with nitrogen, plants yield healthy, full-grown ears (*bottom right*).

It is photosynthesis that creates the world's food supply. And when plants form starch, oxygen is given off to the air. It is photosynthesis, therefore, that keeps the air breathable and prevents us from ever using up the world's oxygen supply.

Until 1945 practically nothing was known about photosynthesis. Now the details are being revealed at a fast rate. If biochemists can learn enough about photosynthesis, they may be able to bring about the same chemical reactions. Then they may be able to learn ways of making food out of air, water, and sunlight so that we will depend less on rainfall and good harvests.

Using modern techniques, biochemists have been able to develop plants with special characteristics, such as these thornless blackberries.

Genetics

The other exciting development involves the study of the way in which the pattern of chemical change in a body is inherited. Children inherit far more than outward appearance from their parents. Many of the internal substances and processes that make us what we are—the diseases we may have or how long we live—are determined by our inherited chemical patterns. The study of these patterns is called **genetics.**

This science takes its name from the genes, tiny elements in certain body cells that determine heredity. Biochemists have discovered that the genes are made up of special proteins called nucleic acids. Each nucleic acid brings about the formation of a particular enzyme by what is called the "genetic code." In the 1950's and 1960's biochemists began to work out the genetic code.

Once the code is fully understood, scientists may be able to correct many human conditions that cannot now be helped. It may become possible to assure health and long life from the beginning.

ISAAC ASIMOV
Boston University School of Medicine

See also BIOLOGY; BODY, HUMAN; BODY CHEMISTRY; CHEMISTRY, HISTORY OF; GENETICS; LIFE; PHOTOSYNTHESIS.

BIOGRAPHY, AUTOBIOGRAPHY, AND BIOGRAPHICAL NOVEL

Biography is both a craft and an art. As a craftsman the biographer begins with research, gathering all the available information about a person's life. There are first the surface facts about a chosen subject. Then the biographer looks beneath the surface for evidence of inner truths—what the man or woman thought, felt, desired, suffered.

The biographer as an artist sets down the meaning of a person's life. With his research at hand, the writer chooses the facts he will use. Sometimes it is the bulk of detail; sometimes it is the essence, or pith. With this task of selection comes the task of writing the story in a clear, convincing way. The artist must so construct his book that every portion of the person's life fits into an understandable, moving whole. The writing must have style; the structure must have architectural form. That is the meaning of art.

▶ BIOGRAPHY OLD AND NEW

Modern biography, as an independent and popular literary form, is fairly new. Writing about individual lives, however, is an old practice. The Bible is full of stories about the prophets and saints. The earliest Greek biographical writing was done by Xenophon, who wrote about Socrates in the 4th century B.C. Plutarch's *Parallel Lives* (about A.D. 100) is still famous. The best-known Latin biographer is Suetonius, author of *Lives of the Caesars* in A.D. 120. Tacitus set down an account of the life of his father-in-law, Agricola, in A.D. 97–98. The purposes of these early Greek and Roman biographers were mixed. Some tried to tell the history of a dynasty or of a war. Others attempted to justify a moral or philosophical system. As a result the human story was sometimes lost.

Modern biographers' aims are varied. Some wish to tell an exciting, dramatic, and often inspirational human story. Others study the life of a person so that we can profit by another's experience and better understand ourselves and the world about us. Still others wish to make the past more alive. Instead of writing about the impersonal forces of history, the biographer tells of the impact of an individual on the life of his times. There is Lytton Strachey's *Eminent Victorians,* which describes an interesting age in England. Douglas S. Freeman's *George Washington* portrays the beginning of the American nation. Hendrik Willem van Loon's *R.v.R.,* a biography of Rembrandt, serves as an introduction to art. René Jules Dubos' *Louis Pasteur* gives us a picture of the scientist at work.

Biography may be written out of love or hate but never out of indifference. It may take years to write. It may require thousands of hours of study in libraries, law courts, halls of records, city halls, museums, family archives. Frequently many miles must be traveled to visit the places where the subject lived and worked, to interview men still alive who can add to the body of knowledge. This concentrated effort can be achieved only by people who love deeply—such as the biographers of Jefferson or Michelangelo or Edison—or by those who hate deeply, such as the biographers of Torquemada or Hitler or Mussolini.

Often the search is frustrating. For a conscientious biographer the easily available material won't be half enough. A researcher is a detective. He hunts down clues, pursues scraps of evidence, never gives up looking for material he senses must exist. In his hero's life there are always blank spaces that must be filled in if the biography is to be complete and true. To a good biographer everything is findable. When he comes up empty-handed, he must return to the quest with fresh ideas and renewed courage. For it is not enough to know everything a man did. It is also important to know why he did what he did—his reasoning, his fears, his failures before he achieved something important.

Once all his material is collected, the biographer faces a new challenge. The reader must feel that he is in the hands of a thorough and honest workman. Therefore, the biographer has to be objective. He has to tell the complete truth, based on his findings. He must not conceal his hero's faults, omit his shortcomings, bury his failures. He must not allow his own prejudices to take over. What is known as his "principle of selection," that is, his choice of materials to use, must be strictly ethical. Otherwise the reader will sense that something is wrong. He will feel that he is being deceived.

But when he reads an honest, well-balanced biography, such as Benjamin Thomas' *Abraham Lincoln* or Muriel Rukeyser's *Willard Gibbs* or Carl Van Doren's *Benjamin Franklin,* he will know that the strands of each story are accurately woven.

Biography is one of the most enjoyable forms of reading and learning. While reading biographies, one can sit at home yet roam the realms of time and space with *Genghis Khan* (Harold Lamb), *Napoleon* (Emil Ludwig), *Aristotle* (W. D. Ross), and *Madame Curie* (Eve Curie). A good biographer will become as one with the person he is writing about. This union enables the reader, in turn, to live another's life in his imagination.

▶ AUTOBIOGRAPHY

Autobiography is a very different medium. "Auto" comes from the Greek for "self," "one's own." An autobiography is the story of a person's life written by himself. Sometimes an autobiography is ghostwritten, that is, written by someone else, frequently with journalistic experience. Sometimes the real writer is completely unknown. Sometimes there is an "as told to . . ." approach.

Autobiography is a difficult art form, yet it looks easy. Perhaps that is what tempts so many thousands to try it.

A man sometimes writes his own story because he has experienced some kind of self-discovery. The discovery may be about his relationship to life, to his fellow man, or to God. Others write about their struggles against great odds and their eventual success. The autobiographies of Alfred E. Smith and Helen Keller show a refusal to be held down or defeated. Some autobiographies, like those of Booker T. Washington and Jane Addams, glow with an individual's dedication to a life of serving mankind. Greatness of character, which seems to spring from selflessness and courage, often reveals itself in an autobiography. The best of these life stories raise the stature of the human race. They inspire the reader and deepen his understanding.

Not all autobiographies are written for noble purposes. Many are written for selfish reasons—to get money, attention, sympathy, or revenge. Yet all too often the writer of autobiography conveys the exact opposite of the impression he had hoped to impart.

Every kind of American has written an autobiography. As a group, clergymen are more interested in writing about themselves than any other single category. Authors and politicians follow close behind. Industrialists, scientists, and engineers tend to remain silent. In between come the educators, the reformers, the military and the professional men. It has become fashionable for actors and athletes to have their stories ghostwritten.

▶ THE BIOGRAPHICAL NOVEL

In recent years a third biographical form has become increasingly popular and important. It is called the biographical novel. This is biography presented in the form of a novel, with dialogue, suspense, and plot structure. The biographical novelist can use his creative imagination to develop these aspects of the novel. But he must do so only within the framework of truth. The novelist will have found the truth in documents—diaries, letters, journals, notes, recorded deeds.

The biographical novel is thus the fruit of a marriage between the research of biography and the fictional devices of the novelist. Books like *I, Claudius* (Robert Graves) and *The Romance of Leonardo da Vinci* (Dimitri Sergeevich Merezhkovski) are fine examples of the biographical novel. It offers a more emotional approach to life, with more personal interpretation by the author. Facts can be forgotten, but rarely an emotional experience. The biographical novelist tries to catch up his readers in the emotions of his hero. Emotions felt while reading a biographical novel can be almost as unforgettable as the emotions one experiences in real life.

Not every life will fit into the form of the biographical novel. Dramatic elements must be present, along with an overall pattern into which the parts can be fitted. Many lives, important in their achievement, do not lend themselves to the nature of the novel. Other lives seem to have been lived as though the subject were constantly aware that he was creating a dramatic structure.

Biography, autobiography, and the biographical novel are personal books. They tell the story of men's lives, in order to help us understand mankind.

IRVING STONE
Author, *Lust for Life, The Agony and the Ecstasy*

BIOLOGICAL CLOCK

As the sun rises on a warm, sunny day, the trumpet-shaped flowers of the morning glory unfold. It is in the afternoon, as the morning glories close, that the buds of moss roses uncurl. When darkness comes, moss roses curl shut. Only then do evening primrose flowers open, pale and ghostly in the night. In the morning, before daylight, they close again.

The opening and closing of the flowers is one of the natural cycles, called **biological rhythms**, that occur in living things. The biological rhythms of the morning glories, moss roses, and evening primroses occur within a single day. Such rhythms are called *circadian rhythms*, from the Latin words *circa* and *diem*, meaning "about a day." But not all biological rhythms are based on a day. Some, such as the beating of the heart, occur every few seconds. Other rhythms are repeated each month and still others are repeated each year.

Scientists use the term **biological clock** to describe the internal timing mechanism that controls biological rhythms. Where is this biological clock and what is it? In animals, the brain is thought to play a role; however, plants, fungi, and microscopic organisms lack brains and still exhibit biological rhythms. There is increasing evidence that chemicals produced by living things trigger the cycles. These chemicals, in turn, are controlled by factors outside the living organism including the light-dark cycle of a day and the changing seasons of a year. Yet, even if an organism is shut off from all clues in the environment, it will still display biological rhythms.

▶ BIOLOGICAL CLOCKS IN NATURE

The biological rhythms of seashore organisms are often linked to the rise and fall of the ocean's tides. Clams, mussels, and barnacles feed by filtering food from the water. When the tide is in, their shells open and they feed. As the tides go out, the shells close and the animals are protected from the drying air.

The migration of animals is an event that is triggered by a signal from an animal's biological clock. One of the most dramatic examples of a migration is the journey some birds make in spring and autumn. These migrations are associated with changes in day length. As days grow longer, birds leave their winter feeding grounds in the south. By the time they reach their northern destination, the plants they depend on for food are flourishing there. When the birds reach their summer feeding grounds, another biological rhythm is triggered: They are ready to mate and raise young. As autumn approaches, days shorten, temperatures drop, and plants begin to die. Birds' biological clocks signal the return to the south where there is food and warmth.

Like flowers, birds, and other animals, humans have biological clocks that control their biological rhythms. Humans have daily, weekly, monthly, and seasonal biological rhythms. Body temperature, blood pressure,

The jimsonweed, which blooms at night, is a desert flower with a biological rhythm opposite that of most flowers. *Right:* Throughout the hours of daylight, the flower of the jimsonweed remains tightly closed. *Far right:* After the sun has set, the funnel-shaped flower slowly opens.

sleeping and waking, and the levels of many chemicals in the body have a 24-hour rhythm. Many illnesses appear to have a yearly rhythm. Colds, flu, and pneumonia are most common in autumn and winter. Measles most often occur in spring and summer.

▶ CHANGES IN BIOLOGICAL CLOCKS

When people travel by plane across several time zones, their internal clocks are no longer in tune with where they are. This is called jet lag. Its effects are worse when people travel to a place with a later time (that is, west to east) than when they travel to a place with an earlier time (east to west). People with jet lag feel cranky and tired. They may also be clumsy and forgetful. It takes several days for the body's biological clock to reset to the new time zone.

People who work night shifts also experience problems with their biological clocks. They are generally not as productive or alert as people who work during the day, and they have more accidents on the job. They also have more health and sleep problems than people who work day shifts.

In recent years, scientists have made important discoveries about what controls circadian rhythms. The hormone melatonin, for

At a signal from their biological clocks, monarch butterflies gather in huge swarms to make a yearly migration that covers thousands of miles.

example, has been found to play a key role in resetting the body's clock. Sleeping aids containing artificially made melatonin are now available to help people overcome the effects of jet lag and shift work.

Scientists have also discovered that exposure to bright light can change the body's natural production of melatonin. Such change affects not only sleep-wake cycles but also a person's mood. Light-sensitive chemicals in the eyes and perhaps even in the skin appear to be involved.

▶ MEDICAL APPLICATIONS

Other exciting breakthroughs are being made with new medical treatments. Certain medical problems are associated with different times of the day. Heart attacks and strokes happen most often during the waking hours before noon. Asthma and ulcer attacks occur most often between midnight and 8 A.M. Thus, heart medication taken right after waking may help protect a person with heart disease. Medication for asthma and ulcers is available in time-release tablets. When these tablets are taken at night, an individual is helped most during the high-risk time.

Biological clocks control the many familiar rhythms of life. As scientists learn more about these rhythms, especially those in humans, new solutions can be found to make travel more comfortable, working conditions safer, and medical treatment more effective.

KARIN L. RHINES
Coauthor, *Discover Science*

See also HIBERNATION; HOMING AND MIGRATION.

Workers who switch between day and night shifts, such as these firefighters, experience problems with their biological clocks similar to the effects of jet lag.

BIOLOGY

You only have to look around and listen to see and hear the evidence of life. Outside, squirrels romp among the trees gathering nuts, bees dart busily in and out of flowers carrying their valuable cargo of nectar and pollen, and birds fly from ground to nest, chirping as they go. Besides those plants and animals that are readily seen, there are countless tiny living creatures in the soil, water, and air. For centuries, people have been interested in the lives of organisms around them. This interest and the observations that were generated from it were the foundation for the science of biology. Biology is the study of living things in all their forms.

▶ THE STUDY OF LIFE

Biology is a creative, dynamic, and constantly changing science. It is influenced by our social, cultural, and historical settings. Our concerns about global warming, AIDS, and overpopulation did not concern early **biologists**, the scientists who study living things. They just wanted to know which plants and animals were present in different parts of the world.

But no matter what period of time they live in, biologists examine their environments. In their searchings, they are stirred by their curiosity to ask similar questions: How do living and nonliving things differ? How was such a variety of living things produced on Earth? What makes something able to survive in its environment and reproduce? How are creatures such as a massive elephant and a microscopic bacterium alike, and how do they differ? How do all the organisms on Earth interact with one another to make the Earth what it is? How will human beings be affected by changes in the world? Wherever the search for answers to these and other questions leads biologists, it always begins with the same question: Is it a living thing?

▶ HOW BIOLOGISTS DETERMINE WHAT IS LIVING

We somehow know that a human being, a rose, and a worm are living things, while a rock and a cloud are not. Yet what are the differences between them that determine which is living and which is not? Biologists have identified a common set of characteristics that are shared by all organisms.

The world around us vibrates with the pulse of life. Biologists have identified 1.5 million species and estimate that there are perhaps as many as 50 million species of living things populating our Earth.

Organisms Are Made of Cells. All organisms are composed of the same building blocks called cells. Most cells are so small that they can be seen only with a microscope. A cell is truly the basic unit of life—it contains all the necessary components to carry on the activities of life. Like a tiny factory, a cell constructs its own tools, machinery, rooms, and even its own building. It can even repair itself and generate its own energy or power. Some simple life-forms, such as bacteria, consist of a single cell and are called unicellular. In contrast, complex life-forms, such as a whale or an oak tree, have trillions of cells and are called multicellular organisms.

Organisms Need Energy. An organism needs energy to perform the vital tasks that keep it alive. It gets that energy from its environment. Just as you eat food to get energy, other living things use materials in their environment for energy.

Ultimately, the sun is the main source of energy. Its energy flows through nearly all forms of life. Green plants and certain microorganisms capture the energy of sunlight. Through a process called **photosynthesis**, they convert the light energy into food for themselves, into energy-rich sugar molecules, and into new cells. We see the effects of this process as trees grow and produce new leaves.

Many living things, including human beings, cannot perform photosynthesis. They get their energy by eating plants and animals that have eaten plants. The chemicals, or nutrients, in the food are broken down to release the trapped energy using chemical reactions. The released energy can then be used to do work and make new cell parts. The sum of all these chemical reactions that fuel the activities of a cell is called **metabolism**.

Organisms Maintain Their Internal Environment. To stay alive and work efficiently, an organism must keep the conditions within its body in a consistently steady state. In multicellular organisms, this process is called **homeostasis**, from the Greek words meaning "to stay the same." Cells must continuously adapt to preserve this steady state. For example, cells cannot function if the temperature changes drastically. Your heart and brain cells must be kept at the proper temperature to work even if the temperature outside is very hot or very cold. Your body can sweat to release heat if you are hot and can metabolize more food to generate additional heat energy if you are cold.

Changes do occur in the life of an organism, such as growth and development, but these processes do not happen because homeostasis has failed. They are changes that are programmed into the life cycle of an organism. Amazingly, an organism can grow, develop, and change, yet all the while maintain a constant environment in which its cells can function.

Organisms Grow and Develop. An organism, whether it is a baby chick, a pet dog or cat, or your brother or sister, grows and develops as it ages. As living things grow, they increase in size. This occurs because of an increase in the size of cells, the number of cells, or both. Most plants and animals start out very small and grow until they reach adult size. If you measure your height over several years, you know that you are changing and getting taller. Some organisms, such as most trees, grow continuously through life, though they grow at a slower rate as they get older.

Growth of an organism is not constant throughout its life, nor do all parts of an organism grow at the same rate. Most organisms do not become adults, however, just by growing taller and larger. An adult chicken or rooster does not look like a baby chick. The chick changes its appearance as it develops, or matures. Growth and development occur in a characteristic way for each type of organism. Some changes are obvious: We see plants sprouting from seeds, or tadpoles losing their tails as they mature into frogs. You started life as a single fertilized egg, then grew and developed many specialized types of cells that formed heart, muscle, bone, or brain. The specialized jobs of these different cells are an important part of development.

Organisms Reproduce. For life to continue on our planet, new organisms must be produced constantly to replace those that die. This process of producing new individuals of the

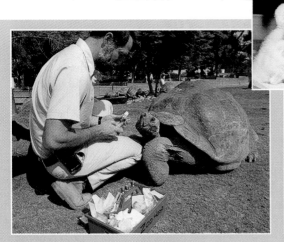

The work of biologists, whether it is (*counterclockwise from left*) breeding captive birds, identifying species through genetic testing, searching for medicinal plants, digging for evidence of ancient ancestors, or testing life-forms to see how they survive in different environments, is concerned with living things.

Once hatched, this green mamba snake will grow to resemble its parents. Appearance is just one of its inherited characteristics. Its ability to adapt and evolve, a trait that is necessary for a species to continue, is also part of its genetic heritage.

same kind, or offspring, is called reproduction.

A fundamental principle of biology is that life comes only from living things. In simple creatures, such as bacteria and amoebas, reproduction is usually asexual, or not sexual. A bacterium grows to twice its size, and then it usually reproduces by splitting in half to form two new bacteria. During this process, the bacterium copies its hereditary material, or genes, and directs one complete set of genes into each new daughter cell. The passing on of the genetic material is similar to passing a blueprint of the organism's characteristic traits from one generation to another.

Most plants and animals carry out sexual reproduction, in which an egg (the female sex cell) and sperm (the male sex cell) unite to form a fertilized egg that can develop into a new organism. Sexual reproduction produces offspring that show traits contributed by both the mother and father. While we all have inherited the general characteristics of a human being, the details may differ. We may have inherited the hair color of our mother and the eye color of our father. This slight variation or diversity in life is essential for the processes of adaptation and evolution to take place.

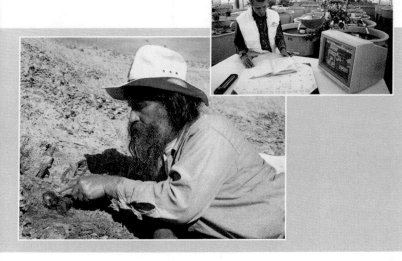

Organisms Adapt and Evolve. Organisms can sense and respond to changes in their world. If you touch something hot, you move your hand away quickly. If a baby hears a loud noise, it cries. If a plant is placed in a room with only one window, it grows toward the sunlight. Even simple, single-celled bacteria living in your intestine will make different molecules if you drink milk rather than eat bread.

Special sensing molecules and organs help us respond to light, sound, chemicals, and other signals in our environment. A response may protect you against some danger or discomfort. For example, you know to run for cover if it starts to rain heavily when you are outside. Changes in our environment can be sudden and dramatic, such as those that occur when a flash flood or earthquake rips apart the landscape, but usually they occur much more slowly. In order to survive, an organism must adjust, or adapt, to such changes. As winter sets in, you will see the fur of the arctic fox turn white and thick. This change in coat color is an adaptive response, so that in a snow-covered environment the fox will not be as easily seen by its enemies.

Some variations or differences occur in each organism that affect its ability to adapt. In a den of polar bears, there may be one animal with changes in its genes that spur the production of a fur coat that is thicker than that of the other bears. If the climate becomes colder, as it did in the ice ages, these changed animals will be more likely to survive and leave offspring. A selection process occurs in which nature determines who will survive and reproduce. This process is called **evolution**.

If changes in nature occur more rapidly than do genetic changes and adaptations, a species may become extinct. The giant trees in the petrified forests are examples of organisms that could not adapt when desertlike conditions occurred. We must remember that our activities can sometimes change an environment faster than nature can adapt. Destruction of the rain forest, global warming, and pollution of our air, soil, and water are all concerns because of their impact on living things.

Organisms Are Organized. Within the structure and function of a living thing, there is an orderly arrangement. This can be observed when examining the structure of an organism: An organism is made up of molecules that make up cells; the cells make up tissues, and the tissues make up organs. A pattern emerges as we look at the levels of life's structures. The various components of life become increasingly complex in their organiza-

tion and interactions. We find that the complex levels build on the simpler ones.

All members of a species that live in one area are called a population. When different populations living in the same area interact with one another, they make up a **community**. The various plants, fish, insects, and frogs that live in a lake are an example of a community.

Biologists who study **ecosystems** are examining how communities of living things interact with the nonliving parts of their environment. Over time, the organisms and the environment can be changed by these interactions. A coral reef is an example of a marine ecosystem. It is made up of corals, sponges, fish, algae, and many other populations. Ecosystems can be grouped together

The populations that make up a community vary depending on its environment. For example, the living things that form the community inhabiting an African savanna (*right*) are very different from those of a garbage dump (*above*). However, each community functions in much the same manner, as members interact and fight for survival.

into still larger units. The **biosphere** is the most complex, since it makes up all of the ecosystems on Earth. You are part of the biosphere since it includes all of the organisms and their environments. We must remember that no individual can function at a single level. What we learn and do can affect all life on Earth.

▶ **BIOLOGISTS AT WORK**

The diversity of living things offers scientists a variety of career options and a broad range of work settings. In their work, biologists can focus on specific types of living organisms. **Botanists** study how plants grow and reproduce. They do important work in such areas as agriculture, forestry, conservation, landscaping, and botanical gardening. For example, biotechnological research has developed plants that resist drought, disease, and insects. **Zoologists** study animals. Some zoologists specialize, or focus, their work and study only certain types of animals. For example, **ornithologists** study birds, while **marine biologists** study animals that live in the oceans. Another branch of biology includes scientists called **microbiologists**. They study microscopic organisms. Their research on

Each living thing is fashioned in the same orderly manner, from the simple to the complex. This biological organization can be seen in a tree. Many atoms make up a chlorophyll molecule (1), the light-absorbing green pigment that drives the food-making process of photosynthesis. Chlorophyll and other molecules necessary for photosynthesis are organized within a chloroplast (2). Chloroplasts and other structures are found within the functioning unit called a cell (3). Similar cells are grouped within an organism to form tissues (4) that perform specific functions. Many different tissues are organized to form the leaves (5) and other parts of a tree (6).

bacteria, fungi, and viruses, which are all micro-organisms, has a great impact on what is known about diseases in plants and animals, food production, recycling of chemicals in nature, and pollutants.

Some biologists study parts of organisms. **Biochemists** study the molecules and chemical reactions that occur in organisms. These scientists identify the substances in plant and animal cells that affect processes such as metabolism and disease. Other scientists who look at normal and diseased cells and tissues include **cytologists** and **pathologists**. The study of inheritance and genes is the work of

geneticists. With new sophisticated instruments and techniques, the DNA molecule, which forms the genetic code, can be studied, changed, and transferred among cells. **Molecular biologists** are scientists that use this new technology in their work.

The functions of organs and systems in organisms are studied by **physiologists**. Because living creatures have many organ systems, it is not unusual that physiologists will specialize. For example, a **neurophysiologist** studies the nervous system, while a **cardiovascular physiologist** studies the functions of the heart and circulatory system.

Other biologists study living things in their natural environments. **Ecologists** study how living organisms relate to each other within their environment. Their work affects our natural resources, such as forests, water, and wildlife. Scientists who are interested in creatures that lived in prehistoric times, when the ecology of our world was different, are **paleontologists**. **Evolutionary biologists** study the diversity and history of living things resulting from evolution.

Different biologists often work together to get a more complete understanding of an organism—how its parts work together and how the organism interacts with its environ-

People and Events in the Early Development of Biology

Ancient Times
Left: An Egyptian tomb painting of a grain harvest shows the work of early biologists. Agriculture develops as people observe and experiment with living things, such as plants, to ensure a steady supply of food.

● *Left:* Declaring that "every natural event has a natural cause," the Greek physician Hippocrates (460–377 B.C.) challenges the ancient belief that events, such as diseases and other occurrences, are punishments from the gods or spirits.

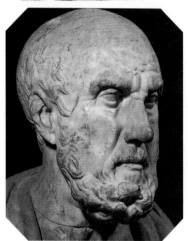

● *Above:* The Greek philosopher Aristotle (384–322 B.C.), later considered the founder of biology, searches to find out all that can be known about the natural world. Dedicated to observation, logic, and objectivity, he creates theories that dominate the natural sciences for close to 2,000 years.

Early 1500's
Left: With his contribution of more than 750 sketches of the body in all its stages, including the developing fetus, Italian artist and scientist Leonardo da Vinci (1452–1519) leads the way in the study of human anatomy.

---

ment. One example would be a partnership formed by a paleontologist and an evolutionary biologist who are studying the same dinosaur. The findings of the paleontologist may reveal what the dinosaur looked like, what it ate, and where it lived, while the findings of the evolutionary biologist may disclose how different circumstances forced the dinosaur to change and evolve over time.

▶ THE HISTORY OF BIOLOGY

From the earliest written records, we know our ancestors observed nature and learned how to use plants and animals in beneficial ways. They trained, or domesticated, certain animals for food and tasks, such as moving loads, and developed techniques for planting crops. The early Chinese, Egyptians, and Arabs also learned how to prepare medicines from plants. A fascination with the human body is evident from historical drawings that show common practices, such as the Egyptian practice of embalming the dead.

The Golden Age. The golden age of the Greeks, about 2,400 years ago, was a time of major advances in biology. While others around them believed that natural events were caused by gods or spirits, the ancient Greeks explained their world by looking at the patterns and laws of nature. The teachings of the Greek physician Hippocrates, who lived in the 400's B.C., greatly affected the practice of medicine. He described many conditions and procedures, from the noises in the chest associated with infections to dramatic surgery on the head. Hippocrates emphasized the importance of recording both successes and failures of a treatment and, most important, the responsibility a physician has to care for people. Physicians today still take a modern version of the Hippocratic oath—an oath that was written in Hippocrates' honor and reflected his high ideals.

Another important Greek scientist and philosopher was Aristotle (300's B.C.). He very accurately described and classified many plants and animals and their behaviors. Galen, a Greek physician who practiced medicine in Rome about 100 B.C., extensively described the anatomy and functions of the

1543 *Left:* With *On the Structure of the Human Body*, Belgian physician Andreas Vesalius (1514–64) produces the first scientific anatomy text. The book, which is based on Vesalius' dissections of the human body, revolutionizes the study of both anatomy and medicine.

1628 *Left:* Stating his conclusions about how blood circulates in *On the Motion of the Heart and Blood in Animals*, English physician William Harvey (1578–1657) solves an ancient puzzle and ushers in a new age of medicine and biology.

1665 *Top:* In *Micrographia*, English scientist Robert Hooke (1635–1703) publishes his observations made using a compound microscope, describing the minute compartments of cork tissue as "cells."

1683 *Left:* The Royal Society publishes the pictures of "little animalcules" made by Dutch naturalist Anton van Leeuwenhoek (1632–1723). He is the first to see and describe single-celled microbes.

human body. He obtained this knowledge from treating the gladiators who had been injured during their battles and by dissecting animals. Progress in science slowed after the Greeks' early contributions. During the Dark Ages and most of the Middle Ages, little scholarly work occurred that added to what was known about the nature of life.

The Renaissance. The Renaissance, meaning "rebirth," was a period (A.D. 1300–1600) of intense interest in science and nature. Naturalists described and classified many plants and animals on the Earth. Great artists contributed beautiful and accurate drawings of various organisms that are still available for us to see today. Among them were the Italian artists Botticelli, Michelangelo, and Leonardo da Vinci. This was also the time when the first scientific textbook on human anatomy appeared. Written by Andreas Vesalius, *On the Structure of the Human Body* was published in 1543. One of the most important contributions of the time was made by William Harvey, an English physician. It was in 1628 that he published the results of his experiments showing how blood is pumped by the heart and how it circulates throughout the body. Up until that time, it was thought that blood ebbed and flowed out of the heart, much like a tide.

Microscopic Discoveries. The invention of the microscope opened up a whole new world for exploration. During the middle and late 1600's, great discoveries were made by those who pioneered in the use of the microscope. Among the pioneers were Marcello Malpighi, the Italian anatomist who observed blood moving through the capillaries, and Robert Hooke, an English scientist who published the book *Micrographia* (1665), in which he made detailed drawings of the many creatures he had studied using the microscope. More than any other person of his time, Dutch biologist Anton van Leeuwenhoek furthered the use of the microscope, making more than 400 microscopes himself. Using one of the simple microscopes he made, Van Leeuwenhoek was the first person to observe single-celled organisms. His drawings of small life-forms in pond water and his studies of cells influenced many scientists.

1735 *Left:* With the publication of his *Systema Naturae*, Swedish botanist Carolus Linnaeus (1707–78) transforms biology. In the book, he classifies the living world according to shared characteristics and relatedness, giving each plant and animal its own scientific name made up of two words.

Late 1700's *Below left:* The oxygen experiments of French chemist Antoine Lavoisier (1743–94) expand the understanding of body processes, including respiration and the conversion of food to energy.

1839 *Below:* Working independently of each other, German scientists Theodor Schwann (1810–82) and Matthias Schleiden (1804–81) develop the cell theory, proposing that all plants and animals have the same basic unit of life—the cell.

1856 *Above right:* Austrian monk Gregor Mendel (1822–84) begins experiments in genetics using garden peas. Through his work in the monastery garden, he discovers the basic laws of heredity.

1859 *Right:* British naturalist Charles Darwin (1809–82) offers a new theory of nature in *On the Origin of Species*, stating that new species evolve from more primitive species through a process he calls natural selection.

The Cell Theory. It was in the 1830's that two Germans, working separately, came to the same conclusion about the makeup of living things. Botanist Matthias Schleiden and physiologist Theodor Schwann established a general theory about cells. The cell theory recognized that cells are the basic units of life and that all organisms are made of cells and all cells come from pre-existing cells. This revolutionary idea made biologists rethink how organisms are made and how they function.

Classifying Life. With the beginning of world travel in the mid-1700's, biologists searched for previously unknown forms of life. Thousands of new plants and animals were collected each year. However, problems arose among these naturalists because there was a variety of ways to name new discoveries. This made it very difficult for biologists to communicate among themselves about their discoveries. A Swedish botanist named Carolus Linnaeus developed a new system of classification that solved many of these problems.

He described the rules and characteristics to use for the grouping of plants and animals. Linnaeus put organisms with similar characteristics in the same group and suggested that the group be called a **species**. He also suggested that similar species be linked into a larger group, called a **genus**. For example, lions, tigers, and jaguars each represent a different species. However, they are similar enough to be considered members of the same genus.

▶ **THE GROWTH OF MODERN BIOLOGY**

As biologists studied more animals and plants, they saw that there was some order in living organisms—from simple to more complex. They began to question the belief that each species in life had remained unchanged since the world began. The scientists saw that farmers could make new varieties of plants and animals by breeding two different types of organisms. Biologists also wondered why there were so many species with few differences. Eventually biologists realized that species can change over time and that some species had gradually developed or evolved from other species.

The Theory of Evolution. Several biologists in the early 1800's contributed to the understanding of how species evolved. In 1859, the British naturalist Charles Darwin presented his explanation. Darwin described his ideas on evolution in his widely read book, *On the Origin of Species*. His ideas came largely from the variation among species of plants and animals that he observed during his expeditions to the Galápagos Islands. For example, Darwin saw 13 species of finches on different islands of this group. Each bird resembled those on the other islands in general appearance, but each had a differently shaped and sized beak. The beak of each type of bird was well suited for getting the food found on its island. Darwin proposed that evolution had occurred among the birds, and he tried to explain how the changes resulted. His theory of evolution proposed that inheritable traits can vary among individuals of the same species. An organism will produce more offspring than the available natural resources. The offspring will compete for food and other necessities of life. Those born with favorable traits will survive and reproduce. The environment will select organisms with beneficial traits, a process he called **natural selection**. This theory became the theme that unified biology in the twentieth century.

The Principles of Heredity. Also occurring in the mid-1800's was the development of the principles of heredity. Gregor Mendel, an Austrian monk, performed experiments using pea plants that showed there is a pattern to how traits are passed from parents to offspring. Mendel's choice of pea plants was important because he could easily get the seeds, the plants grew fast, and many offspring were produced. Mendel also carefully thought through his experiments and kept good records. He showed that traits are produced by basic hereditary units that can be transmitted from generation to generation.

▶ **BIOLOGY TODAY**

Only in the 1900's have scientists learned that hereditary traits are passed on by means of information stored in cellular molecules called **deoxyribonucleic acid (DNA)**. We now know that the traits are due to DNA segments, called genes. These genes affect protein molecules in the cells and thus the properties and processes of cells. The structure of the DNA molecule was discovered in 1953 by James Watson, an American biologist, and Francis Crick, a British biophysicist. Knowing the structure of DNA molecules helped biologists understand how changes in these molecules, called **mutations**, could affect genes and their functions.

Many exciting breakthroughs in genetics and molecular biology have occurred since the 1950's. An understanding of DNA has made it possible to change genes and use them in beneficial ways. New laboratory instruments allow scientists to identify the many genes that are present in the DNA of living things. Potential benefits of this knowledge include the correction and prevention of diseases in organisms. With careful safeguards, biologists can change bacteria into "chemical factories" by adding new genes that can produce useful substances such as hormones, drugs, and vaccines. Today's developments in molecular biology are as exciting as the discoveries of new organisms by our early naturalists.

Scientists are also getting a better understanding of how cells and organs work and "talk" with each other. Neurobiologists are exploring the brain and its signaling system of nerve cells and chemicals. The study of the immune system is another area of intense biological research. Immunologists are studying how immune cells and molecules interact to

James D. Watson (left) and Francis H. C. Crick (right) worked together to unravel the mystery of DNA structure, paving the way for the understanding of life processes at the molecular level.

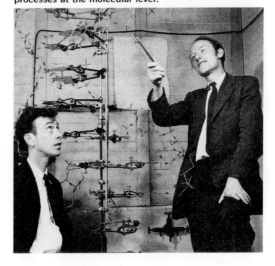

How a Biologist Explores Nature

See For Yourself

Some biologists observe nature, either directly or with instruments, and compare the general patterns or changes they see. The scientists may then think and wonder about what their observations mean. These thoughts can lead to a **hypothesis**, or an "educated guess," as scientists attempt to explain their observations. A hypothesis is tested using further observations or experiments. The results are analyzed to see if they support or reject the hypothesis, and then a conclusion about the experiment can be made. Scientists may ask new questions based on the results of their investigations and test other factors or variables that might affect their results.

But biologists are not the only people who examine nature; nature influences the work of many different people. The artist Leonardo da Vinci was a keen observer of nature. He studied the shape and design of living things, especially human beings. One of his famous studies of the human form is the drawing of a Vitruvian man. In it he showed the proportions that he believed to be typical for most people. The results of his work are

still used today, not just by artists, but by people in such diverse fields as architecture and medicine. We can use Leonardo's observations to form a hypothesis, test it, analyze the results, and come to a conclusion in much the same way a biologist would.

1. **Forming a hypothesis.** In Leonardo's drawing, the Vitruvian man is set standing inside a square with his arms outstretched to the sides. Knowing that the length of a square is the same as its width, we can develop a hypothesis about the human proportions depicted: The height of a person is equal to the distance across the individual's body with arms extended out to the sides.

2. **Testing the hypothesis.** In order to test the hypothesis, the height and width measurements of a group of people, such as your classmates, need to be taken. You will need a ruler or tape measure as well as paper and a pencil to record your data. For each individual, measure the height (for the

most accurate height measurement, shoes should be off) and then the width across the body with arms outstretched and hands open. Record your findings (in inches) for each member of your group.

3. **Analyzing the data.** After you have recorded all your data, you need to analyze it and find out if the results support the hypothesis. If there is 5 percent or less difference between the measurements, they can be considered equal. To determine this for an individual using 60 inches for height and 58 inches for body width, the calculations would be 60 − 58 = 2, then 2 ÷ 60 = .033, or 3 percent difference. This individual's measurements would be considered equal.

4. **Reaching a conclusion.** When you examine the results of your experiment, do they support or reject the hypothesis? What is your conclusion? Does the height of a person equal the distance across the individual's body with arms extended out to the sides?

Sample Calculations

Height = 60"
Body width = 58"

$$60 \quad \text{then} \quad \frac{.033}{60 \overline{)2.000}} = 3\%$$

$$\begin{array}{r} 60 \\ -58 \\ \hline 2 \end{array}$$

$$\begin{array}{r} .033 \\ 60\overline{)2.000} \\ \underline{180} \\ 200 \\ \underline{180} \\ 20 \end{array}$$

defend the body. Basic research in this area will provide a better understanding of organ transplant rejections and of diseases such as AIDS. Understanding the brain and the immune system will be some of the great challenges for future biologists.

. As the human population continues to grow, the work of biologists becomes even more important. Understanding human beings and how they interact with their environment will help us better manage our world so that life on Earth can continue to exist.

CYNTHIA V. SOMMER
University of Wisconsin at Milwaukee

See also BIOCHEMISTRY; CELLS; DARWIN, CHARLES ROBERT; EVOLUTION; FOSSILS; GENETICS; HARVEY, WILLIAM; KINGDOMS OF LIVING THINGS; LIFE; MEDICINE, HISTORY OF; MICROBIOLOGY; PHOTOSYNTHESIS.

Left: Vividly colored glowing corals are animals that live on the Great Barrier Reef off the eastern coast of Australia. *Above:* Some species, or kinds, of fireflies have light-emitting glands in their abdomens that are used to flash mating signals.

BIOLUMINESCENCE

Light from fireflies and other living things is called **bioluminescence**. There are many bioluminescent things in nature—plants, animals, and bacteria.

The glowing plants include only a few kinds, such as certain toadstools and molds. But animals that light up are more numerous; they range from tiny one-celled sea creatures to sponges, clams, worms, and insects. The most numerous glowing forms of life are found in the salt water of oceans. The most familiar forms are found on land—fireflies, glowworms, and fox fire fungus.

Bioluminescence is called "cold" light to distinguish it from incandescence, or heat-giving light. (For example, electric light bulbs, oil lamps, and candles give off "hot" light.) Living plants and animals could not produce incandescent light without being burned up. Their light is caused by chemicals combining in such a way that little or no measurable heat is given off.

The substance that gives off the light in living things is called luciferin. This "glowing" chemical was named in 1887 by one of the earliest scientists to study living light, Raphaël Dubois, of France. Dubois named this chemical substance "luciferin," meaning "light bearer." Through his experiments using the glowing fluid taken from a clam, Dubois found that the light was caused by a team of chemicals working together. Luciferin would not light up except in the presence of a second chemical, which Dubois called "luciferase."

Scientists have since learned that living light is produced when luciferin and oxygen combine in the presence of luciferase. Other substances are also needed to produce light in some living things, such as adenosine triphosphate (ATP) in fireflies. It is the additional substances that give the light a range of color from yellow to blue, green, and red.

In some cases, the function of the light seems obvious. Marine fireworms use glowing light as mating signals. During the mating season, the female fireworms come up from deep waters to the surface of the sea and glow. Seeing the light, the males join the females. A mating dance follows and then both sexes release their reproductive cells into the water.

Bulblike organs, called photophores, on the bodies of many deep-sea fish attract mates or prey and illuminate the search for them in the darkness of the ocean depths. Some luminescent fish zigzag through the water with lights flashing to confuse predators and escape being eaten. In other cases, such as the many blind light-emitting deep-sea species, the light seems to have no function.

Much remains to be learned about the chemistry of bioluminescence. Perhaps some day enough will be known to produce this cold light for everyday use instead of the energy-wasting electric light we use now.

W. D. McElroy
Author, *Light: Physical and Biological Action*

Large herds of zebras and wildebeests roam across the vast grasslands, or savannas, of Africa, grazing on the abundant plant life that includes a variety of grasses.

BIOMES

The hot, humid rain forest, the dry desert, and the icy tundra all have something in common: Each one is a biome. A biome is a community of specific types of plants and animals that covers a large area of the earth's surface. Each biome is made up of many **habitats**—the places where a particular plant or animal normally lives and grows. The type of biome in a region is generally determined by the kind of climate in that region. Deserts cover dry regions. Rain forests cover hot, humid regions. Tundras cover cold and dry regions.

On every continent except Antarctica, most of the different kinds of biomes can be found. Each place has unique species of plants and animals, yet the plants and animals of a particular biome, all around the world, tend to be similar. For example, spine-covered cacti are common plants in the deserts of the American Southwest. In African deserts, similar prickly plants called euphorbs grow in abundance. Euphorbs and cacti have both adapted to living in the hot, dry desert biome. Similarities among plant species in biomes around the world allow scientists to identify the different kinds of biomes. Scientists also study a biome's **ecology**; that is, the interactions of living things with the environment and with each other.

▶ KINDS OF BIOMES

This article covers the major land biomes—grasslands, deserts, chaparral, deciduous forests, coniferous forests, tundra, and tropical rain forests. Aquatic biomes also exist in rivers, lakes, and oceans. You can find out more about the organisms in these biomes in the articles ALGAE, FISH, OCEAN, and PLANTS.

Each biome (except deserts) is named after a **climax vegetation**—one that has become dominant over a long period of time. The plants and animals that it supports together make up a **climax community**.

Grasslands

Known as prairies in North America, savannas in central Africa, steppes in central Asia, and pampas in South America, grasslands are among the richest biomes. Major agricultural crops, including corn, wheat, oats, and barley, were all bred from grasses—the main plants in the grassland environment.

Grasslands are found in climates slightly drier than the climates that support deciduous forests. Average rainfall in the grasslands varies from 10 to 40 inches (254 to 1,016 millimeters) annually. Fires, which can destroy deciduous forests, cause grasslands to thrive. Burned grasses enrich the soil and allow new plants to grow. Some grassland wildflowers cannot sprout unless their seeds are exposed to a fire's searing heat. Fires also keep certain plants from growing that would change the grassland environment, such as deciduous trees.

Grasslands that receive the most rain produce tall, dense grasses, as in America's tall-grass prairies. Grasses there can reach heights of 12 feet (3.7 meters). Early settlers riding through the grasslands had to stand up in the stirrups of their saddles to spot their cows grazing in these tall grasses. Grasslands that receive the least precipitation have short grasses. Short-grass prairies are dotted with clumps of grasses that grow less than 2 feet (0.6 meters) tall. Grasslands also include wild-flowers, which add vibrant color to the green backdrop. An occasional shrub or tree dots the landscape, springing up in places where there is adequate moisture.

The dominant grassland animals are grazers. In Africa, millions of gazelles, zebras, and wildebeests migrate across the savannas, each grazing on a different part of the grass plant. Predators, including lions, tigers, and hyenas, stalk the old and sick grazing animals. Vultures feed on the decaying carcasses while insects strip the bones clean. In their natural state, grasslands support the largest herds of animals in the world.

Deserts

Regions that receive less than 10 inches (254 millimeters) of rain each year are generally classified as deserts. Desert rains are infrequent. Sometimes it will only rain once or twice a year. When it does rain, a great quantity of rain may fall so rapidly that a quick, heavy flood (called a flash flood) occurs. Deserts also tend to have extreme variations in temperatures. Days are very hot, but temperatures plummet at night, sometimes dipping down below freezing. Desert plants and animals have to be quite hardy to adapt to these difficult conditions.

Succulents, plants that store water in their leaves or stems, are among the major plants of the deserts. Cacti and euphorbs are two different types of succulents. Shrubs with small leathery or waxy leaves also thrive in some desert environments. These plants may shed their leaves and remain dormant through the desert's harshest seasons. Some desert plants live short lives, sprouting, flowering, setting seed, and dying in the few days during and after a heavy rain. The seeds of these plants lie dormant in the sand for months or years until adequate rain once again falls.

Desert animals must also find ways to adapt to the extreme dryness and heat. Many rest in their underground burrows during the day and only come out at night. Others, such as certain iguanas and other types of lizards, are active during the day. They spend most of their time out of the sun, venturing from the shade of one plant only to scurry to the shade of another. Some animals can survive with very little water. The kangaroo rat is one animal that does not need water to drink. It gets its water from the seeds and leaves it eats.

Chaparral

Scattered along certain coastal areas is the chaparral biome. The Mediterranean coast, the coast of southern California, the coast of central Chile, the southern tip of Africa, and the southern coast of Australia all are covered by chaparral. Like the desert, the chaparral gets little rainfall. Some regions average as little as 10 inches (254 millimeters) of rain a year, all of which falls during the winter months. However, warm, moist air from the oceans helps balance the chaparral environment and prevents conditions from being as severe as those in the desert.

The main plants of the chaparral are tough evergreen shrubs with small leathery leaves. Animals adapted to a dry climate, including lizards, rodents, rabbits, hawks, and owls, inhabit the chaparral. Deer and songbirds migrate to the chaparral during the wet winters, when food is more plentiful.

The scattered evergreen shrubs of the chaparral, which are the plants found most often in this dry coastal biome, help prevent soil erosion.

During the hot, rainless summers, brush-fires often rage across the chaparral. However, chaparral plants are well adapted to what would be a disaster in other places. Many species produce fire-resistant seeds. Others send shoots from the base of charred stumps. It takes as little as ten years for a burned area of chaparral to recover completely.

Deciduous Forests

Spanning eastern North America, central Europe, eastern China, and the southeast coast of Australia, deciduous forests grace the land. Such forests are made up of trees that grow and shed their leaves in a distinct seasonal pattern. In spring the trees bud, in summer they grow, in autumn they lose their leaves, and in winter they stand dormant. Ample rain falls throughout the year, averaging about 40 inches (1,016 millimeters) annually. In this constantly changing environment, many different types of plants and animals flourish.

Deciduous forests, such as the maple-beech forests of North America, tend to have rich soil that supports numerous types of plants. Shrubs grow in the shade of the leafy maple and birch trees. Ferns, flowers, and mosses carpet the floor of the deciduous forest. Mushrooms and other fungi grow on rotting leaves and logs.

Animal life, too, is quite abundant in these woods. Earthworms and insects tunnel through

the dark, moist soil. Songbirds flit among the tree branches and on the ground. Amphibians, such as newts and salamanders, scurry through the thick cover of fallen leaves. Deer browse and rodents burrow. Predators, such as foxes, weasels, and bobcats, stalk their prey. Such activity, especially during the summer months, makes deciduous forests inviting places in which to study wildlife.

In the winter, when the trees have shed their leaves and the woods stand under a blanket of snow, life in the forest slows down. Many living things adapt to the cold by becoming dormant. Some mammals hibernate, burrowing in dens for a long

Snowy owl

Pronghorn antelope

Black bear

American elk

Raccoon

Rufus hummingbird

Bell's vireo

Mountain Biomes

A mountain can create as many as four different communities similar to those found in major biomes around the world. As the climate changes with the altitude, so does the community.

Gray wolf

Caribou

Arctic fox

Tundra

A rocky landscape with scattered short grasses, the tundra blooms only for a few months in the summer. During that time, migrants from down the mountain feed on the abundant blooms.

Coyote

Bald eagle

Grasslands

The coniferous forest meets the grassland at the tree line. In summer, many animals migrate above the tree line. In winter, however, the harsh weather drives most animals down from the grasslands to the forests below.

Mountain lion

Coniferous Forests

The colder, drier coniferous forest lies upslope from the deciduous forest. Many animals shelter in the coniferous forest during the winter months. They move up to the grasslands during the summer.

Red squirrel

Black-tailed deer

Deciduous Forests

The deciduous forest carpets the foothills of the mountain. The forest provides ample food for many types of animals, including hummingbirds, vireos, deer, raccoons, and squirrels.

period of inactivity. Others, including three quarters of the birds, migrate, spending the winter in warmer climates. A few, including sparrows, raccoons, and rabbits, stay through the winter, searching out food as best they can.

Coniferous Forests

Coniferous forests are forests that are largely made up of cone-bearing trees. There are two distinct types of coniferous forest biomes: the temperate coniferous forest and the northern coniferous, or boreal, forest.

The temperate coniferous forest is found in moist, coastal environments, including the northern Pacific coast of North America and the eastern coast of Australia. These forests contain the largest trees in the world—the giant sequoia trees of California, which are also called redwoods, and the towering eucalyptus trees of Australia. The boreal forests are much more extensive than the temperate coniferous forests. They stretch across the northern reaches of North America, Europe, and Asia. In these regions, winters are long and cold. The short, cool summers allow only a brief growing season.

Pine, spruce, hemlock, and fir trees are the most common trees in the boreal forests. All have needle-like leaves that help prevent water loss in the cold, dry winter air. The soil in

During the summer months, a wide variety of animals—elk, moose, birds, rabbits, and insects—populate the coniferous forest, feeding on tree leaves and grasses.

coniferous forests tends to be acidic, and few types of plants can grow in it. Blueberry shrubs and heather plants, however, thrive in the acidic soil.

Many different types of animals live in the boreal forests, especially in the warmer summer months. Moose, elk, and deer browse on tree leaves. Migratory birds eat the plentiful insects, which hatch in the late spring and summer. Porcupines gnaw on pine bark. Snowshoe hares, whose coats change so that they blend in with both summer's fallen leaves and winter's blanket of snow, dart from under cover. Wolverines and bears stalk their prey.

Tundra

North of the boreal forest lies the tundra. Under this treeless region is a layer of frozen ground more than 1,000 feet (305 meters) thick, called permafrost. The soil on top of the permafrost thaws for only eight weeks during the short Arctic summer. The small flowering plants and dwarf trees of the tundra have to grow, bloom, and set seed quickly to survive. The outburst of growth in the tundra during the summer creates a colorful carpet of low-lying flowers that dazzles the eye. Adding to the colorful display are the numerous types of lichens, which are really a combination of algae and fungi living and growing together, that cover the rocky landscape.

Not many animals spend the long winter months in the tundra. Some small rodents, such as lemmings, have adapted to the harsh winter environment. Arctic foxes, wolves, and polar bears also stay feeding on whatever they can find during the quiet winter months.

When summer comes, the tundra once again teems with life. Herds of caribou and also reindeer graze on the tundra's quick-growing grasses. Flocks of migrating birds make the tundra their destination. Many birds feed on the numerous insects that hatch in the ponds and puddles of the tundra's soggy ground. As summer fades away, the caribou and many other mammals travel to the forests and the birds fly south. The tundra again becomes a snowy, silent world.

Tropical Rain Forests

Tropical rain forests are damp, humid places where lush, leafy plants abound. In most tropical rain forests, annual rainfall averages between 80 and 200 inches (2,032 and

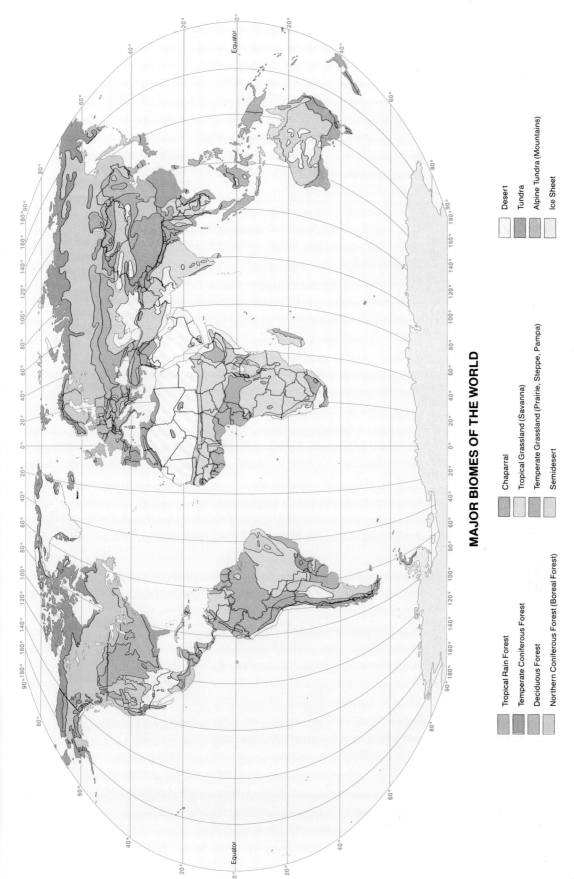

MAJOR BIOMES OF THE WORLD

Legend:

- Tropical Rain Forest
- Temperate Coniferous Forest
- Deciduous Forest
- Northern Coniferous Forest (Boreal Forest)

- Chaparral
- Tropical Grassland (Savanna)
- Temperate Grassland (Prairie, Steppe, Pampa)
- Semidesert

- Desert
- Tundra
- Alpine Tundra (Mountains)
- Ice Sheet

A biome includes a large geographic area that has characteristic plants and animals. The major biomes of the world are shown on the map above. Each biome has a certain type of climate and soil to which plants and animals of the region have adapted.

The continued destruction of the rain forest may lead to such dramatic climate changes that life in all of the other biomes around the world will be threatened.

5,080 millimeters). The rain falls evenly year-round. Temperatures hardly vary, hovering just below 80°F (27°C) day and night. This steady environment has the greatest variety of plant and animal species of all the biomes.

The leafy branches of tall trees, 75 to 100 feet (23 to 30 meters) in height, spread out to form a canopy that shades and shelters the tropical rain forest. Beneath the canopy, lower trees form leafy umbrellas 40 to 60 feet (12 to 18 meters) tall. A few smaller trees grow 20 to 30 feet (6 to 9 meters) above a shrub layer that is at most 10 feet (3 meters) tall. The floor of the rain forest receives so little light that only plants able to grow in almost total shade can live there. Thick jungle growth occurs only along river edges or other places where light easily penetrates to the ground.

The most lively part of the tropical rain forest is the canopy and upper layers of trees. Colorful flowers use the higher tree branches as platforms to reach the sun. These plants, called epiphytes, send no roots into the soil. They get their nutrients from the small amounts of dirt and dust that collect in the forks of tree branches. They gather moisture from the misty air. Some epiphytes, called bromeliads, have overlapping leaves that form a cup at their base. The bromeliad cup can hold several quarts of water to nourish the plant. These miniature ponds are the breeding grounds for snails, insects, and tiny frogs.

Larger animals, including lizards, birds, monkeys, and leopards, inhabit the rain forest. Although a few rain forest animals search for roots and seeds on the ground, most dwell solely in the trees.

▶THE CHANGING BIOMES

These descriptions of biomes apply to regions that have not been disturbed by human activity. But in many places throughout the world, nature's biomes have been altered. Forests are cut down for farms. Domestic animals are set loose on grasslands, crowding out the animals that naturally live there. Desert land is irrigated to grow crops. Oil rigs in the Arctic tundra destroy large patches of the slow-growing plants.

The disruption of the biomes can cause tremendous problems for people living in the regions. In the dry grasslands of the Sahel, in western Africa, domestic goats and sheep have overgrazed the land. The thin layer of topsoil has blown away and the Sahel is becoming a desert. This process, called desertification, threatens other parts of the world.

In other places, disturbing the biomes may cause serious problems in the future. People in Central America, South America, and Southeast Asia have been burning down the tropical rain forests to make farmland and cutting down the trees for lumber. Each year millions of acres of rain forest are destroyed. The loss of these lush lands may seriously disrupt the global climate. Plants need carbon dioxide to grow and they take this gas from the air. Without the rain forests, the amount of carbon dioxide in the air will increase tremendously. This gas holds heat close to the earth, warming the atmosphere and the earth's surface. This warming is called the **greenhouse effect**. With the destruction of the tropical rain forests, the greenhouse effect could cause our planet to heat up at an unhealthy rate.

Environmental groups and government agencies around the world are working to protect the world's biomes. In this way, the earth's precious natural resources can be preserved for future life.

ELIZABETH KAPLAN
Author, *Biology Bulletin Monthly*

See also DESERTS; ECOLOGY; FORESTS AND FORESTRY; GRASSES; PRAIRIES; RAIN FOREST; TUNDRA.

BIOSPHERE. See LIFE (Living Things and Their Environments).

Each day, no matter what kind of environment you are in, you will see some kind of bird. It may be a pair of courting swans (*left*), a proud sparrow hawk with its prey (*below left*), or some helpful oxpeckers plucking parasites off a black rhinoceros (*below*).

BIRDS

Throughout the ages, birds have been a source of wonder to all who have observed their soaring flight or listened to their sweet song. As a group, birds are unique—they are the only animals covered with feathers. This evolutionary development separates birds from all other animals.

Birds can travel faster than any other animal—the fastest bird can fly more than 100 miles (161 kilometers) per hour! Although all birds have feathers and wings, not every bird can fly. Some birds walk, run, or swim instead of flying.

Birds are **vertebrates** (animals with a backbone), as are fish, amphibians, reptiles, and mammals. Like many vertebrates, birds lay eggs from which their young hatch. They are warm-blooded animals; that is, their body temperature always remains about the same no matter what the temperature of their surroundings. They differ from other vertebrates in that they are toothless and have a hard beak, or bill, that they use to get and eat food.

The more than 9,000 kinds, or species, of birds belong to the class of animals called Aves. Because of their superb flying skills, birds have been able to reach virtually every area of the world: forests, mountains, oceans, and deserts. Birds have adapted to a great variety of habitats, living in places too harsh for people or any other animal. The large snowy owl is able to survive in the Arctic, where temperatures dip below −50°F (−46°C) during the long winter. Its thick feather coat even covers its bill and feet. Birds are able to live in the middle of the world's oceans. The albatross family lives most of its life on the wing, soaring over the open ocean searching for food. It only comes to shore to build a nest and to breed.

▶ BIRDS AND PEOPLE

Birds as Food. Humans have hunted birds since prehistoric times. Along with hunting birds, early humans also gathered bird eggs and nestlings (babies).

People eventually learned to tame and raise birds, and over time this has led to the domes-

Probably the greatest use of feathers was by native Hawaiians. Helmets, staffs, and huge feather cloaks (*above left*) were made for royal chiefs from the feathers of native honeycreepers. Since ancient times, people have engaged in the sport of hunting with trained birds of prey, such as the eagle (*above right*). Macaws (*left*) and other brightly colored tropical birds are among the most prized bird pets.

tication of several species: ducks, chickens, turkeys, and pigeons. Domestic ducks, a form of the mallard, appeared in Egypt around 1500 B.C. and spread quickly to Europe. Greylag geese were also domesticated at about the same time. Even earlier, people in Southeast Asia had tamed the red junglefowl, a bird recognized today as a chicken. Native Americans in Mexico and Central America successfully domesticated the wild turkey. Pigeons were domesticated in Europe and were used as food and to carry messages since Roman times. Birds, both wild and domestic, continue to be an important source of food today.

Products from Birds. The people of many societies used, and some still use, the feathers and skins of wild birds. Eagle feathers were exchanged much like money in some native North American tribes. The feather cloak of the Hawaiian king Kamehameha I took at least a hundred years to make and used about 450,000 feathers from more than 80,000 birds! It is not surprising that the king collected taxes from his subjects in honeycreeper feathers. The Inuit people of the Arctic use waterfowl feathers for pillows and clothing. The skins, especially eider skins, are used to make warm and waterproof blankets. On the other side of the world, the aborigines of Australia still wear feathers of cockatoos and emus as decoration.

Birds in Religion, Art, and Literature. Birds are powerful symbols used to represent everything from peace (the dove carrying an olive branch) to wisdom (the wise owl) to politics (the bald eagle that is the national symbol of the United States).

From the earliest times, birds have played almost as great a role in people's religion and art as in their diet. The religious paintings of early humans on the walls of Lascaux Cave near Montignac, France, include birds among the animals depicted. Ancient Egyptians used birds in their art. Painting and sculptures of birds adorn buildings and tombs of royalty.

Birds are also found in early literature. The Bible mentions almost forty species of birds—most often doves—in ways that show a knowledge of their habits and an appreciation of their grace and beauty. The religion of the Egyptians has many gods, including real and imaginary birds. They believed in the legendary phoenix, a bird that serves as a symbol of immortality. The ibis was so sacred that they were often mummified and buried with royalty in their family tombs.

Birds as Pets. Birds are also popular pets. Except for dogs and cats, more people have pet birds than any other animal. People share their homes with an amazing variety of birds, including finches, waxbills, and parrots.

The great horned owl fans its feathers in a defensive threat display. Along with their use as a defense measure, feathers keep birds warm and help them fly.

▶ WHAT MAKES A BIRD A BIRD?

All animals share certain characteristics, such as having the ability to move about and needing food to live. Some animals even share the same methods for performing these tasks and securing those substances that are necessary for life. However, birds are unique. There is no other animal with the same combination of features.

Feathers

Other animals have wings and can fly, but no other creature is covered with feathers. Feathers, which are formed in special skin cells from a protein called keratin, perform many different jobs. Body, or contour, feathers smooth and streamline the bird's body so it can move easily through the air or water. Contour feathers also protect the bird's skin from wind and, sometimes, from water. Beneath the contour feathers are tiny down feathers. Down acts as an insulator to help the bird

maintain its body temperature even in temperatures below zero. In addition to contour and down feathers are filoplume feathers, which provide information on the position of movable feathers, and bristles that form eyelashes, which provide sensory information in much the same manner as a cat's whiskers.

Molting. Molting is a process that involves shedding thousands of feathers, and then growing new ones. Most birds molt twice each year: before the spring migration and after nesting. Replacing all of a bird's feathers is a

The External Body Structures of a Bird

crown
forehead
eye
nostrils
nape
beak
throat
back
bend of wing
breast
wing
rump
abdomen
tail feathers
flank
feet

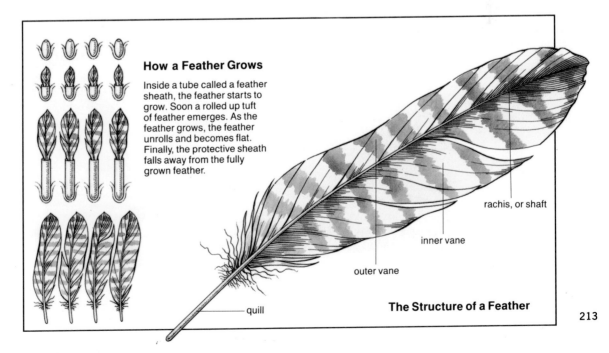

How a Feather Grows

Inside a tube called a feather sheath, the feather starts to grow. Soon a rolled up tuft of feather emerges. As the feather grows, the feather unrolls and becomes flat. Finally, the protective sheath falls away from the fully grown feather.

rachis, or shaft

inner vane

outer vane

quill

The Structure of a Feather

213

major undertaking—it takes a lot of energy to molt. Feathers are so important to birds that many birds do not nest a second time; instead, they save their energy for the molting process.

The spring molt replaces flight feathers that will be needed to make the long journey north to the breeding grounds. The males of many species molt their drab winter plumage and replace it with spectacular breeding colors—bold reds, yellows, oranges, and blues—that will help attract a mate.

After nesting, most species molt for the second time. The bright colors needed to attract a mate and defend a territory are now dangerous. Standing out makes it difficult to hide from and escape from predators. Ducks and geese even lose their ability to fly because they molt all of their flight feathers at once. During this period of flightlessness, and before they grow a new camouflage plumage, they hide in remote marshes.

Flight

The dominant forces that affect a bird's flight are lift and propulsion. The shape of a bird's wings helps create lift: Air moves more quickly over the curved top of the wing than it does under the flattened bottom of the wing. This difference in speed creates lower air pressure over the wing than under the wing. Because air moves from a high-pressure area to a low-pressure area, the higher pressure bottom air moves toward the lower pressure top air, lifting the wing upward. A bird can increase

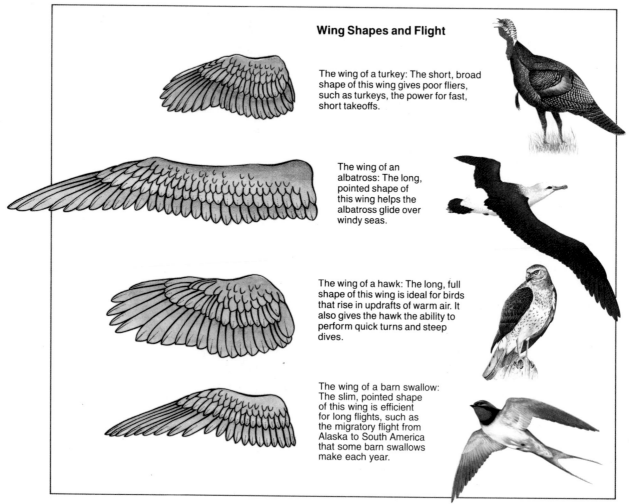

Wing Shapes and Flight

The wing of a turkey: The short, broad shape of this wing gives poor fliers, such as turkeys, the power for fast, short takeoffs.

The wing of an albatross: The long, pointed shape of this wing helps the albatross glide over windy seas.

The wing of a hawk: The long, full shape of this wing is ideal for birds that rise in updrafts of warm air. It also gives the hawk the ability to perform quick turns and steep dives.

The wing of a barn swallow: The slim, pointed shape of this wing is efficient for long flights, such as the migratory flight from Alaska to South America that some barn swallows make each year.

During the flight of the mallard duck, the bird is thrust forward by the flapping wing strokes.

or decrease the lifting force to travel up or down by tilting the forward edge of its wing upward or downward.

Propulsion, which is a forward-moving force, is created by long wing feathers that close together and overlap so air cannot pass through. In much the same manner as a boat paddle pushes against water, the closed structure of the wing pushes down against air, propelling the bird forward. On the return stroke, the wing feathers separate and allow air to pass between them.

Wing feathers are not the only feathers that aid flight. The long, strong tail feathers are used much as the tail fin of an airplane to steer while the bird is flying. The tail feathers also act as a brake when landing.

There are three basic types of flight: flapping, gliding, and soaring. Most birds use flapping flight, that is, after they take off, they continue to fly by flapping their wings. When gliding, birds keep their wings extended and coast downward. During soaring flight, birds use the energy of rising columns of warm air, called thermals, to move without having to flap their wings. With wings extended, a soaring bird circles lazily as the thermal current lifts it higher and higher. Other air movements, such as prevailing winds, are also used by birds to soar.

Walking and Running

When most people think of how birds get from place to place, they think of flight. However, there also are birds that walk, run, hop, or swim. Some birds, such as the ostrich, emu, and rhea, have evolved into flightless, swift-running birds. Typically, birds that nest and feed on the ground walk and run by moving one foot forward at a time. Most birds that nest in trees hop on both feet when they are on the ground. Some birds run and hop.

The snow goose (*above left*) uses its feathered wings for flight. Rapidly beating wings power this pair of grebes (*above*) across the water's surface during a courtship dance. The male peacock (*left*) fans its lush plumage to attract females.

A bird's legs and feet match their habits and environment. Legs serve as good shock absorbers and can launch the bird from the ground during takeoff. There is a great variety in the length of their legs. The swift-running birds have very long legs. Other birds, such as water-loving penguins, have very short legs that make walking on land difficult. Most birds have four toes—three pointing forward and one pointing backward. Some climbing birds, such as woodpeckers, have two toes pointing backward that help them to cling to tree trunks. The osprey has an outer toe that can point either forward or backward. In swifts, all the toes face forward.

Toes for grasping perches, climbing, capturing prey, and carrying and manipulating food are tipped with sharply curved and pointed nails. Strong toes for running and scratching have thick blunt nails. Toes for swimming and paddling are sometimes webbed or they may have fleshy lobes attached to them. South American jacanas appear to walk on water. Their extremely long toes spread out the bird's weight so that the bird can be supported by the underwater weeds growing near the water's surface.

hunting

golden eagle

perching

black-capped chickadee

walking

eastern meadowlark

climbing

pileated woodpecker

The long-legged ostrich (*left*) can reach speeds of 40 miles (64 kilometers) per hour. The blue-footed booby performs a tapping dance during courtship (*below*). On its stilt-like legs, the flamingo (*below right*) wades into deep waters to feed.

swimming, three webbed toes

common goldeneye

running

ostrich

tearing   hammering

bald eagle   yellow-bellied sapsucker

Food and Feeding

Birds use their bills, flexible necks, feet, and ability to fly in order to find, secure, and eat their food. They feed on a wide variety of food—from fruit and seeds to dead animals.

A bird's bill is made up of upper and lower halves, called mandibles. The mandibles are the visible part of the bill and are made of layers of keratin, the same protein found in feathers. In most birds, the bill is black.

Bills come in a variety of shapes and sizes. Birds of prey have powerful, hooked bills to tear apart their victims. Wading birds, such as the heron, have long, sharp, daggerlike bills that they use to spear fish and frogs. Shore-birds have long, slender bills to probe mud for food. Seed-eaters have strong wedge-shaped bills to crack open the hard shells of seeds. The sawlike edges on the bill of a fish-eater, such as the merganser, is ideal for grasping and holding slippery prey.

Along with food, birds need water. Some birds, such as fruit- and insect-eaters, may get the water they need from the food they eat. Others find a water source and scoop water up in their bills. Still others have devised special ways to get water. The sand grouse lives in some of the driest deserts on earth. They travel long distances to a water source, soak the special feathers on their bellies, and carry water back to the nest. The young grouse suck on the feathers to get the water.

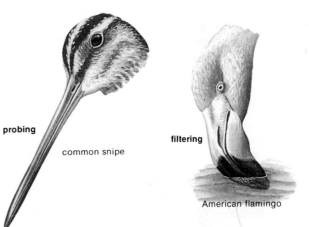

spearing   cracking

       common redpoll

black-crowned night heron

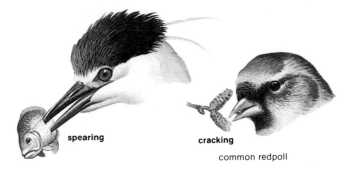

probing   filtering

common snipe   American flamingo

Many birds, such as the blue jay (*left*), feed on seeds and nuts; others, such as the western gull (*below left*), eat small water animals and insects; still others, such as the bald eagle (*below*), prey on larger animals—fish, frogs, and even other birds.

The Skeleton and Flight Muscles of a Bird

The large breastbone (*right*) supports the muscles that power a bird's wings. The large muscles pull the wings down during flight (*below*) while the smaller muscles pull the wings up (*bottom*).

A cross section of a flying bird's wing bone (*below*) shows a hollow cavity reinforced with lightweight struts (supports). In many flightless birds, the bones are solid.

▶THE BODY SYSTEMS OF BIRDS

There are many physical features that are shared by birds and mammals. For instance, both groups of animals have backbones, are warm-blooded, and have four limbs. However, the body systems of birds are adapted to flight.

Bones and Muscles

Over time, the skeleton of the bird has developed into an airy, lightweight, yet strong, frame. Since the earliest birds, many body parts, such as teeth, have disappeared—lightening the frame. Other parts, such as the vertebrae of the back, have become fused (joined)—giving the frame more strength.

While a bird's many neck vertebrae are shaped so that the neck is extremely flexible, most of the rest of the skeleton has become stiffened. Birds have a large breastbone, or sternum, that protects the internal organs and provides strong support for the attached muscles that power flight. The heaviest, strongest bone is the coracoid. Together with the ribs, it holds the sternum and the rigid backbone apart when the flight muscles contract.

The largest muscles in a bird are the pectoral (breast) muscles. These muscles may account for as much as one fifth of a bird's entire weight. They are attached to the long bone of the wing. When they contract during flight, the wings are pulled down. Smaller muscles, called the supracoracoideus, contract during flight and the wings are pulled up.

Digestive System

Since birds have no teeth, the digestive system must grind up food so that the energy stored in it can be used. A hollow digestive tube extends from the mouth through the entire length of the body to an external opening called the cloaca. The tube is divided into the throat (pharynx), esophagus, stomach, small intestine, and large intestine.

Food passes from the mouth through the pharynx into the esophagus. Some birds, such as pigeons, doves, and hawks, have a portion of their esophagus enlarged to form a storage pouch called a crop. The crop allows birds to feed quickly and digest its meal later in safety.

Nearly all birds have a stomach made up of two parts. The first part of the stomach, called the proventriculus, secretes strong digestive juices, which in some birds are strong enough to digest bones! The second part of the stomach, called the gizzard, has strong muscular walls that act like teeth to grind and pulverize foods. In addition to the muscular walls, birds often swallow small pebbles and grit that get trapped in the gizzard and aid in the grinding process.

From the stomach, food passes into the small intestine where the nutritious end products of digestion are absorbed into the bloodstream. The remaining indigestible matter travels into the large intestine where it is stored until it is eliminated from the body through the cloaca.

Metabolic System

A bird's metabolic system guides all the chemical changes that provide energy for vital processes and activities such as new cell growth and maintenance of body temperature. Birds, which have a higher body temperature, a faster heart rate, and a greater need for oxygen than mammals, must eat a great deal of food to get the necessary energy to fuel the body functions. Small birds have a relatively higher metabolic rate, and therefore higher energy needs, than large birds. An ostrich can go several days without food, however, a small hummingbird needs so much energy that it must feed almost constantly during the day.

Birds are endothermal, or warm-blooded. That means they have an internal furnace, fueled by food, that generates heat and allows them to keep their bodies at a constant temperature, even though the temperature of their en-

The tiny hummingbird (*above*) requires between fifty and sixty meals a day to sustain its high metabolic rate. With wings beating at a rate of between fifty and eighty times a second, the hummingbird can hover (*right*) without rest for four hours at a time.

vironment changes. Birds are also able to regulate their body temperature by conserving or losing heat through a variety of ways—feathers help retain heat, while panting helps get rid of heat.

Circulatory System

A bird's circulatory system consists of a four-chambered heart and blood vessels. With each beat, or stroke, of the heart, a large volume of blood is carried throughout the bird's body by vessels called arteries. Blood is then returned to the heart by vessels called veins. Birds are nature's best athletes. With their powerful hearts, they can keep up extraordinary levels of physical exertion for long periods. A ruby-throated hummingbird's heart is about 3 percent of its total body weight, but it is strong enough to supply fuel and oxygen to the flight muscles for a nonstop flight across the Gulf of Mexico.

The high metabolism of birds requires rapid circulation of the blood because waste products build up quickly in the cells and must be removed before they reach a toxic level. Typically, small birds have a higher metabolism than large birds and therefore have a faster heart rate.

The Internal Body Structures of a Bird

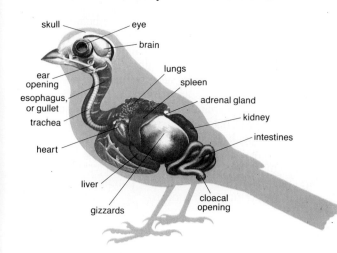

skull
eye
brain
lungs
spleen
ear opening
esophagus, or gullet
adrenal gland
trachea
kidney
heart
intestines
liver
cloacal opening
gizzards

How Birds See

The owl, whose eyes are on the front of its head, has a wide overlapping field of vision in front and good depth perception.

The falcon, whose eyes are on the sides of its head, has a narrow overlapping field of vision in front.

The woodcock, whose eyes are far back on the sides of its head, has a narrow overlapping field of vision both in front and behind.

Respiratory System

The high metabolism and athletic life-style of birds require a great deal of oxygen. Four organs work together to bring oxygen from the atmosphere to the cells: nostrils, trachea, lungs, and air sacs. With each breath, air moves through the nostrils, down the trachea and into the lungs and air sacs. From the lungs, oxygen passes into the bloodstream and then to the body cells. The air that passes into the air sacs cools the internal organs and helps maintain body temperature. Nearly all of the air in the lungs is replaced with each breath. At rest, birds breathe slowly. When flying, birds require ten to twenty times more oxygen than at rest. To supply the extra oxygen, birds increase their breathing rates.

Nervous System

The nervous system of a bird is similar to that of other vertebrates and consists of the brain, sense organs, and nerves. Nerves carry messages from sense organs, such as the eyes, to the brain. Nerves also carry messages from the brain to the muscles.

As a group, birds have the best vision of all animals. Their large eyes, which sometimes weigh more than their brain, provide keen sight and excellent color perception. Birds that are most active at night, or nocturnal, also have well-developed sight. The range of vision that a bird has depends on whether the eyes are located on the sides of the head or on the front of the head.

Hearing is also well developed in birds, with some night birds having especially acute hearing. Only a few birds, such as the kiwi, have a highly developed sense of smell. The kiwi is nearly blind and relies on its sense of smell to find food.

Reproductive System

A bird's reproductive system is composed of the sex organs and a series of tubes, or ducts, which act as passages for the sex cells produced within the organs. The male sex organs, called the testes, produce sperm; the female sex organs, called the ovaries, produce eggs.

When birds mate, sperm from the testes pass from the male to the female. The sperm fertilize the eggs, which have formed in the ovaries. After an egg is fertilized, it begins to travel down a narrow tube called the oviduct toward the external opening, or cloaca. On the way down the oviduct, it first receives a coating of the protein called albumen (the egg white). Further down the oviduct, the albumen is surrounded by a shell composed of calcium. As the egg nears the end of the oviduct and before it is laid, it also may receive various colored pigments.

▶ THE BEHAVIOR PATTERNS OF BIRDS

Birds have many behaviors that help them to survive. Some of these are learned behaviors, but many others are not learned. Behaviors that animals are born with are called instinctive behaviors. Some instinctive behaviors help birds recognize enemies. Great kiskadees display an instinctive behavior related to coral snakes, which eat young birds. Even though they have never seen a snake, hand-raised great kiskadees are frightened by sticks that have been painted to look like coral snakes. Newly hatched herring gulls know by instinct to peck at the red spot on the bill of their parents in order to be fed. Pecking becomes more accurate as the baby gulls learn to anticipate the position of their parents' bills when they return with food.

Bird-watching

Birds are fascinating creatures. You do not have to be an ornithologist to enjoy watching birds. Many amateurs have contributed to the understanding of birds by recording their observations and reporting interesting or significant sightings to their local bird club. Information provided by amateur bird-watchers can then be used to compile information about population changes within a specific area or to document the introduction of a new species into an area.

Some people simply watch birds at a backyard feeder; others hike the forests, fields, and marshes to get a close look at birds. Whichever way you decide to bird-watch, recording what you observe is fun as well as helpful. Information that will help you recall a bird sighting includes the date, time of day, location, weather conditions, and persons with you (if any). Some observations to keep track of are the species, number of birds, and behaviors of the birds you see. Quick sketches of plumage or flight patterns can also be made. Along with a notebook and pencils, supplies such as field guides, binoculars, camera, and tape recorder (for recording bird calls) are all useful.

Birds also learn very well. Young birds learn to recognize predators by observing the behavior of other birds. Many species of birds make loud, scolding calls when they discover predators such as owls, cats, or snakes. Flocks of birds attack and usually drive away the predator—a behavior called mobbing. Inexperienced birds quickly learn to associate danger with mobbing. Some birds learn how to build better nests as they get older and more experienced.

Living in a Community

Flocks. Birds that stay all winter in northern regions have little time to do anything but find food, water, and shelter. Some species form large social groups called flocks. Among these species, some form flocks in the winter, some remain in flocks year-round, and others never form flocks at all. Living in a flock has two big advantages: It is easier for the many eyes of the group to find food and to spot predators. A bird in a flock is much less likely to be killed by a hawk than a lone bird singled out for attack. Usually all the birds in a flock do the same thing at the same time—they sleep together, feed together, and sometimes even breed together.

Dominance. Often winter birds living in small flocks establish a system of dominance, which is sometimes called a **pecking order**. Pecking order is organized so that each bird pecks another bird lower in standing within the group and submits to pecking by birds of higher rank.

In flocks with dominance systems, the highest ranking bird gets first choice of food, water, even mates, while others wait their turn. Dominance helps all the birds in the flock to survive by reducing competition. Being lowest bird in the pecking order is better than fighting over every scrap of food with all the members of the flock.

Defense. Birds use a variety of methods to protect themselves and their offspring against

Birds have different bathing behaviors that keep their feathers free of parasites and dirt. A swan (*above left*) thrashes its wings in water, while the helmeted guinea fowl (*above right*) digs a small pit in the ground and shuffles its feathers in the dirt.

Not all species of birds have the same activity cycle. Great gray owls (*left*) rest during the day and hunt during the night. Egrets (*below*) follow the typical cycle —they feed during the day and rest during the night.

For most birds, defending territory is the focus of the males' day. Threat displays by the sage grouse (*right*) warn intruders that they had better leave the territory. Occasionally, fighting erupts. Brown pelicans (*below right*) use their beaks to peck and grab at the enemy.

enemies. Some birds that are colored or patterned so that they blend with their surroundings can often remain undetected if they stay still. This type of **protective coloration**, or natural camouflage, not only helps a bird avoid enemies, but it also helps a bird get close to prey without being seen.

Other birds may flee or hide. As a last resort and if it cannot escape or hide from danger, a bird will fight using its beak, legs, or wings, depending on its species. Sometimes, a bird will try to distract an intruder from its nest by making a noisy disturbance or pretending to be hurt and, therefore, easy prey. Once the intruder follows the "wounded" bird away from the nest, the "wounded" bird flies off.

Establishing a Territory

In general, male birds migrate north before females. They need to arrive early to stake claim to a territory. A territory is a fixed area that is defended continuously for a period of time. Most birds defend territories during breeding; some defend territories all year long. Both males and females defend territories, but most often it is the male who works hardest to defend the territory. Birds establish, maintain, and defend breeding territories in order to attract mates, find appropriate nest sites, and find enough food to raise hungry nestlings.

Communicating

Bird song may sound beautiful, but birds do not sing to make music; birds sing to attract mates and to tell other males to stay off their territory.

Birds are capable of an enormous variety of vocalizations. Traditionally they are divided into two groups: calls and song. Calls are

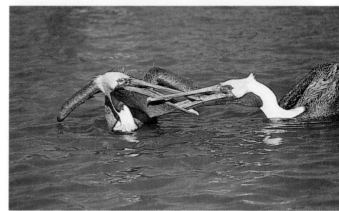

short, simple vocalizations such as calls of distress, feeding, flight, flocking, and warning. Songs are long vocal displays with specific repeatable patterns. Normally only males can sing. However, some females, such as northern cardinal females, sing quite well.

Birds can sing more than just one specific song. Birds generally have between 5 and 14 songs, but some species have many more. Northern mockingbirds and wrens are capable of producing hundreds of songs. Besides helping males to defend their territories and attract mates, songs can warn others about potential dangers; can say "Here I am . . . where are you?"; and can tell other birds the species, age, sex, and experience of the singer.

No two birds sing exactly the same song. Subtle differences in the pitch and timing of songs are used to recognize individuals. Birds are able to identify their mates, young, parents, and neighbors. Penguins returning to nesting colonies that may have tens of thousands of birds are able to locate their mates by picking out their unique call from the deafening chorus of the colony.

During courtship, the male sage grouse (*left*) inflates its neck pouches and lets out booming calls to attract females. The male frigate bird (*right*) seeks the attention of a female by inflating his huge red throat pouch and keeping it inflated, sometimes for many hours, until he has lured a female to his side. During courtship, a pair of great blue herons (*below*) collect twigs and sticks and build their nest together.

▶ THE LIFE CYCLE OF BIRDS

A year in the life of a bird is controlled by a series of rhythms and cycles. Every year birds pass through the phases of breeding, molting, and migrating. What is amazing is that birds do these things with astonishing precision. This is because they have an internal biological clock that controls their daily and annual schedules and regulates when they sleep, feed, migrate, breed, and molt.

Mating

In spring, males arrive at the breeding ground before females. After establishing a territory, they defend it against neighboring males and sing to attract a mate. When the females arrive, they may choose a mate in one of several ways. Northern mockingbirds prefer males with a large number of different songs. Red-winged blackbirds select males with the best territories. Regardless of how the choice is made, a strong tie known as a pair bond is formed between the male and female. Canada geese and bald eagles form pair bonds with their mates that last their entire lives. At the other extreme, ruby-throated hummingbirds form a pair bond for only a few minutes. In most birds, the pair bond lasts the entire summer, as the birds build a nest, incubate eggs, and raise fledglings to adulthood.

Most birds are monogamous, which means they only have one mate at a time. Some birds have more than one mate at a time; they are called polygamous. Promiscuity is a form of mating without bonding. The male and female come together briefly to mate and then part. The female builds the nest and cares for the young alone.

Nesting

All birds lay eggs and care for them in one way or another. The place where birds lay their eggs is called a nest. Nests hold and cushion eggs before they hatch. Some birds, such as murres, do not build any type of nest to hold their eggs. They simply lay them on bare cliff ledges overlooking the sea. Other birds build elaborate structures to hold the eggs. Some nests are used year after year.

Birds must choose the safest possible place to nest if the young and the adults are to survive. The nest must provide protection from predators, who like to eat eggs, nestlings, and even adults sitting on the nest. The nest must also protect the eggs from bad weather.

Types of Nests. Although birds build nests in a variety of places, using many different types of materials, members of the same species generally build similarly styled nests.

The first birds probably built nests that were just a slight depression scratched in the ground or fallen leaves. This type of nest is called a scrape and is still used by many birds today. Shorebirds, terns, nighthawks, and falcons are some of the species that make scrapes. Other birds, like belted kingfishers and petrels, nest in a scrape at the end of long burrows they have dug deep within stream banks or the ground.

When most people picture a bird's nest, they think of a cup-shaped nest. These cup nests are the most common type and can be built almost anywhere. Warblers, American robins, and blackbirds all build cup nests.

Other birds are well equipped to chisel out a home in a dead tree. Woodpeckers, parrots, and hornbills dig nest cavities. Cavity nests are widespread among birds because they provide especially good protection. Male hornbills seal the female into their nest cavity and she does not leave until the chicks have hatched!

Many species build flat platform nests in just about every type of habitat imaginable—from treetops to water environments. Bald eagles build the largest tree nests of any bird. These large platform nests

are used year after year and can be more than 9 feet (3 meters) wide! Great blue herons also make large tree nests and place them close together in what are called colonies. Grebes build floating platforms, anchoring them to plants growing in shallow water. The horned coot of South America even builds its own island! Thousands of small stones are piled up over several years, making a custom-designed nesting island that may weigh as much as a ton.

One of the most unusual nests belongs to the dusky

Nests come in many forms. The northern flicker (*above*) has settled into a cavity it has made in a giant cactus. The nest of the Caribbean flamingo (*left*) is a cone of mud about 1½ feet (.5 meter) high. The eggs are laid in a small depression formed at the top of the cone. Nestlings within their snug cup-shaped nest (*below left*) call for food. The cup-shaped nest is the most common type of nest. At one time the mud nests of the cliff swallow (*below*) were only found at cliff sites; today they can be found under the eaves of buildings and under concrete bridges.

scrub fowl of Australia. Males of this species build gigantic mounds of rotting leaves, sticks, and grass that can sometimes measure 36 feet across (11 meters) and more than 16 feet (5 meters) high! The female lays her eggs in the mound, where they are warmed by the heat generated from the rotting vegetation and by the sun. The male dusky scrub fowl carefully checks the temperature of the mound with his bill and adds or removes layers of vegetation as needed.

Eggs and Egg Laying

Once an egg is fertilized, it develops quickly in the female's oviduct and is surrounded with a protective eggshell. As soon as the egg is fully formed, it is laid before the next one has grown very large. Usually females lay an egg each day, or every few days, until the group of eggs, called a clutch, is complete. Most birds wait until all the eggs are laid, then they sit on the eggs to warm them with their bodies. They will warm the eggs in this manner, in the process called incubation, until the eggs hatch. In this way, all the young birds hatch at about the same time.

Other birds, like owls, start incubating as soon as the first egg is laid. The eggs hatch at different times and the young are much different in size.

Eggs vary tremendously in size and color. The flightless ostrich lays a gigantic egg that can weigh up to 4 pounds (1.8 kilograms). It is so big and the shell is so thick that few animals can break it open. On the other hand, the tiny Cuban bee hummingbird's egg is only ¼ inch (.5 centimeter) long and weighs ¹⁄₁₀₀ ounce (.25 gram). More than 5,000 hummingbird eggs would fit inside an ostrich egg!

Often eggs are perfectly colored to blend in with their background. Ground-nesting birds usually have pastel gray, blue, or green eggs that are speckled with shades of brown or black.

Eggs show countless variations, not only in size and color but in shape. The shape of eggs varies from long and elliptical, or oval, to nearly round. Most eggs are shaped like the familiar chicken egg. Streamlined birds, such as swifts and hummingbirds, lay long, elliptical eggs that help females keep their efficient body shape. Murres, which nest on narrow

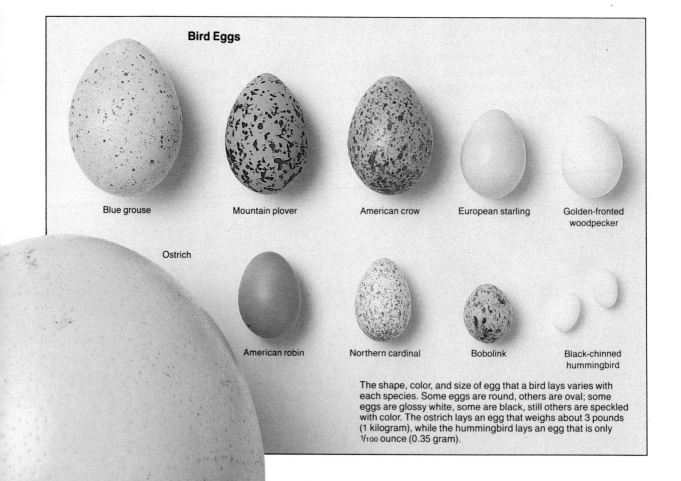

Bird Eggs

Blue grouse   Mountain plover   American crow   European starling   Golden-fronted woodpecker

Ostrich

American robin   Northern cardinal   Bobolink   Black-chinned hummingbird

The shape, color, and size of egg that a bird lays varies with each species. Some eggs are round, others are oval; some eggs are glossy white, some are black, still others are speckled with color. The ostrich lays an egg that weighs about 3 pounds (1 kilogram), while the hummingbird lays an egg that is only ¹⁄₁₀₀ ounce (0.35 gram).

When temperatures soar, the heron (*left*) partially extends its wings to provide cooling shade for the eggs in its nest. The trumpeter swan (*right*) turns the eggs to make sure they are warmed evenly. Eggs may be turned from once every few minutes to about once an hour. The cowbird lays its eggs in other birds' nests. Here (*below*), a yellow warbler cares for cowbird nestlings.

cliffs, have eggs shaped like toy tops. These eggs roll in a tight circle, which is important if rolling out of the nest means a fall of several hundred feet. Cavity-nesting birds tend to lay round eggs that pile neatly in the bottom of the nest hole. Shorebirds lay four pointed eggs that fit together like pieces of a pie.

Incubation. A few days before a bird lays its first egg, the bird loses some of the feathers on its belly. The blood vessels in the area also enlarge and form what is known as a brood patch. When a bird incubates its eggs, it settles itself down so that its brood patch is in direct contact with the eggs. In general, brood patches develop only in the birds that incubate. If both sexes incubate, both develop brood patches.

Birds that nest in places where the temperatures are above 100°F (38°C) need to keep their eggs cool. Some birds will stand over the eggs, shading them with partially opened wings. Mourning doves nesting in Arizona have been found to use their brood patches to cool their eggs down to body temperature. The birds pant heavily while incubating, to get rid of the extra heat.

The incubation period of an egg is the time from the start of incubation until hatching of the egg. In general, larger eggs need longer incubation periods. The wandering albatross, one of the largest flying birds, needs 75 to 82 days of incubation. Small finches and warblers need only 11 to 12 days.

Some birds neither build nests nor take care of their young. Instead, they lay their eggs in the nests of other species, and rely on them to incubate the eggs and rear the offspring. This

behavior is called brood parasitism. Some birds, such as cuckoos, are always brood parasites, while others, such as redhead ducks, are irregular brood parasites.

Redhead ducks are irregular brood parasites, which means that sometimes they have their own nests and incubate their own eggs, and sometimes they lay eggs in the nests of different duck species. Honeyguides, found in Asia and Africa, are totally parasitic and have lost all courtship and nesting behaviors. Honeyguides usually lay a single egg in the nest of a closely related species. Newly hatched honeyguides, while still blind and featherless, will eliminate the other nestlings that compete with them for food. They use the sharp hook on the tip of their beaks to bite and kill the other nestlings or, one by one, they push the host's young out of the nest.

Hatching of a Chick

When the offspring inside the egg is fully developed, hatching begins. The chick uses the egg tooth on the tip of its beak to peck an opening in the shell. Pushing through the opening it has made, the chick tumbles out of the shell. Depending on the species, hatching may take as little as five hours or as long as four days.

The brown-headed cowbird, which is widespread throughout North America, is also a brood parasite. Cowbird eggs have been found in the nests of more than 150 species. The abundance of cowbird parasitism has been an important factor in the decline of some birds, such as the endangered Kirtland's warbler.

Hatching. Inside the egg, the growing bird develops a short, pointy structure on the tip of the upper beak called an egg tooth. When the incubation period is complete, the fully developed offspring uses its egg tooth to break out of the shell. Small birds, such as warblers, finches, and sparrows, may complete the hatching process in five hours. Larger birds, especially seabirds, may take as long as four days.

Imprinting. Birds exhibit a very special type of learning called imprinting. Imprinting only occurs during a critical period early in life, and once something is learned by imprinting it cannot be changed or forgotten. For instance, the moving object that a duckling follows in the first 24 hours after hatching is accepted as its "mother." Usually the moving object is the adult female duck; however, it has been shown that a duckling will follow and imprint on humans or even a moving box with a ticking alarm clock inside.

Later in life, birds will select mates and other members of their flock based on what has been imprinted. Baby birds raised by people do not imprint correctly and never select an appropriate mate for nesting. Birds also imprint on the type of nest and its location, which is important information when they need to select a good spot to build their nest.

Because these peregrine falcon chicks are being raised by humans, they will not learn how to perform some of the tasks necessary for their survival in the wild.

Care of the Young

Feeding. A nestling bird is an ugly thing. It is all belly and head with two large bulging eyes. Almost immediately, a nestling can lift its wobbly head and open its mouth. The inside of the mouth is usually brightly colored, providing a food target for the parents. On either side of the nestling's mouth are sensitive nerve endings. When touched, the mouth automatically snaps shut. The combination of the nestling's wide-open mouth and constant begging for food is powerful stimuli for the adults. The instinct to feed young is so strong that they will occasionally feed other birds' young.

Some birds are altricial—that is, they are helpless when they are born. They are born featherless and blind. At first, altricial nestlings cannot maintain their own body temperature. If the parents are gone too long, they grow cold. Fortunately, in a few days, the nestlings grow a coat of downy feathers. They also take in huge quantities of food and grow very rapidly. A common cuckoo, which is only about 0.07 ounces (2 grams) at hatching, weighs about 3.5 ounces (100 grams) after

three weeks. By the time it leaves the nest, its weight is almost that of the adult female. Young albatrosses and petrels weigh much more than either parent when they leave the nest. Their tremendous fat reserves are slowly used up after the parents abandon them and return to sea. By the time young albatrosses have reached normal adult weight, they are ready to leave the nest and soar over the ocean in search of food.

Precocial birds spend more time in the egg than altricial birds do, so they are better developed when they hatch. However, they grow more slowly than altricial birds after hatching. The killdeer is typical of most precocial birds. It is born with its eyes open, a thick layer of down, and well-developed legs and bill. Shortly after hatching, it is able to run around and find its own food.

In the Nest

Life in the nest is not easy. Very few of the young live long enough to nest themselves. Eight or nine out of every ten birds die during their first year. For most species, weather and predators are the greatest threats to young

To satisfy the seemingly boundless appetite of nestlings, a parent bird makes many trips to and from the nest—sometimes as many as 900 trips per day.

The 27 Orders of Living Birds

Coliiformes
blue-naped mousebird

Psittaciformes
gray parrot

Apodiformes
ruby-throated hummingbird

Passeriformes
blue jay

Coraciiformes
carmine bee-eater

Gruiformes
crowned crane

Rheiformes
common rhea

Tinamiformes
variegated tinamou

Columbiformes
victoria crested pigeon

Casuariiformes
Australian cassowary

Anseriformes
wood duck

Falconiformes
bald eagle

Apterygiformes
brown kiwi

T. BOYER

Piciformes
keel-billed toucan

Trogoniformes
collared trogon

Cuculiformes
white-eared turaco

Procellariiformes
gray-headed albatross

Caprimulgiformes
common nighthawk

Struthioniformes
ostrich

Strigiformes
snowy owl

Ciconiiformes
black-crowned night heron

Charadriiformes
ruddy turnstone

Pelecaniformes
great frigate bird

Galliformes
Lady Amherst's pheasant

Sphenisciformes
king penguin

Gaviiformes
arctic loon

Podicipediformes
western grebe

birds. Bad weather can reduce insect populations and thus reduce the birds' food supply, or it can interfere with the parents' ability to find food for their young. Mammals, especially raccoons, foxes, and squirrels, can be very destructive. Nestlings can also suffer heavy losses from parasites, such as mites and blow fly larvae. These insects attach themselves to the skin of the nestlings and feed on their blood, weakening them so much that they are unlikely to survive.

Regardless of their regular diet, the adults feed their young foods rich in proteins. Young birds, like children, need large amounts of protein in order to grow. Even hummingbirds, which as adults feed mainly on flower nectar, bring small insects to their young. Some birds have unique ways of feeding their young. Pigeons and doves (a member of the pigeon family) feed their young on pigeon's milk, a

The trumpeter swan is an attentive parent that sometimes carries its young, called cygnets, on its back. More often, however, the swan simply escorts its brood from one place to another.

material high in fat and protein that is formed in their crop (the storage portion of their stomach). Pelicans catch and store fish in their huge mouths and let their young dip into the enormous pouch and help themselves to the food there. Cormorants swallow the heads of their young and the young feed right from the adult's stomach.

The large amount of food brought to a nest full of young results in the production of much waste. If not removed, this material would foul the nest, attract predators and parasites, or cause disease. Many young birds eliminate undigested food and wastes in a small membrane called a fecal sac. The sacs are then eaten by the adults or carried away.

Before long, the nest becomes overcrowded with the rapidly growing nestlings and soon it can no longer hold them. Then it is time for the baby birds to leave the nest; this is called fledging. In some birds, the young make their first flight when they fledge. In others, the fledglings (baby birds) simply move out of the nest to a nearby limb.

The masked booby (left) carefully preens its offspring, combing through the feathers to remove dirt and parasites. Spreading its wings to create shade, the egret (below) protects its downy offspring from the hot sun. In a few species of birds, such as the emperor penguin (below right), the male has much of the responsibility for taking care of the offspring. Here, the emperor penguin chick huddles under the warm belly of its parent.

By fall, the young birds that were born in late spring have learned a great deal. They have practiced flying and can now find their own food, although they still may beg for their parents to feed them. In many cases, they have been on their own for months. Many birds nest more than once in a summer. The young from the first nest fend for themselves while the parents start a second brood. In some birds, the young from the first nest stay with the parents and help raise their siblings.

The Migration Cycle

There are ancient records of the appearance and disappearance of birds. Early naturalists did not know if birds migrated or hibernated. People told stories of swallows that were found frozen in marshes and would fly away when thawed. Now we know that billions of birds make astonishing migrations, traveling to distant places to breed and winter. Each spring, an estimated 5 billion birds migrate from the Central and South America to North America in search of nesting sites. An equal number leave the warmth of Africa and set out for breeding grounds in Europe and Asia. The migration of birds is truly one of the most spectacular feats in the natural world.

Residents and Migrants. Some birds never make a long-distance migration. These birds are called residents. Other birds fly incredible journeys to spend winters in tropical areas. These birds are called migrants.

There are advantages and disadvantages to both resident and migrant life-styles. Residents face long, cold winters and scarce food supplies. If a bird cannot find enough food to burn for energy during the long, cold winter night, it will freeze to death. It is much easier to survive the winter in the warm tropical forests of Central and South America. However, long-distance migrations are dangerous. Many birds are killed during migration by storms and man-made hazards, such as radio and television towers. Many forest areas have been destroyed to provide land for construction and development, so good places to stop and rest during migration are harder and harder for birds to find.

Migration. As fall approaches, the days get shorter and the nights grow cooler. With nesting over, things begin to change. The territories that were defended so vigorously in the beginning of summer no longer matter. Many species have urges to join large flocks of birds —for safety and to prepare for the migration to come.

Whether in a flock or not, birds feed heavily at this time of year to build up the fat reserves they will need to fly back to their wintering grounds. Before long, the alarm goes off on their biological clocks and it is time to migrate south.

Some birds migrate by day, others migrate at night. Hawks ride the thermals created as the sun warms the ground below. Humming-

With winter on the way, snow geese leave their nests in high Arctic regions to form large flocks for the journey southward. They fly during the day and night, coming down at regular intervals to rest and feed.

birds migrate alone and during the day, stopping to feed as needed. However, most small land birds, including flycatchers, thrushes, warblers, and orioles, migrate at night when temperatures are cooler and the tremendous quantities of heat generated by flapping flight muscles are quickly lost to the cool night air. Predation is less likely at night and the daylight hours can be used to find food and refuel for the next night's journey. As the day dawns, large flocks of migrating songbirds descend into patches of woods in what is known as a fallout, to rest and feed.

Many birds, especially duck and geese, follow narrow paths as they migrate north and south. These paths are called flyways. The main migration routes in North America run north to south, much as most of the mountain ranges and major rivers do. In Europe and Asia, birds migrate east to west as they travel from their breeding grounds to wintering ground.

In spring the days grow longer, and once again the changing daylight sets off the bird's biological clock. It is time to molt and begin preparations for the migration north. Longer days do more than just trigger the molting process. The increasing day length also triggers an increase in appetite and an increase in fat storage, which help to prepare the bird for spring migration.

After traveling all the way to the tropics, why do birds not stay and nest there? The costs of migration are great, but the benefits

Under clear skies and with a good tail wind, Canada geese can cover many hundreds of miles in a single nonstop flight.

Each year in their migratory journey between the Arctic and the Antarctic, Arctic terns log up to 25,000 miles (40,225 kilometers) of travel.

of returning north to breed are even greater. The tropics are full of predators that would quickly gobble up young birds. In North America, there are not as many reptile and small mammal predators.

Birds also migrate north to breed because there is an extremely large supply of the insects that are needed to feed growing young. In the long days of the northern summer, birds have time to find plentiful amounts of food for their young. In the Arctic, the mid-summer sun never sets, allowing birds to hunt 24 hours a day.

How Birds Migrate

How do birds know where to go? How do they find their way? Why do some birds travel during the day, while others travel during the night? These are questions that **ornithologists** (scientists who study birds) have tried to answer for at least a century. Birds have an astonishing ability to return to an exact location after wintering in South America or Africa. Homing pigeons can return to their home loft from places hundreds of miles away.

Recently ornithologists have started to learn how birds know where they are and navigate during their great migrations. Near your house, it is unlikely that you would ever get lost. You know the way because you recognize landmarks; birds also use landmarks to find their way. But they also have other ways of navigating when they fly out of their neighborhood. They have several sources of information that tell them which way to go. Migrating birds can use the sun by day and the stars by night. Research shows that they can even use the earth's magnetic field (the same field detected by a compass) and that they sometimes use odor clues, and maybe even low-frequency sounds.

However birds find their way, they are rarely very late. One of the extraordinary things about migration is its precision. Birds that travel across a continent, or farther, arrive at their destination within a few days of the same time each year.

A bird's internal clock is mostly responsible for the start of migration, but weather is also a factor. Many species, such as American robins, time their arrival to match the spring thaw. Birds are sensitive to changes in atmospheric pressure. Strong favorable winds cause birds to migrate in large numbers.

The Birds Around Us

Some birds spend most of their lives in deserts, others can be found along seacoasts, still others are found in woodlands and forests. In the following section, a variety of birds are shown in the kind of habitat, or environment, in which they can typically be found. The habitats include seacoasts, deserts, woodlands and forests, grasslands, polar regions, tropics, and residential areas. Below is an alphabetical listing of the birds presented and the habitats in which they live.

Bird	Habitat	Bird	Habitat
American kestrel	Grasslands	Hairy woodpecker	Woodlands and forests
American oystercatcher	Seacoasts	Herring gull	Seacoasts
American robin	Residential areas	Hoatzin	Tropics
Baltimore oriole	Residential areas	Long-billed curlew	Seacoasts
Blue jay	Residential areas	Mockingbird	Residential areas
Bobwhite	Grasslands	Phainopepla	Deserts
Bohemian waxwing	Woodlands and forests	Purple finch	Woodlands and forests
Burrowing owl	Grasslands	Quetzal	Tropics
Cactus wren	Deserts	Red-tailed hawk	Deserts
Chipping sparrow	Residential areas	Ruffed grouse	Woodlands and forests
Common cormorant	Seacoasts	Sandpiper	Seacoasts
Common pigeon	Residential areas	Scarlet ibis	Tropics
Common tern	Seacoasts	Snowy owl	Polar regions
Eastern meadowlark	Grasslands	Tawny owl	Woodlands and forests
Emperor penguin	Polar regions	Toco toucan	Tropics
Gila woodpecker	Deserts	Wandering albatross	Polar regions
Great hornbill	Tropics	Western kingbird	Grasslands
Great skua	Polar regions	Wilson's storm petrel	Polar regions
Greater roadrunner	Deserts	Yellow warbler	Woodlands and forests

Birds of the Seacoasts

Many birds are found along the coasts of the world's continents. Some are shorebirds; that is, they live most of the time on the shore. The most widely distributed and probably the best-known shorebird is the gull. Gulls are scavengers — they forage along the shore for dead animals and even search through garbage dumps for food. They also hunt the shallow waters for fish or clams and other mollusks. The gull must break the mollusk's shell to get to the soft meat inside. It does this by carrying the mollusk aloft, then dropping it on rocks or other hard surfaces. Other birds found along the coasts are seabirds; they live most of the time at sea, coming ashore only to breed and nest. Terns are seabirds that stay at sea for long lengths of time, sometimes months or even years. Some seabirds spend so much time flying that they have lost the ability to walk on land or to swim. Not all of a seabird's time is spent flying; seabirds also soar and glide.

Herring gull

Common tern

Long-billed curlew

Common cormorant

Sandpipers

American oystercatchers

Birds of the Deserts

Only the hardiest of birds survive in the desert. The days are very hot, and during the night the temperatures plunge, sometimes even dipping below freezing. The desert is also a dry place. Because it is so dry, desert birds must get their water from the foods they eat. Rather than eating dry seeds and other plant products, most desert birds eat insects or small animals, such as lizards, snakes, and tree frogs, that supply the moisture they need. It is difficult to escape the hot desert sun. Few birds build nests on the hot ground; most build nests in the scattered thickets of low trees and shrubs. Cacti and prickly, thorny shrubs are the favorite nesting sites of the cactus wren. The nest is built deep among the protective spines of the cactus. Within the nest, the cactus wren is shaded from the sun. The Gila woodpecker excavates a cavity in the giant saguaro cactus. The bird uses the same hole for several years. When the nest is abandoned, other birds take it over.

Red-tailed hawk

Gila woodpecker

Phainopepla

Cactus wren

Greater roadrunner

Birds of the Woodlands and Forests

Woodlands and forests provide habitats to many different kinds of birds. Some birds are found in dense forests of evergreen trees; others prefer the open areas among the scattered thickets of shrubs and leafy trees of the woodlands. Some birds build their nests high in the treetops, while others make their nests in the lower branches or on the ground. The ruffed grouse builds its nest on the ground in thick woods and dense cover — at the base of a tree or rock, under a log, or in dense brush. The hairy woodpecker, which digs a cavity in a tree or tree stump, is a year-round resident whether it is found in woodlands, wooded swamps, or mountain forests. It is active even on the most frigid winter days. One part-time resident of wooded areas is the yellow warbler. It builds its nest in shrubs or low trees close to streams and lakes. After raising its young, it heads for warm southern climates.

Tawny owl

Bohemian waxwing

Purple finch

Ruffed grouse

Yellow warbler

Hairy woodpecker

Birds of the Grasslands

Whether they are called prairies, savannas, pampas, or steppes, grasslands provide an abundant source of food and water for a variety of birds. The rich food supply supports birds that eat plant matter, such as grasses and seeds, as well as those birds that eat small animals, such as insects and spiders. Some birds, such as bobwhites, seek the dense cover provided by the tall grasses to hide their ground nests. While nesting, the bobwhite jealously guards its territory deep within the grassland. The meadowlark is also a ground nester that forms its nest from surrounding grasses. However, it prefers to be in more open areas. Perched at the edge of a field, the meadowlark can be heard singing its cheerful song. The burrowing owl does not burrow into the ground to make its nest; instead, it searches for the abandoned burrow of other animals, such as the prairie dog.

American kestrel

Western kingbirds

Burrowing owl

Bobwhites

Eastern
meadowlark

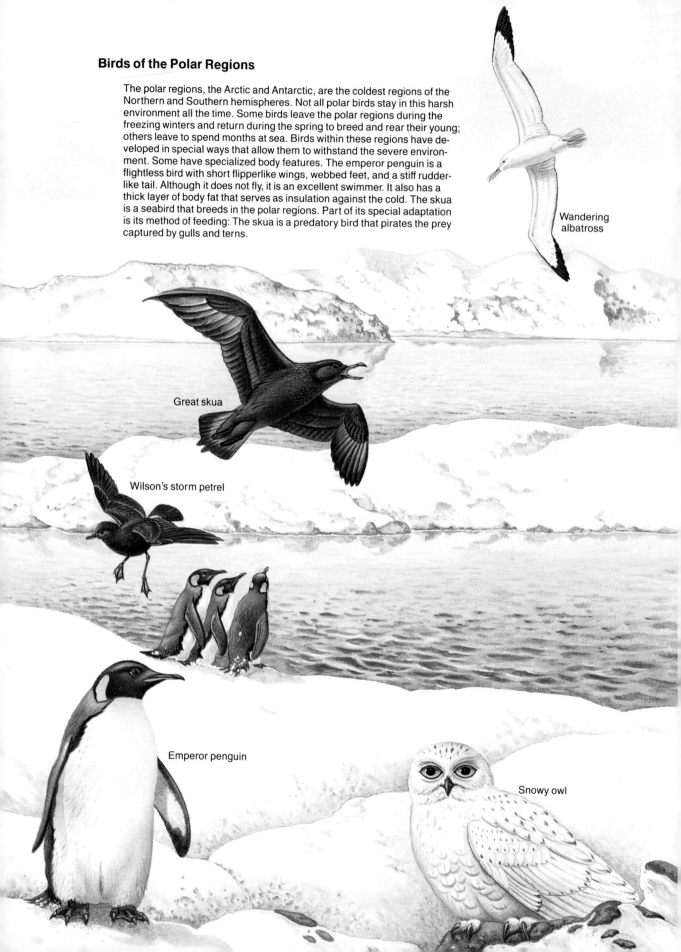

Birds of the Polar Regions

The polar regions, the Arctic and Antarctic, are the coldest regions of the Northern and Southern hemispheres. Not all polar birds stay in this harsh environment all the time. Some birds leave the polar regions during the freezing winters and return during the spring to breed and rear their young; others leave to spend months at sea. Birds within these regions have developed in special ways that allow them to withstand the severe environment. Some have specialized body features. The emperor penguin is a flightless bird with short flipperlike wings, webbed feet, and a stiff rudderlike tail. Although it does not fly, it is an excellent swimmer. It also has a thick layer of body fat that serves as insulation against the cold. The skua is a seabird that breeds in the polar regions. Part of its special adaptation is its method of feeding: The skua is a predatory bird that pirates the prey captured by gulls and terns.

Wandering albatross

Great skua

Wilson's storm petrel

Emperor penguin

Snowy owl

Birds of the Tropics

The tropics are damp, humid places where lush, leafy plants abound. Day and night, the temperatures hover just below 80°F (27°C). This steady environment has the greatest variety of animal species, including birds, of anywhere on earth. The brilliantly colored male quetzal is one of the most beautiful birds in the world. Humid mountain forests are home to the quetzal. Some tropic birds, such as the hoatzin, are found feeding on the plentiful supply of leaves and fruit in the dense vegetation that lines the rivers and streams of South American rain forests. Other tropic birds live in the thick canopy formed by the leafy branches of tall trees. There they feast on a great variety of insects and other small animals such as frogs and lizards. The rain forests of India and Indochina are home to the great hornbill. The ibis, which is a wading bird that can be found in most of the warmer areas of the world, nests in huge coastal colonies.

Quetzal

Scarlet ibis

Great hornbill

Toco toucan

Hoatzin

Birds of Residential Areas

The variety of habitats in which birds are found includes patches of grass
and trees within the noisy city and in the trimmed backyards and gardens
of the suburbs. The mockingbird can be heard singing its varied song,
composed of other birds' songs, animal calls, and other common sounds.
The cooing of pigeons is a familiar sound in cities as well as in less populated areas. Pigeons are quite social and often breed in colonies and
gather in flocks during the nonbreeding season. In some places, the robin
is a year-round sight; in other places it is only a resident during the warmer
months. The blue jay is a big, bold, dashing bird. Its presence does not go
unnoticed. It is a noisy bird that is abundant in backyards and wooded
areas.

American robin

Blue jay

Baltimore oriole

Chipping sparrow

Common pigeon

Mockingbird

▶THE HISTORY OF BIRDS

Since the days when dinosaurs roamed the land, millions of years ago, birds have inhabited the earth. They have become one of the most widely distributed of all the wild creatures. Many evolutionary changes have occurred on the path that has led those first primitive forms to modern-day birds.

The First Birds

If you have ever closely examined a bird's scaly foot or watched an anhinga sunning itself on a mangrove or a roadrunner dashing across the desert, you may have noticed how much birds look and act like reptiles. There is a good reason for the similarities—birds and modern reptiles evolved from a common ancestor.

What did this ancestral bird look like? When did it live? The answer is found in fossils that are more than 200 million years old. At that time there was a group of primitive reptiles, dinosaurs called thecodonts, that were covered with scales, had long, strong hind legs for running and jumping, and had teeth set in sockets. There were many different types of dinosaurs, and competition for food forced some of these animals to live in trees. The trees provided safety and plenty of food for them, and their descendants became very good at climbing among the branches.

Over long periods of time, these tree-living reptiles began jumping from branch to branch, then gliding from branch to branch, and eventually from tree to tree, using skin folds similar to the wings of modern birds. The scales on the outside edge of the wings and along the edges of the tail became modified—they lengthened, widened, and lightened into feathers. Feathers were a big advantage for gliding over long distances. Eventually muscles developed that were able to flap the wings and allow these animals to make the first true flight. The descendants of the thecodonts, over a million or more years, learned to fly; they became birds.

Modern Birds

As the ability to fly evolved, birds developed the higher metabolism necessary to provide the fuel for the flight muscles; they also developed the trait of warm-bloodedness. Some experts believe that feathers may have developed as an insulating covering to conserve body heat and that feathers became an aid to flying later. Others argue that feathers emerged to help primitive birds fly and later became useful in keeping the body at a constant temperature.

By the end of the Cretaceous period, 65 million years ago, the toothed birds had vanished and a wide variety of bird life had evolved. The ancestors of modern birds, such as penguins, rheas, loons, tropic birds, and even some perching birds, were already flying across the skies and swimming in the seas. Fifty-three million years ago there was a marked change in the life on earth. Gone were the dinosaurs and the early reptiles that had dominated the environment. Birds, warm-blooded and able to fly, spread and multiplied quickly, taking advantage of every available habitat on earth.

The Decline of Birds

In the past 20 million years or so, there have been more bird extinctions than evolutions of new species. Humans have caused the decline of many birds, in direct and indirect ways.

Environmental pollution caused by humans is a constant threat to the welfare of birds. This bird is a helpless victim of an oil spill.

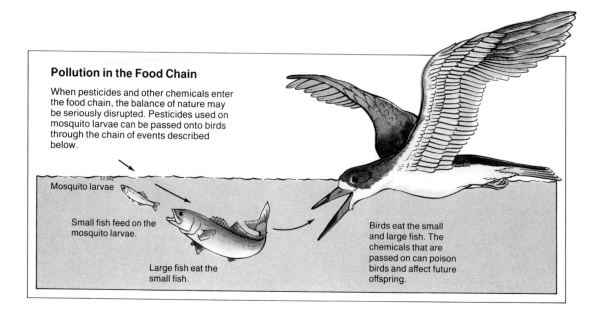

Pollution in the Food Chain

When pesticides and other chemicals enter the food chain, the balance of nature may be seriously disrupted. Pesticides used on mosquito larvae can be passed onto birds through the chain of events described below.

Mosquito larvae

Small fish feed on the mosquito larvae.

Large fish eat the small fish.

Birds eat the small and large fish. The chemicals that are passed on can poison birds and affect future offspring.

At one time, the hunting of birds for food and feathers destroyed a large part of the bird population. Barrel after barrel of salted birds and bale after bale of feathers were shipped to market. In 1878, a single Michigan hunter shipped 3 million passenger pigeons to market. Eleven years later, the passenger pigeon was extinct in that state.

The popularity of bird pets has also contributed to the decline of birds. The international trade in species from Africa, Asia, and South America is one of the major causes of a decline in their numbers—especially hard hit are the world's parrots. Of this beautiful bird family, 78 species are in danger of extinction. Conservationists estimate that for every bird that reaches the pet shop alive, another four perish during the trip to the market.

People have introduced into new lands animals, such as rats, cats, and mongooses, that are bird predators. Cattle, rabbits, pigs, and sheep do not kill birds directly, but they destroy the habitats that birds live in.

The most damage to bird populations has been caused by the human destruction of habitats: Woods and forests have been cut down, marshes drained, and swamps filled to provide more land for development, farming, and grazing.

The Future of Birds

The combination of hunting, destruction of natural habitats, and environmental pollution has proved to be too much for many plants and animals. More than one hundred known birds have become extinct, although many more species must have disappeared before they were even discovered.

Conservationists describing the status of birds categorize them as endangered, threatened, or rare. A species is considered endangered when the population has been so severely reduced that it is unlikely to survive if the cause of the bird's decline is not stopped. Endangered species are in immediate danger of extinction. Threatened species are likely to move into the endangered category in the near future. Rare species have small populations that are not yet in trouble, but could be quickly driven toward extinction.

The need for effective measures on behalf of the world's birds has never been more urgent. Humankind needs birds. We no longer depend on them for food, but we still need them. Birds are part of a healthy, thriving planet. Coal miners used to bring a canary into the mines with them to warn them when the air became too poisonous to breathe. Birds are like the coal miner's canaries for the whole planet. When they can no longer survive, we are in danger. Saving the birds is in our own best interest. By preserving the environment for birds, we take the first steps in saving all life on earth, including our own.

TODD A. CULVER
Education Specialist
Cornell Laboratory of Ornithology

See also ANIMALS; BIRDS AS PETS; ENDANGERED SPECIES; HOMING AND MIGRATION; OSTRICHES AND OTHER FLIGHTLESS BIRDS.

Although ducks are most often raised for their commercial value, their lively manner makes them a popular zoo animal and an affectionate companion.

BIRDS AS PETS

Everyone has a different idea of what kind of animal makes a good pet. Some people want an animal that is friendly and will be a good companion; others want an animal that is entertaining—one that can talk, do tricks, or sing; and still others want an animal that is inexpensive to keep. It is possible to have all these things when the pet you have is a bird.

Birds have been popular pets for centuries. Records show that pigeons were tamed in Egypt nearly five thousand years ago. Canaries were luxury pets of wealthy Europeans about five hundred years ago. Alexander Wilson, a pioneer and scholar of American bird life, kept a Louisiana parakeet as a companion. Wilson even took the bird on long horseback journeys exploring the West. The parakeet rode in Wilson's pocket during the day and perched beside his campfire at night.

One of the best features of keeping a pet bird is that most kinds take up little space. They usually live in cages that fit easily in small homes or apartments. Pet birds keep themselves clean and need little daily care. There are also many unusual and interesting varieties to choose from.

▶ PARAKEETS

The parakeet is among the most popular of all house pets, feathered or furred. It is called by several names. Budgerigar, or "budgie" for short, is its Australian name, for parakeets originally were native to Australia. In the Far East, these birds are known as shell parakeets.

Parakeets belong to the parrot family. There are certain characteristics that help identify such birds. The feet have two toes in front and two behind. The bill is thick, strong, and hooked. The body is short and compact, with a short neck, large head, and thick tongue. The plumage (feathers) comes in a variety of bright colors. Parakeets are hardy birds and long-lived. These pets also have the wonderful ability to imitate a human voice.

The best place to buy a parakeet (or other cage bird) is at a reliable pet store. There you can learn the age and the sex of the bird you are buying. You can also ask for advice on the correct size and type of cage.

These birds can eat boxed mixtures of small-sized seed like wheat, millet, and canary seed. Many of them have tastes for certain snacks. With some it is apples; others enjoy bits of vegetable greens. Drinking water must always be within reach.

▶ PARROTS AND MYNAHS

A parrot or a mynah bird does not have to say anything really funny to be amusing. The way these birds talk is funny enough. They seem to know what they are saying and why they are saying it. Of course this is not true.

WONDER QUESTION

Can people get parrot fever?

Parrot fever, also known as psittacosis, can be passed along to people from infected birds. Although the disease occurs most often in members of the parrot family, it is also found in other birds such as pigeons. In people, the disease is an infection somewhat like pneumonia. It can spread to humans when they handle sick birds or come into contact with infectious articles (bird droppings, perches, cages). The best way to avoid it is to buy pet birds from a reliable dealer, keep their cages clean, and never handle sick birds.

Choosing a Bird

Everyone wants to have a healthy pet. Before selecting a bird, it is important to watch the bird during its normal activities. Look for one that has bright, fully opened eyes and is completely feathered without any bald spots or deformities, such as crooked toenails or overgrown beaks. A bird that looks tamer than the others in its cage may actually be quiet and inactive because it is sick. Other signs that may mean a bird is ill include an unwillingness to eat, runny nose, ruffled feathers, coughing and sneezing, and excessive scratching.

They merely imitate sounds they have heard. But it makes them seem almost human.

Pet parrots need a great deal of attention. They must be given roomy living quarters and a well-balanced diet. As with other pet birds, proper seed foods for them will be found at pet shops. But parrots have a definite need for more than seeds. Greens, fruits, and nuts are all important for a parrot. On their own, parrots are likely to sample any food that is around—meat, eggs, cheese, or cake—even though it may not be good for them.

The Amazon parrot, with blue markings on its face, and the African gray are two of the most popular parrots. Both can be taught to speak clearly and often to sing and whistle.

If you are shopping for a parrot, you will find a wide range in price. Some are young and completely untrained, while others are older and used to talking and living with people. Be prepared to care for a parrot for a long time. Depending on the type of parrot, these birds can live from 25 to 50 years.

The mynah bird is quick to imitate human talk. It is also likely to startle its owner with a piercing squawk or scream. Native to Southeast Asia, mynahs are members of the starling family. There are several kinds of mynahs, some as small as robins, some as large as crows, but all are bright and perky. Again, proper food (mynah birds like a soft mixture) is to be found at pet shops. Once a day they should be given fruit, such as cut up bananas, apples, and grapes.

▶CANARIES

Like parakeets, canaries are mostly seed-eaters. They are easily cared for with foods you find at pet shops, with additional snacks of fresh greens and bits of apple or orange. Since its song is one of the canary's best features, the smart canary shopper will look into this before buying a bird.

There are many kinds of canaries, but all of them may be grouped into two main types of singers—the choppers and the rollers. The choppers are the kind of canary most often found in pet shops. They may be sold when only 5 or 6 months old and without training in singing. The chopper sings loudly with high-pitched, short notes. The rollers are usually older and are often given careful training so that their song is at its best. The roller performs with soft, sweet, rolling trills. The male is always the singer.

With its cheerful yellow color and its soft, sweet trill, the roller canary is one of the most popular of all pet birds. Canaries, which belong to the finch family, are native to the Canary Islands, off the coast of Africa. Over time, breeders have developed different varieties—some are known for their melodious songs, others are known for their distinctive appearance.

Native to Central and South America, the scarlet macaw is a large long-tailed parrot. It is valued as a pet because it is easy to tame and lives a long time.

▶PIGEONS

People who keep pigeons may own dozens of these birds. They are mainly used for racing or to produce the squabs, or young pigeons, that people eat as a luxury food.

Pigeons are kept in many city areas as well as in the country. Pigeon fanciers sometimes keep them in special houses, or lofts, on the roofs of buildings—if city laws permit. From the rooftops the birds can be released for exercise flights. Wherever they are kept, pigeons need air and light and protection from drafts and mice. Seed mix that can be bought from a pet shop is their chief food. If you feed them by hand, they become very tame and friendly. A pair of pigeons may be purchased for a small amount of money, but a single champion racing bird may be expensive.

▶BACKYARD BIRDS

Chickens, ducks, and geese are birds that are usually thought of as farm birds, but any one of them may be tamed and kept as a backyard pet. A chicken is interesting to watch and to hear. It has a varied and unmistakable "language" all its own. Ducks and geese, too, make interesting and unusual pets.

DOROTHY E. SHUTTLESWORTH
Author, *Exploring Nature With Your Child*
Founder, *Junior Natural History Magazine*

BIRTH CONTROL

When a man and a woman have sexual intercourse and do not want the woman to become pregnant, they use birth control, or **contraception**, to try to prevent pregnancy. Knowing how to prevent pregnancy can help them with family planning. Deciding when to have a child and how much time should pass between the birth of one child and the birth of the next is important. It allows parents to have children when they are ready to love and care for them and be responsible for their many needs.

▶METHODS OF BIRTH CONTROL

To understand how birth control works, you must understand some basic facts about how human beings reproduce. About once every 28 days an egg cell, or ovum, is released from one of a woman's ovaries and begins to travel down a narrow Fallopian tube toward the uterus. This is called **ovulation**. If this ovum is not fertilized by a sperm cell from a man, it will quickly die and pass out of the uterus during a normal menstrual period. But if sexual intercourse takes place while the ovum is in the tube, one of millions of sperm cells deposited in the woman's vagina through the man's penis may unite with the ovum. This is called **conception**—fertilization of the ovum. The fertilized egg may then attach itself to the inner lining of the woman's uterus, and a new life will begin to develop—the woman is pregnant. Some nine months later a baby will be born.

There are a number of birth control techniques. This discussion is limited to descriptions of birth control techniques that prevent conception.

Barrier Methods. Barrier methods of birth control prevent pregnancy by blocking sperm from entering the vagina or uterus so conception cannot take place. The **condom** is a tube of thin latex rubber, closed at one end, that is rolled down over the man's penis before intercourse. Latex condoms treated with nonoxynol-9 also protect against the AIDS virus. A

▲ Condom

◀ The Pill

diaphragm is a dome of thin rubber that a woman can insert into her vagina before sex. It covers the opening of the uterus, blocking the entrance of any sperm. Both the condom and the diaphragm are best used with a **spermicide**—a chemical that kills sperm cells. The **vaginal sponge**, which is already treated with spermicide, and the **cervical cap** can be inserted into the vagina; they function much like a diaphragm. Condoms and vaginal sponges can be bought at a pharmacy, or drugstore; diaphragms and cervical caps must be fitted by a doctor. When used properly barrier contraceptives have no bad side effects and they are about 80 to 90 percent effective.

The Pill. Contraceptive pills taken by mouth every day contain tiny amounts of powerful body chemicals known as **hormones**. These hormones prevent the woman's ovaries from producing egg cells so there are none to fertilize as long as the pills are taken. One form of the Pill also makes it hard for any fertilized egg cell to attach itself to the uterus lining and grow.

The Pill must be prescribed by a doctor, who would be able to discuss and monitor any side effects that could occur. The Pill is almost 97 percent effective when used properly. Since ovulation begins again as soon as the woman stops taking the Pill, couples can use it to plan when to have children.

Intrauterine Device (IUD). An intrauterine device is a small coil of metal or plastic that is inserted by a doctor into the woman's uterus. It prevents any fertilized egg cell from attaching itself in the uterus. Younger women who use IUD's sometimes are bothered by cramping or unusual menstrual bleeding. IUD's are more easily used by older women who have already had children. They are over 97 percent effective for preventing pregnancy.

Natural Birth Control. Natural birth control methods attempt to prevent conception without the use of artificial devices. The **Fertility Awareness Method (FAM)**, or rhythm method, depends upon avoiding sexual intercourse on the days before, during, and after ovulation—about 12 days each month—so that no sperm are present to fertilize the egg cell. Unfortunately, because it can be difficult to pinpoint the time of ovulation, the Fertility Awareness Method as well as another natural birth control technique—withdrawing the penis from the vagina just before sperm are ejaculated—are not very reliable.

Other Birth Control Methods. During the 1980's researchers developed **hormonal implants** that prevent ovulation for extended lengths of time by releasing tiny amounts of

▲ Cervical Cap

Intrauterine Device (IUD) ▶

hormones into the woman's body daily. One form is inserted in the uterus, to be replaced yearly. Others are inserted under the skin of the forearm and work even longer. Removing the implant restores fertility. **Sterilization**—surgically cutting and tying off the woman's Fallopian tubes or the man's sperm tubes—is a way to prevent pregnancies permanently. These operations can seldom be reversed once they are performed. Finally, researchers are seeking a reversible pill for men to use to prevent sperm formation as long as the pill is taken. So far, no such "male pill" has been found to work well.

▶ HISTORY OF BIRTH CONTROL

Birth control is a fairly recent idea in human history. Centuries ago large families were important for survival. Many babies died in infancy and childhood, and people had large families to be sure that enough would survive to help gather food and to have children of their own.

In the 1700's and 1800's medical and scientific discoveries enabled many diseases to be controlled and food supplies to be increased. Large families were no longer necessary for survival. People live longer, and the world's population began to grow rapidly.

In 1798 Thomas Malthus (1766–1834), an English economist, predicted that the world's population would quickly outgrow the available food supply. This population increase, he said, would lead to worldwide hunger, wars, and plagues unless people stopped having so many children.

▲ Diaphragm

Spermicidal Cream and Foam ▶

Malthus' prediction proved to be wrong. But as the world population increased rapidly in the early 1900's, the idea of family planning took root. Methods of contraception began to be developed, and a worldwide movement to encourage birth control began.

Margaret Sanger (1879–1966), a trained nurse, became a leader of that movement in the early 1900's. She believed that the poor in America and other countries needed to control the size of their families. Although it was illegal to provide family planning information at that time, Mrs. Sanger published pamphlets and books about it, and eventually helped pass laws that allowed doctors to teach birth control

methods. In 1916, she established the first birth control clinic to advise people, and in 1917 she founded the National Birth Control League. This organization and her clinics were combined to form the Planned Parenthood Federation of America in 1942.

▲ Vaginal Sponge   ▲ Skin Implants

▶ BIRTH CONTROL TODAY

Widespread use of birth control is becoming more important worldwide every year. The world now has more than 6 billion people, and the number is increasing rapidly, especially in the poor underdeveloped countries. Different countries support birth control in different ways. In Europe and the United States, many birth control methods are readily and legally available. In China, rigid laws control family size. In India, vigorous efforts are being made to make birth control available to millions of people. Family planning is also being taught by satellite television in many remote areas.

Not everyone favors the use of birth control, however. The Roman Catholic Church forbids artificial methods of birth control, believing that sexual love in marriage should never be separated from the possibility of conception. Only **abstinence** (refraining from sexual intercourse) or the rhythm method of family planning are considered acceptable. Some people fear that governments may impose birth control in order to obtain political control over their people. Others charge that teaching birth control encourages people to have sex before marriage—an idea that is not supported by scientific evidence.

Doctors and other knowledgeable people you respect can help you understand the different methods and how they may affect your life and your health.

ALAN E. NOURSE, M.D.
Author, *Birth Control* and
Teen Guide to Birth Control

See also REPRODUCTION (Human Reproduction).

BISMARCK. See NORTH DAKOTA (Cities).

BISMARCK, OTTO VON (1815–1898)

Otto Eduard Leopold von Bismarck-Schönhausen—the statesman responsible for bringing about the unification of Germany—was one of the most skillful and practical politicians the world has ever known. He was born on April 1, 1815, at Schönhausen, in the German state of Prussia. His father belonged to the Prussian landowning class known as the Junkers. His mother came from a middle-class family.

As a boy, Bismarck attended a boarding school in Berlin. Later, he studied law at the universities of Göttingen and Berlin. After graduating in 1835, Bismarck worked in the Prussian civil service and served in the army. He then returned home to help his father manage the family estates. He became religious, partly because he married the devout Johanna von Puttkamer in 1847. That same year, he became a member of the Prussian Diet (parliament), where he represented the conservative traditions of the Junkers.

In 1848 a wave of change swept across Europe. Germany was still a collection of independent states. Liberals tried to turn the country into a constitutional monarchy headed by the king of Prussia. But the king refused to accept the crown from an elected parliament.

In 1851, Bismarck was Prussia's delegate to the German Diet at Frankfurt-am-Main. There he spoke for Prussia's interests against those of Austria—then the most powerful German state. In 1859 he was named Prussian ambassador to Russia and, later, to France.

In 1862 the new king of Prussia, William I, clashed with his parliament. When the lower house refused to approve money for military reforms, King William appointed Bismarck prime minister and minister of foreign affairs.

Bismarck skillfully silenced parliament and gained the power to put his ideas on foreign and domestic policy into effect. Prussia and Austria defeated Denmark in 1864 in a war over the tiny northern states of Schleswig and Holstein, which had large German populations but were linked to the Danish crown. Prussia then fought the Seven Weeks' War (1866) against Austria and gained control of both Schleswig and Holstein.

In 1867 Bismarck set up the North German Confederation, dominated by Prussia. As chancellor of the confederation, he soon became known as the Iron Chancellor. The nickname came from an 1862 speech in which he had said that "the great questions of the time are decided not by speeches and majority decisions . . . but by iron and blood."

Bismarck had made Prussia the strongest German state. In 1870 he helped provoke the Franco-Prussian War, which united the German states against a common enemy. In 1871, France was defeated and forced to cede the province of Alsace and most of Lorraine to Germany. The new German Empire was born. It included all the German states except Austria. King William of Prussia became Kaiser (Emperor) William I of Germany.

Bismarck had reached his goal of a united Germany under Prussian leadership. He formed alliances that kept a balance of power in Europe and helped nations settle their differences peacefully. Within Germany, Bismarck played his political rivals off against each other. Although he never accepted democratic views, he put through sweeping social reforms to gain liberal support. But King William II, who came to the throne in 1888, had his own ideas on running the empire. After much conflict, Bismarck resigned in 1890. His retirement from public life marked the end of an era in European history.

Bismarck died on July 30, 1898. His tombstone bears the words "A true German servant of Emperor William I."

Reviewed by GERARD BRAUNTHAL
University of Massachusetts, Amherst

See also FRANCO-PRUSSIAN WAR.

BISON. See BUFFALO AND BISON.

BLACK, HUGO. See ALABAMA (Famous People).

BLACK AMERICANS. See AFRICAN AMERICANS.

BLACKFOOT INDIANS. See INDIANS, AMERICAN (On the Prairies and Plains).

BLACK HAWK. See ILLINOIS (The Black Hawk War).

BLACK HOLES

Black holes are among nature's most bizarre objects. They exist where a dense concentration of matter has produced an enormous gravitational field so strong that nothing—not even light—can escape it. Even though a black hole cannot be seen directly, most astronomers think that black holes litter space and that they may also be lurking in the centers of galaxies.

How Is a Black Hole Created?

The creation of a black hole requires that a lot of matter be squeezed into a small volume. Such enormous compression takes place whenever a star dies, but the result is not always a black hole. As the sun enters old age, billions of years from now, its nuclear fires will cool. It will collapse under its own weight, and gravity will shrink it to a white-hot ball less than 1 percent of its present size—a strange fate, but not a black hole. However, nothing can stop the inward collapse of large dying stars three times the sun's mass or more. Their fate is to become infinitely small.

Although the collapsing mass of the dead star shrivels indefinitely, we do not see it. It is hidden, because its gravity is so strong that the light within it cannot get out. According to Einstein's theory of relativity, once inside this region, there is no possible escape from the black hole, for matter or for light.

Finding Black Holes

Despite the fact that black holes are invisible, it is possible to uncover strong evidence of their presence, at least for the larger ones. Astronomers have looked for black holes where two stars orbit one another. Such double stars are common in our galaxy, and a few of them emit X rays. The most famous X-ray double star is Cyg X-1 in the constellation Cygnus. When astronomers first observed Cyg X-1, they found only one hot blue star. From its motion, they computed that its partner should have about ten times the mass of the sun and be easy to see. But it was not. Instead, Cyg X-1 seemed to be a hot blue star dancing around an invisible partner.

Most researchers now think that the invisible companion is the collapsed mass of a large star, which became a black hole whose

An artist's impression of an X-ray binary star system consisting of a black hole (bottom) and a normal orange-red star (top). Gas is pulled from the atmosphere of the star by the black hole's strong gravitational field, into which it spirals in the form of an intensely hot, X-ray-emitting disk.

strong gravity has been ripping gas off the outer layers of Cyg X-1. The gas swirls into a flattened disk that is squeezed and heated to millions of degrees as it is pulled into the black hole. This produces the X rays that first attracted the attention of astronomers.

Researchers have found evidence of massive black holes inhabiting the centers of galaxies. These black holes could have been formed when the galaxies were young and their inner regions were crowded with large stars. When these stars died, they became individual black holes that joined with one another to create a single, massive black hole that slowly swallows other stars. Just as for double stars, the intense heating of swirling gases that occurs during this process releases energy, which produces the light and radio waves we often see coming from the centers of galaxies.

Seth Shostak
SETI Institute

See also ASTRONOMY; GRAVITY AND GRAVITATION; MILKY WAY; QUASARS; STARS; UNIVERSE.

BLACK KETTLE. See INDIANS, AMERICAN (Profiles).

BLACKMUN, HARRY A. See ILLINOIS (Famous People).

BLACK MUSLIMS. See AFRICAN AMERICANS (Separatism, Militancy, and Black Power).

BLACK PANTHER PARTY. See AFRICAN AMERICANS (Separatism, Militancy, and Black Power).

BLACK SEA. See OCEANS AND SEAS OF THE WORLD.

BLACKWELL, ELIZABETH (1821–1910)

As a young woman, Elizabeth Blackwell earned her living as a teacher. But she was not happy in her work. She longed for independence and became a supporter of women's rights. Searching for a career that would offer her independence and that would also allow her to help people, Blackwell decided to become a doctor.

Blackwell was born on February 3, 1821, in Bristol, England. She and her family moved to the United States in 1832. It was in the United States that Blackwell applied to medical school. However, women were not welcome in the medical profession, and Blackwell was repeatedly turned down by the medical schools to which she applied. Finally she was accepted by the Geneva Medical College in Geneva, New York.

Most of her fellow students respected her, but the doctors at a hospital where she went for training treated her less kindly. "When I walked into the wards they walked out," she later wrote of her experience. Still, Blackwell did not give up. She graduated from medical school in 1849, the first woman in the United States to do so. She then went to Europe to continue her studies.

Blackwell returned to the United States in 1851. However, because she was a woman, no hospital would allow her to practice medicine. In 1853, determined to help the sick, she set up her own small clinic in a poor New York City neighborhood. Four years later Blackwell opened the New York Infirmary for Women and Children, a hospital run almost entirely by women. In 1868, Blackwell expanded the hospital to include the Women's Medical College, the first of its kind in America. In 1869, she returned to England, where she helped found the London School of Medicine for Women. She died on May 31, 1910, at the age of 89.

KARYN L. BERTSCHI
Science Writer

BLAINE, JAMES GILLESPIE.   See MAINE (Famous People).

BLAKE, WILLIAM (1757–1827)

William Blake, the English poet and artist, was born on November 28, 1757, in London. His father was a shopkeeper, and the family lived simply. William was taught at home by his mother. He read poetry and other literature, including the Bible, theology, mystical writings, and philosophy. Sometimes William would speak of visions he had seen. Once he returned home from a walk and told his parents that he had seen angels in the treetops.

When he was 10, William was able to go to a drawing school. He began to write poems at the age of 12. At 14, he was apprenticed to an engraver so that he could learn a trade.

In 1782, Blake married Catherine Boucher. Blake trained his wife to help him produce hand-colored engravings of his poems and drawings. Blake's drawings enlarge and complete the meaning of his poems.

Blake's chief prose work is *The Marriage of Heaven and Hell* (1790–93), a satire. But he is best loved for his collections of poems called *Songs of Innocence* (1789) and *Songs of Experience* (1794). These works contain his two most famous poems, "The Lamb" and "The Tiger." Blake's engraving of "The Tiger" is reproduced in Volume E, page 278.

Blake's comments on the ugliness, cruelty, and injustice of the world as he saw it play as much a part in his works as do his comments on the beauties and joys of life.

Blake believed that the world of the imagination was more real than the world that people could see or touch. And he was able to bring alive, through words and pictures, the world of his own imagination. As time went on, his art and poetry became increasingly filled with symbols from his visions.

After about 1818, Blake did little writing, but he continued to produce engravings and watercolors. He died peacefully on August 12, 1827. The full appreciation of his genius did not come until long after his death.

EDMUND FULLER
Author, *Man in Modern Fiction*

BLEEDING.   See FIRST AID.

BLIGH, WILLIAM (1754–1817)

British naval officer William Bligh commanded the H.M.S. *Bounty*. The scandalous mutiny aboard that ship in 1789 immortalized his name in the annals of maritime history. Bligh was born in the old Devon County seaport of Plymouth, England, on September 9, 1754. At the early age of 22, he became sailing master of the H.M.S. *Resolution* on Captain James Cook's third great Pacific voyage of exploration (1776–80).

In 1787, Bligh was given command of the H.M.S. *Bounty* and ordered to sail to the South Pacific to collect breadfruit plants in Tahiti. The plants were to be transported to the British West Indies and used to feed the slaves on the colonial plantations.

The infamous mutiny on the *Bounty* occurred on April 28, 1789, when Bligh's crew became fed up with his bullying ways. The ship's second lieutenant, Fletcher Christian, took command of the *Bounty* and cast Bligh adrift in a small boat with 18 loyal crew members. After a stormy and miraculous passage that covered 3,900 miles (6,240 kilometers) in 43 days, Bligh and his men landed safely on the island of Timor in Southeast Asia. Christian, in the meantime, had sailed eastward with 8 other mutineers and 17 Tahitians and settled on uninhabited Pitcairn Island (where some of their descendants still reside).

The British searched in vain for Christian and his group, but three of the mutineers who had settled in Tahiti were found and hanged for their crime. Bligh was absolved of all blame for the loss of the *Bounty*. His last important appointment was as governor of the British penal colony in Australia (1805–08). He retired as a vice admiral and died in 1817.

SAM MCKINNEY
Author, *Bligh: A True Account of Mutiny Aboard His Majesty's Ship Bounty*

BLINDNESS

Some people cannot read the words printed on this page. This is because they are blind. People without eyesight face difficulties in everyday life that can be hard for sighted people to imagine. Try putting toothpaste on a toothbrush with your eyes closed. How would you cook a meal if you could not see? Most of the things we learn by watching others must be taught to people without sight.

Blindness is not simply being without eyesight. There are many degrees of blindness. Some blind people can distinguish light and dark. Others can recognize the direction of a light source.

People who have limited eyesight are said to be visually impaired. Their eyesight may be limited in one or more ways. Some visually impaired people can recognize large objects, such as chairs or tables, but cannot see details on those objects. Some individuals cannot see to the left or right, some have several blind spots in their vision, and some individuals cannot distinguish colors or contrasts.

There are approximately 2.5 million people in the United States alone who are severely visually impaired. Three quarters of these people are 65 years of age or older. This is because many of the causes of eyesight loss are associated with aging.

▶ THE DEGREES OF BLINDNESS

People who study eyesight loss have established guidelines for identifying blindness and visual impairment. The guidelines are based on **visual acuity**, which means the amount of details an individual can see. A person is said to be visually impaired if he or she has a visual acuity of 20/70 or less when wearing corrective lenses (eyeglasses or contact lenses). This means that what a person with normal vision can see at 70 feet away, a visually impaired person can see at only 20 feet away.

A person is considered to be blind if his or her visual acuity is 20/200 or less with corrective lenses. This means that what a person with normal vision can see at 200 feet away, a blind person cannot see at all or at no more than 20 feet away.

These measurements are always determined by the stronger eye. Some people have no eyesight in one eye but some vision in the other eye. They are not considered blind or visually impaired unless the stronger eye meets the above guidelines.

There is one additional measure of blindness that has to do with a person's **visual field**. Visual field refers to how great an area a person can see. It is measured in degrees of an angle. If a person with normal vision looks straight ahead, he or she should be able to see nearly all the objects in a half-circle (180 degrees). Individuals who have a visual field of no greater than 20 degrees are considered to be blind.

▶ CAUSES OF BLINDNESS

There are many causes of blindness and visual impairment. Some people are born with this condition. Their blindness or visual impairment is said to be **congenital**, meaning "born with."

Accidents can also cause eyesight loss. Wearing protective eyeglasses or goggles during activities such as using power tools, playing racquetball, or working with chemicals can help prevent such accidents.

Disease is a very common cause of blindness and visual impairment. **Cataracts**, an ailment usually found in elderly people, causes a clouding of the lens in the eye. If you look through a piece of waxed paper, you can experience what some people with cataracts see.

Glaucoma is a disease that causes increased fluid pressure inside the eye. It can cause blindness and also tunnel vision. If you close one eye and look through a paper towel tube with the other eye, you will see what tunnel vision is like. If detected early, glaucoma often can be treated with special eye drops or surgery.

Diabetes causes a swelling and leaking of the blood vessels inside the eye. This can cause blurred vision. If the blood vessels break, the blood interferes with light passing through the eye. This can cause visual impairment or total blindness.

In developing nations, there are additional diseases that cause eyesight loss. **Onchocerciasis**, commonly referred to as "river blindness," is an eye infection caused by a parasite. This disease is common in tropical areas such as Central America and parts of Africa. In some villages, 10 percent of the total population is blind because of this disease.

What to Do When You See a Blind Person

If you see a blind person who seems to need help, offer your assistance. Tell the person who you are and that you are speaking to him or her. If the person says that help is not needed, believe it and simply go on your way.

If the person accepts your help, let him or her take your arm at the elbow. When you lead a blind person, you should always walk slightly in front. If a blind person is using a guide dog, do not pet or distract the animal. The guide dog is a working dog and is not a pet.

Do not be afraid to use words like "see" and "look." Such words do not make blind people uncomfortable. If a person is blind, that does not mean he or she cannot hear. Remember to speak in a normal tone of voice.

When you leave a blind person, tell him or her that you are leaving. Let the person know that you may meet again. "See you soon!"

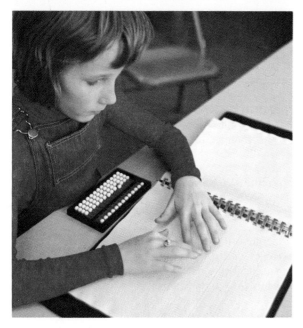

Using an abacus, the student works on math problems from a braille textbook. Braille is a touch method of reading letters, numbers, and other symbols.

BRAILLE ALPHABET AND NUMERALS									
a	b	c	d	e	f	g	h	i	j
k	l	m	n	o	p	q	r	s	t
u	v	w	x	y	z				
1	2	3	4	5	6	7	8	9	0

Xerophthalmia is the major cause of blindness in young children in many developing countries. It is caused by a severe lack of protein and vitamin A in the diet. This disease is found in overpopulated regions of south and east Asia, Africa, the eastern Mediterranean, and parts of Latin America. In India alone, more than 60,000 children under the age of 6 go totally blind each year due to this disease.

▶ COPING WITH BLINDNESS

Two of the biggest challenges that a blind or visually impaired person must face are moving about independently and communicating with others.

Moving about without sight—or with very limited sight—requires a unique set of skills. Blind people must use their sense of hearing, smell, and touch to learn about their environment. This is called **orientation**. For example, a blind person in the city listens for traffic sounds to know when to cross a street. The person may smell flowers in a park or food from a restaurant to help them know where they are.

To move about safely, blind or visually impaired people can rely on a variety of aids. A long cane, also called a prescription cane, is used when walking to warn of objects, stairs, or street curbs in a person's path. Scientists have developed a laser cane, which can also detect objects at head or chest level. When it senses an obstacle, the cane gives out a warning sound.

Blind teenagers and adults can learn to use a guide dog to move about. Both the dog and the handler attend a special school to learn how to work together. Guide dogs serve the same purposes as the long cane. They help the person move around obstacles or stop before stepping up or down.

Blind and visually impaired people have the same need for information about the world as people with sight. To meet that need, there are many useful aids.

Braille is a touch method of reading. The braille alphabet was developed in France by Louis Braille in the 1800's. The letters of the braille alphabet are based on a system of six raised dots that can be read by the fingertips. There are also special braille symbols for mathematical, musical, computer, and foreign language materials. Braille can be produced by using heavy paper with special braille typewriters.

Large-print books and magazines are useful to people with less severe visual impairments. Audio tapes are frequently used for both leisure and educational reading. Some computers have speech devices that can talk to the user, telling what is happening on the screen.

Two recent developments help blind and visually impaired people gain more immediate access to current information. Talking Newspaper programs allow people to call on the telephone and have the newspaper read aloud to them. Audiodescription Services provides a description of the action, mannerisms, and

What is a Talking Book?

The world of books is open to the blind today through books prepared in braille and through long-playing recordings of books, called talking books. The largest producer of braille textbooks is the American Printing House for the Blind in Louisville, Kentucky.

The Library of Congress of the United States, Division for the Blind and Physically Handicapped, in Washington, D.C., has hundreds of thousands of braille volumes and talking books. Hundreds of new library titles are recorded and brailled each year. Throughout the country there are libraries that act as distributing centers for these books and records. They are mailed postage-free.

Technological advances, such as talking computers and electronic braille machines, have opened up new career opportunities for blind and visually impaired individuals.

other nonverbal communications shown on television programs.

▶ **EDUCATION AND EMPLOYMENT**

The first school for children who were blind was founded in France in 1784 by Valentin Hauy. By 1833 there were three special schools for blind children in the United States. Public school began to educate blind children in the early 1900's. Today, about 90 percent of all the children in the United States who are blind or visually impaired are educated in their neighborhood or community schools. Blind and visually impaired children must learn the special skills needed by people without sight. They also must learn basic concepts in special ways. Because so much of what we learn is through observation, visually impaired children need a great deal of hands-on experience. Concepts such as up and down, streets, rainbows, clouds, and stars are meaningless words unless taught with models or accurate verbal descriptions.

Any career that does not depend on sight is open to a blind or visually impaired person. People without sight can become teachers, farmers, computer programmers, government workers, accountants, or lawyers. Young people can work at jobs such as delivering newspapers, counseling children at summer camp, and serving food at fast food restaurants.

▶ **AGENCIES AND ASSOCIATIONS THAT HELP**

The American Foundation for the Blind helps blind and visually impaired people achieve equal access to opportunities that will help them live independent and satisfying lives. This organization helps pass laws that will help people with limited sight, publishes information about blindness, and provides a directory of consumer groups, agencies, schools, and services that can help. Its headquarters is in New York City.

Three United Nations agencies are concerned with blindness in both industrialized and developing nations. These are the United Nations Education, Scientific and Cultural Organization (UNESCO), the World Health Organization (WHO), and the United Nations Children's Fund (UNICEF).

KATHLEEN MARY HUEBNER
Director, National Consultants Department
American Foundation for the Blind

See also EYE; KELLER, HELEN.

BLOOD

A crimson river flows through the human body, carrying materials that are essential to the life of each and every body cell. This river of life is blood. Each beat of the heart propels the vital fluid to the body's cells. Without blood, we could not exist.

The amount of blood in an individual's body depends for the most part on size, making up about 7 percent of a person's body weight. The average 160-pound (73-kilogram) adult has about 5 quarts (4.8 liters) of blood, while the average 80-pound (36-kilogram) child has about 2.5 quarts (2.4 liters).

Blood supplies the body's cells with food and oxygen and carries away carbon dioxide and other cell waste products. It also carries the hormones that help regulate body functions and removes excess heat from cells, which helps keep the body temperature within a steady range. Antibodies and other chemicals produced by blood cells fight infections and heal injuries. In addition, the water that body cells need for their chemical reactions is transported by the blood. The ability to perform all these tasks truly makes blood the river of life.

Every 60 seconds, a life-giving cycle takes place as blood courses through our bodies. Fluid plasma and solid matter—platelets (*right*), red blood cells (*below*), and white blood cells (*bottom*)—form the complex mixture that is blood.

▶ **WHAT BLOOD IS MADE OF**

Blood is a complex mixture of solid matter (cells and cell fragments) and fluid. The fluid portion of blood is called **plasma**. It makes up about 55 percent of the blood volume. The solid matter, which makes up about 45 percent of the volume, consists of **red blood cells** (or **erythrocytes**), **white blood cells** (or **leukocytes**), and cell fragments called **platelets**.

Plasma. Plasma, which is about 92 percent water, is a straw-colored fluid. The majority of substances dissolved in plasma are proteins, such as albumins, globulins, and fibrinogen. Other important substances found in plasma include minerals, nutrients, and waste products.

Red Blood Cells. Red blood cells, shaped like tiny round disks with flattened centers, make up most of the solid portion of blood. It is the **hemoglobin**, an iron-containing protein, found inside these cells that gives blood its red color. There are more red blood cells in an individual's body than any other kind of cell—about 25 trillion in the average adult. If they were stacked one on top of another, they would reach 31,000 miles (50,000 kilometers) into the sky!

White Blood Cells. There are about 5,000 to 10,000 white blood cells in 1/30,000 of an ounce (1 microliter) of blood—about one for each 700 red cells. White blood cells are jelly-like blobs that can change their shape. These large cells ooze along on their own and can even leave the bloodstream, squeezing out through tiny gaps in the blood-vessel walls. There are five main kinds of leukocytes: **neutrophils** make up the largest percentage of white blood cells, followed by **lymphocytes**,

Red blood cells squeeze single file through thin-walled capillaries as they carry their load of oxygen to all the cells of the body.

monocytes, eosinophils, and basophils.

Platelets. Blood platelets are tiny bodies, much smaller than red blood cells. They are formed as broken fragments of **megakaryocytes**, which are giant cells found in bone marrow. Unlike other cellular components of the blood, platelets have no nucleus. There are normally from 250,000 to 400,000 platelets in 1/30,000 of an ounce (1 microliter) of blood.

▶ HOW BLOOD WORKS IN THE BODY

The river of blood that courses through the body journeys along a path that stretches 60,000 miles (97,000 kilometers). As it flows, it functions as a vehicle of transportation, protection, and regulation.

Transportation. Networks of tiny blood vessels called capillaries carry oxygen to the cells. In the lungs, inhaled oxygen passes through the thin walls of capillaries surrounding the air sacs and combines with hemoglobin in the red blood cells. The bright red, oxygenated blood flows into the heart, which pumps it out into a network of blood vessels that go to all parts of the body.

When the blood reaches its destination, the hemoglobin releases its oxygen, which then passes out of the capillaries and into the cells. The cells' waste products, including carbon dioxide and urea, move out of the cells and into the capillaries to be carried away in the bloodstream. When the blood reaches the lungs again, carbon dioxide passes out through the capillary walls and into the air sacs, to be breathed out. Urea, along with salts and other substances, is filtered out as blood passes through the kidneys and leaves the body in the urine.

After a meal, the blood picks up nutrients from food digested in the stomach and intestines: amino acids from proteins, sugars from starches, and small particles of fats, as well as vitamins and minerals. The blood carries these nutrients to cells, where they are used as fuel, to build and repair tissue, or stored for future needs.

Hormones that aid digestion are also carried in the blood. For example, the hormones insulin and glucagon control how much glucose, the body's main fuel, is taken up or released by cells. They also keep the amount of glucose in the blood at a consistent level.

Fighting Disease. The white blood cells help defend the body against disease-causing micro-organisms and other threats. Neutrophils are the first to attack invading mi-

A tear or puncture to a blood vessel triggers a flurry of activity that is dedicated to plugging the wound. Along the way, the plasma protein fibrinogen is converted to fibrin. The sticky, threadlike fibrin gradually spins a loose net (*above*) that catches platelets and blood cells. Platelets (*left*) deliver chemicals that link the threads together, helping to form the clot.

crobes. The neutrophil's body flows around a bacterium and digests it. Eosinophils help fight parasites and allergic reactions. Basophils release chemicals that help in inflammation and healing. Monocytes leave the bloodstream to fight microbes in infected tissues. They mature in the tissues and become macrophages, swelling in size as they gobble up bacteria. Some lymphocytes (**B cells**) make the specialized proteins, called **antibodies**, that help to attack germs. Others (**helper T cells**) release substances that direct the activities of the antibody-producing cells. Still others (**killer T cells**) attack the germs directly. Some T lymphocytes search out and destroy outlaw body cells that could grow into cancerous tumors.

Regulating the Internal Environment. The blood helps to regulate the body temperature by carrying excess heat away from body cells. Heat is radiated out into the air from capillary networks in the skin. In cold weather, these capillaries contract, reducing the amount of heat lost from the body.

▶ **THE BLOOD SUPPLY**

Red blood cells live an average of 120 days before wearing out. Many worn-out red cells are captured and destroyed in the liver and spleen. White blood cells, too, wear out. They also can be poisoned by the microbes they gobble up while defending the body.

New blood cells are formed in the bone marrow. Special blood-forming marrow cells called **stem cells** can develop into red blood cells, one of the various kinds of white blood cells, or platelets. A hormone produced by the kidneys, **erythropoietin**, stimulates the bone marrow to produce new red blood cells. Other hormones help to regulate the volume of blood and the concentration of salts and other substances in the blood plasma.

Blood platelets normally live for only about five to eight days. If a platelet comes in contact with the rough edge of a cut blood-vessel wall, it tears, spilling out chemicals that help control bleeding. Some cause the blood vessel to contract; others start chemical reactions that convert the plasma protein **fibrinogen** to **fibrin**, a jellylike substance. Threadlike strings of fibrin form a sticky mesh on which platelets and blood cells are caught. Together they form a clot, which plugs up the hole and stops the bleeding.

BLOOD TYPES

It was in 1901 that the Austrian doctor Karl Landsteiner discovered that red blood cells have special proteins (antigens) on their surface that can react with antibodies, causing the red cells to clump together. People do not have antibodies to their own red blood cell proteins, but their plasma may contain antibodies to antigens of a different blood type. If blood of different types is mixed, the red cells may clump (*pictured below*), clogging the blood vessels.

Landsteiner found two main types of antigens, A and B, which are transmitted by heredity from parents to their children. There are four possible blood types: A, B, AB (both antigens), and O (neither antigen). In addition to the A-B-O blood groups, researchers have found many other blood groups, including the Rh and M-N blood groups. Those who have the Rh antigen, called the Rh factor, on their red blood cells are Rh positive; those who do not are considered Rh negative.

The other blood groups, such as the M-N, also have red-cell antigens. But unlike the A-B-O and Rh blood groups, these antigens rarely produce a strong antibody response. This means they are much less likely to cause dangerous reactions during transfusion procedures.

DISORDERS OF THE BLOOD

Blood disorders result from a variety of conditions, including too many or too few blood cells. In **anemia**, there are not enough red blood cells to supply the body with the oxygen it needs. A diet lacking iron or B vitamins, both of which are needed to produce hemoglobin, or the lack of intrinsic factor, a stomach protein that helps in the use of vitamin B_{12}, can cause anemia. In **aplastic anemia**, the bone marrow has been damaged, perhaps by radiation or certain drugs, and is unable to produce new blood cells. **Sickle-cell anemia** is a hereditary disorder in which defective hemoglobin causes the blood cells to have a

The deformed cells, rigid and twisted, that are present in sickle-cell anemia are the result of an error in the genetic coding of the hemoglobin molecule.

characteristic sickle or crescent shape. When sickling occurs, cells clump together and block small blood vessels, depriving tissues of blood and resulting in joint pain and fever. Several types of the anemia known as **thalassemia** are also caused by abnormal hemoglobin, resulting in destruction of red blood cells.

Leukemia is a cancer of the bone marrow or lymph nodes, resulting in the production of large numbers of abnormal white blood cells that cannot fight infection. Damage to the bone marrow may stop the formation of white blood cells, producing **leukopenia** (a lack of white blood cells). Without an adequate number of white blood cells to patrol the body, disease-causing invaders can multiply unchecked, causing infections in many parts of the body.

Blood clotting is a very complex process, involving more than a dozen different chemicals. A hereditary lack of one of the "clotting factors" can cause **hemophilia**, a condition in which even a minor cut can result in severe blood loss. Damage to the bone marrow can result in **thrombocytopenia**, a lack of blood platelets. The amount of time it takes for blood to clot increases as the amount of platelets decreases. The person with thrombocytopenia may have many small purplish patches on the skin, due to bleeding from torn capillaries.

In **infectious mononucleosis**, the Epstein-Barr virus infects B lymphocytes. Some of them become abnormal and are attacked by killer T cells, producing swollen lymph nodes and fever. The AIDS virus, HIV, does the most damage to the helper T lymphocytes. As these blood cells are destroyed, the body loses its ability to fight infections.

ALVIN SILVERSTEIN
VIRGINIA SILVERSTEIN
Coauthors, *The Circulatory System*

See also BODY, HUMAN; CIRCULATORY SYSTEM; HEART.

Did you know that...

the first successful blood transfusion was performed more than 500 years ago by the Incas of South America? When an Inca was injured and suffered a great blood loss, the victim was given blood from a healthy individual. Inca doctors used a hollow tube to link the injured person with the blood donor.

Doctors in other parts of the world also tried to perform transfusions, but the recipients often died when they did. Medical experts think the treatment worked for the Incas because it is likely that they all had the same blood type. Having the same blood type would mean that they could give and receive blood among themselves without the risk of a dangerous transfusion reaction.

BLUEPRINT

The blueprinting process was discovered by Sir John Frederick Herschel, an English astronomer, in 1842. It was originally called cyanotype and involved coating paper with a special chemical, which resulted in a print of white lines on a Prussian blue background.

The blueprint was used mainly for copying drawings and other clerical work done by architects, engineers, and shipbuilders who needed quick, long-lasting records of designs and figures. It was the simplest, cheapest, and most permanent photographic print and could be easily made by almost anyone.

To make a blueprint, a chemical coating is applied to a piece of paper. When the sensitized paper has dried to a bronze color, it is placed in contact with a drawing, covered with a sheet of glass, and exposed to sunlight for about an hour. After a final cold-water wash, the paper becomes bright blue and the lines of the image are white.

Blueprints were widely used until the 1960's when other techniques were developed. The sepia print and the whiteprint—an image of blue, brown, or black lines on a

A blueprint like this one serves as a detailed plan for the building of a house. Copies used by everyone in the construction process show both the builder and the owner the exact specifications they have agreed upon.

white background—were faster to make and easier to mark up and read. Architects and engineers continue to use these alternative reproduction methods. No one is sure, however, if they will last as long as blueprints, which survive for many decades without fading.

DONNA ROBERTSON
Director, Barnard College Architecture Program

BLUES. See JAZZ.

BLUME, JUDY (1938–)

The American writer Judy Blume is best known for books that deal frankly with issues and problems confronting young people. Her books consistently appear on lists of young readers' favorites.

Blume was born Judy Sussman in Elizabeth, New Jersey, on February 12, 1938. She was an imaginative child who studied dance and earned high honors at school. After graduating from New York University in 1960, she lived in suburban New Jersey with her husband, John Blume, and two children. Looking for a creative outlet, she tried

Judy Blume's fiction deals frankly with issues confronting young people. Her books are sometimes controversial with adults but always popular with her young readers.

writing pop songs and making banners. Finally, she began to write stories, taking a college course in writing for children.

Her first successful book was *Are You There, God? It's Me, Margaret* (1970). It tells of a sixth-grader's preoccupation with religion and with her own developing body. Blume dealt with the issue of parental divorce in *It's Not the End of the World* (1972) and with teenage sex in *Forever* (1975). In all her works she attempted to be completely honest with her readers, saying, "Problems only get worse when there are secrets, because what kids imagine is usually scarier than the truth."

Other books by Judy Blume include *Superfudge* (1980), *Just As Long As We're Together* (1987), *Fudge-A-Mania* (1990), *Here's to You, Rachel Robinson* (1993); three novels for adults; and *Letters to Judy* (1986), a collection of letters from her young readers.

Reviewed by CHARLES MORITZ
Editor, *Current Biography*

BLY, NELLIE (1864–1922)

Nellie Bly was once the most daring and celebrated newspaper reporter in the United States. She helped pioneer a sensational eyewitness reporting style that broke new ground for women and journalism. Bly acquired international fame by traveling around the world in record time—72 days, 6 hours, and 11 minutes. Her trip, completed in 1890, sought to outdo the fictitious record of Phileas Fogg, the hero of Jules Verne's popular novel, *Around the World in Eighty Days*.

Nellie Bly was born Elizabeth Cochran on May 5, 1864, in Cochran's Mills, Pennsylvania. She began her journalism career in 1885 as a reporter for the Pittsburgh *Dispatch*. It was there she took the pen name Nellie Bly.

As a novice reporter, Bly took many risks for a woman in her day. She wrote controversial articles on divorce, slum housing, and dangerous factory conditions. Newspapers around the country picked up her articles.

In 1887, Bly moved to New York City and joined Joseph Pulitzer's *World*. For her first assignment, she pretended to be insane to gain admission to the notorious asylum on Blackwell's Island. She wrote a blistering account of her experiences and exposed the asylum's appalling treatment of its patients. Her story sparked a statewide reform effort.

Such stunts became Bly's trademark. She later posed as a prostitute and as a criminal to gain firsthand information on prison life. Her most famous exploit, however, was her 72-

News reporter Nellie Bly became an international celebrity when she completed a record-breaking 72-day trip around the world in 1890. This photograph was taken the day she returned from her journey.

day trip around the world. She recorded her adventures in *Nellie Bly's Book: Around the World in 72 days*, published in 1890.

In 1895, Bly married Robert L. Seaman, a Brooklyn industrialist. After his death in 1904, Bly took over his manufacturing company, where she provided health care and equal wages to men and women. At the age of 50 she resumed her newspaper career but failed to achieve a major comeback. Nellie Bly died of pneumonia on January 27, 1922.

ELIZABETH EHRLICH
Author, *Nellie Bly*

BOARDSAILING

Boardsailing is a modern sport that combines features of two ancient activities, sailing and surfing. It is sometimes called windsurfing because the first sailboard, built in 1968, was named Windsurfer by its inventors, Americans Hoyle Schweitzer and Jim Drake.

Certified schools offer one- or two-day boardsailing courses that help beginners learn correct techniques. With six to eight hours of practice, beginners can learn enough of the basic skills at such schools to enjoy sailing in gentle breezes on smooth water.

Experienced boardsailors have many exciting challenges. There are races from local to international level, including the Olympic Games. Freestyle is a form of gymnastics on the sailboard. Wave jumping combines the speed of surfing and sailing to gain enough momentum to fly off the crest of a large wave and then fly or somersault through the air.

Equipment. A sailboard resembles a surfboard. It may be about 12 feet (3.6 meters) long for sailing and racing or shorter for freestyle and wave jumping. It is equipped with a **mast** attached by a **universal joint**—a device that allows the mast to turn and tilt in all directions. A bar, called the **boom,** curves around both sides of the sail at a height at which the sailor can grip it when standing on the board. The triangular sail usually has an area of from 55 to 65 square feet (5 to 6 square meters). It has a clear plastic window, allowing the sailor a view of the water on either side.

Controlling the Sailboard. When the sailboard is at rest, the mast and the sail lie flat on the water. The sailor stands on the board and pulls them upright with an attached line. The sailor then holds the boom. **Tacking** (turning the board toward the direction from which the wind is blowing) is done by tilting the mast toward the back of the board. **Jibing** (turning away from the wind) is done by tilting the mast forward.

Safety. Boardsailors must follow the general rules found in the article SAILING in Volume S. They must know how to swim and should always wear life jackets. It is important to have a companion nearby to give assistance if required.

Boardsailors must guard against hypothermia—chilling of the body that can cause death. This chilling can be caused by exposing the wet body to wind even when the air and water seem warm. The first symptoms are numbness in the hands and feet and uncontrollable shivering. If this occurs, the sailor must immediately get out of the water, dry off, and get warm. Wet suits are worn by most boardsailors. These suits hold a thin layer of water next to the body, where it is warmed and acts as insulation.

Competition. Boardsailing races are held on triangular, slalom, or long-distance courses. Triangular courses are used in Olympic competition (known as sailboarding), which was instituted for men in 1984 and became a part of women's competition in 1992. Slalom racecourses have six marks set close enough together to test the sailors' ability to tack and jibe. Distance races usually cover 5 to 15 miles (8 to 24 kilometers) and test both skill and endurance.

RHONDA SMITH-SANCHEZ
World Champion

BOAS, FRANZ (1858–1942)

Franz Boas was a pioneer of anthropology, the study of the origin and development of people and their cultures. Before Boas, many believed that some cultures were advanced while others were primitive. Boas did not accept this. He believed that cultures were different from one another because of the differences in their environments. He established that each culture should be judged on the basis of its own environment and history, and not by the standards of others.

Boas also had a great influence on how anthropologists work. He established the importance of field work—the recording of data based on personal observation. He showed that information about language, art, folklore, and mythology was as important to one's evaluation of a culture as the physical details about the people and their surroundings.

Franz Boas was born on July 9, 1858, in Minden, Germany. His parents encouraged his interest in science, and he attended the University of Kiel. His interest in anthropology developed during a scientific expedition to Baffin Island in the Arctic (1883–1884), where he had an opportunity to observe the local Eskimo (Inuit) culture. Many of his ideas were shaped by several trips he made to the northwest coast of North America, over a period of time from 1886 to 1931, to study several Indian cultures, including the Kwakiutl.

In 1887 Boas decided to live permanently in the United States and he became a citizen in 1891. At first he worked for the magazine *Science*. Later, he taught and did research at Clark University in Massachusetts and at Chicago's Field Museum of Natural History. Finally, he settled in New York City to work at the American Museum of Natural History and to study and teach at Columbia University. Boas founded a department at Columbia that produced many of the great anthropologists of the 1900's, including Ruth Benedict, Margaret Mead, and Edward Sapir. He also published many books and several important studies on American Indian folklore and art.

Franz Boas died in New York on December 22, 1942.

RACHEL KRANZ
Editor, Biographies
The Young Adult Reader's Adviser

See also ANTHROPOLOGY.

BOATS AND BOATING

Boating is a fast-growing sport. Every year more young skippers pilot their craft on fresh-water lakes and rivers and on the bays and inlets at the ocean's edge. To keep pace with the rapid growth of boating, hundreds of marinas have been built to provide shoreside berths, or places to anchor small craft. *Marina* is a Spanish word meaning "seacoast," and is used in English to describe a modern boat basin with piers and slips for docking boats, launches, and yachts. In a marina large and small boats are repaired, serviced, and stored. Shore electricity, telephones, fresh water, ice, and fuel are available at dockside. Pleasure-boat owners may shop here for supplies and food and drink all within walking distance of their boats. Every type of craft may be seen at a marina. There are sailing dinghies and two-masted schooners, outboard runabouts and big cabin cruisers with facilities to sleep six or more people.

The 14- to 18-foot (4.3- to 5.5-meter) run-abouts are the most popular small powerboats. They are wonderful for fishing or for just having fun on the water. The larger ones, fitted with powerful outboard engines, are used for towing water-skiers.

Before beginners learn to run one of these craft or even go for a ride in a dinghy or other small rowboat, they should know the basic rules of safety for themselves and their boat.

▶ **SAFETY RULES FOR YOUNG SAILORS**

(1) Learn to swim. If you cannot swim, wear a life jacket.

(2) Do not go out in a boat alone. Young children should always be accompanied by an adult.

(3) Do not go out in bad weather, or when a storm is forecast, or in a fog. Beginning boaters should stay close to shore.

(4) Never overload your boat.

(5) Sit quietly when boating. Do not scuffle while aboard a boat. Do not change seats when the water is rough or when the boat is in deep water.

(6) Do not try to swim ashore from an over-turned boat even if you are a good swimmer. Hold on to the boat and wait for help.

(7) Wear sneakers or rubber-soled shoes to avoid slipping, and wear a hat to protect yourself from the sun.

(8) Before diving off a boat into strange water, test for depth, rocks, and weeds. Swim in a safe place.

▶ THE RULES OF BOATING

It is important to know the rules of any sport, but in boating not knowing the rules can mean disaster. The important rules of boating concern whistle signals, the lights for different kinds of boats, and rights of way.

Signal Talk

One blast of a boat's whistle or horn means "I am going right." Two blasts mean "I am going left."

Motorboats are forbidden to respond using a cross signal—that is, answering one whistle with two blasts or two blasts with one. Instead, they are required to answer with the same signal to indicate that the other boat's signal has been understood. Whistle or horn signals, however, are not exchanged between sailboats.

Four or more blasts are the signal for danger. If the skipper disagrees with a signal or does not understand it, the danger signal should be given and the boat stopped. The boat should not proceed until the proper signals have been given, answered, and understood.

Lights Required After Sunset

Class A boats, which are under 16 feet (4.9 meters) long, and Class 1 boats, which are 16 to 26 feet (4.9 to 7.9 meters) long, have a combination red and green light at the front, or **bow** of the boat. The red light indicates the **port**, or left side, and the green light indicates the **starboard**, or right side. Each color should be visible from dead ahead and should show for 10 points around the horizon on each side for a distance of 1 mile (1.6 kilometers). (On a compass, 32 points represent a complete circle.) A white light at the rear, or **stern**, of the boat should show all around the horizon and be visible for about 2 miles (3 kilometers).

Class 2 boats, which are 26 to 40 feet (7.9 to 12.2 meters) long, and Class 3 boats, which measure 40 to 65 feet (12.2 to 19.8 meters), have separate red and green side lights. These boats must also have a white 20-point light at the bow, as well as a white 32-point stern light, which is placed higher than the bow light.

When boats approach head on, one blast of the whistle means "going right" (starboard). It is answered by one blast from the approaching boat. Two blasts mean "going left" (port), and are answered by two blasts.

Right of Way

The first rule of the seaway is "Keep to the right." For instance, when two boats are about to meet head on, each skipper should give one blast on the whistle and turn the boat to starboard (right). The boats will then pass port side to port side (left side to left side). This and other passing situations are shown above and on pages 264–265.

Sailboats always have the right of way over powerboats, unless a sailboat is overtaking a powerboat. In any dangerous situation, even though a boat may have the right of way, it is best to turn or back away to avoid collision. Pamphlets on piloting rules are available from the U.S. Coast Guard office in Washington, D.C., or from local coast guard offices. In Canada, boating information is available from the Canadian Department of Transport, Hunter Building, Ottawa, Ontario.

Good boating safety also requires having certain emergency equipment, including a fire extinguisher, a well-stocked first-aid kit, life jackets, and buoyant cushions. A compass is also important for boats that navigate offshore.

▶THE MANY ACTIVITIES OF BOATING

People swim from all types of boats. Before going swimming, however, the boat should be either moored to a pier or lying at anchor, and the motor must be stopped. The boat should have a boarding ladder placed at one side so that swimmers can climb back into the boat. Someone should always remain on board, ready to throw a life preserver if a swimmer needs help. Children under ten years of age should wear life vests and never swim in water over 5 feet (1.5 meters) deep. Skin diving is another activity that can be done from most kinds of boats. Waterskiing, on the other hand, requires a fast powerboat in order to pull the water-skier rapidly through the water.

Fishing is the most popular activity for boaters. Most fishing from runabouts and other small boats is done with light poles and lines and small reels. The boat can be stopped and the bait cast out into the water, or the bait can be pulled along behind the boat as it is moving —a method called trolling. Deep-sea fishing requires big boats and heavy fishing tackle. A

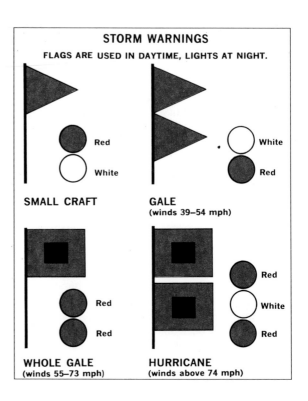

STORM WARNINGS

FLAGS ARE USED IN DAYTIME, LIGHTS AT NIGHT.

Red
White

SMALL CRAFT

White
Red

GALE
(winds 39–54 mph)

Red
Red

WHOLE GALE
(winds 55–73 mph)

Red
White
Red

HURRICANE
(winds above 74 mph)

Left: Sailboats always have the right of way over powerboats. *Center:* Red to red (port to port) means safe to go ahead. *Right:* When you see both red and green lights, blow one blast and pass red to red (port to port).

RED
GREEN

G   R

R   G

BEEP

Left: Green to green means safe to proceed. *Center:* Boat astern asks to pass. Lead boat answers and moves to starboard. *Upper right:* Red to starboard gives other boat right of way; signal and go astern. *Lower right:* Green off your port bow gives you right of way.

boat with a "flying bridge," a piloting platform at the top, is used to fish for large game fish, such as marlin or sailfish. When one of these fish is hooked, the skipper must be able to twist and turn the boat quickly to keep the fishing line tight and prevent it from getting under the boat. The person fishing is often strapped into a special chair and may require several hours to land a large fish.

Camping is another activity that almost every boat owner can enjoy. Even a canoe or small runabout can carry the tent, sleeping bags, portable stove, and supply of food that will make a satisfying trip.

▶POWERBOAT RACING

A more specialized boating activity is powerboat racing. Most racing requires special boats and motors. Racing boats are classified according to the size of the boat and the type of motor. The largest competition boats are the 25- to 40-foot (7.6- to 12.2-meter) **hydroplanes**. (Hydroplanes are light, flat-bottomed boats.) These boats have powerful engines that enable them to reach speeds of 200 miles

(320 kilometers) an hour. Jet-powered speedboats can reach speeds of almost 300 miles (480 kilometers) an hour.

Racing boats compete in a variety of contests in the United States and throughout the world. The famous Gold Cup race, for example, is held at various cities in the United States. The marathon is a long-distance event often raced on a river. Powerboat races are also held on the open ocean. These races provided a rugged test of boats, their equipment, and their drivers.

Racing requires expert boating skills. However, newcomers to boating can have a great deal of fun using their boats for exploring, for nature studies, for photography, and for simply being on the water. As Kenneth Grahame wrote in *The Wind in the Willows*, "There is nothing half so much worth doing as simply messing about in boats. . . . in or out of 'em, it doesn't matter."

TOM BOTTOMLEY
Author, *Cruising for Fun*

See also DIVING; FISHING; ROWING; SAILING; SKIN DIVING; SWIMMING; WATERSKIING.

BOBSLEDDING

How does it feel to shoot down the side of a mountain and around sharp curves at high rates of speed? You would know if you rode a racing bobsled down an ice-packed bobrun. A bobsled is a plank of steel or other metal alloy mounted on two sets of runners. The front runners are steered by means of either a wheel or ropes. The back runners do not turn.

Bobsleds can carry two or four people. The four-person bobsled used in championship races is about 12 feet (3.5 meters) long. The weight of the sled and crew cannot be more than 1,389 pounds (630 kilograms). A two-person racing bobsled is about 8½ feet (2.5 meters) long and combined with its crew its weight cannot total more than 827 pounds (375 kilograms).

The person in the front of a bobsled is in charge of steering. The person in the back is in charge of braking. On a four-person sled, the other two riders sit in the middle. In the early days of bobsledding, these riders would bob back and forth to make the sled go as fast as possible. This is how bobsledding got its name.

The bodies of today's bobsleds are often made of graphite or other very lightweight material. The body of the bobsled helps protect the riders and the steering mechanism. Streamlined design helps cut down wind resistance, making faster speeds possible. Push handles on each side of the sled are used by the crew to help get the sled off to a fast start. Competitive bobsleds are usually painted with the colors and emblem of the club or country that enters the bobsled in a race.

Modern racing bobsleds incorporate some of the most advanced engineering techniques. Many have runners mounted in rubber that act like the shock absorbers on a car to absorb the shock of bumps. Some bobsled racers design and build their own bobsleds, with special features to try to make the sleds go faster.

▶HOW THE SPORT OF BOBSLEDDING GREW

Long ago people discovered that it was easy to travel and carry loads over snow and ice on sleds. The earliest sleds were probably made of flat boards or animal skins stretched over frames. Later, narrow wooden runners were added. This made the sleds faster and easier to control. Indians of North America used a light, flat-bottomed sled that curved up in front. The name "toboggan" came from the Algonkian Indian word for this kind of sled.

During the 1880's, people in the Swiss Alps tried mounting toboggans on runners, which made them go faster. In fact, they went so fast that they often ran off course, out of control. Members of the Toboggan Club at St. Moritz, a famous winter resort in Switzerland, found that by making these sleds much heavier they could be controlled better. This was the birth of the bobsleigh, or bobsled, as it is called today. A special bobrun was built at St. Moritz, and the first race was held there in 1898.

A United States bobsled crew pushes off for a fast start in an Olympic race.

The first national championship bobsled races were held in Austria in 1908, and bobsledding became a world event in the first Olympic Winter Games, held in France in 1924.

▶NORTH AMERICA'S FAMOUS BOBRUN

The 1932 Olympic Winter Games were held at Lake Placid, New York. The Van Hoevenberg bobrun was built for these Olympics, and it became one of several bobruns in the world that qualify for international competition. Some others are at St. Moritz, Switzerland; Cortina d'Ampezzo, Italy; and Innsbruck, Austria.

The Van Hoevenberg bobrun is about 1 mile (1.6 kilometers) long. It has 16 curves with sections in between called straightaways. The walls of the curves and straightaways are made of concrete covered with a mixture of ice and snow. Using concrete eliminates the need for building walls of large ice blocks. The base of the bobrun is also made of concrete. Refrigeration under this concrete base keeps the run very cold. When water is sprayed onto the bobrun, it freezes quickly into ice, making the bobrun very fast.

The largest curve at Van Hoevenberg is called Shady; it is one of the most famous curves in the world. The trickiest curve is Zig-Zag. It is actually two curves, one right after

Spectators watch a two-person bobsled climbing high on the sidewall as it takes a curve.

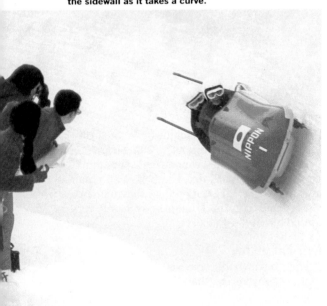

the other in opposite directions. If the bobsledders' timing isn't perfect in Zig, they will have trouble going into or out of Zag.

▶BOBSLED RACING

There is room for only one sled at a time on a bobrun. A bobsled race is therefore a race against time. Each sled is timed with the aid of electronic eyes.

Bobsled racers push their sled from a starting point and leap on it after crossing the starting line. As the sled crosses the starting line, electric eyes cause a clock in the timing booth to start running. Other electric eyes along the bobrun mark the sled's time at intermediate points. At the end of the run a final pair of electric eyes stops the clock in the timing booth. The clock is able to time each run to 1/100 of a second.

Championship races consist of four heats, or runs, for each sled. The sled with the shortest total time for the four heats is the winner. The fastest times on the Van Hoevenberg bobrun are less than 1 minute for a four-person sled and less than 1 minute and 4 seconds for a two-person sled. Bobsleds often reach speeds of about 90 miles (145 kilometers) an hour.

Bobsled racing is governed by the International Bobsleigh and Tobogganing Federation. During races, a jury of three people is in charge of the bobrun and the sleds. If anything should happen to the bobrun during the event, this jury would decide what to do. Bobsled championships are held at the Winter Olympics, as well as at world championship races each year. North American championships are usually held each year also.

▶BOBSLEDDING FOR FUN

It is not necessary to be a racer to enjoy bobsledding. In winter the Van Hoevenberg bobrun at Lake Placid is open for public pleasure riding. Paying passengers can ride with experienced bobsledders who do the steering and braking. People who want to drive a bobsled must have a license. To obtain one, they must first pass a physical examination. They are then taught by expert drivers. If they pass the driving tests, they are granted licenses.

STANLEY BENHAM
Former World Bobsled Champion

Reviewed by JOHN J. FELL
Bobsled Chairman, XIII Olympic Winter Games

There is a magic to being human. Our bodies let us participate in the world around us in ways unlike any other animal. As humans we have a wide range of wondrous abilities: We can move with grace and precision, learn intricate tasks, feel deep emotion, and survive in an ever-changing environment.

BODY, HUMAN

From the earliest times, people have tried to understand how the human body is made and how it works. Scientists have tried to unlock its secrets to improve health and to help fight disease. Artists have used the human body as a source of inspiration to create art. Athletes and performers have studied the human body to better their performing abilities.

Those who have studied the human body often compare it to a machine. Like a machine, the body needs energy to do its work. A machine such as an automobile engine burns fuel, usually gasoline, to obtain energy. The fuel combines with oxygen from the air, and energy is released. The body's fuel is food. The food is combined with oxygen that is breathed in. Energy is released.

There are many other likenesses between machines and the human body. But it is the differences that make us better than machines.

The body can grow. Machines cannot. Cameras can "see" and computers can "learn" in a way. But machines cannot feel, see, think, and learn as humans do. The body can repair worn-out parts and even produce new humans. Most important, the human body has a very special quality—it is alive.

▶BODY CHEMISTRY

The human body consists of chemical elements—substances that cannot be broken down into simpler substances by ordinary means. The most common chemical elements in the body are carbon, hydrogen, nitrogen, and oxygen; the body also contains many others, such as sodium, calcium, iron, phosphorus, and potassium.

Every element is made up of units called **atoms**. When two or more atoms combine, a microscopic structure called a **molecule** is formed. Some molecules are composed of atoms of only one element. For example, a molecule of oxygen (O_2) consists of two atoms of oxygen. When an atom combines with one or more atoms of different elements, **compounds** are formed. Water (H_2O), for instance, is a compound consisting of molecules that contain two atoms of hydrogen joined with one atom of oxygen.

The compounds of the body must be arranged in a very special way to produce life. The most basic compound in the human body is water. It is necessary for most of the chem-

serve important chemical functions. Nucleic acids carry the instructions that pass human traits from one generation to the next.

▶ **THE LIVING CELL**

The cell, which is a collection of compounds, is the basic unit of life in all living things. A cell can take in food, get rid of wastes, and grow. The human body is made up of billions of cells. This tells you something about the size of cells. Most of them are too small to be seen without a microscope. But they are alive. Throughout life, the body continues to grow new cells. These new cells replace those that have worn out.

Most cells have three main parts. A thin skinlike covering, called the **cell membrane**, encloses each cell. Inside the cell is a soft jelly called **cytoplasm**. Within the cytoplasm lies the **nucleus**, which is sometimes called the "control center" because it directs the activities of a cell.

ical reactions that occur. In addition to water, there are four other main compounds in the body: carbohydrates (such as starch), lipids (or fats), proteins, and nucleic acids.

These four compounds are large, complex structures that contain the element carbon. Carbohydrates provide the energy for all of the body's activities. Lipids store extra fuel and serve as building material for the cells of the body. Proteins also perform several duties. Some proteins are used to build cells, others

The cell membrane acts not only as a wrapper but as a sieve: It lets some materials pass into the cell while keeping others out. Food and oxygen carried to the cell must pass through the cell membrane. Wastes given off by the cell when it has burned the food and oxygen pass through the sievelike membrane back into the blood and are carried away.

The cytoplasm makes up most of the cell. Within the cytoplasm are many tiny structures called **organelles**. These are the organs of the

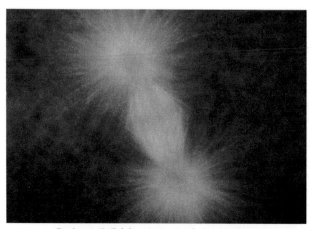

During cell division, two sets of chromosomes are pulled apart toward opposite poles. Completion of the process yields two genetically identical cells.

cell. The **mitochondrion** is one type of organelle. It transforms substances from the food we eat into energy that the cell can use. Cells that are very active such as muscle cells have lots of mitochondria. Another type of organelle is the **lysosome**. It digests and gets rid of unwanted material.

The nucleus is a solid ball in the center of the cell. It contains rodlike structures called **chromosomes**. Each cell has 46 chromosomes —half are inherited from the mother and half from the father. The chromosomes are made up of **genes**. Genes are the basic units of heredity—that is, they carry the characteristics that are inherited from an individual's parents. The fact that a boy has blue eyes like his

mother or brown hair like his father is determined by the genes that he has inherited from his parents.

The genes also control what cells do. The genes carry their instructions, or master plans, in a special language called the **genetic code**. The genetic code is formed using a chemical substance called **DNA** (*d*eoxyribo*n*ucleic *a*cid). All living plants and animals use the same genetic code; however, it is the different master plans carried in the genetic code that make every living thing different from all other living things.

Cells not only grow larger, they also reproduce new cells. New cells serve two functions: They help the body grow and they replace injured or dead cells. Cells reproduce by dividing—one cell divides to make two cells. First the nucleus reproduces by dividing into two parts. Then each part becomes a new cell complete with chromosome-containing nucleus, cytoplasm, and cell membrane. When cells divide, each of the two **daughter cells** are exactly like the **parent cell**.

Cells get their nourishment from blood. They convert some of the nourishment to energy. This is called **energy metabolism**. They may also use part of the food for making new cell materials. In some kinds of cells, such as fat cells, food is stored for later use.

▶ **THE ORGANIZATION OF THE HUMAN BODY**

The human body has more than a hundred different kinds of cells. Each has a special form that makes it fit with the special job it

The Living Cell

The adult human body contains some 100 trillion cells teeming with activity. Although all the cells do not look alike, they do share the same basic structure and some characteristic parts.

Cell membrane
Cytoplasm
Ribosomes
Endoplasmic reticulum
Chromosomes
Golgi apparatus
Mitochondrion
Lysosome
Centriole
Nucleolus
Nucleus

Cells of the Body

Cells are the building blocks of life. The many different kinds of cells that make up the human body come in all shapes and sizes. Cartilage cells (*right*) form the major supporting tissues of the body. The regularly arranged epithelial cells (*below right*) make up the outer surface of the skin. A cross section of bone (*bottom left*) shows the spidery form of bone cells. Each nerve cell (*below left*) has projections that carry electrical signals to the cell and others that carry electrical signals away from the cell to other parts of the body.

has to do. Cells of one kind are usually joined to make **tissue**. Blood cells are an exception. They are not joined. They travel alone through the blood vessels.

A tissue is a fabric of the same kind of cells. For example, muscles are tissue made up of muscle cells; nervous tissue is made up of nerve cells. There are four main kinds of tissue: **Epithelial tissue**, which covers the surface of the body; **connective tissue**, which helps support and join together parts of the body; **muscle tissue**, which makes body movement possible; and **nervous tissue**, which carries nerve signals throughout the body.

Different kinds of tissue are combined in the body's organs. An **organ** is a body part that does one or more special jobs for the rest of the body. The heart, lungs, stomach, brain, and skin are all organs.

A group of organs working together is called a **system**. For example, the heart, blood, and blood vessels make up the circulatory system. The nose, throat, windpipe, and lungs make up the respiratory (breathing) system. The kidneys, bladder, and connecting tubes make up the urinary system. The systems of the body are like members of a team. Each one has a specific job, but together they make it possible for the body to work, play, grow, and carry out many other functions.

What is the largest organ of your body?

Your skin—the only body organ that is exposed to the outside world—is the largest organ of your body. Skin is a tough, elastic, waterproof protection for the entire body. Even your eyes have a transparent layer of skin, called the conjunctiva, covering them. The skin of an average adult covers an area of about 22 square feet (2.04 square meters) and weighs 8 to 10 pounds (3.6 to 4.5 kilograms).

While the skin is the largest organ of the entire body, the liver—which in an adult weighs about 3 pounds (1.4 kilograms)—is the largest organ inside the body. It is also one of the most active organs. Its tasks include processing nutrients, such as proteins and carbohydrates; metabolizing drugs and hormones; and storing blood, vitamins, and minerals.

▶ BODY SYSTEMS AND ORGANS

Body systems help the body remain alive: The skin protects the body; the body obtains oxygen through the respiratory system; the digestive system processes food so it can be used for energy and growth; the heart and blood vessels circulate oxygen and other substances throughout the body; the kidneys eliminate waste materials; and the reproductive system produces offspring. Together the nervous system and endocrine system form a command system that links all of the other body systems.

The Skin

The skin is the largest organ of the body, and it does many jobs. It holds fluids inside the body. It protects the body from air, water, dirt, and germs. By giving off heat, it helps to regulate body temperature. It contains nerves that are sensitive to things such as touch and temperature that provide information about the world around us.

The skin is made up of two layers of tissue. The top protective layer is called the **epidermis**; the inner layer is called the **dermis**. The thickness of the skin varies on different parts of the body. For example, the skin on the soles of the feet is thicker than that on the face.

In addition to forming a protective covering for the body, the epidermis also forms the fin-

The Skin

Skin — the largest organ of the body — contains such structures as sweat glands, blood vessels, and nerve endings and performs many vital functions, including protecting the body from dirt and germs and helping to control body temperature.

Hair shaft

Nerve endings

Melanocytes

Epidermis

Dermis

Nerve fiber

Blood vessels

Muscle

Hair follicle

Sweat gland   Fat cell

Some people, such as the young boy above, are born with clumps of melanocytes in their skin. These people end up with freckles.

The pigment melanin acts as an umbrella to help protect the skin of these sunbathers (*left*) from ultraviolet rays that could damage cells.

gernails and toenails. Fingernails and toenails are collections of dead cells. That is why it does not hurt when you cut your toenails and fingernails.

The outermost layer of the epidermis is called the **stratum corneum**, and it is made up of a tough protective layer of dead cell material called **keratin**. When you look at a person's skin, all you are actually seeing is dead cells. The stratum corneum is thickest on the soles of the feet and on the palms of the hands. Collections of keratin, called corns, form to protect the foot from ill-fitting shoes.

The epidermis also has special cells called **melanocytes**, some 60,000 in every square inch of skin. Melanocytes produce a dark pigment called **melanin**. Melanin gives skin its color. People with black or brown skin have more melanin in their skin than people with white or yellow skin. Melanin protects the body from the damaging effects caused by the sun. When the skin is exposed to sunlight, the melanocytes produce additional melanin. This is what creates a suntan.

The dermis contains sweat glands, blood vessels, nerves, and cells called **hair follicles**. Each hair follicle contains a hair root. The hair root produces hair cells. These cells die and form the hair that projects from the skin's surface. Hair is present on most parts of the body's surface except for the palms of the hands and soles of the feet.

Each person's handprint is a unique pattern of loops, arches, and swirls formed by the ridges and grooves of the skin.

The Skeletal System

The framework that holds the human body erect is the **skeleton**. The skeleton, which is made mostly of bones, has two major jobs. It supports the body—without a skeleton you would be like a jellyfish—and it protects delicate organs, such as the brain and heart.

The skeleton must also be able to move. The parts of the skeleton that let bones move are called **joints**. Bones fit together at joints and are held fast by tough cords or straps, called **ligaments**. Some joints can be moved freely; others cannot be moved at all. When you run, you move your legs at the hip and knee joints. When you throw a ball, you move your arms at the shoulder and elbow joints. The bones in your spine help you stand straight. They do not move as freely as other joints, but they let you bend. Except for the bones in the jaw, the bones in your skull, which protect your brain, do not move at all.

Bone is made up of two types of living tissue. The outer layer of bone is dense hard (or compact) tissue; the inner layer is lightweight spongy tissue. The holes in the spongy tissue are filled with **marrow**. Some of the marrow is yellow and stores fat. Other marrow is red and produces blood cells. Because bone is living, growing tissue, it must be fed. The outside of bone is covered with a thin skin called a periosteum, which holds the tiny blood vessels that carry food to the bone.

The Skeletal System

The human skeleton is a hard, strong, living framework for the body's tissues. It provides the support needed so that we can stand upright and move about freely. It also holds internal organs in place and shelters them from injury.

Cross Section of a Bone

Compact (hard) bone
Periosteum (membrane covering bone)
Cartilage
Spongy bone
Blood vessels
Marrow

Parietal bone
Frontal bone
Sphenoid bone
Maxilla (upper jawbone)
Temporal bone
Occipital bone
Nasal bone
Zygomatic bone (cheekbone)
Clavicle (collarbone)
Mandible (lower jawbone)
Cervical vertebrae (7)
Scapula (shoulder blade)
Ribs
Thoracic vertebrae (12)
Sternum (breastbone)
Humerus
Lumbar vertebrae (5)
Ulna
Radius
Carpals (wrist bones)
Sacrum
Ilium
Coccyx
Pubic symphysis
Ischium
Pubis
Metacarpals (hand bones)
Phalanges (finger bones)
Femur (thighbone)
Patella (kneecap)
Tibia (shinbone)
Fibula (calf bone)
Metatarsals (foot bones)
Tarsals (anklebones)
Phalanges (toe bones)

The Muscular System

Bones are the framework of the body, but they cannot move by themselves. **Muscles** are the body's movers. For every bone that can move, there are muscles called **skeletal muscles**, that move it. Skeletal muscles are firmly attached to the bones by hard, ropelike tissue called **tendons**.

Muscles have the unique ability to contract, or get shorter. They are able to do this because each muscle cell contains special proteins. It is the proteins that are extended or shortened when the muscle relaxes or contracts. The process of relaxing or contracting is controlled by the central nervous system.

When a skeletal muscle shortens, it pulls on the tendons that are attached to the bone, and the bone moves. Muscles pull, but they cannot push. So they must work in pairs. If you bend your arm, one set of muscles contracts and pulls your forearm up. To straighten your arm, you relax the first set of muscles. A second set pulls in the opposite way, straightening your arm.

The skeletal muscles are under a person's control. They work because you decide to walk, pick up a ball, or take off your sweater. The body also has another body system that works without conscious orders from you. These muscles, called **smooth muscles**, contract automatically. They are found in many parts of the body and are not attached to bones. Smooth muscles do jobs like controlling the pupil of the eye and propelling food through the digestive tract.

The Muscular System (Front view)

The body has more than 600 muscles. Every movement, whether it is the lifting of an arm, the beating of the heart, or the opening and closing of blood vessels, starts with the contraction of muscles.

Frontalis—
Orbicularis oculi
Orbicularis oris
Sternocleidomastoid—
Deltoid—
Pectoralis major—
Biceps—
Brachioradialis—
Pectineus—
Gracilis—
Quadriceps femoris—

—Temporalis
—Zygomaticus
—Masseter
—Buccinator
—Trapezius
—Serratus anterior
—Brachialis
—Rectus abdominis
—External oblique
—Ligament (wrist)
—Sartorius
—Patella
—Gastrocnemius
—Soleus

Skeletal muscle (*top*) controls every movement we make; powerful cardiac muscle (*center*) drives blood to every cell in the body; smooth muscle (*bottom*) keeps the internal systems of the body, such as our digestive system, working at all times.

BODY, HUMAN • 275

some 650 muscles cover the body's skeleton? Muscles do more than shape and define the contours of our bodies. They are responsible for all of the body's movements. Muscles are attached to bones by tough, hard tissue called tendons. In response to instructions from the brain, muscles contract and pull on the bones and movement occurs. Usually skeletal muscles work in groups. Even a seemingly simple task such as taking one step involves about 200 muscles! Some muscles lift and move your leg forward, while others in the back, chest, and abdomen help keep you from losing your balance during the motion.

The Muscular System (Back view)

Temporalis
Occipitalis
Masseter
Sternocleidomastoid
Trapezius
Deltoid
Teres minor
Teres major
Triceps
Latissimus dorsi
Flexor carpi
Extensor carpi
Extensor digitorum
Gluteus medius
Ligament (wrist)
Gluteus maximus
Semitendinosus
Semimembranosus
Lumbodorsal fascia
Biceps femoris
Gastrocnemius
Achilles tendon

The heart is made up of another type of muscle, called **cardiac muscle**. Cardiac muscle is made up of fibers that resemble skeletal muscle. However, cardiac muscle also resembles smooth muscle in that it contracts automatically without conscious control.

The Digestive System

To do work, muscles and other tissue need water and fuel to burn. This fuel comes from the foods we eat and drink. But food cannot be used directly as fuel. Foods must be broken up and changed before they can be used as an energy fuel. This process of converting food to fuel is called **digestion** and takes place in the digestive system.

Digestion begins in the mouth where the teeth are used to break food into small pieces. The saliva that is in the mouth gets the food moist and makes the food easier to swallow. Saliva also contains amylase, an enzyme that starts breaking the starch in food into sugar. Then the moist ball of food is carried to the back of the mouth by the tongue.

Swallowing starts food on its journey through the 25- to 30-foot (8- to 9-meter)-long tube that coils through the center of the body and makes up the digestive system. Muscles force the food into the **esophagus**, the section of the digestive tube that connects with the stomach. Other muscles force the food down the esophagus.

Next, the food enters the pouchlike stomach portion of the tube. Here the food is churned and broken down further. Glands in the stomach add the chemical substances hydrochloric acid and pepsin to the food mixture. Pepsin is an enzyme that breaks down meats and other proteins. The acid sterilizes the food and makes the pepsin work better. A mucous slime, which coats the stomach and protects it from injury by the acid, is also secreted. The stomach works on the food for one to four hours. By then, the food is almost liquid.

From the stomach the food is pushed into the **small intestine**. The small intestine is so called because it is about 1 inch (2.5 centimeters) in diameter. However, it can be very long —about 20 feet (6 meters) in length. The small intestine does the main job of digestion. And it is from the small intestine that food starts its journey to the cells.

In the small intestine, more protective mucus is secreted. Food mixes with juices from the liver and pancreas. The liver makes liver bile, which helps to digest fats; the pancreas secretes enzymes that digest protein, fat, and carbohydrates. The small intestine also makes some digestive enzymes. As the food is digested, it becomes liquid. The starches are broken down into simple sugars. Proteins are split into smaller particles. Fats are changed to fatty acids and glycerol.

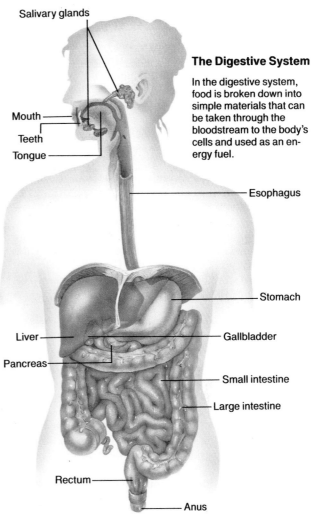

The Digestive System

In the digestive system, food is broken down into simple materials that can be taken through the bloodstream to the body's cells and used as an energy fuel.

Salivary glands

Mouth

Teeth

Tongue

Esophagus

Stomach

Liver

Gallbladder

Pancreas

Small intestine

Large intestine

Rectum

Anus

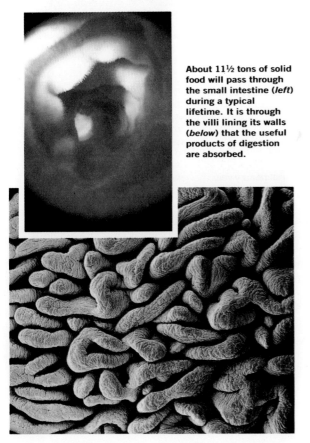

About 11½ tons of solid food will pass through the small intestine (*left*) during a typical lifetime. It is through the villi lining its walls (*below*) that the useful products of digestion are absorbed.

These digested materials pass through the cell membranes of the intestinal cells into the bloodstream. To make sure that none of the small particles are wasted, the small intestine is lined with hundreds of microscopic fingerlike projections called **villi**. These projections reach out and capture the food particles. Because particles can pass through the sides as well as the top of the villi, there is more space for food to be absorbed. Food particles travel from the villi into the bloodstream, then into the cells.

Most of the blood from the intestine passes through the liver before it enters the heart. The liver is like a large chemical factory. It changes many of the food particles. Some of the sugar is changed to a starchy substance called **glycogen** for storage in the body. When body cells need more sugar, the liver changes glycogen back to sugar and releases it into the bloodstream. Other products are used by the liver to manufacture proteins and process fats to be used as fuel. The liver also acts as a storage warehouse. It stores vitamins such as vitamin A and D.

Whatever food is left undigested after its journey through the small intestine moves into the **large intestine**. The large intestine is much wider than the small intestine and also much shorter. It is about 6 feet (2 meters) long. In the large intestine, water and minerals are removed from the undigested material, leaving solid waste material. Most of the body's waste comes from what is left of the food after the body uses what it needs. The solid wastes are then stored in the large intestine until they pass out of the body as bowel movements.

The Respiratory System

Cells have two important needs: They must have oxygen to produce energy, and they must get rid of the waste gas, called carbon dioxide, that forms when energy is produced. The respiratory system provides both of these services for the body's cells.

Oxygen enters the body from the air that is breathed in. Usually the air is taken in through the nose. But at times, when the body needs extra oxygen, air can be also taken in big gulps through the mouth. The moist lining of the nose contains many small hairs that clean the air as it moves through the nose. There are also many blood vessels in the lining of the nose, and the warm blood heats the air.

From the nose, air travels through the **pharynx** (the cavity located behind the nose and mouth), to the **larynx** (or voice box), the **trachea** (or windpipe), and finally, the lungs. Together these structures form the respiratory system.

The larynx contains folds of gristle-like tissue called the **vocal cords**. When air moves through the vocal cords, the cords vibrate and

The life-sustaining exchange of gases, oxygen and carbon dioxide, takes place within the lungs' approximately 300 million tiny air sacs called alveoli.

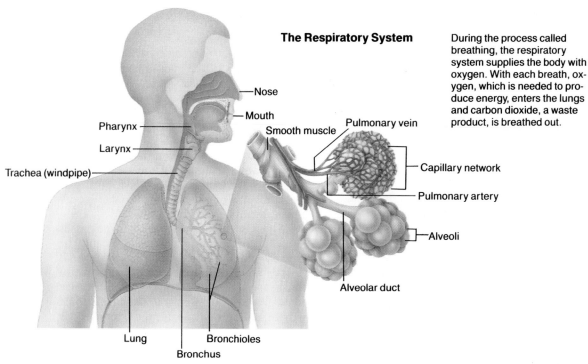

The Respiratory System

During the process called breathing, the respiratory system supplies the body with oxygen. With each breath, oxygen, which is needed to produce energy, enters the lungs and carbon dioxide, a waste product, is breathed out.

Nose
Mouth
Pharynx
Larynx
Trachea (windpipe)
Smooth muscle
Pulmonary vein
Capillary network
Pulmonary artery
Alveoli
Alveolar duct
Lung
Bronchus
Bronchioles

produce sounds, such as talking. Like the strings on a violin, the vocal cords can be tightened or loosened to produce higher- or lower-pitched sounds. The larynx also serves a protective function. When water or other materials enter the throat, the folds close so that the material cannot go into the lungs.

Air moves from the larynx to the trachea. The trachea is a ridged tube that is about 1 inch (2.5 centimeters) in diameter. The ridges, which are made up of firm gristle-like material, keep the trachea from collapsing during the act of breathing. In the upper part of the chest, the trachea divides to form two tubes. Each tube, called a **bronchus**, branches into smaller and smaller bronchial tubes that look like the branches on a tree. Each of the tiniest branches opens into a grapelike cluster of air-filled sacs, called alveoli. The air sacs are covered with a network of capillaries, which are the small blood vessels that connect veins and arteries.

Waste-carrying blood is pumped from the heart into the capillaries of the air sacs. Here a quick exchange takes place. Oxygen moves out of the air sacs into the blood. The waste gas carbon dioxide moves out of the blood into the air sacs and then is breathed out of the body. The oxygen is picked up by the red blood cells and carried back to the heart. From there it is pumped throughout the body.

Aided by the work of muscles, air is moved into and out of the lungs during the process of breathing, or **respiration**. Muscles in the chest wall and a muscle called the **diaphragm**, that separates the chest from the abdomen change the size and shape of the chest. With each breath taken in, the chest muscles contract, lifting the front and sides of the ribs and the breastbone to make a bigger space in the chest. When the diaphragm contracts, it flattens out and makes the space even bigger. As the chest expands, so do the lungs and air rushes in to fill them. With each breath let out, the muscles relax, the space becomes smaller, and air is pushed out of the lungs.

Breathing is automatic. That means you do not have to think about breathing to actually breathe. You continue to breathe even when you are sleeping. People do have some control over their breathing. You can take large or small breaths and you can breathe faster or slower. You can even hold your breath. But you cannot stop breathing altogether.

The Circulatory System

The circulatory system, which includes the heart, blood, and blood vessels (arteries, veins, and capillaries), moves life-giving blood throughout the body. Many thousands of miles of vessels travel through the body, supplying oxygenated blood to the body's tissues and organs.

Blood acts as a transport vehicle, carrying nutrients and oxygen to cells. Blood also picks up unneeded waste materials from the cells, carries important immune cells throughout the body, and picks up and carries heat from the inside of the body out to the skin, where it is released into the air.

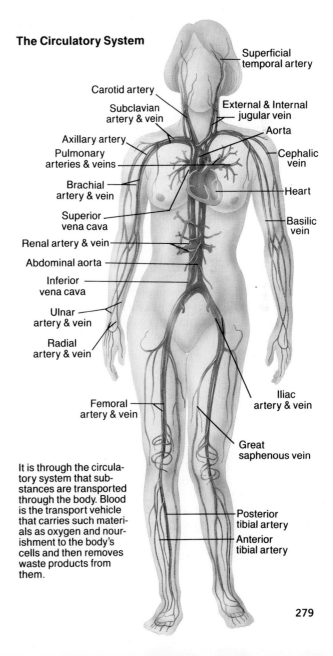

The Circulatory System

Superficial temporal artery

Carotid artery

Subclavian artery & vein

External & Internal jugular vein

Aorta

Axillary artery

Pulmonary arteries & veins

Cephalic vein

Brachial artery & vein

Heart

Superior vena cava

Basilic vein

Renal artery & vein

Abdominal aorta

Inferior vena cava

Ulnar artery & vein

Radial artery & vein

Iliac artery & vein

Femoral artery & vein

Great saphenous vein

It is through the circulatory system that substances are transported through the body. Blood is the transport vehicle that carries such materials as oxygen and nourishment to the body's cells and then removes waste products from them.

Posterior tibial artery

Anterior tibial artery

279

An elaborate and extensive network of blood vessels brings a rich supply of oxygenated blood to the face, head, and brain.

About half of the body's blood is made up of a thin, clear light yellow liquid called **plasma**. It flows through the blood vessels carrying many dissolved materials and solid blood cells. Most of these blood cells are red blood cells. Some 25 trillion red cells move through the bloodstream.

The red blood cells carry out specific jobs. Their main job is to carry oxygen from the lungs to cells in the body. These blood cells have powerful protein molecules called **hemoglobin** that carry the oxygen. Each hemoglobin molecule contains an iron atom that acts as a magnet, snapping up oxygen in the lungs, then clinging tightly to it. When the red cells reach the tissues, the hemoglobin releases the oxygen. Red blood cells also pick up carbon dioxide in the tissues and carry it back to the lungs, where it is removed from the body.

White blood cells are also transported in the blood. These cells kill dangerous bacteria and fight disease. **Platelets** are the third kind of solid material carried in the blood. They are the repair force. More than a trillion strong, platelets start the clotting process when a blood vessel is torn or cut.

The red and white blood cells and the platelets are all made in the bone marrow. Red blood cells live about four months. White blood cells live a much shorter time—some live only a few days. Platelets are not actual cells. They are pieces of larger cells. They live about eight to ten days. The bone marrow replaces blood cells and platelets as they die or are destroyed.

The force needed to push the blood through the many miles of vessels is supplied by a powerful muscular pump: the heart. It lies in the middle of the chest, between the lungs.

The heart is divided into four parts called **chambers**. There are two chambers called **atria** at the top of the heart and two chambers called **ventricles** at the bottom. The atria act as receptacles for blood as it enters the heart and the ventricles act as pumps to force blood out of the heart. The heart pumps the body's 4 to 6 quarts (4 to 6 liters) of blood through many thousands of miles of blood vessels, most of them tiny.

From the heart, blood is pumped into the lungs where carbon dioxide and other wastes are removed, and oxygen from the air breathed in is added to the blood. The oxygen-rich blood returns to the heart to begin its travels to the body's cells.

The Heart

The heart is a hollow muscle that functions as a pump to distribute oxygen-rich blood throughout the body. The round-trip of blood traveling between the heart and a part of the body may take about a minute.

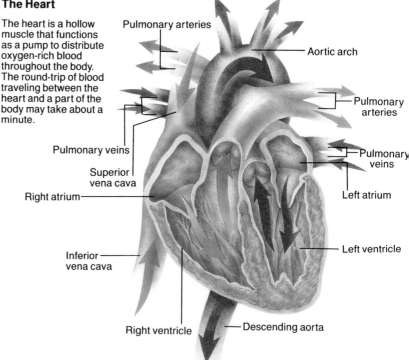

Pulmonary arteries

Aortic arch

Pulmonary arteries

Pulmonary veins

Pulmonary veins

Superior vena cava

Left atrium

Right atrium

Inferior vena cava

Left ventricle

Right ventricle

Descending aorta

there are more red blood cells in the body than any other kind of cell? Some 25 trillion of the plump, round dimpled cells course through the bloodstream. The sole task of these tiny cells is to bring oxygen to all of the body's tissue and remove carbon dioxide.

Each of the cells travels approximately 173,000 times between the lungs and other tissues before it dies. The red blood cell has a life span of about 120 days. At that time, the aging cell is caught by a macrophage (*pictured at right*) and digested.

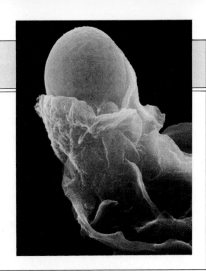

When the oxygen-rich blood leaves the heart, it travels in vessels called **arteries**. The **aorta** is the biggest artery in the body. It travels from the heart through the chest into the abdomen. Other large arteries branch from it, and still other arteries branch from them. Blood flows from the smallest arteries into tiny thin-walled tubes called **capillaries**. The oxygen and nutrients from digested food are carried in the blood and pass through the walls of the capillaries to the cells. In much the same manner, the waste materials from the cells pass back into the blood through the walls of the capillaries.

From the capillaries, the waste-carrying blood moves into tiny vessels called **veins**. The tiny veins lead into bigger veins. The bigger veins lead into still bigger veins until the blood finally flows into the large **vena cava**, the vein that enters the heart. From the heart, the waste-carrying blood is pumped into the lungs where the waste gases are removed from the blood and oxygen is added. The oxygen-rich blood returns to the heart and once again begins its travels.

The Urinary System

In order to function properly, the body must be able to get rid of its gaseous, solid, and liquid waste materials. Carbon dioxide, the waste gas, is eliminated through the lungs; solid wastes are eliminated through the large intestine. Some liquid waste evaporates from the skin as sweat; however, most of the liquid waste is removed by the urinary system as **urine**. The two kidneys, the bladder, and the tubes that connect them are the structures of the urinary system.

The Urinary System

Removing liquid waste and regulating fluid balance are the tasks of the urinary system. Each hour, as blood passes through the kidneys, about 2 ounces (57 grams) of urine are produced.

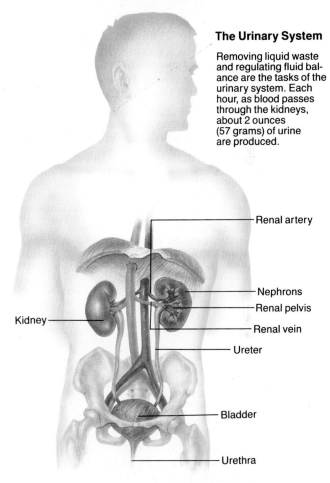

Renal artery
Nephrons
Renal pelvis
Renal vein
Ureter
Kidney
Bladder
Urethra

A **kidney** is bean-shaped and dark red in color. It is about 4 inches (10 centimeters) long. The kidney is like a waste purification system. Within each kidney there are about a million capillary clumps. These capillaries are like sieves. They have small openings that allow water and waste particles, but not blood cells, to leave the blood. The liquid containing waste is collected in small tubes that surround the capillary sieves.

From the tubes, the waste then moves through the kidney and is processed further. Some small particles, such as sugar and salt, are taken back into the body; other waste particles are added to the urine. One familiar substance that is in the waste liquid is water. Water makes up more than 95% of urine. By removing water, the kidneys help keep the balance of water in the blood just right.

After the waste liquid has been processed in the kidney, it moves through the connecting tubes into the bladder. The bladder stores the urine until it is eliminated from the body.

The Reproductive System

The process of reproduction involves the creation of a new human being. It begins when a male's reproductive cell, called a **sperm**, joins with a female's reproductive cell, called an **ovum**. The joining of the sperm and the ovum is called **fertilization**.

Within a fertilized egg are all the instructions that are needed to direct the growth of a new human being. The baby develops as the joined cells divide and form the many organs that make up a new human being. Because the two reproductive cells contain the parents' genes, the baby that is formed will tend to look like both its parents.

The reproductive structures that develop in male babies, both inside and outside, are different from those that develop in female babies. Males and females also produce different chemical messengers, or **hormones**. During puberty and adolescence, these hormones produce noticeable body changes.

In the male, the reproductive structures include the **testes**, two walnut-sized structures

The Reproductive System

The reproductive structures of the male and female, which differ, provide the means to produce a new generation of human beings. The process begins when the male sex cell and the female sex cell unite.

Cross section of testicle

Testicle (sperm made here)

Epididymis (sperm stored here)

Vas deferens (sperm duct)

Bladder

Penis

Epididymis

Testicle Vas deferens

Prostate

Urethra

Cross section of an ovary showing developing egg

Fallopian tube

Ovary

Uterus

Fallopian tube

Ovary

Ovary

Cervix

Bladder

Fallopian tube

Urethra

Clitoris

Vagina

Fertilization takes place when one of the sperm cells thrashing around the egg (*opposite page, far left*) penetrates its gelatinous covering. A new life grows cell by cell as the fertilized egg divides (*opposite page, left*). The fetus floats within a wet, dark world. Now at 4 months (*right*), all its organs have been formed, and the time remaining before birth will be simply a time of growth.

that hang between the legs in a loose skin sac called the **scrotum**. The testes produce and store sperm. The sperm that are produced in the testes are transported through narrow tubes to the **penis**, which is the external reproductive organ of the male. The penis is used for both transporting sperm into the female reproductive system and eliminating urine.

In the female, the internal reproductive structures include the **ovaries** (which produce the ovum) and the **uterus** (which is where babies grow until they are ready to be born). Women have two ovaries. Each ovary is connected to the top of the uterus by a small tube called the **fallopian tube**. At the bottom of the uterus, a canal-like structure called the **vagina** opens to the outside of the body. The external structures of the female are small folds of skin and mucous membranes called **labia**.

Women usually produce only one ovum a month. At the same time that the ovum is developing, changes occur in the uterus. It is preparing a place for the baby to grow. The inside of the uterus gets thicker and forms new blood vessels. If the ovum is not fertilized, the uterus sheds this inside layer. This is called a **menstrual period**. Most women have a menstrual period once a month.

The reproductive process involves an act called **sexual intercourse**. During sexual intercourse, millions of sperm from the penis enter the vagina. The sperm move around and look for the ovum. If an ovum is present, a sperm may join with the ovum and begin the process of creating a new human being.

Communication Systems of the Body

Throughout the body, changes are happening second by second and minute by minute. Even though hundreds of different things are going on at the same time, no part of the body acts alone. For instance, the heart does not just start beating differently. If it did, other systems in the body would act to bring the heart back to the usual rhythm. All of the body systems communicate with each other and work together in the ongoing process called **self-government**. Self-government works whether you are awake or asleep.

When you run, both legs must move at the right time. You breathe more often, your heart beats faster, and your cells use more energy. Messengers travel from one part of the body to another telling each part what needs to be done and when it needs to be done.

There are two types of messenger systems that work together in the body. One system uses electrical signals; the other system uses chemical signals. Most of the body's electrical messages are sent through the **nervous system**. The many kinds of chemical messages are carried in hormone messengers that travel through the bloodstream and other body fluids. The most common are hormones that are produced by the **endocrine system**.

Although each person is a unique mix of genetic information, individuals within a family tend to share a likeness of features.

The Nervous System

The structures of the nervous system include the brain, spinal cord, **neurons** (or nerve cells), and sense organs (such as the eyes and ears). The brain acts as a central computer for the nervous system, processing many types of orders, sensations, emotional feelings, and thinking behaviors.

Neurons have a cell body that contains a nucleus and wire-like projections called **nerve fibers**. They have input fibers that receive information and a single long output fiber that sends information. Nerve fibers from all over the body go to the brain and fibers from the brain go to all parts of the body.

Within the nervous system, electrical signals are used as messengers. Neurons have been programmed to recognize specific incoming signals. When the correct signal arrives, the nerve cell "fires." Some nerves work like calculators—they add up the incoming signals until they get the correct answer and then they fire.

When a nerve fires, information leaves the nerve through the output fiber. Many of these fibers communicate with other nerves, many of which are in the brain. Some communicate with muscle cells; others communicate with glands, blood vessels, and organs of the digestive tract.

The Nervous System

The complicated tasks of detecting, interpreting, and acting on information from the body's external and internal environments are performed by the nervous system.

Cerebrum — Brain
Cerebellum
Brain stem
Spinal cord — Cervical nerves
Radial nerve
Median nerve
Thoracic nerves
Ulnar nerve
Lumbar nerves
Sacral and coccygeal nerves
Femoral nerve
Sciatic nerve

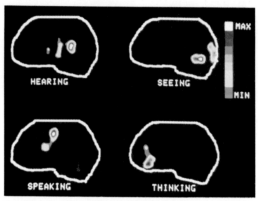

Scans of the brain while an individual is awake show the level of activity in areas of the brain that are dedicated to hearing, seeing, speaking, and thinking.

Different parts of the brain do different things. The **brain stem** is the part of the brain that connects with the spinal cord. Its nerve cells carry messages between the spinal cord and other parts of the brain. These nerves are in charge of the muscles and glands that work day and night. Even as you sleep, nerves in the **medulla**, a part of the brain stem, keep your heart beating and your lungs breathing.

The **cerebellum** controls body movement and balance. Information about many of the habits and skills you have learned is stored there. Once you have learned these behaviors they become automatic. The cerebellum issues orders that enable you to, among other things, walk, ride a bicycle, and play the piano.

The **cerebrum**, the largest part of the brain, is where thinking, learning, remembering, deciding, and being aware occur. Sensations of seeing, hearing, smelling, tasting, and touch-

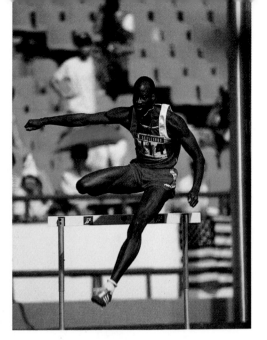

The structures of the nervous system work together to produce conscious and automatic activities. Without the contributions of each part, it would be impossible to engage in such activities as playing the violin (*above*) or jumping hurdles (*right*).

ing are centered there. So are body feelings. The cerebrum enables you to enjoy things, speak intelligently, make up a poem, even design a rocket.

The different parts of the brain work together to accomplish a task. For example, suppose you decide to take a bike ride. The cerebrum, which is the thinking part of your brain, makes this decision. It decides where you will ride, how fast you will pedal. It orders the muscles to work. After that, the cerebellum and other parts of the brain take over. These make the muscles work smoothly and together. The medulla matches the action of the heart and the lungs to the energy needs of the muscles. As you pedal harder, your heart beats faster and you breathe more often.

The Sense Organs. Because we get information about the outside environment through the senses of sight, hearing, smell, taste, and touch, they are often referred to as external senses. Along with the external senses that tell us about the outside world, there are some senses that tell us what is going on inside of our bodies. These senses, called internal senses, let us know such things as when we are hungry or thirsty, whether we are in pain, and if we are sitting up or lying down.

There are **receptors** for every sensation. Receptors are special nerve structures such as those in the eye that let you see. Each receptor processes only one kind of information. That is why you cannot see with your ears or hear with your eyes. The sensory information is sent to the brain through input fibers. The eyes report on a wide range of sensory information, such as the size, shape, color, position, and movement of objects.

The seeing process begins when light coming from an object reaches the eyes. The rays of light go through the **lens** to the **retina**, a sort of screen at the back of the eyeball. From there the message is sent to the brain, and the person sees.

Because the two eyes are a small distance apart, they report slightly different images.

The human eye observes its surroundings as an upside-down image and sends this message along nerve fibers to the brain. The brain interprets this information so that we perceive the world with objects right side up.

The Eye

The eye provides visual information by changing light waves into nerve impulses that are interpreted in the brain.

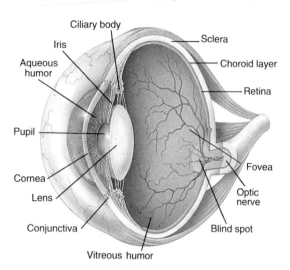

Ciliary body
Iris
Aqueous humor
Pupil
Cornea
Lens
Conjunctiva
Vitreous humor
Sclera
Choroid layer
Retina
Fovea
Optic nerve
Blind spot

The Ear

Sound waves received by the ear are conducted through its structures and converted to nerve impulses before traveling to the brain.

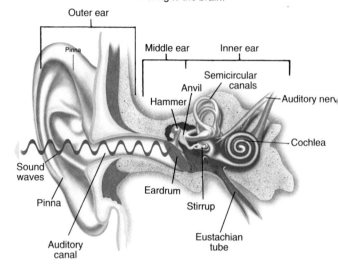

Outer ear
Pinna
Middle ear
Inner ear
Anvil
Hammer
Semicircular canals
Auditory nerve
Cochlea
Sound waves
Pinna
Eardrum
Stirrup
Auditory canal
Eustachian tube

However, the two images merge, and the important result is that we see things in depth and can therefore judge distances.

Having an ear on each side of our head helps us to judge the direction from which a sound comes. We hear when something sends out vibrations called **sound waves**. The sound waves enter the ear and hit the eardrum, causing a vibration that moves some small bones inside the air-filled cavity of the skull's temporal bone. The bones send a message along the hearing nerves to the brain.

Smelling and tasting work closely together, and much of what most people call tasting is actually smelling. Taste is a chemical sense. As food becomes wet in the mouth and dissolves, a chemical reaction takes place and taste receptors are activated. These receptors, usually called **taste buds**, are contained within the small bumpy structures, or **papillae**, on the tongue. Once activated, taste buds send messages to the brain about whether the flavor of the food is sweet, sour, bitter, or salty. Some tastes seem stronger on certain tongue areas. The tongue also has receptors that report on heat, cold, texture, and pain.

Anything that has an odor is giving off tiny particles of gas, which mix with the air. By breathing, you draw these particles into your nose, where the particles of gas are moistened. Nerve cells sense the wet particles and send a message to the brain. Then you smell whatever the odor is.

Through different kinds of nerve cells in the skin, the brain learns about pain, pressure, heat, cold, and touch. The sense of touch tells whether things are rough or smooth, hard or soft, sharp or rounded. When you feel your way through the dark, you are using your sense of touch. The same sense tells you when and how the skin is being stroked and about something that is pulling on the skin.

The nerve cells of the skin are scattered all over the body, but some parts of the body have especially large collections of them. The fingertips are such parts—you can get much more information by feeling something with your fingertips than with your elbow.

Sometimes the information that is reported by our exter-

The tongue's surface is covered with small budlike projections that house the taste buds.

nal senses seems more obvious and important than information reported by our internal senses. However, the internal senses make us aware of feelings such as hunger, pain, movement, and fatigue. The internal senses help maintain a steady, healthy environment inside the body. They do this by responding to specific chemical and physical changes in internal systems, such as the digestive, respiratory, and nervous systems.

None of the senses work alone. We do not see with just our eyes or hear with just our ears. The senses are reporters. They take in information and send it to the brain. Each kind of information reaches a particular part of the brain, and in a way that scientists do not understand, the brain turns nerve impulses into sounds, tastes, and smells. Not until the messages reach the brain do we actually see, hear, taste, and so on.

Sometimes when one sense does not work, other senses tend to become sharper to make up for the loss. People who are blind tend to develop keen senses of hearing and touch. And people who are deaf tend to develop sharper senses of sight and touch.

The Endocrine System

The endocrine system produces powerful chemical messengers called hormones. Similar to the nervous system, the endocrine system works automatically and we cannot control it. Hormones are most often manufactured by patches of cells called **glands**. Glands that are part of the endocrine system include the thyroid, parathyroid, adrenal, pituitary, and sex glands. However, there are hormone-secreting endocrine tissues in organs such as the brain, kidneys, stomach, and pancreas. Wherever the endocrine secretions are produced, they pass directly into the bloodstream and remain in the body.

Some glands do not produce hormones. Instead, they secrete substances such as saliva or sweat. Such glands are called exocrine glands. Substances such as saliva and sweat perform specific tasks close to where they are released. Their secretions leave the body either from the skin or through the digestive tract.

When sense receptors send conflicting messages to the brain, such as during weightlessness, the mechanism that keeps our internal processes stable is disrupted.

The **thyroid gland** is an example of an endocrine gland that keeps the body working normally. It is a rather large gland in the neck. Its hormone stimulates cells to produce more energy. The thyroid hormone controls the rate at which cells burn food and thus the rate at which they produce energy. It also affects growth and development of the mind. Four tiny glands that function as one make up the

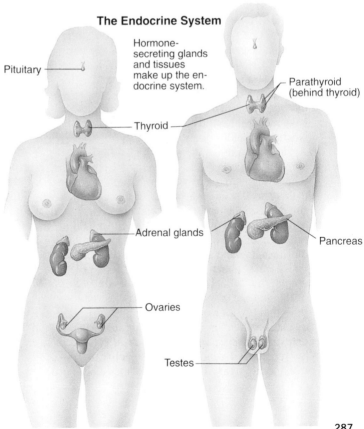

The Endocrine System

Hormone-secreting glands and tissues make up the endocrine system.

Pituitary

Parathyroid (behind thyroid)

Thyroid

Adrenal glands

Pancreas

Ovaries

Testes

Many things contribute to a healthy and well-functioning body and mind, including work, play, and companionship.

parathyroid, which lies close to the thyroid. The parathyroid secretes hormones that control blood calcium and are important in several body processes, such as bone growth and muscle and nerve function.

Another type of endocrine gland is the **adrenal gland**. There are two adrenal glands—one is located on the top of each kidney. Each adrenal gland has two parts, and each part does a different job. Whenever a person is in danger, one part of the gland releases a hormone called **adrenalin** that prepares the body for quick action. Suppose something happens to give you a sudden fright. Your heart begins to pound. Your face turns pale, and the pupils in your eyes open wider. Your muscles tense. You feel "butterflies" in your stomach. This is what adrenalin does to the body.

The other part of the adrenal gland produces hormones too. These hormones help keep your blood sugar up between meals, regulate the salt levels in your blood, and prevent tissue damage due to injury or infection.

The **pituitary gland** is a pea-sized gland at the base of the brain. It is sometimes called the master gland because it makes hormones that control other endocrine glands. For example, one of its hormones controls the action of the adrenal glands. Another makes the thyroid gland work harder.

The pancreas is one of the organs that has endocrine tissue. **Insulin**, which is produced by specialized pancreatic cells, helps to control blood sugar. It carries the message that

tells fat cells and muscle cells to take sugar out of the blood.

Hormones and other chemical messengers act through receptors. The chemical messengers fit into the receptors in a lock and key fashion. Each hormone and chemical messenger (the key) has its own specially shaped receptor (the lock). Insulin has a different shape of receptor than the thyroid hormone. Hormones travel throughout the body but will communicate only with cells that have the right kind of receptor.

▶**YOUR BODY**

The human body is a complex arrangement of separate parts. Each part performs its own specific task, yet each is dependent on the other to maintain one unique living being: you. Learning about the human body and how it works also helps us examine ourselves and the world around us. When we examine the human body, we find that there are differences that make each person unique and special. However, the basic truth is that we are each of us more alike than we are different.

CAROL MATTSON PORTH
Author, *Pathophysiology: Concepts of Altered Health States*

See also BLOOD; BODY CHEMISTRY; BRAIN; CELLS; CIRCULATORY SYSTEM; DIGESTIVE SYSTEM; DISEASES; EAR; EYE; GLANDS; HEART; IMMUNE SYSTEM; KIDNEYS; LIVER; LUNGS; LYMPHATIC SYSTEM; MUSCULAR SYSTEM; NERVOUS SYSTEM; PHYSICAL FITNESS; SKELETAL SYSTEM.

BODYBUILDING

Bodybuilding is a system of exercises for developing the muscles in order to change the body's appearance. It is also a sport in which contestants are judged for their muscular development.

Bodybuilding grew out of weight lifting. Training with weights produces bigger and stronger muscles because of the body's ability to adapt to stress. Lifting a weight heavier than a muscle is accustomed to lifting causes that muscle to get stronger. Once the muscle adapts to the new level of stress, you must increase the amount of weight you are using in your training in order to force the muscle to continue to adapt. This is called **progressive-resistance training**—you progressively increase the weight, or resistance, to keep pace with the increasing strength of your muscles.

The purpose of weight lifting is to lift as much weight as possible. But the aim of bodybuilding is to use weights, or some other form of resistance to muscular effort, to change the way the body looks. The bodybuilder is not concerned with how much weight he or she can lift but rather with the full contraction of each muscle involved in an exercise. Of course, bodybuilding training does make you stronger. But more important to the bodybuilder is the size, shape, proportion, and definition of the muscle structure. These create the unique physique of a bodybuilder.

▶ PRINCIPLES OF BODYBUILDING

There are certain basic principles of bodybuilding training. The first is progressive-resistance training. The bodybuilder also tries to isolate and train each muscle of the body. Using weights or some other form of resistance, the bodybuilder subjects each of the muscles to a series of "sets" that are made up of a specific number of "reps," or repetitions. For example, to build up the biceps, a bodybuilder may do an exercise called "curls," which alternately contract and expand the biceps muscles. Using weights the bodybuilder may do 5 sets of 20 repetitions of curls. Contracting the muscles over and over, with the proper balance of sets and repetitions, is what gives the bodybuilder's muscles the shape and definition that weight lifters lack.

Bodybuilders used to work their whole bodies in each exercise session. Then they

This bodybuilder is doing an exercise called curls to develop her biceps—a muscle in the upper arm. Bodybuilding has become increasingly popular among women.

found that they got better results by training certain body parts one day and others the next. They also learned more about diet and nutrition. They are now able to create maximum muscle mass together with minimum body fat, so that every individual muscle fiber seems to be visible.

Top-level bodybuilding competitors train for many hours each day. As with any athlete, proper rest and nutrition are extremely important. Anything—even emotional factors—can change the way the bodybuilder's physique appears during the day of a contest.

▶ THE FIRST BODYBUILDING CONTESTS

The forerunners of modern bodybuilding contests were "physical culture" competitions, which took place in the United States during the 1920's and 1930's. In these contests a variety of athletes, including swimmers, runners, boxers, gymnasts, and weight lifters, were judged on the look of their physiques and on their ability to perform athletic feats. The weight lifters began to dominate these contests because their huge muscles created such an overwhelming impression. Eventually all the competitors in these events were weight lifters, and the modern bodybuilding competition was born.

A competition called the Mr. America contest was held in 1939, but the first of the modern Mr. America bodybuilding events was held in 1940. Competitors were still required to perform some sort of athletic feat, as in the old physical culture contests. But the mass, proportion, and overall development of the contestants' physiques made it clear that they were really bodybuilders and not just weight lifters or physical culturists.

▶ MODERN BODYBUILDING CONTESTS

In modern bodybuilding contests, the judges look at each competitor in order to evaluate the shape and proportions of the body, as well as how much muscle definition the competitor has achieved. The contestants are asked to do a series of poses that reveal the relative quality of the various parts of their physiques. Each also does a posing routine of his or her own choice. This routine is designed to emphasize the especially well-developed parts of the competitor's body.

Presenting the body properly through posing is a difficult art. It involves more than just flexing the muscles. The way a bodybuilder poses can impress or disappoint the judges. In addition, posing for long periods of time requires great endurance. Bodybuilders must practice posing in order to avoid becoming exhausted on stage.

In the late 1970's, the first bodybuilding contests for women were held. Before that time, contests for women were actually physical-culture beauty contests. Today women bodybuilders are held to the same high standards of physical development as men.

▶ BODYBUILDING ORGANIZATIONS

The world governing organization of bodybuilding is the International Federation of Bodybuilders (IFBB), which has more than 120 member nations. The major events sanctioned by the IFBB are the World Amateur Bodybuilding Championships (Mr. Universe), the men's and women's World Professional Championships, the World Mixed-Pairs Championship (in which men and women compete together as teams), and the Mr. Olympia contest, in which the top champions come together each year to see who is the best.

▶ FAMOUS BODYBUILDERS

The first bodybuilder who became well known to the general public was Steve Reeves, an American Mr. Universe winner who played Hercules in a series of ''muscle movies'' in the 1950's. In the 1970's and 1980's, two other bodybuilders gained celebrity through movies and television: Lou Ferrigno, an American, who played in ''The Incredible Hulk'' on television, and Austrian-born Arnold Schwarzenegger, who won the Mr. Olympia contest seven times. Both men starred in *Pumping Iron* (1977), a movie about bodybuilding.

BILL DOBBINS
Founding editor, *Flex* magazine

Left: Arnold Schwarzenegger strikes a pose, displaying the physique that won him numerous bodybuilding titles. Right: A bodybuilder examines her muscular development.

BODY CHEMISTRY

The body is a complicated chemical machine. The cell is the engine that runs this machine. If we want to learn how the cell engine works, we must take it apart. We must find out what each part looks like and what job it does.

The body is made up of so many cells that it would be impossible to take each one apart to learn how it works. Fortunately, this is not necessary, because cells resemble one another in many ways. A liver cell, a kidney cell, and a brain cell have much in common even though they do very different jobs in the body. Much of what we learn about one kind of cell applies to others as well. Therefore, from now on we will talk about a typical cell. This is a cell that doesn't really exist but that has the properties of many different kinds of cells.

▶ WHAT CELLS ARE MADE OF

The cell is a collection of chemicals called compounds. At first glance these compounds don't seem very unusual. A typical cell is about 65 percent water, 15 percent fatlike material, 15 percent protein, ½ percent carbohydrate, and 4½ percent salt. You could make up a mixture like that for less than a penny's worth of chemicals, but of course you wouldn't have a living cell. These compounds must be arranged in a very special way to produce life.

The most ordinary compound in the cell, water, has several important functions. For one thing, water is a very good solvent, which means it will dissolve many different kinds of chemicals. This is very important because the cell engine runs on chemical reactions. And chemical reactions, in general, take place best when the chemicals are dissolved in some liquid.

Many salts are dissolved in the cell water. Of course, it wouldn't do for all the salts in the body to dissolve in water. If they did, our bones would dissolve and we would collapse like a wet rag. Our bones contain calcium salts, which do not dissolve very much in water.

These simple compounds, water and salts, are found everywhere—in the sea, in the ground, and so on—not just in living cells.

A molecule of water contains two atoms of hydrogen attached to an atom of oxygen. A typical cell is about 65 percent water.

Table salt is one of the simplest compounds known. It contains only two different kinds of atoms, sodium and chlorine. Water is simple, too. It contains two atoms of hydrogen attached to an atom of oxygen.

Not all the compounds in the body are this simple. Some of the most important molecules in the body contain thousands of atoms hooked together in a definite way. The compounds we are most interested in can be divided into four groups. These groups are called: the carbohydrates, the proteins, the lipids, and the nucleic acids.

A compound in a particular group is built on a definite plan. The carbohydrates have a plan, the proteins have another plan, and so on. A chemist can recognize this plan and can tell a carbohydrate from a protein as readily as you can tell an automobile from an airplane.

Within each group there are differences, too, just as there are differences between different makes of automobiles. You must learn a little about these different compounds before we can talk about how the cell works.

▶ CARBOHYDRATES

Carbohydrates are made up of carbon, hydrogen, and oxygen atoms. Lots of other compounds contain these same atoms. But carbohydrates can be recognized by the way the atoms are put together. **Sugars** are the simplest carbohydrates. When sugars were first discovered, scientists thought they were just carbon atoms combined with water. So they named the sugars carbo-hydrates, meaning carbon-water. Actually sugars are more complicated than this, and the carbohydrate group includes many compounds other than sugars.

Left: Long, branched chains of glucose form glycogen. Right: Proteins are very important macromolecules. Amino acids (small dots) link together in complex chains and form huge protein molecules.

The word "sugar" makes everyone think of table sugar. But table sugar is actually a particular kind of sugar, which is called **sucrose**. There are many different kinds of sugar. The most important sugar in the body is **glucose**. Glucose is also called **dextrose**. It is one of the body's most important fuels. It is so important that the body stores up a good supply of it in a form called **glycogen**.

Glycogen is not a sugar itself, but is made up of sugar building blocks. Glycogen is produced when glucose molecules are hooked together into chains. The main glucose chain has many shorter chains that branch off it like the branches of a tree.

Starch is another important carbohydrate. Starch comes from plants, and starch molecules are very similar to glycogen. They are made up of glucose chains, too. Starch is the most important carbohydrate in the diet because it furnishes much of the glucose your body needs to function properly.

Compared to the sugars, starch and glycogen are huge molecules. Biochemists (scientists who study the chemistry of living organisms) have a special name for giant molecules like this. It is **macromolecules**. Macromolecules are so important that there cannot be any life without them.

▶ **PROTEINS**

Starch and glycogen are not the only macromolecules in the body. Proteins are macromolecules, too. Every cell of every living organism has protein in it. In fact, the word "protein" means "of the first importance" in Greek.

There are many different proteins in the body, and they have many jobs to do. Your skin and hair contain a tough structural protein called **keratin**. Keratin and other structural proteins hold the body together. They are like the frame of your house. Another group, the **functional proteins**, are actively working at all sorts of important jobs. **Hemoglobin**, a blood protein, carries oxygen from the lungs to the cells. A large group of proteins called **enzymes** helps the cell carry out hundreds of chemical reactions.

Proteins are made from simple building blocks, the **amino acids**. Like the sugars, amino acids contain carbon, hydrogen, and oxygen, but they also contain nitrogen. There is a common pattern of carbon, hydrogen, oxygen, and nitrogen atoms in the amino acids that sets them apart from other compounds. However, there are also different arrangements within this basic plan. And so there are many different amino acids. Twenty of them are of particular importance in the body.

The amino acids are hooked together in long chains. One or more of these chains makes up a protein. Sometimes the chains are stretched out like string. Many structural proteins, such as keratin, are like this. In other proteins the chains are coiled and folded into a ball-like structure. Hemoglobin and many other functional proteins have this globular form.

Protein chains are complicated, with 20 different kinds of building blocks. Most proteins contain all 20, but a few do not. Our bodies can produce 12 of the 20 amino acids needed to make cell proteins. The other 8 must come from proteins in our food. A prolonged diet deficient in any of these 8 **essential amino acids** causes serious disease.

The chains in even the simplest protein are more than 30 amino acids long. The chains of many proteins are several hundred units long. The order of amino acids in the chains and the way the chains fold up give the protein the special properties it needs to carry out its particular job in the body.

The sum total of all your body's proteins makes you what you are. They are responsible for both the similarities and the differences between you and your parents. You do not inherit your proteins directly from your parents. But you do inherit the information that tells your cells what kind of proteins to make. This hereditary information is carried by another important group of compounds, the nucleic acids.

▶ **NUCLEIC ACIDS**

Like proteins, nucleic acids contain carbon, hydrogen, oxygen, and nitrogen. But nucleic acids also contain phosphorus. And like proteins, nucleic acids are made up of long, chainlike molecules within the body's cells. The building blocks of nucleic acid chains are called **nucleotides**.

Nucleotides are divided into two groups, depending on the sugar they contain. One group has the sugar **ribose**; these nucleotides are called **ribonucleotides**. The other group contains the sugar **deoxyribose**; these nucleotides are called **deoxyribonucleotides**. Deoxyribose has one less oxygen atom than ribose.

Ribonucleotides join together and form one type of nucleic acid—**ribonucleic acid**. It is commonly known as **RNA**. The smallest RNA has about 75 nucleotides in a single chain. The largest RNA chains are thousands of nucleotides in length.

Deoxyribonucleotides join together to form the other type of nucleic acid—**deoxyribonu-**

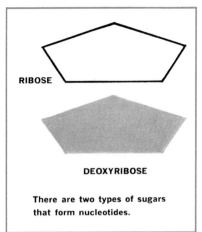

RIBOSE

DEOXYRIBOSE

There are two types of sugars that form nucleotides.

PHOSPHATE

There is only one kind of phosphate bridge.

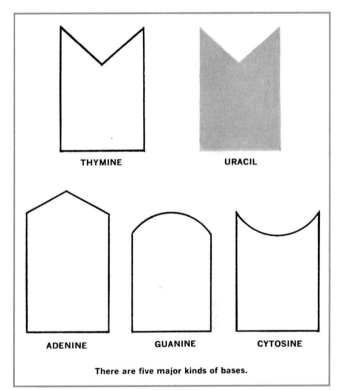

THYMINE

URACIL

ADENINE

GUANINE

CYTOSINE

There are five major kinds of bases.

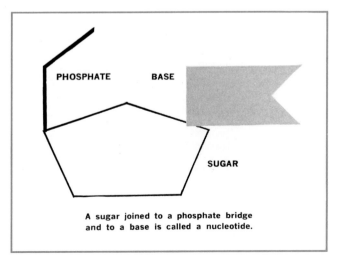

PHOSPHATE

BASE

SUGAR

A sugar joined to a phosphate bridge and to a base is called a nucleotide.

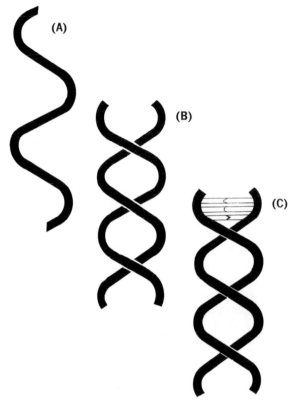

Above: RNA is made of many nucleotides strung together. All the nucleotides in RNA have the sugar ribose. Below: DNA is made of many nucleotides strung together. All the nucleotides in DNA have the sugar deoxyribose.

Above: (A) Nucleotides in DNA and RNA are arranged in a helix. (B) Nucleotides that make up DNA form two helices that wind around each other. (C) The helices are held together by bases that join in pairs. Two bases are always found together, one base on each helix. Below: Model of a DNA molecule.

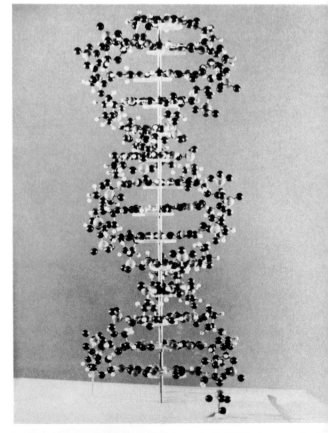

cleic acid, or **DNA**. DNA chains contain many thousands of nucleotides. Usually the DNA molecule has two nucleotide chains exactly the same length. The chains are wound around each other like two strands of rope and form a double helix.

DNA is found only within the nucleus of the cell. DNA carries all the body's hereditary information. All of us inherit DNA from our parents. When the two chains of the DNA helix split apart, each produces a new partner. The result is two DNA molecules exactly like the original one. As this process continues hereditary information is passed on from cell to cell.

Later in this article, you will learn more about the fascinating things nucleic acids do. But there is still one more group of compounds to talk about before we come to how the body machine works.

▶ **LIPIDS**

All the fatlike or "greasy" compounds in the body belong to the lipid group. The simplest lipids are the fatty acids. There are many different fatty acids in the body. They are building blocks for other lipids. For example, **fats** such as beef fat or lard and **oils** such as olive oil are made when three fatty acids become attached to a molecule of glycerol (glycerin). Fats are an important storehouse of energy in the body.

The **steroids** are also fairly simple lipids. Perhaps you have heard about the steroid **cholesterol**. It serves as the raw material for making many other important steroids such as the **sex hormones**. The body can't function normally without cholesterol. But when the amount gets too high, the cholesterol may deposit in the arteries and lead to the disease atherosclerosis (hardening of the arteries).

Not all lipids are simple. In fact, lipid macromolecules are perhaps the most complex (complicated) molecules in the body. They do not have just one building block, as in glycogen, or a few similar building blocks, as in proteins and nucleic acids. Rather, the **complex lipids** may contain many different kinds of building blocks. Fatty acids are almost always part of these lipids, but the lipids may also contain sugars, amino acids, phosphates, and some special compounds.

These complex lipids make up the various membranes of the cell. The membranes hold important parts of the cell machine together. The cell itself is encased in a lipid membrane —without this membrane there can't be a cell. The cell nucleus also has a lipid membrane. These membranes are so constructed that certain kinds of molecules can pass through them easily. For example, building blocks such as sugars must pass through the cell membrane in order for the cell machinery inside to use them. Waste products such as carbon dioxide must pass out of the cell.

There are other molecules that the cell must keep inside the membrane. The liver cell can't store glucose because glucose molecules pass through the cell membrane. But large glycogen molecules will not go through the cell membrane. So the liver can store glucose as glycogen. When glucose is needed, some glycogen is broken down into glucose.

As you can see, the cell is more than a complicated mixture of chemicals. And these chemicals are not just thrown together like nuts in a bag. They are carefully woven into the complicated chemical structures that make up the different parts of the cell machine.

Now that you know a little about the parts of the machine, we can go on to how they work at the chemical level. The cell machine runs on hundreds of chemical reactions. All these reactions, taken together, are called **metabolism**.

▶ **ENZYMES**

Many chemical reactions by themselves are quite slow. For example, if the gases hydrogen and oxygen are mixed, nothing happens. When a little finely ground platinum metal is added, the hydrogen and oxygen combine to form water. Sometimes they react so fast in the presence of platinum that the mixture explodes. When the reaction is finished, the metal can be recovered unchanged.

The platinum speeded up the reaction between hydrogen and oxygen without being permanently changed itself. Chemists call compounds that do this **catalysts**.

The body has hundreds of different catalysts. Almost every chemical reaction that occurs in the body has a special catalyst. These body catalysts are called **enzymes**. Enzymes, then, speed up the body's chemistry.

With all catalysts, including enzymes, a

little bit goes a long way. This is because they aren't changed by the reaction they catalyze. So a single molecule of catalyst can work over and over again. However, enzymes have special properties, which are different from those of other catalysts. First of all, enzymes are proteins. (Now you see one reason why proteins are so important.) Second, enzymes have **specificity**. This means that a particular enzyme catalyzes one particular reaction or, at most, one particular group of reactions. It will not work in any other reactions.

Specificity comes in when the enzyme and its **substrate** meet. The substrate is the substance on which the enzyme does its work. The substrate and the enzyme must fit together in the way that a lock and its key fit together. On the surface of the enzyme, the substrate is changed to some other compound. The new compound separates from the enzyme. And so the enzyme is again free to combine with another molecule of the substrate. This can happen again and again.

Enzyme and substrates fit together like a lock and key. Chemical reaction alters the substrates while the enzyme remains unchanged. Products of reaction on substrates are separated from the enzyme. The enzyme is now free to act on other molecules of substrates.

▶ ENZYME HELPERS

The protein molecules can't always act as catalysts by themselves. Sometimes they need help.

Very often an enzyme has two parts, a protein and a **coenzyme**. A coenzyme is a fairly complicated molecule, but much simpler than a protein. And it is the coenzyme that actually gets the job done. The protein part of the enzyme assures that the job is done on the right substrate.

The body can make coenzymes if it has the right building blocks. The building blocks must be furnished by the diet because the body can't make them. These building blocks are the **vitamins**. For example, vitamin B_2 (riboflavin) is changed into the coenzyme, flavin adenine dinucleotide, or simply FAD. Other vitamins are converted into other coenzymes. Now you can understand why vitamins are important in the diet.

▶ DIGESTION

Enzymes are made inside the cell. Most of them remain in the cell, where they catalyze the complicated cell reactions. A few of them, however, pass out of the cell to do their job. The digestive enzymes are **extracellular** (out-

side the cell) **enzymes**. Let's see how digestion works at the chemical level.

Suppose you have just had a ham sandwich. This sandwich contains protein and fat in the meat. It contains carbohydrate (starch) in the bread. An enzyme called **ptyalin** or **alpha-amylase** is present in your saliva. This enzyme begins to break down the starch chains. In the stomach the enzyme **pepsin** begins to work on the proteins, splitting the chains into shorter pieces. The finishing touches are carried out in the intestine. There still other enzymes finish the digesting. The protein chains are digested into amino acids. Starch is digested into glucose. Fats are converted to fatty acids and glycerol.

All of these are small molecules. They pass through the intestinal wall and are carried by the circulatory system to the various cells of the body. There they serve as fuel and building blocks for the cell engines. Without the digestive enzymes much of our food would remain as macromolecules. Since these are too big to pass through the intestinal wall, we would starve to death.

Unlike the digestive enzymes, most enzymes act inside the body's cells. There are enzymes that hook the glucose molecules together to form glycogen. There are enzymes that string the amino acids together again. The result is not proteins just like the ones in the meat but new proteins that are needed by the particular cell that is making them. Fatty acids and glycerol are combined again to make fat.

Now you can understand why proteins, carbohydrates, and fats are important in the diet. They are the raw materials. Digestion converts them to important building materials, such as sugars, amino acids, and fatty acids. As we shall see, they are also important fuels for the cell engines.

▶ MAKING PROTEINS

It is not too difficult to imagine how cells can make certain vital substances. Enzymes assist in much of the work. Enzymes in the cells can hook glucose units together to form glycogen. Enzymes in the cells can link fatty acids to glycerol to produce fat.

However, making a protein is much more complicated. (The process is called **protein biosynthesis**.) Even the simplest protein contains at least 30 amino acids in a chain. The more complicated proteins contain hundreds of amino acids. Furthermore, the amino acids must be arranged in just the right way if a protein is to carry out its particular job.

The problem of making proteins can best be understood through a comparison. Imagine you are told to make a string of beads representing a chain of amino acids. Each bead (amino acid) is numbered. You are told the string of beads must have a certain length and the numbers must run in a certain order. But you are not told what this length is or what the order of numbers is.

All the parts for solving the problem are set out (Fig. 1). The only information is given by the pattern. In the cell DNA is the pattern. This information is coded in units (nucleotides) of different shapes. There are six units, which means that the string of beads is to be six beads long.

Now the information of the DNA pattern must be decoded to find the order of the amino-acid beads in the chain. Of all the parts, only the shaded blocks (ribonucleotides) fit

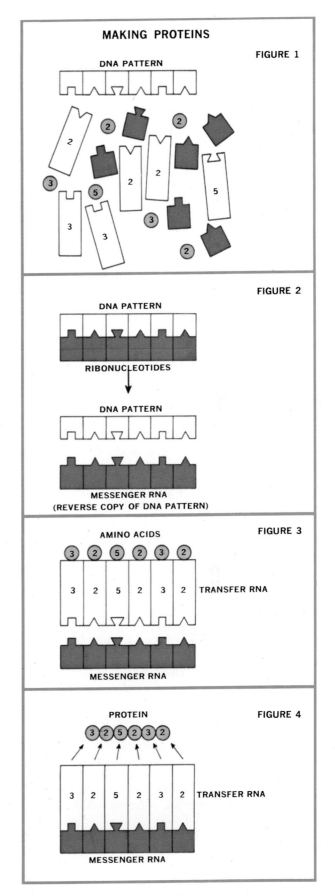

MAKING PROTEINS

FIGURE 1

DNA PATTERN

FIGURE 2

DNA PATTERN

RIBONUCLEOTIDES

DNA PATTERN

MESSENGER RNA
(REVERSE COPY OF DNA PATTERN)

FIGURE 3

AMINO ACIDS

TRANSFER RNA

MESSENGER RNA

FIGURE 4

PROTEIN

TRANSFER RNA

MESSENGER RNA

into the pattern. When the shaded blocks are joined together, the result is a copy of the pattern (Fig. 2). It is not the same as the pattern—everything is reversed. But it contains all the information that was in the pattern. In the cell this reversed copy is called **messenger RNA**.

This reversed copy is like a plaster cast taken of a head or a sculpture. When the proper material is poured into the cast, the original form can be reproduced.

The white blocks represent another kind of RNA, **transfer RNA**. The beads attached to them represent amino acids. There is a different transfer RNA for each different amino acid. When the transfer RNA and its amino acid fit into the messenger RNA copy (Fig. 3), the DNA pattern is reproduced and the order of amino acids is fixed (Fig. 4).

There are 20 kinds of amino acids. Then how does each kind of amino acid hook up with its own kind of transfer RNA and with no other? If a mistake should happen, the order of amino acids in the protein chain would be wrong. Suppose, for example, that a molecule of amino acid 2 becomes attached to a transfer RNA 3. As the protein chain is built, this amino acid will be fitted into a place where an amino acid 3 belongs.

Proteins called **activating enzymes** provide for the correct pairing of transfer RNA and amino acids. A specific activating enzyme links amino acid 2 with transfer RNA 2. Another enzyme does the same for the number 3 pair, and so on.

Arranging the amino acids in the correct order is only part of the problem, however. As you know, it takes work to make something. It requires mechanical work to build a house and electrical work to produce light. It takes chemical work to build proteins and the other compounds the body needs.

▶ FROM FOOD TO ENERGY

Work requires energy. The energy to do the body's work comes from the food we eat. Our food is mainly carbohydrate, fat, and protein. It took energy to make these food molecules. And energy is never really lost—it just appears in different forms. So we should be able to get energy back when our body breaks down these molecules.

Let's take a simple example and see how this energy cycle works. The sugar glucose contains 6 carbon atoms, 12 hydrogen atoms, and 6 oxygen atoms. Plants make glucose from carbon dioxide, water, and sunlight. The carbon dioxide provides the carbon atoms and some of the oxygen atoms. The water provides the hydrogen atoms and some of the oxygen atoms. The sunlight provides the energy that hooks these atoms together in a glucose molecule. (As it turns out, when the glucose molecule is finished, there is some oxygen left over. It becomes the oxygen in our air.)

We call this process **photosynthesis**. And we can summarize it as follows:

(plants)
carbon dioxide + water + energy → glucose + oxygen

If we reverse this process we should be able to produce energy:

(animals)
oxygen + glucose → energy + water + carbon dioxide

And that is exactly what people and animals do. Glucose is oxidized, or combined with oxygen, to give energy and waste products (water and carbon dioxide). This energy is used by the cells to make their macromolecules and to carry out their other work assignments, such as moving muscles.

This process of oxidation also occurs when we burn something. That's why a fire needs oxygen to burn. That's why you will often hear that the body "burns" its food to obtain energy. This "burning" is not exactly the same as a campfire, though. There are no tiny flames flickering inside the cell.

Furthermore, we build a fire to produce heat. We use this heat in many ways—to cook our food, to change water into steam that runs a steam engine, and so on. The body has no way to use heat to do work. It needs heat to keep the cells warm. But much of the heat produced by oxidation is a waste product because the body cannot use it directly.

If the body can't use heat to do work, how does it use its energy? The answer lies in a special molecule called **adenosine triphosphate** or **ATP**. ATP is a nucleotide. It is an RNA building block. But it is also able to trap the chemical energy released by oxidation and convert this energy into chemical work. ATP supplies the energy for building macromolecules. It also supplies the energy for muscle contraction, for nerve transmission, and so on.

THE ENERGY DYNAMO

Actually the cell is more like an electrical dynamo than a furnace. In a dynamo water flows over the turbine blades and turns the turbine. The turbine drives an electrical generator, which produces electricity. The electricity is used to produce light, run electric motors, and so on.

In the cell glucose is oxidized by a series of chemical reactions, which are like the turbine wheel. This chemical wheel turns another chemical wheel, which is like the electrical generator. This second wheel produces ATP, instead of electricity. The energy obtained from the ATP is used to do the cell's work.

So far we have talked only about the oxidation of glucose. But the other sugars are oxidized too. Except for the first few steps where preparation for oxidation occurs, all carbohydrates are oxidized by the same reactions. Fatty acids (from fats) and amino acids (from proteins) are oxidized inside the cell by the same energy dynamo.

Each different kind of food can furnish the cells with a definite amount of energy. Suppose you ate the same weight of each foodstuff in a meal. The fat would furnish one half the energy from that meal. The carbohydrate and protein would each furnish one fourth. In other words, fat can furnish about twice as much energy as the same amount of carbohydrate or protein.

As you remember, energy is never lost. What happens if you take in more potential energy in your food than your body can use up? The answer is simple. The body stores the extra food. The body can only store a certain amount of this food as carbohydrate and protein. The rest is stored as fat. It doesn't make any difference what this extra food is. Extra carbohydrate and protein can be converted to fat.

Clearly, if you eat more than your body needs, you will get fat. If you eat less than your body needs, it must draw upon its energy stores. The fat will be broken down to supply energy, and you will lose weight. When the carbohydrate and fat supplies are low, protein will be used to produce energy. If this break-down of vital proteins continues for very long, a person will die.

CONTROLLING THE CELL ENGINE

When you run a race your muscles work hard. They need a big supply of fuel quickly. Your liver goes to work almost instantly changing glycogen, a carbohydrate that it normally stores, into glucose. The glucose enters the bloodstream, and in seconds it reaches the straining muscles. What controls this process? How does the liver know when to supply glucose for the muscles? Two systems control the work of the body tissues: the **nervous system**, and the **endocrine system**.

The nervous system provides a rapid response to an emergency situation. You know how fast you pull your hand away when you accidentally touch a hot stove. Your nervous system has told your muscles what to do.

The endocrine system acts less quickly, but for a longer time. The eight different glands that make up this system produce special chemicals called **hormones**. These are given off directly into the bloodstream, which carries them throughout the body. Each hormone acts on a particular organ to speed up or slow down its work. For example, the adrenal glands produce epinephrine (adrenaline). This hormone stimulates the liver to change glycogen into glucose. The hormones of the endocrine system act collectively to regulate the body's very complicated chemistry, producing a smoothly running machine.

SUMMARY

As you can see, the body is a complicated chemical machine. Simple chemicals are built into complicated macromolecules. Some macromolecules are woven into various structures that form the cell. Inside the cell hundreds of chemical reactions are going on and these reactions are catalyzed by other macromolecules, the enzymes. The chemical reactions provide the energy to make new cells and to carry out the functions of the body—moving muscles, thinking, and so on. Each cell is an independent unit, but it co-operates with other cells to make the body machine run smoothly and efficiently.

ROBERT WARNER CHAMBERS
New York University School of Medicine
See also BIOCHEMISTRY; CELLS.

BODY SIGNALS

Your body is smart. It knows how to take care of many problems. You do not even have to think about them; your body just acts.

Yawns

No one knows what causes yawns. You yawn when you are tired and when you are bored. Sometimes you yawn just because someone nearby has yawned. Even reading about a yawn can make you yawn. When you exercise, you do not yawn, and you never yawn when you are angry or excited. Probably some yawns are caused by your body's need for extra oxygen. A big yawn brings extra oxygen into your body. However, the need for oxygen does not explain why yawns are contagious.

Snores

People who snore breathe through their mouths when they sleep. Snores occur when soft parts of the mouth and throat wiggle and flop as air goes in and out. Many people snore only when they are lying on their backs.

Blushing

There are more tiny blood vessels, or capillaries, in the skin of your face than anywhere else on your body. When you are embarrassed or angry or overheated, your body sends a message to the blood vessels in your skin to expand, or become larger. When the capillaries expand, more blood flows through them, and your skin looks red. "You're blushing!"

Coughs and Sneezes

Coughs and sneezes are your body's way of reacting to something that is bothering your throat or your nose. When something irritates your throat or when a piece of food goes down your windpipe, you cough to force it out. When you have an itch or irritation in your nose, you sneeze.

Coughs and sneezes are very similar: you take in a big breath, muscles in your chest and abdomen tighten up, your throat closes, and air bursts out. In a cough, the vocal cords close tight, and the exploding sound is the air blasting its way through the vocal cords and out of the mouth. In a sneeze, the air is expelled through your nose as well as your mouth.

Sometimes you keep coughing or sneezing, because the irritation does not go away. That is why you cough and sneeze a lot if you have a cold. During a sneeze, tiny germ particles are forced from the nose at great speeds. This is one of the main ways that colds are spread from one person to another.

Hiccups

You get hiccups when something unusual happens to your diaphragm (the muscle at the bottom of your chest that helps you breathe). When you breathe out, your diaphragm relaxes and bulges up into your chest. That helps push air out of your lungs. When you breathe in, the diaphragm tightens and flattens out. This makes a bigger space in your chest, and air rushes in.

Your diaphragm usually has a regular rhythm of relaxing and tightening. But every so often the diaphragm suddenly jerks itself tight. That sudden jerk is called a spasm.

When your diaphragm is tight, air usually goes into your lungs. But when the diaphragm spasms, a tiny flap at the back of your throat, called the epiglottis, covers up the opening of your windpipe and prevents the air from going down. The "hic" is the sound you make when the air hits the epiglottis. After a "hic" the diaphragm goes back to normal. Then the spasm may happen again.

No one knows what causes the spasms. Sometimes they happen after a scare, or from laughing very hard, or from swallowing food too fast. Hiccups usually just stop after a while, but people have invented many unusual ways to try to cure them.

Burps

Burping is the body's way of getting rid of too much air or gas in the stomach. You swallow air with everything you eat and drink. When you chew food, you mix air with it. When you drink a glass of water, you swallow air. Soda, popcorn, and toast are filled with air. Apples and oranges have gases trapped in them that are set free by the acids in your stomach.

As your stomach digests the food you swallow, the trapped air and gases rise as bubbles and pop, just like the bubbles in soda. As more and more bubbles pop, more and more air presses against the sides of your stomach. Finally the gas pushes up into your esophagus and bursts out your mouth as a burp. The scientific word for burping is eructation.

Stomach Growls

Stomach growls can happen anytime, not only when you are hungry. Usually it is not even your stomach that is growling at all; it is your intestines. When your stomach finishes mashing and grinding your food, it pushes the food into your intestines where muscles then move the food along. It is this squeezing of the liquid food out of your stomach and through the twisted narrow intestines that causes stomach growls.

Gas

Everything you swallow moves into your digestive tract. Your digestive tract is a very long tube that has two openings. One opening is at your mouth; the other is at your anus, through which you expel solid waste and gas. All the air you swallow with your meal goes right to your stomach. The swallowed air that is not burped out goes on from the stomach into your intestines. Other gases are added to this air when millions of bacteria that live in the intestines attack the food.

When air, or gas, comes to the end of the digestive tract, it is held there by a muscle that keeps the exit tightly closed. The muscle is called the anal sphincter. Sometimes a lot of air gets to the anal sphincter and puts so much pressure on it that you cannot hold the muscle tight. The gas just pushes out. Other times you can keep your sphincter tight so the gas will not come out at an embarrassing time. Still other times, you can relax your anal sphincter and push out the gas when you want to.

Goose Bumps

Sometimes you feel chilly or are frightened by something, and you get little bumps all over your body. Those are called goose bumps, or gooseflesh.

If you look closely at the goose bumps, you will see a hair coming out of each one. Each hair on your body sits in a tiny pocket in your skin (called a follicle) with a little muscle attached to it. Usually those muscles are relaxed and let the hairs lie flat on your skin. But when you are cold or frightened, the muscles tighten. That makes the hairs stand up and the skin bunch up into little bumps.

Scientists think that many years ago, people's bodies were covered with lots of thick hair. When all those hairs stood up, warm air from the body was trapped by the hairs and kept the body warm. That thick hair is not there any more, but the muscles still are. And they still pull on the tiny pockets, making hairs stand up and causing goose bumps.

SUSAN KOVACS BUXBAUM
Coauthor, *Body Noises*

BOEING, WILLIAM EDWARD. See WASHINGTON (Famous People).

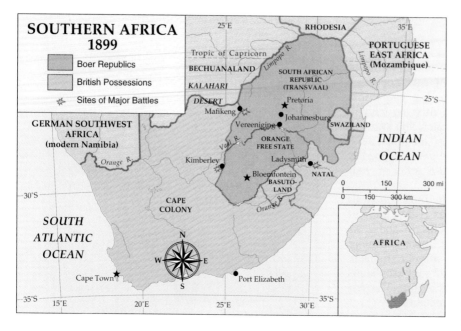

SOUTHERN AFRICA 1899

Boer Republics
British Possessions
Sites of Major Battles

GERMAN SOUTHWEST AFRICA (modern Namibia)

SOUTH ATLANTIC OCEAN

RHODESIA

Tropic of Capricorn

BECHUANALAND

KALAHARI

DESERT

PORTUGUESE EAST AFRICA (Mozambique)

SOUTH AFRICAN REPUBLIC (TRANSVAAL)

Mafikeng

Pretoria

Johannesburg

Vereeniging

SWAZILAND

ORANGE FREE STATE

Kimberley

Ladysmith

Bloemfontein

BASUTOLAND

NATAL

CAPE COLONY

Cape Town

Port Elizabeth

INDIAN OCEAN

AFRICA

Limpopo R.

Vaal R.

Orange R.

BOER WAR

The Boer War—also known as the South African War—took place between 1899 and 1902. It was actually the second of two wars fought between Great Britain, then the world's leading power, and two small African countries—the Orange Free State and the South African Republic (Transvaal).

Background. In the 1600's the southern tip of Africa was settled by employees of the Dutch East India Company. In 1814, following the Napoleonic Wars in Europe, Great Britain acquired the territory from the Netherlands and called it Cape Colony. Not wishing to live under British rule, some of the Dutch descendants, then known as Boers (from the Dutch word for "farmers"), moved northward, settling in Natal, the Transvaal, and the Orange Free State. In 1853, without giving up its sovereignty, Great Britain recognized the independence of the Transvaal, which the Boers then called the South African Republic. The Orange Free State was declared independent the following year.

The First Boer War (1880–81). Diamonds were discovered near Kimberley in 1871, leading Britain to annex the western portion of the Orange Free State. Then in 1877, Britain formally annexed the Transvaal. The Boers revolted and defeated the British in the First Boer War (1880–81). They regained their independence, but their republics remained British sovereign lands.

The Discovery of Gold. The discovery of gold in the Transvaal in 1886 attracted many immigrants, most of them British. Hostility between the British and the Boers increased as the British began to outnumber the Boers.

To assert control, the Boers passed restrictive measures against the newcomers, including refusing them the right to vote. But the British government insisted that the new settlers be granted full political rights.

In 1895 a band of British colonists tried to overthrow the government of the South African Republic. This action convinced the Boers that the British meant to take control of their territory. The two Boer republics formed a military alliance and mobilized their forces. The British sent troops to the border areas. When the British refused to withdraw, the Boers declared war on October 12, 1899.

The Second Boer War (1899–1902). The Boers were not professional soldiers, but their knowledge of the land aided them against the slow-moving British troops. Early in the war the Boers defeated the British in several battles. The British government was embarrassed by the defeats and stung by criticism of the war at home and abroad. It sent more troops and new generals to Africa. By 1900 the superior British force succeeded in capturing the capitals of both Boer republics. But the Boers refused to surrender, and they waged a guerrilla war for over a year. The British retaliated by burning Boer farms and putting Boer families in detention camps.

The Outcome. Finally, on May 31, 1902, the Boers signed a peace treaty at Vereeniging, and the two republics became British colonies. In 1910 they became part of the Union (now the Republic) of South Africa.

Reviewed by JOHN E. FLINT
Dalhousie University

See also SOUTH AFRICA.

BOGART, HUMPHREY. See MOTION PICTURES (Profiles: Movie Stars).

BOGOTÁ

Bogotá is the capital of Colombia and its largest and most important city. Located in central Colombia, on a wide plateau high in the Andes mountains, Bogotá is a city of contrasts, with skyscrapers perched next to historic buildings.

The city, which is more than 8,600 feet (2,600 meters) above sea level, is surrounded by mountains on three sides. For centuries, Bogotá was isolated by these high ranges. Formerly it took eight days to reach the city from the Atlantic coast. Now the trip can be made in one hour by airplane.

Bogotá usually bustles with activity. In the downtown sector, the main commercial district, the narrow streets are crowded with people and cars. Children walk or ride donkeys through traffic. Everywhere there are vendors and *campesinos* (farm laborers), who come to the city looking for work. Well-dressed business people and shoppers stroll by or stop at one of the many coffeehouses.

The people of Bogotá are of European, Indian, and mixed ancestry. The city's rapid growth to a population of about 6 million has

Bogotá, Colombia's capital and largest city, is located high in the Andes. Visitors enjoy a spectacular view of the city from atop the nearby mountain of Monserrate.

caused a housing shortage. Many new apartment houses are being built. But the slums have grown enormously, and unemployment is a problem.

Bogotá's factories process agricultural and dairy products from nearby farmlands and manufacture furniture, household appliances, construction materials, textiles, and chemicals. The city is a world center for emeralds, which are mined north of Bogotá.

Places of Interest. Bogotá has fine restaurants, hotels, and theaters. Concerts and plays are performed in the richly decorated Colon Theater, in the older part of the city. It faces the Palace of San Carlos, where the president of Colombia lived. The city is also home to several universities, including the National University of Colombia, founded in the late 1500's. Among the art galleries and museums, the National Museum and the Colonial Museum are known for collections of colonial art. The Gold Museum houses magnificent gold objects made by Indians before the country was conquered by the Spanish.

History. Bogotá was founded in 1538 by the Spanish conquistador (conqueror) Gonzalo Jiménez de Quesada. It became the capital of New Granada, which was a center of the Spanish empire in South America. The city was liberated from Spanish rule in 1819, and in 1821 it was named the capital of Gran (Greater) Colombia. This federation, which included the present-day nations of Colombia, Panama, Venezuela, and Ecuador, fell apart by 1830. Bogotá then became the capital of the Republic of New Granada, which was later renamed the Republic of Colombia.

ARLENE GOULD
Former correspondent, *Life en Español*
Reviewed by THOMAS E. SKIDMORE
Brown University

BOGS. See WETLANDS.

BOHR, NIELS (1885–1962)

Early in the 1900's a young Danish physicist named Niels Bohr began to study the atom. His studies turned out to be both his life's work and extremely important. First he gave science a new view of the atom's structure. Some years later he helped to release the energy of the atom. Still later he worked to control that energy for peaceful uses.

Niels Bohr was born on October 7, 1885, in Copenhagen, Denmark. His father was a scientist and professor at the university there, and Niels was raised in a home where science was naturally of interest. In 1903 he entered the University of Copenhagen. His chief concern was physics, but he was also an outstanding soccer player. By 1907 Niels had won a gold medal from the Royal Danish Academy for his scientific work.

After receiving his doctor's degree in 1911, Bohr wanted to learn more about the atom. He decided to go to England and study with J. J. Thomson and Ernest Rutherford. Both these men were leaders in atomic physics. Bohr first studied under Thomson at Cambridge University; a year later he worked with Rutherford at the University of Manchester. In 1913 Bohr returned to the University of Copenhagen as a lecturer.

It was during this year that Bohr made his first great contribution to atomic physics. By that time many scientists had attempted to explain the atom. Rutherford, for example, had provided one theory. The great German physicist Max Planck had another.

Working from the ideas of Rutherford and of Planck, Bohr set forth a new theory of his own. It dealt with atomic structure and behavior. Bohr's theory became the basis of the branch of modern physics known as quantum mechanics. For his brilliant work, Bohr received the Nobel Prize for physics in 1922.

Bohr continued teaching at the University of Copenhagen, and in 1920 he became director of the university's new Institute of Theoretical Physics. He made the institute into one of the world's major research centers. Scientists came from all over the world to study with Bohr. He was sometimes so busy with his work that he forgot about his meals. But he always managed to make time for his wife and five sons.

About 1930 the institute began important studies of the nucleus of the atom. In 1936 Bohr made another major advance in atomic physics: he gave the first correct description of a nuclear reaction. This work later helped the United States develop the atomic bomb.

Bohr arrived in the United States in 1939 to work at the Institute for Advanced Study in Princeton, New Jersey. Some of the world's leading scientists were there, including Albert Einstein. Bohr told them of the work going on in Europe in splitting uranium atoms. His reports spurred the United States to conduct research in this field.

Bohr returned to Copenhagen a few months after World War II broke out. In 1940 the Germans conquered Denmark. Bohr refused to cooperate with them and closed his institute. In 1943, when he was threatened with arrest, Bohr fled. He went first to Sweden and then to the United States.

Bohr served as adviser at the first atomic bomb laboratory, near Los Alamos, New Mexico. He soon began to worry about the far-reaching effects of the new bomb. After the first atomic bomb test, in 1945, Bohr went to Washington to plead for immediate international control of atomic weapons.

When the war ended in 1945, Bohr returned to work at his institute in Copenhagen and periodically spoke out on important nuclear issues. In 1955 he became chairman of the newly founded Danish Atomic Energy Commission. Two years later Bohr received the first Atoms for Peace award—a fitting climax to his life. Bohr died November 18, 1962.

JOHN S. BOWMAN
Author and Science Editor

BOILING POINT. See LIQUIDS.
BOISE. See IDAHO (Cities).
BOITANO, BRIAN. See ICE-SKATING (Profiles).

Niels Bohr helped form the modern theory of atomic structure. He later was an adviser on the atomic bomb.

BOLÍVAR, SIMÓN (1783–1830)

For nearly 300 years most of South America was under Spanish rule. Simón Bolívar vowed to free his native land, Venezuela, from Spain. When he died in 1830, he had freed not only Venezuela, but Ecuador, Bolivia, and Colombia as well.

Bolívar was born at Caracas, Venezuela, on July 24, 1783. His ancestors in Spain had belonged to the nobility, and young Bolívar was educated as an aristocrat. When he was 16, Bolívar was sent to Spain to continue his education. For the next seven years he studied and traveled in Europe. The example of the American and French revolutions stirred Bolívar deeply. He swore that he would not rest until he had broken the chains that bound his country to Spain.

In Venezuela a group of patriots, including Bolívar and Francisco Miranda, seized Caracas. On July 5, 1811, they declared Venezuela's independence. But the patriots were crushed by Spanish troops. Miranda died in prison and Bolívar fled from Venezuela.

Years of bloody fighting and heartbreaking defeat followed. Twice again Bolívar was forced to flee into exile. But his stern face and dark, piercing eyes showed a determination to win independence at all costs. In 1819 he boldly marched his patriot army over the snow-covered Andes mountains. It was winter, and in that terrible march many men and all the horses perished. But Bolívar surprised the Spanish Army and defeated it completely at Boyacá, in Colombia. The victory brought independence to Colombia. Two years later, Bolívar liberated Venezuela. And the following year, Ecuador was freed.

Venezuela, Colombia, and Ecuador were united into the republic of Gran Colombia, with Bolívar as its president.

Meanwhile, General José de San Martín, the liberator of Argentina, with Bernardo O'Higgins of Chile, had proclaimed the independence of Peru. Bolívar met with San Martín at Guayaquíl. San Martín generously gave Bolívar command of his army to complete the liberation of Peru. The next year Upper Peru was renamed Bolivia in honor of its liberator.

Bolívar soon had all the powers of a dictator, though his ideals were freedom and jus-

Simón Bolívar led his troops over the Andes mountains in 1819, surprising the Spanish Army. His victories led to the liberation of Colombia, Venezuela, and Ecuador.

tice. He encouraged the creation of constitutional government and urged that more schools and universities be built. There were slaves in South America. Bolívar had freed his, and he insisted that other slave owners do the same.

Bolívar's dream had been to see all the liberated countries united. However, each country wanted its independence. New revolutions broke out and Gran Colombia fell apart. Bolívar's enemies accused him of being a tyrant, and an attempt was made to kill him.

In 1830, weary and ill after years of war and revolution, Bolívar resigned as president of Colombia. On December 17, 1830, he died at the age of 47.

Bolívar's dream of a united South America was a failure. He died a disappointed man, with few friends and many enemies. But to the people of South America he is still *El Libertador*—the liberator.

Reviewed by ERNESTO SÁBATO
Author, *The Graves and the Heroes*

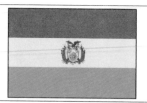

BOLIVIA

Bolivia lies in the heart of South America. Dominated by the great snowcapped peaks of the Andes mountains, it is one of the highest countries in the world. In fact, it is sometimes called the Tibet of South America. The city of La Paz, one of the country's two capitals, is about 3,600 meters (12,000 feet) above sea level. It is the world's highest capital city.

▶THE PEOPLE

Most of the people of Bolivia live in the snowcapped Andes in the western part of the country. Only about one quarter of the people make their home in the east, where the land slopes away into tangled tropical jungles and hot, dry plains.

Bolivia is the most Indian of the South American nations. More than one half of the people are Quechua and Aymará Indians. People of mixed Spanish and Indian descent, or Mestizos, make up one quarter of the population. Only a small fraction of the people call themselves whites. These are mostly descendants of Spanish settlers.

The Indian Way of Life

The Aymará Indians trace their ancestry back more than 1,000 years, to a great Indian civilization that grew up on the banks of Lake Titicaca. Today most Aymará live in the mountain area around Lake Titicaca. They work as farmers, shepherds, and miners.

Bolivia's other major Indian group, the Quechua, are descended from the Inca invaders who came to Bolivia in the 13th century A.D. The Quechua live mostly in the highlands and the deep valleys of the eastern Andes. Like the Aymará, the Quechua have their own language.

The life of the Bolivian Indian is generally harsh and monotonous. Families live in one-room houses of stone or baked mud brick called adobe. Windows are often just slits in the walls. Most Indians are farmers. The government has made many of them owners of their own land; but the life of the Indians is still hard. If they are fortunate, they may have oxen to draw their wooden plows across the fields. After the seed is sown, the children often follow behind to cover the furrows with earth.

The children also tend the herds of llamas and alpacas. These long-necked animals are related to the camel and are found only in the Andes. The Indians use them as pack animals and for their meat and fur.

The foods most commonly eaten are potatoes, corn, and beans. A basic food is *chuño*. It looks like popcorn, but it is really a potato that has been preserved by drying and freezing so that it can be stored for many months.

The life of the Indians who work in Bo-

FACTS AND FIGURES

REPUBLIC OF BOLIVIA (República de Bolivia) is the official name of the country.

THE PEOPLE are known as Bolivians.

LOCATION: West central South America.

AREA: 1,098,581 km² (424,165 sq mi).

POPULATION: 6,000,000 (estimate).

CAPITAL: La Paz (actual), Sucre (legal).

LARGEST CITY: La Paz.

MAJOR LANGUAGES: Spanish, Quechua, Aymará.

MAJOR RELIGION: Roman Catholic.

GOVERNMENT: Republic. **Head of state and government**—president. **Legislature**—Congress (composed of a Senate and a Chamber of Deputies).

CHIEF PRODUCTS: Agricultural—potatoes, corn, beans, wheat, barley, sugarcane, cotton, cacao, coca, coffee, alfalfa, oats, livestock. **Manufactured**—textiles, refined sugar, processed food, lumber. **Mineral**—tin, petroleum, natural gas, zinc, tungsten, silver, antimony, iron ore, copper.

MONETARY UNIT: Bolivian peso (1 peso = 100 centavos).

NATIONAL ANTHEM: *Bolivianos, el hado propicio coronó nuestros votos y anhelo* ("Bolivians, propitious fate has crowned our hopes").

livia's mines is a little better than that of the farmers. Miners live in houses built by the mining companies. They can also shop in special stores that sell low-priced goods. But the miners' work is very dangerous, especially in the tin mines that are at altitudes of 3,600 to 5,500 meters (12,000 to 18,000 feet). They are given a daily ration of coca, which is very important to them. Chewing the leaves of this tea-like plant relieves hunger. In 1952 the mines were nationalized, as the first step toward economic and social reforms for the miners.

Feasts and Fairs. The gayest days in the life of Bolivians are holidays and fairs. They delight in the Alacitas Fair, which is held in La Paz each January. The fair is held in honor of the Aymará god of abundance, Ekeko. Ekeko is a cheerful fellow. He looks a little bit like Santa Claus without a beard. Ekeko carries miniatures of all the things people may want or need: tiny sacks of rice and sugar, a miniature sheep or cow, a house, an automobile, a suit of clothes. According to legend, if a person buys one of Ekeko's miniatures, he will get its life-sized equivalent during the coming year.

Spanish missionaries long ago converted the Indians to Catholicism. But many ancient Indian festivals are still mixed with Christian rituals. For example, at carnival time in Oruro dancers perform the Diablada, or Devil Dance. The dance is dedicated to the Virgin of the Mines. The dance is the miners' way of asking the Virgin's protection against the devil, whom they fear meeting deep in the dark mines.

Religion. The majority of Bolivians are Roman Catholic. Catholicism is recognized as the state religion, but members of all religious groups may worship freely.

Language. Spanish is the official language of Bolivia, and most educated people in Bolivia speak it. Bolivia's Indians are taught Spanish in school. At home they may speak the language of their group, be it Aymará or Quechua.

Education. All children between the ages of 6 and 14 are supposed to go to school. But many Bolivian boys and girls are so busy helping their families that it is not always possible for them to attend school. There may not even be a school nearby. Many Indian

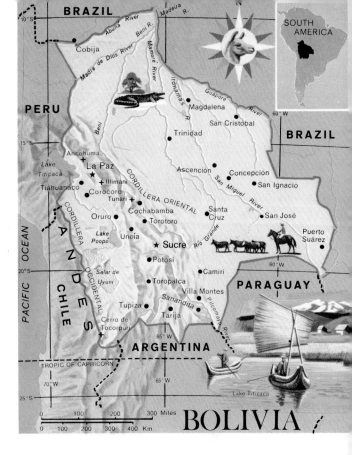

BOLIVIA

children drop their studies after a year or two. Only a few go on to universities. The government is working to increase the number of people who are able to read and write.

In Bolivia's cities many more children are able to attend school. Some schools are modern, especially the private and parochial schools. Boys and girls usually go to separate schools. In addition, there are universities in leading Bolivian cities such as Oruro, Potosí, Cochabamba, and La Paz. San Francisco Xavier University at Sucre was founded in 1624 and is one of the oldest universities in the Western Hemisphere.

▶THE LAND

Bolivia has three major land regions. They are the Andes, the Altiplano, and the lowlands.

The Andes are widest in Bolivia, stretching as much as 640 kilometers (400 miles) across at their widest point. The Bolivian Andes are divided into two main ranges, or cordilleras. The Cordillera Occidental, or Western Range, forms Bolivia's border with Chile. It is the barrier that cuts Bolivia off from the Pacific Ocean. Bolivia's highest mountain, Anco-

Balsas, small boats made of reeds, on Lake Titicaca.

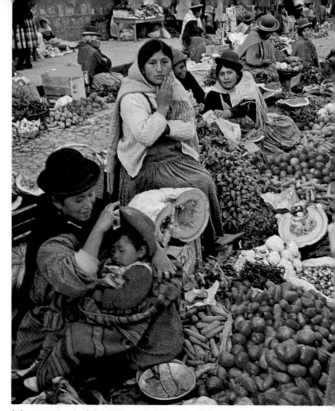

A busy and colorful outdoor market in La Paz.

huma, rises in the Cordillera Oriental, or Eastern Range. Deep valleys called *yungas* have been cut by rushing rivers in the slopes of the Eastern Range. The mild climate of these deep valleys makes them good farming areas.

The Altiplano is the high, bleak, cold, and almost treeless plateau between the mountain ranges. Its average elevation is almost 3 kilometers (2 miles) above sea level. Three out of four Bolivians live in this region, many in La Paz and smaller towns.

The lowlands of Bolivia are entirely different from the highland zone, and much larger. The climate throughout this region is hotter. The northern lowlands are heavily forested. Close to the border of Brazil the jungle grows dense and the rivers are a home for giant crocodiles. The southern lowlands are drier than those in the north. Instead of jungles there are great plains where wild cattle roam. Near the Argentine border there are important oil reserves owned by the Bolivian Government.

Lakes and Rivers. Lake Titicaca, at the northern edge of the Altiplano, is the highest navigated body of water in the world. It lies 3,810 meters (12,500 feet) above sea level, on the border with Peru. Small native boats called *balsas* are used for fishing in the lake. Lake Titicaca drains into Lake Poopó, farther south. There is no drainage from Lake Poopó.

The water evaporates, leaving the lake very salty. Great salt flats dot the lonesome landscape south of the lake.

The Beni River and its tributaries drain the northern *yungas*. They flow north to join the Madeira River in Brazil and finally the great Amazon River. The southern *yungas* are drained by the Pilcomayo River and its tributaries. They are part of a river system that flows southeast to join the Paraguay River and the Río de la Plata in Argentina.

Climate. Because of Bolivia's altitude, there are great differences in temperature between day and night. The average annual temperature at La Paz, on the Altiplano, is only 8°C (47°F). At Trinidad, a city in the lowlands of eastern Bolivia, the average temperature is around 21°C (70°F). In Bolivia there is little difference in temperature between summer and winter. Wet and dry seasons are more important. The dry season lasts from May to November. Between December and February there are heavy rains on the Altiplano and drenching tropical storms in the lowlands.

Natural Resources. Bolivia has been described as "a beggar on a throne of gold." The country's mountainous terrain and its turbulent history have kept Bolivia from making full use of its great natural resources.

The little wealth Bolivia has enjoyed has come from the mines on or near the Altiplano. The Cerro Rico ("rich hill") of Potosí is a mountain that is almost a solid mass of tin, silver, tungsten, and other ores. Zinc, antimony, gold, iron, bismuth, sulfur, and asbestos are also mined in Bolivia. And at Corocoro there is one of the world's rare surface deposits of natural copper. Another increasingly important Bolivian resource is oil, which is found mainly in southern Bolivia.

Timber is one of Bolivia's most valuable and least-exploited resources. Timber covers nearly 40 percent of the land. The most valuable trees—mahogany, jacaranda, rosewood, balsa, and cedar—grow on the eastern slopes of the Cordillera Real.

▶ THE ECONOMY

Agriculture. The leading Bolivian occupation is agriculture. About one half of Bolivia's farms are on the Altiplano. But the crops have been poor because of the high altitude, the lack of rain, and the primitive methods of cultivation. However, potatoes, barley, a grain called quinoa, broad beans, wheat, and alfalfa are grown. Coca, coffee, cacao, and bananas are grown in the *yungas*. From the fertile valleys around Cochabamba, Tarija, and Sucre come corn, wheat, barley, vegetables, alfalfa, and oats. Only a very small portion of the lowlands east of Santa Cruz de la Sierra are under cultivation. Rice, sugar, cotton, corn, yucca, oil plants, and fruit are grown there. Cattle and hogs are raised in the lowlands.

Industry. Large-scale industries, except for mining, are as yet unknown in Bolivia. The chief source of Bolivia's industrial wealth comes now, as it has for centuries, from mining. Tin is mined in larger amounts than any other mineral, and Bolivia has long been one of the leading exporters of tin in the world. Petroleum and petroleum products are of growing importance to the economy.

Transportation and Communication. Bolivia's future as a united and strong country depends to a large degree on its success in improving its transportation network. At present Bolivia must import a great deal of food and lumber because these products cannot be transported cheaply from the lowlands to the cities of the Altiplano. The hardwood trees of the northern forests die of old age while Bolivia imports lumber because there is no road from the forests. Airplanes sometimes fly beef from the city of Trinidad to La Paz —the only way to get the meat to market.

Most of the communications system in Bolivia is privately owned. There is telephone service in the major cities, but more than half the total number of phones are in the city of

The ancient Indian ruins of Tiahuanaco are among the most important archeological sites in South America.

La Paz, Bolivia's largest city, is one of the highest cities in the world.

La Paz. There are many radio stations and a government-operated television network.

▶MAJOR CITIES

Bolivia's two capitals are Sucre and La Paz. Sucre is the legal capital and the site of the Supreme Court. La Paz is the administrative capital and the seat of government. It is the country's largest city and the center of its commerce and culture. Sucre, founded by the Spanish in 1538, was known by several names. It received its present name, after Bolivia's first president, in 1839. La Paz was founded by the Spanish in 1548 on the site of an Indian village. Other major cities include Santa Cruz, the second largest in population; Cochabamba; Ouro; and Potosí.

▶HISTORY AND GOVERNMENT

Early History and Spanish Rule. The magnificent carved stone Gate of the Sun, ruined temples, and a few ancient roads are all that remains of Tiahuanaco, a great Indian civilization that once flourished on the banks of Lake Titicaca. From about A.D. 600 to 900 the Indians of this region reigned supreme. Then mysteriously their civilization vanished. By the year 1300 the powerful Incas of Peru ruled the region. The Inca Empire in turn was conquered by the Spanish in the 1500's. Spain ruled the area for nearly 300 years, exploiting what were then the rich silver mines at Potosí.

Independence. Harsh Spanish rule had led to a number of uprisings in the 1600's and 1700's, but the most important movement toward Bolivian independence began in 1809. It was inspired by Simón Bolívar's liberation of the northern part of the continent from Spain. It was not until 1824, however, that Antonio José de Sucre, one of Bolívar's lieutenants, completely broke Spanish power in this region. The new nation declared its independence on August 6, 1825. It was named Bolívar in honor of the Liberator. Later the spelling was changed to its present form.

Bolivia's first president was General Sucre. He was followed in office by General Andrés Santa Cruz, who tried but failed to bring about a permanent union between Peru and Bolivia. The next half century of Bolivian history is scarred by a succession of military dictatorships.

The most terrible of these dictators was Mariano Melgarejo, who came to power in 1864. He was illiterate, cruel, dishonest, and tyrannical. During the years of his rule Melgarejo sold and leased national territory to neighboring countries. In later years, wars cost Bolivia much of her original territory.

The first 50 years of the 20th century in Bolivia were marked by some advances in industry and transportation. But since the Bolivian economy depended so much on the world demand for tin, events far from Bolivia shaped the course of Bolivian life. During the depression of the 1930's, when the tin demand was slight, Bolivians suffered. World War II brought a rise in the price of tin and some improvement in the Bolivian economy. But at the end of the war, tin prices dropped, and Bolivia was once again in crisis.

Recent History. A revolution in 1952 brought the National Revolutionary Movement (MNR) to power. Victor Paz Estenssoro, an MNR leader, served as president from 1952 to 1956 and from 1960 to 1964. He nationalized (brought under government control) the country's tin mines, began a program of land reform, and extended the right to vote to all adult Bolivians. Paz Estenssoro was overthrown in a military coup in 1964. General René Barrientos Ortuño, who as vice president had led the coup, was elected president in 1966. His death in an accident in 1969 led to a period of political instability as Bolivia alternated between military and civilian rule. From 1971 to 1978 the presidency was held by General Hugo Banzer Suárez. A civilian, Hernán Siles Zuazo, became president in 1982.

Siles resigned in 1985 because of protests against his policies. The winner in new elections was Victor Paz Estenssoro, who thus returned as president after more than 20 years. He was succeeded by Jaime Paz Zamora, who took office in 1989. Gonzalo Sánchez de Lozado was elected president in 1993. No candidate won a majority in the 1997 election, so Congress elected a president, Hugo Banzer Suárez, as called for in the constitution.

Bolivia's government is headed by a president and vice president, who are elected to 4-year terms. Presidents cannot serve two consecutive terms. The legislature is the Congress. It consists of two houses, the Senate and the Chamber of Deputies. Members of each house are elected to 4-year terms.

J. DAVID BOWEN
Author, *Hello, South America*

BOMBAY (MUMBAI)

Bombay, with a population of nearly 10 million, is the largest metropolis in India. Renamed Mumbai in 1995, it is the capital of the state of Maharashtra as well as the major port and industrial center on the west coast of India.

The main part of the city is built on Bombay Island. Greater Bombay, a metropolitan municipal organization that includes Bombay Island, Trombay Island, and part of Salsette Island, was created in 1957. More than 15 million people live in Greater Bombay and its mainland suburbs. A satellite city called

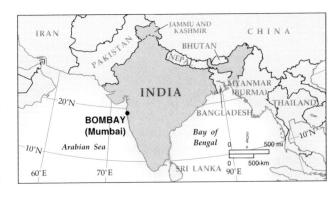

New Bombay is being built to ease the overcrowding.

Bombay is considered India's most sophisticated and culturally varied city. The majority of the inhabitants are followers of the Hindu religion, but the population includes Muslims, Christians, Jains, Zoroastrians, Jews, and Sikhs. The two major languages are Marathi and Gujarati, although more than fifty different languages are spoken.

The City. At the southwestern end of Bombay Island, the coast is indented. It forms a shallow body of water known as Back Bay, which opens into the Arabian Sea. To the west of the bay is a high ridge known as Mal-

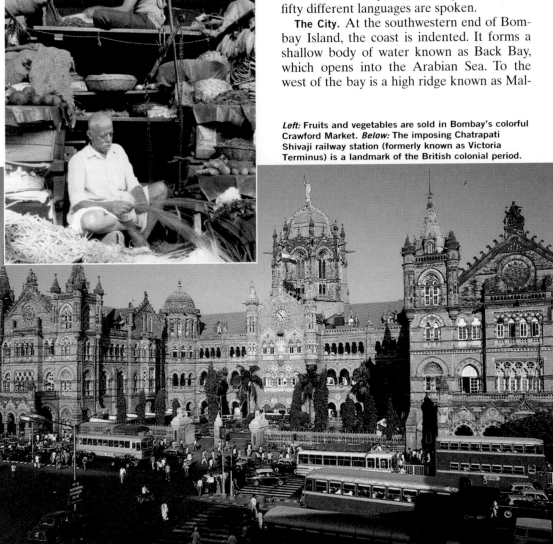

Left: Fruits and vegetables are sold in Bombay's colorful Crawford Market. *Below:* The imposing Chatrapati Shivaji railway station (formerly known as Victoria Terminus) is a landmark of the British colonial period.

abar Hill, where many expensive homes have been built. The Hanging Gardens and Kamala Nehru Park, featuring a giant Mother Hubbard shoe, are also in the Malabar Hill area. The summit of the hill offers a superb view of the city. At night thousands of lights form a sparkling outline of Marine Drive, which runs along the northeastern edge of Back Bay. Marine Drive has rows of modern apartments on one side. On its other side are lovely palms and a wide promenade facing the bay.

At the entrance to the harbor is the Gateway of India, the most familiar landmark of the city. This magnificent stone arch was built in 1911 in honor of King George V and

Modern apartment houses line Marine Drive along the shoreline of Back Bay, an inlet of the Arabian Sea.

Queen Mary of England. Elephanta Island in the harbor is the site of seven magnificent Hindu cave temples built in the 700's. Other special attractions in Bombay include the Prince of Wales Museum, the Jehangir Art Gallery, the National Art Gallery, and many religious temples and shrines. Kanheri National Park, on Salsette Island, contains more than one hundred ancient Buddhist temple caves. Additional places of interest include Victoria Gardens, an aquarium, and a zoo.

Bombay's major commercial center is situated west of the waterfront, in a part of the city known as the Fort. The area includes the famed Chatrapati Shivaji railway station (formerly Victoria Terminus) and the University of Bombay. Most of the older and larger buildings in the Fort are built in Gothic and other European styles of architecture.

Economic Activity. Most of India's foreign trade passes through the port of Bombay, which is situated on the eastern edge of the island in one of the world's finest natural harbors. Its shore is lined with miles of docks, piers, and warehouses. Bombay's factories are generally located in the north, where there are also many overcrowded slums.

Bridges link Greater Bombay to the mainland, where many factories have been relocated. Chemicals, glassware, leather goods, and machinery are among the products made there. Finance, commerce, oil exploration, filmmaking, and publishing are also major activities in Bombay.

History. The Bombay area has been inhabited since prehistoric times. The harbor and islands were ceded to Portugal by the sultanate of Gujarat in 1534.

In 1662 the British king Charles II married a Portuguese princess, Catherine of Braganza. He received Bombay as part of her dowry, and it soon became the leading center of British power on the west coast of India. But the city did not grow rapidly until it replaced the Confederate South as the world's chief source of cotton during the U.S. Civil War (1861–65).

Today Bombay is more than a great port and textile center. Each year the glamour and wealth of what has been called India's most beautiful city attract huge numbers of people seeking a better life. Modern Bombay, with its skyscrapers and slums, has become one of the world's most crowded cities.

DAVID FIRMAN
Towson State University
Reviewed by the Consulate General of India

BONDS. See STOCKS AND BONDS.

BOOKKEEPING AND ACCOUNTING

No business could operate very long without knowing how much it was earning and how much it was spending. Bookkeeping and accounting are the methods business firms use to keep track of their earnings and expenses.

Bookkeeping is a formal, organized system of recording financial transactions. (Volumes in which business records are kept are often called books.) It is done according to standardized rules. These rules make it easier to detect errors in the bookkeeping. The bookkeeper's record shows how much was spent in a certain transaction and how much was gained or lost in the transaction. The information is arranged so that it may be easily analyzed, that is, examined to determine the financial condition of the business or person involved.

A bookkeeper often works under the direction of an **accountant.** While the bookkeeper's duties are mainly to keep a record of the company's business transactions, the accountant's work has a broader scope. In addition to supervising the recording of financial information, the accountant analyzes the information. The company relies on this analysis when making business decisions.

▶ THE DOUBLE-ENTRY SYSTEM

The system used in keeping the financial records of a business is the **double-entry** system. Behind this system is the basic idea that every business transaction affects the company's financial position in at least two ways. In the double-entry system every aspect of a transaction is recorded.

Accounts

The records kept by bookkeepers are called accounts. The three main types of accounts used in bookkeeping are assets, liabilities, and capital.

Assets are anything of value owned by the company. Examples of assets are land, buildings, and equipment. Money in the company's bank account also is an asset, as are services that the company has paid for in advance.

Liabilities are debts owed to persons or to other companies. Examples of liabilities are wages owed to employees, money owed to a bank, unpaid bills for supplies, and stocks that have been sold to obtain money to run the business.

Capital, sometimes called **equity,** is the total value of everything that the company owns free of debt. Capital is equal to the company's assets minus its liabilities. For example, if a company's assets are $100,000, and its liabilities total $45,000, its capital would be $55,000.

Each of the company's assets and liabilities, as well as its capital, is given a separate account. Examples of asset accounts are the "cash" account, which is a record of money that a company owns, and the "accounts receivable" account, the record of money owed to the company. One type of liability account is the "accounts payable" account, the record of money owed by the company for such things as purchases of goods, supplies, and equipment.

In a double-entry system, each account has two sides: the left side, called the **debit** side, and the right side, called the **credit** side. One side is used for increases and the other for decreases. In asset accounts, increases are recorded on the debit side of the account, and any decrease in value is shown on the credit side. In liability and capital accounts, increases and decreases are recorded in the opposite way. These accounts are increased on the credit side and decreased on the debit side. Every business transaction affects two or more accounts—any entry made on the credit side of one account must be balanced by an entry on the debit side of another account. Debits must equal credits. Here are two examples of this system:

(1) Suppose the Acme Company decides to pay off a $25,000 bank loan. Payment of the loan decreases the liability account, so Acme's bookkeeper will debit the liability account $25,000. Acme's "cash" account, an asset account, has also been affected by the transaction. It has been decreased by the $25,000 used to pay off the loan. Thus, in order to record the transaction fully, the bookkeeper must also credit the "cash" account $25,000.

(2) Suppose Acme sells a piece of equipment for $2,000. The buyer pays $500 immediately and will pay the other $1,500 later. Acme's bookkeeper credits the "equipment" account $2,000 and then debits the "cash" account $500 and the "accounts receivable" account $1,500.

ACCOUNT: Checking				
Date	Item	Debit	Credit	Balance
12/1	Balance			4,500.00
12/8	Cash Sales	1,350.00		5,850.00
12/15	Cash Sales	2,000.00		7,850.00
12/15	Old Farms Dairy		830.00	7,020.00

ACCOUNT: Accounts Payable				
Date	Item	Debit	Credit	Balance
12/1	Balance			2,285.00
12/15	Old Farms Dairy	830.00		1,455.00
12/15	Sprinkles 'n' Such		300.00	1,755.00
12/25	Acme Refrigeration Co.		1,500.00	3,255.00

```
                SUE'S ICE CREAM SHOP
                   Balance Sheet
                   Dec. 31, 1989


        ASSETS

Current Assets
    Cash                        10,800.00
    Accounts Receivable          4,500.00
    Materials and Supplies       2,400.00
    Interest Receivable            500.00
                                ---------
        Total Current Assets                18,200.00

Fixed Assets
    Equipment                   20,000.00
    Shop Building               55,000.00
                                ---------
        Total Fixed Assets                  75,000.00
                                            ---------
Total Assets                                93,200.00
                                            =========



        LIABILITIES AND CAPITAL

Current Liabilities
    Accounts Payable             3,500.00
    Notes Payable                6,000.00
    Mortgage Interest Payable      600.00
                                ---------
        Total Current Liabilities           10,100.00
Long-Term Liabilities
    Mortgage Payable            38,000.00
                                ---------
        Total Long-Term Liabilities         38,000.00

Capital                                     45,100.00
                                            ---------
        Total Liabilities and Capital       93,200.00
                                            =========
```

Top to Bottom: Each of a company's assets and liabilities, as well as its capital, has a separate account. A checking account is a type of asset account, while accounts payable is a liability account. A balance sheet shows a company's financial state at a given time. Note that assets equal liabilities plus capital.

The use of the double-entry system maintains an up-to-date record of the assets, liabilities, and owner's equity of a business. At any time an examination of the books will show just what the financial situation of a business is. An accountant periodically checks the books to see that the debit and credit entries are equal to one another. If they are not equal, it shows that an error has been made. This is called preparing a **trial balance.**

Journals and Ledgers

Separate entries of all day-to-day transactions are made in a book known as a **journal.** Typically, a journal contains columns for recording the date, the account title, the amount of money debited, and the amount credited. In modern bookkeeping, journal entries often are entered on a computer, which stores the information until it is needed.

At the end of each month, or more frequently, all journal entries are recorded, or **posted,** in a more permanent book of accounts called a **ledger.**

▶FINANCIAL STATEMENTS

Financial statements use the records kept in the accounts to give a picture of the financial activity of the company. Two types of financial statements are most commonly used to report this information: the **balance sheet** and the **income and expense statement.** (Before these statements are prepared, a trial balance is made to be certain that debits equal credits.)

The balance sheet, sometimes called the statement of financial position, is a summary that represents the financial condition of a business at a given time. It shows the company's assets at that moment, as well as its liabilities and capital.

The income and expense statement, sometimes called the profit and loss statement, shows the income and expenses of a business over a specified period of time, usually one year. From this statement the managers of the business can learn whether the company had a profit or a loss for the period covered by the report.

▶ACCOUNTING SPECIALTIES

The three main fields of accounting are public accounting, industrial accounting, and governmental accounting. Each of these fields has special characteristics.

Public accountants offer their services to the public rather than to one organization. Their work often involves advising businesses about investments or taxes. They may also help individuals prepare their income tax returns. Public accountants also perform **audits**. An audit is an examination of a business's financial record and a report on the findings. Audits are made mainly for the benefit of stockholders, creditors, and the public.

Public accountants can become C.P.A.s (Certified Public Accountants) by fulfilling certain requirements of education and experience and passing a written examination. A C.P.A. certificate is the mark of expert competence in the accounting field. This certificate is required in order to certify financial statements.

Industrial accountants are employed by single business firms. They keep the records and make the reports on which the managers of a business rely in planning the operations of the business. The accounting department is, in effect, the nerve center of a company. A gain or loss in business is almost immediately revealed in the figures of the accounting department's records.

Government accountants hold important positions at all levels of federal, state, and local government. Their duties are often similar to those of public and industrial accountants.

In modern business, accounting has such a variety of duties to perform that there are accountants who specialize in certain types of jobs. **Tax accountants** keep tax records and prepare reports that must be sent to government tax agencies. They also advise management about the taxes that the company may have to pay as a result of a business transaction. Many individuals hire tax accountants to prepare their income-tax returns.

Cost accountants deal with the costs involved in all the operations of a business. These may be the cost of a product, a service, a manufacturing process, or the operating expenses of a business. The information provided by the cost accountant helps management to budget the company's money and to plan its future operations.

More and more financial information is assembled using electronic data-processing equipment. Many personal computers can be equipped with accounting programs, so that even small businesses can have computerized record-keeping systems. Today's accountants should have some familiarity with data processing.

▶ **HISTORY**

People have counted and kept records throughout history. In the ancient world, trade between merchants made necessary the creation of some kind of business records. Ancient clay tablets show that a system of positive and negative entries was used, in which the gain or loss of any business transaction was added to or subtracted from the total worth of the business.

The modern system of bookkeeping originated in medieval Italy. Records were kept according to the modern system in the city of Genoa in 1340. Some historians believe that the origins of the system can be traced as far back as the 13th century. Genoa, Lombardy, and Tuscany were all thriving business centers in Italy, and any one of them could have been the birthplace of modern bookkeeping. Gradually merchants in other countries learned of the new bookkeeping system, and it spread throughout Europe.

As the methods of the new bookkeeping system were developed, some people became specialists in this kind of record keeping. They were known as accountants. With the increase of business activity, some accountants began to offer their services to any individuals or organizations that needed accounting work done. This was the origin of public accounting. Public accounting developed mainly in the British Isles, which were a leading center of trade. As early as 1720 an English public accountant was called in by Parliament to investigate a financial scandal.

During the 19th century, corporations became the most important form of business organization. A corporation has many owners. These are the stockholders, people who have bought shares, or stock, in the business in return for a share of the corporation's profits. The stockholders depended on published financial reports to learn how well their corporations were doing and whether the executives they hired to manage them were doing their jobs properly. During this period the basic principles of modern accounting were worked out to ensure that the stockholders got thorough and accurate reports.

Stockholders soon realized that if the reports were to have any value, there had to be a set of common principles for gathering and reporting the information. Without a standard method of reporting financial information, a misleading idea about the condition of a business could be given by reporting some facts and ignoring others.

Many unqualified people claimed to be accountants and attempted to do auditing work. Just as standard accounting methods were needed, it also became necessary to establish standards by which properly qualified accountants could be trained and measured.

Today a college degree in accounting has become essential for a successful accounting career. The possible rewards make it worthwhile to get the education. The accountant's familiarity with nearly all the basic operations of a business provides a good opportunity for promotion to the management of a company. Many business executives began their careers as accountants.

EUGENE L. SWEARINGEN
Bank of Oklahoma, N.A.
Tulsa, Oklahoma

Reviewed by JOHN PETRO
Accounting Teacher

BOOK REPORTS AND REVIEWS

A **book report** is a discussion or an analysis of a book and it is one of the most common school assignments. It can be either written or delivered aloud. Book reports are helpful both to those who prepare them and to those who read or listen to them. When you are assigned a book report, you pay extra attention when reading your book, and you think carefully about what it says. Doing this helps you understand your book better and remember it longer.

Others benefit, too. By listening to or reading each other's reports, students learn about a variety of subjects and discover new books to read.

Readers outside the classroom also benefit from what others have to say about books. Newspapers and magazines regularly publish **book reviews** for readers who want help deciding what new books to read or information about books they might not have an opportunity to read. In a book review, a knowledgeable person offers comments and criticism on a recently published book.

Keep in mind, then, that your book report is a sharing experience. Even if no one but your teacher reads it, prepare it as though you were addressing a wide audience.

▶ **WRITTEN BOOK REPORTS**

Your book report, whether it is written or spoken, should include five major points of information: (1) the author, title, publisher, and date of publication of the book, (2) the type of book it is, (3) what the book is about, (4) the form and style in which the book is written, and (5) your opinion of the book.

Author, Title, Publisher, and Publication Date. The first thing your readers will want to know about your book is its title and the name of its author. Remember, also, whenever you prepare a written record of a book, to include the name of the publisher and the date the book was published. The publisher's name can be found at the bottom of the title page. The date of publication is usually located on the other side of the title page, following the word "Copyright." Put all of this information in a heading—several lines at the top of the first page of your written report.

CHOOSING A BOOK

Your teacher will probably give you guidelines on what kind of book to choose for your book report. He or she may even assign a specific book for you to read. If, however, some decisions about your book are left up to you, the best thing to do is to spend some time at the library. Ask a librarian to help you find the section that has books at your reading level.

Look for a book about a topic that interests you or that you would like to learn more about. If you are interested, you are more likely to pay attention to what you read. This will help you write a better book report. For example, if you like horses, select a book about riding or about a special breed of horses. Or, read a fictional work about horses, such as *Black Beauty.*

If you are assigned a biography, try to find one about a favorite author, artist, or musician. Do you like basketball, baseball, or hockey? Your library probably has biographies of well-known sports figures.

Do not wait until the last minute to choose your book. Be sure to give yourself enough time to finish reading it and write your report.

Type of Book. All books can be classified as either fiction or nonfiction. In a library, all novels and short stories are called fiction, and all other books nonfiction. Within these two divisions, though, books can be put into narrower categories. The book you report on might be a collection of poems, a biography, a history, or a work of science fiction. Add this information to your heading.

What the Book Is About. The longest portion of your report will be devoted to the subject matter of your book. If the book is a work of fiction, you will reveal something of the story in this section. If it is a factual work, you will deal mainly with the information it contains.

In the case of a novel, your report should cover the plot, the characters, and the time and setting. It is not necessary to discuss all of these at equal length. There are many kinds of novels, and you must decide what is most important about the one you have read. For a mystery or adventure tale, in which the plot is usually the outstanding feature, your main job will be to relate the story.

Do not tell too much of it. For most people, reading a novel is a kind of adventure, where the pleasure comes from not knowing what will happen next. Your role in narrating a story is to tell your audience of readers enough about what is going on to make them want to read the book, but not so much as to take away the surprise.

Use the present tense to re-tell a story. Avoid opening phrases such as "This book is about . . ." Just tell what it is about. Your summary might be something like this:

The day Henry Jameson turns 12, a lot of strange things begin to happen to him. A package arrives in the mail, and he thinks it is a birthday present. But there is no card or return address, and the box contains only a key on a chain.

The following day, he receives another box, this one containing a map with directions to a place he has never heard of. Every day after that,

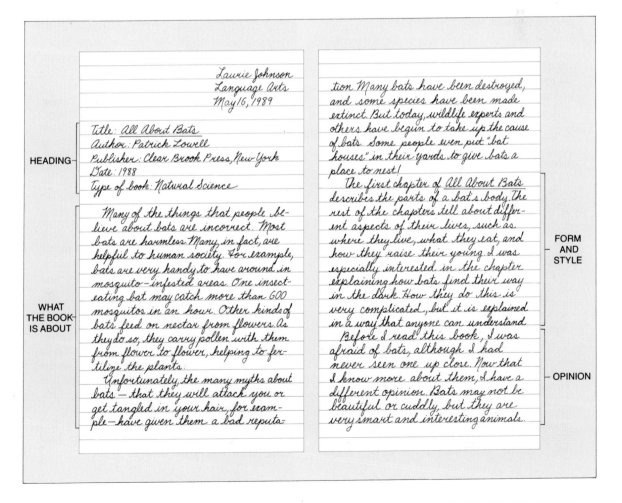

HEADING

Laurie Johnson
Language Arts
May 16, 1989

Title: All About Bats
Author: Patrick Lowell
Publisher: Clear Brook Press, New York
Date: 1988
Type of book: Natural Science

WHAT THE BOOK IS ABOUT

Many of the things that people believe about bats are incorrect. Most bats are harmless. Many, in fact, are helpful to human society. For example, bats are very handy to have around in mosquito-infested areas. One insect-eating bat may catch more than 600 mosquitos in an hour. Other kinds of bats feed on nectar from flowers. As they do so, they carry pollen with them from flower to flower, helping to fertilize the plants.

Unfortunately, the many myths about bats — that they will attack you or get tangled in your hair, for example — have given them a bad reputation. Many bats have been destroyed, and some species have been made extinct. But today, wildlife experts and others have begun to take up the cause of bats. Some people even put "bat houses" in their yards to give bats a place to nest!

FORM AND STYLE

The first chapter of All About Bats describes the parts of a bat's body. The rest of the chapters tell about different aspects of their lives, such as where they live, what they eat, and how they raise their young. I was especially interested in the chapter explaining how bats find their way in the dark. How they do this is very complicated, but it is explained in a way that anyone can understand.

OPINION

Before I read this book, I was afraid of bats, although I had never seen one up close. Now that I know more about them, I have a different opinion. Bats may not be beautiful or cuddly, but they are very smart and interesting animals.

a package arrives with a mysterious object that seems to be connected in some way with what he has received before. He feels as though he is on a treasure hunt, and when, after many weeks, he finally puts all the clues together, he learns something about his ancestors that no one in his family had ever suspected before.

For other novels, you will want to concentrate more on the characters than on the events. To describe a character clearly, imagine that you are telling someone about an old friend. Tell what she looks like and how she behaves. Tell, too, how she feels inside and what she thinks:

Everybody in Maria's family says that she is "the plain one." Her hair is no special color, her eyes are small, her teeth are too big, and her ears stick out. Maria's two sisters, Jane and Laura, are "the beauties." That is what all their aunts call them, adding in a low voice, "Maria is the plain one." After a while, Maria thinks of herself that way, too. She spends most of her time in her room, making up strange fantasies about people she's never met.

In a novel of this type, the plot focuses on changes that cause the character to be different at the end of the book from the way she was at the beginning. Keep this in mind when you tell the story:

When Maria goes to Oklahoma to visit a grandmother she has never known before, she finds herself in a household where what you say is more important than how you look. There are some "beauties" in Grandmama's family, and some "plain ones" like Maria, but nobody cares about any of that. What matters is how you tell a story, and when Maria relates some of the fantasies she had made up, everybody listens. For the first time in her life, Maria is admired, and pretty soon she begins to admire herself.

Some novels are written to inform readers about a specific culture or historic era. When reporting on this kind of book, concentrate on its setting and time:

Raj Sahni lives in a rural village just west of New Delhi, in present-day India. Life is not easy for Raj. In the summer months, the temperature goes over 100°F in the shade, and in the monsoon season that follows, rain falls for days on end. Very little has changed over the generations in Raj's village. Many people live in mud houses with thatched roofs, and goats and water buffalo wander about on the streets. Raj's father plants corn and wheat in the same fields his father and grandfather farmed before him. Raj, though, wants to do something different when he grows up. He wants to be a doctor in the small hospital down the road from his house.

If, instead of a novel, your book is a collection of short stories, mention a common theme among them, if there is one, and then tell about one or two stories in detail:

All the stories in *After and Beyond* tell of supernatural happenings. The most frightening is "The Strange Return of Mr. Jensen," in which a baker disappears from his shop one day in late 19th century London and is not heard from for nearly ten years. During that time, his family, many of his former customers, and the police try to track him down. When a little girl finally discovers where he is and what he has become, they all wish they had never looked for him in the first place. "What Became of Jody?" and "The Lost Butler" are also about people who have disappeared and later return in strange and frightening forms.

Follow the same rules when you report on a collection of poems:

Wingsongs is a collection of poems about things that fly, such as airplanes, geese, bees, angels, and pterodactyls. Some of the poems are funny, some are scary, and some are full of unusual images. In "Washday," a flock of geese is compared to a clothesline of wash flapping in the wind. In "Pterrible Beast," the poet makes up crazy words and spellings to describe a pterodactyl.

For a report on a biography, a history, or a science book, you will be relating facts rather than imaginary events. Works of this sort usually contain a great deal of information, and you may have difficulty remembering it all. Keep a notepad at your side as you read, so that you can write down important points and their page numbers as you come across them. Do not attempt to report on all the material in the book. Offer a general statement about the subject, and follow that with a few specific details.

If your book is a biography, begin by explaining why its subject was important and what he or she accomplished. Use the past tense when you report on real events:

Harriet Tubman was often called "Moses" during her lifetime because she led her people out of slavery and into freedom. A runaway slave, she returned to the South over and over to help hundreds of other slaves escape to a new life.

A report on a book of history or science should also open with a general statement, this time offering an introduction to the subject:

The Boston Tea Party of 1773 was an act of rebellion engaged in by Boston citizens who opposed British taxation of tea.

Or, for a science book:

Many of the things that people believe about bats are incorrect. Most bats are harmless. Many, in fact, are helpful to human society.

Use your notes to provide further details about your subject. You might conclude this section of your report on a biography this way:

Harriet Tubman lived to be more than 90 years old, and she devoted most of these years to helping other blacks. Before the Civil War, she worked with the Underground Railroad to rescue slaves. During the war, she helped the Northern army locate enemy camps in the South, and she nursed runaway slaves and black soldiers in hospitals. After slavery was abolished, she set up the John Brown Home in Auburn, New York, where she took care of sick and poor blacks.

Form and Style. Every book has a form and style all its own. The form of a book refers to its structure, or the way it is organized. A novel, for example, might be written in the form of a diary. A biography might be written in the form of an exchange of letters. The style refers to the way the author expresses himself or herself. Styles vary from book to book the way personalities vary from person to person. Some books are written in very formal prose, others in the language you hear around you all the time. You can combine a discussion of the form and the style in a single paragraph:

Each chapter of *The Plain One* is introduced by a letter written by Maria to her grandmother, long after she has returned home from her visit to Oklahoma. The chapter then tells in detail what the letter refers to. The letters are written in simple, everyday language. The chapters often sound like poetry, with long descriptions of cornfields and the Oklahoma sky.

Your Opinion. There are many reasons for liking or disliking a book. The plot of a novel may be exciting, or it may be slow moving. The dialogue may sound authentic, or it may sound false. The facts in a history book may be clear and understandable, or they may be hard to follow. At times, you will like some aspects of a book and dislike others. Whatever your opinion, be specific in stating it. Do not say only that the book was interesting or boring. Tell why:

When I read *The Plain One*, I felt that I myself was Maria. I suffered with her when her family ignored her at home, and I triumphed with her when her storytelling won her so much admiration in Oklahoma. The other characters, though, seemed much less real. They all spoke alike, and they sounded like people on a television show, not like people in the real world.

▶ **ORAL REPORTS**

When you present an oral book report, you should give the same basic information that you would provide in a written report. This time your audience will be listening to, rather than reading, what you have to say. However, you will still have to write out in advance everything you want to tell them. Do not read this written report word for word to your audience. Instead, prepare index cards, each containing a few phrases that will remind you of what your full-length report said. Make one card for each major idea in your report. An index card for the biography of Harriet Tubman might read like this:

Harriet Tubman often called Moses
Led her people to freedom
Runaway slave
Returned to South over and over
Helped hundreds of slaves escape

Glance down at your cards when you need to, but look at your audience as much as you can. Stand up tall and speak in a slow, clear voice. Keep reminding yourself that your audience wants to hear what you have to say. Those who have not read your book will want to hear about something new. Those who have read it will want to compare your understanding of it with their own.

SYLVIA CASSEDY
Author, *In Your Own Words:*
A Beginner's Guide to Writing

BOOKS

It is difficult to imagine a civilization without books. Their importance in human history cannot be exaggerated. Valuable ideas and discoveries throughout our history have been recorded in books. Using information from books, scholars and scientists have explored and expanded almost every subject known to us. Without books there would be no modern medicine, no modern science or technology, no television, no space flights to the moon, no teachers, and no schools. In short, without books, life as we know it would not be possible.

Information about fields and crops are etched on this clay tablet, which dates from about 2800 B.C. Clay tablets could be moved from place to place but they were heavy and not very practical.

▶BEFORE BOOKS

The human need to record and pass along stories and information is as old as the human race. For thousands of years, some of our early ancestors preserved their beliefs, legends, and daily activities by painting pictures on walls of caves and other rock surfaces protected from the weather. Unfortunately, in order to "read" these stories, one had to go to the source—a wall could not be carried or placed on a library shelf.

The Need for Books

About 10,000 years ago, people began raising crops in addition to hunting animals and gathering edible plants. As farming expanded and became more complicated, there was a need to count, measure, and record holdings —sheaves of grain, numbers of cattle, bins of rice, and so on. Therefore, people developed simple symbols to help them count and keep track of their animals and crops.

Over time a creative people called the Sumerians, who also built the world's first cities, invented a simple form of writing that was made up of three-cornered marks. This form of writing is called **cuneiform**, which means "wedge-shaped." Using sticks, the Sumerians drew their farm and business records on small slabs, or tablets, of soft, damp clay that were then hardened in the sun. The tablets could be stored and carried, and when they were no longer useful, they were simply thrown away.

The more important Sumerian texts were baked in ovens much like fine pottery and then stored in the world's first libraries. In recent times, thousands of these clay tablets have been discovered; many were found in perfect condition under the dry desert sands.

▶THE FIRST BOOKS

The next advance in the history of books occurred in Egypt, around 3500 B.C. The ancient Egyptians had developed a lovely, but complex, picture writing called **hieroglyphics**, or "sacred writing." In order to reproduce this complicated writing, they invented papyrus sheets. These thin cream-colored sheets were made from the papyrus plant—a tall reed that grew in flooded marshes along the Nile River. To make the sheets, the reeds were split open

This Egyptian papyrus, which dates from about 2500 B.C., illustrates the creation of the universe.

and cut into strips. Then the strips were flattened and joined together. Brushes and reeds were used to illustrate and write on the long rolled pieces of papyrus, which were called **scrolls**.

Papyrus-making became a major industry in Egypt; blank rolls and scrolls were exported to every corner of the known world, especially to Rome and Athens. Although Egypt was the largest producer, excellent quality papyrus was also grown in other places in the eastern Mediterranean.

Ancient Greece—Books Begin to Travel

The best customers for Egypt's papyrus were the Greeks, particularly the people of Athens, then the world capital of learning. Scribes, people who made copies of scrolls, were busy individuals in Athenian communities, and their work required large amounts of papyrus.

Greek scholars, teachers, actors, and musicians, who often traveled from job to job and from town to town, usually carried with them

many Greek ideas, seized large numbers of Greek books, and moved entire Greek libraries to Rome.

The Romans also wrote their own books on thin wooden boards. Eventually, they decided to join several boards together by punching holes along one side and passing rings through the holes to connect the pages. This kind of wooden book became known as a **codex**, which in Latin *(caudex)* means "tree trunk."

In order to write in an early codex, the pages were first coated with gesso, a liquid mixture of chalk and glue. When the gesso dried to a hard finish, a thin coat of black wax was applied. Then with a pointed instrument called a stylus, the writer scratched the lettering through the wax. The early codices were used mainly as notebooks.

The crude early codices made of wood were soon replaced by ones made of flat papyrus pages that were cut to uniform sizes and bound between two boards. These codices were very popular, largely because they were so easy to use and to carry. When an opened codex was

Wooden boards were spread with gesso and a thin coat of black wax. Using a sharp, pointed tool, it was easy to scratch symbols on the waxed surface. The tablets could be joined together, making a wooden book, or codex. These codices replaced the clay tablets and papyrus scrolls of earlier times.

the latest papyrus scrolls of poetry, geometry, philosophy, music, manners, and morals.

The Greeks greatly advanced writing and the making of books by inventing an alphabet of 24 symbols, called letters. Each letter represented a particular sound in the spoken language. It is far easier to write down a language made up of letters than one based on pictures.

Moving Toward Modern Books

Around 146 B.C., the expanding Roman Empire conquered Greece. The victorious Romans were dazzled by the cultural richness of classical Greece, and they readily adopted

placed on a table, it stayed open, unlike a scroll, which had an annoying tendency to roll back up the moment it was put down. It was also easier to locate sections of a text in a codex. Today, codex is the technical term for any book made up of many pages bound together and not in the form of a roll or scroll.

Parchment Replaces Papyrus

The next step toward the modern book was the use of **parchment**, or processed and stretched animal skin. Parchment was not a new material, but its potential was realized with the invention of the Roman codex.

A "page" from an Indian palm-leaf book. People in India, China, and Nepal sometimes wrote on the backs of palm leaves. When the leaves were fastened together, they could be spread for reading.

Parchment is actually a very smooth thin leather. It is prepared from a sheep's or goat's skin that has been carefully cleaned, bleached white, stretched flat, and then rubbed smooth with pumice, a lightweight volcanic material that works like a fine sandpaper. An especially desirable creamy white parchment called vellum was made from calfskin.

Parchment was more expensive than papyrus, which was made from a plant that grew wild and required much less preparation. But parchment had several advantages over papyrus. It was a tougher material and less likely to tear or decay. Ink could be erased from parchment, unlike papyrus, and parchment could be painted and decorated with bright colors and gold leaf. Parchment also had two usable sides. A single page of parchment could carry twice as many words as a page of papyrus, which had only one usable side.

The codex, with its double-sided parchment pages, was in many ways the first truly modern book—one of Rome's many gifts to the world.

▶ BOOKS OF THE ORIENT

Thousands of miles east of Egypt, Greece, and Rome was the "celestial kingdom" of China. The Chinese developed their language, writing, and books in ways similar to those of their Western counterparts, even though there was very little contact between the two widely separated areas.

The ancient Chinese, like the Sumerians and the Egyptians, began to write with pictures instead of an alphabet. Over the centuries Chinese writing developed into elegant **pictograms** with thousands of separate characters. With some changes, this writing system is still used by the Chinese people today.

The earliest Chinese books were written on the backs of palm leaves and on flattened pieces of wood and bamboo. The Chinese never used the roll or scroll. Instead, their palm-leaf and bamboo books were strips fastened at one end much like a fan and then spread like a fan to be read. The Chinese did not use pens or styluses. They painted their pictograms with brushes and shiny black ink.

The Chinese had no papyrus or parchment, and they desired a better, more practical material than palm leaves or bamboo as a writing surface. They tried using panels of silk cloth for their finest poetry, but silk pages were not durable and were very expensive. Their search for a better material finally ended in A.D. 105 when a Chinese dignitary named Ts'ai Lun invented the world's first sheets of real paper. He concocted a pulp of wood chips, silk and cotton rags, hemp rope, and even old fishing nets, and then molded it into sheets. The Chinese were immediately aware of the great value of paper and they kept the art of papermaking a secret for hundreds of years. Eventually, however, the technique was carried east in the 100's and west in the 200's.

Using their paper, the Chinese at first made books that were written by hand. Later, they developed a printmaking technique, called **woodcut**, which enabled them to illustrate their texts more easily and also allowed them to make multiple impressions of the pages.

The invention of paper changed the format of Chinese books—full-size pages were glued together and accordion-folded. This style of book was the Chinese standard for well over a thousand years, until the introduction of the printing press from Europe.

This illustration of a man collecting bamboo pulp is from a Japanese edition of a Chinese encyclopedia on traditional technology, written about 1637.

▶MEDIEVAL MANUSCRIPTS

After the fall of Rome in 476, nearly all the making and selling of books stopped as a cultural and political decline, called the Dark Ages, occurred throughout Europe. Later, books began to be made again in small Christian communities called **monasteries**.

Dedicated monks of religious orders began to make exact, handwritten copies, or **manuscripts**, of the most significant Greek and Roman books that had survived. The monks diligently copied the old books—mostly Bibles and other religious and philosophical works—from dawn to dusk, six days a week, year after year. They worked in rooms called **scriptoria** whose windows faced the sun. The presence of such rare manuscripts made the monks very fearful of fire, so the scriptoria were unheated and candles were not allowed.

By the Middle Ages, around the year 1100, monks were making beautiful **illuminated manuscripts**—radiantly colored codices with ornamental borders of animal and plant designs. Nuns sometimes inked in the delicate, perfectly formed letters. But hand-copying, however beautiful, was a very slow process. Even the most diligent monks could not produce enough books to satisfy the growing demand for them.

▶THE PRINTING PRESS

At the height of the Middle Ages, the first colleges and universities were opening in cities across Europe. Students wanted and needed books. Secular professional copyists, called **stationers**, began to make hurried, unattractive manuscripts for the students, but still there never seemed to be enough books. This situation changed—rapidly and forever—with the invention of the printing press.

The printing press was invented by Johann Gutenberg in the small city of Mainz in Germany around 1450. Gutenberg's press used tiny pieces of metal type to print each letter of the alphabet. The printing press soon replaced the slow work of the manuscript copyist. The printer with his ink-stained hands could create thousands of copies of a book in the time it would take a copyist or stationer to make just one.

The next 50 years were explosive. By 1500 there were printing presses in some 300 European cities. More than 10 million copies of thousands of books had been printed. In order

Illuminated manuscript pages like this one from the *Belleville Breviary* (1343) are as colorful and hauntingly beautiful as the stained-glass cathedral windows of the same period.

to illustrate so many books quickly and easily, Europeans adopted the Chinese woodcut technique. A drawing was carved into a block of wood, and the block was locked into the press with the text. Then the text and illustration were printed as a complete page again and again.

For the first time in history, books were plentiful and popular. Millions of ordinary people developed an intense desire to learn to read now that books were available.

All of the books printed before 1501 are called **incunabula**, the Latin word for "cradle," because this was the infancy of modern bookmaking. By 1500 the printing press itself was so mechanically perfected that it would change very little over the next 400 years.

The form, look, and feel of the books we read today were also worked out and adopted worldwide during the late 1400's. Italian book designers and printers were especially adept at creating typefaces, layouts, and illustrations that were pleasing to look at and to read.

Left: Some unusual types of books include large-print books for the visually impaired, and talking books, shape books, and pop-up books. *Below:* Children's books in braille, such as this one, are available in many bookstores and libraries.

MODERN BOOKS

Most modern books resemble those made 450 years ago—paper pages are bound between a front cover and a back cover. There have been, however, a few variations in the materials, and even in the format, used in books over the last 200 years.

In the 1800's the first paperback books were published. Printed on cheap paper with paper covers, they only cost a dime. Just about anyone could read about the exploits of cowboys in the Wild West and other adventurers. Paperback editions of the classics as well as popular fiction and nonfiction were also printed. The paperback book industry is still a big business today.

Since the 1930's when they were first introduced, books on audio tape have become increasingly popular. Well-known actors and sometimes the authors themselves are recorded as they read entire novels or nonfiction books. More recently, children's stories have been recorded to give pre-readers more exposure to language and literature.

Other innovations in children's books have included cloth books with pages that cannot be torn; plastic books that can be taken into the bathtub; wipe-off books that can be colored with crayons and then wiped clean with a cloth; and pop-up story books with flat pages that become three-dimensional when they are turned.

The newest types of books are electronic books. These are books that can be read on a computer screen. Researchers are even de-

veloping electronic paper and electronic inks. These will be used to create books whose content can be changed completely when connected to the Internet or cued by a radio signal. Imagine owning books with ever-changing stories!

BOOKMAKING TECHNOLOGY

The technology involved in making books has changed dramatically with the advent of phototypesetting, computers, and four-color printing processes used in reproducing illustrations and photography. The paper used for the pages of books has also been improved to ensure its durability and longevity.

JACK KNOWLTON
Author, *Books and Libraries*

See also GRAPHIC ARTS; ILLUMINATED MANUSCRIPTS; ILLUSTRATION AND ILLUSTRATORS; LIBRARIES; PRINTING; WOODCUT PRINTING.

BOOKS: FROM AUTHOR TO READER

Books are one of the miracles of humanity. They make our thoughts, our feelings, our dreams, and our knowledge permanent, and they make them available to everyone.

Millions of books are printed each year in the United States. Have you ever wondered how these books were made? Let us look at the bookmaking process for the type of book you might buy in a bookstore or borrow from your local library. We will begin with the author's manuscript.

▶ FROM AUTHOR TO PUBLISHER

Imagine that you have written a story called *It Rained Every Day,* about a family on vacation. Like most authors today, you have used a word processor to prepare your manuscript. In the past when authors wrote poems, stories, novels, or other material, they prepared handwritten copies of their work. Typewritten copies or printed copies from word processors or computers are much easier to read, and the people who make books prefer them.

You have worked very hard and long on your story and think it is good. Friends and family who have read it agree. They urge you to try to have *It Rained Every Day* made into a book. Fine! But now that the story is finished and you have prepared the manuscript, what do you do?

▶ FINDING A PUBLISHER

When your manuscript is finished, you must find a publisher who is interested in making it into a book. The best way to find a publisher is to go to the library and look at *Literary Market Place (LMP).* This reference book lists hundreds of different publishers with their addresses, phone numbers, and the names of some of the people who work there. You want to find publishers who publish children's trade books. **Trade books** are fiction and nonfiction works sold in bookstores, and that is where you want your book to end up. Other publishers listed in *LMP* may specialize in textbooks, reference books, or other types of publishing.

February 9, 1992

Ms. Julia Lee, Editor
Children's Book Department
Crabapple Publishing Co.
669 Fifth Avenue
New York, NY 10020

Dear Ms. Lee:

I am enclosing my manuscript, IT RAINED EVERY DAY, which I would like you to consider for publication.

IT RAINED EVERY DAY is about a brother and sister who fight all the time. When they go on vacation with their family, the weather is bad every day. The brother and sister learn that if they keep fighting each other, their vacation will be really ruined. This is the story of how the vacation is saved.

I hope you will enjoy reading the manuscript. I look forward to hearing from you.

Sincerely,

Mary Smith

Mary Smith
8 Lafayette Street
Belmar, NJ 07719
(908) 555-6704

MS/ms
Enc: ms and SASE

Above: Be sure to enclose a one-page letter and a self-addressed, stamped envelope with any manuscript you send to a publisher.

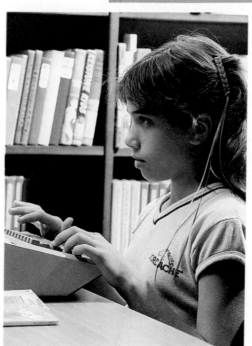

Left: A young author works on her manuscript. Changes in her manuscript are easy to make on a word processor.

Contacting a Publisher

After selecting a number of trade book publishers, the next step is to write a short, one-page letter to the children's book editor at one of them. In this letter you should tell the editor a little about yourself and your book. Send the letter and a copy of your manuscript to the editor in a sturdy envelope. Include a stamped, self-addressed envelope so that the editor can return your manuscript if he or she decides not to publish it.

A book contract is carefully checked before it is sent to an author.

Publishers receive thousands of manuscripts every year, so months may go by before you hear from the editor. The manuscript may be returned with a rejection note, saying that the publisher is not interested. If so, send it to another publisher. Imagine, however, that the editor wants to publish your manuscript as a book. What happens next?

Book Contracts

If the editor is interested in your book, one of the first things he or she probably will do is telephone you and offer you a contract. At this point the editor will want to discuss an advance and a royalty, as well as some of the other terms of a contract.

Advances and Royalties. An **advance** is an amount of money the publisher agrees to give you before your book is published. Usually, the publisher pays half the advance when a contract is signed and the other half when the manuscript is delivered and the editor agrees that it is acceptable. Advances for first novels usually range from $1,500 to $4,000. Well-known authors receive advances many times greater than that.

A **royalty** is a percentage of the price of each copy of your book that is sold. Part of the royalty is used to pay off the money you received as an advance. When the advance has been paid off, an author begins to receive royalty payments twice a year based on the sales of the book.

Contract Clauses. A book contract contains many clauses, or conditions, dealing with such things as territorial and subsidiary rights, warrants, and permissions. It will also include the date on which you, the author, promise to deliver the final manuscript.

Clauses dealing with **territorial rights** specify the countries in which your book can be sold. The contract may state that you agree to sell "world rights," or the rights to sell your book in any country. Or it may agree to sell rights for only certain countries.

Subsidiary rights allow your book to be sold for such things as a paperback edition, a book club edition, a movie or television version, translations into foreign languages, a large print edition, or a serialization in a newspaper or magazine.

Contracts also include **warrants**, or guarantees. One warrant states that you guarantee your work to be original and of your own creation. Another states that the book contains no recipe, formula, or instruction that may be harmful to someone reading your book. Suppose, for example, that you write about a person eating a particular wild plant. If someone reads your book, eats this plant, and becomes ill because the plant is poisonous, this person might sue. The warrant helps protect the publisher from such a lawsuit, and reminds you, the author, of your responsibility to be sure such information is carefully checked and that appropriate warnings are included in your book when they are necessary. The contract will also include a warrant stating that you have not invaded the privacy of another person or written anything that is libelous—that is, that discredits someone's character.

Contracts may also include clauses concerning permissions. **Permissions** are written consents from others saying that you may use materials they have created. Songs, poems, photographs, and excerpts from interviews are all examples of materials that usually require written consent for their use. Contracts normally state that the author must pay any fees required to obtain such permissions.

The Importance of Agents

Dealing with publishers and book contracts can be quite complex. For this reason, it is usually advisable for writers to hire literary agents to represent them in negotiations with editors and publishers. Agents often are able to get better terms in contracts than writers can get negotiating alone. In return for their services, agents will charge commissions of 10 to 15 percent of the income writers earn from their books.

Literary agents are professionals who know the publishing business and the people who work in it. Because of this, the manuscripts of writers with agents are usually given more careful consideration by publishers than ones by writers without agents. Getting an agent is not easy, however. It is almost impossible to find an agent who will take on a young, unknown writer before he or she has been published. Once a writer has been offered a contract, it is much easier to get an agent. Nevertheless, unknown writers can try to find agents by submitting letters of inquiry and samples of their work to them.

▶ **THE EDITORIAL AND DESIGN PROCESS**

Once a contract has been signed, the publisher begins work on your manuscript of *It Rained Every Day* to make it into a book. The publishing process is quite complex. It involves many stages and a variety of people both inside and outside the publishing company. Since several parts of the process may be going on at the same time, the people involved in making a book work closely together to ensure the book's completion.

The two divisions of a publishing company that are initially involved in creating a book from manuscript are the editorial department and the art department. The publishing professionals working in these departments include the editors, managing editors, copy editors, proofreaders, art directors, designers, and illustrators.

The Editor

Most manuscripts undergo changes after they have been submitted to the publisher. The person responsible for improving a manuscript is the editor. The edi-

tor will read the manuscript and then return it to the author with suggestions for changes, or revisions. These constructive suggestions are not meant as criticisms but are aimed at making the book better. The editor will point out flaws or errors and propose ways the manuscript could be improved. Perhaps he or she will suggest a different ending, or question whether a character's actions make sense. The editor might even suggest that certain parts of the manuscript be rewritten.

Although editing is their primary role, good editors do more than just edit. They must be knowledgeable about new trends, new ideas, and what is being written elsewhere. They must also be on the lookout for new, talented writers and must encourage published writers to continue working. They might also develop ideas for books themselves and try to find writers who can turn those ideas into books.

After a manuscript has been revised and approved, the editor prepares to put it into **production**. The editor estimates the length of the book; sets a date for publication; and determines other specifics, such as the size of each page (the **trim**), the kind of binding, and the

On this page of the copyedited manuscript, note the content changes—"fork" to "spoon" and "plate" to "cereal bowl"—as well as the corrections in grammar and punctuation.

```
                    CHAPTER ONE

      Paula Jones grit her teeth.  The screen door slammed.

Her brother Pete was gone, and she was left at the breakfast

table with her parents and her little brother, Ted.

      She slammed down her fork.  "It isn't fair," she said.

"It's Pete's turn to do the dishes.  I did them last night."

      Her mother stood up.  "It's not fair, you're right.  I'll do

the dishes, but I hope you'll help us with unpacking and

setting things up.  It's a shame to waste our first day of

vacation working, but we have to get organized before we can

have fun."

      "I'll help."  Ted stood up, his plate in his hand.  He

reached for his half-full glass of milk, grabbed it tightly,

and set it on the plate.  Holding the plate and glass of milk

with one hand, he began piling silver on to the plate.  It

wobbled, and the milk sloshed against the sides of the glass.

A knife fell onto the floor.  Ted lurched for it, but the glass

tilted, and milk splashed onto the table.

      Ted looked miserable, Paula thought.  He's always trying

to help and makes a mess because he's so little.  Paula

remembered when she was six...
```

Handwritten marginal notes: *au: they had cereal... see changes below*; *spoon*; *cereal bowl*; *in*; *bowl*; *into*; *bowl*; *how many "sides" does a glass have?*

quantity of books to be printed. The editor also prepares a brief description of the book—to be used later for advertising purposes—and a brief biographical note about the author.

The editor's responsibility does not end when a book goes into production. He or she generally reviews the progress of a manuscript during the publishing process to see that everything is proceeding as planned.

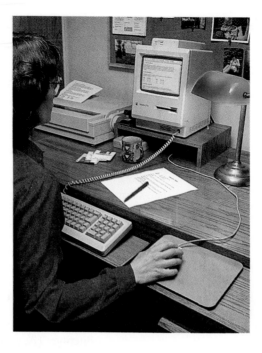

An editor often uses a word processor to make changes the author has agreed to in the manuscript.

The Managing Editor

When an editor puts a manuscript into production, the first person to receive it is generally the managing editor. Managing editors are familiar with all aspects of the bookmaking process. Although their duties may vary from publisher to publisher, they are usually in charge of **trafficking** the manuscript. This means making sure that the manuscript is complete, sending it to the appropriate people at the right time, and keeping track of schedules and deadlines. It often takes from nine months to a year for a manuscript to be made into a book and placed in bookstores. The managing editor makes sure that each person involved in the process does his or her job properly and on time.

The Copy Editor

One of the first people to receive a manuscript from the managing editor is the copy editor. Copy editors are responsible for checking a manuscript for accuracy and style—that is, consistency in spelling, grammar, and word usage. The copy editor's most important tools are a collection of specialized reference books that he or she refers to while working.

While working on a manuscript, the copy editor keeps an alphabetical list of proper names and unusual spellings on a piece of paper called a **style sheet**. This style sheet will be used later to double check the accuracy of the manuscript. The copy editor rewrites passages that are not grammatical, corrects misspellings, and punctuates the book according to accepted rules of punctuation. The copy ed-

itor also checks for consistency, making sure that words are spelled the same way throughout the book.

Copy editors are trained to doubt every fact in a manuscript and to check these facts in a variety of source books. For example, if a manuscript says that a character caught a rainbow trout in the ocean, the copy editor will suggest that the author choose another type of fish after checking and learning that rainbow trout are only found in freshwater streams.

In making corrections and changes, copy editors use marks called proofreader's marks. These are special marks used throughout the bookmaking process to ensure that instructions are conveyed accurately.

The Proofreader

One member of the editorial staff—the proofreader—does not become involved in the bookmaking process until much later. The proofreader begins working on a book after the manuscript has been set into type by a typesetter. At that point the proofreader will carefully check typeset copies of the manuscript against the copyedited manuscript to catch any errors and mark them so that they will be corrected. You will read more about typesetting and the job of proofreaders later in the section on composition.

The Art Director

The art director in a publishing house is responsible for overseeing all aspects of a book's design. This includes assigning artists to work on a book, supervising design staff, and often choosing a design for a book's cover. The art director, as well as other artists involved, works with the editorial staff to make sure that the design of a book is appropriate for its content and its intended audience. The art director becomes involved in the publishing process when he or she is given a copy of the manuscript by the editor. At that point, the art director assigns the work to staff members of the art department or to outside artists.

The Book Designer

The design of a book—the physical arrangement of all the materials that make up the book—is the responsibility of the book designer. The primary goal of the book designer is to translate an author's words into a visual design that helps a reader understand the author's ideas.

Determining Book Length. One of the first things the book designer does with the manuscript of *It Rained Every Day* is make a **cast off** or **character count**. A character is any letter, numeral, space, and punctuation mark in the manuscript. A cast off is necessary for calculating how long the finished book will be. An average young person's novel of 160 to 192 pages may contain more than a quarter of a million characters!

Choosing Type. Once the cast off has been done, the designer chooses a typeface and type size that he or she considers most appropriate. The designer also considers the length of each line of type, the space between the words, the space between lines, and the margins around the outside of the type. These elements all help to determine how easy or difficult the book will be to read.

Baskerville

Size 14 pt.   ABCDEfghijklmno

Size 18 pt.   ABCDefghijkl

Size 24 pt.   ABCdefghi

Helvetica

Size 14 pt.   ABCDEfghijklmno

Size 18 pt.   ABCDefghijkl

Size 24 pt.   ABCdefghi

Above: Baskerville and Helvetica are two of the many typefaces used for books. Note the differences in the shapes and sizes of the letters in these examples.

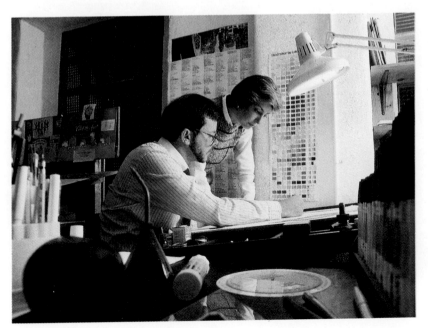

Left: A designer discusses the layout of a book with the art director.

One

Paula Jones grit her teeth. The screen door slammed. Her brother Pete was gone, and she was left at the breakfast table with her parents and her little brother Ted.

She slammed down her spoon. "It isn't fair," she said. "It's Pete's turn to do the dishes. I did them last night."

Her mother stood up. "It's not fair, you're right. I'll do the dishes, but I hope you'll help us with unpacking and setting things up. It's a shame to waste our first day of vacation working, but we have to get organized before we can have fun."

"I'll help." Ted stood up, his cereal bowl in his hand. He reached for his half-full glass of milk, grabbed it tightly, and set it in the bowl. Holding the bowl and the glass of milk with one hand,

he began piling silver into the bowl. It wobbled, and the milk sloshed against the side of the glass. A knife fell onto the floor. When Ted lurched for it, the glass tilted, and milk splashed onto the table.

Ted looked miserable, Paula thought. He's always trying to help and makes a mess because he's so little. Paula remembered when she was six.

This two-page layout shows how the text and art will look when the manuscript for *It Rained Every Day* is printed into a book.

The placement of the title, the author's name, and the name of the publisher on the book jacket is important because the book may be placed on a shelf rather than on a table or in a window of a bookstore.

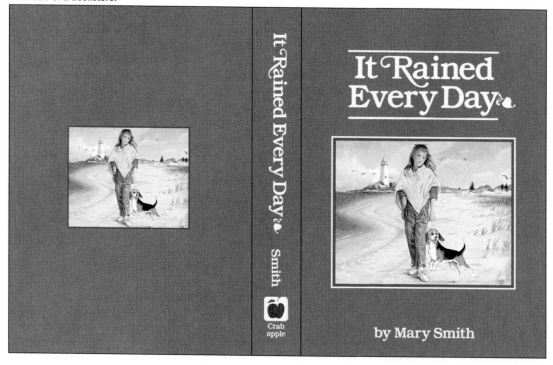

It Rained Every Day

Smith

Crab apple

It Rained Every Day

by Mary Smith

Front Matter and Back Matter. The book designer is not only concerned with the main text, or body, of the book. He or she also designs the material that comes before, and sometimes after, the text. The material at the front of the book, called the **front matter**, normally includes a half-title page, a title page, a copyright page, and often a dedication page. Some books may have additional front-matter pages such as a frontispiece (a page with a map or illustration), a preface, an author's note, a table of contents, or an introduction. Nonfiction books often include **back matter**, such as an appendix, a glossary, a bibliography, and an index.

Layouts. After a design has been created, the designer prepares special sheets, called **layouts**, that show how the book will look. Layouts include detailed plans for every element of the book. Frequently, the designer will ask the **compositor**—the person setting the type—to provide samples that show how these different elements will look after the book is printed. After reviewing the layouts and samples, the designer and editor may decide to make changes in the design.

Preparing for Typesetting and Printing. When the design has been finalized, it is the designer's job to mark the manuscript with coded instructions for setting type. These instructions tell the compositor exactly how to set all the type throughout the book, including the main text, page numbers (folios), headings at the top or bottom of the page, and all front- and back-matter materials.

Before a book is printed, the designer may sometimes be asked to prepare a mechanical. A **mechanical** is a detailed assembly of the book, with every element in place. The mechanical is then photographed and the film is used in the printing process.

The Jacket Designer

While *It Rained Every Day* is being edited and designed, artists are creating its artwork. This could include art for the cover of a paperback book and for the paper dust jacket that protects the cover of a hardcover book.

The cover or dust jacket of a book is very important. It protects the book and serves as an advertisement. The person responsible for designing the cover is the jacket designer. Working with the art director of the publishing house, the jacket designer tries to create an

WONDER QUESTION

What information is on a copyright page?

The copyright page contains a copyright notice, which indicates that the rights of the book are reserved as of a specific year. It also lists the full address of the publisher, the edition number, and the Library of Congress Cataloging in Publication (CIP) notice. The CIP is the official catalog card information to be used at the Library of Congress in Washington, D.C., and at many other libraries.

Another important piece of information on the copyright page is the International Standard Book Number (ISBN). This is an identification number, assigned to every book published, that is used in ordering books. Several parts of the ISBN stand for specific things. The first digit indicates the language of the book; a zero stands for English. The next three digits indicate the publisher; each publisher is assigned a three-digit code. The next group of five digits is the number of the book. The last digit is a checking number.

attractive, eye-catching, and informative cover that is appropriate for the book and conveys all necessary information, including the title and the author's name.

When the jacket designer has created a design, he or she often prepares a **comp**, a mock-up of what the design will actually look like after it is printed. If the editor and art director approve the design, the jacket designer will then prepare a mechanical to be used in the printing process.

The Illustrator

Many books, especially those for young readers, have artwork in the interior of the book as well as on the cover. The artist who creates the original art to be used in the interior of a book is called an illustrator.

While the manuscript of *It Rained Every Day* is being prepared, the editor and art director choose an illustrator to work on the art. Following their guidelines, the illustrator prepares sketches to show what the finished art will look like. These sketches are checked by the editor or an assistant to make sure they are appropriate to the text and that all the details are correct. For example, a section of a story may say that a girl has red hair, wears blue jeans, and is walking with her dog, so the illustration for this portion of the story should show the same things.

If an illustration does not match the text, something will have to be changed. Sometimes the art can be changed. However, since it is often costly and time-consuming to change a piece of art, the editor might ask the author to revise the text as long as it will not hurt the author's storyline or ideas.

▶ THE PRODUCTION PROCESS

After the editorial and art and design departments have completed their work, the actual production of a book begins. This part of the bookmaking process involves several stages, including composition, or typesetting, color separation, printing, and binding. Most of the work at these stages is done outside the publishing house.

Control over the process during these stages is maintained largely by the publishing house's production department and a production manager or supervisor. The role of the production manager or supervisor is a complex and very important one. It is that person's responsibility to select outside groups to work on various production aspects of the book, to act as liaison between these groups and the publishing house, to choose the paper to be used for the book and its cover, to coordinate production schedules, and to maintain control of production budgets.

Composition

During the composition process a compositor, or typesetter, changes a typewritten manuscript into pages of type that can then be printed and made into a book. In the past, typesetting was done manually and involved arranging individual pieces of metal type to create a page. Today, computer technology has made most typesetting much easier, as well as faster and cheaper.

As the typesetting proceeds, the compositor prepares **galley proofs**, which are long sheets of paper showing the typeset material. These galley proofs are sent to the publisher for approval. A proofreader compares a master set of galley proofs against the original, copy-edited manuscript to find any errors. The author receives a set of galley proofs as well and may request certain changes. These changes are added to the master set, which is then sent back to the compositor for corrections.

The compositor then prepares other stages of typeset material to be checked by the editor and designer. These stages include page proofs, repros, and blues. **Page proofs** are corrected galley proofs that have been broken up into pages. They show how the type on each page of the book will appear. The editor checks page proofs for any additional changes or corrections. **Repros**, or reproduction proofs, show any further changes in typesetting. They are printed on a special coated paper that will be photographed and used in the printing process. Repros are used by the designer to make any mechanicals that might be required. **Blues**, or blueprints, are the last stage in the typesetting process. They are made from photographic film that has been prepared for use in the printing process. Blues show how all the parts of each book page will be assembled, with art, text, and any other

On this galley proof, note the proofreader's correction marks. A "pe" indicates a printer's error; an "aa" indicates an author's or editor's change in the text.

One

Paula Jones grit her teeth. The screen door slammed. Her brother Pete was gone, and she was left at the breakfast table with her parents and her little brother Ted.

She slammed down her spoon. "It isn't fair," she said. "It's Pete's turn to do the dishes. I did them last night."

Her mother stood up. "It's not fair, you're right. I'll do the dishes, but I hope you'll help us with unpacking and setting things up. It's a shame to waste our first day of vacation working, but we have to get organized before we can have fun. help." Ted stood up, his cereal bowl in his hand. He reached for his half-full glass of milk, grabbed it tightly, and set it in the bowl. Holding the bowl and glass of milk with one hand, he began piling silver into the bowl. It wobbled, and the milk sloshed against the side of the glass. A knife fell onto the floor. Ted lurched for it, but the glass tilted, and milk splashed onto the table.

Ted looked miserable, Paula thought. He's always trying to help and makes a mess because he's so little. Paula remembered when she was six.

elements in place as they will appear in the finished book. Corrections can be made at this stage, but they are very expensive.

Color Separation

Printing colored illustrations in a book or on a cover is a much more complicated and expensive process than printing black type. In order to print color, it is necessary first to separate a color image into four process colors—yellow, magenta (red), cyan (blue), and black. The principle behind this is the same as mixing paints. Mixing the three primary colors—red, yellow, and blue—produces all other colors. Black is used to add highlight and depth.

Records or separations of the different hues of each color illustration or photograph are made. They are produced by a process that uses photographic film or by one that uses an electronic scanner and a computer program. The separations are then used to make printing plates that, when printed, will produce a full-color image on the printed pages of the book or cover.

A designer carefully checks the color plates. If the colors are not right, the color separator can change color hues.

A color illustration or photograph is first separated into four process colors—yellow, cyan (blue), magenta (red), and black.

yellow   cyan (blue)   magenta (red)   black

When the four colors are printed together, they make up more colors. For example, a combination of yellow and blue produces green, and a combination of blue and red produces purple.

yellow blue / green   yellow red / orange   blue red / purple   yellow blue / green

red   purple   black   orange   brown

This example shows how 32 pages are printed on one sheet of paper. Sixteen pages are printed on each side. Some pages are upside down. They are arranged so that they will fall into the proper sequence when the sheet is folded. This arrangement is called an imposition.

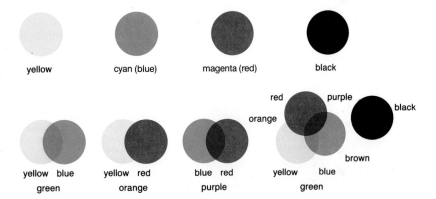

25	8	5	28	27	6	7	26
24	9	12	21	22	11	10	23
29	4	1	32	31	2	3	30
20	13	16	17	18	15	14	19

When the separation has been done, the separator will send a proof to the publisher for approval. If the colors do not seem right, the color separator can make adjustments and change color hues.

Printing

The printing process involves transferring all typed images and art onto large sheets of paper, which can then be folded and bound into a finished book. In the past, printing was done by hand on manually operated printing presses. Today, modern machines do the work.

When the printer receives the film prepared by the compositor, the film is exposed to flexible metal sheets. This process is similar to the way a photograph is developed from a negative. The images on the film are transferred to the metal sheets, which are then treated with chemicals. When these sheets are placed on cylinders in the printing press and passed by ink, the images are transferred to the sheets of paper that become the pages of the finished book.

The pages of a book come off the printing press on large sheets of paper. From 4 to 64 pages may be printed on each side of these sheets, but the usual number is 16 or 32. The pages do not follow each other in order. In-stead, they are arranged so that they will fall into the proper sequence when the sheets are folded. This arrangement is called an **imposition**. When all the pages have been printed, the book is ready for the next stage of the production process.

Binding

Binding is the final stage of the production process. After printing is finished, the printed sheets are sent to a bindery where they are folded, arranged in the correct sequence, and put within the book's cover.

At the bindery, the large printed sheets are put into a folding machine to be folded, gathered, and trimmed by special knives. Each folded section is called a **signature** and is usually made up of groups of 16 or 32 pages. Putting the signatures together in the proper sequence is called **gathering**.

Next, the signatures are sewn together by a large sewing machine. There are three methods of sewing a book. In **saddle sewing**, the book is stitched only through the center from back to front. With this method, books will open flat, but they are not very strong. In **Smyth sewing**, each signature is first individually sewn through its fold. Then the signatures are placed next to each other and sewn together across the back. Smyth-sewn books

Left: Two press operators check the color printing press. *Below:* The signatures—folded groups of 16 or 32 pages—are sewn or glued together before they are bound into a book.

open flat, and they are much stronger than saddle-sewn books. In **side sewing**, stitching runs through all the signatures from the side. Side-sewn books cannot open flat, but they are the strongest type of books.

Some books, such as paperbacks, are not sewn. Instead, a method called **perfect binding** is used. In this method, the folded rear edge of each signature is trimmed and the pages are glued directly to the cover. Perfect binding is not always durable.

After sewing comes smashing and gluing. In **smashing**, a powerful compressor squeezes all the signatures so that the sewing does not cause a bulge along the rear edge of the book. Smashing is usually followed by gluing, in which a mechanical roller and brush force glue between the rear edges of the signatures. This increases the book's strength.

After smashing and gluing, the pages of the book are trimmed and cut again in preparation for attaching the cover. The covers for most books are made of special cloth that can withstand wear and tear and be cleaned easily. This cloth is attached to heavy cardboardlike material called **binder's board**, which acts as a backing to stiffen the cover. After the covers are attached and the book's dust jacket is put on, it is ready to be shipped to the publisher's warehouse.

▶**MARKETING AND SELLING**

After a long complicated process, your book, *It Rained Every Day*, has finally been published. Congratulations! Soon you will receive your first copy, hot off the press.

Long before you see this first copy, however, your publisher will have begun planning how to market and sell your book. It was listed in the publisher's catalog with a photograph of the book jacket and a summary of the story. Advance news about the book was sent to book reviewers and booksellers, and plans were made to exhibit the book, along with other new books, at special conventions and traveling exhibits throughout the country.

When the first copies of *It Rained Every Day* are available, some are sent to book reviewers. Book reviews in newspapers, magazines, or on radio and television are free advertising and can be very important in generating interest in the book. Copies may also be sent to groups, such as library associations, that include booklists in their publications.

Most bookstores have a department where you can find many kinds of books for young readers, including picture books, storybooks, books on special topics such as history, science, or sports, and dictionaries and encyclopedias.

Publishers employ other techniques to market books as well. These may include paid advertisements in magazines and newspapers, posters that are displayed in bookstores or other places where books are sold, special bookmarks, and public appearances by the author (if he or she is well known).

Marketing promotes your book and creates interest in it. Selling the book is what earns money for you and the publisher. Several months before your book was published, it was presented at one of the publisher's sales conferences. At this conference your editor enthusiastically described your book to sales representatives, whose job it is to sell it to bookstores and other booksellers. Once in the hands of booksellers, the long process of publishing *It Rained Every Day* is finally over.

OLGA LITOWINSKY
Executive Editor, Books for Young Readers
Simon & Schuster

See also CALDECOTT AND NEWBERY MEDALS; CHILDREN'S LITERATURE; PRINTING; PROOFREADING; PUBLISHING.

BOONE, DANIEL (1734–1820)

Daniel Boone has become a legend as one of America's greatest pioneers and frontier heroes. He was a dead shot with a rifle and a skillful hunter who could glide through forests as swiftly and silently as an Indian.

Daniel was born on November 2, 1734, at Oley, a frontier settlement in Pennsylvania. By the age of 12, he was hunting game for the dinner table with his first rifle. Indians roamed the nearby woods. Daniel knew that if he were caught by Indians on the warpath against intruders on their land, he would either be tomahawked or taken prisoner. So he learned how to walk through the forest without making a sound.

In 1751 the Boones settled in North Carolina. In 1755, during the French and Indian War, Daniel joined British General Edward Braddock's expedition against the French. The British, who were unused to Indian ways of fighting, were ambushed and slaughtered, but Daniel and a hunter named John Finley (or Findley) escaped into the woods. Finley told Daniel about a mysterious land, west of the Appalachian Mountains, that the Indians called Kentucky. He said its forests were thick with turkeys, bears, and deer, and buffalo thundered across its prairies. These stories inspired Daniel to go to Kentucky.

First Daniel returned to North Carolina to marry 17-year-old Rebecca Bryan, whose family lived near the Boones. For the next ten years they rarely lived very long in one place.

Daniel often was away hunting deerskins and beaver pelts, which he sold to support his growing family.

Finally, in 1769, Daniel set out across the Appalachian Mountains, and for the next two years he explored Kentucky. Then he went back to North Carolina to gather several families who would return with him to establish a settlement. On the journey back to Kentucky, the pioneers were attacked by Indians, and Daniel's son James and several others were killed. The settlers turned back.

In 1775, still determined, Daniel cleared the Wilderness Road, through the Cumberland Gap, into Kentucky and built a fort called Boonesborough on the Kentucky River. Then he returned home to lead another group of pioneers across the mountains to settle there. Daniel's wife and daughter were among the first women settlers in Kentucky.

In 1778, Daniel was captured by Shawnee Indians. Their chief, Blackfish, was so proud to have caught the famous frontiersman, he "adopted" Daniel as his son and named him *Shel-tow-ee*, meaning "Big Turtle." For several months, Daniel lived among the Indians. One day he overheard the Indians plan a raid on Boonesborough, but he was able to negotiate a plan with the Shawnee to surrender his men as prisoners. His quick thinking saved the lives of countless numbers of other settlers. Later, when Daniel discovered the Indians were planning yet another attack on Boonesborough, he made a daring escape and reached the fort in time to warn the settlers.

Daniel later held several public offices, including lieutenant colonel of the militia and representative of the Kentucky state legislature. However, he lost all claim to the land he had been the first white man to explore and settle, because he had not followed the proper procedures to obtain legal title to it.

In 1799, feeling Kentucky had become too crowded with people, he moved westward to Missouri to find, as he put it, "more elbow room." He died in Missouri on September 26, 1820, at the age of 86.

Reviewed by DANIEL ROSELLE
State University College (Fredonia, New York)

BOOTH, JOHN WILKES (1838–1865)

John Wilkes Booth, the infamous assassin of President Abraham Lincoln, came from one of America's most famous theatrical families. His father, Junius, and his brother, Edwin, both were actors of considerable reputation, and John followed in their footsteps.

Booth was born in 1838 near Bel Air, Maryland, on a farm worked by slaves. As a young man during the Civil War, he strongly sympathized with the Confederate cause. In 1864, as the war turned ever more in favor of the Union, Booth and several other conspirators hatched a plan to kidnap Lincoln and strike a blow against Union morale. They also hoped to exchange the president for Confederate prisoners of war. However, nothing came of their immediate plans. After Confederate General Robert E. Lee's surrender at Appomattox on April 9, 1865, Booth and his followers' kidnapping plot turned toward murder. In addition to Lincoln, their targets included Vice President Andrew Johnson and Secretary of State William H. Seward.

On the evening of April 14, Lincoln, his wife, and two young friends attended the play *Our American Cousin* at Ford's Theatre in Washington, D.C. Booth entered their private box with a small pistol and shot the president in the back of the head at point-blank range. Witnesses reported that Booth then jumped down to the stage, shouting, *"Sic semper tyrannis!"* (Thus always to tyrants), Virginia's state motto. Lincoln never regained consciousness and died the next morning in a rooming house across the street from the theater. As the president drew his last breath, his Secretary of War Edwin Stanton uttered, "Now he belongs to the ages."

In his leap to the stage, Booth had broken his left leg above the ankle, but he managed to escape with one other conspirator. Union soldiers caught up with him several days later and cornered him in a barn near Port Royal, Virginia. Refusing to surrender, Booth was shot to death. His last reported words were, "Tell mother I died for my country."

For the murder of President Lincoln, eight conspirators were quickly brought to trial and sentenced. Four were hanged: George Atzerodt, Davy Herold, Lewis Paine, and Mary Surratt (owner of the boardinghouse in which the conspiracy reportedly took place).

After shooting President Abraham Lincoln on April 14, 1865, John Wilkes Booth leapt to the stage of Ford's Theatre and escaped. Lincoln died the following morning. Booth was later captured and killed.

The other four were sentenced to life imprisonment, including Dr. Samuel Mudd, who had set Booth's fractured leg after his escape from Ford's Theatre.

Many conspiracy theories regarding Lincoln's assassination cropped up after his death. One story, for example, implicated Secretary of War Stanton as a co-conspirator; others claimed repeated "sightings" of Booth as late as the 1890's. Such stories take advantage of the fact that, unlike in detective mysteries, many questions regarding historical events can never be answered with certainty.

It is possible that the Confederate government was involved in the assassination plot, but Lincoln's murder was more likely the work of a small group of conspirators living in a society deeply disturbed and divided by war. Many Southerners could not accept defeat and the changes that were to be imposed on them. In Lincoln's last speech, he made reference to extending to blacks the right to vote. For John Wilkes Booth, it appears that this was a consequence he could not endure.

GABOR S. BORITT
Director, Civil War Institute
Gettysburg College

BORAH, WILLIAM EDGAR. See IDAHO (Famous People).

BORDEN, SIR ROBERT LAIRD. See CANADA, GOVERNMENT OF (Profiles).

BORGLUM, GUTZON. See IDAHO (Famous People).

BORLAUG, NORMAN. See IOWA (Famous People).

BORNEO

Borneo is the world's third largest island. Only Greenland and New Guinea are larger. With an area of about 287,000 square miles (743,000 square kilometers), Borneo is larger than many nations of the world.

Borneo straddles the equator at the western end of the Pacific Ocean. To the north, across the South China Sea, is the mainland of Asia.

Politically, Borneo is divided among three separate nations—Indonesia, Malaysia, and Brunei. Kalimantan, the largest region of Borneo, belongs to Indonesia. Sabah and Sarawak belong to Malaysia and together are known as East Malaysia. Brunei, a tiny, oil-rich nation, is situated on the northwestern coast of the island.

▶ PEOPLE

Borneo has a population of more than 14 million. The great majority are Dayaks, a native people who belong to a number of different tribes. Malays and Chinese make up the next largest ethnic groups. Many people from the crowded nearby island of Java, encour-aged by the Indonesian government, have re-settled on Borneo in Kalimantan.

Language. Major languages spoken in Borneo include Bahasa Indonesia and Bahasa Malaysia (the official languages of Indonesia and Malaysia). Various Dayak dialects, English, and Chinese are also spoken.

Religion. Many Dayaks practice traditional native religions. Most of the other people of Borneo are Muslims.

Rural Life. The Dayaks, who form the majority of residents in the interior, tend to follow older, more traditional ways of life. The people hunt, fish, and plant crops on small plots cleared from the forest.

▶ LAND

Land Regions. Borneo consists of a flat, swampy coastal lowland and a mountainous interior, with dense tropical rain forests and many rivers. Mount Kinabalu, the island's highest peak, rises 13,455 feet (4,101 meters) above sea level. The Kapuas mountain chain, which runs generally east and west, forms the backbone of the island. The Schwaner Mountains run in a northeast and southwest direction.

Rivers and Coastal Waters. The island of Borneo is located in the western Pacific Ocean. The South China and Sulu seas lie to the north, the Celebes Sea to the east, and the Java Sea to the south. The Karimata Strait separates Borneo from the island of Sumatra in the west.

Borneo's many rivers include the Baram, Kayan, Mahakam, Barito, Kahayan, Kapuas, and Rajang. Since travel is often difficult in the rugged interior, the rivers provide an important means of transportation.

Climate. Borneo has a tropical climate, with generally high temperatures and humidity and considerable rainfall. The temperature seldom falls below 70°F (21°C), except in the cooler highland areas, and often reaches a high of 96°F (36°C). Depending on elevation and exposure to rain-bearing monsoon winds, Borneo receives from 100 to 200 inches (2,500 to 5,000 millimeters) of rainfall a year.

Wildlife. Borneo is famous for its wildlife. Hundreds of species of birds add brilliant color to the forest. Reptiles include several varieties of poisonous snakes; crocodiles live in the rivers. The larger forest animals include two-horned rhinoceroses, honey bears, wild

Borneo

Many houses along the coast of the island of Borneo are built on stilts because the land is low and easily flooded.

pigs, wild oxen, deer, elephants, monkeys, and gibbons. One of the shiest creatures is the orang-utan, a large ape whose name means "man of the forest" in Malay.

Natural Resources. Forests cover most of the island. The trees, which may grow to a height of 120 feet (37 meters), grow so thickly that little sunlight can penetrate their cover. Timber is one of Borneo's most valuable natural resources. Teak and other valuable hardwoods grow in the interior.

Petroleum and natural gas are Borneo's most important minerals. Brunei is the single most important petroleum-producing area on the island. Coal, bauxite, iron, gold, and other minerals are also mined.

▶ **ECONOMY**

Agriculture and Forestry. The majority of Borneo's people earn their living from agriculture. Rice is the most important food crop; other crops include corn, sweet potatoes, yams, cassava (manioc), and beans. Clearing land for cultivation frequently is carried out by the slash-and-burn method, in which vegetation is first cut and then burned away. In 1997–98, many such fires raged out of control when the normal monsoon rains did not arrive, destroying thousands of acres of forest and blanketing Borneo with dense smoke.

Borneo's chief commercial agricultural product is rubber. Copra (dried coconut), tobacco, pepper, and hemp (for making rope) also are produced in large quantities.

Manufacturing and Mining. Borneo has limited industry. Most of it involves the drilling for and refining of petroleum and the processing of agricultural products and timber.

▶ **MAJOR CITIES**

Almost all of Borneo's cities and towns are located in the coastal areas. Banjarmasin in Kalimantan is Borneo's largest city. Other large cities, also in Kalimantan, are Pontianak, Balikpapan, and Samarinda. Kuching is the capital of Sarawak, and Kota Kinabalu the capital of Sabah. Brunei's capital city is Bandar Seri Begawan.

▶ **HISTORY**

Borneo has a long history. Traders from India arrived in Borneo at least 2,000 years ago. Chinese settled on the island in succeeding centuries. There were also early contacts between Borneo and what are now the Indonesian islands of Java and Sumatra.

Europeans first arrived in the region in the 1500's. The Dutch became the most successful colonizers, gaining control of what is now Kalimantan by the early 1800's. By the mid-1800's the British were dominant in the northwestern quarter of the island, in what are now Sabah, Sarawak, and Brunei.

During World War II (1939–45), Japanese troops occupied most of the coastal areas of Borneo. When Indonesia gained its independence from the Netherlands in 1949, it acquired Dutch-controlled Borneo. Sabah and Sarawak became part of Malaysia in 1963. Brunei remained a British protectorate until 1984, when it won complete independence.

PHILLIP BACON
University of Houston
Author, *Golden Book Picture Atlas of the World*

See also BRUNEI; INDONESIA; MALAYSIA.

BOSNIA AND HERZEGOVINA

BOSNIA AND HERZEGOVINA

Bosnia and Herzegovina (sometimes spelled Hercegovina) was formerly one of the six republics making up the nation of Yugoslavia. In 1992, Bosnia and Herzegovina declared its independence, becoming the fourth Yugoslav republic to do so. Following independence, however, it was torn by more than three years of bloody civil war among its three main ethnic groups.

The People. Bosnia and Herzegovina has a population of about 4.4 million. Its people are nearly all South Slavs, but they are sharply divided into three main ethnic communities.

According to the last census, nearly 32 percent of the people are Serbs, who belong to the Eastern Orthodox Church. Slightly over 17 percent are Croats, who are Roman Catholics. The largest group, nearly 44 percent of the population, are Muslims, who may be Serbs or Croats in terms of nationality and language. This is a reminder of the long period of rule by the Muslim Ottoman Turks. The official language is Serbo-Croatian. The country's rugged landscape with its few natural resources has produced a people of generally hardy and vigorous character.

Sarajevo, the capital and largest city, had a metropolitan population of about 500,000. Mostar is the second largest city.

The Land and Economy. Bosnia and Herzegovina's area of about 19,800 square miles (51,280 square kilometers) is largely mountainous. Bosnia, the northern part of the country, takes its name from the Bosna River. Herzegovina, in the south, derives its name from *Herzog*, the German word for "duke," the title of its onetime rulers.

Roughly half the land is covered with forests, while only about one-quarter is suitable for farming. Most of the remainder is used as pasture for livestock. Historically, the rugged nature of the terrain has made transportation difficult. The country's economy is based chiefly on agriculture. Wheat and other grains are major food crops. A variety of fruits are also grown. The forests provide timber and other wood products.

Early History. An independent Bosnian state emerged in the 1300's, but in the late 1400's, it fell to the Ottoman Turks, who ruled it for some four centuries. In 1878, the two territories were placed under the administration of Austria-Hungary. Complete annexation by Austria in 1908 fanned the flames of Bosnian nationalism.

Creation of Yugoslavia. In 1914 a Bosnian Serb student, Gavrilo Princip, assassinated the heir to the Austrian throne at Sarajevo, triggering World War I. After the war's end in 1918, Bosnia and Herzegovina became part of an independent Yugoslav kingdom. From 1941 to 1945, during World War II, the region was under Nazi German occupation. In 1946 it became a republic of a newly established Communist Yugoslav state.

Independence. Yugoslavia began to break apart in 1991, following the collapse of other Communist regimes in Eastern Europe. Bosnia and Herzegovina's proclamation of independence in 1992 led to an immediate outbreak of fighting by Serbs opposed to independence. Supported by Serb-led Yugoslav forces, they expelled large numbers of Muslims and by 1993 had gained control of about two-thirds of the region's territory. But in 1995, airstrikes launched by the United States and other members of the North Atlantic Treaty Organization (NATO) against Bosnian Serb forces compelled them to agree to a cease-fire. Under the 1995 Dayton peace accord, the country was divided into separate Muslim-Croat and Serb parts.

ARTHUR CAMPBELL TURNER
University of California, Riverside

BOSTON

Boston is the capital of the Commonwealth of Massachusetts. The city is located in the northeastern United States on a peninsula, where the Charles River flows into a large, well-protected bay of the Atlantic Ocean, forming one of the world's finest natural harbors. Founded in 1630, Boston is at once an old city and a new one. Because many of the major events of the American Revolutionary War took place in or near Boston, it has come to be known as the "Cradle of Liberty."

With a population of about 575,000, Boston is New England's largest city. The city encompasses 46 square miles (119 square kilometers), which is more than 35 times its original colonial size. This growth is due in part to a clever landfill project that was undertaken in the late 1800's to reclaim much of the swampland along the Charles River basin. The project took soil from Boston's hills to create the Back Bay section and the waterfront area. Boston's growth is also due to the annexation of several bordering towns. The modern city of Boston is made up of many neighborhoods, including Downtown Boston, Charlestown, Dorchester, Roxbury, South Boston, East Boston, Back Bay, Beacon Hill, the North End, Brighton-Allston, the Fenway, Jamaica Plain, Roslindale, West Roxbury, Mattapan, and Hyde Park.

Boston's average temperatures range from 31°F (−1°C) in the winter to 71°F (22°C) in the summer. The average yearly precipitation is 43 inches (1,080 millimeters).

Business and Industry

Boston was one of the first industrial cities in the United States. Today it maintains a number of strong industries, including the processing of fresh and frozen fish; electronics assembly; video and film production; the manufacture of medical and dental instruments; printing and bookbinding; and the manufacture of stone, clay, and glass products. An expanding service economy and the success of high technology of defense-weapons manufacturing have contributed to Boston's economic health and high rate of employment.

Major components of Boston's service industry include financial services (banking, insurance, and real estate), health care, education, and tourism.

Transportation

Boston's public transportation system, the oldest in the United States, provides a crisscross of subway lines, trolleys, buses, and trains, which makes it easy for residents of outlying neighborhoods to travel into the center of the city.

Boston is also the major seaport and air terminus for Massachusetts and New England. The port of Boston, with its 25 miles (40 kilometers) of docking space, handles about 26 million tons of cargo annually. Logan Airport, the twelfth busiest in the world, services 20.5 million passengers and 335,000 tons of cargo annually.

Urban Renewal

In the 1960's an extensive project was undertaken to bring new life to the decaying

Modern skyscrapers and historic landmarks grace the Boston skyline. Many high-rise buildings were erected in the 1960's as part of an urban renewal project.

Colorful Quincy Market is a lively place where residents and tourists alike go to shop, dine, and be entertained. Both the market and Faneuil Hall (rear) were successfully restored in the late 1970's.

this day maintains a national reputation for academic excellence. In 1636, across the Charles River in neighboring Cambridge, Harvard University opened its doors.

Today, there are more than 65 colleges and universities serving 250,000 students in the Greater Boston Area. Among these are Harvard University, Radcliffe College, the Massachusetts Institute of Technology (MIT), Boston University, Boston College, Northeastern University, Brandeis University, Emerson College, Tufts University, and the University of Massachusetts.

Libraries. Many world-class libraries are located in Boston. Among them are the Athenaeum, which owns George Washington's book collection; the Boston Public Library, considered one of the finest in the United States; and the library at Harvard, the world's largest university library, with more than 9 million volumes.

Museums. Famous Boston museums include the Museum of Fine Arts, the Children's Museum, the Museum of Science, the Computer Museum, the John F. Kennedy Presidential Library and Museum, and the Isabella Stewart Gardner Museum.

Music and Dance. The Boston Pops Orchestra and the Boston Symphony Orchestra delight audiences at Symphony Hall. The Boston Opera and the Boston Ballet have earned worldwide recognition and perform regularly to full houses.

downtown area. Today, Boston's skyline includes many new skyscrapers and prominent landmarks, such as the Prudential Center, the Government Center, and the John Hancock Mutual Life Insurance Company tower.

Education, Culture, and Recreation

For its size, Boston has an unusually large number of educational, cultural, and recreational facilities. It is a major center for the publication of books, textbooks, and magazines. The city's major newspapers are the *Boston Globe*, the *Boston Herald*, and the *Christian Science Monitor*, which is distributed internationally.

Schools. In 1635, Puritan settlers established the Boston Latin Academy, the first free public school in the United States, which to

---

BOSTON "FIRSTS"

A partial list of many "firsts" that occurred in Boston illustrates the city's importance in American tradition, culture, and technological development.

1639	First post office.
1653	First public library.
1686	First schoolbook printed.
1704	First American newspaper published, the *Boston News-Letter*.
1776	First proclamation of the Declaration of Independence, Old State House, July 18.
1845	First sewing machine.
1846	First anesthesia demonstration.
1857	First American literary magazine published, the *Atlantic Monthly*.
1873	First university to open all departments to women (Boston University).
1874	First words spoken by telephone.
1897	First subway for trolley car operation.
1900	First Davis Cup tennis match.
1903	First modern World Series, won by the Boston Red Sox over the Pittsburgh Pirates.
1929	First computer, developed at MIT.
1944	First automatic digital computer, patented at Harvard.

Parks. Boston Common (the oldest public park in the United States), the Public Garden, the Arnold Arboretum, the Charles River, and Boston Harbor provide beautiful settings within the city for outdoor activities, such as bicycling, jogging, picnicking, and sailing.

Sports. Fenway Park is the home of Boston's professional baseball team, the Boston Red Sox. The city also supports professional teams in basketball (the Boston Celtics), football (the New England Patriots), and ice hockey (the Boston Bruins). Perhaps the one sporting event most identified with the city is the Boston Marathon. Held on Patriot's Day (the third Monday in April), it is the oldest sporting event in the United States and attracts more than 6,000 competitors every year.

HISTORY

Ten years after the Pilgrims arrived at Plymouth on the *Mayflower*, English Puritans followed them to New England in search of religious freedom. In 1630, under the leadership of John Winthrop, the first governor of the Massachusetts Bay Colony, the Puritans founded Charlestown and later Boston on the other side of the Charles River.

Although the Indians who inhabited the area called it "Shawmut," the Puritans first re-named it "Trimountaine" for the three hills that dominated the landscape. (To this day, the official symbol of the city includes the "trimount.") The name Boston was later adopted because many of the Puritans had come from a town by that name in England. In 1632, Boston became the capital of the Massachusetts Bay Colony.

For two hundred years after the Puritans arrived, Boston remained populated almost exclusively by their descendants. However, beginning in the 1840's, great waves of European immigrants voyaged to the United States in search of a better life. Many of those who settled in Boston came from Ireland to escape the great famine caused by a four-year blight to their potato crops. Today the Irish form the largest ethnic group in Boston, followed by the Italians. Blacks account for about 22 percent of Boston's population.

Throughout the 1800's, Boston witnessed many religious, literary, philosophical, and social changes. The Christian Science religion was established at The Mother Church, and King's Chapel was the birthplace of American Unitarianism. William Lloyd Garrison made his first antislavery speech in 1829 at the Park Street Church. The Old Corner Bookstore became a favorite meeting place for distin-

Every year millions of people take a walk along the famous "Freedom Trail" to visit Boston's most important historic landmarks, many of which date from colonial days.

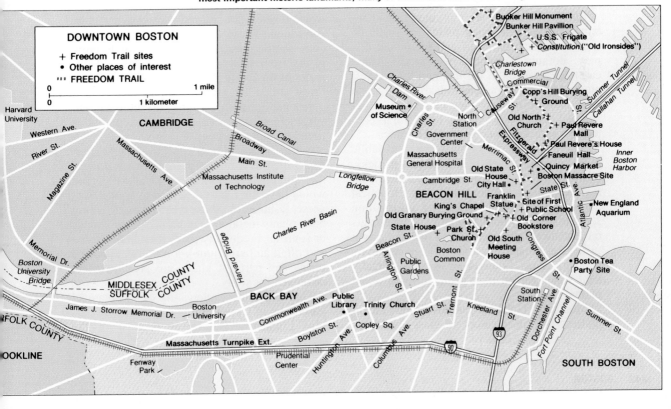

guished writers, such as Henry Wadsworth Longfellow, Ralph Waldo Emerson, and Henry David Thoreau.

Places of Interest

Each year more than 2 million visitors—as well as countless area residents—take a 2-mile (3.2-kilometer) walk along a well-marked path called the "Freedom Trail" to visit the Boston of old. Colonial Boston seems to come alive when one visits the sites of many of the events that led up to the American Revolutionary War (1775–83). Of special interest are the site of the Boston Massacre (1770), where British troops fired at a crowd of American colonists, killing five; the Old South Meetinghouse, where in 1773 the "Sons of Liberty" planned the infamous Boston Tea Party; and Christ ("Old North") Church, where in 1775 Robert Newman hung the "two if by sea" lanterns that sent Paul Revere and William Dawes on their famous midnight rides to warn the Minutemen.

Other sites along the Freedom Trail include Paul Revere's house, the site of Benjamin Franklin's birth, the Old State House, and Fan-

euil Hall. Since 1742, Faneuil Hall has been used as an all-purpose marketplace (first floor) and meeting hall (second floor). In front of Faneuil Hall is Quincy Market. Today, more than 14 million residents and tourists every year come to visit its 175 shops, restaurants, food markets, and art galleries.

Boston also has a "Black Heritage Trail," a walking tour that explores the history of Boston's black community. The trail begins at the Museum of Afro-American History and includes visits to the African Meeting House (the oldest church established by blacks in the United States) and the Robert Gould Shaw and 54th Regiment Memorial, a monument to one of the black regiments that fought for the North during the Civil War.

Boston's rich historic and cultural heritage makes it an exciting city for its residents as well as its 10 million annual visitors. The unusual variety of attractions makes Boston deserving of another of its popular nicknames— the "Hub of the Universe."

ANNE N. BONNER
Director of Communications and Public Relations
Greater Boston Chamber of Commerce

BOSTON MASSACRE. See REVOLUTIONARY WAR.
BOSTON TEA PARTY. See REVOLUTIONARY WAR.

BOTANICAL GARDENS

Botanical gardens are museums that maintain collections of living plants for scientific and educational purposes and for public display. **Botanists** (scientists who study plants) carry out research in the laboratories and test plots of botanical gardens to learn more about how plants grow, how new plants can be developed, and how plants can be useful to people as a source of food and other products.

Sharing knowledge of plants with the public is an important function of botanical gardens. Visitors will find all the plants labeled with their scientific and common names. Botanical gardens may have libraries and information services and may publish books and pamphlets on botanical subjects. School classes might visit local botanical gardens for guided tours or workshops. Sometimes students actually tend small garden plots there to learn about plants.

Most large botanical gardens include greenhouses or conservatories—glass buildings

where temperature, humidity, and light can be controlled. These artificial environments can copy natural ones, making it possible to grow plants from many different regions and climates of the world. In one room a tropical rain forest might be created; in another, desert plants can grow in a sunny, dry climate; and yet another room can display the conditions found in a marshy bog.

Some botanical gardens have theme gardens, such as a butterfly garden with flowers that attract those insects. A Japanese garden would have the plants arranged in typical Japanese fashion. A Shakespeare garden would have plants mentioned in Shakespeare's plays or sonnets. Frequently there is an herb garden and often an herbarium—a place where dried plants and parts of plants are preserved and cataloged for study.

One of the most interesting of all botanical gardens is in Uppsala, Sweden, home of Carolus Linnaeus. This great botanist of the

1700's devised a system of classifying and naming plants and animals. He managed the Uppsala Gardens from 1742 to 1777. Today the gardens display plants in beds that Linnaeus himself laid out. A biography of Linnaeus is included in Volume L.

One of the greatest botanical gardens in the world today is the Royal Botanic Gardens at Kew, near London, England. The facility is sometimes known as Kew Gardens. In the 1800's it introduced plants brought back from the voyages of Captain Cook, including coffee, cotton, and cinnamon trees.

One of the best-known botanical gardens in the United States is the New York Botanical Garden in the Bronx, New York, which has more than 13,000 species of plants. The Missouri Botanical Gardens in St. Louis is the oldest in the United States.

Canada has a number of well-known botanical gardens, among them the Montreal Botanical Gardens in Quebec and the Royal Botanical Gardens in Ontario.

LUCY E. JONES
Director of Education
Brooklyn Botanic Gardens

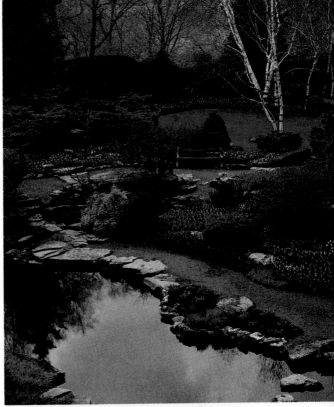

Carefully arranged and labeled gardens offer an opportunity to study as well as to enjoy plants in a natural setting. The Royal Botanical Gardens in Hamilton, Ontario, is known for its late-blooming tulip collection.

BOTANY

Have you ever wondered what is inside a flower? Or what the veins in a leaf are for? If you have, you have asked the same sorts of questions as those asked by a botanist. A botanist is a scientist whose field is botany—the study of plants.

Plants form the basis of all life on earth. Only plants can capture the energy of the sun and use it—in a process called photosynthesis —to make food. Animals cannot do this and so must depend on plants for food. We also depend on plants for the oxygen they give off during photosynthesis.

This essential world of plants is a large and varied one. There are about 300,000 different kinds of plants that have been identified. They range in size from tiny mosses as small as $\frac{3}{8}$ inch (1 centimeter) to the giant redwoods, the largest living things on earth. Some plants, such as carrots, are rooted in soil. Others— orchids, for example—grow in air. Some plants reproduce from seeds, others from underground stems.

Botany includes every aspect of plant life. A botanist may study the plant itself—its structure and the function of its various parts. Other botanists may study the development of plants on earth—when they first appeared, how they changed over long periods of time, and how they are related to one another.

Some botanists study plants in relation to their environment. They may, for example, try to determine how soil and water affect the growth and reproduction of plants.

A botanist may specialize in one area of botany, but whatever his or her specialty, the work can benefit people. Thus, botanists may discover plants that yield important new medicines, or they may help to improve crops by developing new and better varieties of plants.

Reviewed by NANCY R. MORIN
Missouri Botanical Garden

See also ALGAE; BACTERIA; CACTUS; CELLS; FERNS; FLOWERS; FUNGI; GENETICS; GRASSES; KINGDOMS OF LIVING THINGS; LEAVES; LIFE; MOSSES; PHOTOSYNTHESIS; PLANT PESTS; PLANTS; REPRODUCTION; TREES; WEEDS.

BOTSWANA

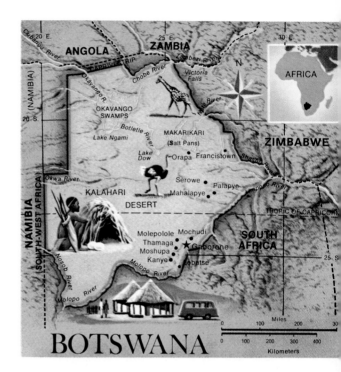

Botswana is an arid, landlocked country in southern Africa. Formerly known as Bechuanaland, it was a British dependency before gaining independence in 1966. Much of Botswana's land is desert or grassland suitable only for grazing cattle.

▶ PEOPLE

Most of the people are Tswana, who belong to the large Bantu family. The Tswana are cattle herders and farmers. A number of San, a distinct people of southern Africa, inhabit the Kalahari Desert, where they live primarily as hunters and food gatherers. Many of the people practice traditional African religions. Others are Christian. The most widely spoken languages are Setswana, a Bantu language, and English, which is the official language. Botswana has few cities. The largest city is Gaborone, the capital. Most of the people live in villages, some of great size.

▶ LAND AND ECONOMY

Most of Botswana is a vast plateau. In the northwest the Okavango River overflows to create an area of large swamps. Southern Botswana forms part of the great Kalahari Desert.

FACTS and figures

REPUBLIC OF BOTSWANA is the official name of the country.

LOCATION: Southern Africa.

AREA: 231,804 sq mi (600,372 km²).

POPULATION: 1,500,000 (estimate).

CAPITAL AND LARGEST CITY: Gaborone.

MAJOR LANGUAGES: English (official), Setswana.

MAJOR RELIGIOUS GROUPS: Traditional African religions, various independent Christian churches.

GOVERNMENT: Republic. **Head of state and government**—president. **Legislature**—National Assembly.

CHIEF PRODUCTS: Agricultural—cattle, sorghum, millet, corn. **Mineral**—diamonds, copper, nickel.

MONETARY UNIT: Pula (1 pula = 100 thebe).

The north and east receive most of the slight rainfall and generally have the only land suitable for cultivation. Most of the population is concentrated in the east.

Botswana's economy is based on cattle raising and mining. Meat and hides, diamonds, copper, and nickel are the chief exports. Farming is limited to a few food crops.

▶ HISTORY AND GOVERNMENT

Europeans knew little about what is now Botswana before the early 1800's, when British missionaries arrived there. For many years the region was torn by tribal warfare and by clashes between the Tswana and the Boers of South Africa. In 1885 the native chiefs asked Great Britain for protection against the Boers, and the territory—then called Bechuanaland—became a British protectorate. Botswana gained its independence in 1966.

The government consists of a president and a legislature called the National Assembly. There is also an advisory body, the House of Chiefs. Elections are held every five years.

Since independence, Botswana has had continuously elected democratic governments. It has followed a moderate course in African affairs and a policy of non-alignment in its international relations.

HUGH C. BROOKS
St. John's University (New York)

BOTTICELLI, SANDRO (1444?–1510)

The poetic paintings of the Renaissance master known as Botticelli often describe the beginnings of things. With grace and delicacy Botticelli depicted not just love but the birth of the love goddess, not simply faith but the birth of Christ, not only the beauty of nature but the blooming of spring. He turned for subject matter to history and religion, to poetry and legend.

Botticelli's life is somewhat like a legend. Little about it can be proved since much of what we know has come down through the ages by word of mouth. He was born in Florence and died there when he was about 65. His real name was Alessandro Filipepi, but he took the name Botticelli from his older brother, whose nickname was *Botticello,* meaning "little barrel." By 1460 he was probably studying with the well-known artist Fra Filippo Lippi. By the time he was 25, Botticelli had already become teacher to Lippi's son and was considered one of the best painters in Florence.

Among his many admirers was Pope Sixtus IV. In 1481 the Pope invited Botticelli to Rome to help decorate the Sistine Chapel, which had recently been completed. Botticelli's contributions to the chapel include wall paintings illustrating the life of Moses.

The Medici family, rulers of Florence, were the greatest supporters of artists and scholars in all Italy. Botticelli received encouragement from them and may even have lived in the Medici palace. The scholars there were fascinated by the poetry and philosophy of ancient Greece. As his painting the *Primavera* shows us, Botticelli, too, was entranced by the creators of ancient mythology. The spiritual quality of his religious paintings can also be seen in his portrayals of the gods and heroes of ancient Greece.

In his later years Botticelli was influenced by the monk Savonarola, who preached against the vanity and extravagance of the Florentines. Botticelli became very religious and painted only religious subjects.

Botticelli's paintings are famous for their dancing lines, flowing forms, and delicate details, admirably represented in the *Primavera*. His golden-haired Venus, goddess of love, has in her eyes the faraway look of one lost in a daydream, which appears so often in Botticelli's work.

Reviewed by ARIANE RUSKIN BATTERBERRY
Author, *The Pantheon Story of Art for Young People*

Primavera ("Spring") by Sandro Botticelli, painted around 1478. This famous picture, on a huge, rectangular wooden panel, hangs in the Uffizi Gallery, Florence.

Bottling is an automated process. Conveyor belts carry bottles to washing, filling, capping, and labeling machines. Machines also pack the bottles in cartons, which are conveyed to shipping areas.

BOTTLES AND BOTTLING

Bottles are made in an endless variety of forms—tall, squat, round, and slender. They range in size from tiny perfume bottles that hold less than an ounce to large industrial bottles that hold many quarts. Some bottles are designed from a practical standpoint. They have very broad bases to keep from being toppled over or long, narrow necks to make pouring easy. Other bottles are shaped in odd and interesting ways for advertising purposes. Many bottles are so beautifully designed that they may be used solely as ornaments.

Glass bottles came into use very slowly over a span of many hundreds of years. The Egyptians learned how to make glass before 3000 B.C. Around 1500 B.C. they began to make bottles by forming molten (melted) glass around a core of sand or clay. When the object had been fashioned and decorated, the core was scraped out. Making bottles in this way was so difficult and expensive that glass bottles were a luxury item for 1,500 years. Then the Romans developed cheaper and quicker methods of production. Using blowpipes, skilled Roman workers blew the molten glass into bubbles. By blowing the bubble inside a mold, they found they could produce bottles of uniform size and shape.

After the fall of the Roman Empire in the 5th century A.D., glass bottles again became a scarce and sought-after luxury in Europe. They were collected and displayed like prize paintings.

Bottles became more of an everyday item in the 18th century, but they were still made by hand by the same methods the Romans used

nearly 2,000 years before. Even with the help of molds, an experienced glassblower and a crew of assistants could only turn out about 250 bottles a day.

Some of our most familiar glass containers date from the 19th century. The first baby bottle was patented in 1841. John L. Mason put his famous mason jar on the market in 1858. Dr. Hervey D. Thatcher perfected the milk bottle in the mid-1880's.

Glass manufacturers experimented with various ways to automate the bottle-making process. In 1865 the pressing and blowing machine was invented. In this machine a plunger forces the molten glass against a mold. Then compressed air blows the glass into its final shape.

The first fully successful automatic blowing machine was invented in 1903. The Owens Bottle Machine, invented by Michael Owens, was the first real advance in the manufacture of glass containers since the invention of the blowpipe. Today, modern versions of blowing machines make a variety of products—including jelly glasses, fruit jars, and soft-drink bottles—efficiently and inexpensively.

Bottling

After bottles have been made, they must be filled and prepared for shipment to stores. This task, called bottling, involves a number of steps. These are washing, filling, capping, labeling, and packing. Today almost all the work is done by machines. Conveyor belts move the bottles from one machine to another in an orderly parade, like marching soldiers.

The bottles must first be cleaned. This is especially important with returnable glass containers that are used over and over again. Some soft-drink, milk, and beer bottles are reused as many as 30 times before they are broken or lost.

The clean bottles move along a conveyor belt to a rotary filling machine. Rotary filling machines can fill up to 2,000 containers per minute. A platform lifts each bottle up and presses it tightly against one of many filling valves. The contents pour in. The full bottle is then lowered and moved on to the capping machine. The capping machine presses a cap onto the mouth of each bottle. These may be cork- or plastic-lined caps or screw caps. One type of cap used in the soft-drink market is a closure made of aluminum and rolled onto the lip of the bottle. Other bottles have corks inserted in the neck. After capping comes labeling, if required. This is done by a labeling machine that has sets of automatic "fingers." The fingers pick up a label, put glue on it, and press it onto the correct place on the bottle.

After being washed, filled, capped, and labeled, bottles are ready to be packed for shipment to stores. Packing is done by machines that drop the bottles into cases or cartons, seal the boxes, and send them on their way to the shipping platforms.

Recycling

Glass bottles have been replaced for some uses by plastic, metal, and cardboard containers that are not breakable and can be discarded. However, government legislation in many states has discouraged discarding glass, plastic, and metal beverage containers by requiring that deposit fees be paid at the time of purchase. The fees are refundable only if the container is returned.

Bottles and other glassware that are not reusable can be recycled and used to make new glass containers. The used glass is sorted by colors. It is crushed into small pieces and added to a mixture of sand, limestone, and soda ash. This mixture is melted in a furnace and formed into new bottles and other products. By recycling bottles, we conserve the energy resources used in making new bottles. We also limit the costs and other problems of disposing of discarded bottles.

Reviewed by JANET F. FLYNN
Glass Packaging Institute

BOUTROS-GHALI, BOUTROS. See UNITED NATIONS (Profiles).

BOW AND ARROW. See ARCHERY.

BOWELL, SIR MACKENZIE. See CANADA, GOVERNMENT OF (Profiles).

BOWIE, JAMES (1796?–1836)

James (Jim) Bowie was a fighter in Texas' struggle for independence from Mexico. Much folklore has been passed down about his adventures. It has been said that he rode alligators, speared wild cattle, and smuggled slaves for profit along the Gulf Coast with the pirate Jean Laffite.

Born about 1796, Bowie grew up in the backwoods of Louisiana. He was said to have invented the bowie knife after he cut his hand on a butcher knife while fighting Indians. He had a crosspiece placed between the handle and the blade to prevent the hand from slipping forward.

In 1828, Bowie settled in San Antonio, Texas, which then belonged to Mexico. About 1832 he joined the Texas independence movement and later became a colonel in the Texas army. In 1836 he and fewer than 200 other Texans were besieged at the Alamo by Mexican General Santa Anna and

Folklore credits Jim Bowie with the invention of the bowie knife. A metal guard, or crosspiece, separates the blade and handle. Frontiersmen nicknamed this razor-sharp, all-purpose tool the "Arkansas Toothpick."

his large army. Although sick with pneumonia, Bowie killed several of the attackers before he was fatally wounded on March 6, 1836. All of the other defenders of the Alamo lost their lives there as well.

Reviewed by DANIEL ROSELLE
State University College (Fredonia, New York)

Attractive, modern alleys with electronic pinsetting and scoring equipment have helped bowling become the largest organized competitive sport in the United States. More than 64,000,000 people enjoy the challenge of the game in which they attempt to knock down ten pins by rolling a ball down a 60-foot wooden lane.

BOWLING

The game of bowling has been played for more than 7,000 years. Objects similar to our modern tenpins were discovered in the grave of an Egyptian whose burial has been placed at 5200 B.C.

Just how the sport came to be called bowling is not known. The word "bowl" may have come from the Saxon *bolla* and the Danish *bolle,* meaning "bubble," and through usage, "round."

In its earliest form bowling was a crude recreation and was played with primitive equipment in any space that provided suitable conditions. Today we have automatic pinsetters, automatic scorers, and smooth, well-balanced balls and pins. We bowl in air-conditioned centers amid attractive surroundings. Bowling is very popular with people of all ages.

▶ EQUIPMENT FOR THE GAME

The basic idea of bowling is to roll a ball down a wooden lane and knock down the 10 pins set in a triangle. The American Bowling Congress sets the following standards for the equipment used in bowling tenpins.

The length of a bowling lane is 60 feet from the foul line to the head pin. The width of the lane is 42 inches, and the approach must be 15 feet from the rear edge to the foul line. Tenpins are 15 inches in height and must weigh not less than 3 pounds 6 ounces. The distance between pins set for play is 12 inches from center to center. A bowling ball cannot weigh more than 16 pounds. Its circumference must be 27 inches.

The correct clothing for bowling is important. Since the sport involves activity of the entire body, clothing should allow freedom of movement of arms, shoulders, and legs.

Special bowling shoes should be worn on the lanes. One of these shoes has a leather sole and one a rubber sole. The leather sole allows you to make the necessary slide on the last step of your approach. The rubber sole is used as a brake to control the slide. The shoes can be rented for a nominal fee. The use of a bowling ball is included in the price of the game.

FOUR-STEP APPROACH: (A) Face pins, holding ball just above waist. **(B)** Step 1, right foot, is short. Push ball forward smoothly. **(C)** Step 2 is a half step, ball passes right leg. **(D)** Ball is at top of backswing on a full-size Step 3. **(E)** On Step 4, left foot glides to foul line, ball is released well beyond foul line. **(F)** Follow through.

A three-finger ball, preferred by most bowlers, is especially recommended for beginners. Grip is very important. If the distance between the holes is too wide or too narrow, it strains or cramps the hand, reducing ball control. Bowling balls come in weights of 6 to 16 pounds. Use a ball weight with the right feel. Never use a ball that is too heavy, for it will tend to make you drop your shoulder and thus put you off balance before you release the ball. Start with a lightweight ball and gradually work up to the heavier weights.

▶ THE FOUR-STEP APPROACH

The most popular style of bowling is called the four-step approach. Although five-step and three-step approaches are used, the four-step has proved to be the best for most bowlers.

Champions agree that every bowler eventually develops his or her own style, but for beginners the illustrated way to learn the four-step delivery is strongly recommended.

To determine where you should begin your approach, go to the foul line and place your left foot so that the toes are from 2 to 6 inches on the near side of the line. Then turn around, take one long step, one full step, one half step, and one small step. Again turn around and face the pins. This position indicates approximately where you should start your four-step delivery. If you are left-handed, start with your right foot on the near side of the line.

▶ TIMING

To excel in bowling, as in other sports, you must develop good timing. For example, in baseball a batter will hit the ball far only if his bat connects with the pitched ball at exactly the right moment. If his timing is off, he will miss the ball or merely pop it to the infield.

In bowling, timing is equally important. It consists of the ability to co-ordinate the forward motion of your body with the pendulum swing of your arm. Develop your timing and your bowling scores should improve.

To understand better the value of timing, study some fast-action-sequence photographs of champion bowlers. Be sure to note the smooth, rhythmic flow of their delivery as ball and body work together.

▶ CONVERTING SPARES

In each turn you are allowed to roll your ball at the pins twice if necessary. If you knock down all the pins on your first try, it is scored as a strike. If you knock down all 10 pins with two balls, it is scored as a spare. Spares are important in bowling, both to be-

DELIVERING BALLS: (1) Straight: Thumb on top, fingers underneath. **(2)** Hook: Twist wrist left, remove thumb first, lift and spin with fingers. **(3)** Curve: Same as hook, less twist of wrist.

ginners and to expert bowlers. They can make the difference between a 190 and a 90 bowling average.

Spares fall into four categories: right-side spares; left-side spares; spares that can be converted with your strike ball; and splits, the most difficult spares. Study the illustrations that show how to convert spares—that is, to knock down all the pins that remain standing after your first bowl. In spare situations where your strike-ball delivery is required, you should take the position you normally apply to your first ball. Splits are very difficult, but with the proper determination and concentration, and confidence in your bowling style, you will find yourself converting more spares than you are missing.

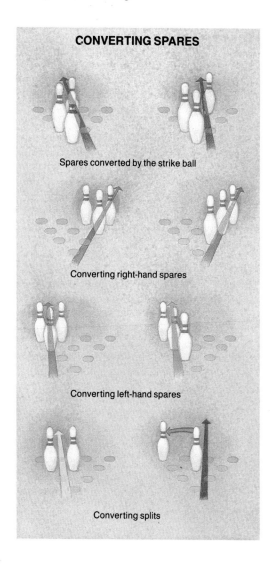

CONVERTING SPARES

Spares converted by the strike ball

Converting right-hand spares

Converting left-hand spares

Converting splits

A game consists of 10 frames. Each bowler rolls two balls per frame unless he strikes, which makes a second ball unnecessary. The symbols used for scoring are **X**, strike; /, spare; —, possible spare not converted; **O**, split that is difficult to convert; and **Ø**, split that has been converted.

For a strike a player receives 10 pins plus the total number of pins knocked down (called a **pinfall**) by his next two balls. A spare entitles a player to 10 plus a pinfall on the next ball. Now let us score a game you might bowl.

In the first frame you spare.

1	2	3	4	5	6	7	8	9	10
/									

In the second frame you roll your first ball into the pocket for a strike. This gives you 20 in the first (a spare in the first plus a pinfall on the next ball).

1	2	3	4	5	6	7	8	9	10
/	X								
20									

In the third frame you split, but you **bring in** (knock down) one with your second ball for a pinfall of 9. Score in the second is 39 (10 from a strike in the second plus a pinfall of the next two balls, added to the score in the first frame). Add your 9 for a third-frame total of 48.

1	2	3	4	5	6	7	8	9	10
/	X	O							
20	39	48							

In the fourth frame you strike.

1	2	3	4	5	6	7	8	9	10
/	X	O	X						
20	39	48							

In the fifth frame you strike. No score is recorded in either the fourth or fifth frame because for a strike you receive 10 pins plus the pinfalls of the next two balls.

1	2	3	4	5	6	7	8	9	10
/	X	O	X	X					
20	39	48							

In the sixth frame you bring in 8 on your first ball. You then knock down the two standing pins with your second ball for a spare. The score, which is 48 from the third, plus 10 for a strike in the fourth, plus 10 for a strike in the fifth, plus 8 for a pinfall of the first ball in the sixth, totals 76 in the fourth. Score in the fifth frame, which is 10, plus a pinfall from two balls in the sixth, which was 10, makes the total score 76 plus 20, which is 96.

1	2	3	4	5	6	7	8	9	10
20	39	48	76	96					

In the seventh frame you bring in 8 on your first ball, then miss two standing pins on your second ball. Score 96, plus 10, plus 8 pins on the first ball, giving you a score of 114 as of the sixth frame. Add 8 for a score of 122 in the seventh frame.

1	2	3	4	5	6	7	8	9	10
20	39	48	76	96	114	122			

In the eighth frame you spare.

1	2	3	4	5	6	7	8	9	10
20	39	48	76	96	114	122			

In the ninth frame you bring in 7 on your first ball and then knock down the 3 standing pins for a spare. Score 122, plus 10, plus 7, for a total of 139 in the eighth.

1	2	3	4	5	6	7	8	9	10
20	39	48	76	96	114	122	139		

In the tenth frame you throw a strike, adding 10 pins to your spare and giving you a total of 159 points for the ninth frame. Striking in the tenth frame allows you to throw two more balls, of which you make good use and spare. To your 159 from the ninth frame you add 10 for your strike plus 10 for your extra two balls, giving you a final score of 179 for the game.

1	2	3	4	5	6	7	8	9	10
20	39	48	76	96	114	122	139	159	179

BOWLING ORGANIZATIONS AND COMPETITION

Bowling is played in more than 100 countries and in the Olympic Games. More than 10,000 bowling tournaments are conducted in the United States each year. There is competition for bowlers of all ages and all degrees of ability, from beginner to top professional. Prizes range from tiny 2-inch trophies to $250,000.

The Professional Bowlers Association sponsors more than 35 tournaments each year with over $6,000,000 in prizes. At most of these events, young amateur bowlers can compete with the pros in junior Pro-Am competitions. There is also a tournament circuit for a women's bowling association, the Ladies Pro Bowlers Tour (LPBT).

The American Bowling Congress (ABC) is the official organization for adult male bowlers. Standards set by the ABC govern all sanctioned bowling in North America and most of the world. The Women's International Bowling Congress is the counterpart of the ABC for adult women bowlers. The Young American Bowling Alliance regulates youth and collegiate bowling in the United States. All three organizations are headquartered in Greendale, Wisconsin. With more than 5,000 local associations, bowling is the largest organized competitive sport in the United States. There are more than 64,000,000 people who bowl in the country.

OTHER BOWLING GAMES

Germans of the Middle Ages played a game in which balls were rolled to knock over wooden clubs, or *kegels*. The players were called *keglers*. From Germany this game spread to other parts of Europe. Varying numbers of pins were used, but the most common game in Germany and Holland was (as it is today) ninepins. The pins were set up to form a diamond.

Early Dutch settlers in New York played ninepins. This is the game that made the sound of thunder Rip Van Winkle heard in the famous story by Washington Irving. By about 1840 ninepin bowling had become such a popular gambling game that some states actually issued laws against playing it. In order to get around the laws against playing ninepins, a tenth pin was added. The ploy was successful because tenpins is the most popular form of bowling in the United States today.

Fivepins is a favorite form of bowling in Canada. The pins, 12⅜ inches tall, are arranged in a V. Balls are 5 inches in diameter and weigh 3½ pounds. A bowler rolls three balls in each of the 10 frames.

Another bowling game, popular in New England and eastern Canada, is candlepins. It is played with long, tapering pins.

Skittles is a game sometimes confused with bowling. It is like ninepins but is played on a smaller scale and with disks instead of balls. The disks are tossed or slid toward the pins.

▶ DUCKPINS

Duckpins is a variation of bowling in which smaller pins and smaller balls are used. It is popular in the eastern part of the United States from New England to Baltimore, Maryland.

The game is played on a regulation bowling alley, but the ball used in duckpins is no more than 5 inches in diameter and weighs 3 pounds 12 ounces. It is completely smooth, without grooves for the player's fingers. The 10 bottle-shaped pins are 9¹³⁄₃₂ inches high. Some duckpins have a band of rubber around the middle, but the game using all-wooden pins is considered the real test of skill.

Each player bowls three balls in a frame, rather than two. Even though there are three chances to score in each frame, the total score is usually lower than in regular bowling because the ball is so much smaller and lighter.

In duckpins you hold the ball comfortably and firmly, but not very tightly. You must be able to let it go easily. The ball is rolled straight off the tips of the fingers, without any twisting motion. After the ball has been bowled, the back of your hand should be turned down.

▶ BOWLS, OR LAWN BOWLING

The game called bowls is the most popular form of bowling in Britain, Australia, New Zealand, and some other Commonwealth lands. In the United States and Canada, where it is also widely played, it is called lawn bowling, or bowling on the green, to avoid confusion with the tenpin game.

Bowls is usually played on a smooth, level grass court. The object is to roll balls, which are themselves called bowls, as close as possible to the jack, a white ball 2½ inches in diameter. Bowls are made of a composition material or very hard wood and weigh not more than 3½ pounds each. They are about 5 inches in diameter. One side of a bowl bulges less than the other, giving it what is called **bias.** This causes the bowl to lean to one side and curve as it loses rolling speed. A player can roll his bowl so that it will approach the jack in a curve from either side.

In singles or doubles games each player uses four bowls; in triples, three bowls. When full teams of four play, each person rolls two bowls. To start, the first player rolls the jack from a rubber mat at one end of the rink, a division of the green on which the game is played, at least 75 feet toward the other end. In team play two opposing players, called the leads, roll their bowls alternately. Then two other opposing players bowl. Last to bowl are the skips (captains) of the teams, who have been directing the play of their teammates. If a bowl touches the jack, it is marked with chalk to show that it is still alive, even if it goes into the ditch at the end of the rink. Any other bowl going into the ditch is out of play.

When all players have bowled, an end (inning) is over. The team that then has a bowl closest to the jack scores a point for every bowl that it has closer to the jack than the nearest of the opponents' bowls. (Each set of bowls has a special marking so they can be identified.) The players then bowl toward the opposite end of the rink, the side that scored last bowling first. A game consists of 21 points in singles, or in team play a number of ends (usually 21) agreed on at the start.

Similar games were played with balls of stone in very early times. One called "bowles" was popular in England in the 13th century or earlier. The bowls used were generally of wood, and by the 1500's they were made with bias. From England the game spread to Scotland and to the British colonies.

Bowls was played in Jamestown as early as 1611. It was also enjoyed by early New Yorkers in a small area at the lower end of Manhattan that is still called Bowling Green. Lawn bowling grew in popularity in the United States during the 1900's. The American Lawn Bowling Association was formed in 1938.

ARTHUR K. SERBO
Brunswick Division, Brunswick Corporation

Reviewed by CHUCK PEZZANO
Author, *PBA Guide to Better Bowling;
Sports Illustrated Bowling*

Dempsey Through the Ropes (1924), by George W. Bellows, depicts 1923 heavyweight championship fight. Jack Dempsey climbed back into the ring to knock out Luis Firpo.

BOXING

Boxing is a sport in which two opponents battle (or fight) each other with their fists. Each boxer tries to score more points than his opponent by the intelligent use of skills in which he has been trained. In amateur boxing, especially, skill is more important than strength.

Boxers wear gloves made of soft leather padded with sponge rubber. Gloves usually weigh from 8 ounces (230 grams) to 10 ounces (280 grams). A boxer's hands are wrapped in soft cotton or linen for protection from the impact of his own blows. Amateur boxers may wear headgear to protect their heads and ears from injuries. All boxers use a rubber mouthpiece that helps prevent injuries to the teeth.

The space in which a boxing match (bout) takes place is called a ring. It is generally 16 to 20 feet (4.9 to 6.1 meters) square, closed in by lengths of muslin-wrapped rope. The ropes are 2, 3, and 4 feet (0.6, 0.9, and 1.2 meters) above the floor of a platform on which the ring is mounted. A canvas floor covering is laid over thick padding. The cornerposts and turnbuckles that hold the ropes are also heavily padded.

The length of a round in both amateur and professional boxing is 3 minutes. There is a 1-minute rest period between rounds. During this period the fighters go to corners of the ring opposite one another and are tended by their cornermen. Most amateur matches are scheduled for three rounds. Professional championship bouts can be as many as twelve rounds. A timekeeper marks the beginning and end of each round by sounding a bell.

The referee is a very important third person

in the ring during a bout, seeing that the rules are obeyed and separating the boxers if they clinch one another. Blows below the beltline, on the kidneys, or on the back of the neck (rabbit punches) are fouls. So too are pushing, head-butting, or hitting an opponent when he is down (on the floor, getting up, or outside, between, or hanging helpless over the ropes).

If a fighter is knocked down, his opponent must go to a neutral corner—a corner of the ring not occupied by either fighter between rounds. The fighter who is down must get back on his feet within the ring before the referee counts to 10 at 1-second intervals. If he does not do this, his opponent is declared the winner by a knockout (KO). Until 1963, if a round ended before the count reached 10, the man who was down was said to have been "saved by the bell" because he could recover between rounds and continue. In 1963, though, the rules were changed. The count continues despite the bell and the fight can end if the count is completed. The count may not continue after the bell has sounded ending the final round. If a downed boxer gets up before the count of 10, he is usually forced to wait for a count of 8 before action can continue.

The referee is expected to stop a fight any time he feels that a boxer is too badly hurt to continue. A fight ended in this way is called a technical knockout (TKO). A physician must be on hand to determine whether an injured fighter should continue. It is also a TKO if a fighter is knocked down three times in one round. But this rule does not apply to professional championship bouts.

If there is no knockout, usually two judges and the referee decide the bout's winner on a basis of rounds won or points. They note how effectively each man punches his opponent, how well he defends himself, and how aggressive he is. They also allow for knockdowns and for fouls and such minor faults as hitting in a clinch. The decision may be based on the number of rounds won or on total points. In case of a tie, a bout is declared a draw.

▶ BOXING AS AMATEUR AND PROFESSIONAL SPORT

In boxing, as in any physical contact sport, there are bound to be injuries. In 1938 the Society of State Directors of Physical and Health Education adopted an official policy disapproving of boxing as an interscholastic sport. A few years later boxing was dropped from collegiate competition.

Supporters of amateur boxing claim that when it is conducted under proper rules and supervision, it is a safe competitive sport.

Many youth and athletic clubs provide instruction in basic boxing skills. They stress sound body condition, proper training, knowledge of the rules, and principles of fair play. They match only opponents of nearly equal size and experience.

Olympic and other amateur boxing competition around the world is governed by the International Amateur Boxing Federation. In the United States, the Amateur Athletic Union is the chief governing body. The Golden Gloves Association conducts amateur tournaments throughout the country, and the winners compete in national championships.

The activities of professional boxers—people who fight for cash prizes—are regulated by the World Boxing Association (WBA), the World Boxing Council (WBC), and the International Boxing Federation (IBF). However, these organizations do not have the power to control boxing. They often disagree on which boxer is champion of his division. Professional boxing in Canada is regulated by the Canadian Professional Boxing Federation and by various provincial and local boards.

▶ BOXING PAST AND RECENT

The people of Sumer in ancient Mesopotamia made many carvings in stone. Archaeologists have found one of these that shows

---

SOME IMPORTANT BOXING WEIGHT LIMITS

	International	A.A.U. World Amateur	Professional
Light Flyweight	48 kg	106 lb	108 lb
Flyweight	51 kg	112 lb	112 lb
Bantamweight	54 kg	119 lb	118 lb
Junior Featherweight	55.5 kg	—	122 lb
Featherweight	57 kg	125 lb	126 lb
Junior Lightweight	59 kg	—	130 lb
Lightweight	60 kg	132 lb	135 lb
Light Welterweight	63.5 kg	139 lb	140 lb
Welterweight	67 kg	147 lb	147 lb
Light Middleweight	71 kg	156 lb	154 lb
Middleweight	75 kg	165 lb	160 lb
Light Heavyweight	81 kg	178 lb	175 lb
Heavyweight	Over 81 kg	Over 178 lb	Over 175 lb
Super Heavyweight	Over 91 kg	Over 201 lb	—

In professional boxing, light welterweight is called junior welterweight, and light middleweight is called junior middleweight.

1882–92	John L. Sullivan	1930–32	Max Schmeling	1960–62	Floyd Patterson	1987–90	Mike Tyson
1892–97	James J. Corbett	1932–33	Jack Sharkey	1962–64	Sonny Liston	1990	James Douglas
1897–99	Robert Fitzsimmons	1933–34	Primo Carnera	1964–67	Muhammad Ali	1990–92	Evander Holyfield
1899–1905	James J. Jeffries	1934–35	Max Baer	1968–70	Disputed	1992–93	Riddick Bowe
1905–06	Marvin Hart	1935–37	James J. Braddock	1970–73	Joe Frazier	1993–94	Evander Holyfield
1906–08	Tommy Burns	1937–49	Joe Louis	1973–74	George Foreman	1994	Michael Moorer
1908–15	Jack Johnson	1949–51	Ezzard Charles	1974–78	Muhammad Ali	1994–95	George Foreman
1915–19	Jess Willard	1951–52	Joe Walcott	1978	Leon Spinks	1996	Mike Tyson,
1919–26	Jack Dempsey	1952–56	Rocky Marciano	1978–79	Muhammad Ali		Evander Holyfield
1926–28	Gene Tunney	1956–59	Floyd Patterson	1979–85	Larry Holmes	1997–99	Evander Holyfield
1928–30	None	1959–60	Ingemar Johansson	1985–87	Michael Spinks	1999–2000	Lennox Lewis

*Various champions have been recognized by the World Boxing Association (WBA), World Boxing Council (WBC), and International Boxing Federation (IBF). Those listed are considered to have the best claims to the title.

two boxers in combat. Greek and Roman athletes fought with their hands wrapped in a kind of leather covering called a cestus. To this the ancient gladiators attached murderous metal studs or spikes. A Roman boxer was called a *pugil*, from which we get "pugilism," another name for boxing.

Revival in England. Little more is known about fistfighting until the 1600's. Then in England the name "boxing" was given to a contest in which men boxed, or beat, one another with their bare fists. In 1719, James Figg became the first British champion. Figg opened a boxing school in London, and interest in the sport spread. Men often fought for prizes, hence the term "prizefighting." Jack Broughton, a champion from 1743 to 1750, drew up the first London Prize Ring Rules.

Boxers of the bareknuckle era stood toe to toe and wrestled, shoved, or struck each other until one man was knocked down. That marked the end of a round. After a brief rest the fight began again. When one man could no longer fight, his opponent was the victor.

If a boxer's second, or assistant, in his corner decided to give up the match for his boxer, he could inform the referee by throwing a towel into the ring. From this practice comes the saying that a person who gives up some effort is "throwing in the towel."

In 1865 the Marquis of Queensberry drew up rules that are the basis for those used today. The rules provided for 3-minute rounds with a 1-minute rest period between rounds. They required fighters to wear "fair-sized" boxing gloves, banned wrestling holds, and set the 10-second count for a knockout. With the adoption of these rules, boxing gradually became acceptable in the United States, where prizefighting had been illegal. Heavyweight bouts were the most popular.

The Modern Era. In 1892, John L. Sullivan, the last of the bareknuckle champions, was defeated by James J. (Gentleman Jim) Corbett in the first heavyweight title bout fought with gloves under the Queensberry rules. Two other great heavyweight champions of the early modern era were James J. Jeffries, who retired undefeated in 1905, and Jack Johnson, who became the first black champion in 1908.

William Harrison (Jack) Dempsey launched the "golden age" of boxing by knocking out Jess Willard in 1919. His bouts began to draw huge crowds. James J. (Gene) Tunney won the title from Dempsey in 1926. The next year Dempsey knocked Tunney down in the seventh round; but because Dempsey did not go at once to a neutral corner, the referee did not start the count for several seconds. Tunney got up and went on to win by a decision.

Joe Louis knocked out James J. Braddock in 1937 to capture the heavyweight crown. Louis went on to a brilliant career with many knockouts. Unbeaten in 26 title bouts, he retired in 1949. Rocky Marciano retired as an undefeated champion in 1956. Floyd Patterson gained the title that year but lost to Ingemar Johansson in 1959. When Patterson defeated Johansson in 1960, he was the first modern heavyweight to regain the title.

Muhammad Ali first captured the crown in 1964. Three years later he lost it, but regained it in 1974. Leon Spinks defeated Ali in 1978. When Ali defeated Spinks later that year, he became the first boxer to win the heavyweight title three times. During the 1980's Larry Holmes and Mike Tyson dominated the heavyweight division. In 1990, Tyson lost the title to James (Buster) Douglas, who later lost it to Evander Holyfield. Holyfield was then defeated in 1992 by Riddick Bowe, and one year later, Holyfield took the title back from Bowe. In 1994, Michael Moorer defeated Holyfield in a twelve-round majority decision. Seven months later, George Foreman knocked out Moorer, but Foreman was stripped of his crown within a year. In late 1995, Mike Tyson won the WBC crown by knocking out Frank Bruno, and in September 1996, he won the WBA title by knocking out Bruce Seldon. Tyson later gave up the WBC title by refusing to fight Lennox Lewis, the top contender, but he pursued a WBA title fight with Evander Holyfield for November 1996. Tyson lost the fight and the title to Holyfield. Tyson and Holyfield fought again for the title in June 1997, but Tyson was disqualified for biting him after the third round.

There have been notable champions in other weight classes too. Lightweights Joe Gans (1902–08) and Benny Leonard (1917–25) are two of boxing's greats. Henry Armstrong was the first boxer to win three titles, featherweight, lightweight, and welterweight (1937–38). Sugar Ray Robinson held the middleweight title five times (1951–60) and he was also a welterweight champ (1946–51). Rivals Willie Pep and Sandy Saddler ruled the featherweight class (1946–57). Roberto Durán won lightweight, welterweight, and junior middleweight titles between 1972 and 1984. Sugar Ray Leonard held the welterweight, junior middleweight, middleweight, super middleweight, and light heavyweight titles.

ROCKY MARCIANO
Former World Heavyweight Boxing Champion
Updated by BILL BRADDOCK, *The New York Times*

BOYD, BELLE. See SPIES (Profiles).

BOYLE, ROBERT (1627–1691)

Robert Boyle was a self-taught scientist who during the 1600's carried out experiments that helped to found modern chemistry and modern physics. Boyle was born on January 25, 1627, at Lismore Castle in Ireland. His father was a wealthy, land-owning Englishman who had been made Earl of Cork.

Robert went to Eton, the famous boys' school, at the age of 8. When he was 11, he went abroad with a tutor. He spent most of the next six years in Switzerland and Italy. During this time Boyle developed an interest in science and began to study the works of Galileo.

When his father died, Robert Boyle inherited a rich estate in England. In 1644 he returned there. He was now in a position to do anything he wanted. Having what he called "an unsatisfied appetite for knowledge," he decided to explore the unknowns of science. Since there were no textbooks and few teachers, Boyle had to proceed on his own. He set up a laboratory and worked alone, but hired assistants when he needed help. One assistant was Robert Hooke, who became an important scientist himself.

Boyle investigated questions in biology, chemistry, and physics. He studied how animals breathe and how blood circulates. He showed how matter burns, boils, and freezes. His investigations ranged from the barometer and crystals to light and sound. The results of these experiments are no longer important.

What matters is that Boyle was among the first to use careful scientific methods.

Boyle's work with the air pump is probably best known. The pump was a new device that could both compress air and produce near vacuums. With it Boyle could control the quantity of air in a closed container. His experiments demonstrated the role of air in burning, breathing, and sound. During these experiments Boyle discovered that when pressure on a given quantity of air is increased, the volume of air becomes smaller. This finding became the basis of what is now known as Boyle's law: If the temperature and quantity of a gas remain constant, the volume varies inversely with the pressure.

By 1645, Boyle had begun to meet with other scientific researchers in London. The Royal Society, which is still one of the world's leading organizations for the encouragement of science, grew out of these meetings.

Boyle, a deeply religious man, learned Greek and Hebrew in order to read the Bible in the original, and he wrote books on religious matters. He also financed translations of the Bible and supported missionary work abroad.

Boyle never married. He tended to be sickly, but his interest in science was so strong that he worked steadily almost until his death, on December 30, 1691.

JOHN S. BOWMAN
Author and Science Editor

BOYS & GIRLS CLUBS OF AMERICA

Boys & Girls Clubs of America is a national federation of clubs that offer a wide range of programs and activities for young people. More than 2,200 clubs are located in communities throughout the United States. Each year, these clubs assist some 3 million children, many of whom are from underprivileged backgrounds.

Clubs are located in cities, suburbs, and rural areas. Some clubs are in specially designed centers equipped with swimming pools, learning centers, computer laboratories, and gymnasiums. Other clubs operate programs for young people in schools, homeless shelters, shopping malls, reservations, and military bases.

Programs

Boys & Girls Clubs provide programs for children 6 to 18 years of age, conducted by a full-time professional staff. (A small fee is charged for joining the club.) Programs emphasize character and leadership development, educational enhancement, career preparation, health and life skills, the arts, and sports, fitness, and recreation.

SMART (Skills Mastery and Resistance Training) Moves, an alcohol, drug, and pregnancy prevention program, provides girls and boys with the information and skills they need to be able to make smart choices in their everyday lives. Kids in Control is a safety awareness program focusing on safety habits and skills. Torch Clubs are leadership development groups for youth ages 11 to 13. In this program, youngsters elect officers and plan and carry out their own activities and community service projects. In the Career

Boys & Girls Clubs offer members a broad range of recreational and educational activities, including arts and crafts.

Explorers Club, youngsters visit various businesses, government agencies, and colleges while receiving information about career choices. Through the National Fine Arts Program, members can create art using techniques such as pastels, watercolor, collage, and sculpture. Other programs provide instruction on arts and crafts, music, and sports.

History

The first Boys Club was established in 1860 in Hartford, Connecticut. The national organization, originally named Federated Boys' Clubs and later Boys' Clubs of America, was founded in 1906. The purpose was to provide leadership and programs for its member clubs, while helping to establish new clubs in disadvantaged communities. In 1956, the organization was chartered by Congress. In 1990, the organization's name was changed to Boys & Girls Clubs of America.

Boys & Girls Clubs of America headquarters are located in Atlanta, Georgia. The organization continues to work across the country, reaching more and more young people as new branches are opened.

ANDREA K. JOHNSON
Boys & Girls Clubs of America

Did you know that...

many famous personalities are former Boys & Girls Club members? Well-known alumni include newscasters Bernard Shaw and Dan Rather; actors Denzel Washington, Bill Cosby, Jennifer Lopez, and Danny DeVito; sports figures such as football's Randall Cunningham, Junior Seau (Tiana Seau, Jr.), and Wayne Chrebet; baseball's Joe DiMaggio, Alex Rodriguez, and Frank Thomas; basketball's Michael Jordan, Shaquille O'Neal, Anfernee "Penny" Hardaway, and Earvin "Magic" Johnson; and track and field's Jackie Joyner-Kersee.

Camping is one of the many ways in which Boy Scouts work and play to develop mental and physical fitness. Approximately 16,000,000 Scouts and leaders participate in Boy Scout programs throughout the world.

BOY SCOUTS

Not long ago, a 12-year-old Boy Scout was leaving a tidal pool when he saw two small children bobbing helplessly in the water. The Scout rescued the children from the pool and began mouth-to-mouth resuscitation. One child began to breathe, but the other did not. The Scout instructed people on the beach to continue working on the second child while he called for an ambulance. Both children lived, thanks to the Scout's actions.

This is but one of hundreds of real cases in which Boy Scouts have saved lives by using the skills they learned in Scout training. This worldwide organization teaches young men leadership and good citizenship. It teaches them the skills that enable them to live up to their Scout motto, "Be prepared."

Boys get much more from Scouting besides training for emergencies. They find fun and fellowship with other boys and the men who lead them. They find adventure in hiking, camping, boating, and other outdoor sports. They gain useful knowledge and skills and have many chances to take part in the life of their community and nation.

▶ THE BOY SCOUTS OF AMERICA

The Boy Scouts of America has more than 5,000,000 members. The organization provides a long-term program for a boy from the time he enters the first grade until his 21st birthday. In the first grade, a boy may become a Tiger Cub; in the second grade a Cub Scout; at age 11 a Boy Scout; and at age 14 a Varsity Scout or Explorer.

Tiger Cubs

Introduced by the Boy Scouts of America in 1982, the Tiger Cub program is for boys in the first grade. They join with an adult partner, usually a parent, and they participate together in a program of activities and fun with the family and as part of a Tiger Cub group. Group leadership is shared among all of the adult partners.

Tiger Cub Promise: "I promise to love God, my family, and my country, and to learn about the world."

Tiger Cub Motto: "Search, discover, share."

Cub Scouts

Cub Scouting is a program for boys in second through fifth grades.

Many of a Cub Scout's activities and achievements take place in the home with the encouragement of adults in the household. He starts out as a Bobcat. By completing twelve achievements, he earns his Wolf Badge. Then, for earning credits in a variety of activities of his choice, he receives arrow points to wear below his badge. When he completes the second grade (or is 9 years old), he begins to work for the Bear rank. On completion of the third grade (or when he is 10 years old), he may join a Webelos den and earn the Webelos badge and the highest Cub Scout award, the Arrow of Light. Webelos activity badges are awarded for learning special skills. "Webelos" stands for "*We'll Be Loyal Scouts.*"

A Cub Scout belongs to a den with boys from his neighborhood. The den meets each week under the guidance of its adult den leader, who is helped by a Boy Scout called the den chief. Several dens make up a Cub pack, which has an adult leader called the Cubmaster. The pack meets once a month, often in the form of a group outing.

The Cub Scout uniform is dark blue with yellow trim. A different color neckerchief is worn by the Cub Scout to designate his grade or age. Yellow indicates second grade; blue, third grade; and plaid, fourth- and fifth-grade Webelos Scouts.

Cub Scout Motto: "Do your best."

Cub Scout Promise: "I, [name], promise to do my best to do my duty to God and my country, to help other people, and to obey the Law of the Pack."

Law of the Pack: "The Cub Scout follows Akela. The Cub Scout helps the pack go. The pack helps the Cub Scout grow. The Cub Scout gives goodwill." ("Akela" means "good leader.")

Boy Scouts

A boy may become a Boy Scout at age 11. By understanding the Scout Oath and Law and by passing a few simple tests, he may join and be called a Boy Scout. Skill awards and merit badges lead him on to Tenderfoot, Second Class, and then on to First Class rank. Scouts may earn merit badges in any of more than 100 different fields. Certain merit badges help him achieve the ranks of Star (6 merit badges), Life (11), and Eagle Scout (21), the highest rank in Scouting.

SCOUT UNIFORMS, INSIGNIA, AND BADGES

CUB SCOUT

Hat
Yellow: Second and Third Graders
Blue: Fourth and Fifth Graders

Neckerchief
Yellow: Second Graders
Blue: Third Graders
Plaid: Webelos

Bobcat Badge
Wolf Badge
Bear Badge
Webelos Badge

Gold and Silver Arrow Points

Council Patch
Pack Number
Patrol Emblem

SALUTE
SIGN
HANDCLASP

BOY SCOUT

Troop Neckerchief

Shoulder Loops
Red: Boy Scout
Green: Explorer Scout
Silver: District or Council Leader
Gold: Regional or National Leader

Den Chief Cord
Council Patch
Troop Number
Service Pin
Badge of Rank
Arrow of Light Award

Skill Award Belt Loops

SALUTE
SIGN
HANDCLASP

Scouts wear insignia showing their rank, den or patrol, and service and achievement awards. Webelos Scouts may wear blue or khaki and tan uniforms.

Agribusiness	American Business	American Cultures	American Heritage	American Labor	Animal Science	Archery	Architecture	Art	Astronomy
Athletics	Atomic Energy	Aviation	Backpacking	Basketry	Beekeeping	Bird Study	Botany	Bugling	Camping
Canoeing	Chemistry	Citizenship in the Community	Citizenship in the Nation	Citizenship in the World	Coin Collecting	Communications	Computers	Consumer Buying	Cooking
Cycling	Dentistry	Dog Care	Drafting	Electricity	Electronics	Emergency Preparedness	Energy	Engineering	Environmental Science
Farm Mechanics	Fingerprinting	Firemanship	First Aid	Fish and Wildlife Management	Fishing	Forestry	Gardening	Genealogy	General Science
Geology	Golf	Graphic Arts	Handicap Awareness	Hiking	Home Repairs	Horsemanship	Indian Lore	Insect Study	Journalism

A Scout must earn a number of awards, or merit badges, in order to qualify for each new rank. The colorful badges can be earned in many different subject areas.

A small group of Boy Scouts forms a patrol. Several patrols make up a troop. The troop usually meets once a week with its adult leader, the Scoutmaster. Hiking and camping are part of the adventure that Scouts enjoy. They learn how to take care of themselves in the open and how to help others in case of accidents. They also learn to be useful citizens.

Scout Oath or Promise: "On my honor I will do my best to do my duty to God and my country and to obey the Scout Law; to help other people at all times; to keep myself physically strong, mentally awake, and morally straight."

Scout Motto: "Be prepared."

Scout Slogan: "Do a good turn daily."

Scout Law: A Scout is trustworthy, loyal, helpful, friendly, courteous, kind, obedient, cheerful, thrifty, brave, clean, and reverent.

Varsity Scouting

Varsity Scouting is a new Boy Scouts of America program for young men 14 through 17 years of age. It is the "varsity" of Boy Scouting, just as the varsity is the senior team in school sports.

Varsity Scouts are members of a Varsity Scout team. They are under the leadership of an adult Varsity Scout coach. The youth leader of the team is the Varsity Scout team captain. There are youth squad leaders and a youth program manager for each of the five program fields of emphasis.

The fields of interest—advancement, high adventure, personal development, service, and special programs—challenge a young man to use the basic skills learned in Boy Scouting. Participation in Varsity Scout activities and requirements lead to earning the Varsity Scout letter. Advancement toward the Eagle Scout rank is continued in Varsity Scouting.

Varsity Scouting ideals are the Scout Oath or Promise, Law, Motto, and Slogan.

Varsity Scout Pledge: "As a Varsity Scout, I will: Live by the Scout Oath (Promise), Law, Motto, and Slogan; Honor the dignity and worth of all persons; Promote the cause of freedom; and Do my best to be a good team member."

Landscape Architecture · Law · Leatherwork · Lifesaving · Machinery · Mammal Study · Masonry · Metals Engineering · Metalwork · Model Design and Building

Motorboating · Music · Nature · Oceanography · Orienteering · Painting · Personal Fitness · Personal Management · Pets · Photography

Pioneering · Plant Science · Plumbing · Pottery · Public Health · Public Speaking · Pulp and Paper · Rabbit Raising · Radio · Railroading

Reading · Reptile Study · Rifle Shooting · Rowing · Safety · Salesmanship · Scholarship · Sculpture · Shotgun Shooting · Signaling

Skating · Skiing · Small-Boat Sailing · Soil and Water Conservation · Space Exploration · Sports · Stamp Collecting · Surveying · Swimming · Textile

Theater · Traffic Safety · Truck Transportation · Veterinary Science · Waterskiing · Weather · Whitewater · Wilderness Survival · Wood Carving · Woodwork

Exploring

Exploring is a division of the Boy Scouts of America for young men and women from high school age to 21. Young adults—and they need not have been Scouts—may join a general- or special-interest Explorer post or Sea Explorer ship. Exploring offers a choice of activities and a chance for adventure, career experience, education, and recreation. Explorers plan their own programs with the help of an adult adviser or skipper. Young women became full members in 1971.

More than half of all posts are organized around a career interest such as law enforcement, medicine, banking, space exploration, computer programming, or other occupation.

▶THE BOY SCOUT ORGANIZATION

There are about 16,000,000 Scouts and leaders in the world today. They are found in 116 countries. They have different uniforms, badges, and customs, but their aims and ideals are alike. The motto ''Be prepared'' is known in many languages. The headquarters of the Boy Scouts World Bureau is in Geneva, Switzerland.

World jamborees are held every four years. These are huge camps that bring Scouts from many nations together in friendship. The first world jamboree was held in England in 1920. Many countries also hold national jamborees. The Boy Scouts of America held its first jamboree in 1937. Canada held its first in 1949.

United States

The National Council of the Boy Scouts of America is made up of representatives who come from more than 400 local councils across the country. This body elects an Executive Board, which is the governing body of the Boy Scouts of America. The national office is in Irving, Texas. A full-time staff, headed by the Chief Scout Executive, publishes handbooks and magazines for boys and leaders and prepares video and other materials for training leaders. It also controls the manufacture and sale of uniforms and equipment through local Scouting distributors.

The staff of the national organization provides assistance to local councils made up of volunteers who offer to help Scouting in a city, county, or larger area. The council must have, among other things, a camp for its members. A group of professional Scouting administrators work full time in area councils.

Scouting reaches boys and young men and young women through churches, schools, and other organizations. Each group that receives a charter to operate a troop or other Scouting unit offers a meeting place, good leaders, and other needed support.

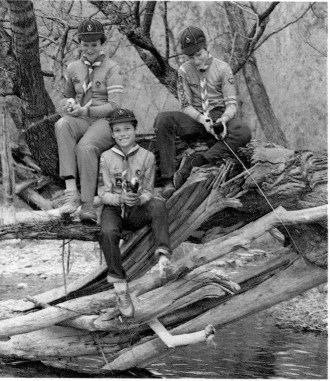

Although uniforms and customs in different countries may vary, the aims of Scouting are alike worldwide. Here a group of Canadian Wolf Cubs enjoy a fishing trip.

Today there is an active interest in Scouting in the inner cities. Many city youngsters join Scouting for its outdoor activities, such as camping and water-safety programs.

Scouting for the Handicapped. Today about 100,000 physically or mentally disabled Scouts are active in various programs throughout the United States. Anyone who has been certified as disabled by a proper medical authority may enroll in Scouting and remain in its program beyond the regulation age limits. This provision allows all members to advance in Scouting as far as they wish.

Canada

In 1914, the Canadian General Council of the Boy Scouts Association was formed. In 1961 this name was changed to Boy Scouts of Canada. In 1990, the organization began accepting girls and was renamed Scouts Canada. Today there are more than 200,000 Canadian scouts divided into five age groups: (1) Beavers, age 5 to 7; (2) Wolf Cubs, 8 to 11; (3) Scouts, 11 to 14; (4) Venturers, 14 to 17; and (5) Rovers, 18 to 26 years old. The mission of Scouts Canada is "To contribute to the development of young people in achieving their full physical, intellectual, social, and spiritual potential as individuals, as responsible citizens, and as members of their local, national, and international communities ...."

▶ **HISTORY OF SCOUTING**

Boy Scouting was started by Robert Stephenson Smyth Baden-Powell, an Englishman born in 1857. As an army officer, Baden-Powell made up many training games and contests, which he later described in a book called *Aids to Scouting*. He became a hero during the Boer War in South Africa (1899–1902). On his return to England, he found that some leaders of boys had started using his scouting games and contests. He then worked out a scouting program for boys that was built around the ideals of the Scout Promise and Law. Guided by Baden-Powell's *Scouting for Boys* (1908), troops of Boy Scouts were formed in many countries.

In 1910, Baden-Powell, Chief Scout of the world, retired from the British army to devote all his time to Scouting. He died in Kenya in 1941.

Shortly after Scouting started in Britain, William D. Boyce, a Chicago publisher, became lost in a London fog and was aided by an English Scout. This led Boyce to become interested in Scouting. On February 8, 1910, he founded the Boy Scouts of America.

Reviewed by Boy Scouts of America

BRACES, DENTAL. See ORTHODONTICS.

BRADBURY, RAY. See SCIENCE FICTION (Profiles).

BRADFORD, WILLIAM. See MASSACHUSETTS (Famous People); PLYMOUTH COLONY.

BRADLEY, OMAR. See MISSOURI (Famous People).

BRADLEY, THOMAS. See LOS ANGELES (Famous People).

BRADY, MATHEW. See NEW YORK (Famous People).

BRAHE, TYCHO (1546–1601)

Tycho Brahe, the great Danish astronomer, was born on December 14, 1546. He grew up in Knudstrup, a village in Denmark that is now part of Sweden. In 1559, his aristocratic family sent him to Copenhagen to study law. But after witnessing an eclipse of the sun, he went against his family's wishes and began studying astronomy on his own.

Brahe was not only stubborn but also hot-tempered. In his student years, he fought a duel with another young nobleman, who cut off part of his nose. Brahe replaced the part with one of gold and silver.

In 1572, Brahe became the first European to sight a supernova—a star that suddenly explodes and becomes brilliant. The star was in the constellation of Cassiopeia. Brahe's fame as an astronomer drew the attention of King Frederick II of Denmark, who built him an observatory, called Uraniborg, and paid him a salary. There, for 21 years, Brahe made careful observations of the stars, sun, moon, and planets—all without the use of the telescope, which had not yet been invented. In 1599, Brahe was invited by the Holy Roman emperor, Rudolph II, to continue his studies in Prague.

Brahe died there two years later, on October 24, 1601. But his work lived on, thanks to his assistant, a young German astronomer named Johannes Kepler. Brahe believed that the sun revolved around Earth, and the other planets revolved around the sun, all in perfectly circular paths, or orbits. However, using Brahe's measurements, Kepler was able to show that all planets in the solar system, including Earth, revolve around the sun, in oblong, or elliptical, orbits.

JOHN S. BOWMAN
Author and Science Editor

See also KEPLER, JOHANNES.

BRAHMS, JOHANNES (1833–1897)

Johannes Brahms was one of the most important composers of the 1800's, producing works in nearly all the forms of music popular in his day. During his life he composed chamber music, numerous works for piano, four symphonies, and over 100 songs. In his music, Brahms combined classical traditions with the warmth of the romantic style.

Brahms was born on May 7, 1833, in Hamburg, Germany. At an early age he showed unusual musical ability. By the time he was 16, however, Brahms decided that his chief interest was composing music rather than performing it.

In his early 20's, Brahms met the great composer Robert Schumann, who recognized his talent as a composer. In 1853 Schumann wrote a famous magazine article entitled "New Paths" in which he hailed Brahms as the coming genius of German music. Schumann also had great influence as a music critic, and his praise of Brahms helped the young composer become better known.

Passed over for a conducting position in Hamburg, Brahms moved to Vienna, Austria, in 1862. His abilities were quickly recognized there, and he soon won an appointment as a choral conductor. During the 1860's, Brahms composed the *German Requiem*, which brought him much recognition. From 1872 to 1875 Brahms was musical director of the famed Viennese Society of the Friends of Music.

In 1876 his first symphony, which he had begun to compose 22 years before, was finally performed. Three years later Brahms introduced his violin concerto. The great second piano concerto was finished in 1881, and in 1885 Brahms completed the fourth and last of his symphonies.

In 1894 Brahms was offered the post he had wanted all his life, conductor of the Hamburg Philharmonic Orchestra. But he felt he was too old for the position and declined the offer. He died on April 3, 1897.

Reviewed by KARL GEIRINGER
Author, *Johannes Brahms*

BRAIN

Inside your head is a spongy, jelly-like organ that allows you to throw a ball, taste a pizza, talk to a friend, and remember your telephone number. This organ is your brain: It controls just about everything you do.

The brain is your body's most complicated organ. It receives and processes sensory information from the outside world and sends messages to control muscles and glands. Your brain is also where you plan ahead, learn, and experience thoughts and emotions.

This computer-enhanced view of a person's brain was created using an MRI scanner. The device detected active areas (shown above as bright spots) as the person thought about a series of letters.

► CELLS OF THE BRAIN

The brain is composed of two main types of cells: nerve cells, or **neurons**, and glial cells, or **glia**. Neuroscientists—researchers who study the brain and nervous system—estimate that the brain has 100 billion neurons and ten to fifty times as many glia.

Neurons and glia have different functions. Neurons are responsible for sending information throughout the nervous system. Neurons are some of the oldest cells in the body because they can last a lifetime. Some neurons are the longest cells in the body, stretching all the way from the tip of your toe to your brain. Glia, from the Greek word for "glue," do not transmit information. Instead, they insulate neurons, clean debris away from them, carry nutrients to them, and provide structural support for the nervous system.

The basic types of neurons are the same in humans and other vertebrates (animals with a backbone). These types can be classified according to their function. **Sensory neurons** respond to a stimulus (plural: stimuli) such as light, temperature, sound, smell, or touch. **Motor neurons** are responsible for controlling muscles. **Interneurons** relay information between sensory neurons and motor neurons.

Although neurons vary in size and shape, depending on their location in the nervous system, they all have four specialized features: a cell body (or soma), dendrites, an axon, and a synaptic terminal.

The **cell body** is the central part of a neuron. It contains a control center, called the nucleus, and other structures, called organelles, that are important for the cell's function. Cell bodies can vary in size from 4 microns (millionths of a meter) to 120 microns in diameter—about the width of a human hair.

Threadlike extensions called **dendrites** branch out from the neuron's cell body. Dendrites, from the Greek word meaning "tree," contain structures called **receptor sites** for detecting signals, or impulses, coming from other neurons. The dendrites bring information to the cell body.

Also extending from the cell body is a single **axon**. The axon carries nerve impulses away from the cell body toward the **synaptic terminal**. At the synaptic terminal, information from one neuron is transmitted to another neuron. This area is called the **synapse**. An axon can branch several times to form synapses with many different neurons.

► NERVE CELL COMMUNICATION

Neurons send messages using an electrochemical process—that is, one that involves both electricity and chemistry. For instance, when you throw a ball, neurons in your brain send messages to the spinal cord, which then relays the messages to the nerves and muscles in your arm. These messages are electrical signals that travel on electrically charged chemicals called **ions**. In the nervous system, important ions are sodium, chloride, calcium, and potassium. When there are different numbers of ions inside and outside a nerve cell, there is a difference in positive and negative electrical charges called a **potential difference**. If some of these ions switch places and move inside or outside the cell, the potential difference can be reversed. When this happens, the neuron generates a brief electrical signal. This signal is called an **action potential**, or a nerve impulse.

Action potentials travel down the axon without a change in the electrical signal. Depending on the size of an axon and whether it is insulated with glial cells, action potentials can travel down an axon at rates between 0.4 mile and 268 miles per hour (0.2 meter and 120 meters per second). That is as slow as a turtle or as fast as a race car! A single neuron can generate hundreds of action potentials each second. It is the pattern of these signals that makes up the messages transmitted throughout the nervous system.

At the synaptic terminal, action potentials cause the release of chemicals called neurotransmitters, such as dopamine, norepinephrine, epinephrine, acetylcholine, and serotonin. These chemicals are released from tiny sacs, called **vesicles**, at the end of a neuron's axon and float across the synapse to the dendrite, cell body, or axon of another neuron. There they may attach themselves to receptor sites. In response to this chemical signal, the receiving neuron's **excitability** changes. In other words, the neuron will be either more or less likely to pass on the signal.

▶ **BRAINS AND NERVOUS SYSTEMS**

Single-celled organisms, such as the amoeba, do not have a nervous system or a brain. However, these types of animals do react to light, heat, and food. Simple multicellular animals, like the sea anemone and jellyfish, have a primitive nervous system but no collection of cells that can be called a brain. Instead, the nervous system of these animals is made up of a collection of interconnected nerve cells called a nerve net.

In general, larger animals have bigger brains. In adult humans, the brain measures about 3.1 pounds (1.4 kilograms) in weight, 5.5 inches (14.0 centimeters) in width, 6.6 inches (16.7 centimeters) in length, and 3.7 inches (9.3 centimeters) in height. For a per-

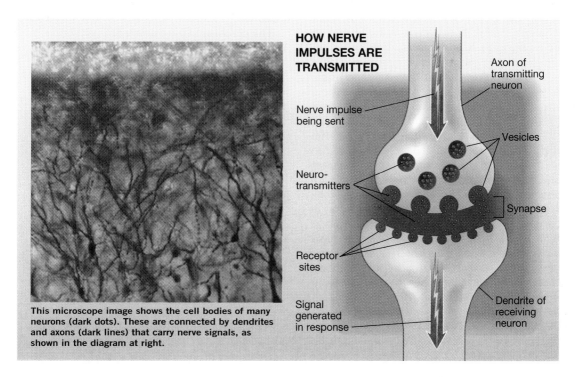

This microscope image shows the cell bodies of many neurons (dark dots). These are connected by dendrites and axons (dark lines) that carry nerve signals, as shown in the diagram at right.

HOW NERVE IMPULSES ARE TRANSMITTED

Axon of transmitting neuron

Nerve impulse being sent

Vesicles

Neurotransmitters

Synapse

Receptor sites

Signal generated in response

Dendrite of receiving neuron

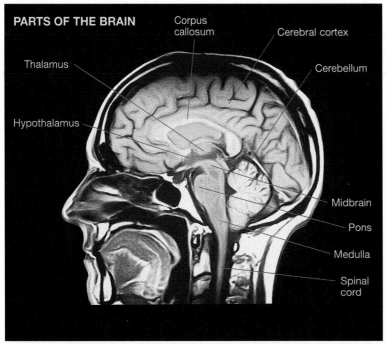

PARTS OF THE BRAIN

Corpus callosum

Cerebral cortex

Thalamus

Cerebellum

Hypothalamus

Midbrain

Pons

Medulla

Spinal cord

The brain's three main parts—the cerebrum (brown), cerebellum (green), and brain stem (blue)—can be seen in this colored image. Other structures within these parts and the beginning of the spinal cord are also visible.

First, there is the skin of the head—the scalp. Under the scalp are the bones of the skull. Between the skull and the brain are three special coverings called the **meninges**. The outermost layer is called the dura mater, which is tough and thick. The middle layer is called the arachnoid. The innermost layer, located on top of the brain, is called the pia mater. A clear, colorless liquid called the **cerebrospinal fluid** flows between the pia mater and arachnoid. This fluid supports the brain, cushions it against sudden impacts, removes waste products, and distributes chemicals called hormones to other parts of the body. The fluid also flows through cavities in the brain called ventricles.

The brain consists of three main parts: the cerebrum, the brain stem, and the cerebellum. Although different areas of the brain may play a role in specific functions, areas in these three parts interact to coordinate how we perceive, move, think, and feel.

Cerebrum

The cerebrum (the Latin word for "brain") is the largest part of the brain, making up about 85 percent of the total brain weight in humans. It looks like a large pinkish-gray walnut that is wrinkled and divided into left and right halves, or **cerebral hemispheres**. It includes the cerebral cortex, the basal ganglia, the amygdala, and the hippocampus.

The **cerebral cortex** makes up the outermost layer of the cerebrum. It is rather thin, varying in thickness from about $1/16$ to $3/16$ of an inch (1.5 millimeters to 4.5 millimeters). The cerebral hemispheres are connected by a thick band of over 300 million nerve fibers called the **corpus callosum**. The wrinkles of the brain are the result of bumps and grooves on the cerebral cortex. Each bump on the brain is called a gyrus (plural: gyri), also called a convolution. Each gyrus is separated by a groove called a sulcus (plural: sulci).

Although most people have the same patterns of gyri and sulci, no two brains are exactly alike. The folding of the cerebral cortex

son who weighs 154 pounds (70 kilograms), the brain makes up 2 percent of the total body weight but uses about 20 percent of the body's total oxygen supply.

On average, men's brains are larger than women's brains. However, it is important to note that there is no relationship between intelligence and brain size: A genius does not necessarily have a larger-than-average brain. In fact, the great physicist Albert Einstein had a brain that weighed just over 2.7 pounds (1.2 kilograms).

The brain connects with the rest of the body's nervous system, which is divided into two main parts: the **central nervous system** and the **peripheral nervous system**. The brain and spinal cord make up the central nervous system. The peripheral nervous system is composed of twelve pairs of cranial nerves that extend from the brain, 31 pairs of spinal nerves that extend from the spinal cord, and nerves that connect to all parts of the body. (For more information, see the article NERVOUS SYSTEM in Volume N.)

▶ ORGANIZATION OF THE BRAIN

The brain is isolated and protected from the outside world by several layers of tissue.

increases how much of it can fit in the skull. The total surface area of the human cerebral cortex is about 2½ square feet (2,200 square centimeters), about the size of a full page of newspaper.

Each hemisphere of the cerebrum is divided into four regions, or lobes, by various sulci and gyri. The **occipital lobes** are located at the back of the brain and are concerned with vision. The **temporal lobes**, located on the lower sides of the brain, play a role in hearing. The **parietal lobes**, found on the upper sides of the brain, are responsible for perceptions related to touch, pressure, temperature, and pain. The **frontal lobes** are found in front of the temporal and parietal lobes and are important for reasoning, planning, parts of speech, movement, emotions, and problem solving.

Deep inside the cerebrum are a group of structures called the **basal ganglia**. These areas are important for controlling movement. The **amygdala** is sometimes included as part of the basal ganglia. It is important for memory and emotional behavior. Another structure within the cerebrum is the **hippocampus**. It is important for transferring memories from short-term memory to long-term memory.

The amygdala and the hippocampus are sometimes grouped together with other brain structures and referred to as the **limbic system**. It was once thought to be the seat of all emotions, but scientists now know that it interacts with other parts of the brain (notably the cortex) in forming memories and emotional responses. The limbic system also shares various types of sensory information, such as smell, with other parts of the brain. That is why smelling something familiar, such as perfume or fresh-baked bread, often brings back strong memories and emotions associated with it.

Brain Stem
The brain stem is subdivided into many parts, including the thalamus, hypothalamus, midbrain, pons, and medulla.

Located at the front end of the brain stem, the **thalamus** is a group of structures that processes information from all of the senses except smell (which is processed by an area in the brain just above the nose called the olfactory bulb). This sensory information passes through the thalamus before it reaches the cerebral cortex. The thalamus also contains cell groups important for motor function, or movement.

Below the thalamus at the base of the brain lies the **hypothalamus**. The hypothalamus is responsible for regulating basic functions such as drinking and feeding, body temperature, sleep, and emotions. The pituitary gland extends down from the hypothalamus and acts as a master-control organ for other glands in the body.

The **midbrain** contains areas important for auditory (hearing) and visual reflexes. It constricts the pupils in our eyes when we step out of a dark room and into the bright sunlight, for instance. Other parts of the midbrain are involved with pain and movement. The **pons** (Latin for "bridge") contains areas that relay motor information from the cerebral cortex to other places in the nervous system. The **medulla** regulates certain invol-

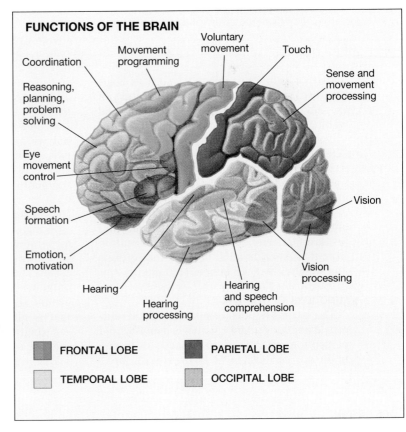

FUNCTIONS OF THE BRAIN

Coordination

Movement programming

Voluntary movement

Touch

Reasoning, planning, problem solving

Sense and movement processing

Eye movement control

Speech formation

Emotion, motivation

Hearing

Hearing processing

Hearing and speech comprehension

Vision

Vision processing

FRONTAL LOBE   PARIETAL LOBE

TEMPORAL LOBE   OCCIPITAL LOBE

KEEPING YOUR BRAIN HEALTHY

Here are some simple tips and good advice to keep your brain functioning at top efficiency:

1. Eat a well-balanced diet. The brain requires energy and proper nutrients to work efficiently.

2. Get enough sleep. To avoid drowsiness and irritability, get a good night's rest. Your brain will react faster and be better at performing complex mental tasks.

3. Avoid head injuries by wearing a helmet when you bike, skate, snowboard, or ski. Head injuries account for almost two-thirds of all bicycle-related deaths. Bicycle helmets reduce the risk for head injury by as much as 85 percent and reduce the risk for brain injury by as much as 88 percent. Also, always wear a seat belt in the car. Seat belts significantly reduce the severity of injury and decrease the number of deaths in car accidents.

4. Never use illegal drugs. Drugs such as cocaine, marijuana, heroin, LSD, and amphetamines alter the function of neurotransmitters in the brain and often lead to addiction and other mental and physical problems.

untary, or autonomic, functions such as heart rate, breathing, and digestion. Other areas of the medulla are important for sleeping and waking.

Cerebellum

The cerebellum (Latin for "little brain") is found at the back of the brain above the pons and midbrain. It plays a role in movement and the learning of motor skills. To coordinate movement and maintain balance and posture, the cerebellum receives information from the senses. In adult humans, the cerebellum weighs about 5.3 ounces (150 grams).

▶ FUNCTIONS OF THE BRAIN

The brain's billions of interconnected neurons make movement, language, memory, and perception possible. Some functions of the brain are established at birth. For example, babies are born with a set of reflexes that help them survive. Other more complicated behaviors develop as we grow, learn, and communicate with other people.

The Senses

The nervous system is equipped with special receptors to provide the brain with information about the environment. These receptors convert outside signals such as light, sound, and pressure into electrical impulses. Receptors are specialized for one particular type of signal. For example, receptors in the eye respond to light, but not to sounds. Electrical impulses generated by receptors are relayed to the central nervous system, where a perception of the signal is formed.

It is often said that humans have only five senses: touch, taste, sight, hearing, and smell. However, the inner ear has receptors that provide information related to balance, and joints and muscles have receptors that provide information about body position. Some animals have additional sensory systems or a greater sensitivity to particular information than humans do: fish can detect changes in water pressure; snakes can see infrared light; the platypus can detect electrical currents; bats can hear high-frequency sounds.

The nervous system also monitors sensory signals inside the body. Sometimes we are not aware of such internal sensory signals. For example, information related to body temperature and blood pressure is sent to the brain, but we are often not conscious of such signals. These signals are monitored by the brain and used to maintain a normal internal environment in the body.

Motor Behavior

A major function of the brain is to control movement, or motor behavior. Incoming sensory information sent to the brain can be processed by the brain and converted into outgoing signals to control muscles and glands. It is the pattern of outgoing signals that is ultimately responsible for an organism's behavior.

Some movements do not require the brain. These automatic movements, called spinal reflexes, require processing only in the spinal cord. For example, when an area on your knee is lightly tapped, your leg will kick before the message is relayed to your brain. Although the information eventually does get to the brain, it is not required for the kick to occur.

More complex movements, such as talking, throwing a ball, or dancing, involve multiple areas of the brain. These brain areas include those involved with memory, perception, and planning. Neurons in an area of the cerebrum called the primary motor cortex send signals to neurons in the spinal cord to control muscles.

The basal ganglia and cerebellum are two other brain areas important for movement, particularly planned movements and those requiring smooth control.

Learning and Memory

The brain is in a constant state of change. As we learn new skills and make new memories, we actually change the physical structure of the nervous system, as our neurons make new connections. This is true not just in humans but in other animals as well. While exploring their environment, organisms learn about the world around them and form memories of events that have taken place. The ability to form new memories is essential for an organism's survival.

Memories are stored in the brain in stages. Small pieces of new information are processed in short-term memory for only a few minutes. Memories may then be transferred to a more permanent form in long-term memory.

The hippocampus, within the cerebrum, plays an important role in this transfer. Although damage to the hippocampus does not affect old memories, it can result in the inability to form new memories. For example, people with damage to the hippocampus can remember their own names, but they cannot remember the names of people whom they have just met.

The exact mechanisms by which the brain stores information are not known. It is likely that other areas of the brain, especially those in the cerebral cortex, are also important for memory. Electrical stimulation of parts of the cerebral cortex can evoke memories of past experiences.

Sleep

About one-third of your life is spent sleeping. During sleep, you are not conscious of the world around you. Although you appear to be inactive, your brain is not at rest. Using a machine called an **electroencephalograph** (EEG) to measure brain activity, scientists have discovered that at times during sleep, the brain displays patterns of activity similar to those when we are awake.

Sleep follows a predictable pattern of stages each night. There are two basic forms of sleep: slow wave sleep and rapid eye movement (REM) sleep. After falling asleep, people pass through a series of stages of slow wave sleep, each characterized by different patterns of brain activity. People then enter REM sleep, which is characterized by brain activity similar to wakefulness. This cycle is repeated at intervals of about 90 minutes. During REM sleep, most skeletal muscles are completely paralyzed. In the 1950's, scientists found that during REM sleep, people's eyes dart back and forth rapidly. Also, if people were awakened during REM sleep, they often reported that they were dreaming.

WONDER QUESTION

Is it true that we use only 10 percent of our brains?

No. This is a common misconception. Although different parts of the brain are more or less active during different activities, there is no evidence that we use only a small portion of our brains. Damage to a small area of the brain can cause devastating effects, such as amnesia, paralysis, or loss of language. This suggests that every part of the brain serves an important function, upon which other parts of the brain depend.

On the other hand, some people—especially children—can recover after suffering major damage to the brain or even losing part of it. Such remarkable recoveries do not suggest that we need only a fraction of our brain, however. Rather, they illustrate the tremendous capacity of the brain to "rewire" itself: Cells in the remaining parts of the brain form new connections and take over the functions of those parts that were removed.

as many as 250,000 new nerve cells can be formed each minute during a baby's development inside its mother? By the time the baby is born, the brain will have almost all the nerve cells, or neurons, it will ever have. However, a child's brain continues to increase in size after birth as other brain cells, called glia, grow around the neurons, insulating them and carrying out various "housekeeping" functions in the brain. A baby is also born with trillions of connections, or synapses, between neurons. As the child learns various skills, many of these synapses are stimulated and become permanent connections.

Although all of the brain mechanisms responsible for sleep are not known, circuits involving the brain stem, hypothalamus, and cerebral cortex are important for sleep and wakefulness. (For more information, see the articles SLEEP in Volume S and DREAMING in Volume D.)

▶ DETECTING BRAIN DISORDERS

Brain disorders affect millions of people and have a tremendous impact on society. Some disorders such as Parkinson's disease, Huntington's disease, and Alzheimer's disease cause neurons in parts of the brain to break down, or degenerate. Epilepsy, which affects about one out of every hundred people, is caused by the massive release, or discharge, of electrical signals by neurons. This discharge can result in seizures, often characterized by periods of unconsciousness or uncontrolled shaking of the body. Brain tumors are caused by the rapid growth of cells and can be life-threatening.

Also life-threatening are strokes, or "brain attacks." Strokes are the third leading cause of death in the United States. A stroke occurs when the blood supply to part of the brain is blocked. The lack of nutrients and oxygen to the brain causes neurons to die. People who suffer a stroke may have memory problems, lose their ability to speak, or become partially paralyzed.

Mental illnesses such as schizophrenia, depression, and anxiety disorders affect mood and thought patterns. These illnesses are also brain disorders. Although the causes of these disorders are not completely understood, many drugs that target specific neurotransmitters have been developed to treat people suffering from mental illnesses.

Mapping the Brain

A variety of methods are used to diagnose brain disorders. Early neuroscientists learned about the human brain by observing the behavior of people who had brain damage. In the 1860's, for example, French surgeon Paul Broca discovered the importance of the left cerebral hemisphere in language by examining the abilities of people with damage to specific areas of the brain.

The electroencephalograph (EEG) was used in human subjects for the first time in the

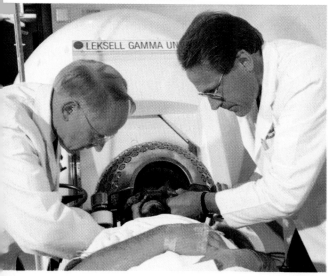

Doctors prepare a patient for entry into a machine that will destroy a life-threatening brain tumor with precisely aimed beams of radiation.

1920's by German psychiatrist Hans Berger. It is an important tool that measures the electrical activity of the brain through contacts called electrodes taped to the scalp. The EEG is still used today in sleep research and in the diagnosis of illnesses such as epilepsy.

In the 1940's and 1950's, the pioneering American-Canadian neurosurgeon Wilder Penfield applied small electrical shocks to the human brain. These shocks caused different sensations, movements, and even memories in the patients. Experiments by Penfield provided detailed maps of the workings of the cerebral cortex. These maps aid surgeons during the removal of brain tumors.

Seeing Inside the Brain

Technological advances now allow scientists to peer inside the living human brain to see the brain in action. These procedures are safe and painless. Scientists using these methods can determine which part of the brain is damaged after an injury or because of disease, and they can develop new methods to treat brain disorders. Brain imaging methods also help scientists understand normal brain behavior as well as mental illnesses such as schizophrenia and depression.

In the 1970's, researchers began using computers to help visualize the structure of the brain. **Computed tomography**, or CT, scanning (also called computerized axial tomography, or CAT, scanning) provides images of the brain formed by multiple beams of X rays that pass through the various tissues of the brain. The CT method has been used to locate brain tumors and other structural abnormalities in the brain. The structure of the brain can also be viewed using **magnetic resonance imaging** (MRI). MRI uses powerful magnets to detect small changes in the atoms of the brain and provides a more detailed view of the brain than CT can.

Unlike CT and MRI, **positron emission tomography** (PET) provides a functional image of the brain—that is, one that shows how the brain functions. During a PET scan, a small dose of a radioactive substance is injected into a person's bloodstream. Scanners around the head detect a form of radiation called gamma rays produced by the radioactive substance. Areas of the brain that contain more of the substance emit more gamma rays. Therefore, PET can be used to determine which parts of the brain are more active than other parts.

▶ UNDERSTANDING THE BRAIN

Scientists have learned a great deal about the brain. Nevertheless, some of the most basic questions about the brain remain unanswered: Why do we sleep? What is consciousness? What is the best way to treat neurological and mental disorders? How do we remember, and why do we forget? What

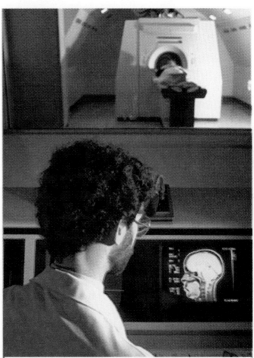

A technician looks at a computer screen showing the brain of a patient whose head is positioned inside an MRI scanner (in the background).

is the neural basis of drug addiction? These and other questions promise to challenge scientists as they attempt to understand the workings of the most complicated structure in the world: the brain.

ERIC H. CHUDLER
Editor, *Neuroscience for Kids* Web site
Research Associate Professor
University of Washington

See also BODY, HUMAN (The Sense Organs); MENTAL ILLNESS; NERVOUS SYSTEM.

BRAKES. See HYDRAULIC AND PNEUMATIC SYSTEMS; RAILROADS.

BRANCUSI, CONSTANTIN (1876–1957)

Constantin Brancusi was one of the great sculptors of the 1900's. His life was outstanding in its simplicity and devotion to art. For many years he lived alone in his studio in Paris, surrounded by his work.

Brancusi was born in a village in western Romania on February 19, 1876, the son of land-owning peasants. When he was 11 years old, he left his home to seek his fortune. He worked at odd jobs for five years and then went to Craiova.

In 1895 he entered the Craiova School of Arts and Crafts and studied sculpture for the first time. From then on, his education was paid for by scholarships and grants. He graduated from the Bucharest School of Fine Arts in 1902 and in 1905 enrolled in the École des Beaux-Arts (School of Fine Arts) in Paris. His work quickly gained respect.

Brancusi's first sculptures showed the influence of the French sculptor Rodin. Brancusi worked in Rodin's studio in 1906 but left after a short time, stating, "Nothing can grow in the shade of a great tree." His work became personal and inventive. In much of his sculpture, natural shapes are reduced to simpler forms.

He sometimes produced multiple versions of a theme—a smooth, simple egg or a bird with elegant lines—seeking to express its purest form. *Bird in Space* was one such example. Brancusi created several variations of this sculpture, in marble and bronze, over a number of years.

From 1908, Brancusi's work was almost entirely of wood or stone—carved often in large, simple shapes—and of bronze cast from the carvings and frequently polished to a mirror finish.

Brancusi died on March 16, 1957. His studio in Paris, as he left it, serves as a museum of his work.

Reviewed by MARK ROSENTHAL
Philadelphia Museum of Art

BRANDEIS, LOUIS D.   See KENTUCKY (Famous People).
BRANDO, MARLON.   See MOTION PICTURES (Profiles: Movie Stars).

BRANT, JOSEPH (1742–1807)

Joseph Brant was a Mohawk Indian chief and war chief of the Six Nations of the Iroquois. He is known for the help he gave the British during the Revolutionary War.

Joseph, the son of a Mohawk chief, was born in 1742 in what is now the state of Ohio. His Indian name was Thayendanegea, which means "he places two bets." When Joseph was 12, he met Sir William Johnson, the British superintendent of Indian affairs. The next year he accompanied Johnson in a French and Indian War campaign. A few years later,

Johnson sent him to school in Connecticut. Joseph became a member of the Anglican Church and began to translate religious works into the Mohawk language.

When the Revolutionary War began, Brant and most of the members of the Six Nations remained loyal to Britain. Brant received the rank of captain in the British Army. He plunged into the conflict and led Indian forces against settlements on the New York frontier. After the war he led members of the Mohawk tribe into Canada, seeking a new home for his people. The British Government granted him a large tract of land in what is now Ontario.

Brant made two trips to England and was presented to King George III. In 1793 he attended a great conference of Indian tribes. He urged the Indian people to live in peace with the settlers. But many of the tribes deserted him and continued to wage war.

Brant died on November 24, 1807. Brantford, Ontario, was named for him.

JOHN S. MOIR
University of Toronto

BRAQUE, GEORGES (1882–1963)

Georges Braque's interest in art began when he was a child in Argenteuil, France, where he was born on May 13, 1882. His father was an interior decorator and an amateur painter. Georges watched and copied his father, and art became the center of his life.

The Braque family moved to the city of Le Havre in 1890, and Georges continued to draw and paint and study. Ten years later he went to Paris, where a great revolution in art was taking place. Braque's first paintings were done in the Impressionist style, but by 1906 he was exhibiting with a new group called *les fauves* ("the wild beasts").

In 1907, Braque met the great young painter Pablo Picasso. They became close friends and for years worked together, experimenting with modern techniques. They helped develop **cubism,** a kind of painting that shows many sides of an object at once. In 1912, Braque invented *papier collé,* or **collage,** a technique of gluing scraps of paper and other objects onto a flat surface, as part of a picture.

During World War I, Braque was seriously wounded while serving in the French Army. After the war he began to work more slowly and thoughtfully. After 1917 he struck out on his own, although he continued to work with cubism, simplifying it as the years passed. He painted many still lifes, often using the table in his studio as a subject.

Braque did not limit himself to painting. He also created stage scenery, book illustrations, and sculpture. In the 1950's he designed a ceiling for the Louvre museum in Paris. Braque died in Paris on August 31, 1963.

Reviewed by PHILIP LINHARES
Director, Mills College Art Gallery

BRASS. See BRONZE AND BRASS.
BRASS INSTRUMENTS. See WIND INSTRUMENTS.

Le Guéridon ("The Pedestal Table") is one of several paintings by Braque using a small, round-topped table as the center of a still life.

BRAZIL

The faces of Brazil reflect the country's ethnic and cultural diversity. *Clockwise from below:* University students in Rio de Janeiro; women of Bahia state in traditional dress; a group of youngsters in São Paulo; brokers at São Paulo's stock exchange; a man from a Japanese community in São Paulo; and an Awa Gaja Indian in Maranhão state.

Brazil is one of the world's giant nations. It is the largest and most populous country in South America, containing almost half the continent's area and more than half its people. Among the nations of the world, Brazil ranks fifth in area, after Russia, Canada, China, and the United States. It ranks sixth in population.

When Portuguese traders arrived in the 1500's, they found certain trees with wood the color of live coals—*brasa* in Portuguese. They called the trees brazilwoods and named their country after them. Brazilwood yields red and purple dyes, which were highly prized in Europe for coloring cloth.

Brazil was ruled by Portugal for over 300 years before gaining its independence peacefully in 1822. Following the reign of two emperors, Brazil dissolved the monarchy in 1889. Today it is a federal republic, made up of a number of states, territories, and the federal district of Brasília, the national capital.

Brazil is a land of great variety and contrast. Vast jungles and tropical rain forests, great rivers, and mountains cover much of the interior of Brazil, while rapidly growing modern cities crowd the long coastline of the Atlantic Ocean.

▶ PEOPLE

Brazil's population is unevenly distributed. Most of its people are concentrated on the eastern edge of the country along the Atlantic coast between the Amazon River and the border with Uruguay and Argentina.

Most Brazilians are of mixed European, African, and Indian ancestry, although many people have come from Japan, the Middle East, and Europe, especially Portugal. People of mixed racial ancestry, called mestizos, are found mostly in the small towns and rural areas of the interior, although in recent decades, thousands have migrated to the cities in search of work and a better way of life. A small number of Indians still live in remote areas of the tropical rain forest.

Language. The Spanish greeting "*Buenos días*" is the way to say "good morning," "hello," or "good day" in every South American country except Brazil. In Brazil, people say "*Bom dia,*" which is Portuguese for the same greetings. Brazil is the only Portuguese-speaking nation in the Western Hemisphere. But because there are many Brazilians, Portuguese has become a major world language. Brazilian Portuguese is much like the language spoken in Portugal except that it is spoken with a different accent and intonation. A visitor from Portugal would also have to learn new words that have been added to the language by Africans and Indians.

Many educated Brazilians also speak Spanish, and many are fluent in English and French. German and Italian are spoken by several million in the southern states.

Religion. Most Brazilians are Roman Catholics. This gives Brazil the distinction of having the largest Catholic population of any nation in the world. There are also many Protestants in Brazil. In fact, Evangelical Protestants represent the country's fastest-growing religious group. Smaller numbers of Buddhists and Jews make their homes in

Brazil. An unusual mixture of African religions and Roman Catholicism known as *candomblé* is practiced by many Brazilians of African descent in the cities and the Northeast.

Education. Brazilian law requires all children to attend elementary school for at least three years. Elementary school pupils can be recognized easily by their uniforms. Boys

Above: A *candomblé* ceremony takes place in Bahia state. Many Brazilians of African descent practice *candomblé*, which is a mixture of African religions and Roman Catholicism. *Left:* Evangelical Protestants are the fastest-growing religious group in Brazil.

wear khaki or white shirts and navy-blue shorts. Girls wear navy-blue skirts and white blouses. They study Brazilian history, arithmetic, science, social studies, and Portuguese. English and French are taught as second languages in the higher grades.

Secondary school consists of four years of junior high school, called *giná-sio*, and three years of senior high school, called *colégio*. Most secondary schools are privately run, and only affluent Brazilians can afford to send their children to them.

Advanced education is available at technical schools, state colleges, and at national and Catholic universities. State and federal universities charge no tuition, and admission is based on results of a nationwide competitive

Carnival is a four-day holiday celebrated in all Brazilian cities and towns. The best-known festival is held in Rio de Janeiro and draws people from all over the world.

remote villages. However, because many of the people of Brazil are under 18 years of age, more schools are needed every year.

Food and Drink. The national dish of Brazil is called *feijoada*. It contains black beans, pork sausage, tripe (stomach of cow or other cud-chewing animal), spices, and greens, and is served with rice. Brazilians also use farinha as a condiment. This is made from the root of cassava, or manioc, a tropical plant that is native to Brazil. When it is cooked and dried, people sprinkle it on soups, meat, and stews and use it as flour in bread and puddings.

Every region of Brazil has its own special foods. *Charque* (dried and salted beef) is traditional in southern Brazil. In the Northeast and along the Amazon River, fish dishes are popular. The cowboys (*gaúchos*) of the southern grasslands eat a form of barbecued beef. Oranges, pineapples, bananas, papayas, mangos, and other varieties of tropical fruit are plentiful and popular.

Coffee is Brazil's main beverage. Brazilians like to drink *cafezinhos*, tiny cups of sweet, steaming hot coffee several times a day. Another beverage is *maté*, an herbal tea. It is sometimes served in a hollowed-out gourd and drunk with a straw.

Holidays and Other Special Events. Brazilians share in the many Catholic holidays, such as saints' days, when festivals, pageants, and dances are held. The most famous of these holidays is Carnival— the four-day festival that occurs just before

Maté, an herbal tea, is a popular Brazilian beverage. In the far south, it is traditionally served in a hollowed-out gourd and sipped through a silver straw.

examination, the *vestibulário*. Students often take a year off after graduating high school to prepare for this entrance examination. Once admitted to the university, students specialize at once, choosing among schools of architecture, business, law, medicine, engineering, and humanities. Some students enter military academies; others prepare to be diplomats in Brazil's highly regarded Foreign Ministry school.

There are still not enough schools for the fast-growing population. The number of people who are able to read and write has been increased greatly through a massive government program of school construction and teacher training. In addition, adult education courses are being given in some of the larger cities. There are also mobile schools that bring teachers, books, and school supplies to

Futebol (soccer) is Brazil's national sport. Thousands of fans watch the game at Maracanã Stadium in Rio de Janeiro.

Lent. Carnival is celebrated in all Brazilian towns and cities. The best-known festival is held in Rio de Janeiro. Schools and businesses close, and the whole city is given over to parades, street dances, and masked balls. Strolling musicians play music such as samba, *marcha*, and *frevo*. Confetti and streamers fill the air. *Cariocas*, as the people of Rio are called, and tourists join in this huge citywide celebration during which no one sleeps and nearly everyone dances to the throbbing samba rhythms.

Sports. Nearly all Brazilians are sports fans. Boating, sailing, and swimming are popular activities, but Brazilians delight in a good *futebol* ("soccer") match. *Futebol* is the national sport, and every school and town has its own team. Professional soccer players are national figures in Brazil, just as baseball players are in the United States. In recent years, however, the biggest stars have left to play in Europe, although every four years they return to form the *Seleção Brasileira*, the all-star Brazilian World Cup team. Brazilians have also excelled internationally in automobile racing and yachting, as well as in basketball and volleyball.

Libraries, Museums, and the Arts. Brazil has very few public lending libraries although large cities have libraries that house both books and archives of documents. Of the country's museums, São Paulo's Museum of Modern Art has a fine collection, as does the Museum of Contemporary Art. In Rio are the National Historical Museum and National Museum of Fine Arts. The National Museum in Brasília displays historical artifacts. In Belém, at the mouth of the Amazon, the Goeldi Museum displays anthropological artifacts. Rio's Municipal Theater features opera, ballet, and concerts. Manaus, in the heart of the Amazon Basin, has an opera house that was built in the late 1800's and has been restored as a tourist site.

Urban and Rural Life. Approximately three-quarters of the people live in urban areas. Affluent Brazilians live in luxurious high-rise apartments or houses surrounded by high walls. They can afford to buy a variety of goods and almost always have maids and servants. For other city dwellers, however, the problem of poverty is severe.

Rural areas, which are mostly poor, consist of small, sleepy towns surrounded by farm-

FACTS and figures

FEDERATIVE REPUBLIC OF BRAZIL (République Federativa do Brazil) is the official name of the country.

LOCATION: Eastern South America.

AREA: 3,286,478 sq mi (8,511,965 km²).

POPULATION: 165,000,000 (estimate).

CAPITAL: Brasília.

LARGEST CITY: São Paulo.

MAJOR LANGUAGE: Portuguese (official).

MAJOR RELIGIOUS GROUP: Christian (Roman Catholic, Evangelical Protestant).

GOVERNMENT: Republic. **Head of state and government**—president. **Legislature**—National Congress (consisting of the Chamber of Deputies and the Federal Senate).

CHIEF PRODUCTS: Agricultural—soybeans, coffee, beans, rice, cassava, cacao, sugar, corn, oranges, bananas, pineapples, tobacco, cotton, livestock and livestock products. **Manufactured**—processed foods, textiles, steel, motor vehicles, chemicals, television sets, paper and other wood products. **Mineral**—iron ore, manganese, bauxite, chrome, nickel, gemstones, uranium, salt, lead, gold.

MONETARY UNIT: Real (1 real = 100 centavos).

Brazil

land on which people live in huts or tiny houses.

Although the family remains the center of everyday life in Brazil, widespread poverty has changed the ways many families are organized. Many families, especially in the *favelas*, or slums, are headed by single mothers. The pressures of crime, drugs, and economic hardship has forced thousands of children to live on the streets.

Poor families tend to have many children. The older children are given the responsibility of taking care of the smaller ones. Because of a housing shortage, many families—including cousins, aunts, uncles, and grandchildren—often live together under one roof. Middle- and upper-income families are usually smaller. Legal adoption is not widely practiced but families will sometimes take in children of relatives or neighbors whose parents cannot raise them. Fathers are traditionally heads of Brazilian households, but women are assuming increasingly important economic roles.

A farmer in Minas Gerais, in Brazil's eastern region, takes a moment to contemplate the sloped valley below him.

▶ LAND

Brazil, like all large countries, has a varied landscape. The country can be divided into uplands and lowlands. The two main upland areas—the Brazilian Highlands and the Guiana Highlands—cover more than one-half of Brazil. The three major lowland areas are the Amazon Basin, a small area in southern Brazil drained by the Rio de la Plata system, and the small area of the upper Paraguay river system in the southwest. There are not many high mountains.

Brazilians usually divide their country into five regions. These are the Northeast, the East, the South, the Central West, and the Amazon Basin. Each region contains several states.

The Northeast. In the region known as the Northeast are the states of Maranhão, Piauí, Ceará, Rio Grande do Norte, Paraíba, Pernambuco, Alagoas, Sergipe, and Bahia. This area, along the upper Atlantic coast, has rich, fertile soil, but the inland area, called the *sertão*, or "backland," is quite

rocky. Many unusual plants grow in the *caatinga*, a tropical thorn forest of the Northeast. One, the carnauba palm, is found only in Brazil. Its leaves yield a widely used commercial wax.

The East. The eastern region is made up of the states of Rio de Janeiro, Espírito Santo, Minas Gerais, and São Paulo. A combination of favorable climate, rich soils, and abundant natural resources has made these states, with the exception of Espírito Santo, the richest and most important in Brazil.

The South. The three southern states are Santa Catarina, Paraná, and Rio Grande do Sul. This region consists of a narrow coastal plain and fertile, rolling grasslands in the interior. The coastline has many beautiful beaches. The Great Escarpment is a steep slope along the southern coast. Huge rolling grasslands are located in the south of this region, near Uruguay.

The Central West. Brazil's frontier states are Goiás, Mato Grosso ("Great Forest"), Mato Grosso do Sul, and Tocantins on the western plateau. This is a vast, thinly populated area. It is rich in plant and animal life.

Cattle are raised on the rolling grasslands of southern Brazil. These *gaúchos* (cowboys) are driving cattle across Brazil's border into Argentina.

Left: The Amazon River, which crosses northern Brazil, is the world's second longest river, after the Nile. The Amazon rain forest, the world's largest, is home to some of the rarest animals on Earth. *Below:* Workers unload fruit from boats in Belém, one of the few large cities on the Amazon River.

The Amazon Basin. The six states of Amapá, Acre, Amazonas, Pará, Rondônia, and Roraima are situated in this enormous basin formed by the Amazon River and its tributaries. It is a rich area filled with rain forests, jungles, and swamps. So much rain falls in the Amazon Basin that Brazilians divide the seasons into the "time of the big rains" and the "time of the little rains."

Rivers and Rain Forests. The Amazon River, which flows across northern Brazil, is the world's second longest river, after the Nile. Brazil has the world's largest tropical rain forest, the Amazon. The *selva*, or rain forest, is home to many rare forms of wildlife, including endangered butterflies, giant spiders, huge beetles, snakes, boa constrictors, and other animals. More than 1,000 different species of fish live in the river. One of these is the *pirarucú*, a codfish that often grows to 5 feet (1.5 meters) in length. Another is the piranha, a small, flesh-eating fish.

A second important river is the São Francisco River, which runs from the coast to the mountainous highlands of Minas Gerais. This river has provided a means of transportation to and from the eastern interior of Brazil.

Climate. Most of Brazil has a tropical climate. The Amazon basin is extremely humid; in Acre, near the border with Bolivia, temperatures hover near 95°F (35°C) most of the time. The climate along the Atlantic coast, however, is mild, aided by ocean breezes. South central Brazil has mild winters. In the far south, snow has fallen and there have been frosts that have killed coffee trees and other crops.

Natural Resources. Brazil's largest gold deposits and a mountain of iron ore have been discovered in Pará. The Amazon Basin also contains large reserves of bauxite (aluminum ore), copper, manganese, and tin. However, scientists fear that opening the Amazon to large-scale development would destroy the fragile balance of the tropical rain forest.

The country has tremendous iron reserves at Itabira and a wealth of industrial diamonds, aquamarines, beryls, topazes, and tourmalines elsewhere in the region.

▶ **ECONOMY**

Throughout Brazil's history, the economy has depended mainly on one product at a time. During the early years of settlement, sugar was the main export. When the soil on the sugar plantations began losing fertility, large deposits of gold were discovered. Throughout the 1700's, Brazil was gripped by "gold fever." As the profits from gold lessened, Brazil turned to agriculture again as the basis of the economy. But services, including tourism, are becoming an increasingly important part of the economy.

Services. Service industries employ many people and account for almost half of Brazil's economy. Leading service industries include education, finance, health care, domestic service, and businesses relating to tourism. Tourists come from all over the world, especially to Manaus, Salvador, and Rio de Janeiro.

Manufacturing. Brazil is the leading industrial nation in Latin America. Many foreign companies have built factories in Brazil, although most industrial plants are owned by Brazilians.

Food processing and textiles are the industrial giants. Industry is centered in São Paulo and Rio de Janeiro but is expanding rapidly in many other cities. Volta Redonda, for example, was once a tiny village. Today it has one of the largest steelworks in Latin America. The manufacture of automobiles, commercial vehicles, television sets, chemicals, and consumer goods is also growing rapidly in Brazil.

The most serious obstacle to industrial growth is the lack of mineral fuels such as coal and petroleum. The building of hydro-

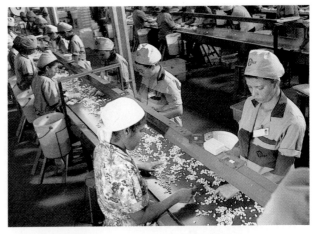

Workers sort through cashew nuts in a Brazilian factory. Food processing is one of the country's most important industries.

electric plants on Brazil's rivers has helped provide electricity. The country is also turning to nuclear power as a source of energy.

Agriculture. Agricultural products are Brazil's chief export. The nation is among the world's leading producers of soybeans, coffee, cacao (the source of cocoa and chocolate), sugar, corn, cassava (manioc), oranges, bananas, pineapples, tobacco, and cotton. Cotton is grown in the South for export and in the East to supply Brazil's textile industry. Beans, rice, and cassava are grown widely for local use. Jute, used for making burlap, sacking, and twine, was introduced by Japanese immigrants. In spite of Brazil's rich agriculture, however, some foods must be imported.

Brazil is now a major cattle-raising nation. It exports large quantities of meat and other animal products. Hogs are also raised extensively, as are horses and other animals.

Mining and Forestry. Iron ore is Brazil's leading single export. Manganese, bauxite, chrome, and many other minerals are mined, and new mineral discoveries are constantly being made. Wood is cut for export and is also processed into wood pulp, paper, and other products. However, be-

An iron mine and smeltery in the Amazon rain forest. Brazil is one of the world's chief producers of iron ore, which is the country's leading single export.

Bruno Giorgi's *Warriors* stands in front of the Congress Building, designed by Oscar Niemeyer, in Brasília.

cause of the pollution problems from paper manufacturing, environmentalists are debating whether limits should be placed on this industry.

Fishing. Because meat, not fish, is a staple in the Brazilian diet, most fish is exported to other countries. Tuna, sardines, lobsters, and shrimp are caught in the Atlantic Ocean off Brazil's eastern coast.

Energy. Brazil has some offshore oil but otherwise must import petroleum. It relies on hydroelectric energy and nuclear power. The Itaipu hydroelectric power plant, on the Paraná River between Brazil and Paraguay, is one of the most powerful in the world.

Trade. Brazil sells its products to other countries to pay for imports of fuels and lubricants, machinery, chemicals, foods, and technology. Imports come mainly from western Europe, Japan, the United States, and Venezuela. Brazil is a partner with Argentina, Paraguay, and Uruguay in Mercosur, an economic common market established in 1991 that eliminated tariff barriers and

made it easier for member nations to trade with one another. Many exports go to western Europe, Japan, and the United States. Brazil supplies many kinds of raw materials and consumer goods to other Latin American countries.

Transportation. Transportation in Brazil has always been difficult because the country is very large. Settlements, towns, and cities are far from one another, and mountains and forests often separate them. The Great Escarpment has made the construction of roads and rails slow. When Brazilians travel long distances, they have to travel by airplanes or buses because passenger railroads are inadequate. Roads on the coasts are good but crowded with traffic.

Air travel links all parts of Brazil. Brazil's domestic air network has become one of the world's busiest. There are many excellent harbors that are busy centers of world trade.

Communication. All major cities are linked by telephone. The country's telegraph system is being replaced by use of electronic mail. Brazil has hundreds of radio stations. The *Globo* television network is the fourth largest in the world, and many Brazilians receive cable programs by satellite from all over the world.

▶ MAJOR CITIES

Brazil has many large and bustling cities.

Brasília is the chief city of the Central West as well as the national capi-

São Paulo's cathedral is located in the Praça da Sé, the oldest part of the city. São Paulo is Brazil's largest city.

Boats dot a harbor in beautiful Rio de Janeiro, Brazil's second largest city. Cone-shaped Sugarloaf Mountain rises in the background.

tal. It is considered an outstanding example of modern large-scale city planning. The city is shaped roughly like a giant airplane. The buildings of its central area are bordered by a V-shaped artificial lake.

São Paulo, in the state of São Paulo, is the chief industrial city of Latin America and the largest city in Brazil. This bustling, modern city is the center of the nation's textile industry. A separate article on São Paulo can be found in Volume S.

Rio de Janeiro, in the state of Rio de Janeiro, is considered one of the world's most beautiful cities. Its fine harbor, steep mountains, and magnificent modern apartment houses strung along the beaches and wide, tree-lined avenues have made Rio one of the most visited and most often photographed cities in the world. For more information, see the article on Rio de Janeiro that appears in Volume Q-R.

Belo Horizonte, in the state of Minas Gerais, is Brazil's third largest city and a major commercial and industrial area. Its name means "beautiful horizon" in Portuguese.

Salvador, in the state of Bahia, is one of the chief cities of the Northeast. **Forteleza**, in the state of Ceará on Brazil's northeastern coast, is a commercial center. **Nova Iguaçu**, in the state of Rio de Janeiro, is an industrial suburb of Rio de Janeiro city. **Curitiba**, in the state of Paraná, is a leading city and rivals São Paulo as a center of coffee production. **Pôrto Alegre**, is one of the leading cities in the state of Rio Grande do Sul in the South. **Recife**, in the state of Pernambuco on Brazil's eastern coast, has a flourishing port. **Belém**, in the state of Pará, is one of a few large cities on the Amazon River. **Manaus**, a free-trade port on the central Amazon, was very important during the 1800's, when the Amazonian forest was the world's leading source of natural rubber. The opera house and mosaic sidewalks of Manaus are reminders of the city's prosperous past.

Many operas and ballets are performed at the Teatro Amazonas, or Amazon Opera House, in Manaus. The opera house was built in the late 1800's.

The dramatic capital city of Brasília is the work of Brazil's leading designers—the city planner Lúcio Costa, the architect Oscar Niemeyer, and the landscape architect Roberto Burle Marx.

Music and Dance. Brazilian dances and music, such as the samba, *baião*, bossa nova, and *lambada*, are known by millions all over the world. Several Brazilian musicians have won international fame. One is Antônio Carlos Gomes, a composer of the 1800's whose opera about a proud Indian is called *Il Guarany* (1870). Heitor Villa-Lobos composed more than 2,000 works based on the folk music of the Brazilian Africans and pioneers. Guiomar Novaes was a noted pianist.

Literature. Brazil has produced many distinguished writers. Joaquim Maria Machado de Assis is considered one of the greatest South American writers. His portrayals of life in Rio de Janeiro during the early 1800's are found in *Epitaph for a Small Winner* (1881), *Dom Casmurro* (1900), and *Quincas Borba* (1891).

Euclides da Cunha is another of Brazil's better-known writers. His most famous book, *Rebellion in the Backlands* (1902), is an essay on people and the land in the Northeast. Distinguished Brazilian writers of the 1900's include the poets Carlos Drummond de Andrade, Manuel Bandeira, and novelists Guimarães Rosa, Graciliano Ramos, Erico Veríssimo, Rachel de Queiroz, and Nélida Piñón. The sociologist-historian Gilberto Freyre is well known in other countries. His classic works are *The Masters and the Slaves* (1933) and *The Mansions and the Shanties* (1936).

▶ **CULTURAL HERITAGE**

The Portuguese brought a love of music and art from their home country that has become a vital part of Brazilian life. As the colony grew into a nation, many Brazilians won fame in the arts.

Sculpture and Painting. One of the first well-known Brazilian artists was a sculptor of the 1700's, Antonio Francisco Lisboa, who was known as O Aleijadinho—"The Little Cripple." Aleijadinho had leprosy. When he could no longer use his hands, he had his tools strapped to his wrists so that he could go on sculpting. His most famous works are the statues of the twelve prophets on the steps of a church in Congonhas do Campo, a small town in Minas Gerais. One of the statues is pictured in the article LATIN AMERICA, ART AND ARCHITECTURE OF in Volume L of this encyclopedia.

Brazilian painters only began to win worldwide fame in the 1900's. Among the best known are Emiliano di Cavalcanti, Lasar Segall, and Cândido Portinari, whose murals can be seen not only in Brazil but also at the Library of Congress in Washington, D.C., and at the United Nations headquarters in New York City.

Architecture. In the field of architecture, too, Brazilians have won international fame.

GOVERNMENT

Brazil is a federal republic, consisting of 26 states and the Federal District of Brasília. Each state has its own elected legislature and governor.

Brazil's legislative body is the National Congress, which is composed of the Chamber of Deputies and the Federal Senate. Deputies are elected, on the basis of population, for a term of four years. Senators serve 8-year terms, with three senators elected from each of the states.

From 1964 to 1985, the military controlled the government under a succession of generals, who suspended constitutional guarantees of rights. Civilian government was restored in 1985, and a new democratic constitution took effect in 1988. It provided for direct elections of a president and vice president to 6-year terms. The president is the head of both state and government.

HISTORY

Brazil's earliest inhabitants were the Indians. More than one hundred native tribal groups inhabited the land. They did not plant crops, but hunted and gathered fruits and berries.

The Portuguese navigator Pedro Álvares Cabral claimed Brazil for Portugal in 1500. However, for some thirty years after Cabral's historic voyage, the Portuguese paid little attention to their new colony, and only a few trading posts grew up along the coast. Portugal's main interest still lay in trade with the Far East. But Portugal's attitude changed after 1530 for two reasons. A new source of wealth was needed, and other European powers were threatening to take Brazil.

Portuguese Settlement. The Portuguese king started the settlement of Brazil by giving favored

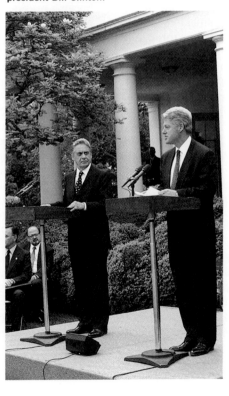

During a visit to the United States, Brazil's president Fernando Cardoso met with U.S. president Bill Clinton.

nobles grants that stretched far inland from the coast. The early settlers had difficulties with the Indians. The settlers also had to face a new and strange tropical environment and unfamiliar soil conditions. The large landowners soon discovered that if they were to run successful settlements, they needed more farm laborers. Black slaves were brought from Africa to work on plantations in the Northeast.

Meanwhile, in the East and the South, groups of people called *bandeirantes* roamed the interior in search of gold. They also sought Indians to sell as slaves to the plantation owners of the north. The *bandeirantes* found both gold and slaves. In doing so, they opened large regions for more exploration and settlement in the present states of Minas Gerais, Mato Grosso, Goiás, and Mato Grosso do Sul.

By the early 1800's, Brazil's first gold mines had been nearly exhausted, but a large part of the country was permanently settled. Farming was the major occupation. The descendants of the Portuguese settlers now thought of themselves as Brazilians rather than subjects of the king of Portugal.

Just as the first movements for Brazilian independence were developing, troops sent by French emperor Napoleon invaded Portugal. In 1808 the Portuguese royal family and more than a thousand members of the court fled to Brazil. For the next 14 years Rio de Janeiro was the capital of the Portuguese empire. At last, in 1821, the king returned to his native land and left his son, Dom Pedro, to rule Brazil. The next year Dom Pedro, following the advice of José Bonifácio de Andrada, his minister of the interior, declared Brazil independent of Portugal. Peaceful change became the pattern of Brazil's political life.

Independence. Brazil remained an empire from 1822 until 1889. Dom Pedro was emperor for nine years and then turned over the throne to his 5-year-old son, Dom Pedro II, who became emperor in 1840 at the age of 14. Dom Pedro II ruled Brazil for 49 years, during which the nation became larger and richer. Wars with Argentina (1851–52) and with Paraguay (1865–70) were finally settled peacefully. Railroads were built. Rubber from the Amazon jungle doubled foreign trade. Thousands of immigrants swelled Brazil's population between 1874 and 1889. But much of the nation's wealth depended on slavery.

This growth ended in 1888, the year that slavery was abolished. Many of the large landowners and slaveholders called for an overthrow of the government. But some wanted a republican form of government. The army itself, which was republican in spirit, favored the change. And in 1889 the old emperor peacefully left Brazil to avoid conflict. Ruy Barbosa, a jurist from the state of Bahia, prepared the first constitution of republican Brazil in 1891.

The Republic. During the early years of the republic, when the army ruled Brazil, there was civil war and political upheaval. But by 1895 order had been restored and Brazil had a civilian government. Brazil became increasingly important in world politics. It fought with the Allies during World War I (1914–18). However, the years between the two world wars were troubled ones. The overproduction of coffee and the fall of world coffee prices during the Great Depression brought new difficulties to the country. In 1930 the president was overthrown, and Getúlio Vargas became dictator of what he called a "disciplined democracy." Under Vargas' rule living conditions improved and trade grew. During World War II (1939–45), Brazil was an ally of the United States and sent troops to Italy. Vargas offered benefits in exchange for passive acceptance of his government, which was patterned after the fascist regimes of Benito Mussolini in Italy and Oliveira Salazar in Portugal. He also encouraged a spirit of nationalism and worked to accelerate economic development.

The Second Republic. The army forced Vargas to resign in 1945. General Eurico Gaspar Dutra was elected as his successor. But in 1950, Vargas ran for office and was elected. In 1954, at the end of a very serious political crisis, Vargas took his own life. Juscelino Kubitschek de Oliveira then became president.

Kubitschek told the Brazilians that they would "enjoy in 5 years the progress of 50 years." He worked hard to live up to his promise. A new capital was built. And the government helped develop hydroelectric plants and some industries. But inflation and falling world coffee prices brought new economic and social problems.

In 1960, Jânio Quadros was elected president, but his attempts to improve conditions were blocked. Quadros resigned within a year, and his vice president, João Goulart, took his place. By 1964, however, Goulart's leftist policies had brought the Brazilian economy to a crisis. Discontent with his government led to a revolution, supported by the United States, which brought the military to power. Until 1985, Brazil's presidents all came from the armed forces. In 1985, Tancredo de Almeida Neves, a civilian, was elected president. Neves died before his inauguration, and the vice president, José Sarney, became president.

The 1989 elections were the first since 1960 in which Brazilians voted directly for the president. Fernando Collor de Mello won the presidency after a runoff election. But his term was marked by controversy, and in 1992 he was impeached on charges of corruption. He resigned and was succeeded by his vice president, Itamar Franco. In 1994 Fernando Henrique Cardoso became president. In 1998 he won re-election to a second term, becoming the first president in Brazil's history to do so. As president he favored policies that made Brazil attractive for foreign investment while at the same time addressing some of Brazil's most pressing social needs. By the century's end, Brazil faced the future supported by faith in its restored democracy but still in need of major social reforms.

PETER O. WACKER
Rutgers, The State University of New Jersey
Updated by ROBERT M. LEVINE
University of Miami
Author, *Brazilian Legacies*

See also AMAZON RIVER.

BRAZING. See WELDING AND SOLDERING.

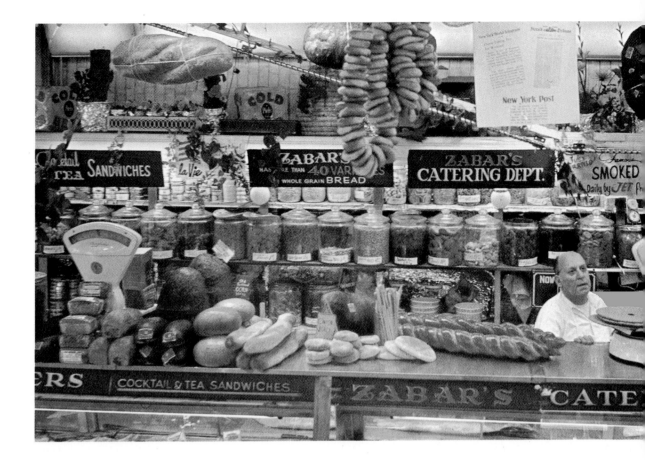

BREAD AND BAKING

Bread in some form is eaten almost everywhere in the world. It is called "the staff of life" because it can go far in meeting people's need for food—in supporting human life. (A staff is a long stick that is used for support in walking.) And the word "bread" has taken on other special meanings. "Breaking bread" (sharing a meal) is a sign of friendship. "More bread!" (a demand for the basic necessities of life) has been the slogan of many revolutions.

Most North Americans and Europeans tend to think of bread as a food that is moist and crumbly on the inside and crusty on the outside. But breads have many different forms. In Greece, for example, bread is often *pita,* a wheat-flour bread that is simply a thin pocket of crust with a hollow inside. In Mexico, the common bread is a delicate cornmeal pancake known as a *tortilla.*

The breads of the world are of two main kinds—flat and leavened. Flat breads are those such as the Greek *pita* and the Mexican *tortilla.* They also include religious breads—the matzoth eaten by Jews during Passover and the wafers used in Communion in Christian churches.

Leavened breads are lighter than flat breads because they contain a rising, or leavening, agent. They include white or whole wheat bread, rye bread, muffins, and rolls. There are many other bakery products that can be considered forms of bread, such as cakes, cookies, crackers, and pretzels.

In most of its forms, bread is an important source of carbohydrates, which provide energy, and protein, which the body uses in building and repairing its cells. Most breads also contain B vitamins and some minerals.

▶ **BASIC INGREDIENTS**

Most breads and baked goods made in Canada, Europe, and the United States are leavened products. These products always include four basic ingredients—flour, a leavening agent, salt, and liquids and fats.

Flour. Bread contains more flour than any other ingredient. There are many different types of flour. Most are made from grains such as wheat, rye, barley, oats, corn, and rice. White flour is made from wheat that is milled (crushed and sifted) repeatedly until the outer covering has been completely removed.

Different flours produce breads of different flavors. They also produce breads of different textures. This is because the flours contain different amounts of gluten. Gluten is a mixture of proteins found in grain. When it comes in contact with a liquid (such as milk or water) and is pushed about by stirring or some other action, it develops long, elastic strands. The stretchable bands of gluten form an invisible structure that enables a loaf of bread to hold its shape. It is because of the elastic nature of gluten that bread will bounce back if you poke it gently with your fingers.

Leavening Agent. Yeast was the first leavening agent, and it is still the most important. Yeast is a tiny one-celled plant that is present all around us. It is found in the air, on trees, in the soil, and on the skins of fruits. Yeast cells feed on sugars and starches. They change the starch of bread dough into sugar, which they then digest. As they do this, they give off carbon dioxide gas as a waste product. (This chemical change is called fermentation.) Tiny bubbles of carbon dioxide are trapped by the strands of gluten in the dough. The gas blows the gluten into bigger and bigger bubbles and makes the bread rise.

In the early days of baking, the chief source of yeast was the foam that bubbled on the tops of vats in which ale or beer was brewing. This liquid yeast was called barm. (Today, in dry form, it is known as brewer's yeast.) Before modern times, most housekeepers did their own brewing, and ale barm was readily available. But too often it was bitter and unpleasant tasting. To improve the taste, the foamy barm had to be "cleaned" (soaked in several changes of water over a period of days). A steady supply of clean yeast was always kept on hand in a corked jug.

Nowadays, people can easily buy yeast in a food store. Some yeast is compressed into tiny blocks. Other yeast, called active dry yeast, is sold as a powder in small packets.

These little beads of yeast have been stripped of all moisture and remain in a dormant (sleeping) state until they come in contact with liquid.

Breads leavened by yeast are called yeast breads. Those leavened by other agents are often called quick breads because they can be baked immediately, without waiting for fermentation to take place. Baking powder is one leavening agent used in quick breads. Its active ingredients are bicarbonate of soda and an acid such as tartaric acid. When the baking powder is moistened, the bicarbonate of soda reacts with the acid to form new substances. In the process, carbon dioxide is produced and released. The result is a dough that is light and airy.

Baking powder is used chiefly in cookies, crackers, biscuits, and pretzels. It makes these baked goods rise just enough to be light and crumbly. Another leavening agent is a mixture of baking soda and an acid food, such as buttermilk, molasses, or lemon juice. This mixture is often used in making muffins and other quick breads.

Salt. Salt is an important ingredient in most breads and other baked goods. It adds vitality to the flavor. In yeast breads, it helps control the speed at which the yeast works. The rate of yeast growth, in turn, helps determine the texture and crustiness of the loaf.

Liquids and Fats. For plain, ordinary bread, water is the only liquid required. Because of its fat content, milk is sometimes used in addition to, or instead of, water. Milk creates a richer-tasting loaf with a soft crust. For this reason it is often the preferred liquid for making sweet rolls, muffins, cakes, and cookies.

To make a rich dough, butter, margarine, or another fat is added. These ingredients are called shortenings because they often make baked goods "short" (crisp and flaky).

Other Ingredients. There is a great variety of baked goods because many other ingredients can be added to the basic dough. Sugar adds a sweet flavor. It also provides extra nourishment for yeast cells and speeds up their manufacture of gas bubbles. Sugar also helps in the browning of the crust.

Eggs generally are not used in breads, but they are often included in rich cakes. Some cake recipes call for egg whites. The whites are beaten until they are stiff. Then they are carefully folded into the cake batter. Because they contain so many little pockets of air, the whites help to create a very light cake. Angel food cake is made in this way.

Raisins, currants, prunes, dates, and other dried fruits often are included in coffee cakes and holiday cakes. So is the candied peel of citrus fruits such as lemons and oranges. Fresh fruits may be mixed into dough—banana bread is an example. Finely ground nuts are sometimes mixed with flour for an especially moist cake or quick bread with a nutty flavor. Spices such as caraway, dill, cumin, fennel, and aniseed are often used to give breads a crunchy texture or tangy flavor. Sweet spices such as cinnamon, cloves, nutmeg, and allspice are used in cakes.

▶ MAKING YEAST BREAD

Two common ways of making yeast bread are the sponge method and the straight-dough method. In the sponge method, the yeast is first mixed with water and some of the flour. This mixture, called a sponge, is allowed to ferment before the rest of the ingredients are added. In the straight-dough method, all the ingredients are mixed at once.

After the ingredients are mixed together in the proper amounts, several steps remain— kneading the dough, letting it rise, releasing the trapped gas, allowing the bread to rise again, and baking the bread.

For the gluten to develop properly, most breads made at home require about 10 to 20 minutes of kneading. The purpose of kneading is to work the dough into a uniform texture. To knead bread dough, put the dough on a lightly floured board and flatten it with the palm of your hand. Pick up the edge farthest from you and fold it over the edge nearest you. Push the edges together with the heel of your hand. At the same time, push the mass of dough away from you. Then turn the dough a quarter of the way around and repeat the process. This folding, pushing, and turning process is repeated until the dough is smooth and shiny and has lost all of its stickiness.

Next, the dough is allowed to rise until it has doubled in bulk. For this step, the kneaded dough must be placed in a warm, preferably moist place, away from any cold drafts. The temperature should be about 27 to 29°C (81 to 84°F). An ideal spot is an unlighted oven.

MIXING INGREDIENTS

KNEADING THE DOUGH

LETTING THE DOUGH RISE

RELEASING TRAPPED GAS

BAKING THE LOAF

Today bread can be mixed, baked, and wrapped in a completely automatic process. Dough is turned out by the revolving paddles of the mixing machine (1). After fermenting in a trough (2), the dough is transferred to the divider (3), which divides the mass of dough into loaf-sized pieces. The rounder (4) forms the dough into balls. From the rounder the dough passes to a proof box (not shown), where it rises. Conveyor belts carry the

The dough is covered with a sheet of waxed paper or a clean towel. This prevents a dried crust from forming on the outside.

Depending on the recipe and the amount of yeast used, some kneaded doughs take close to 24 hours to double in bulk. Others take as little as 1 hour. To test whether a dough has doubled in bulk, press the tips of two fingers lightly and quickly about 1.5 centimeters (½ inch) deep into the dough. If the dent remains, the dough has doubled.

After the dough has risen, it is necessary to release the gas trapped within it. For hand-kneaded dough, this is done by plunging a fist into the dough to collapse it and then kneading it for a few minutes. Then the bread is allowed to rise again, so that it will have a light and even texture.

Baking is the final stage in the breadmaking process. The dough is placed in a preheated oven. Most wheat bread is baked in pans. Some breads, such as French bread, are formed into loaves and placed directly on baking sheets. It is important that the bread be heated evenly from all sides.

The heat of the oven gives the yeast its last chance to work, and most loaves will rise about 5 centimeters (2 inches) while baking. The yeast is not killed until the inside temperature of the loaf exceeds 54°C (130°F). It takes longest for the center of the loaf to reach that temperature, and the yeast in the center has the longest time to work. As a result, most baked breads have the shape of a gently sloping hill.

▶ **MANUFACTURING BREAD**

Today, approximately 95 percent of all bread eaten in the United States is produced commercially. In large commercial bakeries, the entire process is carried out by machinery. Machines mix thousands of kilograms of flour into dough every hour and are automatically switched off when the dough is of the proper consistency. Machines also divide the dough into pieces of the desired weight, shape it into loaves, and put it into pans. Conveyor belts move the dough from step to step in the bread-making process.

The baking itself takes place in a huge oven. The oven may be 23 meters (75 feet) long—big enough to hold almost 3,000 loaves at dough from machine to machine. In the molding machine (5), rollers flatten the dough into pancake shape, then form it into loaves. The loaves rise once more in a final proof box (6), then move into a traveling oven (7). When the bread comes out of the oven about ½ hour later, it is fully baked. The loaves are sliced by the steel blades of a slicing machine (8), then wrapped automatically (9).

one time. After they are baked, the loaves are sent on conveyor belts to be cooled, sliced, and wrapped. The slicing and wrapping operations, like the other steps in the breadmaking process, are performed by machines.

Frozen baked goods and brown-and-serve rolls are usually put out by specialty companies. They give people the chance to serve a variety of fresh baked goods without spending hours making them. Brown-and-serve rolls are baked in a few minutes in a hot oven. A frozen cake needs only to be defrosted.

Some cakes and breads are sold in cans. Canned bread was developed to solve a practical problem—armies had to find a way to keep the bread in combat rations from going stale. Canned bread is made by baking the dough in the can rather than in baking pans. The lid is loosely clinched onto the can to permit steam and leavening gas to escape during baking—otherwise, the can would explode. As soon as the can leaves the oven, a machine seals it hermetically (airtight). This keeps out bacteria and molds that cause decay. The can is then cooled rapidly to protect the flavor and color of the bread.

▶ **HISTORY OF BREADMAKING**

No one knows for sure when people first began to make bread. But many scholars believe that bread was first made more than 10,000 years ago, in the Middle East. Around that time, people made a thick porridge of crushed wheat or barley and water. They shaped the mixture into flat disks. Then they baked it in ashes or on hot stones.

The first leavened bread was probably made by accident. Perhaps a mixture of crushed grain and water was left longer than usual and began to ferment before it was baked. But bread that rises with the aid of wild yeast may turn out quite differently each time because different kinds of yeast may fall on it. The ancient Egyptians learned to control the kind of yeast in their bread. Each time they baked, they set aside some of the leavened dough to mix with the next batch. In this way they could be sure of having the same taste and texture. (The sourdough carried by prospectors in the California and Klondike gold rushes of the 1800's served the same purpose.)

The Greeks were the master bakers of antiquity, with more than 70 different recipes for bread. The Romans turned baking into a large-scale industry and passed many laws governing the quality of bread. Poor people generally ate coarse, dark bread. Fine, white bread was only for the wealthy.

In Europe during the Middle Ages, white bread was also the bread of the rich and privileged. Dark, often sour rye bread was the mainstay of most of the people. This continued to be so until the 18th and 19th centuries, when the Industrial Revolution brought many changes in baking. Large bread factories took the place of neighborhood bakeries. As standards of living rose and wheat became more abundant, people demanded more refined bread. They thought that whiter bread was better in quality. This is not actually true, because the milling that produces white flour removes most of the vitamins and minerals present in wheat. Since 1940, most white bread baked in the United States has been enriched by adding some of the vitamins and minerals lost during milling.

▶ OTHER BAKED GOODS

During the Middle Ages, French travelers, soldiers, and sailors carried a strange, hard bread. The bread had been cooked twice to keep it from spoiling. No one needs to cook bread twice today, but we still eat hard biscuits. The name "biscuits" comes from the early French word for twice cooked. Another form of hard bread—hardtack—was the traditional fare for British sailors.

Cookies, crackers, and pretzels do not look or taste alike, but they are alike in many ways. All are small and crisp, and they keep well. All are made with the same basic ingredients—flour, leavening, shortening, and liquid. Usually the leavening in these products is baking powder.

Crackers appeared in the United States about 1860. Soon every grocery store had a cracker barrel filled with square soda crackers or round butter crackers. Grocery stores were one of the popular centers of social life in small towns during the 1800's and early 1900's. The people who gathered there to exchange news and opinions were called cracker-barrel philosophers.

Part of the fun in eating cookies is their shape. The dough for some cookies is simply dropped by the spoonful onto a baking sheet.

These are called drop cookies. For other cookies, the dough is rolled out into a sheet. Then cookie cutters of various shapes cut out pieces of dough, which are placed onto the baking sheet. Still other cookies are made by forcing the dough through a nozzle shaped like the design of the cookie.

Pretzels date back to the early Christians in the Roman Empire. At that time, they were used solely for religious purposes. Fat, milk, and eggs were forbidden during the Lenten season, and people ate dry pretzels instead of bread. They were especially popular on Ash Wednesday. It was only in modern times that pretzels became snacks to nibble on.

In northern Europe and the Scandinavian countries, the pretzel has become the sign of the baker. A large golden pretzel is usually seen hanging outside each bakery.

The Roman honey bread and the later medieval sweet cakes were the forerunners of the iced layer cakes and sponge cakes of today. Pies were made by medieval cooks. But often these were filled with combinations of meat or fish and fruits and eaten as a main course. Gradually pastry cooks began to use pies as sweet desserts. During the 1800's, desserts became elaborate. The Viennese and French made such artistic and tasty desserts that people traveled to Vienna and Paris just to try their pastries. Today many home bakers use packaged dry mixes or bake from scratch.

The size, shape, and contents of baked goods are forever changing. The basic ingredients—flour, leavening agent, water, and salt—can produce a long crusty loaf of French bread, a soft roll, a crispy pretzel, or a crunchy cracker. Knead in a little oil for pizza dough. Leave out the leavening agent and add some butter, and you have a flaky pie pastry. Stir in a few eggs, some sugar and spice, and you have a pound cake. The possibilities are truly endless.

LORNA J. SASS
Author, *To the King's Taste*

See also FLOUR AND FLOUR MILLING; FOOD AROUND THE WORLD; GRAIN AND GRAIN PRODUCTS; WHEAT.

BRECKINRIDGE, JOHN C. See VICE PRESIDENCY OF THE UNITED STATES.

BRENNAN, WILLIAM J. See NEW JERSEY (Famous People).

BREYER, STEPHEN G. See SUPREME COURT OF THE UNITED STATES (Profiles).

BREZHNEV, LEONID (1906–1982)

Leonid Ilyich Brezhnev was the leader of the Soviet Union from 1964 until his death. He was the first Soviet leader to be head of state and head of the Communist Party at the same time.

Brezhnev was born in Dneprodzerzhinsk (formerly the village of Kamensk) in the Ukraine, on December 19, 1906. His father was an ironworker. Brezhnev's education exposed him to the two fields in which Communist Party leaders usually have some working knowledge—industry and agriculture. He studied first at a boys' secondary school. Later, at an agricultural school, he learned surveying. He graduated from a technical institute as a metallurgical engineer.

Brezhnev's rise in the Communist Party followed the same pattern as that of Nikita Khrushchev, who was party chief before him. Brezhnev became a member of the Young Communist League in 1923 and joined the party in 1931. He attended party schools and gained experience in agricultural and industrial positions in various parts of the country. He worked in the Ukraine with Khrushchev, who was in charge of reorganizing the party there. He was a political officer in the Red Army during World War II.

After the war Brezhnev held several high-level party positions. From 1953 to 1957, he directed an effort to open the dry regions of Soviet Central Asia to farming. When he returned to Moscow, he was named to the party's ruling Presidium. In 1960 he became chairman of the Presidium of the Supreme Soviet (head of state of the Soviet Union). This position is less powerful than that of general secretary of the Communist Party.

Brezhnev was involved in Khrushchev's dismissal in October, 1964. He had resigned his position as head of the Presidium earlier that year, and he replaced Khrushchev as party general secretary. He later strengthened his leadership. A constitution adopted in 1977 elevated the office of head of state, which he resumed and held with his party job. He died on November 10, 1982, in Moscow.

In his domestic policies, Brezhnev favored the military, and he built up Soviet forces. He also tried to improve production in industry and agriculture. He pushed some projects—such as the Baikal-Amur Mainline railroad, in Siberia—despite difficulties in construction.

Brezhnev showed both a mailed fist and a silk glove in dealing with Eastern Europe. In 1968, reform programs in Czechoslovakia seemed to threaten Soviet control there. He ordered Soviet troops to invade Czechoslovakia and dismiss its liberal leaders. The reason given was that the interests of the Soviet bloc outweighed the right to self-rule of any member country. (This policy became known as the Brezhnev Doctrine.) In contrast, when riots broke out in Poland in 1970 and 1976, Brezhnev ensured that the party leader was removed in the first case and that food prices were lowered in the second. But Soviet pressure encouraged the Polish Government to declare martial law in 1981, after workers had formed independent unions and demanded more political freedom.

Under Brezhnev, the Soviets remained on unfriendly terms with China. They gave aid to pro-Communist forces in other countries. In 1979, Soviet troops entered Afghanistan to support a Communist government.

Brezhnev expressed a policy of détente (easing tension) with the West. The Soviets negotiated on arms control. In 1975, they joined in talks in Helsinki, Finland, that set goals of peace, security, and justice for Europe, the United States, and Canada. But relations with the West were often strained.

ROBERT H. DODGE
Washington and Jefferson College

BRICKS AND MASONRY

Brick is one of the most common and useful building materials. It is also one of the oldest. Bricks are made of fired (baked) clay and can be used to build almost any type of structure.

Early forms of brick were sun-baked and were not as durable as fired bricks. Bricks have been made in many sizes and shapes since they were first used almost 10,000 years ago. At the present time, the standard brick in the United States is a rectangular block measuring about 2¼ inches (5.7 centimeters) thick by 3¾ inches (9.5 centimeters) wide by 8 inches (20 centimeters) long. Bricks are produced in many other sizes, as well as in some special shapes, including curved and sloped brick.

Bricks range in color from nearly white, through tan, red, and red-brown, to dark purple. The color is determined by the type of clay used as well as the amount of iron and other impurities in it. The method of firing is also a factor. Generally, the higher the firing temperature, the darker the brick. Bricks, like pottery, may also be glazed in various colors. Finally, coatings and mechanically applied textures can also change the color and appearance of the brick.

Bricks are extremely durable. Ordinary brick can stand the direct flames of a fire with little damage, and refractory brick (a special brick used for lining fireplaces and furnaces) can stand temperatures as high as 4000°F (2200°C). Because brick is not easily damaged by acids, it resists the chemicals created by air pollution and various industrial processes better than some kinds of stone and painted metal.

The strength of brick also varies a great deal. Brick has high compressive strength; that is, it can withstand forces that press in on it. The average brick can take a load of about 10,000 pounds (4,500 kilograms) a square inch before it is crushed. Several types of brick can stand a load as high as 20,000 pounds (9,000 kilograms) a square inch. However, brick does not have tensile strength—it cannot withstand forces that tend to pull it apart.

▶FROM CLAY TO BRICK

Bricks are made from clay, which is a common mineral substance. Some types of clay are formed by the disintegration of rocks by weathering. Other types of clay were formed during the Ice Age by the action of glaciers grinding boulders to fine powder. Clay is found over most of the earth's surface, often in lake beds and riverbeds. It is frequently mixed with other substances, such as sand and silt. Clay becomes slippery and plastic (easily molded) when it is wet. When it is dry, it becomes hard and stony.

Workers in Madagascar set bricks out to dry in the sun. Most modern bricks are machine-formed and baked at high temperatures in large ovens.

When clay is heated to about 850°F (450°C), it changes chemically so that it no longer becomes plastic when it is wet. This means that bricks of fired clay will not soften and lose their shape when they become wet, and a wall made of these bricks will not collapse into a sticky heap during a heavy rain. Bricks are baked, or burned, at 1600 to 2200°F (870 to 1200°C). At about 1000°F (540°C) the brick turns from greenish gray to its matured color (for example, red, buff, or white).

Until the 1800's bricks were made by hand. In one common method clay was dug up from the ground and exposed to the air from fall to spring. After the clay was thoroughly dried, the brickmaker spread a small quantity of it on the ground, added a little water, and mixed it into a paste. He pressed the mixture into wooden forms, or molds, which gave the bricks the correct size and shape. Then he removed the sides of the mold and laid the moist brick on the ground to be dried and hardened by the sun. In biblical times chopped straw was usually mixed with the clay to help hold it together.

Because rain might slow up the process or even ruin the soft clay, brickmakers realized that they had to find a better process of drying. As early as 2500 B.C. the technique of baking the brick in ovens, or kilns, was being used in Mesopotamia and India. (Sun-dried bricks, or adobe, are still used in regions where it seldom rains.)

Over the centuries a number of different types of kilns were invented. In older types of kilns only one batch of brick could be made at one time. Most bricks today are made in continuous kilns. Continuous kilns are designed so that they can turn out bricks 24 hours a day, all year long, if necessary. The tunnel kiln, a heated tunnel through which the bricks are pushed or pulled slowly on small railroad cars, is a leading type of continuous kiln.

A mason places a brick in a bed of wet mortar and taps it into place with the handle of his trowel. Mortar holds bricks together and makes the wall watertight.

Some Brick Bonds

Running bond — stretchers (bricks' long sides) are laid in overlapping courses

Flemish bond — stretchers and headers (bricks' short sides) alternate in each course

Common, or American, bond — a headers course is placed at every sixth stretcher course

English bond — a course of stretchers and a course of headers alternate up the wall

Herringbone bond — often used for paving; bricks may be laid flat or on edge

Basketweave bond — used for paving; bricks may be laid flat or on edge

391

Stonemasons carefully select rocks and fit them into this dry stone wall (built without mortar). Strings are used as guides for building the wall straight and level.

Basically the manufacture of bricks has changed little since ancient times, except that machines now perform most of the tasks that were once done laboriously by hand. The clay is now dug by power shovels. After drying, it is ground in power-driven mills and screened to get particles of uniform size.

In the **stiff-mud** process the clay is mixed with water into a stiff paste and then forced out under pressure through nozzles called **dies**. As it comes out, the clay resembles a giant square-cornered strip of toothpaste. The strip is automatically cut into pieces of the proper size by knives or wires. The soft ''green'' brick is then dried in heated holding areas. Finally the brick is carried on small, flat railroad cars through the kilns for firing.

The **soft-mud** process is older than the stiff-mud process. More water is mixed with the clay than in the stiff-mud process. This produces a softer paste. The soft paste is shaped in individual molds either by machine or by hand. The soft-mud process is usually slower than the stiff-mud process and is used to produce bricks that cannot be formed by other brick-making methods.

In the **dry press** process the ground-up clay is moistened with just enough water to hold it together. Powerful hydraulic presses squeeze the clay into brick shape. Bricks made by this method are as durable as bricks made by the stiff-mud process and usually shrink very little during the drying process. This process is used to make most refractory brick.

▶ **MASONRY**

Masonry is the name for walls, pillars, arches, and other structures made by laying bricks, stone blocks, and other stonelike materials, such as concrete blocks, in a cementing material called **mortar**.

Long ago, primitive people discovered that they could pile naturally occurring stones together to make a rough wall. Later came the idea of trimming the stones so that they would fit together better. This made a firmer and more solid wall. At about the same time, people in regions where stone was scarce discovered how to turn clay into artificial stones—bricks. Bricks were easy to handle and build with because they were the same size and shape and did not need trimming to fit together. An important step in the development of masonry was taken when builders learned that they could use various materials to cement bricks or stone blocks together. In this way they could build rigid walls and more complicated structures, such as arches and vaults.

Brick Masonry

To make a rigid wall of brick, individual bricks are laid together in horizontal layers, or **courses**. The bricks are bound together with mortar.

The mason spreads a layer of mortar with a wide, flat tool called a trowel. The bricks are set on the mortar and pressed down lightly. If a brick is out of line, it is tapped gently into place with the handle of the trowel. Mortar is

Some Stonework Patterns

Examples of ashlar masonry

Examples of rubble masonry

also placed between each brick in a course. When the first course is laid, the mason spreads mortar on top of it and lays the second course on this mortar. This process is repeated until the wall is built.

It is important to make each course level and the wall straight. An uneven wall is not only unsightly but weak. The mason uses a straight level to make sure that the bricks are set level in the mortar. A plumb line (a string with a weight at one end) is used as a vertical guideline. A string stretched tightly from one end of the wall to the other helps the mason line up the bricks horizontally.

The thin horizontal and vertical layers of mortar between the bricks are called the **joints**. The early masons learned that they could build a stronger wall by staggering the joints, or overlapping the bricks so that the vertical joints of one course do not line up with the joints of the course below. The different arrangements or patterns in which the bricks are laid are called **bonds**. A brick laid so that its long end is exposed to view is called a **stretcher**; a brick laid with its short end exposed is called a **header**. Many builders use brick as a facing, or veneer, over the wooden frames of houses and the concrete or steel frames of large buildings.

Stone Masonry

Stones vary widely in size, shape, and composition. The two main types of modern stonework are **ashlar** and **rubble**. Ashlar masonry is constructed of cut and squared stones. They may be set in regular courses, similar to brick, or in random courses where different sizes of stone are used. Rubble masonry is composed of rough, irregularly shaped stones. Rubble stones are usually set in random patterns.

A person who works with stone is called a stonemason. The stonemason's work is more difficult and exacting than the bricklayer's. The stones have rough, jagged edges. To get a smooth surface, the stonemason trims off the projections. This is called dressing the stone and requires experience and skill.

Setting the stones in place in the walls is an art in itself. Because building stones are usually cut in large sizes (to save labor in trimming), they are very heavy. For example, a granite block 6 feet (1.8 meters) long by 3 feet (0.9 meter) wide by 1 foot (0.3 meter) thick weighs about 3,060 pounds (1,377 kilograms) —more than a ton and a half.

Obviously, such stones are too heavy to lay by hand. They must be lifted by powerful derricks and guided into place by the stone setter as they are gently lowered. If the stone is out of line, it cannot simply be tapped into line like a brick. It must be lifted up and lowered into place again.

Stone, like brick, was once a major structural material. It was used where great strength and weight were required, as in dams, bridges, fortresses, foundations, and important buildings. Today steel and concrete have taken the place of stone as a basic construction material. However, stone is still important as sheathing (outside covering) for buildings, as flooring

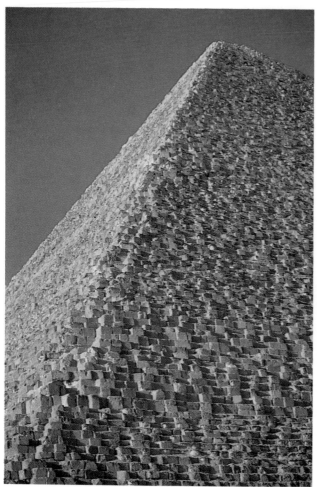

Built some 4,500 years ago, the Great Pyramid, in Egypt, contains more than 2 million close-fitting stone blocks averaging 2.5 tons (2.3 metric tons) each.

to the building sites that stone was used only for temples, palaces, and monuments. Ordinary buildings were made of sun-baked brick.

From Egypt brick making spread to other countries around the Mediterranean Sea. The Romans became the master brickmakers of ancient times. Roman bricks were relatively thin and broad, and they were made in a variety of different shapes: rectangular, square, triangular, and semicircular.

One of the biggest problems faced by builders in the ancient world was the lack of a strong mortar to bind their bricks and stones together. Despite this, ancient builders constructed some remarkable brick temples and palaces, with walls 10 to 20 feet (3 to 6 meters) thick. The builders depended mainly on the weight of the walls to hold the bricks in place.

Masonry construction was revolutionized by the Roman discovery of concrete in the 100's B.C. With this strong cementing material, builders no longer needed to make their walls enormously thick to keep them from toppling over. In fact, the Romans' concrete was so strong that most important Roman buildings were made of concrete with a thin decorative facing of brick or stone.

Perhaps the most famous examples of ancient stone masonry are the pyramids of Egypt, some of which are more than 4,500 years old. These huge stone structures were built as tombs for rulers of ancient Egypt.

Other ancient civilizations besides the Egyptians developed great skill in handling very large blocks of stone. The Myceneans, who lived in central Greece between 2100 and 1300 B.C., built fortifications and tombs of rough stone blocks that weighed several tons apiece. The Greeks became the master stone workers of the ancient world. They were especially skilled at designing and trimming stone blocks.

The Gothic cathedrals of the late Middle Ages are the most complex structures in pure stone ever attempted. The skill of those who built these cathedrals has never again been equaled.

CARL W. CONDIT
Coeditor, *Technology and Culture*
Reviewed by CHARLES N. FARLEY
The Brick Institute of America

See also ARCHITECTURE; BUILDING CONSTRUCTION; CEMENT AND CONCRETE.

BRIDGER, JIM. See WYOMING (Famous People).

where there is heavy traffic, and for many decorative uses. It is valued for its many colors and textures.

▶ HISTORY OF MASONRY

The history of masonry goes back as far as that of civilization. Archaeologists have unearthed bricks that authorities have dated as 9,000 to 10,000 years old. These bricks were discovered at the site of an ancient settlement beneath the biblical city of Jericho. The Old Testament of the Bible contains the earliest written record of brick making.

In Egypt brick making began about 3100 B.C. Although the Egyptians had vast supplies of fine building stone, it took so much labor to quarry the stone, cut it to size, and transport it

Bridges allow easy passage across rivers and other obstacles. In a city like Pittsburgh, Pennsylvania, bridges are lifelines, allowing people and goods to move into and out of the downtown area.

BRIDGES

Imagine life without bridges. Even the smallest river would be a barrier to travel and trade. To cross a broad river we would have to wade across or wait for a ferry boat. To cross a steep canyon would require trudging down one side and climbing slowly up the other. Before bridges were built, cars and trains lined up at busy crossings, waiting for traffic going in other directions.

There are more than 500,000 bridges in the United States today. Most of them are designed to carry automobile or railroad traffic, but some are intended for pedestrians only. Without bridges we would not have a modern system of highways and railroads. Most bridges are so short that they do not have names, and most travelers do not even notice going over them. There are some bridges, however, that are famous for their length, for their outstanding design, and for their beauty.

▶TYPES OF BRIDGES

A bridge must be strong enough to support its **load**, which includes its own weight as well as that of any traffic it may carry. It must have the stiffness and stability to withstand natural forces such as temperature changes, wind, and earthquakes. A bridge must also stand up to corrosion caused by moisture, polluted air, and road salt.

People have developed a variety of structures that meet these requirements. These structures include beam bridges, truss bridges, arch bridges, cantilever bridges, suspension bridges, cable-stayed bridges, and movable bridges. When deciding which kind of bridge to build, engineers consider how far the bridge must span, how deep in water or earth they must go to find solid support, and how much traffic the bridge must carry. These considerations help them choose the type of bridge and the right materials.

Beam and Truss Bridges. The simplest way to bridge a stream or other obstacle is to lay a beam across the stream so its two ends rest on opposite banks. The first bridges were probably natural bridges formed by fallen trees.

The beam may be made of wood, steel, or concrete reinforced with steel. Beam bridges resting on **abutments** (supports at each end of the bridge) are used to span fairly short distances. Longer beam bridges have additional supports, called **piers** and **trestles**, between the abutments.

Beam bridges are simple and relatively inexpensive to build. They can be found on most highways and expressways, where they are widely used at crossings.

| Beam | Truss |

Adding a framework called a truss to a beam bridge creates a **truss bridge**. The parts of a truss are connected in a series of triangles. The truss may lie under the bridge **deck** (roadway). Or large truss arrangements may extend above both sides of the bridge deck. Truss bridges are used to span longer distances than beam bridges. Timber trusses helped support wooden covered bridges built in the 1800's.

Arch Bridges. Bridge builders can span greater distances with arch bridges than they can with beam or truss bridges. The roadway can be built above the gracefully curved arch (a **deck-arch bridge**) or be suspended from it (a **through-arch bridge**). Foundations support the load of the arch, which pushes outward and downward on them.

Arch bridges have been constructed of stone, brick, timber, cast iron, steel, plain concrete, and reinforced concrete. The construction of beautiful stone masonry arch bridges reached a peak in the early 1900's, but they are rarely built anymore. Almost all modern arch bridges are constructed of steel, reinforced concrete, or timber.

Most of the great Roman bridges were supported on arches. In the city of Rome alone, six of the eight arch bridges built over the Tiber River almost 2,000 years ago are still standing.

Cantilever Bridges. In its simplest form, a cantilever is a beam that extends or projects beyond its vertical support. A wall bracket is a familiar example of a cantilever. When secured firmly at one end (bolted to the wall), a wall bracket can support a heavy weight. To make a bridge, two cantilevers are ordinarily built projecting toward each other from opposite sides of a waterway. Each cantilever rests on a pier and is anchored to the waterway bank behind the pier. The cantilevers do not meet until they are connected in the center by a truss.

The Forth Rail Bridge in Scotland, opened in 1890, is a cantilever bridge constructed of enormous steel tubes. Some of the tubes are 12 feet (3.7 meters) in diameter. More recently, very strong reinforced concrete has been used to build cantilever bridges.

Suspension Bridges. All of the world's longest and many of the best-known bridges are suspension structures. Suspension bridges are built to span the longest distances—more than 4,600 feet (1,400 meters) between support towers. And with their tall towers and swooping cables, suspension bridges are among the most beautiful bridges.

All suspension bridges have three common parts: towers, anchorages, and cables. The majestic towers are built on firm foundations near either shore. Some stand more than 700 feet (210 meters) above the water.

The anchorages are placed on land at each end of the bridge and are where the main cables are secured. The cables may be anchored in bedrock or huge blocks of reinforced concrete. The anchorages hold the main cables against tremendous forces.

The main cables themselves are made of thousands of strong steel wires bound together. From one anchorage, the cables soar to the top of a tower, then swoop gracefully almost to road level and back up to the top of the next tower. Finally, they swoop down again to the end anchorages.

Once the main cables are in place, smaller support cables are attached to them. These support cables, called **suspenders**, hold up the framework for the roadway.

The first primitive suspension bridges were probably made with vines in a tropical region. Ropes replaced vines as civilization progressed. Bridges were later supported by wrought-iron chains strung over towers. Eventually, cables made of woven strands of iron or steel were developed, making possible the construction of modern suspension bridges.

The first modern suspension bridges were introduced by the German-American engineer

Left: The Sydney Harbour Bridge in Australia supports its roadway by a graceful steel arch. The roadway of an arch bridge can run through the arch or sit completely above it.

Below: The Forth Rail Bridge—a massive cantilever structure in Scotland—crosses the Firth of Forth, an inlet of the North Sea. The spans of a cantilever bridge project toward one another from piers and are connected by shorter truss spans.

Arch

Cantilever

Robert Browning's *Pied Piper of Hamelin*
is based on an old legend. The following excerpt tells how the rats followed the piper out
of the town of Hamelin.

Into the street the Piper stept,
Smiling first a little smile,
As if he knew what magic slept
In his quiet pipe the while;
Then, like a musical adept,
To blow the pipe his lips he wrinkled,
And green and blue his sharp eyes twinkled
Like a candle-flame where salt is sprinkled;
And ere three shrill notes the pipe uttered,
You heard as if an army muttered;
And the muttering grew to a grumbling;
And the grumbling grew to a mighty rumbling;
And out of the house the rats came tumbling.
Great rats, small rats, lean rats, brawny rats,
Brown rats, black rats, gray rats, tawny rats,
Grave old plodders, gay young friskers,
Fathers, mothers, uncles, cousins,
Cocking tails and pricking whiskers,
Families by tens and dozens,
Brothers, sisters, husbands, wives—
Followed the Piper for their lives.
From street to street he piped advancing,
And step by step they followed dancing,
Until they came to the river Weser
Wherein all plunged and perished
Save one, who, stout as Julius Caesar,
Swam across and lived to carry
(As he the manuscript he cherished)
To Rat-land home his commentary,

Which was, "At the first shrill notes of the pipe,
I heard a sound as of scraping tripe,
And putting apples, wondrous ripe,
Into a cider press's gripe;
And a moving away of pickle-tub boards,
And a drawing the corks of train-oil flasks,
And a breaking the hoops of butter casks;
And it seemed as if a voice
(Sweeter far than by harp or by psaltery
Is breathed) called out, Oh, rats! rejoice!
The world is grown to one vast drysaltery!
To munch on, crunch on, take your nuncheon,
Breakfast, supper, dinner, luncheon!
And just as a bulky sugar puncheon,
All ready staved, like a great sun shone
Glorious scarce an inch before me,
Just as methought it said, come, bore me!
—I found the Weser rolling o'er me."

You should have heard the Hamelin people
Ringing the bells till they rocked the steeple.
"Go," cried the Mayor, "and get long poles!
Poke out the nests and block up the holes!
Consult with carpenters and builders,
And leave in our town not even a trace
Of the rats!"—when suddenly up the face
Of the Piper perked in the market-place,
With a, "First, if you please, my thousand
    guilders!"

BRUEGEL, PIETER, THE ELDER (1525?–1569)

The painter Pieter Bruegel (or Brueghel) the Elder is best known for landscapes and peasant scenes. He was born in the Netherlands sometime between 1525 and 1530. Very little is known about his early life, but he became a master in the Antwerp Painters Guild in 1551.

Bruegel looked to Italy for inspiration. He was in Rome in 1553 and returned home across the Alps by 1555. He had always been interested in landscape painting, but his travels in the Alps led him to portray nature in a grander and more unified way.

In Antwerp, Bruegel made drawings for engravings. The drawings often portrayed serious ideas in humorous form. They showed his interest in popular subjects, his observations on the foolishness of people, and his concern for freedom of religion. Bruegel's paintings were usually made for private patrons. They dealt with many themes. He was interested in the human figure. In many of his paintings, crowds of people cover the canvas, creating a brightly colored pattern. But he was also concerned with nature and how it affects people's lives. This can be seen in the five paintings that remain of a series called the *Months. Hunters in the Snow* (1565) is a winter scene from the series, probably representing January.

In 1563 Bruegel married and moved to Brussels. He died there on September 9, 1569. Two of his sons also became famous painters. Pieter the Younger (1564–1638) made many copies and variations of his father's works. Jan (1568–1625) was a painter whose elegant style earned him the nickname Velvet Bruegel.

LOLA B. GELLMAN
City University of New York

In *Hunters in the Snow*, the hunters are part of a vast, wintry landscape. Bruegel arranged the elements in this scene to show how nature dominates people's lives.

BRUNEI

The small Asian nation of Brunei is located on the northwestern coast of the island of Borneo. Except for its border on the South China Sea, Brunei is entirely surrounded by the territory of Sarawak, a state of the nation of Malaysia. Although small in area and population, Brunei has considerable deposits of petroleum and natural gas, which have given it one of the highest incomes per person in the world.

The People. The majority of Bruneians are Malays. Chinese make up about 25 percent of the population. The remainder include native ethnic groups and people who have come from elsewhere in Asia to work in Brunei. Most of the people live in the capital, Bandar Seri Begawan, and in towns along the coast.

Brunei's official language is Malay. English, Chinese, and native dialects also are spoken. Islam (the religion of the Muslims) is the official state religion, although other religions are permitted.

The Land. Brunei is divided into two unconnected parts, separated by the Limbang River valley off Sarawak. Dense forests cover about 70 percent of the country. The climate is tropical, with high temperatures and humidity and heavy rainfall.

Economy. Brunei's economy is dependent on its petroleum and natural gas. These account for nearly all its exports and more than 75 percent of its wealth. The traditional economic activities of agriculture and fishing have declined, and Brunei must import most of its food. About half of the workforce is employed by the government, which also provides free education and medical care and many other social services. Brunei has no income tax.

History and Government. Brunei's first sultans, or rulers, date from the 1200's. By the 1500's Brunei was the dominant state in the region, but it soon declined in size and power. In 1888, Brunei became a British protectorate.

Petroleum was known to exist in Brunei by the early 1900's. But it was not until 1929 that the first large oil field was discovered and commercial production of oil began. Brunei's oil attracted the Japanese, who occupied the region during World War II. After the war ended in 1945, Britain resumed its protectorate over the territory. Brunei became self-governing under its own constitution in 1959. It regained complete independence in 1984. That year, Brunei also joined the Association of Southeast Asian Nations (ASEAN).

Brunei is ruled by Sultan Sir Muda Hassanal Bolkiah, who succeeded his father in 1967. Although he governs with the aid of a cabinet, the Sultan holds complete power as both head of state and government.

ROBERT O. TILMAN
North Carolina State University

BRUNHOFF, JEAN DE. See CHILDREN'S LITERATURE (Profiles).

FACTS and figures

BRUNEI DARUSSALAM (Brunei, Abode of Peace) is the official name of the country.

LOCATION: Southeast Asia, on the northwestern coast of Borneo.

AREA: 2,226 sq mi (5,765 km²).

POPULATION: 300,000 (estimate).

CAPITAL AND LARGEST CITY: Bandar Seri Begawan.

MAJOR LANGUAGES: Malay (official), English, Chinese.

MAJOR RELIGIOUS GROUPS: Muslim, Buddhist, Christian.

GOVERNMENT: Sultanate (monarchy). **Head of state and government**—sultan.

CHIEF PRODUCTS: Petroleum, natural gas.

MONETARY UNIT: Brunei dollar (1 dollar = 100 cents).

BRYAN, WILLIAM JENNINGS (1860–1925)

William Jennings Bryan was a leader of the Democratic Party for more than 20 years. He was also one of the most powerful speakers of all time. Known as the silver-tongued orator, he is best remembered for his moving Cross of Gold speech and for his work as a prosecutor in the famous Scopes "monkey" trial.

Bryan was born in Salem, Illinois, on March 19, 1860. In 1887 he moved to Nebraska, where he became interested in politics. In 1890 he was elected to the U.S. House of Representatives.

Toward the end of the 1800's, a great argument existed over what kind of money the nation should use. Silver-mine owners and farmers wanted the government to issue silver as well as gold. The farmers felt that free (unlimited) silver coinage would put more money into circulation and raise prices for crops. But people in business wanted money backed by a gold standard. At the Democratic convention of 1896, Bryan, a Free Silver Democrat, excited quarreling delegates to applause with these words from the Cross of Gold speech, "We will answer their demand for a gold standard by saying to them . . . you shall not crucify mankind upon a cross of gold." Bryan's speech won him the Democratic presidential nomination. But he lost the election to Republican William McKinley.

In 1900, Bryan again lost the presidential election to McKinley. In 1908 he ran against William Howard Taft and was defeated for a third time. Yet Bryan still had great influence, and he used it to help Woodrow Wilson win the presidential nomination in 1912. When Wilson became president, he appointed Bryan secretary of state.

In 1925, John Scopes, a high school biology teacher, was brought to trial in Dayton, Tennessee, for teaching Darwin's theory of evolution in violation of state law. Many people felt that Darwin's theory denied the biblical story of creation. A deeply religious man, Bryan went to Dayton to help in the case against Scopes. Bryan won the case. Five days after the trial, he died in Dayton on July 26, 1925.

Reviewed by PAOLO E. COLETTA
Author, *William Jennings Bryan*

BRYANT, PAUL WILLIAM (BEAR). See ALABAMA (Famous People).

BRYANT, WILLIAM CULLEN (1794–1878)

The American poet and editor William Cullen Bryant was born on November 3, 1794, in Cummington, Massachusetts. His father was a doctor, who encouraged his son Cullen to write. When the boy was only 13, he published a long satirical poem, "The Embargo." He wrote his most famous poem, "Thanatopsis," a meditation on death, while he was a student at Williams College.

Bryant had to leave college because he lacked funds to support himself. He was apprenticed to a lawyer and passed his bar examination before he was 20. After moving to Great Barrington, Massachusetts, he pursued a successful law career. In 1821 he married Frances Fairchild. He celebrated their romance in "Oh Fairest of the Rural Maids."

Bryant wrote sensitive descriptions of nature and the American landscape in such poems as "To a Waterfowl," "The Yellow Violet," and "Green River." Collections of his poems issued in 1821 and 1832 established Bryant as the leading American poet of his time.

In 1825, Bryant moved to New York City to begin a new career in journalism. He rose to editor in chief on the *New York Evening Post* by 1829. He worked for the *Post* for over 50 years. On its editorial pages, Bryant supported such causes as abolition and the labor movement. He helped form the Republican Party and elect Abraham Lincoln.

Bryant also continued to compose poems. In "The Flood of Years," he pondered life after death, and in "The Prairies," he described the vast American West. After his wife's death in 1865, Bryant began his popular translation of the *Iliad* and of the *Odyssey*, published in 1870 and 1872. He lived an active life until his death on June 12, 1878.

JOHN B. PICKARD
University of Florida

BUBONIC PLAGUE. See DISEASES (Descriptions of Some Diseases).

JAMES BUCHANAN (1791–1868)

15th President of the United States

FACTS ABOUT BUCHANAN

Birthplace: Cove Gap, Pennsylvania
Religion: Presbyterian
College Attended: Dickinson College, Carlisle, Pennsylvania
Occupation: Lawyer
Marriage: None
Political Party: Democratic
Nickname: "Old Buck"
Post Held Before Becoming President: Minister to Great Britain
President Who Preceded Him: Franklin Pierce
Age on Becoming President: 65
Terms Served: One
Years in the Presidency: 1857–1861
Vice President: John C. Breckinridge
President Who Succeeded Him: Abraham Lincoln
Age at Death: 77
Burial Place: Woodward Hill Cemetery, Lancaster, Pennsylvania

James Buchanan [signature]

DURING BUCHANAN'S PRESIDENCY

Minnesota (1858), Oregon (1859), and Kansas (1861) became states. *Below:* The first transatlantic telegraph cable was laid between Newfoundland and Ireland (1858). *Left:* John Brown, attempting to start a slave rebellion, attacked the U.S. arsenal (1860) at Harpers Ferry, Virginia (now West Virginia). Brown was hanged. *Above:* The Pony Express was established (1860) to carry mail from St. Joseph, Missouri, to Sacramento, California. The first Japanese delegation arrived in the United States (1860). South Carolina seceded from the Union (1860), followed by other Southern states that together formed the Confederate States of America.

BUCHANAN, JAMES. James Buchanan, the 15th president of the United States, also served his country as a congressman, senator, ambassador, and secretary of state. But many people remember mainly two things about him: that he was the only president who never married; and that the Civil War followed his administration.

▶EARLY LIFE

Buchanan was born on April 23, 1791, in a log cabin near the frontier settlement of Cove Gap, Pennsylvania. His father, a Scotch-Irish immigrant, had come to America in 1783. When James was 6, the family moved to Mercersburg, Pennsylvania, where his father opened a general store. James's mother had little schooling, but she loved to read and she inspired her son with a love of learning.

James was able to go to school in Mercersburg. When he was not studying, he helped his father in the store. James's father was fond of his son, but he made him work hard and pay close attention to business. Mr. Buchanan taught James that he must be ready to care for his nine younger brothers and sisters if their parents should die. In later years, after his father died, James Buchanan became responsible for the care of his mother and four of his brothers and sisters.

When James was 16, his father sent him to Dickinson College in Carlisle, Pennsylvania. Young Buchanan was a serious student, but he also wanted to have a good time. He began to drink and smoke with some of the other students. Even though his marks were excellent, he was expelled for bad conduct at the end of his first term. James pleaded to be taken back and promised to turn over a new leaf. He was allowed to return and went on to graduate with honors.

Buchanan then went to Lancaster, Pennsylvania, to study law. Hard work and intelligence made him a very good lawyer. Before long he was earning more than $11,000 a year, a huge sum in those days.

In 1814, Buchanan became a candidate for the Pennsylvania legislature. But the War of

Buchanan's birthplace as it now stands at Mercersburg Academy, Pennsylvania.

Ann Coleman (1796?–1819).

1812 was raging, and the British had just burned Washington. Buchanan felt that the United States should not have gone to war against Great Britain. However, he knew it was his duty to serve his country, and he joined a volunteer cavalry company.

Buchanan returned in time for the election and won his seat in the legislature. He served a second term and then returned to Lancaster to continue his law practice.

▶A TRAGIC LOVE STORY

As his practice grew, Buchanan became an important figure in town. He was invited to parties at some of the best homes in Lancaster. At one party he met and fell in love with beautiful Ann Coleman. In 1819 Ann and James were engaged to be married, but their happiness was destined to end quickly.

During the fall of 1819 Buchanan often had to be out of town on business. While he was away rumors spread that he wanted to marry Ann only for her money. There was gossip about another woman. All of this was untrue, but Ann was heartbroken. Because of a misunderstanding, she broke her engagement to James.

A short time later Ann died. Buchanan was so grief-stricken that he vowed he would never marry. Years later, after his death, a package of Ann's letters, yellow with age, was found among his papers. They were burned, according to his last wishes, without being opened.

▶HE RETURNS TO POLITICS

Buchanan turned to politics to forget his sorrow. The Federalist Party was looking for a candidate for Congress. Buchanan agreed to run, and in 1820 he was elected to the House of Representatives, where he served for 10 years. During his years in Congress, Buchanan changed his political party. He joined the Jacksonian Democrats (named for Andrew Jackson), and became a leader of the Jacksonians in Pennsylvania.

In 1831 President Jackson asked Buchanan to become minister to Russia. Buchanan went to Russia the following year. While there he negotiated the first trade agreement between Russia and the United States.

On his return to the United States, Buchanan was elected to the Senate. He served until 1845, and became chairman of the important committee on foreign affairs.

Buchanan applied all his training as a lawyer to his work in the Senate. The Constitution, he said, was the basis of all political power. But the Constitution also strictly limited the powers of the federal government. Buchanan believed that a constitutional republic could adjust serious differences between its people only by compromise and legal procedure.

▶SECRETARY OF STATE

By 1844 Buchanan had become an important political figure. Though he hoped for the presidential nomination, he gave his support to James K. Polk, who won the nomination and the election. President Polk appointed Buchanan secretary of state.

During Polk's term as president, war broke out between the United States and Mexico. Buchanan, as secretary of state, helped to arrange the treaty of peace in 1848. By this Treaty of Guadalupe Hidalgo the United States purchased from Mexico the region

Photograph of President Buchanan, taken about 1859.

President Pierce made Buchanan minister to Great Britain in 1853. Shortly thereafter Pierce instructed the American ministers in Europe to draw up proposals to "detach" Cuba from Spain. This led to the Ostend Manifesto, named after the Belgian city where the ministers met. The Manifesto defined a plan to purchase Cuba. But it also included a proposal many people condemned: that the United States would be justified in seizing Cuba if Spain refused to sell the island. Buchanan's political opponents severely denounced the Ostend Manifesto, and nothing ever came of the plan. Buchanan wrote of it: "Never did I obey any instructions so reluctantly."

While Buchanan was in England, Congress passed the Kansas-Nebraska Act, permitting slavery in regions of the Northwest from which the Missouri Compromise of 1820 had formerly excluded it. This new law marked the beginning of the Republican Party, which vowed to prevent any further expansion of slavery, and it split the Democratic Party into northern and southern groups. As Buchanan had been in England during the Congressional fight over the Kansas-Nebraska bill, he remained friendly with both sections of his party. When the Democrats met in 1856 to pick a new candidate for president, they needed someone who would be accepted by both the North and the South. Buchanan proved to be the man. This time he won the nomination and the election.

▶PRESIDENT BUCHANAN

On March 4, 1857, Buchanan was inaugurated as president. Since Buchanan had no wife, his 27-year-old orphan niece, Harriet Lane, acted as his hostess. She was very popular, and Buchanan's administration was a great social success. White House guests included the first Japanese representatives to the United States and the Prince of Wales (who later became King Edward VII of England). The Prince arrived with such a large party that the President had to give up his own bed and sleep on a couch.

The Dred Scott Decision

But the political situation was getting worse. Two days after Buchanan's inauguration, the Supreme Court gave its historic

extending west from Texas to the Pacific Ocean.

Another problem concerned the vast Oregon territory, which both Great Britain and the United States claimed. The dispute became so bad that war threatened. But Buchanan arranged a compromise, and the Oregon Treaty of 1846 settled the Northwestern boundary between Canada and the United States.

When Polk left office, Buchanan also retired. For 4 years he lived the life of a country gentleman. He bought the famous mansion, Wheatland, near Lancaster, Pennsylvania, partly to have a suitable place to entertain political guests, but mainly to care for a growing family. Although Buchanan remained a bachelor, he had over the years become a kind of foster father to a score of nephews and nieces, seven of them orphans. They often visited him at Wheatland, and two made their home with him there, cared for in his absence by his faithful housekeeper, Miss Hetty Parker.

But Buchanan could not stay out of politics for long. In 1852 he was again a candidate for the presidential nomination. He was beaten by a little-known candidate, Franklin Pierce.

President Buchanan received the first Japanese delegation to the United States in 1860.

decision in the case of the slave Dred Scott, who sued for his freedom because he had been taken to a nonslave territory. However, the court decided that Congress could not outlaw slavery in United States territories. Buchanan thought slavery was wrong, but unfortunately the Constitution then recognized it. He hoped the Dred Scott decision would calm the country. Instead, people in the North refused to accept the court's decision. Thus the North and South became more divided than ever.

South Carolina Secedes from the Union

The crisis came in December, 1860. Abraham Lincoln had just been elected president, but he did not take office until March, 1861. Until that time Buchanan was still president.

When the news of Lincoln's victory reached the South, the state of South Carolina seceded from the Union, declaring that it was no longer a part of the United States. By February, 1861, six more southern states had broken away from the Union. The split in the nation that Buchanan feared had taken place.

In this crisis Buchanan wanted to keep the remaining slave states loyal to the Union. He said he would do nothing to provoke a war but he would try to protect federal property and enforce the laws in the South. He asked Congress to call a Constitutional Convention and to vote him the men and money needed to enforce the laws. But Congress refused.

▶ THE COMING OF WAR

On March 5, 1861, Buchanan left Washington and returned to Wheatland. He was happy to leave the presidency and hopeful that the president who followed him could maintain peace and restore the Union. But 5 weeks after Lincoln's inauguration, the South fired on Fort Sumter and the Civil War began.

Buchanan spent his last years writing a book about his term as president. He died at Wheatland on June 1, 1868.

Could Buchanan have prevented the Civil War? Historians do not agree. Some say that a stronger president, one with more imagination, could have prevented the war. Others argue that the Civil War was inevitable: it would have happened no matter who was president, and if Buchanan had used force against the southern states, the war would only have started earlier.

Buchanan tried to solve the problems of the United States by acting within its laws. He failed. Whether any man could have succeeded will never be known.

Reviewed by PHILIP S. KLEIN
Author, *President James Buchanan*

See also DRED SCOTT DECISION; KANSAS-NEBRASKA ACT; MISSOURI COMPROMISE.

BUCHAREST

Bucharest (Bucureşti in Romanian) is the capital and largest city of Romania as well as its economic and cultural center. It has a population of more than 2 million. The city is situated amid the fertile plains of Walachia, one of the country's historic regions. It lies on both banks of the Dimboviţa River, a tributary of the Danube.

The City. Much of modern Bucharest was laid out and built in the late 1800's and early decades of the 1900's, in a style that owed much to French influence. During the 1930's, in fact, it was known as the Paris of the Balkans. Many changes were made to the city, however, during the long period of Communist rule after World War II.

From the northwest, a number of broad streets and boulevards lead to the city's center. Among the chief ones are Calea Victoriei and the Bulevardul Bălcescu. Other thoroughfares run in an east–west direction. Where the two intersect, there are usually large, handsome squares. The most notable are Republic Square, the nearby Palace Square, and University Square, where many of the faculties of the University of Bucharest (founded in 1694) are located. Spacious parks add to the city's attractiveness.

Bucharest's museums include the National Museum of Art; the Village Museum, with its examples of village homes from different regions; and the Georges Enesco Museum, dedicated to Romania's most famous composer. The city's vigorous cultural life is also reflected in its numerous theaters, its opera, and its symphony orchestra.

Economic Activity. Bucharest lies astride one of the major trade routes of the Balkans and has a long commercial tradition. The city and surrounding areas (where most of the factories are located) account for about one-fifth of Romania's total industrial output. The major manufactured products include various kinds of machinery, motor vehicles, electrical equipment, and consumer goods.

History. The name of the city first appears in written documents in the mid-1400's. Bucharest was destroyed by the Ottoman Turks in the late 1500's but rebuilt soon after. Proclaimed the capital of the first Romanian state, consisting of Walachia and Moldavia, in 1862, it remained the capital when Romania won complete independence in 1877–78.

Bucharest flourished in the years after World War I, and its population increased substantially after World War II. A considerable area of the city was destroyed in an earthquake in 1977, and under the Communist dictator Nicolae Ceauşescu, in power from 1965 until his overthrow in 1989, many older buildings were torn down to make way for redevelopment. Although the lights of Bucharest were dimmed under Communism, a slow but steady recovery took place in the 1990's, reviving the aspects of the city that made it so attractive in the past.

ARTHUR CAMPBELL TURNER
University of California, Riverside

Calea Victoriei is one of Bucharest's main streets. The spired Palace of the Republic, completed in 1937, now houses the national art museum.

BUCK, PEARL (1892–1973)

Pearl Sydenstricker Buck, American author, was born on June 26, 1892, in Hillsboro, West Virginia. Her parents, Presbyterian missionaries in China, were home on leave. They returned to China five months later.

China was Pearl Buck's home for 42 years. She learned to speak Chinese before she learned English. All her schooling was in China until she attended Randolph-Macon College and, later, Cornell University.

Her marriage to Dr. John Buck, an agricultural missionary, took her to a small town in northern China. She described the region in her best-known novel, *The Good Earth* (1931). After five years she moved to Nanking and taught English literature to university students. When revolutionary soldiers invaded Nanking in March 1927, she was rescued by an American gunboat and went to Japan. The next winter she returned to China, but by 1934 the situation was so dangerous for foreigners that she knew she must leave. She decided to make her home in Pennsylvania. She was divorced from Dr. Buck in 1935 and married Richard J. Walsh, her publisher.

Pearl Buck received many honors for her writing. *The Good Earth* won the Pulitzer Prize in 1932, and in 1938 she became the first American woman to win the Nobel Prize for literature. Her humanitarian activities were also numerous. In 1949 she founded Welcome House, an adoption agency for American children of Asian ancestry. In 1964 she established the Pearl S. Buck Foundation, which aids neglected American-Asian children living overseas. Pearl Buck died in Danby, Vermont, on March 6, 1973.

Reviewed by Paul A. Doyle
Author, Pearl S. Buck

▶ **THE GOOD EARTH**

Pearl Buck's most famous novel, *The Good Earth*, describes the daily life of a Chinese peasant family. In the following passage, Wang Lung and his wife O-Lan face disaster in the form of a plague of locusts.

And as if to cure him of the root of his ceaseless thought of his own troubles, there came out of the south one day a small slight cloud. At first it hung on the horizon small and smooth as a mist, except it did not come hither and thither as clouds blown by the wind do, but it stood steady until it spread fanwise up into the air.

The men of the village watched it and talked of it and fear hung over them, for what they feared was this, that locusts had come out of the south to devour what was planted in the fields. Wang Lung stood there also, and he watched, and they gazed and at last a wind blew something to their feet, and one stooped hastily and picked it up and it was a dead locust, dead and lighter than the living hosts behind.

Then Wang Lung forgot everything that troubled him. Women and sons and uncle, he forgot them all, and he rushed among the frightened villagers, and he shouted at them,

"Now for our good land we will fight these enemies from the skies!"

But there were some who shook their heads, hopeless from the start, and these said,

"No, and there is no use in everything. Heaven has ordained that this year we shall starve, and why should we waste ourselves in struggle against it, seeing that in the end we must starve?"

And women went weeping to the town to buy incense to thrust before the earth gods in the little temple, and some went to the big temple in the town, where the gods of heaven were, and thus earth and heaven were worshipped.

But still the locusts spread up into the air and on over the land.

Then Wang Lung called his own laborers and Ching stood silent and ready beside him and there were others of the younger farmers, and with their own hands these set fire to certain fields and they burned the good wheat that stood almost ripe for cutting and they dug wide moats and ran water into them from the wells, and they worked without sleeping. O-Lan brought them food and the women brought their men food, and the men ate standing and in the field, gulping it down as beasts do, as they worked night and day.

Then the sky grew black and the air was filled with the deep still roar of many wings beating against each other, and upon the land the locusts fell, flying over this field and leaving it whole, and falling upon that field, and eating it as bare as winter. And men sighed and said, "So Heaven wills," but Wang Lung was furious and he beat the locusts and trampled on them and his men flailed them with flails and the locusts fell into the fires that were kindled and they floated dead upon the waters of the moats that were dug. And many millions of them died, but to those that were left it was nothing.

Nevertheless, for all his fighting Wang Lung had this as his reward: the best of his fields were spared and when the cloud moved on and they could rest themselves, there was still wheat that he could reap and his young rice beds were spared and he was content.

BUCKLEY, WILLIAM F. See New York City (Famous People).

BUDAPEST

Budapest is the capital, largest city, and economic heart of Hungary and the center of the country's cultural life. It lies on the Danube River, which divides it into two main parts, Buda and Pest. The two sections were once separate cities. Buda, the older part, is situated on the steep hills of the Danube's western bank. Pest, the much more heavily populated of the two, is spread out along the flatter eastern bank of the river. Eight bridges link the two sections. The population of the city is more than 2 million.

The City: Buda. Buda was once the residence of Hungarian kings and the seat of their governments. It is dominated to a great extent by its hills. Two of the most notable are Castle Hill and Gellért Hill.

Castle Hill is a walled residential district, dating from the Middle Ages, where the nobility formerly made their homes. Its most impressive monuments are the Royal Palace and the Coronation Church, more commonly known as the Matthias Church. The Coronation Church, where Hungary's monarchs were crowned, was completed in 1269 and is the oldest building in Buda. Nearby is the Fisherman's Bastion, which provides an unequaled view of the opposite bank of the Danube.

Gellért Hill, to the south, has at its summit a citadel, or fortress. This was constructed by the Austrian authorities after a failed revolt by Hungarians against Austrian rule in 1848. The hill itself was named for St. Gellért (or Gerard), who, according to legend, was thrown to his death here in 1046 by opponents of Christianity.

At the northern edge of Buda is the district of Óbuda (Old Buda).

It, too, was once a separate city but is now a part of Budapest.

Pest. By contrast, the layout of Pest is distinguished by wide boulevards and avenues. Many of these extend from the Inner City, the oldest and most famous part of Pest. Within the Inner City and overlooking the Danube is the neo-Gothic Parliament building, one of Budapest's most striking landmarks. Nearby is the National Gallery, a fine arts museum. The Academy of Sciences, St. Stephen's Cathedral, the National Museum, and the various colleges of Eötvös Loránd University, the country's oldest and largest university (founded in 1635), are all situated in the Inner City.

Pest has many other museums and institutions of learning. Numerous theaters, two opera houses, and several concert halls also

Budapest, the capital of Hungary, lies on the Danube River. The domed Parliament building is in Pest, on the river's eastern bank.

reflect its rich cultural life. The Margaret Bridge links Pest with Margaret Island, a resortlike area in the Danube.

Economic Activity. Budapest is Hungary's transportation hub and an important river port as well as its industrial center. It produces a wide variety of manufactured products, including transportation and electrical equipment, machine tools, precision instruments, agricultural machinery, textiles, clothing, and pharmaceuticals.

History. Settlements have existed at or near the site of Budapest since earliest known times. The Magyars, the ancestors of the Hungarians, established the cities of Óbuda and Pest during the late 800's. In 1255, King Bela IV built his royal residence in what is now the Castle Hill section of Buda. The city reached the height of its splendor during the reign of Matthias Corvinus (1458–90). But in 1541, Buda fell to the Ottoman Turks, who ruled the region for some 145 years. During this period, Pest developed as a separate city.

Ottoman Turkish rule was replaced by that of the Austrian Habsburgs, who dominated both Hungary and Budapest for the next 200 years. The union of Buda and Pest in 1873 marked the beginning of the modern city, while the breakup of the Austro-Hungarian Empire in 1918, at the end of World War I, made Budapest the capital of a Hungarian republic.

The city suffered enormous damage in 1944–45, near the end of World War II, when many of its historic landmarks and public buildings were destroyed and its eight bridges blown up by retreating German soldiers. In 1948, after Hungary came under Communist rule, Budapest, as it had been under the Turks and Austrians, became a center of resistance to oppression. When a revolt against Communist rule erupted in 1956 and was put down with great severity by Soviet troops and tanks, the city once again suffered considerable damage. However, a peaceful revolution in 1989 led to the collapse of Communism in 1990, and a democratic government was re-established.

HELMUT KOENIG
Travel Writer

BUDDHA AND BUDDHISM

More than 2,500 years ago, a man in India made a discovery. He discovered the cause of unhappiness and its cure. The man was named Siddhartha Gautama, but he is much better known as the **Buddha**, which means "the wise one" or "the enlightened one." The Buddha's teachings are the basis for one of the world's great religions, Buddhism.

▶ **HOW SIDDHARTHA BECAME THE WISE ONE**

Siddhartha Gautama was born about 563 B.C. His father ruled a small state in northern India near the Himalayas. Strangely enough, the man who discovered the cause of unhappiness knew little about it when he was young. His father tried to protect him from all knowledge of sickness, pain, suffering, and death. Siddhartha spent his early years within palaces and gardens where everything was beautiful and pleasant. When he left the palace grounds, his father sent servants to clear the road of any painful sights. As a result, the young Siddhartha knew nothing about unhappiness.

In spite of all his father did, Siddhartha did eventually learn of unhappiness. Once as he was riding in his chariot he came upon a frail old man. Then he saw another man suffering from a dread disease. Later he met some men carrying the body of one who had died. When Siddhartha asked about those who suffered from old age, disease, and death, he was told: "This happens to all men." For the first time Siddhartha understood that unhappiness was a part of life.

Siddhartha thought about what he had learned. He realized that he could no longer live cut off from the sight of all suffering, as he had in the past. Now that he had begun to learn about life, he could never be content until he understood the whole truth. One night Siddhartha left his father and his wife and child and gave up his great personal fortune. He wanted nothing to interfere with his search for understanding.

At first Siddhartha tried to learn wisdom from some holy men, but after six years he realized that this was not the way. He then decided to look for the truth within himself. He seated himself beneath a tree (which Buddhists now call the Bo Tree) and vowed that he would not leave until he understood the whole meaning of life. He sat there for 49 days, and then the truth came to him. Siddhartha, the seeker for wisdom, had become the Buddha—the wise one.

The Buddha spent the next 45 years teaching men what he had learned under the Bo Tree. He died about 483 B.C., when he was 80. Shortly before his death he reminded his followers that they should not grieve because "everything must die."

▶ WHAT THE WISE ONE TAUGHT

The Buddha wrote no books. He taught his followers, and they taught their followers, who in turn did the same. For hundreds of years the Buddha's teachings were passed on by word of mouth. When men did finally try to write down the teachings in books, they no longer agreed about them. Some had learned one thing; some had learned another. For this reason there is no single collection of writings that serves as a Buddhist bible.

However, most Buddhists do agree about certain teachings. They agree that the Buddha taught that pain, suffering, and unhappiness must be expected as a natural part of life. They tell of a woman who came to the Buddha hoping that he could bring her dead son back to life, for she had heard that he had remarkable powers. The Buddha told her to borrow a cup of mustard seed from a family that had not known of death. The woman went from door to door, but, of course, she could find no such family. She then understood what the Buddha was trying to teach her. No one could escape death and unhappiness. We must expect it and accept it. Men expect only happiness and they are disappointed when they do not receive it. To avoid disappointment, the Buddha taught that one should expect nothing.

If one knows the cause of unhappiness, the Buddha said, one also knows its cure. One can escape unhappiness by getting rid of all selfish desires. How can this be done? By thinking as much of others as we do of ourselves. The man who understands the whole truth and accepts it will understand that he should never steal or cheat or grow angry. He will

A golden statue of the Buddha in the city of Mandalay, Burma.

not stir up trouble by repeating hurtful things. The man who understands what the Buddha taught will "bear the burdens of those who are tired and weary," and he will "harm no living thing."

Once a man completely overcomes all selfishness, he will know a kind of freedom from care that the Buddhists call **nirvana**. The word "nirvana" means "the going out of fire," especially the fire of anger, greed, and desire. It is evidently hard to describe nirvana to those who do not know it. It is like trying to explain how salt tastes to someone who has never tasted it.

▶ DIFFERENT KINDS OF BUDDHISM

A hundred years after the Buddha's death, men already had different ideas about what he had taught. Each man believed what he had learned from his own teacher, and he taught this to his own students.

One group insisted that they remain true to the **Theravada**, which means "the way of the elders." The Buddha had taught, they said, that each man must find his own way to nirvana. No one can help him, not even the gods and spirits. The Buddha did all that one person can do for others; he showed them what they must do for themselves.

Young Burmese pupils study Buddhist scriptures in a monastery school.

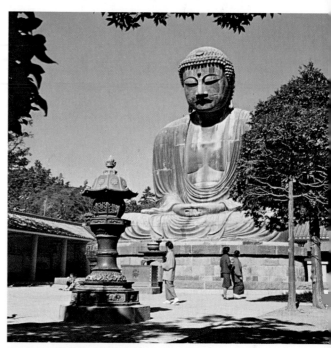

The Great Buddha, at Kamakura, Japan. The huge statue is visited by thousands of pilgrims each year.

Another group said that the Theravada was only a part of the Buddha's teachings. He taught these "lesser ideas" first, but to those able to understand them he gave a greater teaching called the **Mahayana**, which means "the greater vehicle." Mahayana Buddhists refer to Theravada teachings as the **Hinayana**, "the little vehicle."

Mahayana Buddhists also teach that men should follow the Buddha's example of doing good to others. But they believe that the Buddha did more than provide an example. Mahayana Buddhists believe that the Buddha is a god who aids and protects those who pray to him and call upon him. They also believe that men can call upon a number of good spirits, called **Bodhisattvas**, who devote themselves to helping suffering mankind.

From these two divisions of Buddhism have come a number of others. It is said that there are more than 60 different Buddhist groups in Japan today. The differences among the various kinds of Buddhism are great. There are Buddhists, such as those of Tibet, who combine belief in the Buddha with a belief in a large number of spirits and demons. They believe that these spirits and demons can be controlled by magic. Other groups, such as Zen Buddhists of Japan, say very little about gods and spirits. Zen Buddhists, in fact, say

that it is impossible to explain Buddhist teachings in words at all. Either you understand what enlightenment is, or you do not. If you do not, there is nothing that can be said to make it clear to you.

Since Buddhism includes such a variety of branches, it has been described as a group of religions and of ways of thinking rather than a single religion.

▶ BUDDHIST MONKS

During the Buddha's lifetime some of his followers gave up all they had and shared their master's way of life. They spent their time learning the teacher's words and trying to do as he did. We call these men **monks** and the houses they live in **monasteries**.

Some men still choose to live as Buddhist monks. A Buddhist monk owns nothing except his yellow or orange robe, his bowl, his razor, and a few other personal items. Many monks depend entirely upon gifts of food for their living. They spend their time learning and reciting the Buddha's teachings. Monks also teach others, both by their words and by the example of their lives. Some monks care for the sick, for the Buddha once said, "He who would care for me should care for the sick."

Some monks spend their entire lives in the

monasteries. Others may live as monks for a short time. This has been true in Burma, where many boys have spent a few weeks or months living as monks.

BUDDHISM IN THE WORLD TODAY

It is impossible to say how many Buddhists there are in the world today. All that can be said for sure is that Buddhism is one of the world's major religions. A Buddhist is simply a person who believes that there is truth in some form of Buddhism.

Almost all Buddhists live in Asia, but only a small number live in India, where Buddhism began. Most Buddhists are found in Sri Lanka, Burma, Thailand, Cambodia, Tibet, China, and Japan. There are only a few people practicing Buddhism as a religion in Europe and America. But many Europeans and Americans have read and studied Buddhist teaching.

The Buddhists of the country of Sri Lanka follow the Theravada—the way of the elders. They take pride in the fact that Buddhism has been in their country for a long time. Buddhist missionaries went to Sri Lanka 2,200 years ago, bringing with them a cutting from Buddha's sacred Bo Tree. Sri Lankan Buddhists say that the cutting grew into a tree that still stands.

In Tibet the everyday life of the people revolves around a form of Buddhism known as Lamaism. The lamas, or monks, were once very powerful. The highest monk of one order, the Dalai Lama, was both the spiritual and political head of Tibet for several centuries. Although he was forced to leave Tibet for political reasons, the present Dalai Lama is still a spiritual leader.

Travelers carried Mahayana Buddhism to China before A.D. 100, where it became one of the three main religions. The Chinese adopted Buddhist teachings without giving up their old Confucianist beliefs. Some persons might consider themselves both Buddhists and Confucianists. This is why it is so hard to decide how many Buddhists there are.

In about A.D. 372 Buddhist monks carried their teachings to Korea, China's eastern neighbor. About 200 years later Buddhists from both Korea and China carried Buddhist books and images to the island kingdom of Japan. Today Buddhism is one of Japan's two major religions.

KENNETH S. COOPER
George Peabody College

BUDGETS, FAMILY

Most families have far more money than they realize. The ones who get the most from their money seem to have learned how to manage the money they have very well.

A plan for spending the money is called a budget. You, as a member of a family, share in the money spent for food, shelter, clothing, medical care, education, and recreation in your family. It is well to know how much thought and planning often has to be done to provide for the family's basic needs and the individual wants of each member.

Each family must decide for itself exactly how much planning it wants to do. However, there are useful steps that any family can follow for this purpose.

Step 1. Decide whether to divide the budget into periods of 1 week, 2 weeks, or 1 month. Most people find that the time between paydays is the best budgeting period.

WEEKLY BUDGET	
Fixed Expenses	Cost
Rent and Mortgage	
Insurance	
Transportation	
Taxes and Savings	
Time payments	
Living Expenses	
Food	
Clothing	
Utilities	
Recreation	
Contributions	
Medical	
Automobile	
Others	
Total	

Step 2. List all fixed expenses. Include every bill for which the exact amount is known in advance, such as payments for rent, mortgage, insurance, the car, and any other installment purchases.

Step 3. List all regular living expenses for which the amounts vary. Estimate how much each costs during a pay period. Accurate estimates will require time and experience since the amount spent on living expenses depends on such things as how much care is shown by the shopper and the time of year it is. For example, food costs can be kept down by the person who shops and cooks wisely; more water is used in summer, and more fuel and electricity in winter. The cost of clothing and its care can be spread out over the whole year instead of spending large amounts in the fall and spring. The homemaker who knows what to look for in selecting clothing, who has a wardrobe plan that will prevent unwise purchases, and who can sew, will need less money than another person.

Step 4. List any expected major expenses too large to be paid in a single pay period.

Decide how much should be set aside each payday to meet such expenses when they occur. Taxes can usually be estimated in advance, and enough money saved to pay them. Home appliances and furnishings can be bought with savings.

Step 5. Total all expenses. Compare this total with the family's income for the budgeting period. If the expenses are too high, look for ways to cut them. If there is money left, some of it should be set aside regularly in an emergency fund and some in a savings or investment program.

Step 6. Use a budget book or make a chart. Write down the family's plans for using its money. In the following weeks and months, compare this budget with what is actually spent and make any necessary changes.

Even a good budget will not help the family control its spending unless all family members co-operate. Young people who get experience in good money management as they grow up will have little difficulty in working out a family budget of their own.

KATHERINE R. CONAFAY
Author, *Family Budgets*

BUENOS AIRES

Buenos Aires is Argentina's largest city, its capital, and its gateway to the world. It is situated on the Río de la Plata (the River Plate), about 275 kilometers (170 miles) from the sea. Buenos Aires is one of the largest ports in the Americas. Greater Buenos Aires has about 9,000,000 people—over one third of Argentina's total population. The city itself has about 3,000,000 people. Most of the country's roads, railroads, manufacturing plants, ocean shipping, and commerce are centered in Buenos Aires.

The name of the city was given to it by the early Spanish explorers. Buenos Aires means "good airs." A first settlement in 1536 failed because of Indian attacks. A permanent settlement was finally achieved in 1580.

Buenos Aires was a modest city until the end of the 19th century. In time thousands of immigrants—Italians, Germans, Swedes, and people of other nationalities—made it the wonder city it is today. Buenos Aires is set

on a flat plain like a huge, sprawling giant. Its highways and streets stretch out in all directions as far as the eye can see. Seen from above at night, with its countless lights stabbing at the darkness, the city looks like a vast field of glittering diamonds.

On a sunny day the center of the city bustles with sound and movement. Automobile horns honk sharply, and river freighters whistle mournfully. Cheerful, busy people go about their errands, talking in Spanish

Buenos Aires is the bustling capital and commercial center of Argentina. Above: The Palace of the National Congress. Below left: Shoppers throng the city streets. Below right: Avenida 9 de Julio, one of the widest streets in the world.

and as many other languages as are likely to be heard in New York. There is also the dull rumble of the subway trains from deep beneath the sidewalk.

Buenos Aires is a great port whose ships go all over the world. Cement docks line the Río de la Plata. Warehouses, meat-packing plants, grain elevators, and the smokestacks of oceangoing ships loom against the sunny sky. Long freight trains pull into busy yards. Some of these trains have come hundreds of kilometers across the pampas, or plains, with wool to be shipped to distant countries. Most imports also come through the city.

Buenos Aires is a city of sunny plazas and wide boulevards. It is a city of pleasant living. People stroll to the many sidewalk cafés, sit at outdoor tables, and sip black coffee. Many of the streets and avenues are bordered with flowers.

Buenos Aires is the home of the tango. It is a city of music, of drama, of fine libraries and modern schools. World-famous opera stars come to the luxurious Teatro Colón to perform. Open-air performances of ballet are given at the Palermo Gardens. And here a symphony orchestra plays for crowds of appreciative listeners.

It is a city that loves to watch and play sports—golf, tennis, swimming, rowing, polo, and above all soccer, car racing, and horse racing. Champion sports figures become national heroes. One of the largest stadiums in the world, said to have a capacity of about 100,000 people, is in Buenos Aires.

These are some of the sights and sounds of the largest city in the Southern Hemisphere. This is Buenos Aires.

Reviewed by Ernesto Sábato
Author, *On Heroes and Tombs*

BUFFALO. See New York (Cities).

BUFFALO AND BISON

Buffalo and bison are big, strong animals. They have horns on their heads. Their feet have cloven hooves. Buffalo and bison are members of the large group of animals called hoofed mammals. Cows and oxen are hoofed mammals, too. Cows, oxen, buffalo, and bison are all in the cattle family.

Like other cattle, buffalo and bison eat only plants. Those that live on plains eat mostly grass. Those that live in forests eat leaves.

Cows and oxen have been tamed for several thousand years. But only one kind of buffalo has ever been tamed. That is the Asian water buffalo. Bison have almost never been tamed and put to work for people.

▶BUFFALO

Buffalo live in Asia and Africa. They look a lot like oxen except for their horns. For instance, two kinds—the Asian water buffalo and the African Cape buffalo—have big, sweeping horns. These are broad and flat at the base, where they grow out of the head.

The water buffalo is used in India and Southeast Asia to pull plows and do other heavy work. It likes to spend time in the water

The water buffalo (*left*) is very tame when it is in familiar surroundings. In parts of Asia, even very young children handle this huge beast with ease. In contrast, the bison (*right*) has little patience with human beings and will charge quickly if disturbed.

or to wallow in the mud, probably to keep flies away. These buffalo are also raised for milk, meat, and hides.

The Cape buffalo lives in Africa. Hunters have called it the world's most dangerous hoofed animal. Two kinds of forest buffalo also live in Africa.

Pygmy buffalo live in the Philippines and certain islands of Southeast Asia. They are just under 1 meter (about 3 feet) high at the shoulder.

▶BISON

A bison is a large, dark, shaggy animal. It has a thick growth of hair on its head, neck, shoulders, and front legs. It also has a beard and short, curved horns. There is a hump of fat on its shoulders. Bison may stand as high as 1.8 meters (6 feet) at the shoulder.

The American bison once ran in huge herds across the plains and prairies of North America. As the land was settled, people hunted these animals until the big herds were nearly wiped out. Then some people decided that the bison must be saved. There are now thousands of American bison. Most of them live in national parks and wildlife refuges. These animals are often called "buffalo," but "bison" is the correct name for them.

The European bison, or wisent, once ranged throughout Europe. Like its American cousin, it also faced extinction before efforts were made to save it. Today there are fewer than 2,000 of these animals. Most of them live in a protected forest in eastern Europe.

Reviewed by ROBERT M. MCCLUNG
Author, science books for children

See also HOOFED MAMMALS.

BUFFALO BILL (WILLIAM FREDERICK CODY) (1846–1917)

COL. W. F. CODY

Buffalo Bill was the last of the famous American frontier scouts. He was a sharpshooter and an expert guide and hunter. His Wild West shows did much to establish the popular image of the Old West.

Buffalo Bill, whose real name was William Frederick Cody, was born in Le Claire, Iowa, on February 26, 1846. At the age of 14 he was carrying mail for the Pony Express. During the U.S. Civil War, he was a Union Army scout. Later he hunted Bison (often called buffalo) to supply meat for workers building a railroad across Kansas. It is said that Cody killed 69 bison in one day, and over 4,000 in 8 months. He became known everywhere as

Buffalo Bill. When war with the Sioux and Cheyenne Indians broke out in 1875, Cody again became a scout for the cavalry. He is said to have fought a hand-to-hand duel with Yellow Hand, the son of a Cheyenne chief, and killed him.

In 1883, Cody organized his famous traveling Wild West shows. These shows included a huge cast of cowboys, Indians, and sharpshooters, as well as herds of bison, elk, ponies, steers, and wild horses. Historic events such as Custer's Last Stand were re-enacted. Sitting Bull, the Sioux chief whose warriors had helped defeat General Custer's soldiers, traveled with the show in 1885. Annie Oakley, the famous sharpshooter, was another star. Thousands of people in the United States, Canada, and Europe saw the show before Cody lost it in 1913 because of debts.

Cody died on January 10, 1917. His grave and the Cody Memorial Museum are on top of Lookout Mountain in Colorado. Other Cody museums include the Buffalo Bill Historical Center in Cody, Wyoming, where scenes from the old Wild West shows are re-created every summer, and Buffalo Bill's Ranch State Historical Park in North Platte, Nebraska.

Reviewed by THOMAS B. MORRISON
Buffalo Bill's Ranch State Historical Park

The 110-story **World Trade Center** towers in New York City are among the most impressive buildings in the world. New skyscrapers are constantly being built.

BUILDING CONSTRUCTION

The construction of a building requires the talents and skills of many people who work with a variety of materials and processes. Architects and engineers design buildings. Workers in forests, quarries, mills, and factories produce the materials from which buildings are made. Contractors bring together the materials and the workers to assemble the buildings, and building inspectors make sure each building is constructed so it will be safe and healthy for the people who use it. Working together, these people create the fabric of our cities—buildings ranging from simple sheds to skyscrapers.

Materials of Construction

Two basic types of materials are used in buildings: structural and nonstructural. Structural materials hold up the building against such forces as gravity, wind, and earthquakes.

Such materials include stone, bricks, concrete blocks, concrete, wood, and steel. Nonstructural materials keep out the weather and finish the building in useful and attractive ways. There are many nonstructural materials used in buildings, but the most important are roofing materials, thermal insulation, glass, and gypsum.

Structural Materials. The major kinds of stone used in construction are granite, sandstone, limestone, and marble. Quarry workers cut large pieces of stone from the earth. At factories these pieces are sawed into blocks and slabs that will be used to make buildings. Stone is expensive because it is hard to cut and heavy to transport. But with its many colors and patterns, it is among the most beautiful of materials. It is also very durable.

Bricks are molded from moist clay. After drying, they are put into a kiln (a kind of oven), where they are heated to very high temperatures and converted into hard, stonelike blocks. Concrete blocks are molded from fresh concrete. Then they are hardened in a steam chamber.

People who work with stones, bricks, and concrete blocks are called masons. Any construction that uses these materials is called masonry. To make a masonry wall, masons set the blocks or stones in a thick layer of mortar, which is a mudlike mixture of sand, portland cement, and water. (Portland cement is a fine gray powder made from clay and limestone.) The mortar soon hardens into a rocklike material that holds the wall together and makes it weathertight.

Concrete is a mixture of sand, crushed stone, and portland cement. When blended with water, the cement powder hardens into a very strong adhesive that binds the sand and crushed stone into a rocklike material.

Masonry and concrete stand up well against pressing or squeezing forces known as **compression.** These materials are used in walls and columns that must withstand the compression created by the building's weight, or **load.** But masonry and concrete are brittle; they break when exposed to stretching forces, or **tension.** Nonbrittle materials that retain their strength when stretched are also necessary in building construction. Wood and steel, for example, are materials that can be used for beams and slabs that span horizontally between walls and columns.

Wood is used for structures of small or medium size. It is also used for the walls of small structures such as houses. Because wood can burn, however, it is not used in the construction of large buildings. Wood used in buildings must be kept dry and off the ground so it does not rot or become infested with insects.

Steel is a form of iron. Because of its great strength, steel is used for the frames of the tallest skyscrapers. Although it will not burn, steel will lose its strength at very high temperatures. In a large building, steel is covered with fire-resistant materials such as gypsum to protect it from becoming too hot should a fire occur in the building.

The brittleness of concrete can be overcome by embedding steel rods in it. This forms **reinforced concrete.** Beams and slabs of reinforced concrete can also span horizontal distances and are very resistant to fire.

Nonstructural Materials. Many nonstructural materials are just as important as structural materials. Roofing materials prevent rain and snow from leaking into the rooms below and causing structural damage. Buildings with sloping roofs, such as houses, typically are roofed with shingles. These are small, overlapping squares or rectangles of wood, slate, or asphalt. Flat roofs tend to hold rather than shed rainwater and snow. Because shingles have many seams, they are not watertight when used on flat roofs. Seamless sheets of asphalt or synthetic rubber must be used on flat roofs to keep water out.

Thermal insulating materials are also extremely important. They make buildings more comfortable and greatly reduce the amount of energy needed for heating and cooling. Insulating materials include loose mats of mineral fibers and lightweight boards of plastic foam.

Glass, another important nonstructural material, is made by melting sand, soda ash, and lime together. It is cast into large, smooth sheets that are cut into squares for use in windows. Gypsum is a common mineral that is made into plaster and plasterboard for walls and ceilings inside a building. Gypsum creates hard, smooth surfaces and is very resistant to fire. Gypsum plaster and plasterboard play a very important role in protecting structural materials from fire and preventing the spread of fire from one room of a building to another.

Constructing a House

Most houses are built by small crews of builders working with relatively simple tools and methods. The plans for a house may be specially drawn by an architect or team of architects to meet the needs or desires of a homeowner or builder. For an ordinary house, the builder may draw the plans or buy standard predrawn plans from a catalog. After the builder receives a building permit from the city or town building inspector, construction can begin. The first step is for an excavator to dig a hole for the foundation. Then workers construct the foundation, using concrete that has been poured into forms, concrete blocks, or wood treated with chemicals to prevent decay. The foundation must be strong enough to support the weight of the house.

Building a house: The first steps include digging for a foundation (*left*) and pouring concrete foundation walls and floors (*right*). Workers must spread and smooth the concrete for the floor before it hardens.

Sometimes the ground floor of the house is a concrete slab poured directly on the ground. More often it is made of wood. To make a wood floor, carpenters first bolt planks of wood, called **sills,** to the top of the foundation. Then horizontal pieces of lumber called **joists** are nailed to the sills. The joists are covered with sheets of plywood to create a level unfinished floor called the **subfloor.**

Walls of a house are framed with vertical pieces of lumber called **studs.** The subfloor is

Building a house: The foundation has been "capped" with a subfloor. *Above:* Workers are putting up wall frames. *Right:* The wall frames are up and the slanting roof beams—rafters—are in place. A worker is nailing sheathing to the frame. *Below:* A diagram shows the main parts of a house.

A WOOD-FRAME HOUSE: SOME PARTS

Ridge board
Roof sheathing
Shingles
Rafter
Ceiling joist
Wall plate
Overhang
Fascia
Header
Header
Insulation
Gypsum wallboard
Window opening
Door opening
Rough sill
Air infiltration barrier
Plywood subflooring
Exterior sheathing
Floor joists
Siding
Solid concrete foundation wall
Stud
Beam
Sill plate
Band joist
Concrete footing
Concrete basement floor

used as a kind of table on which sections of wall framing are assembled. Carpenters tilt finished sections of wall framing up into place and nail them to the floor frame. If the house is to be two stories high, the second floor joists rest on top of the first floor walls. Then the second story walls are assembled on the second floor, tilted up, and nailed down.

The attic floor and the sloping roof **rafters** are the last pieces of the house frame to be installed. The roof and all the outside walls are covered with a **sheathing** of wood boards, plywood, or sheets of wood composition board. Then carpenters can begin finishing the exterior of the house. First the roof is made watertight by nailing on the shingles. Then windows and doors that have been preassembled at a factory are installed in wall openings left for them. Finally, wood, vinyl, or aluminum siding is applied to the wall sheathing. Brick, stone, or stucco can also be used as siding.

Building a house: When the main frame is up, there is much left to do. *Below:* Pipes for water and wires for electricity must be run throughout the house. *Bottom:* A worker nails siding on the outside. *Below left:* Insulation is installed and large sheets of gypsum wallboard cover the framing inside. *Left:* Overlapping layers of shingles make the roof watertight.

433

Building a house: Finishing work (*above*) includes filling each wallboard joint with plaster and installing decorative trim. Painting or staining the house outside (*right*) makes the house look nice and protects it from the weather.

Why is a tree or an American flag sometimes placed on the highest part of a building under construction?

A tree or flag placed on, or nailed to, the highest part of a building under construction is a modern version of the ancient "topping out" ceremony. Topping out, still practiced in many parts of the world, is meant to indicate that the frame of the structure has been completed. During a topping out ceremony of long ago, a barrel of beer might be drunk while a tree or wreath was attached to the ridge of a building's newly completed roof. Today, finishing the frame of a building is still cause for celebration.

Even before the exterior of the house is finished, work inside begins. Masons may construct a fireplace and chimney. Electricians, plumbers, and sheet metal workers install the electrical wiring, the pipes and plumbing fixtures, and the heating and air conditioning systems. Workers stuff blankets of insulation into all the spaces between the exterior wall studs and ceiling joists. Insulation helps keep heat inside the house during cold weather. The interior walls are then covered with gypsum plaster or sheets of gypsum wallboard. Decorative wood trim is nailed around interior windows and doors. Finish flooring, cabinets, and lighting fixtures are the last items to be installed. Unfinished surfaces are painted, stained, varnished, and wallpapered. Driveway, sidewalk, and landscaping work can take place outside. After a final cleanup the house is ready to live in.

Constructing Larger Buildings

A larger building is much more complicated than a house. Each one is specially designed by a team of professionals that includes both **architects** and **engineers.** Architects design the exterior form, interior spaces, and surfaces of the building. Engineers, who work closely with the architects, design the foundations, the structural skeleton, the heating and cooling system, the electrical wiring, and the plumbing. The design work is complicated and takes many months. The architects and engineers work with the owner of the building to design a structure that is attractive and sturdy, and meets the owner's requirements. They also work with the city building inspector to be sure that the building is constructed according to the building code, which is a set of rules for making buildings safe and healthy. The building code may require that the building is made of fireproof materials; that enough toilets and lavatories are provided for everyone in the building; and that there are at least two safe ways for people to escape from the building in case of fire. Even in buildings that are made from materials that will not burn, the contents of the rooms may burn, causing dangerous fires. The designers must always take fire safety into account.

After the design work has been completed, the architects and engineers make blueprints of their final drawings and give them to the **building contractor.** He or she is responsible for seeing that the building is constructed exactly as it was designed. The contractor buys the materials for the building, hires many kinds of workers to put the materials together, and manages the entire construction process.

Larger buildings are much, much heavier than houses and need larger and stronger foundations. If the soil beneath a building is very firm and the building is not too tall, the foundations may be ordinary concrete **footings,** which are the flat strips and squares of concrete that lie in the ground and support the walls and columns of the building. If the soil is not so firm or the building is tall, more elaborate kinds of foundations have to be built. Sometimes the building is placed on one giant concrete footing that is as broad as the building; this is called a **mat** or **raft** foundation. Sometimes large drills may be used to bore holes several feet in diameter straight down through softer layers of soil until solid rock or a very firm soil is reached. This may lie a hundred feet (about 30 meters) or more beneath the surface of the ground. Then each hole is filled with concrete to make a type of foundation called either a **pier** or a **caisson.** It takes dozens of caissons to support a building; each one can support a single column or a part of a foundation wall. **Pile foundations** are used in some types of soft soil. Workers hammer **piles** into the ground using machines called pile drivers. Piles are long, slender pieces of wood, steel, or concrete. After the pile has been pounded firmly into the soil like a giant nail, it can support a considerable amount of weight. A cluster of piles can support each column of the building. Many clusters of piles in a line can hold up a wall.

Buildings larger than houses must be built of stronger, more fire-resistant materials than those used in houses. Large wood beams and columns can be used in structures less than five stories high. The frames of most large buildings, however, are built entirely of stronger materials such as steel or concrete.

In some large buildings, masonry or concrete walls support floors made of steel beams or concrete slabs. In smaller buildings, the floors might be made of wood joists or beams. This type of construction is called **bearing wall construction** because the walls bear, or support, the weight of the floors and roof. This weight is finally transferred to the foundation, on which the bearing walls are built.

Large buildings need sturdy foundations. Some rest on hundreds of piles, which are driven deep into the ground by powerful machines called pile drivers.

Most large buildings are held up by an open framework of vertical columns and horizontal beams. This type of construction is called **skeleton construction** because it resembles the bony structure that holds up a human body. A building's skeletal frame may be made of steel or concrete. Steel building frames are put up by people called **ironworkers.** Ironworkers use cranes to lift the heavy beams and columns into place. Then they bolt and weld the parts of the frame together. Diagonal braces are also installed to prevent the building from swaying due to wind or earthquakes.

Why don't tall buildings blow down in a strong wind?

Tall buildings must be braced throughout their height with cross-bracing, rigid connections, or stiff structural walls called shear walls. Most tall buildings are constructed of steel or reinforced concrete. These materials are flexible—that is, they can bend slightly without breaking. When strong winds blow, the steel and concrete buildings give way to the force of the wind by bending a little. For example, the World Trade Center towers in New York City were designed to sway as much as two feet (0.6 meters). If the buildings did not sway, they could be snapped in two by violent wind. The buildings are not pulled out of the ground because they are firmly anchored in strong foundations.

Reinforced concrete can be used to make bearing walls, columns, beams, and flat floor structures called slabs. The simplest kind of concrete structure is made up of columns and flat slabs, without any beams. For buildings with greater distances between columns, or where heavier weights must be supported, beams are used to hold up the slabs. In order to span longer distances, slabs are sometimes made with a ribbed or a waffle-like pattern underneath. These slabs are very strong and stiff without being too heavy or using too much concrete.

There are two ways of making a concrete building. One is called **sitecast construction.** In this method, workers construct wooden molds, or forms, into which steel rods are placed. Then wet concrete is poured, or "cast," into the forms, surrounding the steel reinforcing rods. After a few days the concrete has hardened and the forms are pulled off and re-used for another portion of the building.

The other way of making a concrete building is to cast the concrete in large pieces at a factory. The finished pieces of concrete are brought to the building site on trucks and are assembled in almost the same way as steel beams and columns. This is called **precast concrete construction.**

As soon as the steel or concrete frame of the building is finished, roofers apply a waterproof roof surface to keep out rain and snow. Crews of plumbers, electricians, and sheet metal workers install pipes, wires, air ducts, and elevators. Other workers install the exterior walls, which they bolt to the building frame. These walls are called **curtain walls** because they hang on the building (by means of the bolts), much like a curtain hangs on a wall. Curtain walls can be made of masonry, thin slabs of stone, panels of precast concrete, or light frames of aluminum holding sheets of glass and metal. Thermal insulation materials are put in the walls to make the building easier and more economical to heat and cool.

Once the outside walls are in place, interior partitions, ceilings, and floors can be installed. Interior partitions divide the inside of a building into separate spaces but do not bear any of the building's weight. Painters and a cleanup crew complete the construction.

Some kinds of structures, like basketball arenas, exhibition halls, and auditoriums, need roofs that span very long horizontal distances between the supporting walls or columns. Even steel beams may not be strong enough to safely span such distances. Instead, architects and engineers design other types of

The frame, or skeleton, of a skyscraper is made of sturdy steel columns and beams. The steel is lifted to the top by huge cranes or derricks. Thin "curtain walls" can be hung on the finished frame.

- Guy derrick
- Beams
- Curtain wall
- Soil
- Piles
- Rock

Cloth used in the construction of this airport at Riyadh, Saudi Arabia, makes it look like a huge tent. Air flowing through the waiting area cools people while hot air escapes through openings in the roof.

structural systems that are able to span longer distances. Domes or arches of reinforced concrete or heavy timbers can be designed to span hundreds of feet. Steel can make not only domes and arches, but also trusses and cable-supported roofs. A truss is used like a beam and is made up of slender pieces of steel that are connected together to make a series of open triangles. Cable-supported roofs are held up by strong wire ropes. A new type of long-span roof has been used in recent years on a number of covered stadiums. It is a thin, air-tight fabric reinforced with steel cables and held up by slight air pressure from within the stadium. The air pressure needed to hold the roof up—created by blowers in the heating and air conditioning system—is so slight that most people do not even notice it.

How We Learned to Build

Our earliest ancestors built from whatever materials were easily available. In forested areas tree trunks, branches, and saplings were fashioned into shelters of many kinds. Where stone was abundant, it was gathered and stacked into walls, with mud sometimes used between the stones. In regions with no stone, buildings were made of mud. Mud could be smeared over loosely woven mats of sticks, vines, or reeds to make thin walls. Or it could be mixed with straw and piled up to make very heavy, thick walls. Mud could also be molded into bricks that were dried by the sun. The bricks, joined by wet mud, could then be stacked into walls.

Although materials of construction (mud, stone, and wood) did not change for many thousands of years, people gradually learned how to build better buildings from them. These buildings were warmer, dryer, longer lasting, and more beautiful. People found that by raising the floors of their buildings off the ground, they could stay dry even during wet seasons. They learned to protect wooden building parts from water so they would not rot. They discovered ways to build sloping roofs from shingles or thatch (bundles of grass, reeds, or palm leaves) that would shed water without leaking. In cold climates, they discovered ways to build fires inside their buildings to keep warm in the winter, using holes in the roofs to let out the smoke. In hot, dry climates they learned that thick, heavy walls and roofs of stone or mud keep rooms cool even in the hottest weather. In humid tropical climates, where heavy walls would be damp, people developed light, airy houses on stilts so cooling breezes could pass through the rooms.

As time passed, builders became more skilled at cutting stone from quarries and carving it to the exact shapes they wanted for their buildings. They learned to make their mud bricks hard and durable by heating them to high temperatures in wood-fired kilns. Fireplaces and chimneys were developed to heat buildings better and remove smoke from the rooms. With metal saws and axes, tree trunks were squared into heavy posts and beams and sliced into thin boards for exterior and interior

Prefabricated buildings are those that were partly made in a factory. Large sections are transported to the site and assembled there to make a complete structure.

surfaces. Such metals as bronze, lead, and iron gradually came into use for fastening stones and timbers together and for covering roofs of public buildings.

More than 2,000 years ago the ancient Romans discovered how to make concrete, which they used to construct their enormous temples, baths, markets, and law courts. During the Middle Ages, the knowledge of how to make concrete was lost, but masons continued to develop their skills, building impressive churches, mosques, and public buildings that were covered with soaring domes and vaults (arched ceilings or roofs) made of brick or stone.

The Industrial Revolution began in the 1700's. During that time, people began using iron for columns and beams in buildings, especially factories. In the late 1800's, Gustave Eiffel built his famous iron tower in Paris. The making of concrete was revived, and glassmakers learned how to make larger and clearer sheets of glass for windows. Skyscrapers were built in Chicago and New York City using frames made of iron and steel. The first true skyscraper was the ten-story Home Insurance Building in Chicago, completed in 1885. Architects and engineers began using mathematics to make sure that their building frames were strong enough to stand up safely.

During the 1900's there have been many changes in building construction. Many kinds of machines are used on the construction site to cut, shape, lift, and install building materials. The use of mathematics in building design has increased so much that engineers now use computers to do most of their calculations. Much building construction is now done in factories rather than at the building site. Whole finished pieces of buildings are transported to the site and assembled rapidly in a process called **prefabrication.** Prefabrication saves money and time because it is faster and easier for the work to be done in a factory than out in the open.

Over the last century, ways have been developed to keep buildings well lighted and comfortable year-round. Electric lights, telephones, and computer networks are made possible by copper wiring run through buildings. Buildings are heated and cooled with many machines and devices designed to heat or chill air and control humidity. Sunlight is also better used to heat and light buildings. Modern plumbing systems enable people to wash, bathe, and cook in complete comfort and convenience. Computers are now used to control heating and cooling systems in many buildings. Computers will continue to be used more and more, not only to design buildings but to manage every aspect of their operation as well.

EDWARD ALLEN
Author, *Fundamentals of Building Construction*

See also ARCHITECTURE; BRICKS AND MASONRY; CEMENT AND CONCRETE; IRON AND STEEL.

BULGARIA

BULGARIA

Bulgaria is situated on the Balkan Peninsula of southeastern Europe, a location that has played an important role in the nation's history. For although it is now a small country, Bulgaria was a great power in the region during much of the Middle Ages. In the late 1300's, however, Bulgaria was conquered by the Ottoman Turks, who ruled it as part of their empire for nearly 500 years. A self-governing Bulgarian state, greatly reduced in size, was re-established in 1878. A fully independent kingdom of Bulgaria, with borders similar to the country's present-day borders, was proclaimed in 1908.

Bulgaria remained a kingdom from 1908 until 1946. In 1946, after the end of World War II, the monarchy was abolished and the Communist Party took control of the government. The Communists ruled the country as a dictatorship until 1989, when they yielded to demands for reform and accepted the idea of a multiparty political system. A new, democratic constitution was adopted in 1991, and the first free elections in many years were held soon after.

▶THE PEOPLE

Migrating Slavic tribes settled in what is now Bulgaria during the A.D. 500's. In the 600's, the Bulgars, a nomadic people from Asia, conquered the Slavs and established a Bulgarian kingdom. The Bulgars eventually were absorbed into the much larger Slavic population. Little trace of them remains today, except for their name and a few words in the Bulgarian language.

Most of the people are Bulgarian Slavs. Turks form the largest minority group, making up about 9 percent of the population. Bulgaria also has smaller numbers of Gypsies, Armenians, Greeks, and Russians.

Bulgaria is a land of rugged mountains and fertile plains. The Rhodope Mountains, shown here, are the highest in the Balkans and form Bulgaria's boundary with Greece. The woman at right wears the traditional dress of Bulgaria's Plovdiv district.

Left: Blue denims are as popular with young Bulgarians as they are with teenagers the world over. *Below:* A bishop of the Bulgarian Orthodox Church blesses a parishioner. Religious observance was discouraged during the years of Communist rule, but today Bulgarians of all religions are free to practice their faiths.

stored. The constitution proclaims Orthodox Christianity the traditional religion of the nation but gives it no special privileges. Bulgarians of other religions are free to practice their own faiths.

Way of Life. Before World War II, Bulgaria was mainly an agricultural country. Only about one quarter of the population lived in urban areas (cities and towns). After the Communists came to power, Bulgaria experienced vast changes in its way of life. The economy was nationalized, or brought under government control. Private farms were transformed into large, state-run collective farms, which

Language and Religion. Bulgarian, the official language of the country, belongs to the South Slavic group of the Slavic languages. Bulgarian is closely related to Russian. Like Russian, it is written in the Cyrillic alphabet.

Historically, most Bulgarians have belonged to the Bulgarian Orthodox Church, an independent branch of the Eastern Orthodox Church. The head of the Bulgarian church is the Patriarch. Most of the Turks in Bulgaria, and also some Bulgarians, are Muslims. Bulgarian-speaking Muslims are called Pomaks. There are also small communities of Jews, Roman Catholics, and Protestants.

During the era of Communist rule, the government discouraged the practice of religion and regulated the conduct of the clergy. The policy of the new government includes respect for the independence of the country's religious institutions, and customary Christian holidays such as Christmas and Easter have been re-

FACTS and figures

REPUBLIC OF BULGARIA is the official name of the country.

LOCATION: Balkan Peninsula in southeastern Europe.

AREA: 42,823 sq mi (110,912 km²).

POPULATION: 9,000,000 (estimate).

CAPITAL AND LARGEST CITY: Sofia.

MAJOR LANGUAGE: Bulgarian (official).

MAJOR RELIGION: Bulgarian Orthodox.

GOVERNMENT: Republic. **Head of state**—president. **Head of government**—prime minister. **Legislature**—National Assembly.

CHIEF PRODUCTS: Agricultural—wheat, corn, and other grains, sugar beets, grapes and other fruits, tobacco, sunflower seeds, roses. **Manufactured**—processed agricultural products, machinery, chemicals, metal products. **Mineral**—lignite (brown coal), iron ore (limited amounts), copper, zinc, lead, petroleum (limited amounts).

MONETARY UNIT: Lev (1 lev = 100 stotinki).

needed fewer workers. Industrialization led to the rapid growth of urban areas, where about two thirds of Bulgarians now live.

Major Cities. Sofia is Bulgaria's capital, commercial center, and largest city, with a population of more than 1 million. Although Sofia first became the national capital after it was freed from the Turks in 1878, the city has been a site of settlement since ancient times. Its oldest structure, the Church of St. George, was built on the remains of a public bath dating from Roman times.

Plovdiv is Bulgaria's second city, both in population and economic importance. Other major Bulgarian cities include Varna, Ruse, and Burgas.

▶ THE LAND AND CLIMATE

The Major Regions. Bulgaria has four major geographic regions: the Balkan Mountains, the Danube Plateau, the Thracian Plain, and the Rhodope Mountains.

The Balkan Mountains run east and west and split Bulgaria in two. They act as a divider between the two main climatic regions. North of the mountains the Danube Plateau slopes gradually to the Danube River, which separates Bulgaria from Romania. The Danube Plateau is an important agricultural area. It has a continental climate, marked by hot summers and cold winters. Between the Balkan Mountains and the Rhodope Mountains lies the Thracian Plain, drained by the Maritsa River, which has an especially fertile valley. The Rhodope Mountains, highest in the Balkan Peninsula, form the southern boundary between Bulgaria and Greece.

The Maritsa Valley is protected by the Balkan Mountains from the cold winds of the Russian plains. The valley has a Mediterranean climate, with mild but rainy winters and dry, hot summers.

The famous Valley of Roses, which lies in the heart of the country, is the center of Bulgaria's rose-growing industry. It produces attar of roses, an oil used in making perfumes. Bulgaria has nearly a world monopoly in the production of this attar.

Natural Resources. About one third of Bulgaria is covered with valuable forests. Some three quarters of the forests in the mountains are broadleaf; the rest are coniferous. Beech trees and evergreen scrub plants are found along the Maritsa Valley and the Turkish border. The country's wild animal life includes bears, wolves, foxes, elk, and wildcats, which roam the mountain forests.

Bulgaria has a variety of mineral resources, including coal, iron ore, copper, zinc, and lead. But most of its coal is a low-grade kind called lignite (brown coal), and its iron deposits are limited. Some petroleum is produced in the Black Sea region, but not enough to meet the country's energy needs.

Sunshine barely penetrates the winter mist covering Sofia, Bulgaria's capital and largest city. Although the site dates from ancient times, Sofia first became the national capital after it was freed from Turkish rule in 1878.

THE ECONOMY

Until recently, Bulgaria, like other Communist nations, had a centrally planned economy, under which the government determined what the country's economic goals would be. After 1989, however, the country's leaders decided to abandon this system, which had led to severe economic problems, in favor of a market economy with large elements of private enterprise.

Agriculture. About half of Bulgaria's land is suitable for agriculture. The rest is too dry, too marshy, or too mountainous. Much of the farmland, however, is very fertile. The chief crops are wheat, corn, and other grains, grapes and other fruits, tobacco, sunflower seeds, and roses.

Under the Communist system, most of the country's agricultural production came from large agricultural complexes operated by the government. Individuals were permitted to cultivate only small plots of their own, which were usually devoted to raising livestock and animal feed. In 1991 the government adopted a law providing for the return of most of the land to private ownership.

Industry and Trade. Before the end of World War II, Bulgaria was one of the least industrialized countries in Europe. Emphasis by the government on this sector of the economy brought about the rapid development of industry, which is now the most important sector of the economy. The main categories of manufactured goods are processed agricultural products, machinery, chemicals, and metal products.

Most of Bulgaria's foreign trade traditionally had been with the former Soviet Union and other Communist nations, those of Eastern Europe in particular. During the 1990's, Bulgaria sought expanded trade relations with the countries of Western Europe and the United States. The country's main exports are machinery, foods, wine, rose oil, and metal products. Its chief imports include fuels, iron ore, and other raw materials.

GOVERNMENT

Bulgaria is a republic governed under the constitution adopted in 1991. It provides for a president, elected for a 5-year term, as head of state. The president is assisted by a vice president, elected jointly with the president. The legislative body is the National Assembly, made up of 240 members elected for 4-year terms. The government is led by a prime minister, who heads the Council of Ministers. The prime minister is chosen by the political party or coalition of parties having the largest number of seats in the National Assembly.

The third branch of government is the judiciary, or court system, which includes two supreme courts. There is, in addition, the Constitutional Court, which is responsible for interpretations of the constitution. It is composed of twelve justices, four each appointed by the president, the National Assembly, and the justices of the supreme courts.

Below: Bulgaria's Valley of Roses is the world's chief source of attar of roses, used in making perfume. *Right:* Industry, including steel production, is now the most important sector of the Bulgarian economy.

The First Bulgarian Empire. The Bulgars arrived in the region from Central Asia in the A.D. 600's and conquered the part of the Balkan Peninsula inhabited by Slavs from the Byzantine Empire. In 681, Byzantium recognized the first Bulgarian empire, which lasted until 1018. Although they ruled the country, the Bulgars adopted the language and most of the customs of the conquered Slavs.

Bulgaria in the Middle Ages was a great military power. It fought many wars against the Byzantine Empire and against other neighbors and invaders. In 865 the Bulgarian ruler Czar Boris I accepted Christianity. He established the independent Bulgarian church and introduced the Cyrillic alphabet. This alphabet and the Orthodox religion were spread from Bulgaria to other parts of eastern Europe, including Russia. Boris' son Czar Simeon I (reigned 893–927) was one of Bulgaria's greatest rulers. During his reign, Bulgaria flourished as a center of Slavic culture and learning. Simeon I also conquered many new territories. At his death in 927, Bulgaria stretched from the Black Sea on the east to the Adriatic Sea on the west.

Byzantine Rule and the Second Empire. Bulgaria declined in importance after Simeon's death. In 1018 the Byzantine emperor Basil II conquered the country and ended the first Bulgarian empire. Bulgaria remained part of the Byzantine Empire until 1186.

In 1186, John Asen I and his brother Peter regained Bulgaria's independence. Their descendant Czar John Asen II (reigned 1218–41) established the second Bulgarian empire, which included most of the Balkan Peninsula. Art and literature flourished, and many new churches were founded. But in 1396, along with the rest of the Balkan states, Bulgaria was conquered by the Ottoman Turks.

Turkish Rule. Bulgaria remained a part of the Ottoman Empire for nearly 500 years. During that time the Bulgarian nobility disappeared, and Bulgarian farmers were made serfs to Turkish masters. The Bulgarian church, too, lost its independence and was placed under the control of the Greek Patriarch in Constantinople (now Istanbul).

The Bulgarians almost lost their national identity, for the ability to read and write had declined and few could remember the history of their people. However, a Bulgarian national

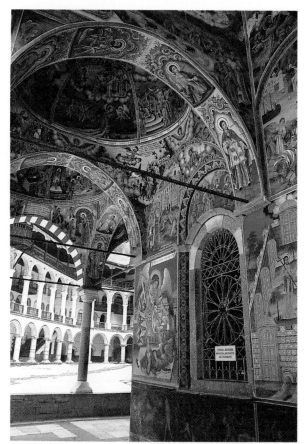

The Rila Monastery is one of the glories of Bulgaria's past. Originally built in the A.D. 900's, it was destroyed and rebuilt several times over the centuries.

revival began in the 1800's. An independent Bulgarian church was restored in 1870. Some Bulgarians took to the mountains and began a guerrilla campaign against Turkish rule.

Independence. Russia helped Bulgaria to win political independence from the Turks in the Russo-Turkish War of 1877–78. But the western European powers feared possible Russian expansion. Therefore, only the northern part of Bulgaria was made independent. In 1885, however, the southern part of the country, called Eastern Rumelia, broke away from Turkey and was reunited with Bulgaria.

The European powers did not believe that the Bulgarians were experienced enough to govern themselves in a fully democratic way, so they required the country to accept a foreign monarch. Its first prince was Alexander Battenberg, but he gave up the throne in 1886. That same year, Prince Ferdinand of Saxe-Coburg-Gotha was chosen as the new ruler.

Balkan Wars. In 1908, Ferdinand took the title of Czar and claimed the rest of the areas

Pro-democracy demonstrators in Sofia signaled "V" for victory after Bulgaria's Communist government yielded to demands for political and economic reforms. A new, democratic constitution was adopted in 1991, and the first free elections in many years were held soon after.

of old Bulgaria, especially Macedonia. A Balkan alliance between Bulgaria, Serbia, Montenegro, and Greece was formed. This alliance fought against the Turks in the First Balkan War, in 1912. Victorious over the Turks, the Balkan allies quarreled among themselves. In the Second Balkan War, in 1913, Bulgaria was defeated by an alliance of Greece, Serbia, Romania, and Turkey, and was forced to give up its claims to Macedonia.

Two World Wars. In World War I (1914–18), Bulgaria, as an ally of Germany and Austria-Hungary, found itself on the losing side and was compelled to give up more territory. Ferdinand was forced to abdicate, and the throne was inherited by his son Boris III. Heavy war reparations (compensation Bulgaria had to pay) and a flood of refugees from Macedonia caused economic and political instability during the 1920's and 1930's. In 1934, Czar Boris and the Army outlawed the country's political parties and made Bulgaria a dictatorship.

In 1941, during World War II, Bulgaria again allied itself with Germany. But although it declared war on the United States and Britain, Bulgaria did not declare war on the Soviet Union. Boris III died in 1943. The following year the Bulgarian government opened peace talks with the Allies.

Communism to Democracy. But the government had moved too slowly. While the talks were underway, the Soviet Union declared war against Bulgaria, and Bulgarian Communist leaders seized power. In 1946 the monarchy was abolished. The young czar, Simeon II, went into exile and Bulgaria adopted a Communist form of government.

During their years of rule, the Communists stressed the rapid growth of industry, but they allowed little political or cultural freedom. By the late 1980's, however, the far-reaching political changes that were sweeping the Soviet Union and other Communist nations of Eastern Europe had also affected Bulgaria. In 1989, Todor Zhivkov, who had led the Bulgarian Communist Party since 1954, was removed from power by his fellow Communist leaders. The new leadership allowed the formation of opposition political parties.

The first elections under the new constitution were held in 1991. They were won by the Union of Democratic Forces, an alliance opposed to the Communists, who promised to maintain political democracy and build a free-market economy. In 1994 the Bulgarian Socialist Party, made up of former Communists, won a majority in legislative elections. But in the 1997 elections, the Union of Democratic Forces regained its majority.

GEORGE W. HOFFMAN
University of Texas at Austin

Revised and updated by JOHN D. BELL
University of Maryland (Baltimore County)
Author, *The Bulgarian Communist Party from Blagoev to Zhivkov*

BULIMIA. See DISEASES (Descriptions of Some Diseases).

BULLETIN BOARDS

A bulletin board is a board for posting notices and other bits of information. A bulletin board of your own can serve many purposes. Perhaps it can make you smile by reminding you of the wonderful vacation you had last summer. It might make you feel proud by displaying your very best school papers. Maybe it can help keep you organized by providing a place to put important schedules and reminders. However you might use it, a bulletin board is a decorative showcase for your interests and accomplishments.

Ready-made bulletin boards are available at hardware and stationery stores. They come in a variety of sizes, ranging from the very large ones usually used in classrooms to the more usual 60- by 90-centimeter (2- by 3-foot) home size. Most bulletin boards are made out of cork. They can be purchased with a plain wood or metal frame or with no frame at all.

Bulletin boards are easy to make. Cork squares found in a hardware or decorating supply store can be used singly or in groups. A sheet of fiberboard (a material sometimes used to make walls), available at building supply stores, makes a good bulletin board. You can even use layers of cardboard glued together. Cover them with fabric or any of the other materials suggested below, and you have an attractive bulletin board at little or no cost.

Bulletin boards are usually hung like pictures on walls. But there are other places where bulletin boards can be just as effective. Try putting a large one behind your bed as a headboard. Or tack cork to the back of a bookcase or a dresser. In this way you can turn a piece of furniture that has an unfinished back into a free-standing piece that makes an excellent room divider.

Just as a bulletin board does not have to be on the wall, neither does it have to be a rectangle. You can easily cut cork or cardboard to any shape. Perhaps you can pick up a decorative shape, such as a flower or a star, from a fabric in your room. Or you can reflect an interesting hobby in the shape of your bulletin board. A car shape, baseball bat shape, or even the letters of your name or initials, cut out of cork and mounted, can provide a decorative touch to your room.

Background Material. There are many materials that can give a nice texture or design to the background of your bulletin board. Paper is a good choice because it can be changed easily when you change your board display. Try large sheets of poster board, construction paper, wallpaper, gift wrap, adhesive-backed paper, or shelf paper. Effective for certain themes are road maps, newsprint, or even aluminum foil. For a more permanent covering, fabrics are a good choice. Burlap, felt, leather, suede, or even fake fur lend good texture to the surface.

Borders. Borders give a finished look to your bulletin board. There are many ways to make effective borders. Pieces of braided or twisted yarn, crepe paper, ribbon, or paper chains can be used. Try stringing halves of paper plates or paper doilies together. See Diagram A on the following page for the technique of making cut-paper borders.

Lettering. If you want to label your bulletin board display, letters can be cut from magazines or made freehand. They can be made from paper or fabric. Diagram B on page 447 shows how to fold and cut paper to make letters.

Fasteners. Use straight pins, map pins, push pins, or double-faced tape to put materials on your bulletin board. Or try gluing magnets to the back of pictures. The magnets will stick to thumbtacks on the board.

On the following two pages, you will find some sample bulletin boards. They should give you some ideas for possible themes and techniques to make your bulletin board exciting and attractive.

ESTHER FINTON
Author, *Bulletin Boards Should Be More Than Something to Look At . . .*

BORDERS

1. Cut large sheets of colored construction paper into strips of 46 X 8 cm (18 X 3 in). Make as many as you need to surround your bulletin board.

2. Fold each strip in half, and in half again.

3. Select a pattern from the examples at right. You may want to make a cardboard sample of your pattern to trace onto each of your folded strips. Cut along the pencil lines indicated in your pattern.

4. Use straight pins to place the unfolded strips around your bulletin board.

Sample Borders

ABOUT THE BULLETIN BOARDS

Left: Reminders of summer camp include badges, a camp hat, and perhaps some photos of friends. The trunk-shaped board makes an appropriate background for any travel display. **Above right:** The food theme board decorated with heart borders is a handy place to keep school lunch menus or recipes. **Above far right:** A board cut into the shape of a fish is as decorative as an aquarium — and the cut paper fish do not have to be fed! **Right:** A semicircle bordered with paper umbrellas serves as a weather reporting station.

dieta

LETTERS

Cut pieces of paper or fabric to the letter size you want. Fold each piece as indicated by the dotted line on the letter you wish to make. Some letters require a vertical fold; others a horizontal; and letters G, J, N, Q, S, and Z require no fold at all. Using the entire paper, cut the shape for your letter, unfold — and enjoy the professional-looking results. You can change the style of your letters by rounding the edges or by changing the shape of the paper.

First fold in half to cut letter. Fold again to cut out center. Cut off bottom to make P.

Cut an O. Unfold and cut for a C.

Cut an E. Make it a straight line for an I. Cut off top and middle for L. Cut off bottom for F.

Cut the R unfolded. Fold top to cut opening.

Do not fold to cut G, J, N, Q, S, Z.

BULLFIGHTING

Bullfighting has been called Spain's favorite sport. But to call it this is wrong for two reasons: first, soccer (called *fútbol* in Spain) is the most popular sport; and second, bullfighting cannot really be called a sport. It should be called, more properly, a spectacle, an exhibition, or a performance, like a ballet. However, this ballet is like dancing on a tightrope, because if the bullfighter makes a mistake, he is likely to be injured or killed.

A bullfight is not really a contest between a man and a bull. Actually it is a contest between a man and himself. The audience goes to the ring to see a man conquer his own fear of the horns and take as many chances with the bull as possible. The men who most gracefully execute the most daring maneuvers become the stars.

Bullfighting is one of the few ways a poor boy can become rich and famous in Spain and Latin America—and many *matadores* have become millionaires. But for every successful *matador*, there are hundreds who have fallen by the wayside and are forgotten. Many do not have the necessary grace and skill. Some are crippled by the bulls, and some are killed.

▶ HOW DID BULLFIGHTING BEGIN?

Bullfighting has existed in one form or another for more than 2,000 years. The ancient Cretans used to perform what they called bull dancing. Both men and women would leap over the bulls' horns in graceful, reckless exhibitions.

One of the reasons that Spain has been the leading place for bullfighting is that the fighting bull first lived there. Bullfighting cannot be done with ordinary animals. It requires the special *toro de lidia,* or *toro bravo,* which is as different from a domestic bull as a cobra is from a gopher snake, or a wolf is from a dog. For centuries, herds of these fierce bulls roamed wild over Spain. The Romans imported them for their savage battles against men and other animals in the Colosseum. The bulls usually won, even when pitted against lions and tigers. The Arabs in Spain helped make bullfighting popular around the early 12th century. In those days the spectacle consisted of a skillful horseman killing a wild bull with a lance while guiding his horse so as to avoid injury both to his mount and to himself. It is said that the famous cavalier El Cid was the first Spaniard to take part in organized bullfighting in an arena.

Bullfighting quickly became very popular, and for centuries rich Moors and Christians, nobles, and even kings practiced it. No feast day was complete without a *corrida de toros.*

The common people used to help the nobles fight the bulls, but they did so on foot. They used capes to distract the bull and keep it from charging at their bodies. Little by little this became the more exciting part of the act, and the ritual developed as we know it today.

Left: *Paseo,* or entrance parade, into the bullring in Madrid. Each *matador* leads his *cuadrilla,* or team of assistants. Right: The *matador* performs a classic *verónica.* The bull charges hard, passing before the *matador,* who swings the cape in front of its nose.

THE ARENA AND THE TOREROS

The first thing a person sees in the *plaza de toros,* or arena, is the gaily dressed and excited crowd. When the band strikes up, *toreros* stride into the arena and parade around it while the *aficionados,* or fans, cheer.

All people who fight bulls are called *toreros.* The *matadores* are the stars of the show, and there are usually three in an afternoon's program. Each one has two *picadores* and three *banderilleros* to help him. It is old-fashioned and incorrect to refer to bullfighters as *toreadores.* (The "toreador" of Bizet's opera *Carmen* is actually a *matador.*)

THE CONTEST

The men stride across the sand of the arena, and then the ring is cleared and the bull charges in. The bull has not been trained or tortured or starved; yet, because of its centuries of breeding, it knows it is supposed to fight. A *banderillero* will run out and swirl his cape a few times in front of the animal to demonstrate to his *matador* how this particular animal charges, since each bull has a different style of fighting.

Now the *matador* goes out. Where the *banderillero* was awkward and stayed safely away from the bull's horns, the *matador,* being the star, must stand very close to the animal. He swings the cape gracefully and lets the horns slice just by his legs. On each pass that the *matador* performs well, the crowd yells and cheers. If the *matador* bends over awkwardly and steps back out of the path of the bull as the *banderillero* did, the crowd boos loudly. The audience would like to see the bullfighters behave exactly opposite from the way they would behave if they had to stand in front of a huge bull with only a cape for protection. The bull goes at the cloth not because it is red, but because the *matador* knows just how to shake the cape to attract the animal and make it go at the lure instead of his body. The cape is yellow on one side and red on the other, but because bulls are color-blind, it makes no difference which side the *matador* presents to the animal.

After the *matador* does several passes, called *verónicas,* a trumpet blows and the *picadores* enter on horseback. They prick the bull with their lances in order to weaken his neck muscles. They do this so that at the end the *matador* will be able to reach over the horns and place the sword blade where it should go—between the bull's shoulder blades. The horses have been safely padded since 1930, so there is less chance that they will be injured by the charging bull.

Next, each of the three *banderilleros* places two *banderillas* ("barbed sticks") in the animal's shoulders. These further weaken the bull's neck muscles.

Finally the *matador* goes out with the sword and a little cape called the *muleta.* This is the most dangerous time of the fight, in spite of the fact that the bull is tired. There have been about 125 great *matadores* since 1700, and 42 of them have been killed, generally during this part of the bullfight. This is because the little cape is so small, the bull has learned so much during the course of the fight, and the man must make his most dangerous passes at this time.

THE KILL

Killing the bull, called "the moment of truth," is the most dangerous maneuver of all. The man must run at the bull at the same time that the bull runs at him, and plunge the sword between the shoulder blades. When this is done correctly, the bull will drop over dead almost instantly.

If the *matador* has done his job well, the crowd applauds, and he is awarded the ear of the bull as a trophy. If he has done a superior job, he is given both ears and the tail. The meat of the bulls is sometimes given to the poor, but usually the animals are butchered in back of the arena and sold for steaks.

Joselito and Manolete, two of the greatest bullfighters of the 20th century, were killed by bulls. Joselito died when he was only 25; Manolete at the age of 30. Many other *matadores,* like the great Antonio Ordóñez and El Cordobés of Spain, have been severely injured in the bullring. The ambition of most bullfighters, who usually come from poor families, is to make enough money to buy a bull ranch and retire at about the age of 30.

The best fights in Spain are held in Madrid, Seville, Valencia, and Málaga during the spring and summer. In Latin America the best fights can be seen in Mexico City or Lima, Peru. In Portugal the only ring of importance is in Lisbon.

BARNABY CONRAD
Author, *La Fiesta Brava, The Death of Manolete*

BUNCHE, RALPH (1904–1971)

Ralph Bunche was the first African American awarded the Nobel Peace Prize. He received this honor in 1950 for his work as a United Nations mediator in the Middle East.

Bunche, the grandson of a slave, was born in Detroit, Michigan, on August 7, 1904. His parents died when he was 13, and he and his sister went to live with their grandmother in California. He received a scholarship to the University of California but still had to take odd jobs to pay for his books, meals, and carfare. Nevertheless he managed to play on three basketball championship teams and to graduate with highest honors. He continued his education at Harvard University, receiving an M.A. degree in 1928.

Bunche began his career teaching political science at Howard University and, soon after, married Ruth Harris, who had been one of his students. The couple had three children. Bunche left Howard for a time to continue his studies at Harvard and received a Ph.D. degree in 1934.

From 1938 to 1940, Bunche worked as chief assistant to the Swedish sociologist Gunnar Myrdal on a survey of race relations in America. The result was an important book titled *An American Dilemma* (1944). He later worked for the U.S. government, becoming the first black to head a division of the State Department. In 1946 he accepted a permanent post at the United Nations.

In 1948, war broke out between Israel and its Arab neighbors. Count Folke Bernadotte was appointed by the United Nations to help end the dispute. When Bernadotte was assassinated, Bunche took his place. He received the Nobel Peace Prize for his role in persuading the warring countries to stop fighting.

He continued to serve the United Nations in various troubled parts of the world, including what is now the Democratic Republic of Congo, Cyprus, and the Middle East. From 1967 until his retirement in 1971, he was the undersecretary-general of the United Nations. Bunche died on December 9, 1971.

Reviewed by MARGUERITE CARTWRIGHT
Hunter College, City University of New York

BUNKER HILL, BATTLE OF. See REVOLUTIONARY WAR.

BUOYANCY. See FLOATING AND BUOYANCY.

BURBANK, LUTHER (1849–1926)

Luther Burbank once remarked: "I shall be contented if because of me there shall be better fruits and fairer flowers." In 50 years of work, he more than achieved his goal. He developed 618 new varieties of plants.

Burbank was born on a farm near Lancaster, Massachusetts, on March 7, 1849. At 15 he entered Lancaster Academy, where he received some instruction in science. But it was in the Lancaster library that Burbank—at the age of 19—discovered the writings of Charles Darwin. From Darwin, Burbank learned how better varieties of plants could be developed. The secret was to select seeds from those plants with the most desirable traits and to breed for those traits.

A few years later, in Lunenburg, Massachusetts, Burbank set about developing his first "new creation," a larger and firmer potato. He planted potato seeds and selected the best potatoes from the resulting crop for replanting. The variety he developed in this way is still known as the Burbank potato.

In 1875, Burbank sold his farm and moved to Santa Rosa, California. There he set up a small nursery garden, greenhouse, and orchard, where he grew and sold plants to support his research. He continued his selection process and also developed new plants, such as the Shasta daisy, by crossbreeding.

Burbank bought more acres and established a world-famous experimental farm. His yearly catalog, *New Creations*, issued from 1893 to 1901, described his experiments. He used scientific principles and methods, but his main interest was in practical results.

Burbank died on April 11, 1926. Although he left behind little documentation of his work, Burbank is considered a significant contributor to the field of science.

JOHN S. BOWMAN
Author and Science Editor

BURGER, WARREN. See MINNESOTA (Famous People).

BURGOYNE, JOHN. See REVOLUTIONARY WAR (Profiles).

BURKINA FASO

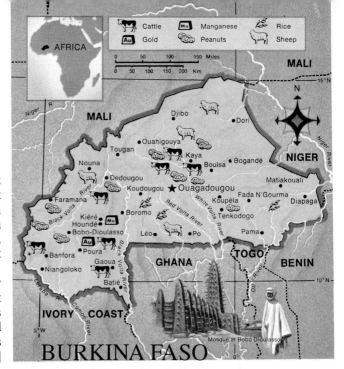

Mosque at Bobo Dioulasso

BURKINA FASO

Burkina Faso is an inland nation of West Africa. For centuries it was the site of a great empire ruled by the Mossi people. The Mossi are still the most numerous people of Burkina Faso. But their empire has long ceased to exist, and Burkina Faso today is one of the poorest nations of Africa.

In 1896, Burkina Faso became a colony of France as part of French West Africa. It gained its independence in 1960. It was called Upper Volta until 1984, when it adopted the name Burkina Faso, which is sometimes translated as "land of the honest [or upright] people." Politically, "Faso" has the approximate meaning of People's Republic.

▶ PEOPLE

Most of Burkina Faso's people live in the central and southwestern parts of the country. The Mossi, who inhabit the central region, make up about one third of the population. Other ethnic groups include the Bobo, Lobi-Dagari, Senufo, Gurunsi, and Mande. The sparsely settled northeast is the home of the Songhai, Fulani, and Tuareg.

Language. French is the official language, but each of Burkina Faso's peoples has its own language or dialect. Moré, the language of the Mossi, is widely spoken in central Burkina Faso.

Religion. The majority of the people practice traditional African religions. About 25 percent are Muslims and some 10 percent Christian.

Way of Life. The Mossi way of life still reflects the discipline enforced by early Mossi rulers. The actions of every individual must conform to a strict code of behavior. The family is the most important unit. Each family lives in a walled compound containing several small, round clay-and-mud huts. Most Mossi are farmers. The family fields surround the compound.

The Bobo, like the Mossi, are family-centered. Their dwellings, however, are larger than those of the Mossi and are built together in compact villages and towns.

The Fulani and Tuareg of the northeast are nomadic herders, who travel with their livestock seeking grazing land.

▶ LAND

Most of Burkina Faso is a vast plateau consisting of savanna, or grassland. The northeast is part of the Sahel, a region of sparse vegetation on the edge of the Sahara desert. The country's three principal rivers are the Red Volta, the Black Volta, and the White Volta.

The soil is generally poor, although crops can be grown where there is adequate rainfall. When the rains are long delayed, however, drought results.

Climate. Burkina Faso has a hot, dry climate, with an average daytime temperature of 82°F (28°C). Rainfall is heaviest in the southwest and scantiest in the northeast. During the hottest season, from about March to May, the harmattan, a dry, searing wind, blows south from the Sahara.

Cities. Ouagadougou, which lies in central Burkina Faso, was once a capital of the Mossi empire. It is now Burkina Faso's capital and largest city, with a population of more than 240,000. Bobo-Dioulasso, the second largest city, is located in the southwest.

▶ ECONOMY

Burkina Faso's economy is based on agriculture and the raising of livestock, particularly cattle, sheep, and goats. The chief food crops include millet, sorghum, peanuts, cassava, and rice. The major exports are livestock and livestock products, gold, and cotton. Severe droughts periodically devastate the economy.

Industry is limited, and young Burkinabe men often seek work in neighboring countries. The country depends heavily on foreign aid.

▶ HISTORY AND GOVERNMENT

The ancestors of the Mossi probably arrived in Burkina Faso in the 1000's. They founded several kingdoms, the most important centered at Ouagadougou.

Europeans first arrived in the region in the late 1800's. France subdued the Mossi kings and became the dominant power. The colony of Upper Volta was created by the French in 1919. It was divided among the other colonies of French West Africa in 1932 but was restored as a separate territory in 1948. Upper Volta gained self-government in 1958 and complete independence in 1960.

Since Independence. The country's history since independence has been stormy. The first president, Maurice Yaméogo, was deposed in 1966 in a military coup led by Lieutenant Colonel Sangoulé Lamizana. Lamizana remained in power until 1980, when economic woes led to his overthrow.

Young radicals led by Captain Thomas Sankara seized power in 1983. The popular Sankara encouraged local efforts to build schools, clinics, and agricultural cooperatives. In 1984 he changed the name of the country to Burkina Faso to end a link to its colonial past.

FACTS and figures

BURKINA FASO is the official name of the country.

LOCATION: West Africa.

AREA: 105,869 sq mi (274,200 km²).

POPULATION: 11,300,000 (estimate).

CAPITAL AND LARGEST CITY: Ouagadougou.

MAJOR LANGUAGES: French (official), Moré, other African languages.

MAJOR RELIGIOUS GROUPS: Traditional African religions, Muslim, Christian.

GOVERNMENT: Republic. **Head of state**—president. **Head of government**—prime minister. **Legislature**—National Assembly.

CHIEF PRODUCTS: Agricultural—livestock (cattle, sheep, goats), cotton, sorghum, millet, peanuts, cassava, rice. **Manufactured**—livestock products, processed foods. **Mineral**—gold.

MONETARY UNIT: African Financial Community (CFA) franc (1 franc = 100 centimes).

In 1987, Sankara was killed by one of his associates, Captain Blaise Compaoré, who then seized power. A multiparty constitution adopted in 1991 reduced the powers of the presidency and allowed for the president and members of the legislature to be elected directly by the people. Compaoré was elected president in 1991 and again in 1998.

H. R. JARRETT
Author, *Physical Geography for West African Schools*

The distinctive architecture of the people of southwestern Burkina Faso is shown in this mosque (Muslim house of worship), located near the city of Bobo-Dioulasso.

BURMA (MYANMAR)

Burma is a nation of Southeast Asia and the largest of the mainland Southeast Asian countries. It has sometimes been called the Land of Pagodas, because of the many pagodas, or Buddhist shrines, that dot the landscape.

Although it shares borders with a number of countries, Burma has been isolated for much of its long history. It was shut off first by the mountains that enclose it on three sides, but also by the choice of its ancient kings and some of its recent political leaders. In 1989, Burma's leaders changed its name to Myanmar, which is "Burma" spelled in Burmese, the national language.

▶THE PEOPLE

Ethnic Groups. The people of Burma come from many different ethnic groups, but the Burmans are the most numerous, making up about two thirds of the population. Their ancestors migrated to what is now Burma from the mountains of southern China more than a thousand years ago and mixed with the people already living in the region.

The main non-Burman peoples include the Chin, the Kachin, the Shan, the Karen, and the Mon. They mostly occupy the mountains and hills and border areas, and some live in neighboring countries as well. Many have never been under the complete control of the central Burmese government. There are many smaller groups, each of which has its own culture. There are also ethnic Indians, Bangladeshis, and Chinese.

Burma has been called the Land of Pagodas, because of the many pagodas, or Buddhist shrines, found throughout the country. Burmese pagodas are distinctive for their cone-shaped spires, which are often covered in gold leaf.

Language and Education. More than 120 different languages and dialects are spoken, but Burmese, the language of the Burmans, is the country's official language. Since it is taught in the schools, it is spoken or understood by most of the people. Burmese is related to Tibetan, which in turn is related to Chinese. English is used as a second language, particularly by educated Burmese. It is a reminder of the time, from the late 1800's to 1948, when Burma was ruled by Britain.

Basic education consists of one year of kindergarten, followed by four years of primary school, four years of middle school, and two years of high school. However, since government budgets are limited and the country is large, there are still shortages of schools and teachers in the smaller and remote areas. The

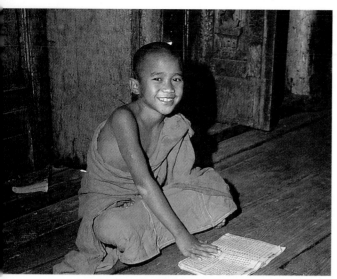

A young Burmese boy wears the saffron-colored robes of a Buddhist monk. Burmese boys traditionally spend a period of time serving as novice, or beginning, monks.

At one time, before the advent of public education, most village children went to monastery schools, where they learned to read and write and studied Buddhist scriptures. Because of this, traditional Burma had one of the highest literacy rates (the percentage of people able to read and write) in Asia.

The Farm Village. Most Burmese live in villages and are farmers. Farm houses are often built on poles with walls of matting and roofs made of palm-leaf thatch. Houses usually have a porch, which serves as both a living and dining area. The houses are grouped together, along dirt paths, with each having a small garden where vegetables and fruits are grown and where domestic animals may be kept. Most farmers plow their land with water buffalo.

Since generous giving and helping others is a part of Buddhist belief, visitors are always offered something to eat, and wayfarers can be assured of water to ease their thirst.

Food and Dress. The Burmese eat their meals at low tables while seated on woven mats on the floor. Rice is the staple food and is eaten at every meal. Burmese use spoons as eating utensils, but do not usually use forks. Rice is rolled into small balls with the fingers and dipped into various dishes.

country's major universities are located in the cities of Rangoon (Yangon), the capital, and Mandalay.

All formal education is government sponsored. But because schools are crowded and standards have fallen, many families in the cities and towns send their children to private tutoring schools in addition to public schools.

Religion. The first Burman kings adopted the Buddhist religion (which originated in India) from the Mon people, whom they conquered in the A.D. 1000's. Today almost all Burmans are Buddhists, as are the Shan and Mon. Some of the hill peoples still follow ancient tribal religions, while others were converted to Christianity by British and American missionaries. Burma also has substantial Hindu and Muslim minorities, chiefly the Indians and Bangladeshis.

▶**WAY OF LIFE**

The Role of Buddhism. Buddhism plays an important role in the life of the people. Burmese boys between the ages of 6 and 13 serve as novice (beginning) monks for a short time, and some remain in the monkhood. Almost every village has a monastery, headed by a monk who is a teacher as well as a spiritual leader. The monastery is the center of village life. In addition to providing for the religious needs of the people, it often serves as a school, a social center, a place for the traveler to rest, and even as a hospital or clinic.

FACTS and figures

UNION OF MYANMAR is the official name of the country. Historically, it has been known as Burma.

LOCATION: Southeast Asia.

AREA: 261,218 sq mi (676,552 km²).

POPULATION: 46,800,000 (estimate).

CAPITAL AND LARGEST CITY: Rangoon (Yangon).

MAJOR LANGUAGES: Burmese (official), English, numerous other languages.

MAJOR RELIGIOUS GROUP: Buddhist.

GOVERNMENT: Republic, under military rule: Since 1997, the government has been led by the Peace and Development Council.

CHIEF PRODUCTS: Agricultural—rice, sugarcane, beans, peas, peanuts, sesame, corn, bananas. **Manufactured**—processed foods, lumber (particularly teak), cement, textiles, paper, consumer goods. **Mineral**—gypsum, copper, lead, tin, jade, silver, rubies, sapphires.

MONETARY UNIT: Kyat (1 kyat = 100 pyas).

Burmese food is tasty and spicy. Curries (dishes spiced with curry powder), vegetables, and fish are particularly favored. A sauce or paste made from fish or shrimp is commonly used as a seasoning. Since Buddhism discourages the killing of animals, meat is eaten only rarely. Coconut and coconut milk are also important ingredients in Burmese cooking, as are fruits such as mangoes, papaya, and bananas.

Most Burmese wear a sarong-like skirt called a *longyi* (or *lungyi*), with men's and women's garments differing in patterns and the way they are tied. On formal occasions men wear a colorful cloth headdress called a *gaungbaung*. Women go bareheaded but often wear flowers in their hair, especially young, unmarried women who frequently tie their lustrous black hair in a ponytail. Married women traditionally wear their hair in a bun.

Names and Social Attitudes. Burmese have given names, but no family names. The first syllable of the given name is usually determined by the day of the week on which one is born. Titles of respect are related to concepts of family, so that an older woman of good reputation is called *Daw,* or "aunt," rather than Mrs. (or Miss or Ms.). A man is addressed as *U* (pronounced 'oo'), meaning "uncle," rather than Mr. Male friends may refer to each other as "elder brother" or "younger brother."

In general, Burma has had a very open social system, without great landed wealth or restrictions based on birth or occupation. One may rise socially through education, the monkhood, the military, and politics. Women have always been treated with respect in Burmese society and traditionally have kept their own property when they married. They are active in business and in many professions, and include an opposition political leader.

Holidays. Some Burmese holidays commemorate national events, but the most important are religious in nature. The Burmese New Year, or Water Festival (*Thingyan*), occurs in April. This is a time when the heat is intense, and celebrants sprinkle water on images of the Buddha as well as on one another as a blessing. This often becomes an excuse for good natured water fights. The Festival of Lights, or *Thadingyut*, comes in October. It celebrates Buddha's return to earth from the realm of the gods and is marked by the lighting of thousands of candles in pagodas and homes.

BURMA (Myanmar)

THE LAND

Mountains and Seas. Burma shares mountainous or ruggedly hilly boundaries with China on the north and northeast, Thailand and Laos on the east, and India and Bangladesh on the west. In the north the mountains form part of the high Himalayan range and some are permanently snowcapped. Even the less mountainous areas are difficult to cross, although the tribal hill peoples do so for purposes of trade. In the south, Burma has a long coastline on the Bay of Bengal and Andaman Sea, arms of the Indian Ocean.

The River System. Burma's major river is the Irrawaddy, which rises in the far north. The Irrawaddy is the chief communications link between central and southern Burma. It was the "road to Mandalay" in Rudyard Kip-

Right: Most of Burma's rice, its chief crop, is grown in the fertile area drained by the major rivers. Some of the mountains that enclose Burma on three sides can be seen in the distance. *Below:* Water buffalo haul logs of teak, a valuable hardwood that is the country's main export.

ling's famous poem *Mandalay* (see Cities section). The Salween River to the east is less important, because it is not navigable (usable by ships) for most of its length. The Sittang River drains the eastern part of central Burma.

Most Burmese live in the area drained by the Irrawaddy, its western tributary (branch), the Chindwin River, and the Sittang. Sediment deposited by the rivers in flood have enriched the soil, creating Burma's most fertile region.

A Monsoon Climate. Burma has three seasons, based on the monsoon winds. From October through February the winds bring dry weather with warm days and cool nights. In March the hot dry season begins. The rainy season begins in June, as humid winds sweep in from the Bay of Bengal, bringing up to 200 inches (5,080 millimeters) of rainfall along the coast. The rains are dissipated by the mountains, however, and central Burma remains relatively dry. It is after the first rains that the hard, dry, compacted earth is moistened and farmers can plow and plant their rice and other crops.

▶ THE ECONOMY

Compared to other Asian countries, Burma has an abundance of fertile land and is not overpopulated. Although the people have fewer goods than in wealthier nations, there are also fewer differences between rich and poor than in most societies. Whatever its problems, Burma has rarely suffered from a shortage of food.

Economic Experiments. From independence in 1948 until 1988, Burmese governments were socialist in ideology, and much of the country's industry was state-controlled. This was a reaction against the domination of the economy by foreigners—British, Indians, and Chinese—during the colonial period. An extreme period of state control over the economy was begun in 1963 under military rule. This economic system failed, and the potentially rich country became even poorer. Since 1988 the government has encouraged private enterprise in many fields, as well as foreign investment, although certain industries remain a state monopoly.

Agriculture. The country's basic crop is rice, which is grown in wet, irrigated fields on the plains and in dry fields in the highlands. At one time, Burma was the world's leading exporter of rice, and rice remains a principal export. Sesame, peanuts, peas, beans, sugarcane, peppers, cotton, and various fruits are also grown in the lowlands.

In the highlands, *swidden* (slash and burn) agriculture is practiced among certain tribes. Trees and brush are felled and burned, and crops are planted. The soil is enriched this way for a few years. Then, as crop production diminishes, these fields are abandoned and new ones found. As populations increased, this system became wasteful and caused damage to the environment.

In remote regions, where government influence is limited, opium poppies are grown. The opium is made into heroin, which then enters the world drug market. The government has tried to control this illegal practice, but with little success.

Manufacturing, Forestry, Mining. Chief manufactured products include processed foods, lumber, cement and other construction materials, textiles, and fertilizers. Consumer goods were often smuggled, or brought into the country illegally. This was because Burmese industry could not produce them efficiently and they could not legally be imported. Many of these goods came overland through the mountainous regions of Thailand and China. The government has since legalized this trade.

Forests, which cover nearly half the land, are one of Burma's most valuable natural resources. Burma has about 75 percent of the world's reserves of teak and is the leading supplier of this valuable hardwood, which is used chiefly in making furniture. Teak is now the country's main export.

Burma has extensive mineral deposits, including lead, tin, tungsten, zinc, silver, copper, coal, and natural gas. It is also famed for such gemstones as jade, rubies, and sapphires. Although once an oil-exporting nation, Burma must now import some of this fuel.

▶**CITIES**

Rangoon (or Yangon), in the south, is the country's capital, largest city, and chief seaport. It has a population of more than 2.5 million. One of the city's most impressive sites is the thousand-year-old Shwe Dagon Pagoda, the most revered Buddhist shrine in Southeast Asia. Most of Burma's industry is located in the city and nearby.

Mandalay, the second largest city, lies on the Irrawaddy River in central Burma. The capital of the kingdom of Burma from 1860 to 1885, it is the country's cultural center. Other important cities are Moulmein, a port on the Salween River in the southeast; Bassein in the delta region in the south; and Pegu, a city near Rangoon that was once a Mon capital.

▶**HISTORY AND GOVERNMENT**

Early History. After migrating south from China in the A.D. 700's, the Burmans unified the country beginning with King Anawratha (1044–77). Their magnificent capital on the banks of the Irrawaddy River, Pagan, a city of some 5,000 pagodas, remains one of the most important historical sites of Southeast Asia. The classical age of Burma collapsed when Pagan fell to the troops of China's Mongol emperor Kublai Khan, in 1287.

Following a period of Shan rule, two powerful Burman kingdoms arose. The Toungoo dynasty (1484–1752) controlled Burma and northern Thailand. The Konbaung dynasty (1752–1885) pushed into eastern India, bringing Burma into conflict with Britain and its Indian colony.

British Rule to Independence. Beginning in 1824, three wars were fought by the British and Burmese. Known as the Anglo-Burmese wars, they gradually eliminated Burma as an independent kingdom. In 1886, Burma became a British colony, governed from India.

Although in ruins, Pagan, capital of the first Burman kings, reflects the splendor of Burma's past.

Anti-government demonstrations, begun by students and monks (*right*), forced Burma's military rulers to hold multiparty elections in 1990. But the results, a victory for the opposition, led by Aung San Suu Kyi (*above*), were ignored by the military, which held on to power. For her efforts, Aung San Suu Kyi was awarded the 1991 Nobel Peace Prize.

Burmese resistance to colonial rule never really ceased. After demands for more control over its own affairs, Burma was separated from India in 1937 and given limited self-government within the British Empire. In 1941, during World War II, the Japanese invaded Burma, drove out the British, and established a Burmese state under Japanese rule.

Burma was reoccupied by the British in 1945, aided by Burmese nationalists. General Aung San, considered the father of independent Burma, negotiated his country's independence from Britain. Although Aung San was killed in 1947, an independent Burma came into existence the next year. U Nu was its first prime minister.

Recent History. From 1948 until 1958, the Union of Burma was a parliamentary democracy. The union was a weak one, however. Some ethnic groups, along with Communists and other dissidents, were in revolt against the central government.

In 1958 the military led by General Ne Win overthrew U Nu and took control of the country. They relinquished power to U Nu after elections in 1960, but seized control of the government again in 1962, ruling by decree. In 1974 a new constitution established a highly centralized government under a single political party, the Burma Socialist Program Party (BSPP), dominated by the military in civilian clothes.

Military rule created social and economic inequality as well as political repression. In 1988 student unrest triggered massive demonstrations that forced the abandonment of the single party system, the end of the BSPP, and the opening up of the economy. As continuing demonstrations were about to topple the regime, a new military group seized power in September 1988. The new military rulers governed as the State Law and Order Restoration Council (SLORC).

Multiparty elections for the National Assembly were held in 1990. The opposition, led by Aung San's daughter, Aung San Suu Kyi, who had been placed under house arrest, won 80 percent of the seats. But the election results were ignored by the military. Aung San Suu Kyi was awarded the Nobel Peace Prize in 1991 and was released in 1995. SLORC was disbanded in November 1997, but the military remained firmly in control. Earlier that year, the country was admitted to the Association of Southeast Asian Nations (ASEAN).

THOMAS F. BARTON
Indiana University
Revised and updated by DAVID I. STEINBERG
Georgetown University
Author, *Burma's Road to Development*

BURNS. See FIRST AID.

BURNS, ROBERT (1759–1796)

Robert Burns, Scotland's greatest poet, becomes the world's favorite each New Year's Eve with the traditional singing of his "Auld Lang Syne." It is fitting tribute to a poet who loved good company, good song, and simple pleasures.

Robert was born on January 25, 1759, in Ayrshire, Scotland. His father was a poverty-stricken farmer, but a man of great character who valued education and strict morality. Although Robert's help was needed on the farm, his father encouraged him to read and gave him as much schooling as he could.

Robert read everything he could, from collections of songs to Shakespeare and Milton. He carried small volumes in his pocket and studied them while he was in the fields or at the table. He began writing his own verses and collected them in a scrapbook.

When his father died in 1784, Robert and his brother Gilbert tried to make a success of farming but failed. Robert fell in love with Jean Armour, but her father, a prosperous builder, refused to have him as a son-in-law. Robert then planned to seek his fortune in Jamaica. But first, he published *Poems, Chiefly in the Scottish Dialect* (1786). The poems were a great success.

In 1787 a second edition of Burns's poems appeared. He began to collect, adapt, and compose lyrics of folk songs for a publication called *The Scots Musical Museum*. For this and for George Thomson's *Select Collection of Original Scottish Airs* (1793), Burns composed over 300 lyrics. Some of his best-known poems are "Sweet Afton," "To a Mouse," "John Anderson, My Jo," and the patriotic "Scots, Wha Hae."

In 1788, Burns began a new life of farming, at Ellisland, near Dumfries, and finally married Jean Armour. But he failed again at farming. He took a government position as a tax officer and moved to Dumfries in 1791. His outspoken sympathy for the French Revolution damaged his popularity. Illness added to his troubles. He died on July 21, 1796, a broken and bitter man. But his poems found a permanent place in literature.

Reviewed by GEORGIA DUNBAR
Hofstra University

BURNSIDE, AMBROSE EVERETT. See RHODE ISLAND (Famous People).

Robert Burns wrote in both standard English and the dialect of the Scottish farmers and villagers he had known all his life. Some of his poetry was written in a mixed language, using English grammar and Scottish vocabulary. Sometimes he simply spelled English words in the Scots fashion. In the following poem, the Scottish word "gang" means "go," and "weel" means "well."

A RED, RED ROSE

O, my luve is like a red, red rose,
That's newly sprung in June
O, my luve is like the melodie,
That's sweetly played in tune.

As fair art thou, my bonie lass,
So deep in luve am I,
And I will luve thee still, my dear,
Till a' the seas gang dry.

Till a' the seas gang dry, my dear,
And the rocks melt wi' the sun!
And I will luve thee still, my dear,
While the sands o' life shall run.

And fare thee weel, my only luve,
And fare thee weel a while!
And I will come again, my luve,
Tho' it were ten thousand mile!

Aaron Burr was a Revolutionary War hero and a leading lawyer and politician whose career was destroyed by poor judgment and uncontrolled ambition.

BURR, AARON (1756–1836)

Aaron Burr was a brilliant lawyer, a hero of the Revolutionary War, and a vice-president of the United States. But most Americans remember Burr only as the man who killed Alexander Hamilton in a duel.

Burr was born in Newark, New Jersey, on February 6, 1756. His father was president of the College of New Jersey (now Princeton University). Aaron was admitted to the college when he was 13 and graduated with honors at 16. Later he studied law.

At the outbreak of the Revolutionary War, Burr joined the Continental Army. He served in the American march on Quebec in 1775. Later he was a staff officer under George Washington. Once, by disobeying orders, he saved an entire brigade from capture by the British. But poor health cut short his military career, and Burr left the army in 1779.

In 1782, Burr married Theodosia Prevost, the widow of a British officer. They had one child, a girl named Theodosia after her mother. Burr carefully educated his daughter since he believed girls should be as well educated as boys. Burr's wife lived only 12 years after their marriage, but she was a steadying influence on her husband.

Burr was a leading figure in the legal, social, and political life of New York. He served in the U.S. Senate and in the New York State Assembly. In his early years in New York, Burr had become friendly with another prominent young lawyer, Alexander Hamilton. But political rivalry soon turned the two men into bitter enemies.

In the presidential election of 1800, Burr and Thomas Jefferson both received the same number of votes. So the election was decided by the House of Representatives. After 36 ballots, Jefferson was elected president, and Burr became vice-president.

Hamilton had led the fight to block Burr's election. The hatred between the two men finally led to a duel near Weehawken, New Jersey, on July 11, 1804. Hamilton fired into the air, but Burr's bullet hit home. Hamilton died the next day, and Burr fled to escape arrest.

After leaving the vice-presidency in 1805, Burr found private life dull. He could not live in New York again because of the duel. He began to plan an expedition against Spain's Mexican possessions. In 1805 and 1806 he traveled down the Mississippi River, but his real reasons for this journey are still a mystery. Some people said that he planned to set up his own empire in the Southwest, with himself as emperor.

In 1807, General James Wilkinson, who was secretly in the pay of the Spanish, denounced Burr to Jefferson. The President ordered Burr's arrest for treason. He was tried at Richmond, Virginia, with Supreme Court Justice John Marshall as judge. Burr was accused of trying to separate the western states from the Union. Marshall ruled that there was no clear proof of treason, and Burr was freed. But his reputation was ruined.

Burr went to Europe and did not return to the United States until 1812. He had hoped to devote his declining years to his daughter and grandson. But both Theodosia and her son died within a year of each other.

Burr spent his last years practicing law. He died, almost forgotten, on Staten Island, New York, on September 14, 1836, and was buried at Princeton, near his father.

Perhaps Thomas Jefferson best summed up the fatal flaw in Burr's character when he wrote: ''No man's history proves better the value of honesty. With that, what might he not have been?''

Reviewed by RICHARD B. MORRIS
Columbia University

See also HAMILTON, ALEXANDER.

BURROUGHS, JOHN (1837–1921)

One of America's greatest nature writers was John Burroughs. He delighted in exploring the quiet world of nature and then sharing his appreciation and knowledge with others through his lyrical prose.

Born on April 3, 1837, John Burroughs was one of ten children. His youth was spent on a small family farm near Roxbury, New York. It was there that he began his lifelong study of nature as he tramped along the untamed Rock Creek, observing the flowers and animals around him.

At various times in his life, Burroughs was a teacher, treasury clerk, and bank examiner. But it was as a naturalist and author that he became well known. Burroughs began his publishing career by contributing essays to the *Atlantic Monthly* and other magazines. A biography of his close friend Walt Whitman, *Notes on Walt Whitman as Poet and Person* (1867), was his first book to be published.

Never comfortable with the clamor and noise of city life, Burroughs made his home in the Catskill Mountains. "Where cattle and woodchuck thrive, there thrive I," he once

wrote. For much of the time, he lived in a log house, called Slabsides. As he gained recognition for his work, friends and important men of his day came to visit "the Sage of Slabsides."

During his long life, Burroughs completed 27 books. They include *Wake-Robin* (1871), *Winter Sunshine* (1875), *Fresh Fields* (1884), *Signs and Seasons* (1886), *Ways of Nature* (1905), and *The Breath of Life* (1915). He also received honorary degrees from several universities and was elected a member of the American Academy of Arts and Letters.

John Burroughs died on March 29, 1921. Each year in his honor, the John Burroughs Society presents awards for outstanding nature essays and books for young people and adults.

BARBARA TUFTY
Conservation Editor, Audubon Naturalist Society

BURTON, SIR RICHARD (1821–1890)

Sir Richard Burton was a man of extraordinary and varied gifts. He was one of the preeminent explorers of his time, an unequaled linguist who is said to have mastered 35 languages, and the author of dozens of books on his travels and other subjects. His most famous literary achievement is a 16-volume translation of *The Arabian Nights*.

Richard Francis Burton was born near Elstree, England, on March 19, 1821, and taken abroad by his parents at an early age. Although he received almost no formal education, he everywhere learned the local languages and dialects. He attended Trinity College, Oxford, but was expelled, and at 21 he joined the army of the British East India Company.

In India, Burton added to his knowledge of languages, learning Hindi, Farsi (Persian), and Arabic and living with native peoples. On

his first great journey, in 1853, he made a perilous trip to the Muslim holy cities of Medina and Mecca, disguised as a Muslim pilgrim. The next year he and John Speke explored East Africa, seeking the source of the Nile River. On a second expedition, in 1858, Burton discovered Lake Tanganyika. But, ill with malaria, he did not accompany Speke north and so did not share in the discovery of Lake Victoria, a main source of the Nile.

In 1861, Burton married Isabel Arundell. She was a devoted wife but had little sympathy for many of his chief interests. Burton's remaining years were spent as a British consular official, at posts around the world, exploring and writing. He was knighted in 1885. He died in Trieste (now in Italy) on October 20, 1890.

ARTHUR CAMPBELL TURNER
University of California, Riverside

BURUNDI

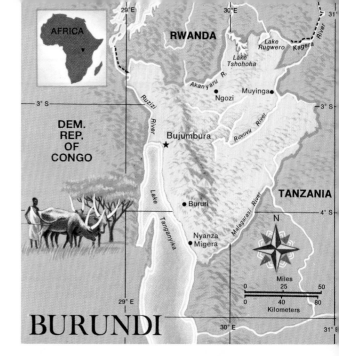

BURUNDI

Burundi is a small, densely populated nation located in the heart of east central Africa. Formerly known as Urundi, it was at one time a colony of Germany. Later, it was governed by Belgium. Burundi gained its independence as a kingdom in 1962. It became a republic in 1966.

▶ **THE PEOPLE**

The people of Burundi belong to three major ethnic groups—the Hutu, the Tutsi (also known as Watusi), and the Twa.

Most of Burundi's people are Hutu. The Hutu live mainly by farming. Tutsi, who make up about 15 percent of the population, are cattle raisers. Many Tutsi are quite tall. In the past they were the warriors who controlled and defended the land, dominating their Hutu neighbors. The Twa are Pygmies who live by hunting and fishing. They were the earliest inhabitants of the region. Today they make up a small part of the population.

The most widely used language is Kirundi. French, which dates from the time when Belgium governed Burundi, is also spoken. Both are official languages of the country. Over three-quarters of the people are Christians, mostly Roman Catholics. Some of the people are Muslims. Others practice traditional African religions.

Some children do not receive an education because of a shortage of neighborhood schools or because they are needed at home. Even very young children herd cattle, sheep, and goats in the mountain pastures. But the educational system is expanding. There is a university in Bujumbura, the capital city.

While many of the people wear European-style clothing in Bujumbura, outside the capital traditional dress is more common. Women usually wear long, colorfully patterned garments. Tutsi men traditionally wear full-length white cotton robes. Almost all the people live in rural areas, often in large family groups. Houses have a distinctive beehive shape, with high, pointed thatched roofs. The houses are sometimes grouped to form villages.

▶ **THE ECONOMY**

Burundi is a poor country whose economy is based largely on agriculture. Coffee, cotton, and tea are the main commercial crops. Coffee is the leading export. Great numbers of cattle, sheep, and goats also are raised. Cattle are especially valued, not only for their meat, milk, and hides, but as signs of importance and wealth. The chief food crops include sweet potatoes, corn, manioc, and sorghum.

FACTS and figures

REPUBLIC OF BURUNDI is the official name of the country.

LOCATION: East central Africa.

AREA: 10,747 sq mi (27,834 km²).

POPULATION: 5,500,000 (estimate).

CAPITAL AND LARGEST CITY: Bujumbura.

MAJOR LANGUAGES: Kirundi, French (both official).

MAJOR RELIGIOUS GROUPS: Christian, traditional African religions, Muslim.

GOVERNMENT: Republic. **Head of state**—president. **Head of government**—prime minister. **Legislature**—National Assembly.

CHIEF PRODUCTS: Coffee, cotton, tea, sweet potatoes, manioc (cassava), corn, sorghum, livestock.

MONETARY UNIT: Burundi franc (1 franc = 100 centimes).

The extent of Burundi's mineral resources is still unknown. But deposits of several minerals, including tin ore and nickel, have recently been discovered.

THE LAND

Burundi is situated in the mountains that form one side of Africa's Great Rift Valley. Lake Tanganyika borders the country on the southwest. Most of Burundi rises more than 5,000 feet (1,500 meters) above sea level. The high elevation makes the climate generally quite pleasant, even though the country lies so near the equator. Rainfall varies, however, and long droughts often cause crop failures.

Bujumbura, the capital, is Burundi's principal city. Located on Lake Tanganyika, it is also the country's chief port. The second largest town, Gitega, is situated in the central part of the country.

HISTORY AND GOVERNMENT

Burundi was one of the last African lands to become a European colony. Annexed by Germany at the end of the 1800's, it became part of the colony of German East Africa. After Germany's defeat in World War I, the League of Nations placed Burundi and what is now the country of Rwanda under the administration of Belgium. The territory was then known as Ruanda-Urundi. Belgium continued to govern the region, as a trust territory of the United Nations, until 1962, when Ruanda-Urundi gained independence as the separate nations of Rwanda and Burundi.

Since Independence. Following its independence, Burundi was a constitutional monarchy ruled by a *mwami* (king). In 1966 the *mwami* was deposed by the prime minister, Michel Micombero, who proclaimed Burundi a republic with himself as president. An unsuccessful attempt to restore the monarchy in 1972 led to the massacre of some 150,000 Hutu by the Tutsi. In 1976, Micombero was ousted in a military coup led by Colonel Jean-Baptiste Bagaza. Bagaza was himself overthrown in 1987 by Major Pierre Buyoya. Ethnic hostilities erupted again in 1988.

In 1992 voters approved a new, democratic constitution, and in 1993, in the first open elections in many years, Melchior Ndadaye, a Hutu, was chosen president. Following his election, however, rebels in the Tutsi-dominated army overthrew and murdered him. Cyprien Ntaryamira, a Hutu, was elected to replace him in 1994. But later that year he was killed in a plane crash. His successor, Sylvestre Ntibantunganya, was himself overthrown, in 1996, by the army, which again installed Pierre Buyoya as president. Meanwhile, new ethnic violence has caused the death of hundreds of thousands of people and the flight of many more out of the country.

ANN E. LARIMORE
Michigan State University

See also RWANDA.

Burundi is a small, densely populated country. To utilize all the available land, farmers often cultivate crops on terraced hillsides (*left*). Burundi women in colorfully patterned traditional garments (*right*) sell food at a local market.

BUSES

Every day, buses carry millions of people to work from their homes in the cities or the suburbs and back again in the evening. Thousands of other passengers take long bus trips for business or pleasure, and millions of children rely on buses to get to school.

The bus is relatively new as a means of travel. Motor buses came into use only when automobile travel began to gain popularity in the early 1900's. But the bus has ancestors much older than the automobile.

In the 1820's, twelve-passenger horse-drawn carriages began carrying people along Broadway in New York City. This marked the start of public transportation in the United States. Similar vehicles, called omnibuses, began to be used in other cities as well. *Omnibus* is a Latin word that means "for all."

Motorized bus lines were operating in some cities as early as 1905. The early buses, built by truck manufacturers, were designed to transport heavy loads rather than to provide for the comfort of passengers. The buses were dirty, bumpy to ride on, and lacked heating systems to keep passengers warm in winter.

In the following years, buses were improved with more comfortable seats, a lower floor for easier boarding, safety features such as shock-absorbing bumpers, and other features for easier maintenance. Today, buses are the most common form of public transportation in the United States and around the world.

▶ BUS SERVICES

There are many kinds of buses, and they are used in many different ways.

Public Transportation. The bus is an important part of the public transportation systems. Hundreds of bus routes may crisscross a single city. Special routes may link city hotels with shopping areas, museums, and other points of interest.

Many cities are able to offer bus service within 1/4 mile (0.4 kilometer) of nearly all their residents. Today's public-transit buses offer improved comfort and convenience. On some buses, a ramp or lift makes boarding easier for elderly riders and people with disabilities. In some areas, door-to-door services called "Dial-a-Ride" use small buses or vans to carry older people or others who may have trouble using the regular system.

Vehicles called articulated buses have been popular in Europe and are now seen in some cities in the United States. These buses are actually two units connected by a hinge mechanism that looks somewhat like a giant accordion. This mechanism makes it easier for the bus to turn corners.

In many areas, public-transit buses are part of special systems that make getting from place to place easier. Express buses for commuters run on special lanes on some major highways so that they can bypass traffic and get into town very quickly. In some downtown areas, automobiles have been banned from certain streets to create transit malls. Buses and pedestrians move freely through these malls.

The long-distance bus that travels the highways today is designed to be comfortable and

A public-transit bus in Portland, Oregon, slows as it comes to one of its designated stops. These buses are an important means of transportation in many cities in the United States and around the world.

convenient. The passengers sit in upholstered chairs that can be tilted back for resting or sleeping. Each seat has its own reading light, so that a passenger can read while the person alongside, who may wish to sleep, is not disturbed. The large windows are tinted to keep out the sun's glare. Most long-distance buses

Above: Riding a school bus is part of the daily routine for millions of children.
Right: With picturesque scenery in the background, a tour bus travels on a quiet highway. These buses, used for long trips, are specially designed for passenger comfort.

have washrooms with hot and cold running water. They also have television screens for video movies. Under the floor is a huge baggage compartment.

Bus companies operate long-distance lines all over the United States and Canada. Their routes extend from coast to coast and from Alaska to Mexico. Some terminals resemble railroad stations, with checkrooms, restaurants, barbershops, and newsstands.

School Buses. The school bus has changed the lives of schoolchildren. Once there were thousands of small one-room schools with one teacher for all the grades. This was because every child who lived on a farm had to be near enough to a school to walk to it. These one-room schoolhouses have been replaced by large central schools that serve a wide territory. School buses pick up children each day at their homes and take them back when school is over. School buses are usually painted bright yellow or orange so that they can be seen easily. As a further safety measure, most states forbid automobile drivers to pass a school bus that has stopped to pick up children or let them off. In addition, many communities have passed local laws requiring seat belts on school buses because it has been proved that seat belts reduce the risk of injury in traffic accidents.

Specialty Buses. Other types of buses include tour buses, charter buses, and airport buses. On a tour bus, people may take short sight-seeing trips to local historic landmarks or other places of interest. They may also take long bus tours that can last several

weeks and tour one or more countries. On long bus tours, bus companies will usually make all the arrangements for the passengers' daily needs, such as meals and hotel room accommodations.

Charter buses are hired by specific groups of people who wish to travel together. Airport buses are small buses that operate between various airport terminals and hotels.

GAIL E. WILLIAMS
Public Affairs Specialist
Urban Mass Transportation Administration
U.S. Department of Transportation

GEORGE BUSH (1924-)

41st President of the United States

FACTS ABOUT BUSH

Birthplace: Milton, Massachusetts
Religion: Episcopalian
College Attended: Yale University
Occupation: Businessman, public official
Married: Barbara Pierce
Children: George W., John (Jeb), Neil,
   Marvin, Dorothy (Robin, died 1953)
Political Party: Republican
Office Held Before Becoming President:
   Vice President
President Who Preceded Him:
   Ronald W. Reagan
Age on Becoming President: 64
Years in the Presidency: 1989-1993
Vice President:
   James Danforth (Dan) Quayle
President Who Succeeded Him:
   William (Bill) Clinton

DURING BUSH'S PRESIDENCY

U.S. troops ousted Panama's dictator, General Manuel Noriega (1989). A U.S.-led military alliance, authorized by the United Nations, liberated Kuwait from Iraqi occupation in the Persian Gulf War (1991). The Soviet Union broke apart (1991) into 15 independent countries. The United States, Canada, and Mexico signed the North American Free Trade Agreement (1992). *Left:* U.S. Marines were sent to Somalia (1992), to ensure that emergency food supplies reached Somalis threatened with starvation. *Above:* Bush and Russian president Boris Yeltsin signed (1993) the second Strategic Arms Reduction Treaty (Start II).

BUSH, GEORGE. Few presidents in recent years have entered the White House with as much broad experience in government as George Bush. He served as a member of Congress and as U.S. representative to the United Nations. He was one of the first officials to represent the United States in the People's Republic of China. He is a former director of the Central Intelligence Agency (CIA). And he was vice president under President Ronald Reagan for eight years, before winning the presidency himself in 1988. Bush was the first sitting vice president to be elected president since Martin Van Buren won office in 1836.

▶ EARLY YEARS

George Herbert Walker Bush was born in Milton, Massachusetts, on June 12, 1924. His parents were Prescott Sheldon Bush and Dorothy Walker Bush. His father was a Wall Street investment banker and later served as a U.S. senator from Connecticut. Four other children, three sons and a daughter, were born to the Bushes. George was named after his maternal grandfather, George Herbert Walker, who established the Walker Cup trophy for American and British amateur golfers.

When George was still an infant, the Bush family moved to Greenwich, Connecticut. There he was raised amid wealth. Three maids tended to the needs of the family. A chauffeur drove young George to the Greenwich Country Day School. The Bushes spent the summers at their vacation home in Kennebunkport, Maine, where George loved to go boating and fishing for mackerel in the waters of the Atlantic Ocean. Bush still maintains a summer home in Kennebunkport.

Bush attended an exclusive prep school, Phillips Academy, in Andover, Massachusetts. He was captain of the basketball and soccer teams, played on the baseball team, and was elected president of his senior class. During his senior year, on December 7, 1941, the Japanese attacked Pearl Harbor, Hawaii, drawing the United States into World War II. Bush was impatient to graduate in 1942 so that he could volunteer for the Navy air service.

▶WAR SERVICE, MARRIAGE, AND COLLEGE

On his 18th birthday, Bush enlisted in the Navy as a seaman second class. Following flight training, he was commissioned as an ensign in 1943 and became a torpedo bomber pilot. At age 19, he was the youngest pilot then serving in the U.S. Navy. During 1943 and 1944, he took part in 58 combat missions in the Pacific. His worst wartime experience occurred in 1944, when his plane was hit by Japanese anti-aircraft fire over Chichi Jima, one of the Bonin Islands. His two crewmen were killed. Bush parachuted to the water. He lay helpless in a rubber raft until he was rescued by a U.S. submarine.

In 1945, while still in uniform, Bush married Barbara Pierce, the daughter of a magazine publisher. The Bushes had five children who lived to maturity, George W., John (known as Jeb), Neil, Marvin, and Dorothy. Another daughter, Robin, died in 1953.

When the war ended in 1945, Bush was discharged from the Navy with the rank of lieutenant, junior grade. He had won the Distinguished Flying Cross and three Air Medals.

Bush resumed his education at Yale University, where he majored in economics. Still interested in sports, he played first base on the Yale baseball team. In 1948, during the home game against Princeton University, Bush got a chance to meet one of his baseball heroes, Babe Ruth. In one of his last public appearances before his death that year, Babe Ruth presented Bush, then the team captain, with the manuscript of his autobiography, which he was donating to Yale.

▶OIL AND POLITICS IN TEXAS

On his graduation from Yale in 1948, Bush was offered a job in his father's investment banking firm. But Bush preferred to make it on his own. With his wife and young son, he headed for Texas. His first job was painting oil rigs. But soon he was selling oil drilling equipment. In 1950 he and a partner formed a company that bought land in hopes of finding oil or natural gas. Three years later, Bush merged the company with the operations of other oil speculators, founding the Zapata Petroleum Corporation. From 1953 to 1966, Bush was the head of the Zapata Off Shore Company, which was a supplier of the drilling equipment used to explore for oil beneath the ocean floor.

A U.S. Navy pilot during World War II, Bush later graduated from Yale University, where he played on the baseball team.

The Bush family gathers at their summer home in Kennebunkport, Maine. The President and Mrs. Bush (in dark sweater) are seated to right of center. The eldest son, George W., is at far right, with his wife and daughter. Seated at left front are sons Neil and Marvin (in white sneakers), with their wives and children. Son John, known as Jeb, is at rear left (in dark shirt). Daughter Dorothy is to John's left, with her husband and children.

Above: Bush served as vice president in Ronald Reagan's administration, from 1981 to 1989. *Right:* President and Mrs. Bush visited U.S. troops in Saudi Arabia on Thanksgiving 1990, two months before the successful allied ground offensive against Iraqi forces in Kuwait.

Meanwhile, Bush had settled his family in Houston, Texas, and had become active in Republican Party politics. In 1964 he ran for the U.S. Senate, but was defeated. Setting his sights a little lower, Bush won election to the U.S. House of Representatives in 1966. He was the first Republican to represent Houston in Congress. He was re-elected in 1968. In 1970, Bush again ran for the Senate and again was defeated.

▶ APPOINTIVE OFFICES

United Nations Representative. In 1971, President Richard M. Nixon appointed Bush U.S. Permanent Representative to the United Nations. It was a crucial time for the world organization. The United States had agreed to allow the admission of the People's Republic of China to the United Nations for the first time since 1949, when the Communists took over the mainland of China. Bush argued forcefully for a so-called "two-China" policy. Under this compromise, a special seat would have been created for the Republic of China (Taiwan), which had held the China seat since the founding of the United Nations in 1945. But the United Nations rejected the two-China plan and expelled the Taiwan government in favor of the People's Republic.

Party Chairman. In 1973, Bush was named chairman of the Republican National Committee. At this time, President Nixon and the Republican Party were under the cloud of the Watergate scandal. For a long time, Bush defended Nixon, because he believed the president when he said that he had taken no part in attempts to cover up illegal activities by some members of his administration. But when the White House tape recordings were made public and exposed Nixon's involvement, Bush, acting for the Republican Party, asked Nixon to resign. Nixon did so on August 9, 1974.

Envoy to China and CIA Director. The new president, Gerald R. Ford, appointed Bush to what was then the top diplomatic post in the People's Republic of China, chief of the U.S. Liaison Office, in 1974. He remained in China until he was called home at Ford's request to become director of the Central Intelligence Agency (CIA). Bush served in that post from late January 1976 until the beginning of Jimmy Carter's administration in January 1977.

▶ VICE PRESIDENT

Bush lost the Republican presidential nomination to Ronald Reagan in 1980 but was named as his vice-presidential running mate. The Reagan-Bush ticket won easily in 1980. They were re-elected overwhelmingly in 1984.

Two Presidential Emergencies. On March 30, 1981, President Reagan was shot in an assassination attempt. While Reagan was recovering, Vice President Bush met regularly with the cabinet, White House officials, and congressional leaders. On July 13, 1985, the powers of the presidency were transferred temporarily to Bush while Reagan underwent cancer surgery.

The Iran-Contra Affair. In 1986 it became known that presidential aides had secretly sold arms to Iran in exchange for the release of American hostages in the Middle East. Some of the arms profits were used, illegally, to help contra guerrillas in their war against the government of Nicaragua. Bush's role in the affair became a point of controversy.

The 1988 Election. In 1988, Bush again sought and won the Republican presidential nomination. In the election, Bush and his vice-presidential running mate, J. Danforth (Dan) Quayle of Indiana, easily defeated the Democratic candidates, Governor Michael Dukakis of Massachusetts and Senator Lloyd Bentsen, Jr., of Texas. The Bush-Quayle ticket won 54 percent of the popular vote and received 426 electoral votes to 111 for the Democrats.

▶ PRESIDENT

Domestic Issues. In one of his first measures as president, Bush proposed legislation to bail out the nation's financially troubled savings and loan institutions. Congress passed a $159 million ten-year plan to rescue the ailing industry, but the scope and cost of the problem grew. The large federal budget deficit, inherited from the Reagan years, was a major concern of Bush's administration. Bush's agreement to a budget-reduction tax package in 1990, which went against his campaign pledge not to raise taxes, cost him considerable popularity, particularly among conservative Republicans.

Following the resignation of U.S. Supreme Court Justice William J. Brennan in 1990, Bush named David H. Souter of New Hampshire to the post. In 1991 he appointed Clarence Thomas, a black federal judge, to the court to succeed Thurgood Marshall, who was scheduled to retire. Thomas was confirmed after much controversy.

Bush signed a compromise civil rights bill in 1991, after vetoing an earlier measure in 1990. He twice vetoed family leave bills, in 1990 and 1992, which would have forced large businesses to grant such leave, preferring voluntary measures. An often-mentioned issue, a constitutional amendment requiring a balanced budget, remained unresolved.

Foreign Affairs. Bush presided during a period of great political change abroad. Between 1989 and 1992, the Communist regimes of Eastern Europe were replaced by representative governments, a divided Germany was reunited, and the Soviet Union broke apart. An activist president in foreign affairs, Bush in late 1989 sent U.S. troops to oust Panama's dictator, General Manuel Noriega, who was tried in the United States on drug trafficking charges and sentenced to prison. When Iraq invaded Kuwait in 1990, Bush led an international effort to counter the aggression. An alliance headed by the United States, and approved by the United Nations, forced the Iraqis' swift withdrawal in 1991. (See the article PERSIAN GULF WAR in Volume P.)

In 1992, Bush signed the North American Free Trade Agreement with Canada and Mexico. The treaty, if approved, would establish the world's largest free trade zone.

Defeat in 1992: Last Measures. But Bush's successes in foreign affairs were offset by an economic recession at home, which became a decisive issue in the 1992 election campaign. Bush's Democratic opponent was Governor William (Bill) Clinton of Arkansas. The entry of a strong independent candidate, H. Ross Perot, a Texas businessman, made it a three-way race. No candidate received a majority of the popular vote, but Clinton won overwhelmingly, with 370 electoral votes to Bush's 168.

Bush's last months in office were busy ones. In December 1992, he dispatched U.S. Marines to Somalia, to ensure that relief supplies reached its starving people, caught up in civil war. In January 1993, he signed the second Strategic Arms Reduction Treaty, or START II, the most extensive disarmament treaty yet, with Russian president Boris Yeltsin. He also authorized new air strikes against Iraq for its violations of United Nations agreements.

WILLIAM A. DE GREGORIO
Author, *The Complete Book of U.S. Presidents*
Updated by JAMES E. CHURCHILL, JR.
Executive Editor, *The Americana Annual*

IMPORTANT DATES IN THE LIFE OF GEORGE BUSH

1924 Born in Milton, Massachusetts, June 12.
1942– Served in the U.S. Navy.
1945
1945 Married Barbara Pierce.
1948 Graduated from Yale University.
1953– Was president and then chairman of the board
1966 of the Zapata Off Shore Company, Texas.
1967– Served in the U.S. Congress.
1971
1971– U.S. Permanent Representative to the United
1972 Nations.
1973– Chairman of the Republican National
1974 Committee.
1974– Chief of the U.S. Liaison Office, China.
1975
1976– Director of the Central Intelligence Agency.
1977
1981– Vice president of the United States.
1989
1989– 41st president of the United States.
1993

GEORGE W. BUSH (1946–)

43rd President of the United States

FACTS ABOUT BUSH

Birthplace: New Haven, Connecticut
Religion: Methodist
Colleges Attended: Yale University, Harvard University School of Business Administration
Occupation: Oil executive, Major League Baseball executive, public official
Married: Laura Welch
Children: Barbara and Jenna
Political Party: Republican
Office Held Before Becoming President: Governor of Texas
President Who Preceded Him: William Clinton
Age on Becoming President: 54
Years in the Presidency: 2001–
Vice President: Richard B. Cheney

BUSH, GEORGE W. With his victory in the 2000 election, George W. Bush became the first son of a president to win the White House since John Quincy Adams, son of John Adams, in 1824. On the road to winning the nation's highest office, he benefited not only from the example of his father, George Herbert Walker Bush, the 41st president, but also that of his grandfather, Prescott Bush, a widely respected U.S. senator. And his victory over Democrat Al Gore, vice president to Bill Clinton, who had ousted Bush's father only eight years earlier, gave the new President Bush the opportunity to restore his family's political reputation.

▶ **EARLY YEARS**

George Walker Bush was born on July 6, 1946, in New Haven, Connecticut, where his father, just returned from World War II, was attending Yale University. Bush's mother, the former Barbara Pierce, later gave birth to three more sons, John (Jeb), Neil, and Marvin, and two daughters, Dorothy and Robin. After George Bush graduated from Yale, he set out for Texas, hoping to make his fortune in the oil business. The Bushes settled in Midland, where young George had a relatively untroubled childhood, apart from the tragic death of his sister Robin from leukemia in 1953.

As he reached high school age, George left Texas to attend the same elite eastern schools as had his father, Phillips Academy and Andover. But his years in the Lone Star State helped shape his life. "I was educated up East, but my heart was always back in Texas," he later told an interviewer. He was not an outstanding student, nor an exceptional athlete. His greatest strength was in getting along with his fellow students.

After high school, George entered Yale University, again following in his father's footsteps. A few months before graduation, he entered the Texas Air National Guard.

George W. Bush, pictured with his parents George and Barbara in 1955, became the first son of a president to win the White House since John Quincy Adams.

Some critics later contended he signed up to avoid combat in the Vietnam War. They also charged that family influence helped Bush advance in the Guard. But Bush claimed he joined up mainly to become a fighter pilot like his father. He was commissioned a second lieutenant, learned to fly fighter jets, and went to monthly guard training sessions until he completed his service in 1973.

Meanwhile George worked for his father in his unsuccessful race for the Senate in 1970. The senior Bush moved on to become Ambassador to the United Nations and then Republican National Chairman. But his eldest son seemed to be drifting, a period he later called "my nomadic years." "I didn't know what I wanted to do, and I wasn't going to do anything I didn't want to do." Afterward, seeking more focus for his life, the young man entered the prestigious Harvard Business School, where he earned a master's degree in business administration in 1975.

▶ EARLY CAREER AND MARRIAGE

Bush decided to make his start in the business world in the same place his father had begun—the oil fields of Texas. Returning to his old home town of Midland, Bush began investing in oil leases and exploration. In 1977 he founded his own oil company, Arbusto Corp.

His personal lifestyle was that of a carefree bachelor. "George had a good time ... a lot of fun and a lot of wise guy remarks," his cousin and friend since childhood, John Ellis, later recalled. Much of that changed in 1977 when he met and married Laura Welch, a librarian, who friends say provided a stabilizing influence. In 1981, Laura gave birth to the couple's twin daughters, Jenna and Barbara, named for their two grandmothers.

Soon after his marriage, Bush plunged into the first political race of his life, for an open seat in the U.S. House of Representatives. He won the Republican nomination easily, but his opponent in the general election, a conservative Democrat named Kent Hance, defeated him by depicting him as a privileged elitist. "Kent Hance gave me a good lesson in country boy politics," Bush later recalled. "He was a master of it, funny and belittling. I vowed never to get out-countried again."

Following that setback, Bush returned to the oil business but found he could not achieve the success his father had years earlier. In his frustration he began to drink heavily, until he realized it was "interfering with my energy level." On his 40th birthday in 1986, he quit drinking abruptly and permanently. "I made a lot of mistakes when I was young and I learned from my mistakes," Bush explained to a reporter. "I've asked people to adhere to a higher standard than I did."

On the campaign trail during his unsuccessful run for Congress in 1978, Bush met with oil refinery workers in West Texas.

He soon made other changes in his life. He sold off his oil business and went to Washington, D.C., to take up a post as an adviser to his father in the 1988 presidential campaign. After his father entered the White House, he took advantage of an opportunity to enter a new field, major league baseball. He assembled a group of investors, who bought the Texas Rangers and installed Bush as managing partner.

Not all of Bush's decisions as a baseball executive worked out well, but he did well financially. When the team was sold, his original $600,000 investment repaid $15 million. The experience acquired at the helm of the Rangers helped fill an important gap. As Bush told *Time* magazine, the biggest liability to his running for office in Texas was that people would think he was simply trading on father's name. "Now I can say, 'I've done something—here it is.'"

▶ GOVERNOR OF TEXAS

In 1993, after his father's defeat for re-election as president, Bush announced his candidacy for the governorship of Texas. He faced a formidable opponent in the Democrat incumbent, Ann Richards, known for her aggressive style and sharp tongue. Although Bush certainly benefited from his father's fame, he had also learned from his father's weaknesses. The senior Bush had been criticized for appearing out of touch with everyday life. His son tried to demonstrate how politics affected ordinary people. He concentrated on four issues: welfare, education, juvenile crime, and legal reforms to limit damages from lawsuits. In November 1994 he defeated Ann Richards and won a 4-year term as governor.

Once in office, Bush gained approval for most of his campaign platform. To fight crime, he signed a law allowing Texans to obtain permits to carry concealed weapons. He initiated educational reforms that gave more independence to local school districts and helped raise test scores. He also challenged schools to stop moving children ahead to the next grade regardless of their ability to learn. "This business of passing children through our schools who can't read has got to end,"

he declared. "You either believe that people can learn or not. And I refuse in my state to condemn anybody to failure." Bush also argued for large cuts in local property taxes—the main source of school funding—intending to replace the lost revenue with state funds. But the legislature resisted and finally approved a reduced cut in property taxes.

Although his policies generally won approval from conservatives, Bush also gained a reputation as a moderate. One reason was his effort to reach out to Hispanic Americans, who usually vote Democrat. Unlike other Republicans, Bush opposed cutting off aid to legal immigrants. He also kept an open mind on the idea of schools offering some courses in both English and Spanish, an approach many others in his party rejected. "My deal on bilingual education is that if it works, if it teaches children, we ought to support the program," he said.

With his wife, Laura, at his side, Bush addressed supporters during the 2000 presidential race. The theme of his candidacy was "compassionate conservatism."

Bush and his family gathered for an informal snapshot during his first term as governor of Texas. From left are wife Laura and twin daughters Jenna and Barbara.

At the end of his first term, Bush was so popular that Democrats had a hard time finding a candidate to oppose him. In 1998, Bush was re-elected with nearly 70 percent of the overall vote and almost half the Hispanic vote. He was the first Texas governor to win two consecutive 4-year terms.

▶ THE 2000 CAMPAIGN

During Bush's first term as governor, Texas Republicans began urging him to run for president. His re-election in 1998 as governor of the nation's second largest state gave his prospects a big boost, as did his brother Jeb's election as governor of Florida.

Bush's presidential candidacy got off to a fast start. He collected more endorsements from Republican leaders than any other candidate. He also raised far more money. Despite his financial advantage, Bush faced several difficulties. Rivals charged that he lacked experience, particularly in foreign policy. He also confronted persistent allegations that he had used illegal drugs as a young man. His most serious challenger was Arizona senator John McCain, who defeated him in the New Hampshire primary. But Bush rallied and won a series of primaries in the South, which assured him the nomination.

At the Republican National Convention in Philadelphia, Bush reinforced his promise of "compassionate conservatism," a major theme of his candidacy. Accepting the nomination for president, he pledged "to extend the promise of prosperity to every corner of this country" and to "tear down that wall" between wealth and ambition on one side and poverty and despair on the other.

▶ THE 2000 ELECTION

The 2000 presidential election turned out to be the most dramatic in living memory. Late into election night, November 7, it became apparent that the state of Florida, with its 25 electoral votes, would determine the winner. The Florida race was so close, however, that Gore was first declared the winner, then Bush. Gore requested a recount of the votes, but after five tense weeks of both sides appealing to the court system, the U.S. Supreme Court ruled on December 12 that uniform standards would have to be agreed upon before a recount could proceed. There was no time for this, though, because the deadline for the certification of Florida electors—also December 12—had essentially passed. Bush was then recognized as the president-elect.

ROBERT SHOGAN
Author, *The Double-Edged Sword: How Character Makes and Ruins Presidents, from Washington to Clinton*

IMPORTANT DATES IN THE LIFE OF GEORGE W. BUSH

1946	Born in New Haven, Connecticut, July 6.
1968	Graduated from Yale University.
1975	Graduated from Harvard Business School.
1977	Married Laura Welch.
1977	Started his own oil company, Arbusto Corp.
1978	Ran unsuccessfully for Congress.
1987–92	Served as aide to his father, President Bush.
1989–94	Served as managing general partner of Texas Rangers baseball franchise.
1994–01	Served as governor of Texas.
2001	Inaugurated as 43rd president of the United States.

The fortunate individual who owns and operates this business is able to work outdoors, surrounded by the beautiful flowers and colorful balloons he sells.

BUSINESS

How do your parents earn their living? How will you earn your living? Chances are that the answers to both questions will involve a business. Most people earn their livelihood either by working for a business owned by someone else, or by operating their own business.

There are many kinds of businesses, from small shops owned and operated by one person to large companies owned by many people and employing thousands of workers. A factory is a business. A store is a business. Other examples include beauty salons, professional sports, and all kinds of entertainment.

A business is any establishment that produces or distributes goods and services. Goods are tangible items like clothing and food. Services are intangible things like entertainment and the services of doctors and lawyers.

▶ TYPES OF BUSINESS ORGANIZATION

There are three basic types of business organization: (1) the individual proprietorship; (2) the partnership; and (3) the corporation.

The Individual Proprietorship

An individual proprietorship is a business owned and managed by a single individual. This owner, or **proprietor**, makes all business decisions, receives all profits from the business, and is legally responsible for all of the losses and debts of the business. This legal responsibility for losses and debts, known as **unlimited liability**, is a major disadvantage of an individual proprietorship. It means that if debts cannot be paid, the owner can lose the business and also personal assets such as savings, home, and automobile. While an individual proprietorship can be started rather easily, often with little money, it is usually difficult to raise money for expansion or to improve efficiency. For this reason, it is often difficult for a proprietorship to compete successfully with larger businesses. An individual proprietorship also has a limited life. If the proprietor dies or retires, the business may cease to exist.

The Partnership

A partnership is a business owned by two or more individuals who are called partners. These partners make business decisions together and share all business profits and losses. They also share in unlimited liability for the business. As in a proprietorship, this means that all debts are the responsibility of all of the partners. If debts cannot be paid, they could lose the business as well as their own personal assets.

A partnership is relatively easy and inexpensive to establish. Since more than one person is involved, it is also generally easier to

The partners in an accounting firm meet often to discuss how to attract new clients and make decisions that will affect the firm's profitability.

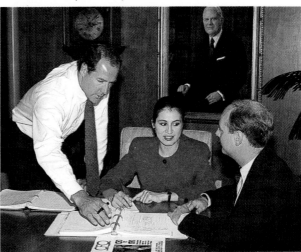

raise money for expansion or other needs. A partnership also provides an opportunity for specialization, allowing one partner to specialize in production, another in finances, still another in sales, and so on. This usually enables a partnership to handle more work than an individual proprietorship. A partnership also has a limited life. If one partner dies, retires, or resigns, the business may be forced to close unless other partners are willing and able to buy out that partner's share of the business.

The Corporation

A corporation is a business that has the legal status of an individual but is owned collectively by many people. Most large businesses that employ hundreds or thousands of workers are corporations.

To establish a corporation, the potential owners must meet various legal requirements of federal, state, and local governments. One basic requirement is a corporate charter, which is a legal document that gives the corporation the authority to operate in a particular state. The charter establishes the corporation as a legal entity that can enter into contracts and make commitments under its own name. This means that the individual owners of the corporation have only a limited liability. No matter what happens to the corporation, the owners can lose no more than their initial investment, and they cannot be held personally liable for corporate debts or losses. This is one of the major advantages of a corporation.

Another advantage of a corporation is its unlimited life. When owners die or choose to leave the business, the corporation continues to operate unchanged because their shares in the company can be sold to other people. A corporation also has the ability to raise large sums of money through the sale of stocks. One disadvantage of a corporation is that because of its size and complexity decision-making may become slow. Sometimes it may not be able to respond as quickly as it should to changing economic conditions.

How a Corporation Works. A corporate charter authorizes the sale of shares of stock in order to raise money for starting a corporation, for expanding its business, or for other needs. The people who buy these shares of stock are called **stockholders**. In return for their investment, stockholders receive **dividends**, or shares of the corporation's profits.

Boards of directors of large corporations establish and review the basic policies their companies will follow and hire the executive officers who will actually manage their businesses.

The stockholders are the actual owners of a corporation and it is their responsibility to vote on major corporate issues. In most cases, stockholders have one vote for each share of stock owned. Stockholders also elect a board of directors, which is responsible for determining basic corporate policies and for hiring executive officers to carry out the decisions of directors and stockholders. These executive officers are responsible for the day-to-day operations of the corporation. To help them do this, they hire managers for specialized departments within the corporation. The number of managers and departments depends on the size of the corporation and the types of goods or services it provides. Most corporations have at least three specialized departments to provide the services of production, finance, and marketing. Corporations may also have personnel, research, and public relations departments.

WONDER QUESTION

What are gross income and net income?

Gross income is the total amount of money a business earns without considering expenses. Net income, also known as profit, is the total amount of money a business earns after expenses and other operating costs have been subtracted.

HOW TO BE AN ENTREPRENEUR

An **entrepreneur** is a person who sees the need for a particular product or service and then creates a business to supply that product or service. There are many opportunities for young people to become entrepreneurs. In some communities there may be a need for services such as babysitting, taking care of pets, or making deliveries. They might produce and sell goods — for example, growing and selling fresh fruits or vegetables or making and selling lemonade. Or they could become involved in woodworking, knitting, quilting, or pottery, and sell their finished products.

Before starting any business, a smart entrepreneur will find out if there is a need or market for a particular good or service, whether or not anyone is already providing it, and the possible costs of running the business. You will probably want to do some research at your local library. Additional information might be available from your town or city hall, chamber of commerce, church hall, or local newspaper. These might also be good places to **advertise** your product or service after your business has been established. Researching such issues is one of an entrepreneur's most important tasks. Now let us look at an example of how to become an entrepreneur.

Suppose your community has many homes with large lawns. You begin to wonder if some homeowners would pay you to mow their lawns. The potential may exist for a lawn-mowing business. You decide to become an entrepreneur.

You begin by asking neighbors if they would like to have their lawns mowed. You might also advertise by posting announcements on bulletin boards in schools, churches, supermarkets, and community centers. After lining up customers, you buy a lawn mower. The money you spend for it is consid-

ered an **investment** in your business. If the money comes from your savings, it is called **capital**. If it is borrowed, it is called a **capital loan**. Of course, if you borrow money you will have to pay it back, perhaps with **interest** — a fee that a lender charges for loaning money.

The income you receive from your business is called **revenue**. Out of this you must pay for fuel and any other costs, called **operating expenses**. If revenue is greater than expenses, your business has made a **profit**. If expenses are greater than revenue, your business has sustained a **loss**.

As your business grows, you decide to buy another lawn mower and hire a friend to help. Now you have become an **employer**, and your friend is your **employee**. The **wages** you pay your employee are part of your operating expenses.

After a few weeks, someone else starts a lawn-mowing service as **competition** to yours. With competition, the price of your service becomes very important. If one person charges less, or **undersells**, the other, the person charging more may begin to lose customers and eventually may be forced out of business. On the other hand, if one person charges too little, the income may not be enough to cover expenses and that business may go **bankrupt**. However, you and your competitor charge similar prices, and there are plenty of customers for both businesses.

As your business grows, you discover that some customers want the grass clippings removed from their lawns. You purchase grass catchers for your lawn mowers and consider paying someone to haul away the clippings. But then you have an idea — grass clippings make good mulch to place around shrubs, flowers, and vegetables. They could, therefore, be considered a product with a potential market. Soon you have found customers who want to buy mulch — you have created a new business and a new source of revenue.

You are a successful entrepreneur and manager of two businesses! The profit you earn is what motivated you to start your businesses, and it is what keeps them in operation. It is the potential for earning a profit that motivates most entrepreneurs.

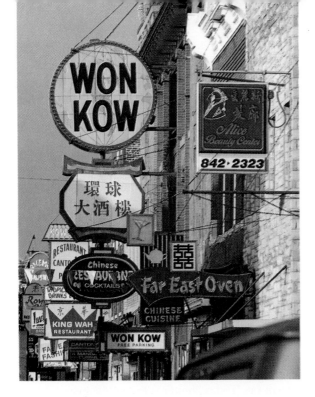

products. For example, laws limit the number of hours people can work and provide workplace safety standards. Product safety is another concern. For example, if a company develops a new medicine, a government agency requires extensive testing to determine the safety and effectiveness of the medicine before it can be sold to the public.

Government regulates business in other ways as well. Antitrust laws are enacted to help prevent companies from merging, or joining together, in order to control the supply and price of a product or service. These laws

By opening restaurants so close together, these businesses face stiff competition from one another. Each business must offer good food and service at low prices to attract and keep customers. They must also be careful not to let costs exceed earnings or they will lose money and be forced to close.

New drugs and medicines must undergo extensive testing before the federal government allows doctors to prescribe them for their patients.

▶ BUSINESS IN A FREE ENTERPRISE SYSTEM

In a free enterprise system, such as the economies of the United States and Canada, businesses produce the goods and services people need and want. While doing this, they also try to make a profit—to have more income than expenses. Profit is essential for a business to remain in operation, and it is one of the most important principles of a free enterprise system.

One of the key factors affecting profit is competition. If a business has competitors—other companies producing and selling similar goods or services—it cannot charge prices that are much higher than those of its competitors without losing customers. However, it cannot charge prices that would result in less income than expenses without jeopardizing the survival of the business. Competition thus helps regulate profits businesses earn and prices consumers pay for goods and services.

Government Regulation of Businesses

Businesses often adjust their operations and their prices in an attempt to increase profits. But in the United States, Canada, and other countries with free enterprise systems, the government often establishes regulations concerning what a business can and cannot do.

The government often enacts laws to promote safe working conditions and ensure safe

help maintain competition among businesses. In certain industries, such as public utilities that supply gas, electricity, and water, the government often grants one company the exclusive right of operating in a specific market but then establishes regulations to ensure that the quality of its services is adequate and its prices are not too high.

Aside from regulations to ensure safety, to promote competition, and to protect consumers, businesses in a free enterprise system are generally left alone to operate according to the laws of supply and demand.

ALLEN SMITH
Author, *Understanding Economics*

See also BANKS AND BANKING; ECONOMICS; STOCKS AND BONDS.

BUTTE. See MONTANA (Cities).

Batutsi see Tutsi
Batwa see Twa
Baudelaire, Charles (French poet)   **F:**441
Baudot, Emile (French inventor)   **T:**51
Baudouin (king of the Belgians)   **B:**135
Bauer, Georg see Agricola, Georgius
Bauer, Wolfgang (German dramatist)   **D:**302
Baugh, Sammy (American football player)   **F:**362 *profile*
   picture(s)   **F:**362
Bauhaus (design school in Germany)
   architecture, history of   **A:**383
   furniture design   **F:**516–17
   industrial design   **I:**214
   influence on decorative arts   **D:**78
   Kandinsky, Wassily   **K:**173
   Mies van der Rohe, Ludwig   **M:**306
   twentieth century German art and architecture   **G:**173
Baule (Baoulé) (African tribe)   **I:**417
   sculpture   **A:**72
Baum, L. Frank (American journalist and author of children's stories)   **N:**276; **S:**326 *profile*
Bauxite (ore of aluminum)   **A:**194c
   Arkansas leads U.S. production   **A:**423
   Australia is the world's largest producer   **A:**510
   France is Western Europe's leading producer   **F:**411
   Guinea is the world's second largest producer   **G:**406a
   Guyana is an important producer   **G:**428a
   Hungary has large reserves   **H:**295–96
   Jamaica is a leading producer   **J:**17
   natural resource   **N:**62–63
   North American mineral resources   **N:**293
Bavaria (Germany)
   Czech way of life influenced by   **C:**608–9
   food specialties   **G:**151–52
   Thompson, Benjamin: service in government   **T:**180
   picture(s)
      Neuschwanstein (castle)   **G:**149
Bavarian Alps (Austria–Germany)   **G:**153–54
Bay (geographic term)   **O:**43 see also the names of bays, as Fundy, Bay of
Bayaderka (ballet)
   picture(s)   **D:**32
Bayamón (Puerto Rico)   **P:**530
Bayar, Celal (president of Turkey)   **T:**349
Bayberry (shrub)   **W:**78
Bayeux tapestry (medieval embroidery)   **N:**100
   picture(s)   **E:**238
Bayezid I (Ottoman sultan)   **O:**261
Baying (of dogs)   **D:**247
Bay Islands (Honduras)   **H:**195
   picture(s)   **H:**197
Bayle, Pierre (French philosopher)   **E:**296 *profile*
Bay leaves (spice)   **H:**114
   picture(s)   **H:**115
Baylor, Elgin (American basketball player)   **B:**95i *profile*
   picture(s)   **B:**95i
Bay lynxes see Bobcats
Bay of Pigs Invasion see Pigs, Bay of
Bayous (marshy creeks)   **L:**314; **M:**352
   picture(s)   **L:**315
Bayou State (nickname for Louisiana)   **L:**315
Bay Psalm Book   **H:**324; **P:**551
Bayreuth (Germany)
   Festival of Wagner's operas   **M:**559; **W:**2
Bay State (nickname for Massachusetts)   **M:**136, 137
Bazaars (Middle Eastern marketplaces)   **S:**550
   picture(s)   **S:**551
Bazán, Emilia Pardo see Pardo Bazán, Emilia
Bazookas (small rocket launchers)   **T:**14
BBC see British Broadcasting Company
B.C. (abbreviation used with dates)   **C:**16
B.C.E. (abbreviation used with dates)   **C:**16
B cells (in the immune system)   **B:**257, 258; **I:**96–97
BCG (vaccine against tuberculosis)   **D:**205
B-complex vitamins   **V:**370c–370d

B.E. 2a (early British airplane)   **A:**562
Beach, Amy Marcy (American pianist and composer)   **N:**162 *profile*
Beach Blanket Bingo (motion picture, 1965)   **M:**495
Beach Boys (American rock group)   **R:**262b *profile*
Beaches see also Seashores
   barrier beaches of Louisiana   **L:**316
   erosion   **E:**319
   Maine places of interest   **M:**44
   picture(s)
      Alabama   **A:**131
      Copacabana (Rio de Janeiro)   **R:**234
      Delaware   **D:**89, 92
      Florida   **F:**261
      Hawaiian black sand beach   **H:**53
      Israel   **I:**371
      Los Angeles   **L:**306
      Puerto Rico   **P:**528
      Rhode Island   **R:**213
      Virginia Beach   **V:**352
      Waikiki (Honolulu)   **H:**205
      Wildwood (New Jersey)   **N:**168
Beach plum   **P:**108
Beacon Hill (Boston, Massachusetts)
   picture(s)   **H:**174
Beaconsfield, Earl of see Disraeli
Beaded lizard   **L:**276
Bead lightning see Chain lightning
Beads (jewelry)
   African sculpture   **A:**72
   early glass articles   **G:**229
   picture(s)
      Indian beadwork   **I:**180
Beads (of a tire)   **T:**209
Beagle (dog)   **D:**250
Beagle, H.M.S. (British ship)   **D:**40; **E:**375
Beagle Channel dispute (Argentina–Chile)   **C:**252
Beaks (Bills) (of birds)   **A:**277; **B:**217
   eagles   **E:**2
   parrots   **P:**85
   waterfowl   **D:**341, 343
Beam bridges   **B:**395
   picture(s)   **B:**396
Beamon, Bob (American track-and-field star)   **T:**259 *profile,* 263
   picture(s)   **T:**259
Beams, steel   **I:**336
Beam trawlers (fishing boats)   **F:**218
Bean, Roy (American judge)   **T:**138 *profile*
Beanies (hats)   **H:**45
Beans   **N:**423; **V:**289 see also Soybeans
   picture(s)
      seed   **P:**307
Bear cats see Binturongs
Bearded collie (dog)
   picture(s)   **D:**250
Bearded seals (animals)   **S:**107
Beardmore Glacier (Antarctica)   **G:**224
Beards (facial hair)
   Vandyke beard   **B:**67
Bear Festival (of the Ainu)   **J:**41
Bear Flag Revolt (California)   **C:**30; **T:**111
Bearings (of machinery)
   made of diamonds   **D:**145
   watches   **W:**45
Bearing wall construction (of buildings)   **B:**435
Bear Paw Battlefield (Montana)   **M:**436
Bears   **B:**104–7
   black bears   **M:**73; **W:**129
   cave bears of the Ice Age   **I:**12
   foot bones   **F:**81
   grizzly bears   **M:**70
   pandas are related animals   **P:**52
   partial hibernation of   **H:**118; **M:**75

Beethoven, Ludwig van (German composer)   B:122; G:186
   chamber music   C:184
   choral music   C:284
   classical age, compositions of the   C:349, 351, 352
   Fidelio was his only opera   C:351; O:144, 154
   picture(s)   G:185; M:546
      studio   M:546
Beetle Bailey (comic strip)
   picture(s)   C:129
Beetles (insects)   B:123–27
   boll weevils   C:560–61, 562
   bombardier beetle   I:243
   carpet beetles   H:263
   plant pests   P:286–87, 289, 290
   strength of   I:241
   used as biological control for weeds   W:106
   vectors   V:284, 285
   picture(s)   I:248
      boll weevil   C:560
      scavenger beetle   I:234
      tiger beetles   I:230
      wings   I:240
Beets   S:485–86; V:289
Beet sugar   S:485–86
B.E.F. *see* British Expeditionary Force
Befana, La (Italian Santa Claus)   C:300
Beggar's Opera (play by Gay)   E:277, 292–93; O:142–43
   musical theater   M:556
   picture(s)
      scene painted by William Hogarth   E:277
Beggar's tick (plant)   P:313
Begin, Menahem (Israeli political leader)   B:127a; I:376
   picture(s)   U:202
Behaim, Martin (German merchant and navigator)   M:98
Behan, Brendan (Irish playwright)   I:328
Béhanzin (king of Dahomey)   B:144
Behavior, animal *see* Animal intelligence and behavior
Behavior, human
   brain function   B:365, 366–67
   effect of drugs on   D:326
   ethics   E:328–29
   etiquette   E:337–39
   gene interactions   G:80
   hypnotism   H:327–29
   identical twins raised apart   T:364
   impulses to take drugs   N:16
   learning   L:98–106
   lie detection   L:193
   lies   L:194
   mental health   M:223–25
   mental illness   M:225–28
   psychology   P:499
   sociology, study of   S:230–31
Behavioral objectives (in education)   P:483
Behavioral sciences
   public health   P:515
Behaviorism (psychology)   P:507, 509
Behavior modification (in psychology)   P:500–501
Behrendt, Jan (German athlete)   O:118
Behring, Emil von (German bacteriologist)   B:127a
Behring, Vitus *see* Bering, Vitus
Beiderbecke, Bix (American jazz musician)   J:61
Beijerinck, Martinus (Dutch scientist)   V:363
Beijing (Peking) (capital of China)   B:127b–127d; C:261
   student demonstrations   C:273
   picture(s)
      "Goddess of Liberty" (statue)   C:474
      Summer Palace   C:267
      Tiananmen Square demonstrations (1989)   C:273
Beirut (capital of Lebanon)   L:121, 122–23
   picture(s)
      Syrian troops patrolling   L:123
Bekaa plain (Lebanon)   L:120
Bel *see* Baal
Béla III (king of Hungary)   H:297

Bela IV (king of Hungary)   B:422b
Belarus   B:128–29; U:34
   Commonwealth of Independent States   C:460
   Minsk   U:43
   picture(s)
      flag   F:235
      horse farm   B:129
Belasco, David (American theatrical producer and playwright)   D:304
Belau (island nation, Pacific Ocean) *see* Palau
Belaúnde Terry, Fernando (president of Peru)   P:165
Belcher Islands (in Hudson Bay)   N:410
Belém (Brazil)   B:375, 381
   picture(s)   B:378
Belém (Portugal)   L:256
Belfast (capital of Northern Ireland)   N:336; U:68
   picture(s)   N:336
Belgian Congo *see* Zaïre
Belgian horse
   picture(s)   H:240
Belgian sheepdog   D:241
Belgium   B:130–35
   Albert (kings)   A:163
   Congo, Democratic Republic of   Z:379–80
   Flemish and Dutch art   D:351–64
   Industrial Revolution   I:224
   medieval fairs   F:18
   Where and what are the Low Countries?   E:356
   World War I   W:278–80, 281, 282
   World War II   W:296, 297, 298, 310, 312, 313–14
   picture(s)
      Bruges   B:130
      Brussels   B:132, 134, 135
      flag   F:235
      flax being stacked to dry   B:133
      hikers   B:131
      people   B:130
Belgium Luxembourg Economic Union (BLEU)   B:133
Belgrade (capital of Yugoslavia)   B:136; S:125; Y:366, 367
   picture(s)   B:136; Y:367
Belinsky, Vissarion (Russian writer)   R:377
Belize (Central America)   B:137–38; C:172, 173, 174
   Latin America   L:50, 59
   nature preserve for jaguars   C:150
   picture(s)
      African Creole man   C:172
      flag   F:241
      Peace Corps activities   P:104
Belize City (Belize)   B:137, 138
Bell, Alexander Graham (Scottish-born American inventor and scientist)   B:139–40; I:285
   airplane research   A:562
   Alexander Graham Bell Museum (Nova Scotia)   N:355–56
   Bell Homestead (Ontario)   O:133
   invented the Graphophone   O:56
   telephone   C:468; T:46
   picture(s)   I:283; T:54
Bell, Currer, Ellis, and Acton *see* Brontë, Anne; Brontë, Charlotte; Brontë, Emily
Bell, Joseph (English doctor and model for Sherlock Holmes)   D:290
Bell, Mabel Hubbard (wife of Alexander Graham Bell)   P:67
Bella Bella (Indians of North America)   I:188
Bella Coola (Indians of North America)   I:188
Belladonna (poisonous plant)   L:117; P:316
Bellange, Jacques (French artist)   F:426
Bellay, Joachim du (French poet)   F:435, 437
Belle Isle, Strait of (north of Newfoundland)   C:126; N:140
Bellerophon (hero in Greek mythology)   G:364
Belleville Breviary (illuminated manuscript)
   picture(s)   B:321; D:68
Bellingrath Gardens (Alabama)   A:138
Bellingshausen, Fabian von (Russian admiral)   A:295; E:414

Bellini, Giovanni (Venetian painter)   **B:**140; **I:**398; **P:**21; **R:**169
Giorgione, influence on   **G:**210
Titian was a pupil of Bellini   **T:**210
picture(s)
Madonna of the Trees (painting)   **B:**140
Bellini, Vincenzo (Italian composer)   **I:**412; **O:**145, 159
Bellini family (Italian painters)   **B:**140
Bellman, Carl Michael (Swedish poet and singer)   **S:**58i
Bello, Andrés (South American educator, statesman, and author)   **L:**68
Bello, Joaquín Edwards (Chilean writer)   **C:**250
Bellow, Saul (American novelist)   **A:**214a; **B:**141; **F:**116; **N:**363
Bellows, George Wesley (American artist)   **C:**444; **P:**30
picture(s)
Cliff Dwellers (painting)   **U:**132
Dempsey Through the Ropes (painting)   **B:**351
Bells   **B:**141–42
Christmas customs   **C:**299
communication, use in   **C:**466
early mechanical clocks   **T:**201
Liberty Bell   **L:**170
orchestra, use in   **P:**149
Bell's vireo (bird)
picture(s)   **B:**206
Bell system (telephone system)   **P:**523
Bell towers *see* Campaniles
Bell X-1 (airplane)   **A:**116
Bell XS-1 (research rocket plane)   **A:**567
Bell XV-15 (airplane)
picture(s)   **A:**121
Bell XV-22 (tilt-rotor aircraft)   **A:**571
Belmont, Alva Smith Vanderbilt (wife of William Kissam Vanderbilt)   **V:**277
Belmont Stakes (horse race)   **H:**232
Belmopan (capital of Belize)   **B:**138
Belo Horizonte (Brazil)   **B:**381
Belorussia *see* Belarus
Beloved (novel by Morrison)   **M:**462
Belshazzar (in the Old Testament)   **B:**167
Belt (to drive an alternator)   **A:**547
Belted-bias tires   **T:**209
Belter, John Henry (American furniture maker)   **F:**514
Beltsville Small White (turkey)
picture(s)   **P:**416
Belugas (whales)   **W:**149
picture(s)   **W:**151
Bely, Andrei (Russian author)   **R:**379
Bemba (a people of Africa)   **Z:**381
Ben (meaning in names)   **N:**5
Benalcázar, Sebastian de (Spanish conquistador)   **E:**69
Ben Ali, Zine el-Abidine (Tunisian president)   **T:**336
Ben & Jerry's (ice cream company)   **V:**318
picture(s)   **V:**312
Benares (India) *see* Banaras
·**Benavente, Jacinto** (Spanish writer)   **S:**391
Ben Bella, Ahmed (premier of Algeria)   **A:**188
Bench, Johnny (American baseball player)
picture(s)   **B:**92
Bench plane (tool)   **T:**228
Bendjedid, Chadli (Algerian political leader)   **A:**188
Bends (knots)   **K:**288
Bends, the (caisson disease)   **B:**400; **H:**106; **U:**22–23
Benedict X (antipope)   **R:**290
Benedict XIII (antipope)   **R:**291
Benedict I (pope)   **R:**290
Benedict II, Saint (pope)   **R:**290
Benedict III, Saint (pope)   **R:**290
Benedict IV (pope)   **R:**290
Benedict V (pope)   **R:**290
Benedict VI (pope)   **R:**290
Benedict VII (pope)   **R:**290
Benedict VIII (pope)   **R:**290
Benedict IX (pope)   **R:**290

Benedict XI (pope)   **R:**291
Benedict XII (pope)   **R:**291
Benedict XIII (pope)   **R:**291
Benedict XIV (pope)   **R:**291
Benedict XV (pope)   **R:**291, 292
Benedictine Cloister Church (Ottobeuren, Germany)
picture(s)   **G:**171
Benedictines (Rule of Saint Benedict) (religious order)   **C:**289; **R:**285
Benedict of Nursia, Saint (Italian monk)   **R:**284; **S:**18d *profile*
Benefice system (in the Roman Catholic Church)   **R:**287
Beneficiary (of a trust fund)   **T:**328
Beneficiation (preparation of coal)   **F:**488
Benefits (part of wage agreement)   **L:**8
Benefit societies (industrial organizations formed to aid members who could not work)   **S:**225
Benefit Street (Providence, Rhode Island)   **R:**220
Ben Eliezer, Israel *see* Baal Shem Tov
Benelux (economic union of Belgium, the Netherlands, and Luxembourg)   **N:**121
Benenson, Peter (British attorney)   **H:**286
Beneŝ, Edvard (Czechoslovakian statesman)   **C:**613, 614; **M:**135; **S:**201
Beneventum, Battle of (275 B.C.)   **P:**558
Bengal, Bay of (arm of the Indian Ocean)   **O:**45
Bengali (Bangla) (language)   **B:**48, 51
Bengalis (a people of Bangladesh and India)   **B:**48, 51
picture(s)   **B:**49
Bengal tigers *see* Indian tigers
Benghazi (Libya)   **L:**189
Ben-Gurion, David (first prime minister of Israel)   **B:**142; **I:**375
picture(s)   **I:**375; **P:**459
Ben-Haim, Paul (Israeli composer)   **I:**373
Benign tumors (of the body)   **C:**92; **D:**190
Beni Hasan (Egypt)   **E:**113
Benin (kingdom in Africa)   **N:**257
art achievements   **N:**254
sculpture   **A:**71
picture(s)
ivory bracelet   **A:**74
Benin (modern African country)   **B:**143–44
picture(s)
flag   **F:**226
village   **B:**144
Benin City (Nigeria)   **N:**256
Beni River (Bolivia)   **B:**308
Benito Bonito of the Bloody Sword (pirate)   **P:**264
Benjamin (in the Old Testament)   **B:**167; **J:**133
Benjamin, Judah Philip (British-born American lawyer and statesman)   **L:**326 *profile*
picture(s)   **L:**326
Bennett, Floyd (American aviator)   **B:**489
Bennett, Richard Bedford (Canadian prime minister)   **C:**77 *profile*
Bennett, William Andrew Cecil (Canadian political leader)   **B:**406d
Bennett's cassowaries (flightless birds)   **O:**247
Ben Nevis (highest mountain in the United Kingdom)   **S:**85–86; **U:**61
Bennington (Vermont)
picture(s)
saltbox house   **C:**415
Bennington, Battle of (1777)   **R:**204; **V:**318
monument   **V:**314
Benny, Jack (American comedian)   **I:**74 *profile;* **T:**326
Benoit, Joan (American runner)   **O:**113
picture(s)   **O:**113
Benoit, Peter (Belgian musician)   **B:**133
Benson, Simon (Norwegian-American lumberman)   **O:**214 *profile*
Bentham, Jeremy (English reformer and philosopher)   **E:**296 *profile,* 297, 328
Benthic (Bottom) environment (of the ocean)   **O:**23, 26
Benthos (organisms living on the ocean bottom)   **O:**26

Benton, Thomas Hart (American artist)   **B:**144a; **U:**132
  teacher of Jackson Pollock   **P:**378
  picture(s)
      Arts of the West   **B:**144a
      Independence and the Opening of the West (mural)
          M:372
Benton, Thomas Hart (American statesman)   **M:**380
Bentonville, Battle of (1865)   **N:**319
Bent's Fort (Colorado)   **C:**438; **F:**378
Benue River (west Africa)   **N:**255
Benz (automobile)
  picture(s)   **A:**541
Benz, Karl (German engineer and automobile manufacturer)
      A:540; **I:**265; **T:**286
Benzene (colorless, highly flammable liquid)   **F:**47; **P:**174
Beograd (Yugoslavia) *see* Belgrade
Beowulf (epic poem)   **B:**144a–144b; **E:**265, 268; **P:**354
  fairy characteristics   **F:**12
  oral poetry later put in writing   **F:**309
Be Prepared (Scout motto)   **B:**358
Bequia (island, Saint Vincent and the Grenadines)   **S:**19
Berber (language)   **A:**56
Berbera (Somalia)   **S:**254
Berbers (people)   **A:**55, 185; **M:**458, 461
  picture(s)   **A:**54; **M:**458
Berceo, Gonzalo de *see* Gonzalo de Berceo
Berceuse (musical form)   **M:**546
Berea College (Berea, Kentucky)   **K:**217
Berg, Alban (Austrian composer)   **B:**145; **G:**189
  chamber music   **C:**184
  expressionism   **M:**548
  modern music   **M:**398
  opera   **O:**148
  Wozzeck   **O:**165
  picture(s)   **B:**145
Berg, Patty (American golfer)   **G:**258 *profile*, 260
  picture(s)   **G:**258
Bergelson, David (Yiddish author)   **Y:**361
Bergen (Norway)   **N:**347
Bergen, Edgar (American ventriloquist)   **V:**302
Berger, Hans (German psychiatrist)   **B:**369
Bergerac, Cyrano de *see* Cyrano de Bergerac
Bergman, Ingmar (Swedish film director)   **M:**493 *profile*, 494
Bergman, Ingrid (Swedish actress)   **M:**486 *profile*
Bergoust, Eric (American skier)   **O:**118
Bergy bits (melted-down icebergs)   **I:**18
Beriberi (disease)   **N:**429; **V:**370c
Bering, Vitus (Danish explorer)   **A:**156; **B:**145; **D:**110; **E:**414
Beringia (Ice Age plain connecting Alaska and Siberia)   **I:**164
Bering Sea   **A:**387; **O:**43–44
Bering Strait (Asia–North America)   **B:**145; **O:**43–44; **P:**2
  divides Asia from North America   **A:**444
Berisha, Sali (Albanian president)   **A:**162
Berkeley, Lord John (English colonial proprietor)   **N:**176
Berkeley, Sir William (English colonial governor)   **I:**202;
      W:136
Berkeley Springs (West Virginia)   **W:**134
  picture(s)   **W:**134
Berkelium (element)   **E:**171
Berkshire Hills (Massachusetts)   **M:**138
Berkshire Music Festival (at Tanglewood in Lenox,
      Massachusetts)   **M:**559
  picture(s)   **M:**559
Berkshire Valley (Massachusetts)   **M:**138
Berle, Milton (American comedian)   **T:**69
Berlin (Germany)   **B:**146–49; **G:**154, 156
  "Cold War" between East and West   **G:**164
  Kennedy administration   **K:**208–9
  Olympic Games (1936)   **O:**111
  World War II   **W:**316
  picture(s)
      American sector border sign   **G:**166
      children play in rubble   **G:**164
      Soviet soldier and flag (1945)   **U:**50

  war memorial   **B:**147
  World War II   **W:**316
Berlin (New Hampshire)   **N:**159
Berlin, Congress of   **U:**47
Berlin, Irving (American songwriter)   **B:**150; **M:**558; **U:**208–9
  Christmas songs   **C:**118
  patriotic songs   **N:**25
  ragtime   **J:**58
Berlin Airlift   **B:**149; **C:**401; **G:**164; **T:**327; **U:**197
  picture(s)   **B:**148
Berlin Blockade   **C:**400–401
Berliner, Emile (German-American inventor)   **P:**195; **R:**123
Berliner Ensemble (theater, Berlin)   **T:**161
Berlin Wall (separating East and West Berlin)   **B:**146, 149;
      C:401; **G:**166
  picture(s)   **W:**275
Berlioz, Hector (French composer)   **B:**150; **F:**446
  band music   **B:**43
  choral music   **C:**284
  harp, use of   **H:**36
  La Damnation de Faust   **F:**73
  opera   **O:**147
  romantic orchestral music   **R:**304
Bermuda (British crown colony of islands in the Atlantic Ocean)
      B:151–52
  What is the Bermuda Triangle?   **B:**152
Bermuda grass   **G:**317
Bermuda onions   **O:**123
Bermuda Triangle   **B:**152
Bermúdez, Juan de (Spanish navigator)   **B:**152
Bern (capital of Switzerland)   **S:**544
Bernadette of Lourdes, Saint   **S:**18d *profile*
Bernadotte, Count Folke (Swedish diplomat)   **S:**529
Bernadotte, Jean Baptiste *see* Charles XIV John (king of Sweden
      and Norway)
Bernal Jiménez, Miguel (Mexican composer)   **L:**73
Bernard, Claude (French physiologist)   **M:**207
Bern Convention (1886)   **C:**547
Bernese Alps (Switzerland)   **A:**194b
Bernhard, Thomas (German dramatist)   **D:**302
Bernhardt, Sarah (French actress)   **T:**160 *profile*
  picture(s)   **T:**160
Bernice P. Bishop Museum (Honolulu, Hawaii)   **H:**55
Bernini, Giovanni Lorenzo (Italian sculptor, painter, and
      architect)   **B:**152; **I:**400
  baroque architecture   **B:**65
  fountains   **F:**394
  high altar in Saint Peter's Basilica   **V:**282
  place in the history of sculpture   **S:**100–101
  picture(s)
      Apollo and Daphne (sculpture)   **I:**400
      David (statue)   **B:**65; **J:**103; **S:**100
      equestrian statue of Louis XIV   **B:**152
      high altar in Saint Peter's Basilica   **V:**281
      Throne of Saint Peter   **I:**400
Bernoulli, Christoph (Swiss naturalist)   **B:**153
Bernoulli, Daniel (Swiss scientist and mathematician)
      A:37–38; **B:**153; **M:**167–68
Bernoulli, Jakob (I) (Swiss mathematician; 1654–1705)
      B:153; **M:**167–68
Bernoulli, Jakob (II) (Swiss mathematician; 1759–1789)
      B:153
Bernoulli, Johann (I) (Swiss mathematician; 1667–1748)
      B:153; **M:**167–68
Bernoulli, Johann (II) (Swiss mathematician; 1710–1790)
      B:153
Bernoulli, Johann (III) (Swiss scientist; 1746–1807)   **B:**153
Bernoulli, Nikolaus (II) (Swiss mathematician; 1687–1759)
      B:153
Bernoulli, Nikolaus (III) (Swiss mathematician; 1695–1726)
      B:153
Bernoulli family (Swiss mathematicians)   **B:**153
Bernoulli's principle (law in physics)   **A:**38, 109; **B:**153;
      M:168
Bernstein, Carl (American investigative reporter)   **W:**65

Bernstein, Leonard (American conductor, pianist, and composer) N:232 *profile*
  dance music D:36
  musical theater M:558
  picture(s) N:232; U:210
Berra, Lawrence Peter (Yogi) (American baseball player) M:378 *profile*
Berries (fruit) G:298–301
  garden fruits G:51
  uses in cooking C:534
Berruguete, Alonso (Spanish artist) S:383
Berry, Charles Edward Anderson (Chuck) (American rock music performer) R:262a, 262b *profile*
  picture(s) R:262b
Berry, Raymond (American football player) F:362 *profile*
  picture(s) F:362
Berryman, John (American poet) A:214
Berry's World (cartoon) C:129
Bertha (Berthrada) (mother of Charlemagne)
  believed to be original Mother Goose N:415
Berthold Missal (illuminated manuscript)
  picture(s) G:167
Berthrada *see* Bertha
Bertin, Rose (French seamstress) C:381
Beryl (gem mineral) G:71
  picture(s) M:314
  table(s) M:315
Beryllium (element) E:171; M:318
Berzelius, Jöns Jakob (Swedish chemist) C:209, 210
Bessarabia (Moldova–Ukraine) M:403; R:300
Bessel, Friedrich Wilhelm (German astronomer) A:474, 476 *profile*
Bessemer, Sir Henry (English inventor of Bessemer steel process) B:154; I:333
Bessemer process (for producing steel) B:154; I:333, 338
Best, Charles H. (Canadian physiologist) B:59
"Best Friend of Charleston" (locomotive) L:287; R:88–89
  picture(s) L:287
Best in Show (dog show award) D:248
Best of Breed (dog show award) D:248
Beta-blockers (drugs) O:116
Beta brass (alloy) B:410
Betancourt, Rómulo (Venezuelan statesman) V:299
Beta particles (of radioactive atoms) R:47, 67
Beta Pictoris (star)
  picture(s) S:249
Beta rays (streams of beta particles of radioactive elements) R:67
Beta video cassette system V:332d
Betelgeuse (star) S:430
Bethlehem (Jordan)
  birthplace of Jesus Christ J:86
  Christmas customs C:300
Bethlehem (Pennsylvania) P:135
  Bach festival M:560
  picture(s) C:413
Bethune, Mary McLeod (American educator) A:79k; B:154; F:274 *profile*
Betrothed, The (novel) *see* Promessi sposi, I
Betsy Ross House (Philadelphia, Pennsylvania) P:180
Bettas (fish) F:196, 204
Bevel gauges (tools) T:230
Bevel gears G:66
  picture(s) G:66
Beverages
  beer B:114–15
  coffee C:396–97
  grain products G:284–85
  tea T:34–36
  what you drink depends on where you live F:330
  whiskey and other distilled beverages W:161
  wine W:190–90a
Beverly Hills Hotel (Los Angeles, California)
  picture(s) L:307
Bewick, Thomas (English engraver) C:232

Beyle, Marie Henri *see* Stendhal
Beyond the Horizon (play by O'Neill) O:122
Béziers (France)
  picture(s) H:179
Bhagavad Gita (Hindu sacred poem) H:130; I:140; P:354
Bhakti (Hindu religious movement) I:141
Bharal (kind of wild sheep) S:145
Bharat *see* India
Bhaskara (Indian mathematician) M:164
Bhopal (India) chemical accident C:197
Bhotes (Bhotias) (a people of south central Asia) B:155
Bhumibol Adulyadej (king of Thailand) T:152
Bhutan (kingdom in the Himalayas) B:155–55a
  picture(s)
    flag F:231
Bhutto, Benazir (prime minister of Pakistan) B:155b; P:40a
  picture(s) B:155b; P:40a
Bhutto, Zulfikar Ali (Pakistani political leader) B:51, 155b; P:40a
Biafra (eastern region of Nigeria) N:258
Bialik, Hayyim (Chaim) Nahman (Hebrew poet) H:101
Bialowieza Forest (Poland) P:358
Bias (in opinion surveys) O:170; S:439–40
Bias-ply tires T:209
Biathlon (sports event) S:184f
Bible B:156–66 *see also* New Testament; Old Testament; Prophets; the names of Biblical characters
  African American spirituals' use of biblical events H:325
  Apostles, The A:328–29
  Bible stories in the Koran K:293
  Biblical dance D:23
  Biblical Hebrew language H:98
  Biblical names N:7
  Biblical origins of the Jewish people J:102–3
  Dead Sea Scrolls contain commentaries on D:47
  Gutenberg Bible C:464; G:427
  Hebrew literature H:99
  Jesus Christ J:85–89
  Judaism, sacred writings of J:142, 145–46
  King James version C:293; E:245, 273–74; R:132
  legends in ancient texts L:129
  Luther's translation C:292
  people in the Bible B:167
  poetry P:354
  prayers P:430
  Protestantism P:490–94
  proverbs (traditional sayings) P:498; Q:19
  Puritans P:550, 551
  Renaissance studies by the humanists R:160
  Roman Catholic Church R:281
  Talmud is a record of Jewish study and interpretation T:13
  Ten Commandments T:72–73
  unicorns, reference to U:28
  picture(s)
    early French picture Bible G:271
    Gutenberg Bible P:474
Bible, people in the B:167
Bible stories B:168–74
  Boy Jesus B:173–74
  Daniel in the Lion's Den B:172–73
  David and Goliath B:169–70
  Jonah B:171–72
  Noah's Ark B:168–69
  scholarly use of word "myth" M:573–74
Biblical names N:7
Bibliography
  national: Cumulative Book Index I:115
  researching reports R:183
  selected children's books, list of C:241–48
Bibliothèque Nationale (Paris) L:173
Bicameral legislature G:276; L:137
  United States, Congress of the U:137
Biceps muscles B:289; M:516
  picture(s) M:517

Bichirs (group of bony fish) F:184, 185
Bickerdyke, Mary Ann Ball (American nurse) O:74 profile
    picture(s) O:74
Bickford, William (English inventor) E:420
Bicuspids (Premolars) (teeth) T:43
Bicycle racing B:176–77; R:33
    picture(s)
        Tour de France F:404
Bicycle Thief, The (motion picture, 1948)
    picture(s) M:494
Bicycling B:175–78
    bicycle camping C:48–49
    gyroscope, properties of G:437
    hosteling H:255
    how gear ratio works G:65–66
    RAGBRAI ride in Iowa I:290
    rubber tires, first use of T:208
    safety S:5
    picture(s)
        plastic bicycling gear P:322
        RAGBRAI ride in Iowa I:291
        stationary bicycle P:226
        transportation in China B:127c; T:288
Biden, Joseph Robinette, Jr. (American public official) D:100 profile
Bidpai, Fables of F:4, 8
Bidwell, John (American pioneer) O:279
Biedermeier style (of furniture) F:513
    picture(s)
        desk F:513
Biennials (plants) F:287; G:29–30, 46; P:311
Bienville, Jean Baptiste Lemoyne, Sieur de (French founder of New Orleans) L:326, 326 profile
Bierce, Ambrose (American writer and journalist) H:290
Bifocal glasses O:179
Bifrost (bridge to Asgard, home of the Norse gods) N:280
Big bands (of the 1930's and 1940's) R:261
    country music, influence on C:563
    guitar G:412
    jazz J:60–61
Big bang theory (of the universe) A:476a; P:232, 239; S:70, 74; U:217–18
Big Bear (constellation) see Ursa Major
Big Ben (clock bell, London) L:293
    picture(s) L:293; U:55
Big Bend National Park (Texas) T:132
    picture(s) T:125
Big Bertha (giant German cannon) G:425
    picture(s) W:279
"Big Bird" (United States spy satellite) see KH-11
Big Black River (Mississippi) M:352
Big Bog (area of Minnesota) M:328
"Big Boys" (steam locomotives) L:288
Big Cypress Swamp (Florida) F:263
Big Dipper (star group) C:523, 524, 525
    Native American folktale about F:317
Big Dog (constellation) see Canis Major
Bigelow, Erastus (American inventor) R:354
Big Foot (Lakota Indian leader) I:182; S:326
Big-game hunting H:300–301
Bigger Splash, A (painting by Hockney)
    picture(s) E:264
Big Hole National Battlefield (Montana) M:436
Bighorn Mountains (Wyoming) W:336
Bighorn River (Wyoming–Montana)
    picture(s) M:430
Bighorns (Rocky Mountain sheep) H:220; M:75; S:145
    picture(s) H:219; M:74
Big M Drug Mart Inc. v. The Queen (Canada, 1985) S:506
Big Muddy (Missouri River) M:382
Bigotry see Ethnocentrism
Big Sandy River (Kentucky–West Virginia) W:128, 133
Big Sioux Falls (South Dakota)
    picture(s) S:315
Big Sky Country (name given to Montana) M:428, 429

Big South Fork National River and Recreation Area (Kentucky–Tennessee) T:82
Big stick (foreign policy of Theodore Roosevelt) R:331
Big Sur (California)
    picture(s) C:20
Big Thicket National Preserve (Texas) T:132
Big top (circus tent) C:307
Bihar (state, India) I:128
Biharis (a people of Bangladesh and India) B:48
Bihzad, Kamal ad-Din (Persian painter) I:357
Bikini (coral atoll in the west central Pacific) M:113
Bilateral treaties (between two nations) T:296–97
Bile (secretion of the liver) B:277; D:161, 162–63; G:227; L:267, 268, 269
Bile ducts (that carry bile to the gallbladder) L:268
Bilingual education E:90; H:137
Bilingual Education Act (United States, 1968) H:137
Bilirubin (bile pigment) L:269
Billboards (used for outdoor advertising) A:30–31
    Ogden Nash poem against H:290
Billets (steel ingots) I:334
Bill Haley and the Comets (rock music group) R:262a
Billiard balls P:327
Billiards B:179–80
Billings (Montana) M:434, 435, 437
    picture(s) M:435
Billings, William (American hymn composer) H:324
Billings Farm and Museum (Woodstock, Vermont) V:314
    picture(s) V:314
Bill of Rights, American B:181–84 see also Civil rights; United States, Constitution of the
    civil rights, historical origins of C:326
    The Federalist, position of F:78
    First Amendment freedoms F:163
    jury, trial by J:163
    Madison was the principal author M:12
    National Archives N:26
    ten original amendments to the Constitution U:147, 155–56
Bill of Rights, Canadian see Charter of Rights and Freedoms
Bill of Rights, English B:184; E:246
    civil rights, historical origins of C:326
    human rights H:284
    jury trial, right to J:163
    taxation T:25
Bill of Rights, French see Declaration of the Rights of Man and of the Citizen
Bill of Rights, Universal see Universal Declaration of Human Rights
Bill of Rights Day B:181
Bills (of birds) see Beaks
Bills (suggested laws) G:276; U:142–44, 166–67, 168
    how laws are made L:86
Billy goats G:244
Billy the Kid (American outlaw) N:192 profile
Biloxi (Mississippi) M:354, 357, 359
    picture(s) M:357
Biltmore House and Gardens (Asheville, North Carolina) N:314
Bimetallic strips (in thermometers) T:163–64
Bimini Islands (Bahamas) B:17
    Ponce de León's search for the Fountain of Youth P:382
Binary fission (of bacteria) B:11
    picture(s) B:11
Binary form (basic design used in writing music) M:537
Binary number system N:409
    automation A:530
    digital sound recording S:267a
    electronics E:160
    fiber optic telephone transmission T:54
Binary stars A:474; S:430, 432, 433
    black holes B:250a
    relativity, theory of R:144
    picture(s)
        artist's impression of X-ray system B:250a
Binchois, Gilles (Flemish composer) D:365; F:444; R:172

Binder's board (for book covers)   B:333
Binding energy (in physics)   S:491
Binding knots   K:288
Binding of books see Bookbinding
Bindweed   W:104
Binet, Alfred (French psychologist)   I:253, 254; P:508
Bingen, Hildegard von see Hildegard von Bingen
Bingham, George Caleb (American artist)
    picture(s)
        Raftsmen Playing Cards   M:380
        Traders Descending the Missouri   O:268
Bingham, Hiram (American missionary in Hawaii)   H:61 profile
Bingham Canyon copper mine (Utah)   U:248–49
Binnie, W. Ian (Canadian Supreme Court justice)
    picture(s)   S:505
Binnig, Gerd (German scientist)   E:164
Binoculars   O:181
    prism binoculars   L:147
    picture(s)   O:180
Binocular vision see Stereoscopic vision
Binomial nomenclature (method of naming living things)
        K:254; T:29
Binomial theorem (mathematical formula worked out by
        Newton)   N:206
Binturongs (Bear cats) (mammals related to mongooses)
        M:419
Biochemistry (study of the composition of living things)
        B:185–88; C:205, 210; S:66 see also Body
        chemistry; Genetics; Photosynthesis
    body chemistry   B:291–99
    careers in biology   B:197
    chemistry, history of   C:211
    life   L:198–200
    medical laboratory tests   M:209
    Pasteur, Louis   P:97
Biodegradable materials   W:66
    detergents and soap   D:141
    plastics   P:327
Biodiversity (variety of species in an environment)   E:53–54,
        55
Biofeedback (method to control body processes)
    picture(s)   D:239
Biogeography (study of geography of plants and animals)
        G:100–101
Biographical novel   B:190
Biography (author's account of a person's life)   B:189–90
    Boswell's Life of Samuel Johnson   E:279; J:125
    children's literature   C:246–47
    English literature   E:288
    library arrangement   L:183
    literature, types of   L:258
    Pulitzer prizes   P:535–36
Bioko (formerly Fernando Po) (province of Equatorial Guinea)
        E:309
Biological clock   B:191–92; L:203–4 see also Rhythm (in
        plant and animal life)
    clock-compass in birds and bees   B:233, 235; H:193
    millipedes   C:169
Biological computers   C:494
Biological control (of pests)   F:57, 482; I:249–50; P:290
    ants used in ancient China   A:321
    mosquitoes   M:471
    vegetable growing   V:288
Biological oceanography see Marine biology
Biological psychology   P:504
Biological rhythm see Rhythm (in plant and animal life)
Biological sciences see Life sciences
Biological warfare (warfare in which living organisms are used
        to transmit disease to an enemy)   D:180
Biology   B:193–202 see also Botany; Evolution; Microbiology;
        Zoology
    biochemistry   B:185–88
    biological clock   L:203–4
    biological oceanography   O:35, 40

cells   C:159–62
crime, theories on causes of   C:575
extinction   E:425–26
genetics   G:77–91
kingdoms of living things   K:253–59
medicine, history of   M:203–8c
Mendel created a new experiment combining biology and
        statistics   M:220
science, milestones in   S:70–71, 72, 74
science, modern   S:72–73
taxonomy   T:27–29
picture(s)
    biologists at work   B:194–95
Bioluminescence (light emitted by living organisms)   B:203
    centipedes and millipedes   C:169
    deep-sea fish   F:183; U:22
    ocean life   O:24, 27
Biomarkers (in genetic engineering)   G:82
Biomedical engineers   E:225
Biomedical sciences (life sciences used in medicine)   S:66
Biomes (communities of plants and animals)   B:204–10;
        G:100
    plants   P:318, 319
    specific regions of the biosphere   L:203
    tundra   T:331
    map(s)
        major biomes of the world   P:318
    picture(s)
        plants   P:320–21
Biondi, Matt (American swimmer)   S:537 profile
    picture(s)   S:537
Biophysics   S:66
Biopsy (examination of living tissue)   C:93; M:209
Bioremediation methods (of cleaning up hazardous wastes)
        H:73
Biorhythm see Rhythm (in plant and animal life)
Biosatellite (satellite that carries living matter into space)
        S:340d
Biosphere   B:196, 204–10; L:201–6
Biosphere 2 (structure where ecology is studied)   T:329
Biostatistics   P:515
Biota (organisms in an environment)   G:100
Biotechnology   G:83–86; S:73
    control of plant pests   P:291
    Japanese industry   J:39
Biotin (B-complex vitamin)   V:370d
    table(s)   V:372
Bipedalism (ability to walk on two feet)   H:280
Bipolar transistors   T:276
Bipropellant (rocket fuel)   R:257
Birch trees
    picture(s)
        paper birch   T:304
        state tree of New Hampshire   N:151
        uses of the wood and its grain   W:223
        white birch   M:328
Bird, Larry (American basketball player)   B:95i profile; I:156
        profile
    picture(s)   B:95i; I:157
Birdbanding
    Audubon made first banding experiments   A:491
    picture(s)   H:187
"Bird Came Down the Walk, A" (poem by Dickinson)   D:153
Bird Day see Arbor Day
Bird in Space (sculpture by Brancusi)   B:370
    picture(s)   S:105
Bird of paradise   A:270–71
Birds   A:266; B:211–44
    acid rain's effects   A:10
    animal communication   A:284
    Audubon's paintings   A:491
    beaks (bills)   A:277; B:217
    biological clocks and compasses   B:191
    caring for their young   B:232

Bit (mouthpiece for a horse) H:228
Bite (in dentistry) O:236
Bites (of animals)
   animal bites, first aid for F:161
   insect bites, first aid for F:161
   mosquitoes M:471
Bitonality (in music) M:398
Bits (Binary digits) (of information) C:481, 491; T:49
Bitter (sense of taste) B:286
Bitterroot (flower)
   picture(s)
      state flower of Montana M:429
Bitumen (hydrocarbon) P:175
Bituminous coal (soft coal) C:388; F:488–89
Bivalves (mollusks with two shells) M:406; O:289–92; S:148
Biwa, Lake (Japan) J:35
Biya, Paul (Cameroon president) C:41
Bizerte (Tunisia) T:336
   picture(s) T:334
Bizet, Georges (French composer) O:152
Bjørnson, Bjørnstjerne (Norwegian writer) N:345; S:58h, 58i
Blab schools L:241
Black (color) C:425
   Christian funeral custom F:494
   symbolism of C:372, 429
Black, Hugo La Fayette (American jurist) A:142 profile
Black, Joseph (Scottish scientist) M:27; S:71
Black, Shirley Temple see Temple, Shirley
Black American literature see African American literature
Black Americans see African Americans
Black-and-tan coonhound (dog) D:250
Black-and-white negative film (in photography) P:204, 205, 210–11
Black Arts Movement A:214
Blackball (to vote against) B:23
Black Bart (British pirate) P:262 profile
Blackbeard (British pirate) P:262 profile, 264
   picture(s) P:262
Black bears B:105–6
   omnivores M:73
   West Virginia's state animal W:129
   picture(s) B:107
Black Belt (area of Alabama) A:132
Black belt (in karate) K:195
Blackberries G:298, 301
   picture(s)
      thornless B:188
Black Boy (book by Wright) W:327
Blackbuck (antelope) A:297
Black Cabinet (of Franklin Roosevelt's administration) A:79k
Black Canyon of the Gunnison National Park (Colorado) C:438
Black-capped chickadee (bird)
   picture(s) B:216
      provincial bird of New Brunswick N:138
Black Caribs (people of Guatemala) see Garífuna
Black cats S:504
Black Codes (laws passed by Southern states just after Civil War) A:79f; J:118; R:118; U:186
Black-crowned night heron (bird)
   picture(s) B:231
Black Death see Bubonic plague
Black-eyed Susans (flowers)
   picture(s)
      state flower of Maryland M:121
Black-figure pottery (of ancient Greece) P:408
Blackfish (Shawnee Indian leader) B:334
Blackfoot (Indians of North America) I:180
Black Forest (Germany) G:153
   picture(s)
      acid rain effects E:304
Blackfriars (London theater) S:132
Black Hawk (Native American chief) I:74–75, 204–5, 303
   Black Hawk Historic Site (Rock Island, Illinois) I:70
   Iowa nicknamed Hawkeye State in his honor I:290
Black Hawk War (1865–1868) I:74–75; U:254; W:205

Blackheads (clogged skin pores) D:187
Black Hills (South Dakota–Wyoming) S:312, 315, 325; W:334
   gold rush G:252
   mineral resources S:317
Black Hills National Forest (South Dakota–Wyoming) S:316
Black Hills spruce trees
   picture(s)
      state tree of South Dakota S:313
Black History Month A:80
Black holes (in astronomy) A:476; B:250a; S:433; U:212–13, 215
   galactic nucleus M:309
   gravitation G:325
   Hawking, Stephen William H:63
   quasars Q:7; U:217
   picture(s)
      artist's impression B:250a
Black homelands (South Africa) see Tribal homelands
Black Iris (painting by O'Keeffe)
   picture(s) U:132
Black Kettle (Cheyenne Indian chief) I:180 profile
Black light see Ultraviolet radiation
Blacklisting (not permitting people to work) U:13
Black lung (disease that comes from breathing coal dust) C:391
Black Madonna (Polish religious symbol) P:358
   picture(s) P:358
Black Mansion (Ellsworth, Maine) M:44
Black market (market in violation of government regulations)
   prohibition P:485
Black Mask (magazine)
   picture(s) M:565
Black Mass (supposed activity of witches) W:208–9
Black Mesa (highest point in Oklahoma) O:82
Black Mountain (highest point in Kentucky) K:212, 213
Blackmun, Harry Andrew (American jurist) I:74 profile
Black Muslims (Nation of Islam) A:79c, 79o, 79p; M:59
Black olives O:101
Black Panther Party A:79o
Black Peter see Swarte Piet
Black plague (disease) see Bubonic plague
Black powder (early gunpowder) E:420, 421; G:415
"Black Power" (slogan of the civil rights movement) A:79o
Black racer (snake)
   picture(s) S:209
Black Reflections (painting by Kline)
   picture(s) M:396a
Black Renaissance see Harlem Renaissance
Blacks see also African Americans; the names of African countries, black leaders, and organizations
   Africa A:55
   Africa, art of A:70–76
   Africa, early kingdoms of A:65–66
   Africa, literature of A:76a–76d
   African Americans A:79a–80
   Caribbean dance D:30
   Haiti H:9, 11
   Jamaica J:15, 18
   Latin America L:49, 50, 58
   music A:77–79; L:72
   sickle-cell anemia D:201
   slavery S:193–97
   Suriname S:516
Black Sea M:213; O:44; U:39
Blackshirts (fascist parties)
   British F:64
   Italian fascists and Mussolini F:63; M:560
Black snake
   picture(s) S:209
Black Sox Scandal (in baseball) B:91
Blackstone, Sir William (English jurist) L:85
   picture(s) L:85
Black Stone of Mecca see Kaaba
Blackstone River (Massachusetts–Rhode Island) R:214

Blackstrap molasses   H:79; S:483
Black tea   T:34–35
Blacktip sharks   S:143
   picture(s)   S:141
Blackton, J. Stuart (American illustrator)   A:290
Blacktop (asphalt for roads)   R:250
Black walnuts   N:435, 436
Black Warrior River (Alabama)   A:132, 133
Blackwater River (Ireland)   I:319
Blackwell, Elizabeth (English-American physician)   B:250b
Blackwell, Rosa (American slave)   S:195
Black widow spiders
   picture(s)   F:161
Bladder   B:282
Bladensburg, Battle of (1814)   W:10
Blades (of broad leaves)   L:112; P:306
Blaese, Michael (American scientist)   G:91
Blaiberg, Philip *see* Barnard, Christiaan
Blaine, James Gillespie (American statesman)   G:54; M:48
   profile
Blair, Bonnie (American speed skater)   I:44 *profile*
   picture(s)   I:42
Blair, Eric *see* Orwell, George
Blair, Tony (British prime minister)   E:255
   picture(s)   E:255
Blair House (Washington, D.C.)   W:166
Blais, Marie-Claire (Canadian writer)   C:87
Blaize, Herbert A. (prime minister of Grenada)   G:379
Blake, Lyman Reed (American shoe manufacturer)   S:158
Blake, Nicholas *see* Day Lewis, C.
Blake, William (English poet and artist)   B:250b; E:278
   book illustration   E:261
   children's literature   C:237
   illustration of books   I:80
   romanticism   R:302
   picture(s)
      engraving from *Songs of Experience*   E:278
      Jacob's Ladder (painting)   R:302
      romanticism   R:303
Blalock, Alfred (American surgeon)   T:24
Blanc, Mont (mountain, France–Italy)   A:194b; F:407; M:504
   picture(s)   A:194b
   table(s)
      first ascent   M:500
Blanchard, Jean-Pierre François (French balloonist)   B:35
Blanchard, Madeline-Sophie (French balloonist)   B:35
Blanco, Salvador Jorge (president of Dominican Republic)
   D:283
Bland-Allison Bill (1877)   H:71
Blanes, Juan Manuel (Uruguayan artist)   L:63
Blankers-Koen, Fanny (Dutch track star)   O:113; T:263
Blanket primary elections   E:129
Blanket toss (Inuit custom)
   picture(s)   I:272
Blank verse (unrhymed verse)   S:133–37
Blantyre (executive and judicial capital of Malawi)   M:53
Blasco Ibáñez, Vicente (Spanish author)   S:390
Blast (of a nuclear explosion)   N:376
Blast furnaces   I:330–32
   fuel   F:489
   picture(s)   O:217
Blasting (in quarrying)   Q:4b
Blasting agents (explosives)   E:421
Blasting caps   E:420–21
Blasting mats (used in construction)   E:423
Blastula (stage in cell division)   E:101
Blatch, Harriot Stanton (American reformer)   W:212a–212b
Blaue Reiter, Die (German art group) *see* Blue Rider, The
"Blazars" (gamma-ray sources)   S:368
Blaze (horse marking)
   picture(s)   H:238
Blazoning (describing arms in heraldry)   H:110, 112
   picture(s)   H:111

Bleaching
   fats and oils   O:78
   hair   H:8
   paper making   P:55
Bleak House (novel by Dickens)   M:564
Blechynden, Richard (English tea merchant)   T:36
Bleeding
   first aid   F:158–59, 160, 161
   hemophilia   D:193
Bleeding Kansas   A:6b; K:176, 188, 191
Blended families   F:37–38
Blenheim, Battle of (1704)   S:377
Blennerhassett Island (West Virginia)   W:134
Bleriot, Louis (French engineer)   A:562
Blessed Virgin Mary *see* Mary, Virgin
Blessings (prayers)   P:430–31
Bless Me, Ultima (book by Anaya)   A:214a
Bligh, William (British naval officer)   B:251; P:295
Blimps *see* Airships
Blindfish   C:158
Blind Man's Buff (painting by Goya)
   picture(s)   G:277
"Blind Men and the Elephant, The" (fable by Saxe)   F:7
Blindness   B:251–54
   cave-dwelling animals   C:158
   computer assistance   C:485
   disabled people   D:176, 177, 178
   dreams and eye movements   D:318
   echoes used by   E:49
   Keller, Helen   K:203
   library service   L:176
   night blindness   V:370b
   public assistance   W:120
   seeing-eye dogs   D:242
   syphilis may cause   D:203
   typewriters for the blind   T:374
   what to do when you see a blind person   B:252
Blindness of Tobit, The (etching by Rembrandt)   G:304
Blind snakes   S:211
Blind spot (in the eye)   E:431
Bliss, Mary Elizabeth Taylor (acting first lady in Taylor's
   administration)   F:170
   picture(s)   T:32
Blister beetles
   picture(s)   B:124, 126
Blithedale Romance, The (novel by Hawthorne)   A:204
Blitz (bombing of England, 1940)   L:298; W:299
Blitzkrieg (sudden military attack)   R:320
Blixen, Baroness Karen *see* Dinesen, Isak
Block, Adriaen (Dutch explorer)   R:224
Blockade (to prevent supplies of war from entering enemy's
   ports)
   Berlin airlift   B:149
   Cuban missile crisis   C:601
Blockhouse (used in spacecraft launchings)   S:340d
Blockhouses (forts)   F:379
Blocking (giving stage directions in a play)   P:336, 337–38
Blocking (in football)   F:353
   picture(s)   F:354
Block Island (Rhode Island)   R:212, 214, 220
   picture(s)   R:215
Block lava   V:383
Block plane (tool)   T:228–29
   picture(s)   T:228
Block printing   P:472
   Chinese printing   C:464
   woodcut printing   W:229
Blocks (rock fragments)   V:383
Bloc Québécois (Canadian political party)   C:75
Bloemfontein (judicial capital of South Africa)   S:271
Blok, Aleksandr (Russian writer)   R:379
Blondie (American rock group)   R:262d
Blondie (comic strip)
   picture(s)   C:129

Blood **B:**255–58
  AIDS transmitted by exchange of blood **A:**100b
  anemia **D:**188
  blood derivatives, medical techniques with **M:**211
  blood tests **M:**209
  calcium needed for clotting **V:**371
  cells are produced in bone marrow **S:**184a
  circulation, studies of **B:**199; **M:**205–6
  circulatory system of human body **B:**279–81; **C:**304–6
  Drew, Charles, and blood storage **D:**323
  Harvey's contribution to studies of circulation **H:**44
  heart **H:**80–85
  hemophilia **D:**184
  insect's blood system **I:**239
  kidneys filter blood **K:**242, 243
  leukemia **D:**196
  liver, functions of the **L:**267–69
  muscles receive fuel from **M:**519
  Red Cross blood service programs **R:**126, 127
  stain removal **L:**82
  transfusion **T:**273
  vitamin K aids clotting **V:**370d
Blood banks **M:**211; **T:**273
Blood clots **D:**189
Blood counts **M:**209
Blood groups (blood types) **B:**257; **R:**28–29; **T:**273
Bloodhound (dog) **D:**241–42, 244, 250
Blood pressure **M:**208f–208g
  hypertension **D:**194–95
  kidneys help control **K:**244
  measurement of **H:**85
Blood tests **D:**207; **M:**209
Blood transfusion *see* Transfusion, blood
Blood vessels **B:**279, 281; **C:**304, 305, 306
  blushing **B:**300
  heart, function of **H:**80–81
  iodine used in taking X rays of **X:**351
  picture(s)
    in human head **B:**280
Bloodworms **W:**320
Bloody Mary *see* Mary I (queen of England and Ireland)
Bloody Sunday (Northern Ireland massacre, 1972)
  picture(s)
    anniversary **N:**337
Bloomington (Minnesota) **M:**335
Blooms (rapid growth of algae) **P:**284
Blooms (steel ingots) **I:**334
Blount, William (American political figure) **T:**86
Blow, Taylor and H. T. (American abolitionists) **D:**321
Blow drying (of hair) **H:**8
Blowhole (of dolphins) **D:**275
Blow molding (plastics manufacturing process) **P:**326
Blowouts (from oil wells) **P:**175
Blowpipes (glassmaking) **B:**346; **G:**229, 233
Blowtorch, oxyacetylene *see* Oxyacetylene blowtorch
Blubber (fatty tissue) **W:**153, 155
  manatees **M:**77
  seals **S:**107
  walruses **W:**6
Blucher (steam engine) **R:**87
Blue (color) **C:**425; **G:**4
Blue and Green Music (painting by O'Keeffe)
  picture(s) **D:**135
Blue babies (children born with defective hearts) **H:**85; **T:**24
Blue-Backed Speller (by Webster) **W:**99
Blue bears *see* Glacier bears
Blueberries **G:**301
  picture(s) **G:**299; **N:**166
Bluebirds
  picture(s)
    state bird of Idaho **I:**47
    state bird of Missouri **M:**367
    state bird of Nevada **N:**123
    state bird of New York **N:**211

Blue Boat, The (painting by Homer)
  picture(s) **U:**130
Bluebonnet (flower)
  picture(s)
    state flower of Texas **T:**125, 126
Bluebottle flies
  picture(s) **I:**244, 245
Blue Boy, The (painting by Gainsborough) **G:**4
  picture(s) **G:**4
Blue cheeses **D:**12
Blue chip stocks **S:**455
Blue crabs (crustaceans) **C:**571
Blue Dancers (drawing by Degas)
  picture(s) **F:**430
Bluefin (fish) **F:**217
Blue-footed booby
  picture(s) **B:**216
Bluegill (fish) **F:**213
  picture(s) **F:**209
Blue goose (bird) **D:**344
Bluegrass Basin (of Kentucky) **K:**214
Bluegrass music **C:**563
  Monroe, Bill **K:**225
  West Virginia festivals **W:**132
  picture(s) **K:**217; **W:**197
    festival **F:**322
Bluegrass State (nickname for Kentucky) **K:**212, 213
Blue-green algae *see* Cyanobacteria
Blue Grotto (Capri, Italy) **C:**156; **I:**363
Blueground (Kimberlite) (diamond-bearing rock) **G:**70
Blue hen chicken
  picture(s)
    state bird of Delaware **D:**89
Blue jays (birds) **B:**242
  picture(s) **B:**217, 230
    provincial bird of Prince Edward Island **P:**460
Blue Lake (New Mexico) **N:**194
Blue laws (legislation on matters of individual conscience or conduct) **L:**88
Blue Licks, Battle of (1782) **K:**220, 225
Blue-light lasers **L:**46d
Blue Mosque (Istanbul, Turkey) *see* Sultan Ahmed Mosque
Blue Mountains (Jamaica) **J:**16
Blue Mountains (Oregon–Washington) **O:**204; **W:**16
Blue Nile River (Africa) **E:**331; **N:**260; **S:**477, 478
Blue notes (in jazz) **J:**57, 58
Blueprint (photographic reproduction method) **B:**259
  picture(s) **B:**259
Blue Riband (award for the fastest Atlantic crossing) **O:**31
Blue Rider, The (modern art group in Germany) **E:**424; **G:**172; **M:**391–92
  Kandinsky, Wassily **K:**173
  Klee, Paul **K:**271
Blue Ridge (mountain range, eastern United States) **N:**285
  Maryland **M:**122
  North Carolina **N:**308
  Pennsylvania **P:**128
  South Carolina **S:**298, 299
  Tennessee **T:**74
  Virginia **V:**348
  West Virginia **W:**128
  picture(s) **G:**133; **N:**104
    Maryland **M:**121
    North Carolina **N:**307
    Virginia **V:**348
Blue Ridge Parkway **N:**314; **V:**354
Blues (in printing) **B:**330–31
Blues, the (music) **J:**58
  contributions to jazz **U:**208
  gospel songs **H:**325
  Memphis (Tennessee) **T:**74
Blue shift (change in galaxy spectrum) **L:**226

Blue spruce trees
   picture(s)
      state tree of Colorado **C:**431
      state tree of Utah **U:**243
Blue supergiant stars **S:**429
Blue whales **W:**151
   krill is the largest portion of whales' diet **P:**284
   largest mammal **M:**66
Blue-winged teal (duck) **D:**341
Bluford, Guion S., Jr. (American astronaut) **A:**79c; **S:**348
   profile
   picture(s) **S:**348
Blum, Léon (French statesman) **F:**418
Blume, Judy (American writer) **B:**259
   picture(s) **B:**259
Blunderbuss (smooth-bore gun)
   picture(s) **G:**417
Blushing (body action) **B:**300
Bly, Nellie (American newspaper reporter) **B:**260
B lymphocytes *see* B cells
BMX (Bicycle motocross) bicycles **B:**175, 177
   picture(s) **B:**176
B'nai B'rith International (Jewish organization) **C:**326
Boadicea (British queen)
   picture(s) **W:**261
Board games **G:**12–15
   video games **V:**332c
Boarding pass (permission to board an airplane) **A:**126, 127
Boarding schools **P:**443
Board of directors (of a corporation) **B:**475
Boardsailing (sport) **B:**260–61
   picture(s) **O:**203
Boars (male pigs) **H:**211; **P:**248
   picture(s)
      wild boar **H:**210
"Boar's Head, The" (English carol) **C:**118
Boas (snakes) **S:**210–11
   picture(s) **S:**216
Boas, Franz (German-American anthropologist) **B:**261; **F:**312
Boat racing **B:**265
   rowing competition **R:**340–41
Boats and boating **B:**262–65 *see also* Canoeing; Rowing;
      Sailing; Water sports
   ancient water craft **S:**151
   canal boats **E:**315
   canoeing **C:**99–101
   Chinese dwellings **C:**264
   dhows of Bahrain **B:**18
   early transportation **T:**281
   floating and buoyancy **F:**253
   houseboats **H:**176–77
   hydrofoils **H:**315
   iceboating **I:**19–20
   inventions in water transportation **I:**280
   kayaks **C:**101
   reed boats on Lake Titicaca **P:**162
   rowing **R:**340–41
   safety measures **S:**5
   sailing **S:**8–12
   snag boats **L:**323
   picture(s)
      Bangladesh riverboats **B:**50
      Dragon Boat Festival (China) **H:**159
      felucca on the Nile **R:**238
      fishing boats in Greenland **G:**373
      Florida fishing boats **F:**268
      Grand Canyon National Park **G:**292
      hydrofoil **H:**315
      Icelandic fishing boats **I:**35
      junks **R:**247
      kayaks **I:**272
      Malaysian ferry boat **M:**56
      Mississippi riverboats **M:**351
      punting on the Cam River **U:**57

      reed boats on Lake Titicaca **B:**308; **P:**161
      toy boats **T:**247
Boats and Sea, Deer Isle, Maine (painting by Marin)
   picture(s) **W:**61
Boats at Argenteuil (painting by Monet)
   picture(s) **M:**411
Bobber (for fishing) **F:**211
Bobbies (English policemen) **P:**118, 368
Bobbin (spool for holding thread) **I:**218
Bobbin lace **L:**19
Bobcats **C:**146, 147; **F:**502
Bobo (a people of Africa) **B:**451
Bobo-Dioulasso (Burkina Faso) **B:**451
   picture(s) **B:**452
Bobsledding **B:**266–67
Bobwhite (bird) **B:**239
Boccaccio, Giovanni (Italian writer) **I:**383, 406; **R:**160
   profile; **S:**161
   humanism **H:**283; **R:**159
   picture(s) **R:**160
Boccherini, Luigi (Italian composer) **C:**184
Boccia (game) **O:**115
Boccioni, Umberto (Italian painter) **I:**403; **M:**391; **S:**104
   picture(s)
      Unique Forms of Continuity in Space (painting) **I:**403
Bock, Jerry (American composer) **M:**558
Bock beer **B:**115
Böcklin, Arnold (Swiss artist) **G:**171
Bode, Johannes (German astronomer) **S:**244
Bode's law **S:**243, 244
Bodhisattvas (Buddhist deities) **B:**424; **S:**18c
Bodleian Library (Oxford University) **L:**174
Body (of an automobile) **A:**546, 551
Body, human **B:**268–88; **H:**281
   adolescence, changes during **A:**23
   aging **A:**82
   air pollution's effects on **A:**122, 123, 124
   antibodies and antigens **A:**313
   bacteria live in human body **K:**259
   biological clock **B:**191–92
   blood **B:**255–58
   bodybuilding **B:**289–90
   body signals **B:**300–301
   brain **B:**362–69
   cancer **C:**92–95
   cells **C:**159
   chemistry *see* Body chemistry
   child development **C:**224–25
   circulatory system **C:**304–6
   defenses against disease **D:**210
   digestive system **D:**161–63
   diseases **D:**181–213
   drawing, history of **D:**314
   dreaming **D:**317–18
   drugs affect **D:**333
   ear **E:**4–6
   energy, source of **E:**214–15
   eye **E:**429–32
   feet and hands, basic pattern of **F:**79–80, 84
   g-forces and weightlessness **S:**340L–341
   glands **G:**226–28
   hair **H:**5–7
   health **H:**74–77
   heart **H:**80–85
   human body is seventy percent water **L:**202
   immune system **I:**95–98
   kidneys **K:**242–44
   Leonardo's studies **L:**153
   lie detection **L:**193
   liver **L:**267–70
   lungs **L:**343–45
   lymphatic system **L:**349–50
   mental health **M:**225
   muscular system **M:**516–19

Body, human (cont.)
    nervous system   **N:**115–18
    osmosis   **O:**242–43
    physical anthropology   **A:**301
    physical examination by a doctor   **M:**208e–208h
    physical fitness   **P:**224–27
    reproductive organs   **R:**178–79
    skeletal system   **S:**183–84b
    smoking, effects of   **S:**207
    teeth   **T:**42–44
    voice apparatus   **V:**377
    water is most important substance in   **W:**50
    What is the largest organ of your body?   **B:**272
    X rays   **X:**350–51
Bodybuilding (exercises for developing muscles)   **B:289–90**
    nutrition   **N:**423
    weight lifting   **W:**107
Body chemistry   **B:291–99**
    aging   **A:**84–85
    biochemistry   **B:**187
    body, human   **B:**268–69
    digestive system   **D:**161–63
    drugs supply hormones   **D:**333
    endocrine system   **B:**287–88
    enzymes   **E:**307
    glands   **G:**226–28
    immune system   **I:**95–98
    liver   **L:**268–69
    living matter, chemical makeup of   **L:**198–200
    nutrition   **N:**423–30
Body drop (automobile assembling)
    picture(s)
        Model T   **A:**543
Body painting
    Africa, art of   **A:**75
    picture(s)
        Australian Aborigines   **A:**7
Body signals   **B:300–301**
    What makes a stomach growl?   **S:**461
Body temperature
    amphibians   **A:**214b
    anesthesia produced by lowering   **A:**258–59
    blood helps regulate   **B:**257
    circulatory system regulates   **C:**305, 306
    dinosaurs   **D:**165, 173
    hibernation   **H:**117–20
    how a nurse takes temperature   **N:**422
    medical examination, techniques of   **M:**208e
    sleep lowers   **S:**198
Body waves (of earthquakes)   **E:**35–36
Boehm, Gottfried (German architect)
    picture(s)
        Cologne building complex   **G:**173
Boeing, William Edward (American manufacturer)   **W:**27
    profile
Boeing 247 (airplane)   **A:**564
Boeing 314 (flying boat)   **A:**565
    picture(s)   **A:**565
Boeing 707 (jet airliner)   **A:**567, 568
Boeing 747 (jet airliner)   **A:**568, 571
    picture(s)   **A:**110, 119, 568
Boeing Company   **W:**20, 27
    picture(s)   **W:**21
Boerhaave, Hermann (Dutch doctor)   **M:**206
Boers (Dutch settlers in South Africa)   **S:**272
    Boer War   **B:**302
    Lesotho, history of   **L:**157
Boer War (1899–1902)   **B:302; S:**273
    England, history of   **E:**251
    use of spy kites   **K:**270
    picture(s)   **S:**272
Bogart, Humphrey (American actor)   **M:**486 *profile*
Bogdan (Moldavian prince)   **M:**403
Boggarts (mischievous fairies)   **F:**9
Bogie wheels (of tanks)   **T:**14

Bogotá (capital of Colombia)   **B:303; C:**404, 406, 408; **S:**289
    picture(s)   **B:**303; **C:**407; **S:**288
Bogs   **N:**63; **W:**145, 146–47
    picture(s)
        cranberry bog   **G:**300
Bog turtles   **T:**355
Bogue Sound (North Carolina)   **N:**308
Bohème, La (opera by Puccini)   **O:**151
Bohemia (historical region in central Europe)   **C:**609, 612
    Habsburgs   **H:**2
    Hus, Jan   **H:**306
    Thirty Years' War   **T:**179
Böhl de Faber, Cecilia *see* Caballero, Fernán
Bohr, Niels (Danish atomic physicist)   **B:304; C:**211; **D:**110; **P:**231
    physics, history of   **P:**237–38
    quantum theory   **L:**223, 224–25
    picture(s)   **B:**304; **P:**237
Bohrium (element)   **E:**171
Boiardo, Matteo Maria (Italian poet)   **I:**406
Boileau-Despréaux, Nicolas (French poet)   **F:**438
Boilers   **H:**96, 97; **S:**445
Boiling (method of cooking)   **C:**533–34
Boiling point   **H:**90–91
    different boiling points make distillation possible   **D:**218–19
    geysers   **G:**193
    liquids, properties of   **L:**254
    liquids boil at lower temperatures in a vacuum   **V:**262
    water   **W:**48
    picture(s)   **H:**90
Boils (skin infections)   **D:**195
Boise (capital of Idaho)   **I:**51, 55
    picture(s)   **I:**55
Boitano, Brian (American figure skater)   **I:**44 *profile*
Bojaxhiu, Agnes Gonxha (Roman Catholic nun) *see* Teresa, Mother
Bokassa, General Jean-Bedel (emperor of the Central African Empire)   **C:**171
Bokher, Eli (Yiddish author)   **Y:**360
Bolas (hunting devices)   **I:**108, 199
Bolden, Charles F., Jr. (American astronaut)
    picture(s)   **S:**341
Bolero (kind of jacket)   **C:**377
Boleyn, Anne (2nd queen of Henry VIII of England)   **C:**292; **E:**242; **H:**108
Bolger, Jim (prime minister of New Zealand)   **N:**242
Bolívar, Pico (highest point in Venezuela)   **V:**296
Bolívar, Simón (South American liberator and patriot)   **B:305, 310**
    Colombia's independence   **C:**408
    San Martín, José, meeting with   **S:**36
    Simón Bolívar's birthday holiday   **H:**152–53
    Venezuela, history of   **V:**298–99
    picture(s)   **S:**294; **W:**270
Bolivia   **B:306–10; L:**48, 49, 50, 55
    Indians, American   **I:**196
    languages   **S:**285, 288
    Tiwanaku civilization   **I:**170
    picture(s)
        Catavi tin mine   **T:**207
        corn being dried   **S:**291
        flag   **F:**238
        La Paz   **B:**308, 309
        Tiahuanaco   **B:**309
        Titicaca, Lake   **B:**308; **S:**280
Bolkiah, Sultan Sir Muda Hassanal *see* Hassanal Bolkiah, Sultan Sir Muda
Böll, Heinrich (German writer)   **G:**182
Bolling, Richard Walker (American politician)   **U:**142 *profile*
Boll weevils   **B:**127; **C:**560–61, 562
    picture(s)   **B:**126; **C:**560; **I:**234; **P:**288
Bologna, University of   **I:**381; **U:**219

Bolshevik Party (in Russian history)   C:473; L:140; R:367;
U:48–49
  Nicholas II executed by   N:249
  Stalin's Great Purge   U:50
  Stalin was an organizer for   S:419
  picture(s)
      1917 coup   R:368
Bolshoi Ballet
  picture(s)   B:30
Bolt-action (of guns and rifles)   G:420–21, 422
Bolter, The (painting by Russell)
  picture(s)   C:569
Bolts (fasteners)   N:3
Boltwood, Bertram (American chemist)   G:111
Bolus (chewed food)   S:460
Bolyai, János (Hungarian mathematician)   G:128; M:168
Bombardier, Joseph-Armand (Canadian inventor of the
snowmobile)   S:218a
Bombardier beetle   B:125; I:243
  picture(s)   B:124
Bombay (Mumbai) (India)   B:310a–310b; I:122
  picture(s)
      Catholic church   R:149
      Marine Drive   B:310b; I:123
      market   B:310a
      railway station   B:310a
Bombay Hook National Wildlife Refuge (Delaware)   D:92, 96
  picture(s)   D:91
Bombers (airplanes)   U:112; W:318
  picture(s)   W:306, 316
Bombings (terrorism)   T:117
  Atlanta (Georgia)   O:113
  Birmingham (Alabama)   A:79n
  Cole, USS   Y:359
  Oklahoma City (1995)   O:94, 95
  Russia   R:369
  Uffizi Gallery (Florence, Italy)   U:3
  U.S. embassy in Kenya   C:368–69; K:233
  U.S. embassy in Tanzania   C:368–69; T:19
  World Trade Center (New York City)   N:234
  picture(s)
      Oklahoma City (1995)   U:205
Bombs *see* Atomic weapons; Bombings; Hydrogen bombs;
Neutron bomb; Nuclear weapons
Bomb shelters
  picture(s)   C:401
Bomb squads (in police departments)   P:365
Bomoseen, Lake (Vermont)   V:309
Bon (kind of nature worship)   B:155
Bonaire (island in the Caribbean Sea)   C:114
Bonanza farms (in North Dakota)   N:335
Bonaparte, Jérôme (king of Westphalia)   N:13
Bonaparte, Joseph (king of Spain)   N:13; S:378
Bonaparte, Louis (king of Holland)   N:13
Bonaparte, Louis Napoleon *see* Napoleon III
Bonaparte, Napoleon *see* Napoleon I
Bonavista (Newfoundland)   N:146
Bond, Edward (English dramatist)   D:303
Bond, James (fictional character)   M:562
Bonding (of adhesives)   G:242
Bondone, Giotto di *see* Giotto di Bondone
Bonds (certificates of loans)   S:454–55; T:294
Bonds, chemical   C:201, 204; M:151–52
  atoms   A:487
Bone china (kind of porcelain)   P:412
Bone marrow *see* Marrow
Bones (of animals and humans)
  anthropological studies   A:301
  babies have more bones than adults   S:184a
  birds   B:218
  body, human   B:274
  broken bones, how to prevent   S:3
  feet   F:80–82
  first aid for broken bones   F:160

  hands   F:83–84
  periodontal disease causes deterioration of bones that
      support the teeth   D:198
  skeletal system   S:183–84b
  X rays, medical uses of   X:350
Bongo (antelope)   A:297; H:220
  picture(s)   H:218
Bongo, Omar (Gabonese president)   G:4
Bongo drums   D:338
  picture(s)   D:337
Bonhomme Richard (ship commanded by John Paul Jones)
      J:127–28; R:205–6
Boniface, Saint (English missionary)   C:290; R:284; S:18d
  profile
Boniface VII (antipope)   R:290
Boniface I, Saint (pope)   R:290
Boniface II (pope)   R:290
Boniface III (pope)   R:290
Boniface IV, Saint (pope)   R:290
Boniface V (pope)   R:290
Boniface VI (pope)   R:290
Boniface VII (pope)   P:182; R:287, 291
Boniface IX (pope)   R:291
Bonin (Ogasawara) Islands (Pacific Ocean)   J:35; P:8
Bon Marché (early department store in Paris)   D:119
Bonn (Germany)   B:146; G:157
Bonnefoy, Yves (French poet)   F:442
Bonnet Carré Spillway (Louisiana)   L:316
Bonnets, feathered (worn by Native Americans)   H:46
Bonneville, Benjamin L. E. de (French-born American explorer)
      O:276
Bonneville, Lake (Utah)   L:28
Bonneville Dam (Oregon–Washington)   D:19; O:216; W:27
Bonneville Power Administration   E:218
Bonneville Salt Flats (Utah)   A:538
Bonney, William H. (American outlaw) *see* Billy the Kid
Bonnin, Gertrude Simmons (American civil rights activist and
      author)   S:326 *profile*
Bonny, Anne (British pirate)   P:262–63 *profile*
  picture(s)   P:262
Bonobos (Pygmy chimpanzees)   A:325, 326, 327
Bonspiel (curling tournament)   C:604
Boobies (seabirds)
  picture(s)   B:216, 232
Book, Shrine of the (Jerusalem) *see* Shrine of the Book
Book awards *see* Awards, literary
Bookbinding   B:332–33; P:471
Book clubs   P:524
Book design   B:327, 329
  encyclopedias   E:206
  medieval books   B:321
  typefaces   T:369–70
Book fair (exhibition of books)
  Frankfurt (Germany)   P:525
Bookkeeping   B:311–12, 313
  checking accounts in banks   B:57
Bookkeeping machines   O:58
Booklist (periodical)   L:181
Book of Common Prayer *see* Prayer, Book of Common
Book of Hours (illustrated prayer book)
  picture(s)   E:362
Book of Kells *see* Kells, Book of
Book of Mormon   M:457; S:205
Book of the Duchess, The (poem by Chaucer)   C:191
Book paper   P:56
Book reports   B:314–17
Book reviews   B:314, 333
Books   B:318–33 *see also* Illuminated manuscripts; Libraries
  from author to reader   B:323–33
  Aztec books had no words   A:577
  back matter   B:329
  bibliographic form   R:183
  binding *see* Bookbinding
  blind, books for the   B:253

Books (cont.)
    bookmaking **B:**323–33
    care of **L:**181–82
    children's literature **C:**228–48
    collecting autographed books **A:**526–27
    commercial art **C:**457–58
    communication, history of **C:**464
    copyright protection **C:**547
    design *see* Book design
    education, history of **E:**77
    encyclopedias **E:**206–7
    etiquette books **E:**337
    Frankfurt Book Fair **P:**525
    front matter **B:**329
    history of bookmaking **B:**318–22
    illuminated *see* Illuminated manuscripts
    illustration and illustrators **I:**79–84
    indexes *see* Indexes and indexing
    invention of **I:**284
    Islamic illustrations **I:**357–58
    layout **B:**329
    manuscript books **C:**463–64
    mass communication tool **C:**471
    Newbery, John **N:**137
    novels **N:**358–63
    paper **P:**53
    paperback books **P:**58a, 524
    prayer books **P:**430
    printing **P:**468–79
    publishing **P:**523–25
    reference materials **R:**129
    reports and reviews **B:**314–17
    on storytelling **S:**464
    What is a talking book? **B:**254
    word origins **W:**241
    writing as a career **W:**332
Boole, George (English mathematician) **A:**184; **L:**290; **M:**169
Boolean logic (used by computers) **C:**487
Boom (of a sailboat) **S:**8
    sailboards **B:**260
Boomerang (throwing stick) **A:**7
Boom operators (for motion pictures) **M:**485
    picture(s) **M:**483
Boomslangs (snakes) **S:**211
Boone, Daniel (American pioneer) **B:334**
    Horn in the West (outdoor drama, Boone, North Carolina) **N:**312
    settlement of Kentucky **K:**225
    West Virginia **W:**135
    westward movement **W:**143
    Wilderness Road **O:**270–71
    picture(s) **K:**224; **W:**142
Boonesborough (frontier fort) **F:**378
Boone's Trace (pioneer road) **P:**260
Boorstin, Daniel Joseph (American historian) **O:**92 *profile*
Booster shots (of vaccines) **M:**210; **V:**261
Booster stage (of multistage rockets) **R:**259, 260
Boot camps (for recruits)
    United States Marine Corps **U:**124
    picture(s)
        juvenile offenders **J:**169
Boot Dance (of South Africa) **F:**302
Boötes (constellation) **C:**525
Booth, Edwin Thomas (American actor) **T:**160 *profile*
Booth, John Wilkes (assassin of Lincoln) **B:**335; **C:**347; **L:**247
    used derringer to assassinate Lincoln **G:**418
    picture(s)
        wanted poster **L:**247
Booth, William (English evangelist) **S:**25
Boothe, Clare *see* Luce, Clare Boothe
Boot Heel (area of Missouri) **M:**366, 368, 369, 374
Boot Heel Museum (Dodge City, Kansas) **K:**184
Bootleggers (in the Roaring Twenties) **C:**539; **P:**485
Boots and shoes *see* Shoes
Bor (Norse god) **N:**279

Bora (wind of Adriatic region) **A:**161; **M:**213; **W:**187
Borah, William Edgar (American lawyer and political leader) **I:**58 *profile,* 59
Borah Peak (highest point in Idaho) **I:**48
Borazon (artificial abrasive) **G:**392
Bordaberry, Juan M. (Uruguayan president) **U:**241
Bordeaux (France) **F:**409
Borden (Prince Edward Island) **P:**460, 462
Borden, Sir Robert Laird (Canadian prime minister) **C:**76
    profile, 84–85
    picture(s) **C:**77
Border states (in the American Civil War) **C:**495
Borduas, Paul-Emile (Canadian artist) **C:**73
Boreal forests **B:**208; **C:**60
Bores (of guns) **G:**415
Bores (tidal waves) **T:**196–97
    Bay of Fundy (Canada) **N:**138
Borg, Bjorn (Swedish tennis player) **T:**96 *profile,* 99
    picture(s) **T:**91, 96
Borges, Jorge Luis (Argentine author and university professor) **A:**393; **L:**70
    picture(s) **L:**70
Borgia, Alfonso de (pope) *see* Calixtus III (pope)
Borgia, Cesare (Italian soldier) **R:**160
Borgia, Lucrezia (Italian duchess) **R:**160
Borgia, Rodrigo (pope) *see* Alexander VI (pope)
Borgia family (in Renaissance Italy) **R:**160 *profile*
Borglum, Gutzon (American sculptor) **I:**58 *profile*
    picture(s)
        Mount Rushmore National Memorial **S:**320
Boring *see* Drilling and boring
Boriquén (name for Puerto Rico) **P:**532
Boris I (czar of Bulgaria) **B:**443
Boris III (king of Bulgaria) **B:**444
Boris Godunov (opera by Mussorgsky) **O:**151
Boris Godunov (play by Pushkin) **D:**300; **R:**377
Borlaug, Norman Ernest (American agricultural scientist) **I:**302 *profile;* **W:**158
Borman, Frank (American astronaut) **S:**347 *profile*
Born, Max (German physicist) **P:**238
Borneo **B:**336–37; **I:**206, 208, 209, 210 *see also* Malaysia
    Brunei, Sultanate of **B:**415
    picture(s)
        houses on stilts **B:**337
        rain forest **S:**331
        wildfire **W:**83
Bornholm (island, Denmark) **D:**110, 112
Borodin, Alexander (Russian scientist and composer) **O:**146; **R:**381
Borodino, Battle of (1812) **N:**13
    picture(s) **U:**46
Boron (element) **E:**171
    California **C:**26
    magnetic qualities **M:**32
    nuclear reactor safety **N:**372
    p-type semiconductors **T:**275, 278
Bororo (Native American language) **I:**197
Borstal Boy (book by Behan) **I:**328
Borzoi (dog) **D:**245, 246
Börzsöny Mountains (Hungary) **H:**295
Bosch, Hieronymus (Flemish painter) **D:**354; **P:**23
    picture(s)
        Temptation of Saint Anthony (painting) **D:**357
Bosch, Juan (Dominican president) **D:**283
Bosc pear **P:**113
Bosnia and Herzegovina **B:**22, 23, **338**
    "ethnic cleansing" **G:**96, 97
    Yugoslavia, history of **Y:**364, 367, 369
    picture(s)
        civilians in wartime **U:**75
        flag **F:**235
        Serbian troops **Y:**369
Bosons (subatomic particles) **A:**489; **F:**366b
Bosporus (strait, Turkey) **I:**377; **T:**345, 347
Bossier City (Louisiana) **L:**323

Bovines (cattlelike hoofed mammals) H:217, 220
  picture(s) H:216
Bovine spongiform encephalopathy *see* Mad-cow disease
Bow and arrow *see* Bows and arrows
Bowdoin College (Brunswick, Maine) M:41
  picture(s) M:41
Bow drill (tool) T:233
Bowe, Riddick (American boxer) B:353, 354
Bowed instruments M:551–52
Bowed kites K:266b, 267
  picture(s) K:268
Bowell, Sir Mackenzie (Canadian prime minister) C:76
  profile; O:135
Bowel movements *see* Feces
Bowen, Elizabeth (English writer) E:290
Bowersox, Kenneth D. (American astronaut)
  picture(s) S:343
Bowhunting (hunting with bows and arrows) A:366
Bowie, James (American soldier and frontiersman) B:347
Bowie knife B:347
Bowker, R. R., Company *see* R. R. Bowker Company
Bow knots K:287
Bowler hats H:45
Bowl games (in football) F:360–61
Bowlines (knots)
  picture(s) K:286
Bowling (game) B:348–50b
Bowling (pitching in cricket) C:573
Bowling Green (Kentucky) K:218
Bowl riding (skateboarding) S:182
Bowls (lawn bowling) B:350b
Bowman's capsules (in the kidneys) K:243
Bowring, Sam (geologist) R:266
Bow River (Alberta)
  picture(s) B:46
Bows and arrows A:364–66
  picture(s) A:364
Bow-steerers (iceboats) I:19, 20
Bow Street Runners (early London police) P:368
Box and whisker graphs G:312
Boxboard (a type of paperboard) P:57
Boxcars (of railroads) R:82
  picture(s) R:82
Boxer (dog) D:245
Boxer, Barbara (American political figure)
  picture(s) W:214
Boxer Rebellion (uprising against foreigners in China) C:270
  Open-Door policy M:194
Boxing B:351–54
  Ali, Muhammad K:224
  Louis, Joe A:143
  related to fencing F:85
Boxing Day H:157
Box jellyfish *see* Sea wasps
Box kites K:266b, 270
  picture(s) K:267, 268
Box turtles P:179; T:356–57
  picture(s) T:355
Box wrenches (tools) T:229
Boyce, William D. (American publisher, organized Boy Scouts of America) B:360
Boycotts
  Martin Luther King's bus boycott A:143; K:251
  Olympic Games O:111–12
  struggle for African American civil rights A:79m, 79n
Boyd, Belle (American Civil War spy) S:408 *profile*
Boyden, Seth (American inventor and manufacturer) N:178 *profile*
Boyer, Herbert (American scientist) G:91
Boyer, Jean-Pierre (Haitian president) H:11
Boy Jesus (Bible story) B:173–74
Boyle, Richard (English architect) A:380
Boyle, Robert (English scientist) B:354; C:207–8; P:234
  gases G:57
  vacuum experiments V:265

Boyle's law B:354; C:207; G:57
Boyne, Battle of the (1690) I:323
Boyne River (Ireland) I:319
Boy Prisoners in the Tower (legend)
  What happened to the Princes in the Tower? E:241
Boys, Charles Vernon (British scientist) F:105
Boys & Girls Clubs of America B:355
Boys' camps *see* Camping, organized
Boy Scouts B:356–60
  picture(s)
    camping B:356
    Canadian scouts B:360
    merit badges B:358–59
    uniforms, insignia, and badges B:357
Boysenberries G:301
Boy's Life (magazine) M:17
Boys Town (Nebraska) N:95
Bozeman (Montana) M:433
Bozeman Trail (frontier trail) O:282; W:344
  map(s) O:273
Bracchae (trousers worn in the Middle Ages) C:375
Brace (tool used to make holes) T:229, 235
Bracelets (jewelry) J:99, 100
  picture(s)
    carved ivory bracelet A:74
Braces (tools of the orthodontist) O:236–37
Brachiopods (ancient animals) F:385, 387
  picture(s) E:26
Brachiosaurus (dinosaur) D:171
  picture(s) D:165
Brackenridge, Hugh Henry (American novelist) A:202
Brackish water (mixture of fresh and salt water) W:148
Bracts (modified leaves of plants) L:117
Bradbury, Ray (American author) S:80 *profile*
  picture(s) S:80
Braddock, General Edward (British soldier) F:464; O:270; W:38
Braddock, James J. (American boxer) B:353
Bradford, Andrew (American printer and magazine publisher) M:19
Bradford, William (American printer) P:58
Bradford, William (governor of Plymouth Colony) A:197; M:148 *profile;* P:347; T:172
  picture(s) T:171
Bradley, Omar Nelson (American army officer) M:379 *profile*
Bradley, Thomas (Tom) (American political figure) L:308 *profile*
Bradstreet, Anne (American poet) A:197; P:551
Brady, Mathew B. (American photographer) N:224 *profile*
Bradycardia (abnormally slow heartbeat) H:83–84
Brady Law (United States, 1993) G:426
Braga (Portugal) P:393
Bragg, Braxton (Confederate general) C:342, 345 *profile*
  Mexican War M:239b
Brahe, Tycho (Danish astronomer) A:472; B:361; D:110
  picture(s) R:162
Brahma (Hindu god) H:129
  picture(s)
    bronze statue H:128
Brahmagupta (Indian mathematician) M:164
Brahman (Atman) (Hindu spiritual principle) H:129
Brahman (breed of beef cattle) C:151
  picture(s) C:152
Brahmans (caste in Hindu society) E:75; H:128
  picture(s) H:130
Brahmaputra River (Asia) G:25; I:124; R:240
Brahms, Johannes (German composer) B:361; G:187
  choral music C:285
  First Symphony O:199–201
  picture(s) B:361
    score for *German Requiem* M:547
Braid, James (English doctor) H:329
Braided rug R:356

Braille (alphabet of the blind)   **B:**253, 254
  picture(s)
      children's book   **B:**322
Braille, Louis (French teacher and musician)   **B:**253
Brain   **B:**362–69
  aging process   **A:**83–84, 85
  Alzheimer's disease   **D:**188
  balance, sense of   **E:**5–6
  biological research   **B:**201
  body's senses   **B:**287
  central nervous system   **N:**118
  cerebral palsy is caused by brain damage   **D:**190
  child development   **C:**225
  damage caused by alcoholism   **A:**173
  damage caused by a stroke   **D:**202
  Did ancient Egyptians understand the importance of the brain?   **L:**104
  disabled people   **D:**177
  Do we use only 10 percent of our brains?   **B:**367
  dreaming   **D:**317–18
  electroencephalograms   **M:**208h–209
  emotions   **E:**203
  epilepsy   **D:**192
  gray matter   **N:**117
  how we hear   **E:**5
  human beings   **H:**280
  learning   **L:**100–101
  mammals   **M:**66
  medical and surgical techniques   **M:**208h–209, 210
  nervous system   **B:**284–85; **N:**115, 116
  operations in hyperbaric chambers   **M:**210
  primates   **P:**456
  psychology   **P:**499–511
  Reye's syndrome affects   **D:**200
  ultrasonoscope detects abnormal conditions   **M:**209
  diagram(s)   **B:**365
  picture(s)
      colored image of brain structures   **B:**364
      computerized image   **D:**206
      magnetic resonance imaging   **B:**362, 369
      nerve cell   **C:**159
Braine, John (English novelist)   **E:**290
Brain stem   **B:**284, 365, 368; **N:**116
Brakemen (on trains)   **R:**84, 86
Brakes
  air brakes   **H:**314; **R:**89
  automobiles   **A:**543–44, 546, 550–51
  dynamic braking   **L:**287
  hydraulic brakes   **H:**313
  railroads   **R:**84
  trucks   **T:**319
  Westinghouse, George, and air brakes   **W:**125
  diagram(s)
      hydraulic brakes   **H:**313
Bramante, Donato (Italian architect)   **I:**397; **R:**167
  picture(s)
      Tempietto of San Pietro Church (Rome)   **I:**397
Bran (of grain)
  flour and flour milling   **F:**277
  rice   **R:**229
  wheat   **G:**281; **W:**156
  picture(s)
      wheat   **W:**157
Branca, Giovanni (Italian architect)   **E:**229; **T:**342
Branches (of department stores)   **D:**119
Branching coral
  picture(s)   **J:**76
Brancusi, Constantin (Romanian-French sculptor)   **B:**370; **F:**432; **S:**103
  picture(s)
      Bird in Space (sculpture)   **S:**105
      Mademoiselle Pogany (sculpture)   **B:**370
      Princesse X (sculpture)   **A:**437
Brandeis, Louis Dembitz (Supreme Court justice)   **K:**224–25
  profile

Brandenburg (former state, Germany)   **F:**461
Brandenburg Gate (Berlin, Germany)   **B:**147
Brandenburg v. Ohio (1969)   **F:**163
Branding (of cattle)   **C:**569–70; **R:**105
  picture(s)   **R:**104
Brand names *see* Trademarks
Brando, Marlon (American actor)   **M:**486 *profile*
  picture(s)   **M:**495
Brandon (Manitoba)   **M:**82, 83, 85
Brandt, Willy (German political leader)   **G:**165; **S:**59
Brandy (distilled beverage)   **W:**161
Brandywine, Battle of (1777)   **P:**139
Brandywine Creek (Delaware)
  picture(s)   **D:**90
Branle (dance)   **D:**29
Branley, Franklyn M. (American science writer)   **C:**240
Bransfield, Edward (British naval officer)   **A:**295
Branson (Missouri)   **M:**366
  picture(s)   **M:**370
Brant, Joseph (Thayendanegea) (Mohawk Indian)   **B:**370–71; **I:**176 *profile*, 204, **R:**205
  picture(s)   **I:**176
Brants (geese)   **D:**343
Braque, Georges (French painter)   **B:**371; **F:**432; **P:**30
  collage   **C:**402
  cubism   **C:**602
  modern art   **M:**390
  Picasso and Braque   **P:**243
  picture(s)
      Guéridon, Le (painting)   **B:**371
      The Portuguese (painting)   **F:**431
Bras d'Or Lakes (Nova Scotia)   **N:**351
Brasília (capital of Brazil)   **B:**372, 375, 380–81
  architecture   **A:**386; **L:**65
  Niemeyer was its chief architect   **A:**386
  work of Brazil's leading designers   **B:**382
  picture(s)   **L:**65
      Congress Building   **B:**380
Brass   **B:**410
  alloys   **A:**190, 191
  antiques   **A:**316b
  buttons   **B:**488
  Waterbury (Connecticut)   **C:**511
  zinc   **Z:**389
Brass band   **B:**42
Brass instruments   **M:**553, 554
  orchestra   **O:**193
  orchestra seating plan   **O:**196
  wind instruments   **W:**184–85
  picture(s)   **W:**185
      orchestra   **O:**197
Brass rubbings   **R:**348b
Brasstown Bald Mountain (Georgia)   **G:**134
Bratislava (capital of Slovakia)   **S:**200–201
Braun, Carole Moseley (American senator)   **A:**79c
Braun, Wernher von *see* Von Braun, Wernher
Brave New World (novel by Huxley)   **E:**289; **H:**309; **S:**81–82
Bray, Thomas (English clergyman)   **S:**301
Brazauskas, Algirdas (Lithuanian political leader)   **L:**263
Brazil   **B:**372–84
  Amazon River   **A:**194e–194f
  art and architecture   **L:**62, 63, 65
  coffee   **C:**397
  coffee, world's largest exporter of   **S:**290
  feijoada is the most popular dish   **F:**337
  forests and forestry   **F:**375
  government, history of   **L:**58
  history   **S:**293, 294
  Lagoa dos Patos   **L:**30
  landforms of South America   **S:**276
  Latin America   **L:**49, 50, 51, 55, 56, 57
  literature   **L:**68
  Marajoara civilization   **I:**170
  origin of name   **D:**371

Brazil (cont.)
Portugal, history of   P:395
Rio de Janeiro   R:234–35
rubber trees   R:344
São Paulo   S:38–39
World War II   W:303
picture(s)
Amazon River   B:378; R:241
automobile industry   S:291
Brasília   B:380; L:65
Cabral taking possession of Brazil   L:58
candomblé ceremony   B:373
Carnival   B:374
Carnival costumes   S:284
Carnival food   F:332
coffee beans being sifted   S:275
factory workers sorting cashews   B:379
farmer   B:377
flag   F:238
gauchos driving cattle   B:377
iron mine   B:379
Itaipu power plant   P:422
Manaus   B:382
people   B:372; S:284
Rio de Janeiro   B:381; C:320; R:234; S:285, 289
Rio de Janeiro soccer fans   B:375; S:284
São Paulo   B:380; S:38, 288, 289
wheatfields   G:98
workers unloading fruit from boats   B:378
Brazil Current (of Atlantic Ocean)   A:479
Brazilein (dye)   D:371
Brazil nuts   N:432–33
Brazilwood (tree)   B:372; D:371
Brazing   W:118
Brazos River (Texas)   T:127
Brazza, Count Pierre Paul François Camille Savorgnan de (French explorer)   C:500
Brazzaville (capital of the Congo)   C:498, 499, 500
picture(s)   C:500
Breach of contract (in law)   L:90
Bread   B:385–88b *see also* Flour and flour milling
black or rye bread   R:386
chemical preservatives   F:342
Egyptians were the first to make leavened bread   C:532
flour from different kinds of wheat   F:276
how to grow bread molds   A:307
mold   F:497, 499
unleavened and leavened compared   F:89
wheat   W:156, 158
picture(s)
Egyptian statue of a baker   A:350
Bread-and-butter notes   L:160
Bread and Butter State (nickname for Minnesota)   M:326, 327
Breadbasket of America (nickname for Kansas)   K:177
Breadfruit (tropical fruit)   F:126; T:317
picture(s)   E:411
Bread mold   A:307; F:497, 499
Bread wheats   W:158
Breakers (giant waves)   S:511
Breakers (hard-coal preparation plants)   C:390
Breakers, The (mansion in Newport, Rhode Island)   V:277
picture(s)   R:220
Breakfast cereals   G:284
Breakfast Club, The (motion picture, 1985)   M:495
Breakfast in Bed (painting by Cassatt)
picture(s)   C:130
Breaking a mirror (superstition)   S:504
Breaking a wishbone (superstition)   S:504
Breaking Home Ties (painting by Rockwell)
picture(s)   R:270
Breaking news (journalism term)   J:135, 140
Breastbone *see* Sternum
Breast cancer   C:93, 94, 95

Breastfeeding (of babies)   B:3
mammary glands   G:227
mother with AIDS can infect baby   A:100b
Breaststroke (in swimming)   S:533
picture(s)   S:534–35
Breastworks (field fortifications)   F:379
Breathing   B:278–79 *see also* Respiration
crocodilian adaptations for staying underwater   C:583–8
dolphins   D:275
emphysema affects   D:192
first aid for stoppage of breathing   F:158
hiccups   B:300
lungs   L:343–45
narcotics, effects of   N:15
oxygen and oxidation   O:287
problems of premature babies   B:2
rescue breathing   F:158
respiratory system of fish   F:191
turtles   T:356
voice training and singing   V:377
What is a yawn?   L:345
Breathless (motion picture, 1959)   M:494
Breccia (rock)   M:453
Brecht, Bertolt (German playwright)   D:302; G:181; T:161
Breckinridge, John Cabell (vice president of the United States)   C:336; V:326 *profile*
picture(s)   V:326
1856 campaign poster   P:370
Breckinridge, Mary (American nurse)   K:225 *profile*
picture(s)   K:224
Breech-loading guns   G:420–21
Breed associations (of dairy farmers)   D:4–5
Breeder reactor (type of nuclear reactor)   N:370
Breeding, animal
advances in agriculture   A:99
cats, purebred   C:137, 139
cattle   C:151, 153, 154; D:4–5
dogs   D:247, 249–51
fur colors and mutation   F:502
genetic engineering   G:82
horses   H:237–38, 241, 244
poultry   P:414, 415, 417
What is artificial selection?   E:379
zoo animals   Z:393, 395
picture(s)
horses   H:239–40
Breeding, plant
advances in agriculture   A:99, 100
Burbank's contributions to   B:450
cereal grains for the future   G:286
genetic engineering   G:82
Mendel, work of   G:90
wheat varieties   W:157–58
Breedlove, Craig (American automobile racer)   A:538
Breed's Hill (Boston, near Bunker Hill)   R:200
Breezes, sea *see* Sea breezes
Breezing Up (painting by Homer)
picture(s)   H:167
Bregenz Festival (Austria)   A:519
Breitenfeld, Battle of (1631)   T:179
Breitling Orbiter 3 (balloon)   B:36
Brel, Jacques (Belgian cabaret singer)   B:133
Bremen (Germany)   G:157
Brendan (Brenainn), Saint (Irish saint)   E:401
Brennan, William Joseph (American jurist)   N:178 *profile*
Brenner Pass (through the Alps)   A:194b
Brent, Margaret (American feminist)   M:132 *profile*
Brenton, Howard (English dramatist)   D:303
Brer Rabbit (character in Joel Chandler Harris stories)   A:76b
Brest-Litovsk, Treaty of (1918)   R:368; U:49; W:289
Brétigny, Treaty of (1360)   E:241; H:292
Breton, André (French poet and surrealist)   F:442; M:394; S:518
Bretons (people)   F:404

Brett, George (American baseball player) **B:**88 *profile*
  picture(s) **B:**88, 94
Brett, Philip Milledoler (American dollhouse maker) **D:**262
Bretton Woods (New Hampshire) **N:**150
Breuer, Lee (American dramatist) **D:**305
Breuer, Marcel (Hungarian furniture designer and architect)
  F:517
Brewer, Margaret A. (American brigadier general) **U:**122
Brewer's yeast **B:**386; **H:**79
Brewis (colonial American dish) **C:**411
Brewster, Sir David (Scottish physicist) **K:**172
Breyer, Stephen Gerald (American jurist) **S:**508 *profile*
Brezhnev, Leonid Ilyich (Soviet political leader) **B:**389; **C:**211;
  R:369; **U:**51
Brian Boru (king of Ireland) **I:**323
Briand, Aristide (French statesman) **P:**106
Briand-Kellogg Pact (1928) *see* Kellogg-Briand Pact
Brices Cross Roads National Battlefield Site (Mississippi)
  M:358
Bricklaying **B:**392–93
Bricks **B:**390–94
  adobe **H:**173–74
  ancient cities built with clay bricks **A:**220
  architecture, history of **A:**370, 371, 373
  building construction **B:**430, 437
  houses **H:**174–75
Bridal rings *see* Wedding rings
Bridalveil (waterfall, California) **W:**63
Bridal Veil (waterfall, New York) **N:**242
Bridal veils **W:**100
Bridge, The (German art group) *see* Brücke, Die
Bridge at Sevres, The (painting by Sisley)
  picture(s) **I:**105
Bridge cranes (Overhead traveling cranes) (machines) **H:**147
  picture(s) **H:**146
Bridge layers (specialized tanks) **T:**15
Bridge of Sighs (Venice, Italy) **B:**401
Bridgeport (Connecticut) **C:**511
Bridger, James (Jim) (American pioneer) **F:**523; **W:**346 *profile*
  Great Salt Lake **U:**254
  national parks **N:**44
  overland trails **O:**277
  picture(s) **O:**276
Bridges **B:**395–401 *see also* Covered bridges
  Chesapeake Bay Bridge-Tunnel **M:**122
  Confederation Bridge (Canada) **C:**66; **P:**462
  Federal Highway Administration **T:**293
  Humber Bridge (England) **U:**66
  New York City **N:**233
  Pittsburgh has over 700 bridges **P:**266
  railroads **R:**79
  reinforced concrete used in **C:**166
  Sydney (Australia) **S:**547
  Why were some of the early bridges in America covered?
    B:401
  picture(s)
    Brooklyn Bridge **I:**329
    federal inspection **T:**293
    railroads **R:**79
    swinging bridge **J:**157
    washed out by flood **F:**255
Bridges (of ships) **O:**32
Bridges, Robert (English poet) **E:**287
Bridget of Sweden, Saint **S:**18d *profile*
Bridge to Terabithia (book by Paterson)
  picture(s)
    Donna Diamond illustration **C:**238
Bridgetown (capital of Barbados) **B:**60
Brig (kind of ship)
  picture(s) **S:**152
Brigade system (for fur trading) **F:**524
Brigantine (kind of ship)
  picture(s) **S:**152
Briggs, Henry (British mathematician) **M:**165
Brigham Young University (Provo, Utah) **U:**247

Brighella (clown) **C:**386
Brightness (of stars) *see* Magnitude
Brighton (England) **U:**59
Bright's disease *see* Nephritis
Brilliance (of pigment colors) **C:**425
Brilliancy (of gemstones) **G:**69
Brimstone *see* Sulfur
Brindle coats (of dogs) **D:**245
Brine (salt and water solution) **S:**22–23
  food preservation **F:**344
  leather process for preserving hides **L:**108
  processing of fish **F:**220–21
  refrigerated warehouses, use in **R:**135
  water desalting **W:**56
Brine shrimps (crustaceans) **C:**591
Bringing Up Baby (motion picture, 1938) **M:**492
Brisbane (capital of Queensland, Australia) **A:**512, 514
  picture(s) **A:**512
Bristlecone pine trees **T:**300
Bristle worms (polychaetes) **W:**320
Bristol (Rhode Island) **R:**217, 220
Bristow, George F. (American composer) **U:**206
Britain (ancient name of England, Scotland, Wales)
  Celtic tribes **C:**163
  discovered by Pytheas **E:**400
  early history of England **E:**235–38
Britain, Battle of (1940) **W:**298–99
Britannia metal **K:**285
British Broadcasting Company (BBC) **R:**57; **U:**59
British Columbia (Canada) **B:**402–7
  Expo '86 (Vancouver) **F:**17
  forestry **C:**61
  gold discoveries **G:**252
  Indians, American **I:**188–90
  Pacific Ranges and Lowlands **C:**55–56
  Vancouver **V:**275
  map(s) **B:**406
  picture(s)
    baling hay **B:**404
    Butchart Gardens **B:**406b
    dam on Kootenay River **C:**61
    Mount Assiniboine **B:**403
    pulp mill **B:**405
    rain forest **C:**58
    Vancouver **B:**406a; **C:**66; **V:**275
    Victoria **B:**406d
    vineyards **B:**404
British Columbia, University of **B:**406a, 406b
British Commonwealth of Nations *see* Commonwealth of Nations
British East India Company *see* East India Company
British Empire **E:**249, 251; **W:**270 *see also* Commonwealth
  of Nations
  extent of (1939) **E:**252
  United Kingdom **U:**55, 66
British Expeditionary Force (B.E.F.) **W:**281, 283, 287, 298
British Guiana *see* Guyana
British Honduras *see* Belize
British Isles (group that includes Great Britain, Ireland, and
  many smaller islands) **U:**66
British Library (national library of Britain) **L:**179
British Mountains (Yukon Territory) **Y:**370
British Museum (London) **M:**521–22, 525
  library **L:**179
British Nationality Act (Britain, 1983) **I:**94
British North America Act (now **Constitution Act**) (Britain, 1867)
  C:75, 83; **M:**2
British Open (golf tournament) **G:**260
British Patent Office **P:**99
British shorthair cat **C:**138
British Somaliland (now **Somalia**) **S:**255
British South Africa Company **Z:**382, 387
British thermal units (BTUs) (measure of heat) **H:**88
British Togoland (United Nations trust territory, west Africa)
  G:194, 198; **T:**215
British Virgin Islands *see* Virgin Islands, British

Britons (early people of England) E:235–37
Brittany (region of France)
   picture(s) W:70
      traditional dress F:405
Brittany spaniel (dog) D:249
Britten, Benjamin (English composer) E:293; O:148, 161
Brittlebush (plant)
   picture(s) N:286
Brittlewood (poisonous plant) L:117
Briullov, Karl (Russian painter) R:373
   picture(s)
      The Rider (painting) R:373
Brno (Czech Republic) C:611
Broadax (tool) T:235
Broadbent, Donald (English psychologist) P:507
Broad-Breasted Bronze (turkey) P:417
Broad-Breasted Large White (turkey) P:417
Broadcasting (of seed) A:98
Broadcasting (radio and television) R:50, 53–54, 55–58;
      T:67–68
   advertising A:30
   Canadian-content ruling C:67
   communication, history of C:469
   hate propaganda G:96
   journalism J:135
   radio programs R:59–61
   television programs T:69–71
Broad jump *see* Long jump
Broadsides (newssheets)
   ballads B:24
   political songs N:24
Broad-spectrum antibiotics A:308, 311
Broadway Boogie-Woogie (painting by Mondrian)
   picture(s) M:410
Broadway theater district (New York City) N:230; T:159
Broadwood, John (English piano builder) P:242
Broca, Paul (French surgeon) B:368
Broccoli (vegetable) V:289
Broch, Hermann (German writer) G:182
Brock, Sir Isaac (British soldier) O:135
Brock, Lou (American baseball player)
   picture(s) B:94
Brockton (Massachusetts) M:145
Broilers (chickens) P:415
Broiling (method of cooking) C:533
Brokaw, Irving (American ice-skating promoter) I:45
Broken Arrow (Oklahoma) O:89
Broken-color technique (in painting) I:104
Brokers (Agents) (negotiators of sales and purchases)
   real estate R:113
   stocks and bonds, dealers in S:457–58
Bromeliads (plants) B:210
Bromine (element) E:171; O:28
Bronchial tubes (of the respiratory system) B:279; L:343
   picture(s) L:344
Bronchioles (small tubes in the respiratory system) L:343,
   345
Bronchitis (inflammation of the bronchial tubes) D:189–90
   acid rain's effects A:10
   emphysema D:192
Broncos (untamed horses) C:569; R:277 *see also* Mustangs
Brong-Ahafo (a people of Africa) G:194
Brontë, Anne (English novelist) B:408; E:286
Brontë, Branwell (English painter and writer) B:408
Brontë, Charlotte (English novelist) B:408; E:286; N:359
Brontë, Emily (English novelist) B:408; E:286; N:359
Brontosaurus (dinosaur) *see Apatosaurus*
Brontotherium (prehistoric mammal)
   picture(s) P:434
Bronx (New York City) N:226, 228
   picture(s)
      apartment buildings N:230
Bronx-Whitestone Bridge (New York City) N:233
Bronx Zoo (New York City) Z:392, 395

Bronze B:409–10
   alloys A:190
   armor A:433
   Babylonian art A:236
   battles with early bronze armor and weapons B:103d
   bell casting B:141
   chemistry, history of C:206
   Chinese decorative arts C:276
   decorative arts D:70, 72, 74, 75, 76
   Japanese gilt bronze sculptures J:48
   metallurgy, history of M:236
   picture(s)
      African sculpture N:254
      decorative arts D:71
      door L:122
      Islamic candlestick I:358
      Persian sculpture P:156
Bronze Age B:409
   metallurgy M:236
   prehistoric people P:442
   time of the Trojan War T:316
   tool use T:233–34
   picture(s)
      tools T:233
Bronze catfish F:204
Bronze Star (American award)
   picture(s) D:66
Brooches (jewelry) J:99
   picture(s)
      gold brooch designed by Leonor Fini D:69
Brooding (of birds) P:86
Brood parasites (birds that use others' nests) B:227–28
Brood patch (in birds) B:227
Brood pouch (of a crustacean) C:592
Brooke, Edward William (United States senator) A:79c;
      M:148 *profile*
Brooke, Sir James (British ruler, White Rajah) of Sarawak
      M:58
Brooke, Rupert (English poet) E:287
Brook Farm (utopian community, Massachusetts) A:204
Brookgreen Gardens (South Carolina) S:304
Brookings (South Dakota) S:318, 319
Brooklyn (New York City) N:226, 227
   aquarium A:337
Brooklyn-Battery Tunnel (New York City) N:233
Brooklyn Bridge (New York City) B:398; N:233
   picture(s) I:329
Brooklyn Dodgers (baseball team) B:92
Brooks, Gwendolyn (American poet) A:79c, 214
Brooks, Phillips (American Episcopal bishop) C:118
Brooks Range (Alaska) A:146
"Brooms" (poem by Aldis) F:124
Brossard, Nicole (Canadian writer) C:87
Brossa Valley (Australia) A:509
Brosse, Salomon de (French architect) F:425
Brotherhood of Locomotive Engineers (BLE) R:86
Brotherhood of Sleeping Car Porters (labor union) A:79k
Brothers Karamazov (novel by Dostoevski) D:287; F:115
Brotulids (deep-sea fish) F:182
Broughton, Jack (English boxer) B:353
Broughton, William R. (English explorer) O:215
Brow-antlered deer D:82
Brown, "Aunt" Clara (American benefactor) C:442 *profile*
Brown, Charles Brockden (American novelist) A:202
Brown, Ford Madox (English artist) E:263
Brown, George (Canadian statesman) B:411; M:2
Brown, Jim (American football player) F:362 *profile*
   picture(s) F:362
Brown, John (American abolitionist) A:6b; B:411; S:196;
      V:360
   events leading to Civil War C:335
   John Brown's Body (song) N:25
   West Virginia W:138
   picture(s) A:6a; C:335; W:138
Brown, John (American Revolutionary leader) R:224 *profile*

Brown, Joseph (American manufacturer and architect)   R:224
profile
Brown, Karen (American ballerina)
picture(s)   B:33
Brown, Kootenai (Canadian conservationist)   G:220
Brown, Marcia (American author and artist)   C:230 *profile*
Brown, Margaret Wise (American author and editor)   C:230
profile
picture(s)
illustration by Clement Hurd for *Goodnight Moon*
C:241
Brown, Moses (American merchant)   R:225 *profile*
Brown, Nicholas (American merchant)   R:224 *profile*
Brown, Robert (Scottish physicist)   A:483–84
picture(s)   A:484
Brown, William Hill (American novelist)   A:202
Brown, William Wells (American reformer, historian, and writer)
A:79c
Brown algae   A:180
Brown Angels (book by Walter Dean Myers)
picture(s)   C:248
Brown bears   B:104, 107
picture(s)   B:106; M:66; U:89
foot   B:105
"Brown Bess" (musket)
picture(s)   G:416
Brown coal *see* Lignite
Browne, Frances (Irish writer)   F:21
Browne, Sir Thomas (English author)   E:274
Brown family (American manufacturers and philanthropists)
R:224–25 *profile*
Brown hyenas (animals)   H:319
Brownian motion (in science)   A:484
Brownie Girl Scouts   G:215
picture(s)   G:214
Brownies (fairies)   F:9
Browning, Elizabeth Barrett (English poet)   B:412; E:284–85
"How do I love thee?"   B:412
Browning, John Moses (American inventor of firearms)   G:423;
U:254 *profile*
Browning, Kurt (Canadian figure skater)   I:44 *profile*
Browning, Robert (English poet)   B:412–13; E:284
"The Pied Piper of Hamelin," excerpt from   B:413
quotation from *Pippa Passes*   Q:19
Brownlee, Don (American astronomer)   C:452
Brownlee particles (dust from asteroids and comets)   C:452
Brown lung (respiratory disease)   O:12
Brown rats *see* Norway rats
Brown recluse spiders   S:406
Brown rice   G:282; H:79; R:229
Brownshirts (Nazi storm troopers)   F:64; N:80–81
Brown sugar   S:483
Brown Swiss (breed of cattle)   C:154
picture(s)   C:153; D:5
Brown thrashers (birds)
picture(s)
state bird of Georgia   G:133
Brown University (Providence, Rhode Island)   R:217
Brown v. Board of Education of Topeka, Kansas (1954)   A:79m;
C:328; E:90; S:114, 509
NAACP   N:28
Browsers, web (computer programs) *see* Web browsers
Broz, Josip *see* Tito
Bruce, Ailsa Mellon (American philanthropist)   N:39–40
Bruce, Blanche Kelso (American political figure)   M:362
profile
Bruce, James (Scottish explorer)   A:66; E:412
Bruce, Robert *see* Robert I (The Bruce) (king of Scotland)
Brucellosis (Undulant fever) (disease)   D:212
Brücke, Die (German art group)   E:424; G:172; M:391
Bruckner, Anton (Austrian composer and organist)   C:284–85;
G:188
Bruegel (Brueghel), Jan (Flemish painter)   B:414

Bruegel, Pieter, The Elder (Flemish painter)   B:414; D:354
picture(s)
Children's Games (painting)   D:356
The Harvesters (painting)   R:170
Hunters in The Snow (painting)   B:414
Peasant Wedding Feast (painting)   W:264
Bruegel, Pieter, The Younger (Flemish painter)   B:414
Bruges (Belgium)
picture(s)   B:130
Bruises (injuries)   F:160
Brûlé, Étienne (French explorer)   G:327, 328; M:269; P:138
Toronto   T:243
Brumidi, Constantino (Italian-American painter)   C:104
Brunei (sultanate on the island of Borneo)   B:336, 337, **415**
Bandar Seri Begawan   S:333
economy   S:332, 333
picture(s)
flag   F:231
Muslims   S:329
Brunel, Isambard Kingdom (British engineer)   T:339
Brunel, Marc (French-English inventor)   T:339
Brunelleschi, Filippo (Italian architect)   A:378; I:395
Foundling Hospital (Florence)   R:164
perspective, rules of   D:311
Renaissance architecture   R:164
picture(s)
Foundling Hospital (Florence)   R:165
Bruner, Jerome (American psychologist)   L:100
Brunhoff, Jean de (French author and illustrator)   C:230
profile
Brünnhilde (in Norse mythology)   O:162–63
Bruno, Frank (American boxer)   B:354
Brunswick (Maine)   M:41
Brushes (for painting)   P:34; W:58
Brushes (of electric generators and motors)   E:134, 153
Brusilov, Aleksei Alekseyevich (Russian general)   W:282
profile, 288
picture(s)   W:282
Brussels (capital of Belgium)   B:130, 132, 134, 135
rug-weaving   R:353
picture(s)
European Union headquarters   B:134
guildhalls on Grand'Place   B:135
seafood market   B:132
Brussels sprouts (vegetable related to cabbage)   V:287
Brussels Universal and International Exhibition (1958)   F:17
Brutus, Dennis (South African poet)   A:76d
Brutus, Lucius Junius (Roman hero)   R:310
Brutus, Marcus Junius (Roman statesman)   A:317; R:316
Bryan, John Neely (first settler in Dallas, Texas)   D:14
Bryan, William Jennings (American politician and orator)
B:416; O:191
Darrow and Bryan   D:38
McKinley and Bryan   M:192
Scopes trial   S:84
picture(s)   N:95
Bryant, Paul ("Bear") (American football coach)   A:142–43
profile
Bryant, William Cullen (American poet and editor)   A:203;
B:416
Bryce, Lord James (British ambassador to United States)
N:56
Bryce Canyon National Park (Utah)   U:250
picture(s)   E:16; U:243
Bryde's whales   W:151–52
Brynhild (in Norse mythology) *see* Brünnhilde
Bryophyte (plant)   M:472–73; P:301, 302
BTUs *see* British thermal units
Bubble and squeak (English vegetable dish)   F:334
Bubble chamber (in physics)   A:194d; C:555
picture(s)
tracks of atoms   A:483
Bubi (a people of Africa)   E:309
Bubka, Sergei (Ukrainian pole vaulter)   T:259 *profile*
picture(s)   T:259

Bubonic plague (disease)
    Florence (Italy)   **F:**259
    medieval England   **E:**240
    Middle Ages   **M:**295
    Norway   **N:**349
    Roman Catholic Church damaged by   **R:**287
    picture(s)   **W:**263
Bucaram, Abdala (Ecuadorian president)   **E:**69
Buccaneers (pirates of the Spanish Main)   **P:**264
    picture(s)   **P:**263
Buchanan, James (15th president of the United States)
        B:417–20
    picture(s)   **P:**447
        1856 campaign poster   **P:**370
Bucharest (capital of Romania)   **B:**421; **R:**297, 298
    picture(s)   **B:**421; **R:**299, 300
Büchner, Georg (German dramatist)   **G:**179
Buck, Pearl (American author)   **B:**422
    The Good Earth, excerpt from   **B:**422
    picture(s)   **K:**208
Buck dancing   **F:**302
Bucket brigades (for fire fighting)   **F:**145
Bucket dredge *see* Ladder bucket dredge
Bucket masks *see* Helmet masks
Buckeye (tree)
    picture(s)
        state tree of Ohio   **O:**61
Buckeye State (nickname for Ohio)   **O:**60, 61
Bucking (in logging)   **L:**339, 341
Buckingham Palace (of Britain's royal family)   **E:**192; **L:**293
Buckland-Wright, John (English artist)
    picture(s)
        Nymphe Surprise II (engraving)   **E:**294
Buckley, William F., Jr. (American writer and editor)   **N:**232
    profile
Bucks (male deer)   **D:**80
Buckskin (leather from deer)   **L:**107
Buck teeth (orthodontic problem)   **O:**236
Buckwheat (grain)   **G:**284
    picture(s)   **G:**283
Bucrania (sculptured ornament)   **D:**74
Buda (section of Budapest)   **B:**422a, 422b
Budapest (capital of Hungary)   **B:**422a–422b; **H:**296
    World War II   **W:**315
    picture(s)   **B:**422a; **E:**287, 359; **H:**294, 297
Buddha, Prince Siddhartha Gautama (founder of Buddhism)
        B:422b–425
    picture(s)
        Buddha Amida (statue by Jocho)   **J:**48
        Great Buddha of Kamakura (Japan)   **A:**444; **J:**27;
            R:147; **S:**90
        sculpture   **I:**135
Buddhism (religion founded by Buddha)   **B:**423–25; **R:**147
    Asian religions   **A:**458
    Burma   **B:**454, 455
    China   **C:**260, 278
    dance combines with religion   **D:**31
    fables and folk tales   **F:**3
    food taboos   **F:**332
    funeral customs   **F:**492
    India, art and architecture of   **I:**135–36
    India, literature of   **I:**141
    Japan   **J:**27, 32, 41
    Japanese art and architecture   **J:**48–49
    Lamaism in Tibet   **T:**189–90
    Laos   **L:**42
    marriage rites   **W:**103
    Oriental sculpture   **O:**222–23, 229
    originated in India   **I:**130
    religious holidays   **R:**154
    Russia   **R:**358
    saints   **S:**18c
    sculpture   **C:**277
    Southeast Asia   **S:**329, 335

Thailand   **T:**148
Union of Soviet Socialist Republics   **U:**35
    picture(s)
        monks   **A:**458; **B:**454; **C:**35; **S:**328
        Oriental sculpture   **O:**226
        temple   **I:**138
        Thailand   **T:**151
Budding (of viruses)   **V:**366
Budding (plant propagation by grafting)   **N:**432
    apple trees   **A:**333
    orange trees   **O:**188
    stone fruit trees   **P:**108
Budding (type of reproduction)   **R:**175
    coelenterates   **J:**74
    sea anemones   **J:**77
Budgerigars (birds)   **B:**245; **P:**86
Budget, national *see* National budget
Budgets, family   **B:**425–26
Budgets, municipal
    diagram(s)   **M:**514
Budgies *see* Budgerigars
Buds (of trees)   **T:**308–9
Buen Aire *see* Bonaire
Buenaventura (Colombia)   **C:**406
Buena Vista, Battle of (1847)   **M:**239b; **T:**32
Buenos Aires (capital of Argentina)   **A:**389, 392, 393, 394;
        B:426–28; **S:**289
    picture(s)   **A:**390, 393; **L:**53; **S:**286
        tango demonstration   **L:**47
Buenos Aires, University of   **A:**389
Buero Vallejo, Antonio (Spanish dramatist)   **S:**392
Buffalo (hoofed mammals)   **B:**428–29; **L:**272
    picture(s)   **H:**216
Buffalo (New York)   **N:**220
    Pan-American Exhibition (1901)   **F:**16
Buffalo, American *see* Bison
Buffalo Bill (William Frederick Cody) (American scout)   **B:**429;
        C:570; **P:**383
    Nebraska state historical park   **N:**90
    Wyoming museum   **W:**339
    picture(s)   **N:**95
        grave   **C:**438
Buffalo National River (Arkansas)   **A:**424
Buffon, Georges-Louis Leclerc, Comte de (French naturalist)
        E:296 *profile*
    picture(s)   **E:**296
Bugaku (Japanese dance)   **D:**32; **T:**162
Buganda (former kingdom, now a region in Uganda)   **U:**6–7
Bugatti Type 41 Royale (automobile)
    picture(s)   **A:**542
Bugging (electronic eavesdropping)   **S:**409
Bugle (musical instrument)   **M:**554 *see also* Trumpet
Bug River (Europe)   **P:**359
Bugs (computer program malfunctions)   **C:**490
Bugs (fly-fishing lures)   **F:**215
Bugs (insects) *see* Insects
Bugs Bunny (cartoon character)
    picture(s)   **A:**289
Bug's Life, A (motion picture, 1998)   **A:**291
Builders (in detergents)   **D:**141
Building code   **B:**434
Building construction   **B:**430–38
    air conditioning   **A:**101–3
    architecture   **A:**368–86a
    bricks and masonry   **B:**390–94
    bridges   **B:**395–401
    castles   **C:**131
    construction engineers   **E:**225
    earth-moving machinery   **E:**30–32
    elevators and escalators   **E:**185–88
    explosives in construction   **E:**423
    heating and ventilating systems   **H:**95–97
    hoisting and loading machinery   **H:**146–47
    invention of tools for   **I:**286

kinds of industry   I:225
landslides can be caused by   A:558
masonry   B:392–94
mechanical drawing   M:200
plumbing   P:339–40
solar energy   S:239
stone masonry   B:393–94
trucks, use of   T:321
Why don't tall buildings blow down in a strong wind?
    B:435
Why is a tree or an American flag sometimes placed on the
    highest part of a building under construction?   B:434
picture(s)   H:270; I:336; P:298
Building materials   B:430–31
acid rain's effects   A:10
adobe houses   H:173–74
bricks and brick masonry   B:390–94
cement and concrete   C:165–66
ceramics   C:177–78
engineering   E:224
fireproofing   B:434
glass as a structural material   G:237
homes   H:171–77
influenced architecture   A:373, 381, 382, 383, 384–85
iron and steel   I:329–38
lumber and lumbering   L:338–42
stone masonry   B:393–94
wood and wood products   W:222–27
Bujumbura (capital of Burundi)   B:462, 463
Buka (island in Pacific)   P:8
Bukhara (early state in Central Asia)   T:11; U:258
Bükk Mountains (Hungary)   H:295
Bukovina (Romania)   M:403; R:297, 300
Bulawayo (Zimbabwe)   Z:386
Bulbs (underground stems)   P:304, 305
gardens and gardening   G:40
garden selection   G:29
houseplants   H:269
leaves, special kinds of   L:117
picture(s)
    gardens and gardening   G:41
Bulfinch, Charles (American architect)   C:104–5; U:128
picture(s)
    Maine State House   M:46
    Massachusetts State House   M:145
Bulgakov, Mikhail (Russian writer)   R:380
Bulgaria   B:22, **439–44**
World War I   W:285, 290, 291
World War II   W:299, 313, 318
picture(s)
    flag   F:235
    Orthodox bishop   B:440
    pro-democracy demonstration   B:444
    Rhodope Mountains   B:439
    Rila Monastery   B:443
    Sofia   B:441
    steel industry   B:442
    teenagers in denim   B:440
    Valley of Roses   B:442
    woman in traditional dress   B:439
Bulgarian Orthodox Church   B:440, 443
picture(s)
    bishop   B:440
Bulgars (people)   B:439, 443
Bulge, Battle of the (1944–1945)   B:135; E:124; W:313–14
picture(s)   W:314
Bulimia (eating disorder)   D:190
Bulk food sales   F:348; S:498
Bull (constellation) *see* Taurus
Bull, John (English composer)   N:22
Bull, Olaf (Norwegian poet)   S:58i
Bull, Ole (Norwegian violinist)   G:380; I:2
Bull dancing (of ancient Crete)   B:448
Bulldog   D:244–45, 251

Bulldozers   E:30
roads and highways   R:249
tanks used for military support   T:15
used on farms   F:53–54
Bulletin boards (for posting information)   **B:445–47**
computer bulletin boards   C:493; L:160b
Bulletproof and bullet-resistant clothing   A:435; F:111; P:329
Bullets (ammunition for guns)   G:414, 418–19, 420
made of lead   L:93
Bullet trains *see* Turbo trains
Bullfighting   B:448–49
Costa Rica   C:557
How did bullfighting begin?   B:448
Mexico   M:243
Nicaragua   N:244
Portugal   P:391
Spain   S:371
picture(s)   B:448
    Mexico   M:244
    Spain   S:371
Bullfrogs   F:477
picture(s)   A:214b
Bullheads (fish)   F:213
Bullion (gold bars)   G:247
Bull leaping (sport of ancient Crete)   A:228
Bull Moose Party *see* Progressive Party
Bullocks *see* Steers
Bull of Minos (in Greek mythology)   G:366
Bullpen (in baseball)   B:83
Bull Run, Battles of (1861, 1862, Civil War)   C:337, 339; J:9
Bulls   C:151
Assyrian art   A:240
dairy cattle   D:5
elephants   E:180, 182
rodeo riding   R:277
picture(s)
    Assyrian art   A:241
Bulls (in stock exchanges)   S:459
Bull sharks
picture(s)   S:141
Bull-tossing (sport in Venezuela)   V:296
Bumblebees   B:121
Bumi (African people)
picture(s)
    traditional hairstyle   H:6
Bumppo, Natty (hero of Cooper's *Leatherstocking Tales*)
    A:202; C:541
Bunche, Ralph (American educator and United Nations
    mediator)   A:79c; **B:450**
Bunching onions (without bulbs)   O:123
Bund, The (street, Shanghai, China)   S:138
Bundesrat (German parliament, upper house)   G:157
Bundestag (German parliament, lower house)   G:157
Bunin, Ivan (Russian author)   R:379
Bunker Hill, Battle of (1775)   R:200
early railroad carried granite for monument   R:87
picture(s)   R:200
Bunny suits (overalls worn by forensic investigators)   F:371
Bunraku (Japanese puppet play)   J:32–33, 53; P:545; T:162
picture(s)   P:548
Bunt (in baseball)   B:83
Buñuel, Luis (Spanish motion picture director)   M:244, 494
Bunyan, John (English writer and preacher)   C:229; E:276
Bunyan, Paul (American folk hero)   G:202
children's literature   C:237
statue in Bemidji (Minnesota)   M:334
Bunyoro (former kingdom, Uganda)   U:6
Buonaparte (Corsican family) *see* Bonaparte
Buonarroti, Michelangelo *see* Michelangelo
Buoninsegna, Duccio di *see* Duccio di Buoninsegna
Buoyancy (upward push on a floating object)   **F:250–53**
Archimedes' principle   A:367
salinity affects   O:17
Buoys (floats)   N:73
Buran (Soviet space shuttle)   S:365

Burbage, James (English actor) **D:**298
Burbage, Richard (English actor) **S:**131
Burbank, Luther (American horticulturalist) **B:450**
Burchell's zebra **H:**244
Burckhardt, Johann (Swiss explorer) **E:**413
Burdock (weed)
  picture(s) **W:**105
Bureaucracy **G:**276 see also Civil service
Bureaus (of the United States government) see individual
  names
Burgan oil field (Kuwait) **K:**307
Burger, Warren Earl (American jurist) **M:**338 profile
  picture(s) **C:**322
Burgess, Anthony (English novelist) **E:**290; **N:**363
Burgess, Gelett (American humorist)
  "I Wish That My Room Had a Floor" **N:**276
Burghers of Calais (statues by Rodin)
  picture(s) **S:**102
Burghley, Lord see Cecil, William
Burglar alarms **P:**197
Burglary (crime) **J:**167
Burgos (Spain) **S:**382
Burgoyne, John (English military commander) **R:**203–4, 208
  profile; **W:**40
Burgundian period (in Dutch and Flemish music) **D:**365
Burgundy (region of France) **F:**405
Buri (Norse god) **N:**279
Burial customs see Funeral customs
Burial mounds (at archaeological sites) see Mounds
Buried treasure **P:**264
Burins (tools used in engraving) **D:**76; **E:**294; **G:**303; **W:**229
Burke, Edmund (English statesman) **O:**191
Burke, Robert O'Hara (British explorer) **E:**411
Burkert, Nancy Ekholm (American illustrator)
  picture(s)
    illustration for Lear's *Scroobious Pip* **C:**237
Burkina Faso **B:451–52**
  picture(s)
    Bobo-Dioulasso **B:**452
    flag **F:**226
Burlesque (form of humor) **H:**290
Burlington (Vermont) **V:**310, 312, 315
  picture(s) **V:**315
Burma (Myanmar) **B:453–58**
  dance **D:**31
  economy **S:**332
  gemstones found in **G:**70
  New Year customs **N:**209
  Rangoon **S:**334
  Thant, U **T:**155
  World War II **W:**303, 304, 315
  picture(s)
    anti-government demonstration **B:**458
    flag **F:**231
    Mandalay Buddha **B:**423
    monk **B:**454
    Pagan ruins **B:**457
    pagoda **B:**453
    pupils in a monastery school **B:**424
    rice growing **B:**456
    water buffalo hauling teak **B:**456
Burma Road **W:**315
Burne-Jones, Sir Edward Coley (English painter) **E:**263
  picture(s)
    Praising Angels (tapestry) **T:**21
Burnett, Peter H. (American pioneer) **O:**277
Burnett, William Riley (American author) **M:**562
Burnham, Forbes (political leader of Guyana) **G:**428a
Burning see Combustion
Burns, Lucy (American reformer) **W:**212b
Burns, Robert (Scottish poet) **B:459; E:**278
  figures of speech **F:**122; **P:**351
  miniature 1786 edition of his *Poems* **D:**262
  quotation from "To a Louse" **Q:**20

"A Red, Red Rose" **B:**459
  picture(s) **B:**459
Burns, Tommy (Canadian boxer) **B:**353
Burns and scalds **F:**148, 161; **S:**4–5
Burnside, Ambrose Everett (American soldier and statesman)
  C:340; **R:**225 profile
Burping (body action) **B:**301
Burr, Aaron (American lawyer and politician) **B:460**
  duels and dueling **D:**346
  Hamilton and Burr **H:**16
  Jefferson and Burr **J:**69, 71
  vice presidency **V:**325 profile
  picture(s)
    duel with Hamilton **D:**345; **J:**70
    as vice president **V:**325
Burritt, Elihu (American advocate of peace) **P:**105
Burros (donkeys) **H:**235
Burroughs, John (American naturalist and writer) **B:461**
  picture(s) **B:**461
Burrowing bees **B:**121
Burrowing owls **B:**239; **O:**285
Burrowing snakes **S:**211
Burrows (of animals) **R:**274
Burr puzzles **P:**553–54
Bursae (fluid sacs in the joints of the skeleton) **S:**184b
Bursters (office machines) **O:**58
Burton, James Henry (American gunsmith) **G:**418–19
Burton, Sir Richard (British explorer) **A:**66; **B:461; E:**412
  picture(s) **A:**66; **B:**461
Burton, Robert (English author) **E:**274
Burundi **B:**135, **462–63**
  picture(s)
    flag **F:**226
    terraced hillside **B:**463
    traditional drum music **F:**327
    women at market **B:**463
Bus and truck tours (of theater groups) **T:**159
Busch Gardens (amusement park, Florida) **F:**270; **P:**79
  picture(s) **F:**270
Buses **B:464–65; T:**288
  airport shuttle buses **A:**126, 128
  bus segregation case **S:**115
  double deckers in London **L:**297
  New York City **N:**233
  United States **U:**102–3
  picture(s) **B:**464, 465
Bush, Barbara Pierce (wife of George Bush) **B:**467, 470;
  F:180a
  picture(s) **B:**468; **F:**180b
Bush, George (41st president of the United States) **B:466–69,**
  470, 471; **R:**112b; **U:**204–5
  Cold War **C:**401
  Iran-Contra Affair pardons **I:**310
  vice presidency **V:**331 profile
  picture(s) **P:**204, 453; **U:**204
Bush, George W. (43rd president of the United States)
  B:470–73
  picture(s) **B:**470, 471, 472, 473; **P:**453
Bush, Laura Welch (wife of George W. Bush) **B:**471; **F:**180b
  picture(s) **B:**472, 473; **F:**180b
Bush balladists (Australian poets) **A:**500
Bushido (Japanese system of conduct) **R:**149
Bushmen (African people) see San
Bushnell, David (American inventor) **S:**473
Bush people (of Suriname) **S:**516
Bushpigs (wild pigs) **P:**248
Bush pilots (of airplanes) **A:**152
Bushwhackers (proslavery men of pre-Civil War days) **C:**335
Business **B:474–77**
  advertising **A:**28–35
  agribusiness **A:**95
  bookkeeping and accounting **B:**311–13
  commercial art created for a business purpose **C:**456–58
  computer graphics, uses of **C:**484

PHOTO CREDITS

The following list credits the sources of photos used in THE NEW BOOK OF KNOWLEDGE. Credits are listed, by page, photo by photo—left to right, top to bottom. Wherever appropriate, the name of the photographer has been listed with the source, the two being separated by a dash. When two or more photos by different photographers appear on one page, their credits are separated by semicolons.

Longridge—Rainbow.

188 © Grant Heilman Photography; © Barry L. Runk—Grant Heilman Photography; © Larry Lefever—Grant Heilman Photography; © Runk/Schoenberger—Grant Heilman Photography.

191 © Dan Suzio—Photo Researchers; © Dan Suzio—Photo Researchers.

192 © Todd Powell—ProFiles West/Index Stock; © Tim Davis—Photo Researchers.

193 © Stuart Westmorland—Photo Researchers; © James Randklev—Stone; © Don Smetzer—Stone.

194 © Peter Menzel; © Frans Lanting—Photo Researchers; © Gary Retherford—Photo Researchers.

195 © Anthony Bannister—Oxford Scientific Films; © Peter Menzel; © François Gohier—Photo Researchers.

196 © Richard Feldmann—Phototake; © Rafael Macia—Photo Researchers; © Mark Newman & Assoc.—Phototake.

197 © Jeremy Burgess—Science Photo Library—Photo Researchers; © Biophoto Associates—Science Source/Photo Researchers; © Jeremy Burgess—Science Photo Library—Photo Researchers; © John Kaprielian—Photo Researchers; © George Ranalli—Photo Researchers; © Mark Newman & Assoc.—Phototake.

198 The Granger Collection; The Granger Collection; © Erich Lessing—Art Resource; The Granger Collection; The Granger Collection.

199 The Granger Collection; The Granger Collection; Archive Photos; The Granger Collection.

200 The Granger Collection; The Granger Collection; Archive Photos; Brown Brothers; The Granger Collection; Archive Photos.

201 © A. Barrington Brown—Science Source/Photo Researchers

203 © Kjell Sandved—Bruce Coleman Inc.; © Raymond Blythe—Animals Animals.

204 © Stephen J. Krasemann—Photo Researchers

205 © Lou Jacobs, Jr.—Grant Heilman Photography

208 © Thomas Kitchin—Tom Stack & Associates

210 © Morley Read—Photo Researchers

211 © Margot Conte—Animals Animals; © Zig Leszczynski—Animals Animals; © Stephen G. Maka—Photo-Nats.

212 The Granger Collection; © Jeff Foott; © Roger and Donna Aitkenhead—Animals Animals.

213 © Ron Austing—Photo Researchers

215 © Ray Richardson—Animals Animals; © Don Enger—Animals Animals; © Peggy Daly—ProFiles West/Index Stock.

216 © Steve Kaufman—Peter Arnold, Inc.; © Jim Nachel—Root Resources; © B. G. Murray, Jr.—Animals Animals.

217 © Jeff Foott; © Gregory Scott; © Jeff Foott.

219 © Jeff Foott; © François Gohier—Photo Researchers.

222 © Ben Goldstein—Root Resources; © Tom McHugh—Photo Researchers; © Jeff Foott; © L. J. Tinstman—ProFiles West/Index Stock.

223 © Jeff Foott (all photos on page).

224 © Jeff Foott; © Sidney Bahrt—Photo Researchers; © Grace DeWolf—Root Resources.

225 © Jeff Foott; © L. L. T. Rhodes—Animals Animals; © Gregory K. Scott; © Mary A. Root—Root Resources.

226 © Rick Wicker—Denver Museum of Natural History

227 © L. J. Tinstman—ProFiles West/Index Stock; © Jeff Foott; © Jeff Foott.

228 © Jerome Wexler—Photo Researchers; © Jerome Wexler—Photo Researchers; © Jerome Wexler—Photo Researchers; © Jerome Wexler—Photo Researchers; © Stephen J. Krasemann—Photo Researchers.

229 © Pat & Tom Leeson—Photo Researchers; © Richard R. Hansen—Photo Researchers; © Gregory K. Scott.

232 © Jeff Foott; © Jeff Foott; © Clarence Postmus—Root Resources; © Doug Allan—Animals Animals.

233 The Granger Collection

234 © Jeff Foott

243 © Alex—Sipa Press

245 © Erika Stone—Photo Researchers

246 © H. V. Lacey—Annan

247 © Tom McHugh—Photo Researchers

248 © Tonya A. Evatt; © John Kaprielian—Photo Researchers; © Tonya A. Evatt; © SIU—Photo Researchers.

249 © Tonya A. Evatt; © Tonya A. Evatt; © Tonya

A. Evatt; © Hank Morgan—Photo Researchers.

250 The Granger Collection

250a © Seth Shostak—Science Photo Library—Photo Researchers

250b The Bettmann Archive

251 The Granger Collection

252 © Martin R. Jones—Unicorn Stock Photos

253 Sally Di Martini—American Foundation for the Blind, Inc.; American Foundation for the Blind, Inc.

254 © James D. Wilson—Woodfin Camp & Associates

255 © Microworks—CNRI/Phototake; © Andrew Syred—Science Photo Library—Photo Researchers; © NIBSC—Science Photo Library—Photo Researchers.

256 © Lennart Nilsson—BonnierAlba (all photos on page).

257 © Lennart Nilsson—BonnierAlba

258 © Walter Reinhart—CNRI/Phototake; The Granger Collection.

259 © Avery Architectural and Fine Arts Library—Columbia University in the City of New York; Courtesy of Penguin USA.

260 The Granger Collection

262 © Charles Moore—Black Star

266 © Myles Adler

267 UPI/Bettmann Newsphotos

268 © Stone

269 © Anthony Edgeworth—The Stock Market; © Jerry Wachter—Photo Researchers.

270 © Gerald Schatten—Science Photo Library—Photo Researchers

271 © Lennart Nilsson—Behold Man, Little Brown and Company; © Lennart Nilsson—Behold Man, Little Brown and Company; © Michael Kevin Daly—The Stock Market; © Lennart Nilsson—Behold Man, Little Brown and Company; © Lennart Nilsson—Behold Man, Little Brown and Company.

272 © Janet Gill—Stone

273 © W. Metsen—H. Armstrong Roberts, Inc.; © Erika Stone—Peter Arnold, Inc.; © H. Armstrong Roberts, Inc.

275 © Michael Abbey—Photo Researchers; © Dwight R. Kuhn; © Biophoto Associates/Science Source/Photo Researchers.

276 © Alon Reininger—Contact Press Images/Woodfin Camp & Associates

277 © Lennart Nilsson—Behold Man, Little Brown and Company; © David Scharf—Peter Arnold, Inc.

278 © CNRI/Science Photo Library/Photo Researchers

280 © Manfred Kage—Science Photo Library—Photo Researchers

281 © Lennart Nilsson—The Incredible Machine, National Geographic Society

282 © Francis Leroy—Biocosmos Science Photo Library—Photo Researchers; © Omikron/Photo Researchers.

283 © Petit Format/Nestle/Science Source/Photo Researchers; © Benser/Z.E.F.A./H. Armstrong Roberts, Inc.

284 © M. Raichle—Peter Arnold, Inc.

285 © Will McIntyre—Photo Researchers; © Jose Azel—Contact Press Images/Woodfin Camp & Associates; © Lennart Nilsson—Behold Man, Little Brown and Company.

286 © Lennart Nilsson—Behold Man, Little Brown and Company

287 © NASA/Science Source—Photo Researchers

288 © Melissa Grimes-Guy—Photo Researchers

289 © R. Mackson/FPG

290 Courtesy of Joe Weider, Photo Library; © Jean-Pierre Laffont—Corbis-Sygma.

303 © Rafael Macia—Photo Researchers

304 © I. Fat—Black Star

305 The Bettmann Archive

308 © Ric Ergenbright—Lenstour; © Jacques Jangoux.

309 © Lenars—Atlas Photo; © Victor Minca—Art Resource.

310a © Catherine Karnow—Corbis; © Porterfield-Chickering/Photo Researchers.

310b © Alain Evrard—Liaison Agency

318 The Granger Collection (all photos on page).

319 The National Archeological Museum of Naples

320 New York Public Library, Spencer Collection; New York Public Library, Spencer Collection; Bibliothèque Nationale

321 © Tonya A. Evatt; © Blair Seitz—Photo Researchers.

322 © Tonya A. Evatt; © Blair Seitz—Photo Researchers.

323 © Jennifer Whitfield—Photo Researchers

324 Grolier photograph by John Kane—Silver Sun Studio

326 © H. Mark Weidman

327 © H. Mark Weidman

331 © H. Mark Weidman

332 © K. B. Kaplan Photography; © H. Mark Weidman.

333 © H. Mark Weidman

334 Washington University Gallery of Art, St. Louis

335 The Granger Collection

337 © Robert Knight—Leo de Wys

339 © Mike Mazzaschi—Stock, Boston

340 © Ellis Herwig—The Picture Cube

343 © W. Griebeling—Miller Services

345 Uffizi Gallery, Florence

346 © Cameramann International Ltd.

347 The Alamo Museum, San Antonio, Texas

348 Courtesy of Fairlanes

351 Collection of Whitney Museum of American Art

355 Courtesy, Boys & Girls Clubs of America

356 © Dick Luria—FPG International

357 © Boy Scouts of America (all photos on page).

358 © Boy Scouts of America

359 © Boy Scouts of America

360 © Boy Scouts of Canada

361 © Corbis

362 Image created by Dr. Leigh Nystrom, Ph.D., in collaboration with Dr. Jonathan D. Cohen, Princeton University and the University of Pittsburgh.

363 © Phototake/PNI

364 Stone

366 © Lori Adamski Peek—Stone

368 Stone; © Jim Sugar—Rainbow/PNI.

369 © Hank Morgan—Rainbow/PNI

370 Philadelphia Museum of Art: Louise and Walter Arensberg Collection

371 © Hubert Josse—Art Resource

372 © Harvey Lloyd—The Stock Market; © Vince DeWitt—DDB Stock Photo; © Mauricio Simonetti—DDB Stock Photo; © Jonathan Kim—Liaison Agency; © Erling Soderstrom—Liaison Agency; © Stephanie Maze—Woodfin Camp & Associates.

373 © Stephanie Maze—Woodfin Camp & Associates; © Claus Meyer—Black Star.

374 © Stephanie Maze—Woodfin Camp & Associates; © Robert Fried.

375 © Peter Read Miller—Sports Illustrated

377 © Viviane Moos—The Stock Market; © Dmitri Kessel—The Stock Market.

378 © Jacques Jangoux—Stone; © Will & Deni McIntyre—Stone.

379 © Paula Lerner—Woodfin Camp & Associates; © Juca Martins—DDB Stock Photo.

380 © Siegfried Tauquer—Leo de Wys; © Charles Bowman—Leo de Wys.

381 © Will & Deni McIntyre—Photo Researchers

382 © Claus Meyer—Black Star

383 © Diane Walker—Liaison Agency

385 © David Sousa

389 © Daniel Simon—Liaison Agency

390 © Art Resource

391 © Bob Burch—SuperStock

392 © Henry J. Ritzer—SuperStock

394 © Bruce Coleman Inc.

395 © Tom Bell

396 © Glen Thomas Brown—Stock Solution; © Bob Daemmrich—The Image Works.

397 © Bill Bachman—Photo Researchers; © Pierre Berger—Photo Researchers.

398 © Tony Freeman—Photo Edit

399 Courtesy, Figg and Muller Engineers Inc.; © MacDonald Photo—Envision.

403 © Kennan Ward—Bruce Coleman Inc.; © Pat Bates—Stone.

404 © Thomas Kitchin—Tom Stack & Associates (all photos on page).

405 © Thomas Kitchin—Tom Stack & Associates

406a © Jim Corwin—Photo Researchers

406b © Chuck O'Rear—Woodfin Camp & Associates; © Lee Rentz—Bruce Coleman Inc.

406d © Sandra Baker—Liaison Agency

408 National Portrait Gallery, London

409 Olin Mathieson Chemical Corp.

413 © Frederick Warne and Co., Ltd., London and New York

414 Vienna Kunsthistorisches Museum

415 The Detroit Institute of Arts

417 The White House Collection, © copyright White House Historical Association

418 Mercersberg Academy; The James Buchanan Foundation for the Preservation of Wheatland, Lancaster, Pa.

419 The Bettmann Archive

420 The Bettmann Archive

421 © Jeremy S. Hibbert—Stone

422a © Grandadam—Louvet—Photo Researchers

423 © Louis J. Somogy